READINGS IN GENERAL PSYCHOLOGY: CANADIAN CONTRIBUTIONS

READINGS IN GENERAL PSYCHOLOGY: CANADIAN CONTRIBUTIONS

Alexander W. Pressey
Associate Professor of Psychology
University of Manitoba

John P. Zubek
Research Professor of Psychology
and Director, Sensory Isolation
Laboratory
University of Manitoba

McClelland and Stewart Limited

The Canadian Publishers
McClelland and Stewart Limited
25 Hollinger Road, Toronto 374

0-7710-9073-0

Printed and Bound in Canada

Contents

13. Applied Problems

14. Physiological Basis of Behaviour

Preface

During the past few years we have been concerned about the total, or almost total, lack of Canadian content in university textbooks and books of readings in the field of psychology, an attitude also shared by some instructors in such disciplines as political science, sociology, and economics. Although many of the books currently in use are excellent and even outstanding in many respects, some of the material covered is not particularly relevant to Canadian experience and therefore not too meaningful to Canadian university students. Furthermore, there exist certain problems and topics which are of special concern to Canadians and which deserve coverage in psychology courses, for example, the English-French problem, research on Indians and Eskimos, life in isolated northern communities, and attitudes towards newly arrived immigrants. It was in the light of these considerations that an attempt was made to prepare a book oriented to Canada for use in the introductory course, a course basic to all further studies in psychology.

In attempting to introduce Canadian content into a beginning book on psychology, two approaches are possible. The first is to write a standard textbook introducing relevant Canadian material wherever possible. This could, of course, be done but because of the limited amount of such material, particularly in the various basic areas of psychology, the question arises as to whether the considerable time and effort involved in preparing a text of high quality is warranted, especially in view of the large number of outstanding introductory books which are currently available. The second approach is to introduce the relevant Canadian material by means of a supplementary book of readings, the articles being so grouped or arranged that the collection could be used in conjunction with any standard textbook in introductory psychology. This alternative approach possesses the virtue of permitting the instructor to select the best textbook available, regardless of its national origin, and, at the same time, allow him to introduce Canadian material by means of a relatively inexpensive book of readings. This is the approach that we favour and have adopted.

In preparing this book of readings, our original intention was to select seventy articles, with approximately one-fourth of them dealing with research conducted in this country, and the remainder being drawn from the world-wide literature. However, as our work progressed it soon became evident that a considerable amount of important research, in all areas of psychology, had been conducted in Canada, particularly during the last five years. In view of this, it was felt than an excellent book of readings in introductory psychology could be prepared, consisting of articles based solely on research conducted in Canada. Such a book, in our opinion, would not only prove to be very meaningful to our students but it would also provide them with an awareness of some of the important research which has been conducted in Canada over the years; too many students, unfortunately, view psychology as largely an American discipline.

Several considerations guided the selection of the articles in addition to those already described.

1. The articles should include a good many classic works as well as those exemplifying contemporary scientific psychology. The emphasis, however, should be on recent advances in psychological knowledge. Of the seventy articles, forty per cent were published within the last five years, and eighty per cent within the last fifteen years.

2. The selections should not be too technical in nature for the beginning student to comprehend. This criterion was in many respects the most difficult of all to achieve. It meant that a number of important articles, particularly in the areas of learning and motivation, had to be excluded because of their highly specialized or complex nature.

3. Most of the articles should have some intrinsic interest or appeal to the student. Included, therefore, were such topics as LSD, sensory isolation, sleep learning, betting at the racetrack, effects of television viewing, and abnormal behaviour and its treatment. Of necessity, some of the selections met this requirement much better than others.

4. Approximately three quarters of the selections should be of an empirical nature with the remainder being devoted to important review articles and theoretical papers. It was hoped that this emphasis on experimental studies might help to correct the misconception held by some beginning students that psychology is a non-empirical "talking" discipline. Furthermore, it will familiarize them with the experimental procedures and observations upon which the general discussions in textbooks and lectures are based. A knowledge of experimental techniques is particularly important in the introductory course since it is rarely accompanied by laboratory exercises.

5. A larger number of articles than is usual in compilations of this kind was selected in order to provide the instructor with flexibility of choice in deciding on the number and type of articles to be assigned to his students. This extensive selection will also indicate to the student the wide range of topics which have been studied experimentally in Canada.

Each of the articles is introduced by a brief essay that sets the context for the selection. In addition, the institutional affiliation of the various contributors at the time the study was made has been given on the title page, a procedure which should indicate to the reader that important psychological research is being conducted throughout the length and breadth of Canada and is not restricted to only a handful of centres. The seventy selections are presented within a framework of fourteen chapters, each of which deals with a basic or major area of psychology. This organization allows the book to be used with any standard introductory text in the field.

We are deeply indebted to the numerous authors who have allowed us to reproduce their works. Without their co-operation, the publication of this volume, of course, would have been impossible. We also wish to thank *Science*, the American Psychological Association, and especially the University of Toronto Press, the publisher of the *Canadian Journal of Psychology*, for permission to reprint many articles. Finally, special thanks are due to Mrs. Lynne Dobbs whose skilful secretarial work materially aided the final preparation of this book.

A. W. PRESSEY

JOHN P. ZUBEK

ONE
THE SCIENCE OF PSYCHOLOGY

1 / Behaviouristics and the Study of the Mind

D.O. Hebb *McGill University*

In this opening article, Professor Hebb, one of Canada's most distinguished scientists and educators and one of the world's foremost psychologists, describes what psychology is and what it tries to accomplish. Professor Hebb is the author of two widely-used and influential books: Organization of Behaviour *(1949) and* A Textbook of Psychology *(1966). He is a Fellow of the Royal Society of England, the only North American psychologist ever to be elected to this world-famous scientific society, and the recipient of honorary degrees from numerous universities.*

Definitions

It is difficult to give a precise and unequivocal definition of psychology, partly because the terms which must be used in a definition are themselves equivocal, meaning different things to different people. To define it as the study of behaviour is not quite satisfactory, because this includes a large segment of physiology. Mouth-watering is behaviour, and so is clenching the fist; to find out how the parotid gland secretes saliva, or how muscle cells produce finger movements, is a problem for the physiologist. (The psychologist is more concerned with the way in which many such small single items of behaviour combine to form complex actions over longer periods of time.) On the other hand, the older definition – that psychology is the study of mind – does not cover the full range of phenomena with which we are concerned. Psychologists for example have traditionally been students of learning, not only in higher species but also in the earthworm and the ant. These organisms do not have the complexity of function which is referred to by the terms "mind" and "mental," so when a psychologist studies learning in the ant he is not dealing with mental processes, in any reasonable use of the term.

With these considerations in mind, we can attempt some definitions, with commentary to avoid misunderstanding.

Psychology is the study of the more complex forms of organization in behaviour, and of processes such as learning, perception or emotion which are involved in the organization. The focal problem is found in the patterns of behaviour shown by the whole animal of a higher species over appreciable periods of time; to say the same thing in a different way, it is found in the mental processes of the higher animal.

Behaviour is the publicly observable activity of muscles or glands of external secretion as manifested in movements of parts of the body or in the appearance of tears, sweat, saliva and so forth. Talking is behaviour; so is a smile, a grimace, eye-watering, trembling, blushing (which is produced by muscular changes in blood vessels), changing one's posture, or following the words of a printed page with the eyes.

The *organization* of behaviour is the pattern, or combination, of separate items in relation to each other and to environmental stimulation. A pattern may be either spatial or temporal, but usually is both. A spatial pattern is the combination of activity in different parts of the body; a temporal pattern is a sequence of activities. An example of a very simple spatial pattern is the simultaneous movement of thumb and forefinger, in opposition, when taking hold of a small object; an example of a spatial and temporal pattern is reaching forward, picking up the object with one hand and, having focussed the eyes on it, touching it or turning it over with the other hand. Far more complex patterns are produced when an animal is looking for food, or when a child plays with a toy.

It is more difficult to specify what behaviour is well organized and what is not. Such distinctions are made in a rough sense only. We may say that behaviour is judged as organized when the various muscle contractions seem to the observer to constitute a smooth flow of movement, or to have a coordinated effect; otherwise, as unorganized, or disorganized.

Most behaviour is not a disjointed series of separate actions but a continuing process, a flow of activity which varies in smoothness or turbulence. For the purpose of analysis and recording it is often necessary to divide the flow into arbitrary units, but this is artificial and theoretical, like describing water as consisting of atoms of hydrogen and oxygen.

Mind and *mental* refer to the processes inside the head that determine the higher levels of organization in behaviour. These are most evident in the higher mammals, and concern the activity of the whole body over periods of minutes, hours or days. In this book we shall assume that mind is an activity of the brain, and that our knowledge of it is chiefly theoretical, inferred from behaviour rather than being ob-

Reprinted, by permission, from D. O. Hebb, *A Textbook of Psychology* (Philadelphia: W. B. Saunders, 1958), pp. 2-18. ©1958.

tained directly from self-observation (i.e., from *introspection,* "looking inward").

There are two theories of mind, speaking very generally. One is animistic, a theory that the body is inhabited by an entity – the mind or soul – that is quite different from it, having nothing in common with bodily processes. The second theory is physiological or mechanistic; it assumes that mind is a bodily process, an activity of the brain. Modern psychology works with this latter theory only. Both are intellectually respectable (that is, each has support from highly intelligent people, including scientists), and there is certainly no decisive means available of proving one to be right, the other wrong.

In these circumstances, we use the mechanistic set of ideas as we would a working assumption, because they are proving – at present, though not in the earlier history of psychology – to be more useful in analysis and research. The student should realize that scientific theories are never regarded as final truth but as subject to possible revision at any time. Working with a particular theory is often on an "as-if" basis, and does not require that the user should believe it.

Saying that our knowledge of mind is theoretical rather than observational means that we study mind in the same way as a chemist studies the atom. Atoms are not observed directly, but their properties can be inferred from observable events. The chemist says in effect, If the atom of hydrogen has such-and-such characteristics, then the gas should behave so-and-so when it is mixed with a certain other gas, let us say, at a particular temperature. He performs this experiment, and if the results agree with expectation his theory of the nature of the hydrogen atom can be retained; if not, the theory is modified and he tries again.

For psychology, our problem is to construct, in imagination, the complex machinery of mind that will account for the phenomena of behaviour. This is the method of *behavouristics* (*behaviourism* is a related term, but is often used to mean a particular kind of theory, which when first formulated denied the existence of mental processes entirely; behaviouristics refers to a method of studying mental processes. See the following paragraphs).

Finally, *public* or *objective evidence* is defined as evidence which might be obtained equally well by any of a number of observers: in most cases, evidence which two or more observers can record at the same time. *Private,* or *subjective,* or *introspective evidence* concerns events within the observer himself, and by the nature of things available to that one observer only. It may happen that there is only one observer of a public event, as for example when there is only one eye in the whole world that is applied to a telescope pointing in the right direction when some unique event occurs in the heavens; even more, there may be only one telescope strong enough so that it is impossible for more than one person to make the observation; but the event is still public, for another observer could have seen it just as well – it is not peculiar to one person. On the other hand, if the reader gets a headache from this text his pain is a private event – no one else can experience it as he does.

But if he describes the pain, aloud or in writing, the description itself is a public event; and so are his facial expressions. That is, speech, writing and facial contortions are behaviour, which others can observe. From such behaviour they can infer, and have theoretical knowledge about, something inside the subject which he calls pain and which makes him behave as he does. As an objective science, therefore, modern psychology constructs its theory of mind from the public data of behaviour.

Sometimes it may seem that private data are being used, especially when there is agreement among different persons concerning their private experiences. Visual after-images are a good example. But the only agreement we know about is in the *reports* of these different persons: in certain conditions they behave in the same way. Speech, and introspective description, is not a sort of pipeline direct to the consciousness of another, giving us first-hand knowledge. It is behaviour, from which we may infer, correctly or incorrectly, the nature of the underlying processes that determined what the subject has said. All that we can know about the conscious processes of another, or about what the psychiatrist calls the unconscious, is *an inference from behaviour,* verbal or nonverbal.

Further, we shall see . . . that a subject's reports may be a most unreliable source of information about what goes on in the mind of another, even though he is entirely honest. Just to ask the colour-blind subject what colours he can see is likely to give most unsatisfactory results. Many subjects report having memory images at which they can "look" just as if a picture or a page of print were being held up before their eyes; but objective test methods show that the actual situation is very different. Where emotions are involved self-knowledge and introspective report become still less satisfactory. When therefore we make behaviour the basis of psychology, and eschew reliance on introspective evidence, we are not necessarily throwing away a superior kind of information about the mind or refusing to take the most direct route to our goal. What we are really saying is that one kind of behaviour, introspective report, is extremely difficult to interpret, and that it is a reasonable procedure to build in the first place on other forms of behaviour in which perhaps we may find more reliable evidence.

This brings us to the large part that animal subjects play in modern psychology.

The Place of Animal Studies in Psychology

There are three reasons why scientists study animals, and all three apply in psychology. The first, as important for pure science as any other, is that animals are fascinating and may be studied for their own sakes. Their behaviour presents some of the most engaging puzzles to be found anywhere, which is quite enough reason for trying to solve them.

The second reason is more crudely practical. One can do experiments on animals that one cannot do on men. If one is interested for example in knowing what would happen to intelligence if a particular part of the brain were destroyed, one's only hope of finding out with human subjects is to wait – perhaps forever – until a patient enters hospital with a brain injury in exactly the right place. But surgical operations can be done with animals, with the same anaesthetics and the same care to prevent infections. It is experimental animal surgery that has led to the skill with which a surgeon can treat human illness, and in the psychological laboratory is now leading to a new understanding of man's behavioural problems, with humanitarian values whose future extent we can only guess at today.

Also, one cannot do breeding experiments with man, or rearing experiments. One cannot bring up children shut off from contacts with the rest of the world to see if the effect is to produce low intelligence, or abnormal behaviour, but one can do the experiment with animals. Man is a poor animal for breeding and rearing experiments anyway, because it takes a child so long to grow; the experimenter would be dead before the experiment got well under way, unless the answer could be had from a single generation of experimental subjects. This difficulty applies to a number of higher animals, and not man alone. The great apes in particular take eight to ten years to grow up; and so nearly all breeding and rearing experiments in psychology have been done with laboratory rats and mice, with which one can readily get two or more generations a year for study.

The third reason for studying animals is less utilitarian, nearer the high philosophical plane of the first. It is the need of *comparative* study, to understand one animal better by setting his behaviour against that of another and seeing how they are similar as well as how they differ. Only in this way does one see how remarkable some features of behaviour are; paradoxically or not, it is only through working with animals that one is likely to gain a proper respect for man's intellectual capacities.

If we knew nothing about animal behaviour, for example, we would never guess what a tremendous intellectual feat is performed by the two-year-old child who can make a sentence and use it to get something he wants. Language is picked up by the child without apparent effort. Even children we think very stupid can use it to good effect, and only the proud parents of a first child are much impressed when the feat is achieved.

But comparative psychology puts a different light on the matter. The rat's intellectual processes we know now are complex (too complex to be well understood yet, despite thirty or forty years of intensive effort); dogs are much more complex, more intelligent, than rats, and chimpanzees still more so – far beyond the rat in many ways; yet no chimpanzee, nor any other animal, is capable of using language as the child does. (The talking birds . . . are no exception.) Only through such comparisons does it become possible to put the intelligence of man in proper perspective. The behaviouristic approach, by applying similar methods to man and animal, does not degrade man but on the contrary dignifies him. It shows, as the introspective method never did, the true enormity of the problem of accounting for his mental processes.

No psychologist would dream of arguing that we should fully solve the problem of animal behaviour before tackling man. But there are great advantages to studying both at the same time. One reason is to be able to use the comparative method, but there is also the hope that it may be easier to unravel the less complex behaviour of lower animals and, in so doing, that we may find new leads to the study of human behaviour. It is quite clear that the anatomical organization of the brains of all mammals is essentially the same; and it seems clear also that the principles of behaviour, or of brain function, are the same in great part if not entirely. Psychology in the twentieth century is not the study of the human mind, but the study of *mind* – when mind is defined as at the beginning of this chapter. It is as proper an occupation for a psychologist to study the chimpanzee as it is to study man; and there is reason to think that the study of both, by similar methods, will be a more profitable enterprise than the study of either alone.

Problems of Human Behaviour: Abnormal Personality

In abstract terms, we have seen what psychology is and what it tries to accomplish. Our definitions will have more meaning if we now begin the study of behaviour by looking at some aspects of personality and, in the following section, of social behaviour. Under these headings come the topics of mental health and mental illness, juvenile delinquency, racial and religious prejudice, and the causes of war (to name a few, but not at random). There is no need to emphasize the importance for human welfare of learning how to deal with such problems. Much of the money and time spent on research in psychology is spent in the hope that it will contribute to their solution. The hope is justified by the fact that a good deal has already been accomplished. But obviously there is much more to be learned than has been to date.

Does this mean, in view of the urgency of the problems, that all research should be concentrated on them directly? The answer certainly is No. A scientific problem is not always solved by attacking it head on, and the present discussion will try to show the student how experiments with learning in dogs, for example, form part of the whole process of understanding human problems. There are different levels of analysis of such complex structures as the nervous system; it is important to study mental illness directly, but if it is to be really understood we need to study normal mechanisms also, and – sometimes in man, sometimes in animals – the separate processes that are involved in the development of normal or abnormal personality.

Personality is a relatively vague term, not susceptible of very precise definition. It refers to the mental characteristics that determine the general pattern of behaviour in a higher animal, especially as it makes the individual distinctive in his relations with others. Some psychologists use the term to include intellectual characteristics; others distinguish, roughly, between intelligence and personality, and use the latter term to refer to the total picture of such emotional, motivational and social characteristics as friendliness, selfishness, sluggishness, initiative, leadership, cheerfulness and so forth, excluding intelligence as far as possible.

In mental illness the whole personality is apt to be affected, in many different ways (it is not quite true that every patient thinks he is Einstein, or the Emperor Napoleon come back to life). Three cases are cited here to show some of the variety that is observed in the clinic.[1]

Mrs. X, 47 years old, had begun with an attack of depression lasting three days. Later the attacks became monthly and increased in length to about two weeks. Still later, these attacks were preceded by periods of exhilaration ("euphoria"). When she was depressed Mrs. X wanted to die (though she did not try to commit suicide), refused to see any visitor, would not speak, and did not eat or dress herself. In the periods of exhilaration she sang and danced, expected unreasonable things of other persons, and was angered by advice or any attempt to get her to behave in a reasonable way. Her behaviour continued to deteriorate and after two years she had to be confined in hospital, for her own protection and that of others. No effective treatment had been found at the time the case was reported.

Dr. Y, 35 years old, was a dental officer in the army. Following an attack of laryngitis he continued to feel weak and tired, and lost all interest in his work. He developed a persistent indigestion, with heartburn, and thought he must have a stomach ulcer, but no evidence of this was found when he was examined medically. His ability to work was interfered with, and he lost his confidence in himself so that difficult cases were handed over to his colleagues to deal with. He did not of course have to be confined in hospital for such symptoms ("contact with reality" was maintained) but his emotional discomfort was severe and his working efficiency was greatly impaired. Psychotherapy (cf. p. 14) did not remove his fundamental emotional problems, which were connected with certain family relations, but did lessen their severity so he could tolerate them and permitted him to go on with his professional work.

Mr. Z, 30 years old, had been a medical student. He had done satisfactory work in his first year but began to have difficulty with the second. He had headaches, could not concentrate, and lost weight. He began to think that his teachers wanted him to fail, in the forthcoming examinations. Then, studying alone one night, he suddenly leaned out of his window and shouted obscene objections at some unknown persons who were, he said, shining a light in his eyes. In hospital, his illness progressed; he often refused to talk to anyone, but sometimes would speak about mysterious persons who were persecuting him. These persons were disarranging his thoughts (which prevented him from studying), calling him obscene names, and directing a mysterious penetrating ray at him which damaged him sexually. He had prolonged periods when he was totally unresponsive, even to pinprick, and had to be fed by stomach tube. In these periods his limbs could be moulded into any kind of bizarre posture and would remain so. No effective treatment was found.

What causes mental illnesses? How can they be cured, or better, prevented? We can go about finding answers in two ways. One is empirical and practical; working directly with mental patients, trying this procedure and that, finding out directly by trial and error which procedures help and which do not. The second approach is more or less theoretical; it sets out to understand the problem first, not to help anyone. The idea is that when we understand both normal and abnormal personality we will see new possibilities for treatment (and prevention) which would never be thought of otherwise.

Both aspects of research are essential. The first has produced immediately practical knowledge of great importance – for example, in the current use of tranquillizing drugs, which have benefited large numbers of patients though no one quite knows how they work nor why – and, in any case, when a patient is seriously in need of help the psychiatrist cannot say, We do not yet really understand your problem; come back in ten years' time and let us see what can be done for you then. He must help now, and in fact he can help a great deal. But for the great majority of cases the available treatments are palliative; they lessen the severity of illness rather than removing it; and the hope of better ones in the future lies mainly in the development of our theoretical understanding.

Fundamentally the question is, What *is* mental illness? At one extreme we have the possibility (1) that it is simply a set of bad habits, wrong ways of thinking, the result of special stresses, of having learned to fear things that need not be feared, or of not learning how to deal with the problems of adult life. This would mean that we are not really discussing an *illness*; it is not a medical problem but an

[1] These cases are paraphrased from Strecker, Ebaugh and Ewalt, *Practical Clinical Psychiatry*, 6th ed., The Blakiston Co., 1947.

educational one. If children are brought up right, so-called mental illness will not occur. At the other extreme we have the possibility (2) that it is truly an illness, a medical problem only, to be treated with drugs or the like (when we know what drugs to use). Some part of the machinery is out of order and repairs are needed before its functioning can return to normal.

Which of the two answers is correct? We do not know certainly, but the answer in all probability is Neither, or Both. Views on this question differ radically, and presumably will do so until we understand the human mind much better than we do now. But there are many indications that mental illness frequently is a combination of undesirable learning or ways of thinking, and some disorder or weakness of a part of the machinery.

Those who have attacked the problem directly have often settled in advance on one of the two answers. (1) Working with the first hypothesis, that the disorder is the result of childhood learning, one can explore the patients' histories to see what particular experiences or what kind of rearing they have had that normal subjects have not had. If this should be successful, one could then prevent mental illness in the future by showing parents how to rear children whose behaviour at maturity will be normal and healthy. Or, with the same hypothesis, one can explore methods of changing what was learned in childhood and replacing it with something more satisfactory, thus correcting behaviour that is already disturbed. *Psychotherapy* is the attempt to correct *disordered* behaviour by talking to the patient, encouraging him to talk, and putting him into situations where relearning is possible, to change underlying attitudes of fear or hatred or whatever is the cause of trouble. The most widely known form of psychotherapy is *psychoanalysis,* which began with the brilliant speculations of Freud about 1890: it is both a theory and a form of treatment.

(2) Working with the second hypothesis, one searches for disease processes in the brain, or in an endocrine gland whose output, secreted into the blood stream, is necessary for brain function; for defects of nutrition (such as lack of some vitamin); or for injuries or inherited defects.

Each of these rather extreme approaches has had some success: the "childhood learning" or psychotherapy school mainly by advancing our knowledge of behaviour, normal as well as abnormal; the "brain disease" school by actually producing some cures. Psychotherapy helps the patient to live with his problems, but the present evidence is that it does not abolish or shorten the disorder. The search for constitutional defect or disease has scored brilliant successes in the discovery, for example, of syphilis of the brain or the mental disorders of beriberi and pellagra (vitamin B deficiencies), for which prevention is fully possible (and cure as well, if the patient is caught in time, before lasting damage has been done). But this approach has added little to our understanding of behaviour problems, and has left us with no clues to the prevention or cure of the large body of other mental illnesses. These include both the *psychoses* (the more extreme disorders of personality) and the *neuroses* (less extreme, but still the cause of a great deal of suffering).

Dogmatism flourishes in direct proportion to ignorance; we are very ignorant of the mechanisms of mental illness and are apt to be correspondingly dogmatic. The student will find that many writers choose one of the two alternatives discussed in the preceding paragraphs, and deny that the other is of any great importance. And this is hard to understand, because there is no reason why past experience and constitutional deficiency should not work together, jointly, as causes of mental illness, and much evidence to indicate that they do work jointly.

We know that brain processes affect what happens in other organs, and that these other organs in turn affect what happens in the brain. Anger or fear interrupts digestion, accelerates the heart, and steps up the production of some glandular substances. The brain of course cannot live in isolation; how it functions depends essentially on the chemical products delivered to it by the blood stream; and each of the changes referred to (digestive, circulatory, hormonal) affects the chemical environment of the brain. The brain both controls and depends on the rest of the body. This makes possible a vicious circle: *A* is upset in function, which upsets *B*, which further upsets *A*, and so on. Normally there are limits to such a cumulative process; the disturbance stays within bounds, and the whole system returns to an even keel fairly quickly when the original source of disturbance is removed. But one weak link in the chain might lead to a very different end result.

Consider the *psychosomatic* ailments (the name is supposed to remind physicians that body and mind form one total entity). These are the cases of stomach ulcer, asthma or skin disease in which the patient's attitudes and emotions are an important cause of the disorder, and the only cause according to some investigators. There is no doubt that the patient's mental state is a major factor in these and other illnesses; but there is real doubt that it is the only one. The difficulty for such a conclusion is always this: Why do other persons, under equal emotional pressure, fail to develop ulcers (or asthma, or heart disease)? The situation would be much easier to understand if, in addition to prolonged emotion, there were also some incipient disorder in the part that eventually shows disease. A man's stomach ulcers might begin with a mild digestive disorder, unimportant in itself until worry or the like sets up the vicious circle. Emotion increases indigestion; indigestion means a possibility, at least, of changes in blood chemistry that might increase emotional responsiveness (e.g., irritability), this in turn increasing or prolonging the indigestion.

It is clear, also, that a person who had learned in childhood to worry about his physical health would be particularly vulnerable to such a process; the first sign of pain from the stomach, or asthma, or irregularity of heart beat, would produce an excessive emotional response, exacerbating the process described. We do not know that this kind of interaction is in fact what happens in the psychosomatic illness; but if it is, it would account both for the role of the patient's emotional sensitivities, and for the disturbance of one particular organ of the body and not other organs.

Or consider this possibility with respect to the occurence of neurosis or psychosis. A woman has some deficiency of the pituitary gland (let us say) such that some part of its output is sufficient in ordinary circumstances, but rapidly exhausted under pressure of emotion. Prolonged irritations, anger which must be suppressed and which thus tends to last, or repeated sexual arousal without satisfaction – any such continued emotional strain might deplete the pituitary output of some component which is necessary to normal brain function. This at once would mean aberrant mental processes: perhaps to a very slight degree, not noticeable to other persons. But if the abnormality should take the form of a further addition to emotional tension ("neurotic anxiety," for example) it would increase the load on the pituitary and tend thus to perpetuate itself. If something of the sort is what happens in some forms of mental illness (though this is a quite hypothetical example), there is an interesting corollary. It is known that heredity is one factor in mental illness, and the possibility just discussed would mean that what the patient had inherited, roughly speaking, was not an inadequate nervous system but an inadequate pituitary or adrenal cortex; the pathologist looking for an "organic" basis of mental illness must not restrict his search to the brain, but must include other organs as well.

The brain and the rest of the body constitute one system. Disorders of behaviour may originate in the glandular system, as we have just seen, but they can also originate in the subject's perceptions and thoughts. It is estimated that *any* human being will break down in the conditions of modern warfare if the strain, the conflict of duty and fear, is continued long enough. Such breakdown is known as "shell shock" or "battle fatigue," but could better be called battle psychosis. Mental strain, therefore, can lead to mental illness: if in the extreme case of battle psychosis this can happen without any predisposing factor of heredity, then in less extreme cases, where predisposing factors do operate, mental strain must often be the decisive cause of breakdown. When we recognize the importance of constitutional deficiencies in mental illness we must not begin to deny the importance of the factors of experience, as if one explanation precluded the other.

What are the features of childhood experience that shape adult personality so as to make the patient a "worrier," or short-tempered, or a troublemaker who inevitably gets himself into trouble, or a perfectionist who is emotionally disturbed when little things go wrong? One man sloughs off his responsibilities when he is away from the job; another does not. One learns how to behave socially (in the broad sense) so as to minimize emotional conflict, another seems to maximize it. One learns easily to adapt himself to new and perhaps unpleasant conditions, another does not and so makes them worse.

How can we understand such differences of personality? They involve, among other things, differences of learning capacity which must to a considerable extent be rooted in the learning of childhood. Again and again such problems of human behaviour bring us back to the fundamental problem of learning, which psychologists still do not clearly understand despite half a century or more of intensive study. A great deal has been learned about learning, but only too often the new information presents us with further riddles for our solution. We crack the outer shell of the nut, which is certainly progress; but within we find a second shell, harder than the outer one.

Consider an important example, which again is relevant to the problem of disordered personality. Pavlov, the great Russian physiologist, found that dogs given a problem too difficult for solution sometimes develop neurosis, or a state very like it. As with some other important discoveries (penicillin is a modern example), the original observation was an accident that occurred in the course of studying something else, but its importance was at once recognized. The experimenter was trying to find out how small a difference the dog could detect between two objects, using the method of conditioned reflexes. He taught the dog that food would be given following the sight of one object, and not following that of another. No punishment was given if the dog failed to discriminate between them. The objects were made more and more alike until, after several days of failing to discriminate, the dog's behaviour changed, suddenly. Instead of coming eagerly to the experimental room the dog struggled to avoid it; instead of standing quietly in the apparatus, waiting for the next signal to appear, he struggled and howled. Discrimination disappeared. The experimenter went back to easier forms of the problem which the dog had solved previously, but this had little effect on the changed behaviour. The disturbance never completely disappeared; even after prolonged rest, there were signs of it when the dog was put back into the experimental apparatus.

Some irreversible learning process seems definitely to have taken place. The whole picture, including the emotional aspects as well as the persistence of symptoms for a long period, has direct relevance to the human problem. We cannot be certain that this "experimental neurosis" and neurosis as it is known in the clinic are really the same, until we understand both better than we do now. But it is of great importance to have demonstrated that a conflict of perceptions by itself, with no pain or other unpleasant consequence following failure to discriminate, can produce such an extensive disturbance of behaviour. If such phenomena do occur in man, it would explain much that is otherwise puzzling.

But the other side of the picture is that we do not understand the breakdown, nor how the learning can be so persistent. We do not know just what kinds of situation would constitute a similar conflict for man. What is a difficult problem for a dog may be no problem at all for a child; and we cannot, obviously, get the answer experimentally. What we must hope instead is that we can discover the principles involved, both with respect to the breakdown and with respect to the learning that is involved. From the dog work alone, of course, we will not be able to generalize directly to man, even when we think we understand what is going on in the dog: the higher levels of man's intellectual processes may mean that other variables enter in and modify our conclusions. What we can do is apply the principles tentatively, and see whether in fact they do lead to better understanding of human phenomena; if they do, splendid; if not, we then search farther to see what other processes need to be taken into account, or whether we have perhaps misinterpreted the animal data.

For some time in psychology a concentrated attack has been directed at learning in the laboratory rat. When a clear-cut answer is achieved, concerning its nature and the specific conditions in which it occurs or does not occur, this will have an immense clarifying significance for other problems, involving higher species. One cannot tell in advance where a scientific breakthrough will occur. We will not solve human problems by the study of lower animals alone, but a combined attack, at different evolutionary levels and from different points of view, holds far greater promise than a narrower attack on a single species, man.

Personality and Social Problems

Our introductory look at the field of psychology, and at the connection between academic and practical problems, can be concluded by considering the relation of "normal" personality to certain social problems; specifically, the problem of group conflict and prejudice.

Suspicion, dislike and hatred of others who differ from him in appearance or beliefs are so common in the human adult as to be almost universal. Whether we like to face it or not, the fact is that persons without such attitudes are a small minority of mankind, and always have been in recorded history. War is not a psychological problem – there are limits to what psychology takes blame or credit for – but unreasoning attitudes, which help to make war possible, certainly are. What can be done about them?

As with mental illness, the first objective is to understand, before we can hope to cure or to prevent. And here too we find that the farther our investigations go the more complicated things become, but also, the more fascinating, considered purely as intellectual riddles posed by society for our solution. If Jew dislikes Gentile without apparent reason, or Protestant fears a Catholic domination of society, or White regards Negro as a potential threat to his own future, one naturally looks first to see whether such attitudes are determined by verbal learning – by the things that members of the one group have been told about the other. And, as we know, such learning does occur. Jewish children are told about the evil things that Gentiles have done, Gentiles are told bad things about Jews, and so forth. But is this the whole story? There are two points that raise some doubt: when one looks for them, one can find examples where such antagonisms seem to arise spontaneously, where prior learning does not seem to explain the attitudes; and secondly, if the attitudes are learned, how is one to explain their strength and persistence? The learning sometimes must have been on the basis of a few casual remarks; yet other things that we try to inculcate in children by verbal training are often achieved only with the greatest effort and then, too often, have little permanence. Such considerations are bound to raise some suspicion that more is involved in the problem.

Let us take a broader view. One is accustomed to think of man as a rational animal, and it is puzzling, consequently, when one finds him afraid or hostile with no good reason. We try therefore to find some special explanation for the social attitudes in question. But *is* man's behaviour so controlled by reason? When we take a wider survey we find some very peculiar phenomena indeed, which suggest that group antipathy is only a special case, a manifestation of something more deep-seated. Fear does not occur only where injury is anticipated. Anger is not caused only by frustration. Man is indeed much more intelligent than any other animal so far studied by scientists, but it appears that the price paid for a higher level of intellect is a corresponding susceptibility to emotional disturbance. Development of *capacity* for rational thought may be paralleled by capacity for bigger and better irrationalities.

Comparative studies in this field have served two purposes. They allow us to study the development of emotions under controlled conditions, so that the animal's previous history is fully known (and verbal learning, of course, is not a complication). They also give us perspective, and draw our attention to significant relations that otherwise might not be seen, partly because the phenomena are so familiar. Fear of strangers – so-called shyness – is normally present in the 6-to-12 month infant; fear of darkness, or imaginary things in the darkness, occurs in a large fraction of children, who experience them at one time or another after the age of 3 years; fear of harmless as well as harmful snakes is very nearly universal after the age of 6 years or so; and this list could be greatly extended. But – perhaps because they are so well known, singly – we do not put these facts together and ask whether man is after all as reasonable as we think him, or, when we are concerned about social hostilities, whether man's attitude toward those who have a different skin colour or different beliefs may not be part of the same broad picture of irrationality. But this is exactly what is suggested by a comparative approach to the problem.

As we go from rat to chimpanzee (from lower to higher animals), we find an increasing variety in the causes of fear. Pain, sudden loud noise and sudden loss of support are likely to cause fear in any mammal. For the laboratory rat we need add only strange surroundings, in order to have a list of things that disturb the animal under ordinary circumstances. With the dog, the list becomes longer: we must add strange persons, certain strange objects (a balloon being blown up, for example, or a large statue of an animal) or strange events (the owner in different clothing, a hat being moved across the floor by a thread which the dog does not see). Not every dog is equally affected, of course, but dogs as a species are affected by a much wider variety of things than rats. Monkeys and apes are affected by a still wider variety, and the degree of disturbance is greater. Causes of fear in the captive chimpanzee make up an almost endless list: a carrot of an unusual shape, a biscuit with a worm in it, a rope of a particular size and colour, a doll or a toy animal, and so on. What one animal fears another may not, but some things, such as a toy animal or . . . a sculptured head or a death mask of a chimpanzee, will terrify nearly all adult chimpanzees.

Similarly, the causes of hostility are more numerous in the higher animal. The rat bites to escape being held or captured, to avoid pain, or in the course of fighting for food or to protect the young, but rarely for any other reason. There is no need, in discussing the rat's behaviour, to make any reference to anger. In the dog causes of aggression are more complex; there are occasionally suggestions of sulking (in man a form of anger), and attacks based apparently on jealousy. In the chimpanzee anger is a frequent phenomenon, aggressions with no apparent cause are common, and the causes when they are evident are extremely varied. A young male had temper tantrums whenever a female, in heat, would not sit where he could watch the lovely creature. Another male was angered when he saw a sexual examination being made of a female in a separate cage. A female took food from a smaller male in the same cage and was then enraged because he had a temper tantrum, and gave him a beating. An offer of food, then withholding it, does not (as with a dog) make the chimpanzee more eager to get the food, but makes him angry – or produces sulking and refusal to accept the food that was originally desired. This list, like the list of chimpanzee fears, could be extended almost indefinitely.

So far, the data are consistent with the idea that the more complex machinery required for higher intellectual function is also capable of more complex aberrations – that is, susceptibility to irrational processes increases with the capacity for rational problem-solving. Furthermore, there are indications that this may be so as intelligence develops in the growing animal. It is certainly true of the dog and the chimpanzee that it is the older animal, rather than the younger, in which the more complex and hard-to-understand causes of fear and aggression are found. This is true as well of children up to the age of five or six. However, it seems not true of adult man in civilized societies: we regard ourselves instead as being free of baseless fears, and unlikely to injure someone else except in self-defence. Is this so?

Is it true that adult civilized man is sweet and reasonable? Or should we see him instead as a dangerous animal, with enough intelligence to try to bring his dangerous propensities under control by means of the social institutions he is able to set up – a process that has gone a long way, but has a long way yet to go? This social machinery would include the prolonged training of the growing child in customs, manners and morals, the elaborate rules of courtesy and propriety for the adult (enforced by ostracism or detention), the emphasis on religious belief and the social practices enjoined by religion, as well as all the apparatus of law and government.

The hostility toward other groups would certainly be an integral part of such a picture, if this is in fact a true account of the behaviour of the human species. We do not know that it is true; but such an account as this deserves serious consideration when one asks how to deal with the problem of war. If man is by nature peaceable and friendly, and hostile to others only because he has learned to be hostile, all we need do to prevent the hostility is to make sure that the growing child is not taught bad ideas about other social or national groups. If man is by nature something else, what we must do is get busy and find out what kind of childhood environment produces the kind of adult personality that can live in friendliness with others who differ in appearance and beliefs. Such persons do exist, so this is by no means a hopeless task; but we do not know at present just what conditions are necessary if the child is to become an adult of this kind.

The questions that are involved include all the topics of psychology. The reader is reminded that we are not primarily concerned with social psychology (or clinical psychology) . . . and that the present discussion is meant to show him why, when there are such pressing problems as mental illness or social conflict, many psychologists devote themselves to the academic study of emotion in chimpanzees, or the learning of nonsense syllables by college students, or the perception of simple diagrams by the rat or cat. If we are really to have a hope of transcending the rule-of-thumb procedures available at present for dealing with social problems, we must ***understand*** human thought and perception and emotions, and such academic studies are aimed at understanding. We know that the way in which a member of another social group is perceived is affected by beliefs about that group; we do not know precisely how. We know that purely intellectual ideas, such as that the earth moves about the sun instead of vice versa, or that man is descended from lower species, can arouse intense emotion and profound hostility. We do not know why, nor how it is that some persons are not so disturbed. We know that attitudes learned in childhood are sometimes permanent, but we do not know how this learning differs from other learning that is more subject to modification.

Psychology . . . is primarily an academic discipline, the study of the more complex aspects of behaviour – or of mind, which determines the behaviour. We may hope, with reason, that it will continue to produce results of practical value in dealing with human problems, as it has done in the past. But in order to do so, it must be aimed primarily at the solution of the fundamental problems; and the student who studies psychology with the hope eventually of contributing to human welfare must master it first as a purely academic discipline, just as much as the one whose interests are scientific instead of humanitarian . . . . Before one can have applied science, one must have a science to apply.

Summary

Psychology used to be called the study of mind; today it is usually called the study of behaviour. If, however, mind is that which determines the complex behaviour of higher animals, both definitions are approximately correct. In modern psychology mind is considered to be some part or aspect of brain activity – though this is held only as a working assumption – and is studied by objective methods. Mental events are known theoretically, being inferred from behaviour. In such a framework the study of animals has a natural part, both for its own sake and for the light it casts on human behaviour.

The most pressing problems of behaviour are those of mental illness and social conflict. These must be attacked at more than one level. Practically, they must be dealt with here and now, by whatever means are available from current knowledge. The "pure-science" approach, the development of theoretical understanding, complements the practical approach by providing the only guarantee of better methods in the future. Mental illness involves perception, memory, emotion, thinking; so does the attitude of hostility to other peoples. But we do not fully understand perception, memory and so on; thus anything that tells us more about these processes, whether it is a study of the eyeblink in man or a study of the mating habits of the rat, is a potential addition to our understanding of mental illness or the causes of social conflict . . . .

2 / Theories, Maps, and Models

Neil McK. Agnew and Sandra W. Pyke *York University*

It is doubtful whether the science of psychology would advance rapidly if it did not have theories to explain various phenomena. Theories are conceptual schemes which attempt to specify how different phenomena are related and how particular facts can be subsumed under more general principles. In this article, the authors discuss why theories are necessary and why they are so prevalent. In addition, they describe the characteristics of a "good" theory. Professors Agnew and Pyke are the authors of The Science Game *(1969) from which this article was taken.*

A theory, or a map, or a model is an abstraction, and abstractions involve representing the part of the world under examination by a model of similar but simpler structure. The important point is that theories are simpler than the data they are designed to represent. Theories are built (1) by squeezing some parts of experience together – all negroes, or all smokers, or all Southern Democrats – and (2) by ignoring or omitting some information, such as the differences that exist between negroes, or between different smokers, or between different Southern Democrats.

Why Bother With Theories?

No Other Choice

We propose that the most important reason for bothering with theories is that we have no alternative. We would have an alternative if we were like some wondrous computer that (1) saw, heard, and felt everything, (2) had a massive and unlimited memory file so we could store each bit of information separately and permanently, and (3) could draw at will from our memory file each bit of information and experience for examination. Obviously, we are not like this. We listen, look, and feel selectively. We also forget, condense, and distort the information we do have. We tie bits of information together in our heads that are not necessarily tied together in the world around us. We are, in fact, information screening, condensing, and relating machines. The end results of this process are theories or mental maps of what goes together and what leads to what. If it were otherwise, we would go crazy from the great avalanche of detailed bits of information and experience to which we are exposed both from the outside and from the inside.

You will recall that when the psychiatrist is faced with too much information or too many alternative suspects he develops biases or theories about what to look at and about what leads to what. Some psychiatrists focus on biochemical information and some on early training. The important point is that by focusing on certain types of information, by developing biases, and through forgetting, we reduce the avalanche of information and experience to manageable size.

Like the psychiatrist, the scientist and the citizen increasingly face information and opinion overload. Like the psychiatrist, we too must develop simplified pictures, stories, models, or theories of what goes together and what leads to what.

Through experience, training, and bias we group together certain people, objects, or events, at the same time ignoring many differences. We may group all negroes together. Even if we do it on the basis of colour, we must ignore the fact that many non-negroes are as dark as many negroes. We may go beyond simple classification and, on the basis of selective experience, bias, or training, conclude that negroes and low intelligence or laziness go together without considering the question of how many exceptions there are to this theory or picture. Others may say that low intelligence and laziness are strongly tied to early environment, ignoring the role which inheritance may play. We develop theories about women, men, communists, Democrats, Jews, WASPS, and Irishmen, the rich, the foreign, teachers, electrons, liquor and LSD. To the extent that we omit critical information, the results of our oversight or error come home to roost, causing us varying degrees of trouble. To the extent we can screen out information contrary to our theory or bias, we continue blithely on our way.

So we propose that the first reason for bothering with theories and maps, those simplified pictures or stories of our world, is that with the information-processing equipment and ability that is built into us, we have no other choice.

Simplify Decision Making

Another reason for bothering with theories, maps, hypotheses, or hunches, is that they simplify our decision making. This point is closely tied to the fact that we have no choice but to develop and act on theory because of the nature of the beast (who distorts, omits, rejects and selectively receives and com-

From Neil McK. Agnew and Sandra W. Pyke, *The Science Game: An Introduction to Research in the Behavioural Sciences*, © 1969. Reprinted by permission of the authors and of Prentice-Hall, Inc., Englewood Cliffs, New Jersey.

bines information) and the nature of the world around us (with the fantastic amount of information bombarding us each second).

All of us base many of our day-to-day decisions on hunches, points of view, biases, or theories that we have developed over the course of time. Some of us have the ability to formulate a point of view very quickly, particularly if we have little information about the issue. It is much easier to develop a theory if you are relatively ignorant about the area in question. As one national leader replied to a reporter, "I would have a ready solution if I didn't know so much about it."

In any case, there is no doubt that theories do simplify decision making by providing us with decision guidelines. These guidelines are generally in the nature of a reduction in the amount and kind of information we consider, and also in the number of possible alternative decisions we might formulate. In other words, the thousand and one potential decisions we might make on any question are reduced to one, two, or three merely because we have a theory which channels our thinking along certain lines and not others.

Theories Are Fascinating

A third reason for bothering with theories is that, for many people, theories are exciting to develop and discuss, regardless of whether the theory concerns why Cathy and Bill split up or why the stock market took an unpredicted and painful downward trend just after we made our purchases. Most of us, when faced with an unexpected event, have a strong desire to explain what caused the event or how it occurred. It's like a puzzle; we worry away at it until we've got some explanation that satisfies us. It's particularly gratifying if our theory is some dramatic or startling recombination and others can be swayed to accept our new interpretation.

Predicting the Future

A fourth reason for bothering with theories is our need to predict the future. We need to predict what will lead to what even when we lack necessary information. The predictions may range from attempting to decide which of three job offers likely gives you the best chance of promotion and development, to predicting the future effects of continued smoking or of air pollution.

Scientist and non-scientist all daily act on predictions. We use the weatherman's predictions to help us decide what to wear and whether to leave earlier because of predicted snow or sleet. We predict that the car will start, or if this prediction, much to our dismay, is not confirmed, we predict that the public transportation system will be operating, that the driver is sober, that the brakes are sound. We predict that the water supply is pure, the cook is clean, the judge is honest. We predict that in our absence our roommates will not die, and our apartment won't be burgled. Thus we're constantly operating on the basis of a variety of predictions of varying probability, often without recognizing it.

Rewards from the Scientific Community

Finally, theories are important for scientists because the academic and scientific communities offer a variety of rewards to people who build acceptable theories and who test them. The eminent men and those to whom the accolades of science are awarded are usually the theory builders.

In summary, we have theories, or simplified pictures of various parts of the world, because we have no choice. Second, we use them as decision making guides through a storm of information, opinion, and experience impinging on us from all directions. Third, for many, constructing stories about the past, present, and future is exciting. Fourth, theories about what is likely to happen assist us to move into the future with some confidence. Finally, the academic and scientific communities reward theory builders and testers.

In the final section of this chapter we will develop some yardsticks which can be used to help us evaluate the adequacy of a theory. Before doing that, however, we will briefly examine one way science can be viewed – as a love affair.

Building Models

Theory building becomes a game of building models, or pictures of the world. Some models are based on how we see the world through our own eyes, other models are based on how we see the world through an ordinary microscope. There are models based on how we see the world through an electron microscope, and models based on how we see the world through a telescope, or how we see the world through the eyes of a protestant biochemist, or how the world looks through the eyes of a Catholic gynecologist. Once a researcher or a theorist has stabilized a picture or a model, it usually requires a great deal of time, data, argument, and turmoil before he changes its superstructure. In other words, if the data coming in through his own research, or the research of others, does not fit his picture or model, he is more likely to question the adequacy of the data, or the competence of the researcher than he is to question the adequacy of his model or picture.

A Love Affair

Since any experiment is open to criticism, the theorist always has a way out in rejecting unwelcome data. The rejection of a theory once accepted is like the rejection of a girl friend once loved – it takes more than a bit of negative evidence. In fact, the rest of the community can shake their collective heads in amazement at your blindness, your utter failure to recognize the glaring array of differences between your picture of the world, or the girl, and the data.

You will perhaps find it easier to understand some of the excitement and despair in the world of science if you view research as a love affair between the investigator and his project. During the initial courting stage he is open to certain kinds of information. But as he invests more time, energy, and money in the courtship, he becomes almost hostile to any information threatening the relationship. Perhaps as the data comes in, he has private moments of uneasiness which he shares with no one – as he analyzes the data he may have moments of agony – but it takes more than one or two lovers' quarrels to break up a love affair, which is just as well. If it were otherwise there would be almost no marriages, just as there would be very few, if any, worthwhile results from research. Fly-by-night relationships in almost any field yield little that is memorable or of lasting interest.

We suspect there are those who would disagree violently with this love affair model of research. They will say that the researcher must be completely dedicated to objectivity, that he is only interested in the truth. Perhaps there are researchers like that. We haven't met enough to fill a phone booth. We have, however, met many researchers who can be brutally objective about someone else's research project, or someone else's girl, but not about their own.

But you are no doubt wondering what happens after a while – does the love affair model shift to the marriage model, Yes, we believe so. After working with a project for a long time we gain some objectivity and can accept some of the limitations and restrictions of our model. Many of us will still keep our serious family quarrels to ourselves. The very senior and established researcher can afford to joke in public about the possible limitations of his model, and speak philosophically about the relativity of truth in science. But if you are wise and humane, you'll no more join him in making fun of his model than you would join him in his very personal game of making pseudo-fun of himself, his wife, or his dog. As you know, making fun of something you love or cherish is one thing, having someone else do it is quite another.

Theory Evaluation

We proposed earlier that we bother with theories for a variety of reasons: (1) we have no choice in that we are theory-manufacturing or information-condensing organisms; (2) theories make decision making simpler; (3) theories are fascinating; (4) theories help us make predictions about the future; and (5) theory production and testing are rewarded by the academic and scientific establishments.

Therefore, while there seems to be a variety of reasons for bothering with theories, how are we to decide on the adequacy of one theory as opposed to another? Generally speaking, a theory is useful to the extent it provides us with acceptable information in a shorthand or economical way, that assists us in making decisions and approaching our goals, or at least appears to help us avoid frequent high cost errors.

More specifically, if we are comparing one theory with another, we can use the following guidelines: (1) Which theory is the simplest to learn and use? (2) Which theory is more readily open to test? (3) Which theory provides us with sufficiently relevant and precise information at each step in our decision making in dealing with the question at hand? (4) Which theory provides us with the most unique and original information, or allows us to predict the most new facts or solutions? (5) Which theory best fits with other accepted facts or theories? (6) Which theory is internally consistent, that is, doesn't contradict itself?

Simplicity

We like simple theories because they are easy to remember and to apply. Scotsmen are stingy, Englishmen are cold, negroes are lazy, Jews are pushy, Wasps are self-righteous, spare the rod and spoil the child, GM products are better than Ford products. While these theories or condensations are simple, they are obviously very imprecise; nevertheless, some are widely held. So, right or wrong, the simplicity yardstick is one of the most important. This is particularly so when, even though the theory is wrong, we personally don't suffer from its application. If, on the other hand, the application of an imprecise theory obviously does lead to our discomfort, we become interested in examining its relevance or its precision. Thus parents come to psychologists saying, "even though I've whaled the daylights out of him, he still misbehaves. In fact, he seems to be getting worse." Such people are then ready for a more precise and more complex theory. Such theories might state, "On some occasions some children respond better to reward than to punishment," and for a more detailed background of this theory we might even be prepared to invest in and study a book on child rearing. Or, if the problem at hand is buying a new car, we may, through bitter experience, be forced to subscribe to the theory that only on certain years are some GM models better than Ford models, and acquaint ourselves with the theories or condensations of such publications as Consumer Reports. Notice, then, that increased precision is usually purchased at the price of increased complexity in our theories. The general rule is: The more accurate we want to be, then usually the more complex the theory, and the more information we have to include in reaching our conclusion.

You can usually spot a simple theory by its emphasis on one or two bits of information: behaviour depends essentially on race, or behaviour depends essentially on early training, or behaviour depends essentially on biochemical factors, or behaviour depends essentially on punishment, or behaviour depends essentially on the institution that you are working for.

While any one of these one-cylinder theories may have some validity, the more precision we want in our solution, the more likely we will need to combine these one-cylinder theories into multi-cylinder theories; behaviour depends on intelligence, and on early training, and on genetics, and on biochemistry, and on work institution.

So we face the problem of reaching a balance between simplicity and precision. If we want to predict the developing behaviour of a child, we may have to combine the series of one-cylinder theories. If, however, we merely want to predict the behaviour of a particular bus driver (e.g., when he will come to our stop), we will usually be adequately accurate by consulting the bus schedule published by the institution that employs him. In most cases it would be irrelevant to worry about his intelligence, his early training, his genetics, and his biochemistry.

Therefore it is not a question of simplicity versus complexity, it is a question of whether a theory or condensation includes enough information to meet our needs or help us make a decision.

If we want to understand or predict complex human behaviour, then theories, of necessity, must be fairly complex because (a) people differ, (b) they learn, (c) their behaviour changes from one situation to another, and (d) they change with age. Therefore any time you encounter a theory about human behaviour which is based on the assumption of stability, you will realize that such a theory leaves out a great deal of information. Examples include theories about introverts and extroverts, depressives and non-depressives, laziness and activity, responsibility and irresponsibility, etc. The reason why these theories have some appeal is: (1) they are simple, and (2) there are a few people who fit them. But they leave out most people. Most people are sometimes extroverted and sometimes introverted, sometimes lazy and sometimes active, sometimes responsible and sometimes irresponsible, sometimes security-seeking and other times risk-taking. Therefore, the next time you hear a speaker describing a theory about human behaviour that divides people into a few simple classifications, you can bet that he is leaving out a great deal more than he is including, and that the major appeal of his theory is on the basis of simplicity.

Testability

While simplicity and personal appeal are two very important yardsticks in theory evaluation, the yardstick of testability is one which is presumably the most important used in science.

Think, for example, how you would go about testing the theory that negroes are less intelligent than whites. It would be a relatively simple matter if we wanted to test the theory that negroes are taller than whites. We could obtain a nonelastic ruler and measure a large, random sample of negroes and a large, random sample of whites. But intelligence tests are elastic rulers – the scores depend on (a) how the tests are administered and by whom, and (b) whether the people being tested and compared have been exposed to similar educational opportunities. Perhaps eventually some researchers will develop an acceptable test of intelligence that is as nonelastic as a tape measure, or at least not as elastic as the tests we now have, but, until better tests are available, the theory is relatively immune to test.

Similarly, if we wanted to test whether GM products are better than Ford products, we need a series of nonelastic yardsticks of what we mean by better, and then we need to measure a large number of different cars manufactured by the two companies. The reasons that make some theories difficult to test or evaluate include the following: (1) lack of nonelastic yardsticks; (2) inability to agree on which of the available yardsticks to use; (3) inability to measure a large, representative sample of the population we are theorizing about; and (4) citizens and scientists who refuse to change their minds even in the face of the new information. With some theories it is difficult to agree how they should be tested, and with others we are not prepared to invest the resources necessary to test them.

Novelty

Theories which lead to surprising or novel information are highly valued. Thus Theory A raises few eyebrows, stating, "Students will get higher marks if they do one hour's study a day for ten days rather than if they do ten hours a day for one day." Eyebrows shoot high, however, if the theory states, "Students will get higher marks if they are exposed to a tape recording of lecture notes for one hour a night while they sleep, for ten nights, than by spending one hour a day for ten days studying the same material." Of course, theories that lead to novel or surprising information are not necessarily readily accepted. Unless such theories lead to an overwhelming amount of evidence, or permit a large number of researchers to test them readily and obtain the same results, these new findings may languish for many years in obscure journals until more and more evidence accumulates, or until the biases and attitudes of a sufficiently large number of the population change so that the new information becomes acceptable.

Goodness of Fit with Other Facts and Theories

As we noted at the outset, a few new facts do not change a well-established theory or lead to the acceptance of a new theory. This is not so merely because some scientists are biased, but rather because we all use familiar theories to evaluate new information – to help us in our decision making. If we gave every new bit of information or theory careful consideration, we would be overloaded with work in ten seconds. For example, drug companies put hundreds of new drugs on the market each year, and only a few can be adequately evaluated merely because of the time and effort required. Furthermore, thousands of research studies are published each year, but only relatively few are repeated by other investigators. Most investigators are busy preparing to publish their own research.

There is no simple solution to this problem other than using our own personally accepted theories, or small modifications of them, as guidelines in helping us decide what we will read and examine carefully.

Internal Consistency

Another way of classifying or evaluating theories is to assess the internal consistency of the theory. This is perhaps one of the minimum conditions a theory must fulfill if it is to be seriously considered. A theory which contradicts itself on any specific question proves embarrassing at times, even though, taken separately, each part is acceptable. Consider the following examples: (1) He who hesitates is lost, and fools rush in where wise men fear to tread; (2) "Colonel Cathcart was conceited because he was a full colonel with a combat command at the age of only thirty-six; and Colonel Cathcart was dejected because although he was already thirty-six he was still only a full colonel."[1]

There are contradictions in the above examples and with such contradictions the theory provides no overall guidelines to aid us in predicting or in making decisions. According to theory (1) we should both buy and not buy the speculative stock, and according to theory (2) we really can't predict whether Colonel Cathcart is happy or dejected. Until we have more information about the conditions surrounding lost opportunity because of hesitation, we can't use theory (1) effectively.

Scientific or philosophical theories, as a rule, do not have such gross or obvious inconsistencies; however, often inconsistencies exist and are fair game for long arguments.

Understanding and Prediction

You will no doubt have heard that the purpose of theories is to help us both understand certain parts of our world and make predictions leading to new information and new solutions.

Understanding is a difficult term to define. Perhaps one of the most common meanings of the term "understanding" is that we develop, sometimes with the help of others, a more satisfying picture of some part of the world. For example, we may ask, "What's University like?" The reply may be, "University is like high school except that no one cares if you come to class, and in most classes you don't get any comments on the work you hand in." Or you may ask, "Why is Harry so cranky?" And you may get the reply, "He had a fight with his girl friend." Typically you will respond, "Oh, I understand." You understand because you can now combine some bits of information that you already have in a new way – you now feel you have a better picture to go on. Our point is that understanding may give you a more acceptable picture about a part of the world, but, nevertheless, that picture may be quite erroneous. Unfortunately, you can walk away feeling you understand from a wide variety of different replies to the same question. It is proposed then that the term "understand" implies a personally-acceptable picture of what goes together or what leads to what, but need not imply an accurate picture. The accuracy is subsequently, if ever, determined by more direct personal experience or by more accurate additional data from another source.

The term "prediction," on the other hand, if stated in testable form, is a more scientifically useful concept. Theories that enable us to understand are personally useful, while theories that enable us to predict are both personally and scientifically useful.

This does not mean that the term "understand" cannot be redefined to include tests of the adequacy of the information; it is merely that the term, as commonly used, does not usually imply such tests whereas the term "predict" more frequently does. Therefore, we propose that theories that predict new information should be ranked more highly than those which lead to understanding, as defined above.

We have stressed the importance of the testability of a theory. Testing a theory can be done in several ways. A theoretician may make a specific prediction growing out of his theory and may state his theory in a testable form which we then subsequently test and support or refute; or he can do an experiment growing out of his theory, and we can attempt to repeat his experiment. Replication in science is probably the foundation of testability, but, as noted earlier, we prefer the concepts of exportability or perishability of data to that of replicability.

Summarizing, we are more and more inclined to view theories as decision-making aids, perhaps not as whimsical as the toss of a coin, nor as crude as a race tout's tip, but decision aids, nonetheless. In the face of ignorance, but forced to act, we build theories – these simplified and crudely drawn maps of the past, present, and future – that give us some semblance of confidence as we race or stagger through life's great maze of alternatives. Are theories true or false? No one knows, since most theories are designed to cover mammoth areas or massive populations, and yet we can usually explore in detail only a tiny corner or a few instances. Thus whether a theory is true or false is anybody's guess, whereas everybody knows that a decision aid is worthy if it helps you make even one decision that is not immediately followed by a disaster.

---

[1] Joseph Heller, *Catch-22* (New York: Dell, 1955), p. 192. Copyright © 1961 by Joseph Heller.

TWO
HEREDITY AND ENVIRONMENT: EARLY EXPERIENCE

3 / Heredity and Environment in Mammalian Behaviour[1]

D.O. Hebb *McGill University*

The relationship between heredity and environment in the development of behaviour is one of the important theoretical issues in psychology. In addition, it is of considerable practical importance to know to what degree behaviour can be modified by altering or manipulating the environment. In this penetrating discussion, Professor Hebb helps to clarify some of the complex problems involved.

A persistent theme in the study of behaviour, one that has dominated psychological thought since Locke and Leibnitz at least, has been the question: What is inborn, what acquired? Is the mind *tabula rasa*? If there are no innate ideas, is there not some framework prior to all experience into which experience is received and by which it must be shaped? Is intelligence inherited, or in what proportion? And so with schizophrenia, visual form and depth, maternal behaviour, gregariousness, pugnacity, even spinal reflex – there is no aspect of behaviour with which this debate has not been concerned at one time or another.

So far as I can now see, even to ask the question, in the form in which it is usually asked, is a symptom of confusion; a confusion, it may be added, to which I have myself contributed as handsomely as I was able. My suspicion is that I am still confused, but I hope that with your criticism and discussion we may jointly make some progress in clarification of the ideas involved, not being concerned if a final agreement among us this afternoon is too much to ask.

In view of what is to follow, it should be said that here my bias is on the nativistic[2] side. If a choice had to be made, I would support – as I have in fact supported – Hobhouse and Kohler against Thorndike and Holt, Lashley against Watson, Kallman against Alexander, as a corrective against the common overemphasis by psychologists and psychiatrists on experience and learning in behaviour. This is what I would be inclined still to do, if I had to choose sides; but the fact is that we have no such choice.

We cannot dichotomize mammalian behaviour into learned and unlearned, and parcel out these acts and propensities to the nativist, those to the empiricist. My first example is from Dennis (1940): "Rage . . . is unlearned in this sense, that when the child has developed a purposive sequence of behaviour which can be interefered with, he will exhibit 'rage' on the first occasion on which this interference occurs." The behaviour is unlearned; but it is not possible without the learning required for the development of purposive behaviour. Again, the first time a chimpanzee baby of a certain age sees a stranger approach he is terrified. The reaction is strongest on the first occasion, it does not have to be practised, and we must say that the shyness is not learned: but it is definitely a product of learning, in part, for it does not occur until the chimpanzee has learned to recognize his usual caretakers. The shyness or fear of strangers appears at about four months of age, or six months in the human baby. The chimpanzee reared in darkness to an age at which the fear is normally at its peak is not disturbed by his first sight of a stranger, but is disturbed by it as soon as he has had sufficient opportunity to learn to recognize those who care for him daily.

Fear of strangers, therefore, or a temper tantrum is not learned and yet is fully dependent on other learning. Do we then postulate three categories of behaviour, (1) unlearned, (2) unlearned but dependent on learning, (3) learned? Perhaps instead we had better re-examine the conception of unlearned versus learned behaviour.

The two examples given are not isolated phenomena. The neurotic disturbances in dog, cat, sheep or goat described first by Pavlov (1928), and studied further by Gantt (1944), Liddell (1938), and Masserman (1943), depend on a conflict between learned modes of response and yet the breakdown itself is clearly not learned. Insight in the chimpanzee, as Kohler (1927) showed, is the occurrence of an unlearned solution to a problem; but Birch (1945) has shown that other experience must precede. I shall not multiply examples, but can refer you here to the finding that mammalian perceptions in general appear to depend, not on formal training, it is true, but on a prolonged period of patterned sensory stimulation (Senden, 1932; Riesen, 1947, 1950, 1951; Nissen, Chow and Semmes, 1951). A paper of my own is on record to the contrary (Hebb, 1937), a clear

---

[1] This is the substance of an address to the Association for the Study of Animal Behaviour, London, May 14th, 1952. The address was made from notes only, not a written text, and in some minor respects the present paper may deviate from what was said at the meeting.

[2] This term may need explanation. The repeated denial that Gestalt psychology is nativistic is unintelligible to me, in view of the powerful Gestalt criticism of empiricistic treatments of perception and intelligence unless "nativism" is considered to have its 19th Century meaning of innate ideas, so it should be noted that my use of the term implies only an opposition to extreme empiricism, or an emphasis on the obvious importance of hereditary factors in behaviour.

Reprinted by permission of the author and publisher from the *British Journal of Animal Behaviour*, 1953, *1*, 43-47.

case of a biased failure to observe, since the same paper included data whose significance I did not see until certain physiological considerations had suggested another point of view (Hebb, 1949, pp. 42, 113). All that a mammal does is fundamentally dependent on his perception, past or present, and this means that there is no behaviour, beyond the level of the reflex, that is not essentially dependent on learning.

It is equally clear that no behaviour can be independent of an animal's heredity: this is so obvious, logically, that it need not be spelt out. Our conclusion then is, that all behaviour is dependent both on heredity and on environment, and all non-reflex behaviour at least involves the special effects of environmental stimulation that we call learning.

Assuming that this is conceded, however, the question may still be asked, to what extent a given piece of behaviour is dependent on one of these influences. Is it fifty-per-cent environment, fifty-per-cent heredity, or ninety to ten, or what are the proportions? This is exactly like asking how much of the area of a field is due to its length, how much to its width. The only reasonable answer is that the two proportions are one-hundred-per-cent environment, one-hundred-per-cent heredity. They are not additive; any bit of behaviour whatever is *fully* dependent on each. What proportion of an animal's behaviour would be left if there had not been, since the moment of fertilization, the highly specialized environment necessary for the growth of the embryo; or what basis is there for thinking of this environment as not causal, but only permissive, in determining the direction of embryonic growth? The newborn mammal is "caused" by a uterine environment acting on a fertilized ovum. Contrariwise, without the fertilized ovum and its special properties no behaviour can result; learned behaviour, further, can never be thought of as something apart from the heredity that made possible a particular kind of sensory structure and nervous system.

The last alternative is to ask how much of the *variance* of behaviour is determined by heredity, how much by the environment. This is a meaningful and useful question, capable of an intelligent answer, but the limits of meaning of the answer must be recognized. If for example by inbreeding we produce a strain of dogs in which heredity is constant and all the variance of behaviour can be attributed to environment, we have not in any way reduced the importance of heredity for the behaviour in question. In other words, such an "analysis of variance" cannot be translated into a statement of causal relations for the individual animal. This is seen best if we classify one of our hypothetical inbred dogs in two ways: (a) as above, treat the animal statistically as one of a group with common heredity but different environments, and (b) as one of a group reared precisely as that one animal was, but with varying heredities (this latter set of conditions might be achieved, including a common uterine environment, by mating a group of inbred bitches to males of diverse breeds). If the proportionate variance is regarded as an estimate of the relative importance of heredity and environment for the individual animal's behaviour, then we should have to conclude (a) that environment is the only important determinant, and (b) that hereditary is the only important determinant, for the same dog's behaviour. If again, eighty per cent of the variance of neuroticism in a particular district of London is due to variations of heredity (Eysenck and Prell, 1951), this does not make environment less important than heredity for the behaviour in question. It may mean only that the relevant environmental influences are much the same throughout that district, and it does not preclude finding another sample of human beings with more similar heredity and less similar experiences, such that the degree of neuroticism varies with environment rather than heredity.

Analysis of variance, in the present sense, is an excellent tool for studying the interaction of heredity and environment, but entirely misleading if it is interpreted as isolating things that are inherited and things that are acquired. We are on solid ground if we think consistently of all behaviour as "caused by" or fully dependent on both environment and heredity, and cast our research in the form of asking how they interact: for each given heredity, asking over what range behaviour can vary, and how it can be manipulated by control of the environment (not only the postnatal environment); or what different heredities will permit survival in each given environment, and how behaviour is correlated with them. To misuse another term of the statisticians', what we want is an analysis of covariance rather than analysis of one variable while forgetting the other.

Here the significance of the theoretical analysis by Haldane (1946) is plain. We cannot generalize freely from one small part of either continuum, hereditary or environmental. The heredity that is "good" in one part of the environmental range may be poor in another, as in Haldane's example of the beef-producing qualities of Aberdeen Angus and Galloway cattle in favourable and unfavourable environments. In the parallel case of man's intelligence and mental health, the heredity that gives best results in an optimal environment may give the worst in a poor one. We can say nothing about such possibilities (obviously of first significance for ideas about eugenics) on the basis of data obtained in a naturalistic study, with a limited sample of heredities and a limited range of environmental variation. The necessary experiments being impossible with man, we clearly need systematic animal studies in which for any given species the widest range of genetic variation is studied over the widest sample of feasible environments, from which for the mental health problem, we must cautiously extrapolate to man.

In all this, of course, we are really dealing with the question of instinct. I am considerably indebted in my discussion to a recent address by Professor Frank Beach, entitled "The De-Scent of Instinct," in which he recants his earlier view that instinct is a scientifically useful conception. Whether his conclusions are accepted or not, some of his points must be reckoned with.

Much of Beach's emphasis is on the consistently negative definition of instinct or instinctive behaviour: instinctive behaviour is what is not learned, or not determined by the environment, and so on. There must be great doubt about the unity of the factors that are identified only by exclusion. There is also a common tendency to identify unlearned with genetically-determined behaviour, and Beach points out that the chemical environment of the mammalian embryo, and nutritive influences on the invertebrate larva, are factors in behaviour which do not fall either under the heading of learning or under that of genetic determinants. (One might cite here the significance of the "royal jelly" in the development of the queen bee, or the fact that the temperature at which the fruit-fly larva is kept determines bodily characteristics such as the number of legs, a feature which of course must affect behaviour). If thus "instinctive" is to be equated with "unlearned," it cannot also be equated with "genetic." Very often when behaviour is attributed to purely genetic determinants no real experimental control of environmental influence has been made; and very often learning is excluded simply on the ground that no obvious opportunity for it was observed by the experimenter.

Let us look at this last point more closely. The crucial but implicit assumption has always been made in the study of instinct that we know what learning is and how it operates. The notion is that learning, if relevant to the instinctive act, is the practice of that act or a closely related one – at the very least, observation of the act by another animal. If therefore there has been no opportunity for such observation, and no practice, and the act is performed effectively when the proper circumstances come along, we say that the behaviour is unlearned and thus instinctive. But, as I have already tried to show, to say that behaviour is unlearned does not mean that it is independent of learning.

For our present purposes, I shall use "learning" to refer to a stable unidirectional change of neural function, resulting from sensory stimulation (including the stimulation that results from response). There is a great deal that we do not know about learning, and we cannot assume that we know what conditions determine it. The occurrence of learning may be far from obvious. There is a great deal of visual learning, in the sense of my definition, in the period when the young mammal first opens its eyes on the world, though nothing but physical growth seems to be going on, and the fact of learning can only be discovered by comparing the normal infant with one reared without pattern vision. The experiment of Nissen, Chow and Semmes (1951) makes the same point concerning somesthetic learning, in the period when the baby seems only to be thrashing about aimlessly. This experiment is very important as showing that the importance of early learning demonstrated by Senden (1932) and Riesen (1947, 1950, 1951) is not restricted to visual function. What Nissen, Chow and Semmes did was to raise an infant chimpanzee with cardboard mailing-tubes over hands and feet, thus preventing normal tactual exploration of the environment and of the chimpanzee's own body. Subsequently, somesthetic learning and localization of tactual stimulation of various points on the body were defective. The conditions of rearing could hardly produce any failure of development in primary sensory equipment of the skin, so it appears that the more or less random tactual experience of the normally reared infant is essential to the development of somesthetic perception.

Such early visual and somesthetic learning must modify all subsequent behaviour; and there are strong indications that this does not apply only to "higher" behaviour but to instinctive and even to reflexive responses as well. The supposedly instinctive grooming of the chimpanzee was not found in Nissen, Chow and Semmes' animal, and responses to pain stimuli, usually considered reflexive, were atypical. The preliminary experiments of Riess and of Birch (cited by Beach, 1951, p. 424) on the relation of early experience to maternal behaviour in rats, Lorenz's studies of imprinting in birds and Thorpe's studies of early environmental influences on the subsequent behaviour of both birds and insects, all imply that the behaviour that ordinarily is "species-predictable," and independent of special experience, is not independent of the experience that is ordinarily inevitable for all members of the species. It has appeared to me in the past that instinctive behaviour, especially in nonmammals, is correlated closely with unvarying genetic factors and not with the varying environment. But is this true? Is the environment so completely variable? It seems to me now that certain essentials of the environment are actually constant – just as constant as the animal's heredity; and therefore that we have no logical basis for giving the one correlation, that with heredity, any greater emphasis than the other correlation, with environment.

I propose consequently that we must study both variables together, in the nonmammalian world as well as the mammalian. My difficulty with the ethological program as laid out by Tinbergen, in terms of first studying the innate before studying learning, is that it is logically impossible. "Innate behaviour is behaviour that has not been changed by learning processes" (Tinbergen, 1951, p.2) and we must know when and where learning occurs before we can say what this behaviour is; just as the "learning theorist" must know what growth processes do to behaviour before he can certainly say what learning does in the growing infant. Evidently we cannot separate the two tasks; they must be carried out together.

It seems to me therefore that the ethologist is in fact studying learning perhaps without always intending to do so, just as the psychologist who works out the rules of learning for the laboratory rat is, again perhaps without intending it, really defining the hereditary potential of this animal's behaviour. Psychologists need the co-operation of the ethologists with their biological background and their demonstrated brilliance in experimental analysis. Psychology in North America has often been narrow, short-sighted, in its emphasis on one factor in behaviour: I should like to urge that ethology should not vie in narrowness, in another direction. Actually, North American psychologists, like their colleagues in England and elsewhere, are now generally alive to the great significance of your ethological studies (although as one might expect there are differences of opinion when it comes to interpretation) and it seems if our lines of communication can be kept open that there are great scientific benefits to be had, in the recognition that in the study of certain variabilities in behaviour (learning) and in the study of certain constancies of behaviour (instinct) it is the same problem that is being attacked. After all, ethology, defined as the scientific study of behaviour (Tinbergen, 1951), is coterminous with psychology, which has the same definition.

Much of the apparent disagreement between the two disciplines is in matters of terminology, in verbal statements of problem or conclusions, so I shall sum up my remarks by returning to this question: what sort of statement can be usefully and logically made about the relationship between environment or heredity, on the one hand, and behaviour on the other?

I would not suggest for a moment that the problems in this area are unreal; I do suggest that they have been poorly stated, inasmuch as we cannot dichotomize behaviour into learned and unlearned, environmentally determined and hereditarily determined. I urge that there are not two kinds of control of behaviour, and that the term "instinct," implying a mechanism or neural process independent of environmental factors, and distinct from the neural processes into which learning enters, is a completely misleading term and should be abandoned. "Instinctive behaviour" may be nearly as misleading, but it might be kept as a convenient designation for species-predictable behaviour, as long as it is thought of, not as determined by an invariant heredity alone, but also by an environment that is equally invariant in most or all important matters. Instinctive behaviour therefore is not valid as an analytical conception, though it may be useful as a rough descriptive term.

However, it is not enough to make destructive criticism alone, especially in a field where it is clear that important theoretical issues are involved. However well or ill-conceived the term instinct may be, or how well-framed the traditional question of environmental or hereditary control of behaviour, there is something here that we must deal with theoretically and about which we must be able to make positive statements.

In distinguishing hereditary from environmental influence, therefore, I conclude that it is reasonable and intelligible to say that a difference in behaviour from a group norm, or between two individuals, is caused by a difference of heredity, or a difference of environment; but not that the deviant behaviour is caused by heredity or environment alone. The fact that we speak English *instead* of French is determined by environment alone; but speaking English is not caused by environment independent of heredity, for no environment can make a dog or cat (or chimpanzee) speak either language, English or French. Making the reference to a difference or deviation really implies, *With environment held constant*, heredity has such and such effects (or vice versa, with heredity constant); it does not say that the behaviour is due to heredity alone. If this is correct, we can also quite accurately speak of the variance due to environment or heredity: variance again being a reference to deviations. We will, I believe, not only pay a proper respect to logic but also plan our experiments better if we speak and think of the effect that environmental influence has on a given heredity, or, in dealing with the differences between heredities, specify the environment in which they are manifested. The behaviour one can actually observe and experiment with is an inextricable tangle of the two influences, and one of them is nothing without the other.

References

BEACH, F. A. Instinctive behaviour: reproductive activities. Chapter 12 in S. S. Stevens (ed.), *Handbook of experimental psychology*. New York: Wiley, 1951. Pp. 387-434.

BIRCH, H. G. (1945). The relation of previous experience to insightful problem-solving. *J. Comp. Psychol., 38,* 367-383.

DENNIS, W. (1940). Infant reaction to restraint: an evaluation of Watson's theory. *Trans. N.Y. Acad. Sci.,* Ser. 2., 2, 202-218.

EYSENCK, H. J., and PRELL, D. B. (1951). The inheritance of neuroticism: an experimental study. *J. Ment. Sci., 97,* 441-465.

GANTT, W. H. (1944). Experimental basis for neurotic behaviour: origin and development of artificially produced disturbances of behaviour in dogs. *Psychosom. Med. Monog., 3,* Nos. 3 and 4.

HALDANE, J. B. S. (1946). The interaction of nature and nurture. *Ann. Eugen., 13,* 197-205.

HEBB, D. O. (1937). The innate organization of visual activity: I. Perception of figures by rats reared in total darkness. *J. Genet. Psychol., 51.* 101-126.

(1949). *Organization of behaviour*. New York: Wiley.

KOHLER, W. (1927). *The mentality of apes.* (2nd Ed.), New York: Harcourt, Brace.

LIDDELL, H. S. (1938). The experimental neurosis and the problem of mental disorder. *Amer. J. Psychiat., 94,* 1035-1043.

MASSERMAN, J. H. (1943). *Behaviour and neurosis.* Chicago: Univ. Chicago Press.

NISSEN, H. W., CHOW, K. L., and SEMMES, Josephine. (1951). Effects of restricted opportunity for tactual, kinesthetic, and manipulative experience on the behaviour of a chimpanzee. *Amer. J. Psychol. 64*, 485-507.

PAVLOV, I. P. (1928). *Lectures on conditioned reflexes*. New York: International.

RIESEN, A. H. (1947). The development of visual perception in man and chimpanzee. *Science, 106*, 107-108. (1950). Arrested vision. *Scient. Amer., 183*, 16-19. (1951). Post-partum development of behaviour. *Chicago Med. Sch. Quart., 13*, 17-24.

SENDEN, M. V. (1932). *Raum- und Gestultffassung bei operierten Blindegeborenen vor und nach der Operation*. Leipzig: Barth.

TINBERGEN, N. (1951). *The Study of Instinct*. Oxford: Oxford Univ. Press.

4 / Effects of Enriched and Restricted Early Environments on the Learning Ability of Bright and Dull Rats[1]

R.M. Cooper and John P. Zubek *University of Manitoba*

The preceding paper indicated that all behaviour is dependent both on heredity and on environment. This interdependence of genetic and environmental factors is clearly demonstrated in the paper which follows in which the heritability of maze learning ability is shown to be influenced by two different types of rearing conditions.

Several recent surveys of the literature (2, 3, 4, 9) reflect the increased emphasis being placed upon study of the relationship between early environment and later behaviour in animals. Learning ability has received particular attention, and several studies have shown that the learning ability of adult animals is affected by the quality of their infant environment. More specifically, they indicate that animals raised in "enriched" or "stimulating" environments are superior in adult learning ability to animals raised in "restricted" or "unstimulating" environments.

These results were obtained with animals possessing a *normal* heritage of learning ability; hence there remains the possibility of differential effects for animals of superior or inferior endowment. The present study was designed to explore this possibility. Its specific object was to test for possible differential effects of enriched and restricted early environments on the problem-solving ability of bright and of dull rats.

Method

Subjects

Forty-three rats of the McGill bright and dull strains (F_{13}) served as subjects. They were divided into 4 experimental groups: a bright-enriched group containing 12 rats (6 males, 6 females); a dull-enriched group containing 9 rats (4 males, 5 females); a bright-restricted group containing 13 rats (6 males, 7 females); and a dull-restricted group containing 9 rats (4 males, 5 females). Normally reared rats served as controls.

Environments

The 4 groups of experimental animals were placed in 4 cages which occupied a grey painted room 12′ x 6′ x 8′. At one end of the room a window allowed diffuse light to pass through. A large rectangular partition, suspended from the ceiling, divided the room lengthways. The two restricted cages were placed on one side of the partition, the two enriched cages on the other side. The side of the partition facing the restricted cages was grey, matching the colour of the room. The side of the partition facing the enriched cages was white with "modernistic" designs painted upon it in black and luminous paint. The partition was so placed that animals in the restricted environment were unable to see the enriched cages.

The 4 cages, each measuring 40″ x 25″ x 13″, were covered with ½-inch wire mesh. Each of the enriched cages contained the following objects: ramps, mirrors, swings, polished balls, marbles, barriers, slides, tunnels, bells, teeter-totters, and springboards, in addition to food boxes and water pans. Some of the objects were painted black and white, and all were constructed so that they could easily be shifted to new positions in the cage. The restricted cages were identical with the enriched ones in size and mesh coverings, but contained only a food box and a water pan.

Test Apparatus

The 12 problems of the Hebb-Williams closed field maze were administered in the manner described by Rabinovitch and Rosvold (8).

Procedure

The 4 groups of animals were kept in their respective environments from the time of weaning at 25 days of age until the age of 65 days, when testing on the Hebb-Williams maze was begun. They were also kept there throughout the testing period.

Since one of the restricted and one of the enriched cages received more light than the other did from the window, the animals were shifted every three days to equate for this difference. In addition, the objects in each of the enriched cages were moved about at random every three or four days. During these moving periods and while the cages were being cleaned all animals were given the same amount of handling.

[1] This research was supported by a grant in aid from the Associate Committee on Applied Psychology of the National Research Council of Canada. The writers wish to acknowledge their indebtedness to Dr. D. O. Hebb for his critical reading of the manuscript.

Reprinted, by permission, from the *Canadian Journal of Psychology*, 1958, *12*, 159-164.

Results

For purposes of statistical analysis and interpretation of the data the performances of the enriched and restricted animals were compared with the performances of 11 bright and 11 dull animals raised in a "normal" laboratory environment. These were the animals that formed two control groups in an experiment by Hughes and Zubek (6).

Effect of the Enriched Environment

In Table I are recorded the mean error scores for the bright-enriched group, the dull-enriched group, and the bright and dull animals raised in a normal environment. It can be seen that the average number of errors made by the bright animals in the enriched environment is only slightly below that of the bright animals raised under normal conditions (111.2 *vs.* 117.0). This difference is not statistically significant (t = 0.715, $p > .4$). On the other hand, the error scores of the dull animals raised in an enriched environment are considerably below those of dull animals reared in a normal environment (119.7 *vs.* 164.0). This difference of 44.3 errors is significant ($t = 2.52$, $p > .02 < .05$). The results indicate, therefore, that an enriched early environment can improve considerably the learning ability of dull animals, while having little or no effect on that of bright animals.

Table I – Mean error scores for bright and dull animals reared in enriched and normal environments

	Enriched environment	Normal environment
Bright	111.2	117.0
Dull	119.7	164.0

Effect of the Restricted Environment

Table II shows the mean error scores of the bright-restricted group, the dull-restricted group, and the bright and dull animals raised in a normal environment. It is seen that the bright-restricted group made many more errors than the normally raised bright animals. The difference of 52.7 errors is statistically significant (t = 4.06, $p < .001$). On the other hand there is no significant difference between the dull-restricted group and the normally raised dull animals (t = 0.280, $p > .7$). Thus the dull animals were not affected by their restricted early experience while the bright animals were significantly impaired in learning ability.

Comparative Effects of Enriched and Restricted Environments

Tables I and II also indicate the degree of improvement produced in the dull animals by their period of enriched experience, and the degree of retardation which the bright animals suffered because of their impoverished experience. Although the dull-enriched group averaged 8.5 more errors than did the bright-enriched, this difference is not significant (t = .819, $p > .5$). In other words, after undergoing a period of enriched experience the dull animals became equal in learning ability to the bright animals. The difference between the bright- and dull-restricted groups in Table II is also obviously insignificant; thus, the bright animals, after a period of early impoverished experience, showed no better learning ability than did the dull animals.

Table II – Mean error scores for bright and dull animals reared in restricted and normal environments

	Restricted environment	Normal environment
Bright	169.7	117.0
Dull	169.5	164.0

Discussion

The results clearly show that both enriched and restricted early environments have differential effects on the learning abilities of bright and of dull rats. A period of early enriched experience produces little or no improvement in the learning ability of bright animals, whereas dull animals are so benefited by it that they become equal to bright animals. On the other hand, dull animals raised in a restricted environment suffer no deleterious effects, while bright animals are retarded to the level of the dulls in learning ability.

Although it had been anticipated that the two extremes of environment would have differential effects on the bright and dull animals, the bright-enriched animals were still expected to perform better than the dull-enriched animals. Bright animals, with their presumably better cerebral functioning, would be expected to make better use of the extra experience afforded by an enriched environment than would dull animals, with their presumably inferior cerebral functioning. The bright-enriched group did in fact make fewer errors, and the difference, though not statistically significant, suggests the possibility of a real difference in learning ability which the twelve problems of the Hebb-Williams test failed to reveal. The ceiling of the test may have been too low to differentiate the animals, that is, the problems may not have been sufficiently difficult to tax the ability of the bright rats. This has happened with tests of human intelligence such as the Standford-Binet (1), on which adults of varying ability may achieve similar I.Q. scores although more difficult tests reveal clear differences between them. It might also be suggested that it is relatively more difficult for the bright animals to reduce their error scores, say from 120 to 100, than for the dull animals to reduce theirs from 160 to 140.

In spite of these possible qualifications of the present results for the enriched environment, it seems reasonable to accept them pending future experimentation.

The effects of the restricted environment are not so difficult to accept. Under such conditions the bright animals, even with their superior learning capacity, would be expected to show an inferior performance. Learning is a function of experience as well as of capacity, and hence, under conditions that severely limit experience, the superior capacity of the bright animals is never fully utilized and they perform far below their potential level. On the other hand, not much decrement would be expected in the dull animals, since they are already functioning at a low level of intellectual capacity.

What physiological mechanism or mechanisms underlie these changes in learning ability? Several theories have attempted to explain the relationship between sensory stimulation and learning behaviour, perhaps the most systematic being that of Hebb (5). Hebb has suggested that neural patterns or "cell assemblies," which he regards as the physiological basis of learned behaviour, are built up over a period of time through varied stimulation coming through specific sensory pathways. This stimulation is especially effective if it occurs during infancy. Others (7, 9) also believe that varied stimulation coming through non-specific projection pathways (e.g., the thalamic-reticular system) aids in the learning process by keeping the brain in an alert state. Thus at the neurophysiological level varied stimulation seems to play a dual role in the learning process; it may act directly on cerebral cells to form cell assemblies, and may also aid learning by keeping the brain "primed" or alert.

If, then, varied stimulation has such an important role in establishing the physiological components (e.g., cell assemblies) underlying learned behaviour, it seems reasonable to assume that a certain level of varied stimulation is necessary if learning (i.e., establishment of cell assemblies) is to occur with maximum efficiency. It may also be assumed that the initial difference in learning ability between the bright and dull rats in some way reflects an underlying neurophysiological difference in their capacity to "utilize" such stimulation. On the basis of these assumptions the present findings might be explained as follows.

In a *normal* environment the level of stimulation is sufficient to permit the building up of cell assemblies (or some other neurophysiological unit underlying learned behaviour) in the superior brains of the bright animals. It is not sufficient, however, to permit them to be readily built up in the inferior brains of the dull animals. In a *restricted* environment the level of stimulation is so low that it is inadequate for the building up of cell assemblies even with the superior cerebral apparatus of the bright rats, who therefore show a retardation in learning ability. The dulls, however, are not retarded further, since the level of stimulation provided by the normal environment was already below their threshold for the establishment of cell assemblies. In the *enriched* environment the level of stimulation is above the higher threshold of the dull animals, who consequently show improvement in learning ability. The brights show little or no improvement because the extra stimulation is largely superfluous, that provided by a normal environment being adequate for the building up of cell assemblies.

Such an interpretation is open to several criticisms. For instance, the assumption that bright and dull rats differ in their inherited capacity to utilize stimulation is open to question. Furthermore, as pointed out above, possible inadequacies of the Hebb-Williams test may throw doubt on the findings for the bright-enriched rats. Nonetheless, although this theoretical interpretation obviously needs a more adequate foundation, it seems best fitted to account for the experimental data in the light of present neurophysiological knowledge.

Summary

Forty-three rats of the McGill bright and dull strains were used as experimental subjects in an investigation of possible differential effects of enriched and restricted early environments on learning ability.

At 25 days of age, 12 bright rats and 9 dull rats were placed in enriched environments, and 13 brights and 9 dulls were placed in restricted environments. At 65 days of age all animals were introduced to the training and testing procedures of the Hebb-Williams maze, their performances being compared with those of normally reared bright and dull controls.

The bright animals reared in enriched environments showed no improvement in learning ability over bright controls reared under normal laboratory conditions. The dull animals, on the other hand, benefited greatly from the enriched experience and attained a level of performance equal to that of the bright animals. Rearing in restricted environments had converse effects. The dull animals suffered no impairment as compared with dull controls, while the bright animals were retarded to the level of the dulls in learning performance.

Possible neurophysiological explanations are suggested.

References

1. ANASTASI, ANNE. *Psychological testing.* New York: Macmillan, 1954.
2. BEACH, F. A., and JAYNES, J. Effects of early experience upon the behaviour of animals. *Psychol. Bull.,* 1954, *51,* 239-263.
3. BINDRA, D. Comparative psychology. In *Ann. Rev. Psychol.* Palo Alto, Calif.: Annual Reviews Inc., 1957, *8,* 399-414.
4. DREVER, J. The concept of early learning. *Trans. New York Acad. Sci.,* 1955, *17,* 463-469.

5. HEBB, D. O. *The organization of behaviour.* New York: Wiley, 1949.
6. HUGHES, K. R., and ZUBEK, J. P. Effect of glutamic acid on the learning ability of bright and dull rats. I. Administration during infancy. *Canad. J. Psychol.,* 1956, *10,* 132-138.
7. MILNER, P. M. The cell assembly: Mark II. *Psychol. Rev.,* 1957, *64,* 242-252.
8. RABINOVITCH, M. S., and ROSVOLD, H. E. A closed field intelligence test for rats. *Canad. J. Psychol.,* 1951, *5,* 122-128.
9. THOMPSON, W. R. Early environment — its importance for later behaviour. Chap. 8 in P. H. HOCH, and J. ZUBIN (eds.), *Psychopathology of children.* New York: Grune & Stratton, 1955.

5 / Effect of Differential Rearing on Photic Evoked Potentials and Brightness Discrimination in the Albino Rat

H.P. Edwards, W.F. Barry, and J.O. Wyspianski *University of Ottawa*

In the preceding experiment, it was shown that rearing animals in either an enriched or a restricted environment can affect their subsequent learning ability. The present article demonstrates that these differential rearing conditions are reflected in measurable changes in the functioning of the central nervous system. Note the relationship of these findings to the results reported in article 70.

When animals whose early experience is impoverished are compared with those whose early experience has been enriched, the former are generally found to be inferior problem-solvers (Forgays and Forgays, 1952; Fuller, 1967; Brown, 1968; Denenberg, Woodcock and Rosenberg, 1968), to explore more and be more easily aroused both behaviourally and physiologically in the presence of novel stimuli (Zimbardo and Montgomery, 1957; Woods, Ruckelhaus, and Bowling, 1960; Melzak, 1962; Melzak and Burns, 1965), and to differ from the latter in some aspects of brain structure and physiology (Rosenzweig, Krech, Bennet and Diamond, 1962; Bennet, Diamond, Krech, and Rosenzweig, 1964. Altman, Wallace, Anderson and Das, 1968; Essman, 1968; La Torre, 1968).

The present investigation consists of two experiments on the effects of rearing in differential environments upon behaviour and electrophysiological characteristics of the albino rat as reflected by the brain's photic evoked potentials. It is based on a previous study by the authors (Edwards, Barry and Wyspianski, 1968), which has reported that enriched rats differ from their impoverished littermates in photic evoked potential latency.

Experiment 1

This experiment is a replication and extension of a previous study Edwards *et al.*, 1968).

Method

Subjects and Rearing

The subjects were 18 Sprague-Dawley albino rats, divided into 2 groups by the split-litter technique at 21 days of age and subsequently reared in differential environments (enriched and impoverished) to the age of 3 months.

Enriched and impoverished environments were patterned after the differential environments described by Hymovitch (1952). The enriched group was housed in a 48 x 30 x 18 in. wire mesh cage containing toys (activity wheel, tunnel, ladder, etc.). Toys were painted black and white, and were changed twice a week. The impoverished subjects were housed in single wire mesh cages measuring 10 x 8 x 6½ in.

Light and temperature were equal for both groups, and all subjects had free access to food and water throughout the experimental period. Contact with the investigator occurred only while cages were being cleaned or food and water replenished.

Apparatus and Procedure

The procedures used in obtaining photic evoked potentials are essentially the same as described elsewhere (Edwards, 1968), with the major exception that in the present study all data were stored on magnetic tape and subsequently analyzed using an Enhancetron computer. As before, the averaged photic evoked potentials were displayed on an oscilloscope screen and photographed with a Polaroid camera prior to latency analysis.

Two photic evoked potential measurements were obtained from all subjects, the first at 21 days of age prior to the period of differential rearing, and the other after 2 months of differential rearing. In all records, a positive-negative-positive complex was identifiable within the 1st 100 msec. The latency of the negative peak was read in milliseconds.

A black-white brightness discrimination test was administered to all subjects at the conclusion of the experimental period, using a 2-choice apparatus patterned after Thompson and Bryant (1955). Criterion performance was set at 8 out of 10 correct trials, and testing was discontinued after 50 trials if criterion performance had not been reached. Testing was preceded by the pretest procedures suggested by Thompson and Bryant, but each subject was tested in a single session. Enriched and impoverished subjects were alternated during testing.

Results

Photic Evoked Potential Data

The latency of the negative peak in the positive-negative-positive complex occurring within the 1st 100 msec was read at 21 days of age, and a 2nd

Reprinted, by permission, from *Developmental Psychobiology*, 1969, 2, 133-138.

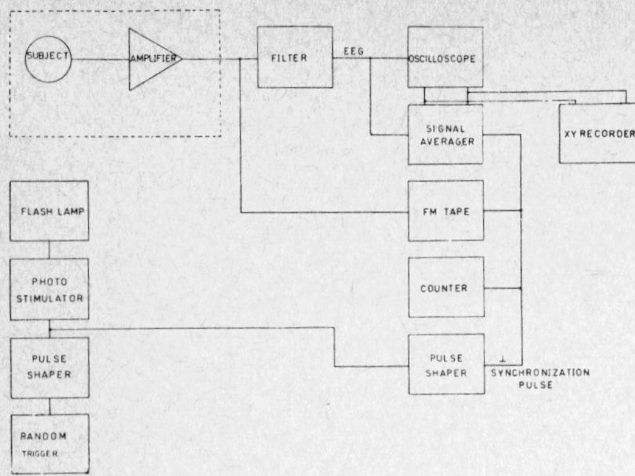

Fig. 1. System diagram for the recording of photic evoked potentials.

time after 8 wk of differential rearing. In each case, the mean latencies of the enriched and impoverished subjects were compared using *t* tests. The results are summarized in Table 1.

Table I – Mean photic evoked potential latencies of enriched and impoverished rats at weaning and after 8 weeks of differential rearing

Age (days)	Group Mean Latencies Enriched	Impoverished	t	p
21	44	44	<1.00	n.s.
80	56	64	3.90	<.01

At 21 days of age, the groups to be designated as enriched and impoverished both yielded a mean latency of 44msec for the negative peak studied. After 8 wk of differential rearing, the mean latency of the enriched group was 56 msec., and that of the impoverished group was 64 msec. (t = 3.90, $p < .01$).

Brightness Discrimination Data

Comparison of enriched and impoverished subjects using a non-parametric rank test shows that the performance of the enriched group was significantly superior to that of the impoverished group when both groups were trained to a criterion of 8 out of 10 correct trials on a black-white discrimination task (Rank Test, $p < .05$).

Experiment 2

This experiment introduces a different approach to the measurement of evoked latencies, presents evoked potential reliability data, and replicates the behaviour testing of *experiment 1*.

Method

Subjects and Rearing

The subjects were 18 Sprague-Dawley albino rats, divided into 2 groups by the split-litter technique at 21 days of age and subsequently reared in differential environments (enriched and impoverished) to the age of 3 months.

Enriched and impoverished environments were set up as described in *experiment 1*, with the exception that all enriched subjects were placed in a multiple T-maze and allowed to explore it for a few minutes each day.

Apparatus and procedure

The apparatus used in obtaining and recording photic evoked potentials is summarized in Figure 1. Restraining procedure and placement of electrodes are described elsewhere (Edwards, 1968). A Mousseau differential amplifier (Model No. SA2a) was used, with filters set 3 db down at 3 and 50 cps. The subject's EEG was constantly monitored on a dual-beam oscilloscope, which served also to display the evoked potential configuration. All data were analyzed on line using an Enhancetron averaging computer and simultaneously stored on FM tape for subsequent re-analysis after a 2nd filtering of frequencies higher than 50 cps. This filtering was done using a Krohn-Hite filter (Model No. 3342). Half-second or 1-sec photic evoked potentials in response to 100 flashes were obtained from all subjects on 3 occasions, first at weaning prior to the placing of subjects in differential environments, then twice during the experimental period at monthly intervals.

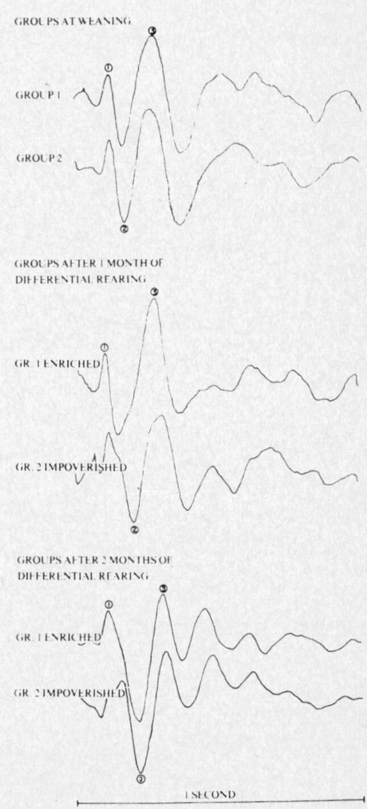

Fig. 2. Group photic evoked potentials obtained from enriched and impoverished groups of albino rats at weaning and on two occasions during the period of differential rearing.

It was decided, prior to latency analysis, to obtain group photic evoked potentials for each occasion. This was done, using the Enhancetron computer, by averaging evoked potentials of all 9 subjects making up a group. Each group was considered as one subject on whom a photic evoked potential had been obtained in response to 900 stimuli. In this manner, the very stable configurations shown in Figure 2 were obtained.

The events labelled as (*1*), (*2*), and (*3*) were then identified visually in all individual records. The latencies of these events were read in milliseconds and form the basis for comparison of enriched- and impoverished-group tests and non-parametric rank tests. The reliability of each event was expressed as a test-retest coefficient, by comparing the latencies obtained from the first 50 as opposed to the second 50 stimuli.

Black-white brightness discrimination testing of all subjects was done at the end of the experimental period, as described in *experiment* 1.

Table II – Comparison of photic evoked potential latencies by t tests and rank tests at weaning and during the experimental period.

Age (days)	Peak[a]	Group Latencies[b] Enriched	Impoverished	t	P^c	(rank test) P
	1	126	123	<1.00	n.s.	n.s.
21	2	185	177	1.67	n.s.	n.s.
	3	284	269	1.71	n.s.	n.s.
	1	115	126	1.80	n.s.	n.s.
50	2	178	191	1.63	n.s.	n.s.
	3	276	304	2.60	<.05	<.05
	1	118	144	2.51	<.05	<.05
80	2	217	225	1.09	n.s.	n.s.
	3	310	309	<1.00	n.s.	n.s.

[a] For peak labels, see Fig. 2.
[b] Group means, in milliseconds.
[c] df = 8.

Table III – Test-retest reliability coefficients of the 3 photic evoked potential events obtained at weaning and after 1 and 2 months of differential rearing

Age (days)	Peak[a]	Reliability coefficient
	1	.90
21	2	.86
	3	.73
	1	.96
50	2	.94
	3	.93
	1	.93
80	2	.80
	3	.82

[a] For peak labels, see Fig. 2

Results

Photic Evoked Potential Data

The mean latencies obtained by enriched and impoverished subjects with respect to peaks labelled *(1)*, *(2)*, and *(3)* on Figure 2 were compared on each of 3 occasions using tests and non-parametric rank tests.

These results are summarized in Table II, which shows that when the groups were formed at 21 days by splitting litters according to weight, there was no significant differences in mean latency, and in fact the group destined for impoverishment had slightly shorter mean latencies in all 3 events. After 4 weeks of differential rearing, however, the impoverished group had longer latencies in all 3 events, and the latency difference between enriched and impoverished subjects was significant with respect to ***event 3*** ($t = 2.60$, $p < .05$; rank test, $p < .05$). After 8 wk of differential rearing, ***event 3*** was no longer significantly different, but *event 1* showed a significant difference between the groups ($t = 2.51$, $p < .05$; rank test, $p < .05$). Again, the impoverished group had the longer latency.

The test-retest reliabilities of the 3 events analyzed in this experiment are shown in Table III. This table shows that the 3 events analyzed in this experiment can be identified reliably from wide-awake restrained subjects both at weaning and during an experimental period of 2 months.

Brightness Discrimination Data

Comparison of enriched and impoverished subjects after 9 weeks of differential rearing using a nonparametric rank test showed the enriched group to be significantly superior (rank test, $p < .05$), when both groups were trained to a criterion of 8 out of 10 correct trials on a black-white discrimination task.

Discussion

The authors demonstrate on two small-sample experiments that rearing young albino rats in differential environments has measurable effects both on photic evoked potential latencies and on black-white discrimination behaviour. They suggest that group photic evoked potentials may be used to facilitate the identification of events from individual records, and they present reliability data for the evoked potentials obtained from awake, restrained, albino rats.

It seems premature at this time to interpret the authors' findings in the context of a specific model of brain functioning, other than to say that they form part of the growing body of evidence that rearing environment, and particularly early environment, has measurable effects on the functioning of the central nervous system. It may be noted that, in these experiments, a lengthening of latency was accompanied by decreased efficiency in solving a brightness discrimination. This is in agreement with findings of longer evoked potential latencies in low-intelligence humans (Chalke and Ertl, 1965; Ertl, in press), and is compatible with the interpretation that both latency and behaviour differences reflect differences in CNS arousal resulting from differential rearing (Melzak, 1965).

Summary

In two related experiments, albino rats were split into enriched and impoverished groups at weaning, and were reared for two months in differential environments, one group in a large cage containing toys, the other in individual cages. Photic evoked potentials were obtained from all subjects both at weaning and after differential rearing, and mean group latencies were compared. At the end of the experimental period, all subjects were tested on a black-white brightness discrimination. It was found that although the groups did not differ in evoked potential latency at weaning, after differential rearing there were significant latency differences. The enriched group developed shorter latencies than the impoverished group. At the end of the experiment, the enriched group obtained superior scores on a brightness discrimination test. It was concluded that differential rearing has measurable effects on certain aspects of the albino rat's behaviour and physiology.

NOTE: This study was partially supported by Ontario Mental Health Grant No. 184. The authors acknowledge the research assistance of J. Chien, a graduate student in their Department, and the assistance of E. Achorn, Departmental technologist.

References

ALTMAN, J., WALLACE, R. B., ANDERSON, W. J., and DAS, G. D., (1968). Behaviourally induced changes in length of cerebrum in rats. *Develop. Psychobiol., 1(2),* 112-117.

BENNETT, E. L., DIAMOND, M. C., KRECH, D., and ROSENZWEIG, M. R. (1964). Chemical and anatomical plasticity of brain. *Science, 146,* 610-619.

BROWN, R. T., (1968). Early experience and problem-solving ability. *J. Comp. Physiol. Psych., 65(3),* 433-440.

CHALKE, F. R., and ERTL, J. P. (1965). Evoked potentials and intelligence. *Life Sciences, 4,* 1319-1322.

DENENBERG, V. H., WOODCOCK, J. M., and ROSENBERG, K. M. (1968). Long-term effects of preweaning and postweaning free-environment experience on rats' problem-solving behaviour. *J. Comp. Physiol. Psych., 66(2),* 533-535.

EDWARDS, H. P., BARRY, W. F., and WYSPIANSKI, J. O. (1968). Early environment effect on rat photic evoked potentials: A preliminary study. *Revista Interamericana de Psicologia, 2(2),* 85-92.

ERTL, J. P., (In press). Neural efficiency and human intelligence. *Journal Educ. Res.*

ESSMAN, W. B., (1968). Differences in locomotor activity and brain-serotonin metalbolism in differentially housed mice. *J. Comp. Physiol. Psych., 66(2),* 244-246.

FORGAYS, D. G., and FORGAYS, J. W., (1952). The nature of the effects of free-environmental experience in the rat. *J. Comp. Physiol. Psych., 45,* 322-328.

FULLER, J. L., (1967). Experimental deprivation and later behaviour. *Science, 158(3809),* 1645-1652.

HYMOVITCH, B., (1952). The effects of experimental variations on problem-solving in the rat. *J. Comp. Physiol. Psych., 45,* 313-321.

LA TORRE, J. C., (1968). Effects of differential environmental enrichment on brain weight and on acetylcholinesterase and cholinesterase activities in mice. *Exp. Neurol., 22,* 493-503.

MELZAK, R., (1962). Effects of early perceptual restriction on simple visual discrimination. *Science, 137,* 970-978.

MELZAK, R., and BURNS, S. K., (1965). Neurophysiological effects of early sensory restriction. *Exp. Neurol., 13,* 163-175.

MELZAK, R., (1965). Effects of early experience on behaviour: Experimental and conceptual considerations. In P. H. HOCH and J. ZUBIN (eds.), *Psychopathology of Perception,* New York: Grune & Stratton. Pp. 271-299.

ROSENZWEIG, M. R., KRECH, D., BENNETT, E. L. and DIAMOND, M. C., (1962). Effects of environmental complexity and training on brain chemistry and anatomy: A replication and extension. *J. Comp. Physiol. Psych., 55,* 429-437.

THOMPSON, R., and BRYANT, J. H., (1955). Memory as affected by activity of the relevant receptor. *Physiol. Psych.,, 1,* 393-400.

WOODS, P. J., RUCKELHAUS, S. I., and BOWLING, D. M., (1960). Some effects of "free" and "restricted" environmental rearing conditions upon adult behaviour in the rat. *Psychol. Rep., 6,* 191-200.

ZIMBARDO, P. J., and MONTGOMERY, K. C., (1957). Effects of "free-environment" rearing upon exploratory behaviour. *Psychol. Rep., 3,* 589-594.

6 / Effects of Stress and Administration of Cortisone on Weight Gain in Gentled Rats[1]

G.J. Mogenson, Gordon A. McMurray, and L.B. Jaques
University of Saskatchewan

A human infant receives a great deal of tactile stimulation from his mother in the form of fondling and cuddling. It has been argued that such stimulation is beneficial to the developing personality. Some support for this point of view is provided by the fact that animals which are handled and petted during infancy exhibit a more rapid growth rate. In the following experiment, the authors attempted to ascertain the physiological mechanisms which mediate the increased weight gain that results from handling. (Professor Mogenson is the Editor of the Canadian Journal of Psychology*).*

Several studies have reported that increased weight gain in growing albino rats results from handling (3, 4, 5, 6, 7) and other treatment involving systematic tactile stimulation (3). This increase, it has been suggested, must be due to improved metabolism and better utilization of food (4), since gentled animals eat no more food than non-gentled and excrete less faeces (4,7). The gentled animals have also been found to be more resistant to certain types of stress applied after the gentling period has ended and the weight differential is well established (5, 6, 7). Little information is available regarding the effect of stress procedures instituted earlier in the growth process.

A satisfactory explanation of the effects of gentling in terms of the mechanisms involved has not been established. Although the threshold of emotional response of gentled rats appears higher than that of the non-gentled animal, it is not clear how the threshold is raised, or how the higher threshold produces the observed effects on growth and resistance to severe stress.

There are two reasons why the somatotrophic hormone (*STH*) of the anterior pituitary should be considered as part of the mechanism explaining the effects of gentling. First, the gentled animals show an increased growth in the size of bones, and thus an increased skeletal length. Their growth is symmetrical, and increased weight is not due merely to deposits of adipose tissue (4, 7). Second, there is better utilization of food. Both the nature of the growth and the improved food utilization strongly suggest increased effects of endogenous *STH* in gentled animals.

Once *STH* is considered as part of this mechanism, the interesting relationship between *STH* and cortisone demonstrated by Kramár and Wilhelmj becomes significant. Kramár (2) found that cortisone and *STH* had opposing effects on both the capillary resistance and the weight of female adrenalectomized rats. Thus daily injections of cortisone (1 mgm./100 gm. of body weight) produced a marked rise in capillary resistance and loss in weight. When *STH* (2 mgm./100 gm. of body weight) was also injected both these effects were counteracted. Wilhelmj (9), using dogs, showed similar opposing effects of these two hormones on a wide variety of functions including systolic blood pressure, pulse rate, capillary resistance, and the level of systolic blood pressure, pulse rate, capillary resistance, and the level of circulating eosinophils. These authors postulate a basic antagonistic action between *STH* and cortisone, the balance of which is the principal determinant of capillary resistance. Disturbance of this balance could result in the phasic changes in capillary resistance that they have found to be a characteristic organismic response to stress (2).

The present study is concerned with the effects of both cortisone and stress on the weight gain normally found in gentled animals. If *STH* is involved in this phenomenon, then cortisone might be expected to nullify the effect. Also, stress procedures resulting in high adrenal cortical activity and increased endogenous cortisone should similarly offset this weight gain.

Method

The subjects were 66 male and 34 female weanling albino rats of Wistar stock. The experiments were

[1] This study was supported by a grant from the Defence Research Board, Canada (Project *DRB* 9350-02).

Reprinted, by permission, from the *Canadian Journal of Psychology*, 1957, *11*, 123-127.

conducted in three stages, each stage starting with a group of newly weaned animals at the age of 21 days, and treatment being identical at each stage except the third, when two further groups were added.

Stage 1. Four groups of eight were treated as shown for Groups 1, 2, 3, and 4 of Table I. *Stage 2.* Four groups of seven were again treated as Groups 1, 2, 3, and 4 of Table I. *Stage 3.* Four groups of five were treated as Groups 1, 2, 3, and 4 of Table I, and two further groups of ten were treated as Groups 5 and 6.

Table I – Size of groups and experimental treatment given each during 21-day period

Group	N (all stages combined)	Treatment
1	20	Gentling ten minutes daily
2	20	Control (no treatment)
3	20	Gentling ten minutes and exposure to sound two minutes daily
4	20	Exposure to sound two minutes daily
5	10	Gentling ten minutes daily; mean dose of ¼ mgm. cortisone acetate administered daily in food
6	10	Mean dose of ¼ mgm. cortisone acetate administered daily in food

All groups used at any one stage were matched for mean weight and sex. However, the animals of Stage 3 were somewhat lighter than those of the other stages. Hence the initial mean weights of rats in Groups 5 and 6 (all from Stage 3) were less than the mean weights of the animals treated as Groups 1, 2, 3, and 4 in the three stages combined.

Each of the six groups thus formed was given the treatment shown for it in Table I during a 21-day period.

Gentling consisted of placing the weanling rats in the fold of the left arm and stroking along the head and back with the right hand. Rats exposed to sound were brought in group cages into a room where a Hartmann whistle was attached to a source of compressed air. The whistle was placed directly above the cages and was turned on for two minutes at a frequency of 9000-12000 c/s and air pressure of 15 lbs. per sq. inch. Since animals in Group 3 were both gentled and exposed to sound, gentling was given in the morning, and exposure to sound in the afternoon.

Rats in Groups 5 and 6 had the regular food removed each morning and were given 10 gm. of powdered feed into which 2.5 mgm. of cortisone acetate in tablet form had been thoroughly ground. This food was given in deep-walled dishes and checked to ensure that all was eaten. Thus the mean dose was ¼ mgm. of cortisone per animal daily. However, as the animals were fed in groups, some variation was possible in the daily dosage received by individuals. Krámar (2) with cortisone injections of 1 mgm. per 100 gm. of body weight used a much heavier dosage. Preliminary tests showed that this amount interfered with normal growth. Consequently, the average daily dose was reduced to ¼ mgm. per animal to reduce the likelihood that the cortisone alone would cause marked loss in weight.

Except for the period of exposure to sound, all animals were kept in group cases in the same room, with the females of each group separated from the males. The animals were weighed every four or five days, these being the only times when non-gentled rats were handled. The final weighing, on which all weight gain figures are based, was made 25 days after the start of the experiments, when the animals were 46 days of age. All groups were supplied *ad libitum* with a diet of ground Quaker calf meal pellets and water.

Results

The results presented in Table II indicate that both the administration of cortisone and exposure to sound nullified the effects of gentling on weight gain. Gentled rats (Group 1) showed the significantly increased weight gain over control animals (Group 2) which other workers have noted. But this enhanced weight gain is not shown in gentled animals which were also exposed to sound (Group 3 compared to Group 2). Similarly, daily administration of an average dose of ¼ mgm. of cortisone had no apparent effect on the weight gain of control rats (Group 6 compared to Group 2). However, it abolished the differential effects of gentling (Group 5 compared to Group 6). Male and female animals appeared to respond similarly to all treatments used.

Table II – Effects of gentling, stress, and cortisone on weight gain in rats

Group	*N*	Initial mean weight (age 21 days)	SE Mean	Mean weight gain (age 21-46 days)	SE Mean
		(gm.)		(gm.)	
1	20	51.1	2.78	96.6*	4.40
2	20	51.8	2.80	84.7	2.94
3	20	51.6	2.80	84.3	3.03
4	20	51.9	2.64	78.3	5.42
5	10	42.0	3.20	85.8	5.26
6	10	42.9	3.20	84.3	3.93

* The difference in mean weight gain for Group 1 vs. Group 2 is significant ($t = 2.24$, $p < 0.05$). All other groups compared with Group 2 yield non-significant differences.

Discussion

The results agree with the hypothesis that the increased weight gain shown in gentled rats is essentially due to the increased effects of endogenous

STH. If gentling or tactile stimulation is considered as resulting in a decreased pituitary-adrenal response, then less cortisone and other corticoids will be elaborated by the adrenal cortex in rats so treated. Consequently, the antagonistic effects of cortisone on *STH* are reduced and the effects of *STH* enhanced. The result is increased weight gain in gentled animals without any necessary increase in endogenous *STH*. Bovard (1) has mentioned the possibility that an increased level of *STH* production could account for superior growth in gentled rats. Our results make it seem more likely that the mechanism operates through the reduction of the antagonistic action of cortisone on *STH*.

Animals exposed to sound do not show the usual effect of gentling, presumably because the intense, high-frequency sound acts as a stressor and keeps the adrenal cortical activity high and hence the level of cortisone. This interpretation is further supported by the fact that raising the level of cortisone by direct means (daily dosage of ¼ mgm.) had the same nullifying effect on weight gain as did the stress agent.

Although a high level of cortisone appears to offset accelerated weight gains, it apparently does not have an equal and opposite effect in reducing growth below that of control animals. Group 4 shows a non-significant reduction in weight gain; Group 6 shows practically no difference in weight gain from the control level. Just why this is so is not clear; but some disparity of effect is to be expected, since the absolute influence of any factor on weight gain would be greater at accelerated growth rates than when rate of growth is slower.

Summary

One hundred albino rats were divided at weaning into six experimental and control groups. The design permitted evaluation of the effects on weight gain of periodic gentling, exposure to high-frequency sound, and ingestion of ¼ mgm. of cortisone daily, over a period of 21 days. Gentling produced the characteristic increase in weight gain; both administration of cortisone and exposure to sound nullified these gentling effects.

It is postulated that gentling reduces the pituitary-adrenal response with consequent reduction in the production of cortisone. This increases the effects of endogenous STH, resulting in greater weight gain.

References

1. Bovard, E. A theory to account for the effects of early handling on viability of the albino rat. *Science,* 1954, *120,* 187.
2. Kramar, J. Endocrine regulation of the capillary resistance. *Science,* 1954, *119,* 790-792.
3. McClelland, W. J. Differential handling and weight gain in the albino rat. *Canad. J. Psychol.,* 1956, *10,* 19-22.
4. Ruegamer, W. R., Bernstein, L., and Benjamin, J. D. Growth, food utilization, and thyroid activity in the albino rat as a function of extra handling. *Science,* 1954, *120,* 184-185.
5. Weininger, O. Mortality of albino rats under stress as a function of early handling. *Canad. J. Psychol.,* 1953, *7,* 111-114.
6. Weininger, O. Physiological damage under emotion stress as a function of early experience. *Science,* 1954, *119,* 285-286.
7. Weininger, O. The effects of early experience on behaviour and growth characteristics. *J. comp. physiol. Psychol.,* 1958, *49,* 1-9.
8. Weininger, O., McClelland, W. J., and Arima, R. K. Gentling and weight gains in the albino rat. *Canad. J. Psychol.,* 1954, *8,* 147-151.
9. Wilhelmj, C. M., Gunderson, D. E., Shuput, D., and McCarthy, H. H. A study of certain antagonistic actions of pituitary growth hormone and cortisone. *J. Lab. clin. Med.,* 1955, *45,* 516-525.

7 / The Effects of Early Experience on the Response to Pain[1]

Ronald Melzack and T.H. Scott *Cornell University, McGill University*

The importance of this paper lies in its demonstration that early experience plays an essential role in the emergence of such basic behaviour as avoidance of noxious stimuli. Note that the effect of a restricted early environment appears to concern the "meaning" of pain, and not the sensation itself.

There has recently been an increase of theoretical interest in the effects of early experience on behaviour, together with an increasing number of experimental studies (1). In one area, however, there is a marked discrepancy between theoretical emphasis and amount of empirical investigation: the area of avoidance behaviour and pain.

Earlier clinical and theoretical formulations of the problem of early experience by Freud and his followers (4, and others there cited) have not led to any experimental studies relevant to pain perception and response, although the importance of early experience as a determinant of adult behaviour was fully recognized. More recently, Scott and his associates (12) have arrived at a new hypothesis of the effects of early experience. They maintain that during the development of the organism there are specific critical periods after which sufficient maturation has occurred for various types of experience to have lasting effects on adult behaviour. Although Fuller (3) has provided evidence for a critical period in the dog for the acquisition of conditioned responses to pain, there is no direct evidence which relates early pain experience with the behaviour of the mature organism.

Hebb's (5) distinction between pain perception as a neurophysiological event and the overt response to pain, such as avoidance, has important implications for any attempt to relate early experience and pain perception in the mature organism. Hebb conceives of pain as a disruption of spatially and temporally organized activity in the cerebrum, this disruption per se constituting the physiological basis of pain. Since aggregates of neurons are assumed to develop their particular spatio-temporal organization as a result of prolonged, patterned sensory stimulation in early life, the theory thus suggests that the degree of pain perceived is, in part at least, dependent on the earlier experience of the organism. Pain, then, in the context of Hebb's theory, is not an elementary sensation, but a complex perceptual process in which a major role is played by all kinds of earlier perceptual learning, including both specific and nonspecific experience involving all the senses. Furthermore, as a result of direct experience with noxious stimuli, the organism tends to repeat and thus acquire any responses which decrease the cerebral disruption (i.e., pain).

That early experience does indeed play an important role in perceiving and responding to pain is strongly suggested by the study of a chimpanzee deprived of normal somesthetic stimulation during infancy and early maturity (11). After removal from somesthetic restriction, the chimpanzee appeared to have a heightened pain threshold, since "he 'panted' as chimpanzees do when they are being tickled" (11, p. 502) when his legs or lower ventral trunk was poked with a sharp pencil point or pin. Furthermore, the animal was found to be strikingly poor in localizing sites of noxious stimulation on its body.

The method of sensory deprivation or restriction has proved successful in ascertaining the effects of early perceptual experience on adult behaviour (7, 14). The present experiment, then, is an attempt to study the effects of early sensory restriction, with special emphasis on the restriction of pain experience, on the adult response to noxious stimuli.

Subjects

Six litters of an inbred Scottish terrier strain were used. Each litter was randomly divided into two groups. One group, containing a total of 10 dogs, was placed in restriction cages. The 12 dogs which comprised the "free environment" or control group were raised normally as pets in private homes and in the laboratory.

Each restricted dog used in the present study was reared in isolation from puppyhood to maturity in a

[1] Part of the results reported in this paper are contained in a thesis submitted by the senior author in partial fulfillment of the requirements of the Ph.D. degree at McGill University. The authors gratefully acknowledge the advice and guidance of Dr. D. O. Hebb throughout this study and the technical assistance of Dr. Peter Milner. This experiment was supported by grants from the Foundations Fund for Research in Psychiatry, the Rockefeller Foundation, and a Fellowship stipend given to the senior author by the National Research Council of Canada.

cage which was specially designed to prevent the dogs from seeing outside, although daylight was permitted to enter through a large air vent at the top of each cage. Each cage contained two compartments, and when the sliding partition between them was opened once a day, the dog was allowed to enter a freshly cleaned compartment. In this way the dogs were deprived of normal sensory and social experience from the time that weaning was completed at the age of four weeks until they were removed at about eight months of age. After the restricted dogs were released from their cages, they received the same opportunities for social and sensory stimulation as their normally reared littermates.

Testing of the dogs began about three to five weeks after the restricted animals were released. Two of the restricted dogs were tested a second time about two years after their release. Since the litters used in this study were born at different times over a three-year period, it was impossible to use all the dogs for all the tests.

Experiment I. Response to electric shock

Method.

Subjects. The Ss were seven restricted and nine free-environment dogs.

Apparatus. A toy car that could be maneuvered by hand through a battery and steering mechanism was connected to a variable electric shock source provided by a variac and transformer circuit. The dogs were tested with the car on a 6-ft. by 3-ft. sheet-metal floor surrounded by a 2-ft.-high wire-mesh enclosure.

Procedure. The toy car was used to pursue the dogs and deliver a 1500-v., 6 ma. shock when it hit them. Each shock was of 1-sec. duration, although the dogs could escape the full shock by moving away rapidly. The car, which had a constant speed, was kept in waiting about 2 ft. from *S*. If *S* were sitting, *E* moved the car directly toward *S*. If *S* were moving, however, *E* moved the car into *S*'s path and pursued *S* up to one of the far sides of the enclosure.

The *E* tried to hit each dog ten times during a testing period. However, if at some time during testing, the dog made five successive avoidances of the approaching car without being hit and shocked, testing was discontinued for that period, and the total number of shocks received by the dog up to that time was recorded. A dog reached the *criterion* of successful avoidance learning when it received no shock during a testing period.

Results.

The restricted dogs received a mean of 24.7 shocks (range: 10 to 40) from the toy car, while the free-environment dogs received a mean of 6 shocks (range: 2 to 11). This difference between the two groups provided a t value of 4.4, which is significant at the .001 level. By the end of the fourth test period all the free-environment dogs had reached criterion. Three of the seven restricted dogs, however, had not yet done so; and two of these had received the full 40 shocks and gave no sign of learning to avoid the toy car. Testing was therefore discontinued at this time. The mean number of shocks received by the restricted dogs, then, would probably be considerably higher than it is if the restricted dogs were tested until all had reached criterion.

Characteristic differences in the behaviour of the two groups were striking. The normal dogs were found to show smooth, precise movements which were oriented directly toward the toy car. They often sat looking at the car, swaying from side to side as it moved toward them, and only at the last moment, when the car was inches away from them, did they jump up and trot out of the way. Although these dogs were excited at first, their behaviour after the first few shocks showed little excitement, and they made only minimal, unhurried avoidance movements of a leg or the tail to avoid being hit.

This behaviour stands in marked contrast with the wild, aimless activity first shown by the restricted dogs. Their typical behaviour consisted of running around in a circular path with excessive, exaggerated movements of the whole body. They often avoided being hit only by virtue of the remarkable rapidity of their action. But there was no difficulty in hitting them if the car were moved into the circular path. They then ran right into it. At other times, they stood up at the side of the testing enclosure, in an attempt to climb out, and received the full ten shocks in this position.

Two years after restriction. Two restricted dogs were tested two years after they had been released from restriction and still showed the same exaggerated behaviour. While one learned after 9 shocks, the other received 23 shocks before it began to avoid successfully. This gave a mean of 16 shocks, which differs significantly from the mean of 6 shocks for the normal animals at the .01 level ($t = 3.5$).

Experiment II. Avoidance training

Method.

Subjects. The *Ss* were 7 restricted and 12 free-environment dogs.

Apparatus. A 6-ft. by 3-ft. testing enclosure, bounded by wire mesh 2 ft. high, was divided lengthwise into two halves by a 3-in.-high barrier. The steel grid floor was connected to a variable electric shock source provided by a variac and transformer circuit.

Procedure. The threshold levels at which the dogs responded to electric shock in the apparatus were first determined by raising the voltage stepwise. The voltmeter reading at which an animal first showed signs of startle or slight jumping was recorded as the threshold value. The behaviour of the animals to this value of shock was then observed for two test periods during which each dog received about ten shocks on both sides of the barrier.

For the avoidance training which followed, the

side which was to be "hot" for a particular animal was the one to which it moved and which it seemed to "prefer" when placed in the apparatus. The first shock on the training days was given 1 min. after the dog was placed on the "hot" side, and a shock was given every 60 sec. thereafter, as long as the dog stayed on the "hot" side, until *S* had received a total of ten shocks. However, when a dog jumped to the safe side during avoidance training, it was placed back on the "hot" side, and *E* waited 60 sec. before shock was again presented. If a dog made three successive jumps from the "hot" to the safe side without receiving shock, testing was discontinued for that period for the animal, and the number of shocks received up to that time was recorded. The shock was of 1-sec. duration, and 1500 v., 6 ma., which was about three times the mean threshold value measured by the voltmeter. The *criteria* for successful avoidance learning were: (a) two successive days with no more than one shock on each day or (b) a training day on which a dog went to the safe side immediately and received no shock.

Results

No significant difference in the thresholds at which the two groups first responded to electric shock was obtained in this experiment. Furthermore, no behavioural differences between the two groups were observed with these minimal values of shock, either in degree of responsiveness or type of response made.

During avoidance training with 1500 v., however, differences in the behaviour of the two groups were obvious. By the end of the third testing period, only 2 of the 12 free-environment dogs had not reached criterion; 5 of the 7 restricted dogs, however, had not reached criterion at this stage, and 3 of these 5 had received the full 30 shocks and gave no sign of learning. Because of the obvious differences between the two groups, and the clearly unpleasant nature of the electric shock used, testing was discontinued at this point. Thus no dog received more than 30 shocks during avoidance training.

While the free-environment dogs received a mean of 5 shocks (range: 1 to 22), the restricted dogs received a mean of 20.3 shocks (range: 1 to 30) during avoidance training. The *t* score of the difference between the means, 5.07, is significant at the .001 level.

The three dogs that received the full 30 shocks showed stereotyped forms of behaviour to the shock. One dog whirled around violently in narrow circles on the "hot" side immediately after getting the first shock in the enclosure and continued to do so until it was removed after getting 10 shocks. The second dog always ran to a particular corner on the "hot" side after the first shock, and sat in a peculiar, awkward position, getting shock after shock without moving. The third dog learned a partial response to the shock, consisting of placing its forelegs on the barrier, while its hindquarters were on the "hot" side, in this way getting repeated shocks without learning the entire response.

Two years after restriction. Two dogs that had been out of restriction for two years, and were reared normally in the laboratory during that time, nevertheless received a mean of 19 shocks during the three testing periods, which differed significantly from the free-environment dogs' mean of 5 shocks at the .02 level of significance ($t = 2.78$). One of these dogs received 25 shocks, and *S* still maintained the same awkward, "frozen" position in the corner that it had assumed when first tested two years previously, giving little sign of learning permanently to make the appropriate response of stepping over the 3-in. barrier to the safe side.

Experiment III. Response to burning

Method.

Subjects. The *Ss* were ten restricted and eight free-environment dogs.

Apparatus. A box of safety matches.

Procedure. Each dog was allowed to roam the testing room freely for 1 min., and the amount of time *S* spent near *E* in an area which had been demarcated previously by a chalk line was recorded. The *S* was then called by *E* to this area. A safety match was struck, and *E* attempted to push the flame into the dog's nose at least three times. Although the dog was held forcibly by *E*, *S* was able to avoid being burned by moving or turning its head away rapidly from the match. The dog was then allowed to move to any part of the room, and the time spent near *E* in the area of the source of burning was recorded during a 2-min. period. The percentages of time *S* spent near *E* before and after presentation of the flame were then compared.

Results.

Of the eight free-environment dogs tested, six spent less time near *E* after he tried to burn them than before. Of the ten restricted dogs, however, nine spent more time in the area near *E after* nose-burning than before. While the restricted dogs spent 27.9 per cent of the time near *E* before stimulation, they spent 51.2 per cent of the time in that area following presentation of the match. The amount of time spent by the free-environment dogs near *E* decreased from 45.1 per cent before to 32.8 per cent after presentation of the match. The nonparametric sign test (9) provided a chi-square value of 5.40 with Yates' correction, which is significant at the .02 level of confidence.

One of the most remarkable features of the restricted dogs was their behaviour during and following presentation of the flame. To the astonishment of the observers, seven of the ten restricted dogs made no attempt to get away from *E during* stimulation, and it was not even necessary to hold them. The sequence of behaviour observed was almost identical for all seven dogs: they moved their noses into the flame as soon as it was presented, after which the head or whole body jerked away, as though reflexively; but then they came right back to their original position and hovered excitedly near the flame. Three of them repeatedly poked their noses into the flame and sniffed at it as long as it was present. If they snuffed it out, another match was struck, and the same sequence of events occurred. The other four did not sniff at the match, but offered no resistance nor made any attempt to get away after the first contact, and *E* was able to touch the dogs' noses with the flame as often as he wished. Only three of the restricted dogs squealed on making contact with the flame and tried subsequently to avoid it by moving their heads. Two of these, however, made no attempt to get away from *E* after stimulation had stopped.

In contrast, the normal dogs moved their heads so rapidly that it was often impossible to hit their noses with the flame. The *E* tried to move the match in from unexpected angles or to distract the *Ss* in order to hit them with the flame. But the normal dogs moved their heads slightly and usually successfully, receiving only one or two very brief contacts with the flame; and they then struggled to escape from *E*'s grasp at their sides.

Experiment IV. Response to pin-prick

Method.

Subjects. The *Ss* were eight restricted and nine free-environment dogs.

Apparatus. A large, sharp dissecting needle.

Procedure. The procedure in this experiment is the same as that used in Experiment III, except the dogs were pin-pricked rather than burned. While the dog was held at the neck, a long dissecting needle was jabbed into the skin at the sides and hind thighs about three or four times.

Results.

Of the eight restricted dogs, six spent more time near *E* after pin-pricking than before. These dogs increased the time spent in the demarcated area from 50.8 per cent before to 58.4 per cent after pin-pricking. The normal dogs, on the other hand, spent a mean of only 8.9 per cent of the time after pin-pricking near *E*, compared with 42.2 per cent before. Of the nine normally reared dogs, eight spent less time near *E* after pin-pricking than before. The sign test provided a chi-square value of 4.74, which is significant at the .05 level.

The behaviour of the restricted dogs in response to pin-prick was almost identical with that observed with the flame: they appeared unaware that they were being stimulated *by something in the environment.* Four of the restricted dogs made no response whatever apart from localized reflexive twitches at the side or leg when they were pricked. The *E* was often able to pierce the skin of these dogs completely so that the needle was lodged in it without eliciting withdrawal or any behavioural indication that pain was being "felt" or responded to other than spasmodic, reflexive jerks. The remaining four restricted dogs pulled their bodies aside a few inches or yipped to *some* of the pin-pricks, but when released two of them stayed right next to *E,* who was able to repeat the procedure and jab them with the needle as often as he wished. The noxious stimulation received was apparently not "perceived" as coming from *E,* and their behaviour subsequently was not oriented or organized in terms of the noxious stimulus in any noticeable way.

The free-environment dogs, however, provided an unmistakable index of perceived pain. They tried to jump aside to escape the pin-prick, yelped, and often struggled for release after two or three pin-pricks. They would then dash away from *E*'s hand and take up a position in the farthest corner of the testing room.

Supplementary observations. The behaviour of the restricted dogs in the four experiments just described is entirely consistent with everyday observations of their behaviour. It was noted, for example, that their aimless activity resulted in some of them frequently striking their heads against water pipes that ran along the walls just above the floor of the testing room. One dog, by actual count, struck his head against these pipes more than 30 times in a single hour. This was never observed in the normal dogs. Similarly, the rapid movement of the restricted dogs and their unpredictability as to direction resulted a number of times in the dogs' having a paw or the tail stepped on. Often there was no sign that the dogs "felt" pain when this happened, though the procedure would have elicited a howl from a normal dog, and the restricted *S* made no attempt to withdraw from the place where injury was received.

Discussion

The outstanding feature of the behaviour of the restricted dogs was their inability to respond adaptively and intelligently to the variety of stimuli which were presented to them. There can be little doubt that the restricted dogs "felt" electric shock: their disturbance by it was marked and unmistakable. Similarly, the behaviour of at least three of the restricted dogs indicates that pin-prick and contact with fire were "felt" in some way. Nevertheless, it was obvious that the restricted dogs did not know how to make the proper avoidance responses which would have prevented further stimulation. The results permit the conclusion, then, that early experience plays an essential role in the emergence of such basic behaviour as avoidance of noxious stimuli.

Sherrington has defined pain as "the psychical adjunct of an imperative protective reflex" (13, p. 286). And many psychologists since then (2, 8, 10) have interpreted pain in terms of imperative reflex responses. Such a view, however, is not consistent with the observations reported here. Most of the restricted dogs did indeed show localized reflex responses to the stimulation, yet their behaviour was clearly inadequate to cope with the intense electric shocks or such grossly injurious stimuli as contact with fire or piercing of the skin. In comparison, their littermates which had been reared normally in a free environment exhibited the ability to avoid prolonged contact with injurious stimuli, and they were able to learn with great rapidity to make highly organized, abiently oriented responses to every form of noxious stimulus that was presented. However, the capacity of the restricted dogs to acquire good, adaptive behaviour to noxious stimulation was notably limited after release from restriction, even with the adequate opportunity that was provided for them to gain varied, normal perceptual experience. Maladaptive behaviour like freezing and whirling also developed, and they were observed as consistent responses as long as two years after release. Thus, it appears that the requisite experience must come at the correct time in the young organism's life. During later stages of development, the experience necessary for adaptive, well-organized responses to pain may never be properly acquired.

The inability of the restricted dogs to cope intelligently with noxious stimuli, however, cannot be attributed to inadequate response mechanisms alone. Thier reflexive jerks and movements during pin-prick and contact with fire suggest that they may have "felt something" during stimulation; but the *lack* of any observable emotional disturbance apart from these reflex movements in at least four of the dogs following pin-prick and in seven of them after nose-burning indicates that their *perception* of the event was highly abnormal in comparison with the behaviour of the normally reared control dogs. Livingston (6) has made the observation that experience with pain in childhood is an important determinant of the manner in which the adult perceives and responds to pain; that is, the "meaning" involved in a perception such as pain, and the attitudes of the individual in situations involving pain, are largely a function of the earlier, related experiences of that individual. The results reported here are consistent with observations such as this and can be interpreted in a similar manner.

The isolation of the restricted dogs prevented them from acquiring experience early in life with severe skin-damage and fire. It is evident, then, that the flame and pin-prick could not have evoked the neural "phase sequences" (memories) acquired during earlier pain experiences (5) that might have been aroused in the normal dogs. The results strongly suggest that the restricted dogs lacked awareness of a necessary aspect of normal pain perception: the "meaning" of physical damage or at least *threat* to the physical well-being that is inherent in the normal organism's perception of pain. The observations of the restricted dogs' poking their noses into fire, or permitting *E* to cause bodily damage by fire and pin-prick without emotional disturbance apart from localized reflexes, indicates that an interpretation such as this is valid. Indeed, to say that these restricted dogs perceived fire and pin-prick as *threatening,* or even painful in any *normal* sense, would be anthropomorphism rather than inference from observed behaviour.

The results which have been reported here then, make it difficult to treat behaviour related to pain simply in terms of frequency and intensity of stimulations or in terms of imperative reflex responses alone (2, 8, 10) without regard to the earlier perceptual experience of the organism. The behaviour of the restricted dogs suggests that perceiving and responding to pain, which is so fundamental to normal adult behaviour and presumably so important for the survival of an individual or species, requires a background of early, prolonged, perceptual experience.

Summary

1. Ten dogs were reared in isolation from puppyhood to maturity in specially constructed cages which drastically restricted their sensory experience. Twelve control littermates were raised normally as pets in private homes and in the laboratory.

2. In two tests using strong electric shock, the restricted dogs required significantly more shocks before they learned to make the proper avoidance responses than their free-environment littermates.

3. In tests using nose-burning and pin-pricking, the behaviour of the restricted dogs was found to be strikingly different in capacity to perceive pain and respond to it when compared to their normal littermates.

4. It is concluded that early perceptual experience determines, in part at least, (a) the emergence of overt responses such as avoidance to noxious stimulation, and (b) the actual capacity to perceive pain normally.

References

1. BEACH, F. A., and JAYNES, J. Effects of early experience upon the behaviour of animals. *Psychol. Bull.,* 1954, *51,* 239-263.
2. ESTES, W. K. An experimental study of punishment. *Psychol. Monogr.,* 1944, *57,* No. 3 (Whole No. 263).
3. FULLER, J. L., EASLER, C. A., and BANKS, E. M. Formation of conditioned avoidance responses in young puppies. *Amer. J. Physiol.,* 1950, *160,* 462-466.
4. GREENACRE, P. The biological economy of birth. In O. FENICHEL (ed.), *The psychoanalytic study of the child.* New York: International Universities Press, 1945.
5. HEBB, D. O. *The organization of behaviour.* New York: John Wiley and Sons, Inc., 1949.
6. LIVINGSTON, W. K. What is pain? *Sci. Amer.,* 1953, *188,* 59-66.
7. MELZACK, R. The genesis of emotional behaviour: an experimental study of the dog. *J. comp. Physiol. Psychol.,* 1954, *47,* 166-168.

8. MILLER, N. E. Learnable drives and rewards. In S. S. STEVENS (ed.), *Handbook of experimental psychology*. New York: John Wiley and Sons, Inc., 1951.
9. MOSES, L. E. Non-parametric statistics for psychological research. *Psychol. Bull.*, 1952, *49*, 122-143.
10. MOWRER, O. H. *Learning theory and personality dynamics*. New York: Ronald Press, 1950.
11. NISSEN, H. W., CHOW, K. L., and SEMMES, JOSEPHINE. Effects of restricted opportunity for tactual, kinesthetic, and manipulative experience on the behaviour of a chimpanzee. *Amer. J. Psychol.*, 1951, *64*, 485-507.
12. SCOTT, J. P., FREDRICSON, E., and FULLER, J. L. Experimental exploration of the critical period hypothesis. *Personality*, 1951, *1*, 162-183.
13. SHERRINGTON, C. S. *Man on his nature*. New York: Macmillan, 1941.
14. THOMPSON, W. R., and HERON, W. The effects of restricting early experience on the problem solving capacity of dogs. *Canad. J. Psychol.*, 1954, *8*, 17-31.

8 / Influence of Prenatal Maternal Anxiety on Emotionality in Young Rats

William R. Thompson *Queen's University*

In this important experiment, the author shows that environmental factors affecting later behaviour begin to operate even before the birth of the organism. Furthermore, the effects persist to a great extent into adulthood.

Professor Thompson is co-author, with J. L. Fuller, of Behaviour Genetics, *1960.*

The purpose of the observations reported in this article[1] was to test the hypothesis that emotional trauma undergone by female rats during pregnancy can affect the emotional characteristics of the offspring. By now, a good deal of evidence favouring this possibility has accumulated from diverse sources, including teratology (1), pediatrics (2), experimental psychology (3), and population biology (4). While none of the studies done has directly confirmed this hypothesis, many of them indicate that such hormones as cortisone, adrenalin, and adrenocorticotropic hormone, injected into the mother during pregnancy, have drastic effects on the fetus via the maternal-fetal blood exchange. Since strong emotion may release such substances into the mother's blood stream, there are grounds for supposing that it may have an important influence on fetal behavioural development. This experiment was the first in a projected series designed to examine this question in detail.

The rationale of the procedure was to create a situation which would predictably arouse strong anxiety in female rats, and to provide them with a standard means of reducing this anxiety; then to expose them to the anxiety-arousing situation during pregnancy, but block the accustomed means of escaping it. The assumption was that strong, free-floating anxiety would be generated in the pregnant females, and that any endocrine changes resulting would be transmitted through the maternal-fetal blood exchange to the fetus. The experiment was done by training five randomly chosen female hooded rats in a double compartment shuttlebox, first to expect strong shock at the sound of a buzzer, and then to avoid the shock by opening a door between the compartments and running through the safe side. When the rats had learned this, the five experimentals, together with five control females, were mated to five randomly chosen males in a large cage. As soon as the experimentals were found to be pregnant (by vaginal smears), they were exposed to the buzzer three times every day in the shock side of the shuttlebox, but with the shock turned off and the door to the safe side locked. This procedure was terminated by the birth of a litter. The controls were placed in breeding cages during the same time.

Possible postnatal influences were controlled by crossfostering in such a way as to yield a design with six cells, each containing ten offspring with two main variables – namely, prenatal and postnatal treatment. The data obtained from tests given to the young were examined by means of analysis of variance. In all tests of significance, three error estimates were used: the within-cell variance, the within-plus-interaction variances, and the within-plus-interaction plus between-postnatal-treatment variances. Thus, as shown in Table I, all tests of significance reported involve three F values.

The emotional characteristics of the 30 control and 30 experimental offspring were compared by two tests given at 30 to 40 and 130 to 140 days of age. In test A, measures of amount and latency of activity in an open field were taken in three daily sessions of 10 minutes each. In test B, emotionality was measured by latency of leaving the home cage, and latency of reaching food at the end of an alley way leading out from the cage after 24 hours' food deprivation. In the second test, the maximum time allowed an animal to reach food was 30 minutes. In the measures used, low activity and high latency were taken as indices of high emotionality.

The results are summarized in Table I. On test A, striking differences between experimentals and controls were obtained in amount of activity, both at 30 to 40 days and at 130 to 140 days. On the first testing, a significant interaction was obtained which probably represents genetic variation. On the second measure, experimental animals showed a much higher latency of activity than controls at both ages of testing. In neither of these activity measures were there any significant differences due to postnatal treatment or interaction besides the one mentioned.

In test B, experimental animals were slower to

[1]This research was done at Queen's University, Kingston Ontario, and supported by grants from the Queen's Science Research Council and the National Science Foundation. Grateful acknowledgement is made to C. H. Hockman for his invaluable aid in helping to build the apparatus and to test the animals.

Reprinted, by permission, from *Science,* Vol. 125, (April 12, 1957), pp. 698-699.

Table I – Comparison of experimental and control animals on two tests of emotionality

Item	Test A: Amount of Activity (Distance)	Test A: Latency of Activity (Seconds)	Test B: Latency to Leave Cage (Minutes)	Test B: Latency to Food (Minutes)
	Tests given at age 30 to 40 days			
Experimentals	86.0	146.3	14.9	23.7
Controls	134.5	56.8	5.2	11.8
F values	(15.79, 14.21, 13.57)	(8.51, 7.91, 8.07)	(16.13, 16.46, 15.62)	(31.73, 25.66, 25.87)
p	$<.001$	$<.01$	$<.001$	$<.001$
	Tests given at age 130 to 140 days			
Experimentals	114.5	71.5	4.8	11.6
Controls	162.3	26.8	2.1	6.2
F values	(9.77, 9.12, 8.76)	(4.95, 4.79, 4.57)	(2.39)	(4.48)
p	$<.01$	$<.05$	$>.05$	$<.05$

leave the home cage than controls at the first age of testing. There was no significant difference between groups in this measure, however, at 130 to 140 days of age. Similarly, experimentals showed a much higher latency than controls in getting to food at the end of the alley way at the first age of testing. The difference was less at the later age of testing. At both ages, significant interaction variances were found. As before, both may well be due to genetic variation. On neither of the measures used in test B were any significant differences found between methods of postnatal treatment.

It is clear from this analysis that the experimental and control animals differ strikingly on the measures of emotionality used, and that these differences persist to a great extent into adulthood. While there is no question about the reliability of these differences, there is some ambiguity regarding their cause. Thus, we do not know exactly how the stress used had effects. It is possible that the buzzer was strong enough to act on the fetuses directly rather than indirectly by causing release of hormones in the mother. Only a more careful repetition of the experiment will throw light on this problem.

A more serious objection than this is that, besides the main factor of prenatal stress, genetic variation could also have been responsible for the offspring differences if there had been inadvertent selection of nonemotional mothers for the control group and emotional mothers for the experimental group. However, several points argue against this possibility. Choice of female animals for the two groups was carried out randomly, and at least some of the genetic variance was included in the error estimates used to test the main effects. Further, an examination of scores within and between individual litters indicates that interlitter variances tend to be smaller than intralitter differences. This means that, in the population used, genetic variation was relatively slight compared with environmental variation. Consequently, it is improbable that even if accidental selection had occurred it could have resulted in an experimental group genetically very different from the control group.

Accordingly, we may state that there are some grounds for supposing that prenatal maternal anxiety does actually increase the emotionality of offspring. This conclusion is offered tentatively until further experimentation has been completed.

References

1. Fraser, F. C., and T. D. Fainstat: *Am. J. Diseases Children, 82,* 593 (1951).
2. Sontag, L. W.: *Am. J. Obstet. Gynecol. 42,* 996 (1941).
3. Thompson, W. D., and L. W. Sontag: *J. Comp. and Physiol. Psychol. 49,* 545 (1956).
4. Chitty, D.: "Adverse effects of population density upon the viability of later generations," in *The Numbers of Man and Animals* (Oliver and Boyd, London, 1955).

THREE
MOTIVATION AND EMOTION

9 / Drive and the c.n.s. (Conceptual Nervous System)[1]

D.O. Hebb *McGill University*

A proper conception of the central nervous system can enhance our understanding of how behaviour is motivated. In this selection, Professor Hebb traces the changing views of neurology and motivation. He focuses on the discovery of an arousal system and shows how such a system may be useful in explaining why, under certain conditions, people seek stimulation whereas under other conditions they may be immobilized by excessive stimulation.

The problem of motivation of course lies close to the heart of the general problem of understanding behaviour, yet it sometimes seems the least realistically treated topic in the literature. In great part, the difficulty concerns that c.n.s., or "conceptual nervous system," which Skinner disavowed and from whose influence he and others have tried to escape. But the conceptual nervous system of 1930 was evidently like the gin that was being drunk about the same time; it was homemade and none too good, as Skinner pointed out, but it was also habit-forming; and the effort to escape has not really been successful. Prohibition is long past. If we *must* drink, we can now get better liquor; likewise, the conceptual nervous system of 1930 is out of date and – if we must neurologize – let us use the best brand of neurology we can find.

Though I personally favour both alcohol and neurologizing, in moderation, the point here does not assume that either is a good thing. The point is that psychology is intoxicating itself with a worse brand than it need use. Many psychologists do not think in terms of neural anatomy; but merely adhering to certain classical frameworks shows the limiting effect of earlier neurologizing. Bergmann (2) has recently said again that it is logically possible to escape the influence. This does not change the fact that, in practice, it has not been done.

Further, as I read Bergmann, I am not sure that he really thinks, deep down, that we should swear off neurologizing entirely, or at least that we should all do so. He has made a strong case for the functional similarity of intervening variable and hypothetical construct, implying that we are dealing more with differences of degree than of kind. The conclusion *I* draw is that both can properly appear in the same theory, using intervening variables to whatever extent is most profitable (as physics, for example, does), and conversely not being afraid to use some theoretical conception merely because it might become anatomically identifiable.

For many conceptions, at least, MacCorquodale and Meehl's (26) distinction is relative, not absolute; and it must also be observed that physiological psychology makes free use of "dispositional concepts" as well as "existential" ones. Logically, this leaves room for some of us to make more use of explicitly physiological constructs than others and still lets us stay in communication with one another. It also shows how one's views concerning motivation, for example, might be more influenced than one thinks by earlier physiological notions, since it means that an explicitly physiological conception might be restated in words that have – apparently – no physiological reference.

What I propose, therefore, is to look at motivation as it relates to the c.n.s. – or conceptual nervous system – of three different periods; as it was before 1930, as it was, say, ten years ago, and as it is today. I hope to persuade you that some of our current troubles with motivation are due to the c.n.s. of an earlier day, and ask that you look with an open mind at the implications of the current one. Today's physiology suggests new psychological ideas, and I would like to persuade you that they make psychological sense, no matter how they originated. They might even provide common ground – not necessarily agreement, but communication, something nearer to agreement – for people whose views at present may seem completely opposed. While writing this paper I found myself having to make a change in my own theoretical position, as you will see, and though you may not adopt the same position, you may be willing to take another look at the evidence and consider its theoretical import anew.

Before going on, it is just as well to be explicit about the use of the terms *motivation and drive. Motivation* refers here in a rather general sense to the energizing of behaviour, and especially to the sources of energy in a particular set of responses that keep them temporarily dominant over others and account for continuity and direction in behaviour.

[1] Presidential address, Division 3, at American Psychological Association, New Yord, September 1954.
The paper incorporates ideas worked out in discussion with fellow students at McGill, especially Dalbir Bindra and Peter Milner, as well as with Leo Postman of California, and it is a pleasure to record my great indebtedness to them.

Drive is regarded as a more specific conception about the way in which this occurs: a hypothesis of motivation, which makes the energy a function of a special process distinct from those S-R or cognitive functions that are energized. In some contexts, therefore, *motivation* and *drive* are interchangeable.

Motivation in the Classical (pre-1930) c.n.s.

The main line of descent of psychological theory, as I have recently tried to show (20), is through associationism and the stimulus-response formulations. Characteristically, stimulus-response theory has treated the animal as more or less inactive unless subjected to special conditions of arousal. These conditions are first, hunger, pain, and sexual excitement; and second, stimulation that has become associated with one of these more primitive motivations.

Such views did not originate entirely in the early ideas of nervous function but certainly were strengthened by them. Early studies of the nerve fibre seemed to show that the cell is inert until something happens to it from outside; therefore, the same would be true of the collection of cells making up the nervous system. From this came the explicit theory of drives. The organism is thought of as like a machine, such as the automobile, in which the steering mechanism – that is, stimulus-response connections – is separate from the power source, or drive. There is, however, this difference: the organism may be endowed with three or more different power plants. Once you start listing separate ones, it is hard to avoid five: hunger, thirst, pain, maternal, and sex drives. By some theorists, these may each be given a low-level steering function also, and indirectly the steering function of drives is much increased by the law of effect. According to the law, habits – steering functions – are acquired only in conjunction with the operation of drives.

Now, it is evident that an animal is often active and often learns when there is little or no drive activity of the kinds listed. This fact has been dealt with in two ways. One is to postulate additional drives – activity, exploratory, manipulatory, and so forth. The other is to postulate acquired or learned drives, which obtain their energy, so to speak, from association with primary drives.

It is important to see the difficulties to be met by this kind of formulation, though it should be said at once that I do not have any decisive refutation of it, and other approaches have their difficulties, too.

First, we may overlook the rather large number of forms of behaviour in which motivation cannot be reduced to biological drive plus learning. Such behaviour is most evident in higher species, and may be forgotten by those who work only with the rat or with restricted segments of the behaviour of (the) dog or cat. (I do not suggest that we put human motivation on a different plane from that of animals (7); what I am saying is that certain peculiarities of motivation increase with phylogenesis and, though most evident in man, can be clearly seen with other higher animals.) What is the drive that produces panic in the chimpanzee at the sight of a model of a human head; or fear in some animals, and vicious aggression in others, at the sight of the anaesthetized body of a fellow chimpanzee, What about fear of snakes, or the young chimpanzee's terror at the sight of strangers, One can accept the idea that this is "anxiety," but the anxiety, if so, is not based on a prior association of the stimulus object with pain. With the young chimpanzee reared in the nursery of the Yerkes Laboratories, after separation from the mother at birth, one can be certain that the infant has never seen a snake before, and certainly no one has told him about snakes; and one can be sure that a particular infant has never had the opportunity to associate a strange face with pain. Stimulus generalization does not explain fear of strangers, for other stimuli in the same class, namely, the regular attendants, are eagerly welcomed by the infant.

Again, what drive shall we postulate to account for the manifold forms of anger in the chimpanzee that do not derive from frustration objectively defined (22)? How account for the petting behaviour of young adolescent chimpanzees, which Nissen (36) has shown is independent of primary sex activity, How deal with the behaviour of the female who, bearing her first infant, is terrified at the sight of the baby as it drops from the birth canal, runs away, never sees it again after it has been taken to the nursery for rearing, and who yet, on the birth of a *second* infant, promptly picks it up and violently resists any effort to take it from her.

There is a great deal of behaviour, in the higher animal especially, that is at the very best difficult to reduce to hunger, pain, sex, and maternal drives, plus learning. Even for the lower animal it has been clear for some time that we must add an exploratory drive (if we are to think in these terms at all), and presumably the motivational phenomena recently studied by Harlow and his colleagues (16, 17, 10) could also be comprised under such a drive by giving it a little broader specification. The curiosity drive of Berlyne (4) and Thompson and Solomon (46), for example, might be considered to cover both investigatory and manipulatory activities on the one hand, and exploratory, on the other. It would also comprehend the "problem-seeking" behaviour recently studied by Mahut and Havelka at McGill (unpublished studies). They have shown that the rat which is offered a short, direct path to food, and a longer, variable and indirect pathway involving a search for food, will very frequently prefer the more difficult, but more "interesting," route.

But even with the addition of a curiosity-investigatory-manipulatory drive, and even apart from the primates, there is still behaviour that presents difficulties. There are the reinforcing effects of incomplete copulation (43) and of saccharin intake (42, 11), which do not reduce to secondary reward. We must not multiply drives beyond reason, and at this

Eng 387 April 16
7pm

Eng 211 April 17
2pm

Eng 471

April 28
9am

Memory
Storage
and
Aging

Schonfeld &
Robertson

point one asks whether there is no alternative to the theory in this form. We come, then, to the conceptual nervous system of 1930 to 1950.

Motivation in the c.n.s. of 1930-1950

About 1930 it began to be evident that the nerve cell is not physiologically inert, does not have to be excited from outside in order to discharge (19, p. 8). The nervous system is alive, and living things by their nature are active. With the demonstration of spontaneous activity in c.n.s. it seemed to me that the conception of a drive system or systems was supererogation.

For reasons I shall come to later, this now appears to me to have been an oversimplification; but in 1945 the only problem of motivation, I thought, was to account for the *direction* taken by behaviour. From this point of view, hunger or pain might be peculiarly effective in guiding or channeling activity but not needed for its arousal. It was not surprising, from this point of view, to see human beings liking intellectual work, nor to find evidence that an animal might learn something without pressure of pain or hunger.

The energy of response is not in the stimulus. It comes from the food, water, and oxygen ingested by the animal; and the violence of an epileptic convulsion, when brain cells for whatever reason decide to fire in synchrony, bears witness to what the nervous system can do when it likes. This is like a whole powder magazine exploding at once. Ordinary behaviour can be thought of as produced by an organized series of much smaller explosions, and so a "self-motivating" c.n.s. might still be a very powerfully motivated one. To me, then, it was astonishing that a critic could refer to mine as a "motivationless" psychology. What I had said in short was that any organized process in the brain is a motivated process, inevitably, inescapably; that the human brain is built to be active, and that as long as it is supplied with adequate nutrition will continue to be active. Brain activity is what determines behaviour, and so the only behavioural problem becomes that of accounting for *in*activity.

It was in this conceptual frame that the behavioural picture seemed to negate the notion of drive, as a separate energizer of behaviour. A pedagogical experiment reported earlier (18) had been very impressive in its indication that the human liking for work is not a rare phenomenon, but general. All of the 600-odd pupils in a city school, ranging from 6 to 15 years of age, were suddenly informed that they need do no work whatever unless they wanted to, that the punishment for being noisy and interrupting others' work was to be sent to the playground to play, and that the reward for being good was to be allowed to do more work. In these circumstances, *all* of the pupils discovered within a day or two that, within limits, they preferred work to no work (and incidentally learned more arithmetic and so forth than in previous years).

The phenomenon of work for its own sake is familiar enough to all of us, when the timing is controlled by the worker himself, when "work" is not defined as referring alone to activity imposed from without. Intellectual work may take the form of trying to understand what Robert Browning was trying to say (if anything), to discover what it is in Dali's paintings that can interest others, or to predict the outcome of a paperback mystery. We systematically underestimate the human need of intellectual activity, in one form or another, when we overlook the intellectual component in art and in games. Similarly with riddles, puzzles, and the puzzle-like games of strategy such as bridge, chess, and *Go*; the frequency with which man has devised such problems for his own solution is a most significant fact concerning human motivation.

It is, however, not necessarily a fact that supports my earlier view, outlined above. It is hard to get these broader aspects of human behaviour under laboratory study, and when we do we may expect to have our ideas about them significantly modified. For my view on the problem, this is what has happened with the experiment of Bexton, Heron, and Scott (5). Their work is a long step toward dealing with the realities of motivation in the well-fed, physically comfortable, adult human being, and its results raise a serious difficulty for my own theory. Their subjects were paid handsomely to do nothing, see nothing, hear or touch very little, for 24 hours a day. Primary needs were met, on the whole, very well. The subjects suffered no pain and were fed on request. It is true that they could not copulate, but, at the risk of impugning the virility of Canadian college students, I point out that most of them would not have been copulating anyway and were quite used to such long stretches of three or four days without primary sexual satisfaction. The secondary reward, on the other hand, was high: $20 a day plus room and board is more than $7000 a year, far more than a student could earn by other means. The subjects then should be highly motivated to continue the experiment, cheerful and happy to be allowed to contribute to scientific knowledge so painlessly and profitably.

In fact, the subject was well motivated for perhaps four to eight hours and then became increasingly unhappy. He developed a need for stimulation of almost any kind. In the first preliminary exploration, for example, he was allowed to listen to recorded material on request. Some subjects were given a talk for 6-year-old children on the dangers of alcohol. This might be requested, by a grown-up male college student, 15 to 20 times in a 30-hour period. Others were offered, and asked for repeatedly, a recording of an old stock-market report. The subjects looked forward to being tested but paradoxically tended to find the tests fatiguing when they did arrive. It is hardly necessary to say that the whole situation was rather hard to take, and one subject, in spite of not being in a special state of primary drive arousal in the experiment but in real need of money outside it, gave up the secondary reward of $20 a day to take up a job at hard labour paying $7 or $8 a day.

This experiment is not cited primarily as a difficulty for drive theory, although three months ago that is how I saw it. It *will* make difficulty for such theory if exploratory drive is not recognized; but we have already seen the necessity, on other grounds, of including a sort of exploratory-curiosity-manipulatory drive, which essentially comes down to a tendency to seek varied stimulation. This would on the whole handle very well the motivational phenomena observed by Heron's group.

Instead, I cite their experiment as making essential trouble for my own treatment of motivation (19) as based on the conceptual nervous system of 1930 to 1945. If the thought process is internally organized and motivated, why should it break down in conditions of perceptual isolation, unless emotional disturbance intervenes? But it did break down when no serious emotional change was observed, with problem-solving and intelligence-test performance significantly impaired. Why should the subjects themselves report (a) after four or five hours in isolation that they could not follow a connected train of thought, and (b) that their motivation for study or the like was seriously disturbed for 24 hours or more after coming out of isolation? The subjects were reasonably well adjusted, happy, and able to think coherently for the first four or five hours of the experiment; why, according to my theory, should this not continue, and why should the organization of behaviour not be promptly restored with restoration of a normal environment?

You will forgive me perhaps if I do not dilate further on my own theoretical difficulties, paralleling those of others, but turn now to the conceptual nervous system of 1954 to ask what psychological values we may extract from it for the theory of motivation. I shall not attempt any clear answer for the difficulties we have considered – the data do not seem yet to justify clear answers – but certain conceptions can be formulated in sufficiently definite form to be a background for new research, and the physiological data contain suggestions that may allow me to retain what was of value in my earlier proposals while bringing them closer to ideas such as Harlow's (16) on one hand and to reinforcement theory on the other.

Motivation and c.n.s. in 1954

For psychological purposes there are two major changes in recent ideas of nervous function. One concerns the single cell, the other an "arousal" system in the brain stem. The first I shall pass over briefly; it is very significant, but does not bear quite as directly upon our present problem. Its essence is that there are two kinds of activity in the nerve cell: the spike potential or actual firing, and the dendritic potential, which has very different properties. There is now clear evidence (12) that the dendrite has a "slow-burning" activity which is not all-or-none, tends not to be transmitted, and lasts 15 to 30 milliseconds instead of the spike's one millisecond. It facilitates spike activity (23) but often occurs independently and may make up the greater part of the EEG record. It is still true that the brain is always active, but the activity is not always the transmitted kind that conduces to behaviour. Finally, there is decisive evidence of primary inhibition in nerve function (25, 14) and of a true fatigue that may last for a matter of minutes instead of milliseconds (6, 9). These facts will have a great effect on the hypotheses of physiological psychology, and sooner or later on psychology in general.

Our more direct concern is with a development to which attention has already been drawn by Lindsley (24); the nonspecific or diffuse projection system of the brain stem, which was shown by Moruzzi and Magoun (34) to be an *arousal* system whose activity in effect makes organized cortical activity possible. Lindsley showed the relevance to the problem of emotion and motivation; what I shall attempt is to extend his treatment, giving more weight to cortical components in arousal. The point of view has also an evident relationship to Duffy's (13).

The arousal system can be thought of as representing a second major pathway by which all sensory excitations reach the cortex, as shown in the upper part of Figure 1; but there is also feedback from the cortex and I shall urge that the *psychological* evidence further emphasizes the importance of this "downstream" effect.

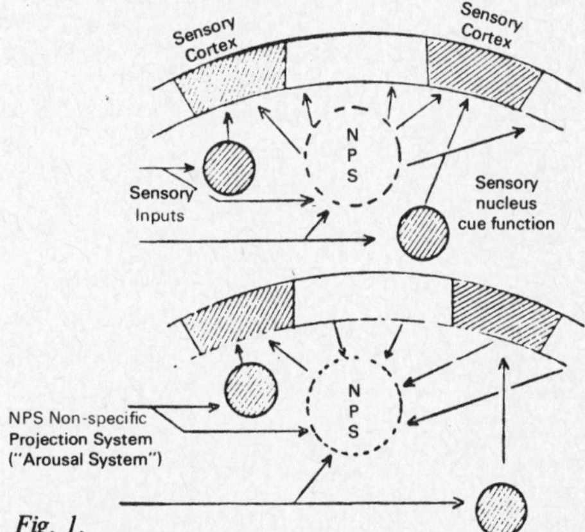

Fig. 1.

In the classical conception of sensory function, input to the cortex was via the great projection systems only: from sensory nerve to sensory tract, thence to the corresponding sensory nucleus of the thalamus, and thence directly to one of the sensory projection areas of the cortex. These are still the direct sensory routes, the quick efficient transmitters of information. The second pathway is slow and inefficient; the excitation, as it were, trickles through a tangled thicket of fibres and synapses, there is a mixing up of messages, and the scrambled messages are delivered indiscriminately to wide cortical areas. In short, they are messages no longer. They serve, instead, to tone up the cortex, with a background supporting action that is completely necessary if the messages proper are to have their effect. Without the arousal system, the sensory impulses by the direct route reach the sensory cortex, but go no farther; the rest of the cortex is unaffected, and thus learned stimulus-response relations are lost. The waking center, which has long been known, is one part of this larger system; any extensive damage to it leaves a permanently inert, comatose animal.

Remember that in all this I am talking conceptual nervous system: making a working simplification, and abstracting for psychological purposes; and all these statements may need qualification, especially since research in this area is moving rapidly. There is reason to think, for example, that the arousal system may not be homogeneous but may consist of a number of subsystems with distinctive functions (38). Olds and Milner's (37) study, reporting "reward" by direct intracranial stimulation, is not easy to fit into the notion of a single, homogeneous system. Sharpless' (40) results also raise doubt on this point, and it may reasonably be anticipated that arousal will eventually be found to vary qualitatively as well as quantitatively. But in general terms, psychologically, we can now distinguish two quite different effects of a sensory event. One is the *cue function*, guiding behaviour; the other, less obvious but no less important, is the *arousal* or *vigilance function*. Without a foundation of arousal, the cue function cannot exist.

And now I propose to you that, whatever you wish to call it, arousal in this sense is synonymous with a general drive state, and the conception of drive therefore assumes anatomical and physiological identity. Let me remind you of what we discussed earlier: the drive is an energizer, but not a guide; an engine, but not a steering gear. These are precisely the specifications of activity in the arousal system. Also, learning is dependent on drive, according to drive theory, and this too is applicable in general terms – no arousal, no learning; and efficient learning is possible only in the waking, alert, responsive animal, in which the level of arousal is high.

Thus I find myself obliged to reverse my earlier views and accept the drive conception, not merely on physiological grounds but also on the grounds of some of our current psychological studies. The conception is somewhat modified, but the modifications may not be entirely unacceptable to others.

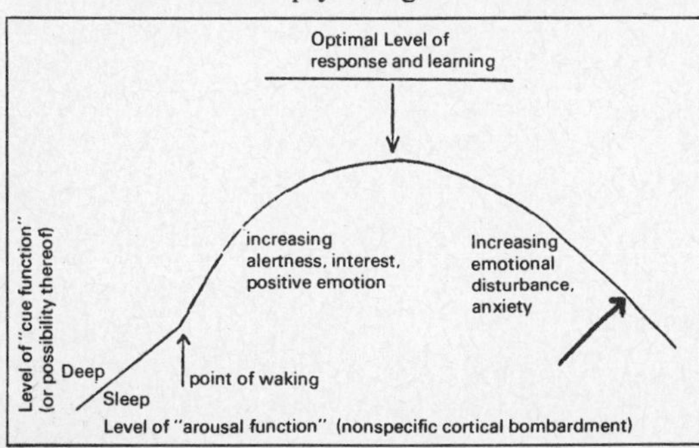

Fig. 2.

Consider the relation of the effectiveness of cue function, actual or potential, to the level of arousal (Figure 2). Physiologically, we may assume that cortical synaptic function is facilitated by the diffuse bombardment of the arousal system. When this bombardment is at a low level an increase will tend to strengthen or maintain the concurrent cortical activity; that is, when arousal or drive is at a low level, a response that produces increased stimulation and greater arousal will tend to be repeated. This is represented by the rising curve at the left. But when arousal is at a high level, as at the right, the greater bombardment may interfere with the delicate adjustments involved in cue function, perhaps by facilitating irrelevant responses (a high *D* arouses conflicting $_{S}H_{R}$'s). Thus there will be an optimal level of arousal for effective behaviour, as Schlosberg (39) has suggested. Set aside such physiologizing completely, and we have a significant behavioural conception left, namely, that the same stimulation in mild degree may attract (by prolonging the pattern of response that leads to this stimulation) and in strong degree repel (by disrupting the pattern and facilitating conflicting or alternative responses).

The significance of this relation is in a phenomenon of the greatest importance for understanding motivation in higher animals. This is the *positive attraction of risk-taking*, or mild fear, *and of problem-solving*, or mild frustration, which was referred to earlier. Whiting and Mowrer (49) and Berlyne (4) have noted a relation between fear and curiosity – that is, a tendency to seek stimulation from fear-provoking objects, though at a safe distance. Woodworth (50) and Valentine (48) reported this in children, and Woodworth and Marquis (51) have recently emphasized again its importance in adults. There is no doubt that it exists. There is no doubt, either, that problem-solving situations have some attraction for the rat, more for Harlow's (16) monkeys, and far more for man. When you stop to think of it, it is nothing short of extraordinary what trouble people will go to in order to get into more trouble at the bridge table, or on the golf course; and the fascination of the murder story, or thriller, and the newspaper accounts of real-life adventure or tragedy, is no less extraordinary. This taste for excitement *must* not be forgotten when we are dealing with human motivation. It appears that, up to a certain point, threat and puzzle have positive motivating value, beyond that point negative value.

I know this leaves problems. It is not *any* mild threat, *any* form of problem, that is rewarding; we still have to work out the rules for this formulation. Also, I do not mean that there are not secondary rewards of social prestige for risk-taking and problem-solving – or even primary rewards when such behaviour is part of lovemaking. But the animal data show that it is not always a matter of extrinsic reward; risk and puzzle can be attractive in themselves, especially for higher animals such as man. If we can accept this, it will no longer be necessary to work out tortuous and improbable ways to explain why human beings work for money, why school children should learn without pain, why a human being in isolation should dislike doing nothing.

One other point before leaving Figure 2: the low level of the curve to the right. You may be skeptical about such an extreme loss of adaptation, or disturbance of cue function and S-R relations, with high levels of arousal. Emotion is persistently regarded as energizing and organizing (which it certainly is at the lower end of the scale, up to the optimal level). But the "paralysis of terror" and related states do occur. As Brown and Jacobs (8, p. 753) have noted, "the presence of fear may act as an energizer . . . and yet lead in certain instances to an increase in immobility." Twice in the past eight months, while this address was being prepared, the Montreal newspapers reported the behaviour of a human being who, suddenly finding himself in extreme danger but with time to escape, simply made no move whatever. One of the two was killed; the other was not, but only because a truck driver chose to wreck his truck and another car instead. Again, it is reported by Marshall (27), in a book that every student of human motivation should read carefully, that in the emotional pressure of battle no more than 15 to 25 per cent of men under attack even fire their rifles, let alone use them efficiently.

Tyhurst's (47) very significant study of behaviour in emergency and disaster situations further documents the point. The adult who is told that his apartment house is on fire, or who is threatened by a flash flood, may or may not respond intelligently. In various situations, 12 to 25 per cent did so; an equal number show "states of confusion, paralyzing anxiety, inability to move out of bed, 'hysterical' crying or screaming, and so on." Three-quarters or more show a clear impairment of intelligent behaviour, often with aimless and irrelevant movements, rather than (as one might expect) panic reactions. There seems no doubt: the curve at the right must come down to a low level.

Now back to our main problem: If we tentatively identify a general state of drive with degree of arousal, where does this leave hunger, pain, and sex drives? These may still be anatomically separable, as Stellar (45) has argued, but we might consider instead the possibility that there is just one general drive state that can be aroused in different ways. Stellar's argument does not seem fully convincing. There are certainly regions in the hypothalamus that control eating, for example; but is this a *motivating* mechanism? The very essence of such a conception is that the mechanism in question should energize *other* mechanisms, and Miller, Bailey, and Stevenson (31) have shown that the opposite is true.

But this issue should not be pressed too far, with our present knowledge. I have tried to avoid dogmatism in this presentation in the hope that we might try, for once, to see what we have in common in our views on motivation. One virtue of identifying arousal with drive is that it relates differing views (as well as bringing into the focus of attention data that may otherwise be neglected). The important thing is a clear distinction between cue function and arousal function, and the fact that at low levels an increase of drive intensity may be rewarding, whereas at high levels it is a decrease that rewards. Given this point of view and our assumptions about arousal mechanisms, we see that what Harlow has emphasized is the exteroceptively aroused, but still low-level, drive, with cue function of course directly provided for. In the concept of anxiety, Spence and Brown emphasize the higher-level drive state, especially where there is no guiding cue function that would enable the animal to escape threat. The feedback from cortical functioning makes intelligible Mowrer's (35) equating anxiety aroused by threat of pain, and anxiety aroused in some way by cognitive processes related to ideas of the self. Solomon and Wynne's (44) results with sympathectomy are also relevant, since we must not neglect the arousal effects of interoceptor activity; and so is clinical anxiety due to metabolic and nutritional disorders, as well as that due to some conflict of cognitive processes.

Obviously these are not explanations that are being discussed, but possible lines of future research; and there is one problem in particular that I would urge should not be forgotten. This is the cortical feedback to the arousal system, in physiological terms: or in psychological terms, the *immediate drive value of cognitive processes*, without intermediary. This is psychologically demonstrable and *has* been demonstrated repeatedly.

Anyone who is going to talk about acquired drives, or secondary motivation, should first read an old paper by Valentine (48). He showed that with a young child you can easily condition fear of a caterpillar or a furry animal but cannot condition fear of opera glasses, or a bottle; in other words, the fear of some objects, that seems to be learned, was there, latent, all the time. Miller (29) has noted this possibility but he does not seem to have regarded it very seriously, though he cited a confirmatory experiment by Bregman; for in the same passage he suggests that my own results with chimpanzee fears of certain objects, including strange people, may be dealt with by generalization. But this simply will not do, as Riesen and I noted (21). If you try to work this out, for the infant who is terrified on *first* contact with a stranger, an infant who has never shown such terror before, and who has always responded with eager affection to the only human beings he has made contact with up to this moment, you will find that this is a purely verbal solution.

Furthermore, as Valentine observed, you cannot postulate that the cause of such fear is simply the strange event, the thing that has never occurred before. For the chimpanzee reared in darkness, the first sight of a human being is of course a strange event, by definition; but fear of strangers does not occur until later, until the chimpanzee has had an opportunity to learn to recognize a few persons. The fear is not "innate" but depends on some sort of cognitive or cortical conflict of learned responses. This is clearest when the baby chimpanzee, who knows and welcomes attendant *A* and attendant *B*, is terrified when he sees *A* wearing *B*'s coat. The role of learning is inescapable in such a case.

The cognitive and learning element may be forgotten in other motivations, too. Even in the food drive, some sort of learning is fundamentally important: Ghent(15) has shown this, Sheffield and Campbell (41) seem in agreement, and so does the work of Miller and his associates (3, 32, 30) on the greater reinforcement value of food by mouth, compared to food by stomach tube. Beach (1) has shown the cortical-and-learning element in sex behaviour. Melzack (28) has demonstrated recently that even pain responses involve learning. In Harlow's (16) results, of course, and Montgomery's (33), the cognitive element is obvious.

These cortical or cognitive components in motivation are clearest when we compare the behaviour of higher and lower species. Application of a *genuine* comparative method is essential, in the field of motivation as well as of intellectual functions (22). Most disagreements between us have related to so-called "higher" motivations. But the evidence I have discussed today need not be handled in such a way as to maintain the illusion of a complete separation between our various approaches to the problem. It *is* an illusion, I am convinced; we still have many points of disagreement as to relative emphasis, and as to which of several alternative lines to explore first, but this does not imply fundamental and final opposition. As theorists, we have been steadily coming together in respect of ideational (or representative, or mediating, or cognitive) processes; I believe that the same thing can happen, and is happening, in the field of motivation.

References

1. Beach, F. A. The Neural Basis of Innate Behaviour. III. Comparison of Learning Ability and Instinctive Behaviour in the Rat. *Journal of Comparative Physiological Psychology, 28,* (1939), 225-62.
2. Bergmann, G. Theoretical Psychology. *Annual Review of Psychology, 4* (1953), 435-58.
3. Berkun, M. M., Marion L. Kessen, and N. E. Miller. Hunger-Reducing Effects of Food by Stomach Fistula Versus Food by Mouth Measured by a Consummatory Response. *Journal of Comparative Physiological Psychology, 45* (1952), 550-54.
4. Berlyne, D. E. Novelty and Curiosity as Determinants of Exploratory Behaviour. *British Journal of Psychology, 41* (1950), 68-80.
5. Bexton, W. H., W. Heron, and T. H. Scott. Effects of Decreased Variation in the Sensory Environment. *Canadian Journal of Psychology, 8* (1954), 70-76.
6. Brink, F. Excitation and Conduction in the Neuron. In *Handbook of Experimental Psychology,* ed. S. S. Stevens, pp. 50-93. New York: John Wiley & Sons, Inc., 1951.
7. Brown, J. S. Problems Presented by the Concept of Acquired Drives. In *Current Theory and Research in Motivation: A Symposium,* pp. 1-21. Lincoln: University of Nebraska Press, 1953.
8. Brown, J. S., and A. Jacobs. The Role of Fear in the Motivation and Acquisition of Responses. *Journal of Experimental Psychology, 39* (1949), 747-59.
9. Burns, B. D. The Mechanism of Afterbursts in Cerebral Cortex. *Journal of Physiology, 127* (1955), 168-88.
10. Butler, R. A. Discrimination Learning by Rhesus Monkeys to Visual-Exploration Motivation. *Journal of Comparative Physiological Psychology, 46* (1953), 95-98.
11. Carper, J. W., and F. A. Polliard. Comparison of the Intake of Glucose and Saccharin Solutions under Conditions of Caloric Need. *American Journal of Psychology, 66* (1953), 479-82.
12. Clare, M. H., and G. H. Bishop. Properties of Dendrites; Apical Dendrites of the Cat Cortex. *EEG Clinical Neurophysiology, 7* (1955), 85-98.
13. Duffy, Elizabeth. An Explanation of the "Emotional" Phenomena without the Use of the Concept "Emotion." *Journal of Genetic Psychology, 25* (1941), 283-93.
14. Eccles, J. C. *The Neurophysiological Basis of Mind.* London: Oxford University Press, 1953.
15. Ghent, Lila. The Relation of Experience to the Development of Hunger. *Canadian Journal of Psychology, 5* (1951), 77-81.
16. Harlow, H. F. Mice, Monkeys, Men, and Motives. *Psychological Review, 60* (1953), 23-32.
17. Harlow, H. F., Margaret K. Harlow, and D. R. Meyer. Learning Motivated by a Manipulation Drive. *Journal of Experimental Psychology, 40* (1950), 228-34.
18. Hebb, D. O. Elementary School Methods. *Teachers' Magazine* (Montreal), *12* (1930), 23-26.
19. ———. *Organization of Behaviour.* New York: John Wiley & Sons, Inc., 1949.
20. ———. On Human Thought. *Canadian Journal of Psychology, 7* (1953), 99-110.
21. Hebb, D. O., and A. H. Riesen. The Genesis of Irrational Fears. *Bulletin of the Canadian Psychological Association, 3* (1943), 49-50.
22. Hebb, D. O., and W. R. Thompson. The Social Significance of Animal Studies. In *Handbook of Social Psychology,* ed. G. Lindzey, pp. 532-61. Cambridge, Mass.: Addison-Wesley, 1954.
23. Li, Choh-Luh, and H. Jasper. Microelectrode Studies of the Cerebral Cortex in the Cat. *Journal of Physiology, 121* (1953), 117-40.
24. Lindsley, D. B. Emotion. In *Handbook of Experimental Psychology,* ed. S. S. Stevens, pp. 473-516. New York: John S. Wiley & Sons, Inc., 1951.
25. Lloyd, D. P. C. A Direct Central Inhibitory Action of Dromically Conducted Impulses. *Journal of Neurophysiology, 4* (1941), 184-90.
26. MacCorquodale, K., and P. E. Meehl. A Distinction Between Hypothetical Constructs and

Intervening Variables. *Psychological Review, 55* (1948), 95-107.

27. MARSHALL, S. L. A. *Men Against Fire.* New York: William Morrow & Co., Inc., 1947.
28. MELZACK, R. The Effects of Early Experience on the Emotional Responses to Pain. Unpublished doctoral dissertation, McGill University, 1954.
29. MILLER, N. E. Learnable Drives and Rewards. In *Handbook of Experimental Psychology,* ed. S. S. STEVENS, pp. 435-72. New York: John S. Wiley & Sons, Inc., 1951.
30. MILLER, N. E. Some Studies of Drive and Drive Reduction. A paper read at the American Psychological Association, Cleveland, September, 1953.
31. MILLER, N. E., C. J. BAILEY, and J. A. F. STEVENSON. Decreased "Hunger" but Increased Food Intake from Hypothalamic Lesions. *Science, 112* (1950), 256-59.
32. MILLER, N. E., and MARION L. KESSEN. Reward Effects of Food via Stomach Fistula Compared with Those via Mouth. *Journal of Comparative Physiological Psychology, 45* (1952), 555-64.
33. MONTGOMERY, K. C. The Effect of Activity Deprivation upon Exploratory Behaviour. *Journal of Comparative Physiological Psychology, 46* (1953), 438-41.
34. MORUZZI, G., and H. W. MAGOUN. Brain Stem Reticular Formation and Activation of the EEG. *EEG Clinical Neurophysiology, 1* (1949), 455-73.
35. MOWRER, O. H. Motivation. *Annual Review of Psychology, 3* (1952), 419-38.
36. NISSEN, H. W. Instinct as Seen by a Psychologist. *Psychological Review, 60* (1953), 291-94.
37. OLDS, J., and P. MILNER. Positive Reinforcement Produced by Electrical Stimulation of Septal Area and Other Regions of Rat Brain. *Journal of Comparative Physiological Psychology, 47* (1954), 419-27.
38. OLZEWSKI, J. The Cytoarchitecture of the Human Reticular Formation. In *Brain Mechanisms and Consciousness,* eds. E. D. ADRIAN, F. BREMER, and H. H. JASPER. Oxford: Blackwell, 1954.
39. SCHLOSBERG, H. Three Dimensions of Emotion. *Psychological Review, 61* (1954), 81-88.
40. SHARPLESS, S. K. Role of the Reticular Formation in Habituation. Unpublished doctoral dissertation, McGill University, 1954.
41. SHEFFIELD, F. D., and B. A. CAMPBELL. The Role of Experience in the "Spontaneous" Activity of Hungry Rats. *Journal of Comparative Physiological Psychology, 47* (1954), 97-100.
42. SHEFFIELD, F. D., and T. B. ROBY. Reward Value of a Non-Nutritive Sweet Taste. *Journal of Comparative Physiological Psychology, 43* (1950), 471-81.
43. SHEFFIELD, F. D., J. J. WULFF, and R. BACKER. Reward Value of Copulation without Sex Drive Reduction. *Journal of Comparative Physiological Psychology, 44* (1951) 3-8.
44. SOLOMON, R. L., and L. C. WYNNE. Avoidance Conditioning in Normal Dogs and in Dogs Deprived of Normal Autonomic Functioning. *American Psychologist, 5* (1950), 264 (abstract).
45. STELLAR, E. The Physiology of Motivation. *Psychological Review, 61* (1954) 5-22.
46. THOMPSON, W. R., and L. M. SOLOMON. Spontaneous Pattern Discrimination in the Rat. *Journal of Comparative Physiological Psychology, 47* (1954), 104-7.
47. TYHURST, J. S. Individual Reactions to Community Disaster: the Natural History of Psychiatric Phenomena. *American Journal of Psychiatry, 107* (1951), 764-69.
48. VALENTINE, C. W. The Innate Bases of Fear. *Journal of Genetic Psychology, 37* (1930), 394-419.
49. WHITING, J. W. M., and O. H. MOWRER. Habit Progression and Regression—a Laboratory Study of Some Factors Relevant to Human Socialization. *Journal of Comparative Psychology, 36* (1943), 229-53.
50. WOODWORTH, R. S. *Psychology.* New York: Holt, Rinehart & Winston, Inc., 1921.
51. WOODWORTH, R. S., and D. G. MARQUIS. *Psychology* (5th ed.). New York: Holt, Rinehart & Winston, Inc., 1947.

10 / Curiosity and Exploration

D.E. Berlyne *University of Toronto*

In considering motivation, early psychologists had emphasized the life-sustaining drives such as hunger, thirst, and sex. The fact that animals and men spend a good deal of their time in exploring their environment and seeking novel stimulation was largely overlooked. It is through the efforts of psychologists such as Professor Berlyne that the significance of curiosity and exploratory behaviour has been elaborated. Professor Berlyne is the author of three books: Conflict, Arousal, and Curiosity, *1960;* Structure and Direction in Thinking, *1965; and* Psychology and Aesthetics, *to be published in 1971.*

Higher animals spend a substantial portion of their time and energy on activities to which terms like *curiosity* and *play* seem applicable (1, 2). An even more conspicuous part of human behaviour, especially in highly organized societies, is classifiable as "recreation," "entertainment," "art," or "science." In all of these activities, sense organs are brought into contact with biologically neutral or "indifferent" stimulus patterns – that is, with objects or events that do not seem to be inherently beneficial or noxious. Stimulus patterns encountered in this way are sometimes used to guide subsequent action aimed at achieving some immediate practical advantage. An animal looking and sniffing around may stumble upon a clue to the whereabouts of food. A scientist's discovery may contribute to public amenity and to his own enrichment or fame. Much of the time, however, organisms do nothing in particular about the stimulus patterns that they pursue with such avidity. They appear to seek them "for their own sake."

Until about 15 years ago these forms of behaviour were overlooked in the theoretical and experimental literature, except for a few scattered investigations. Recently they have been winning more and more interest among psychologists. They constitute what is generally known in Western countries as "exploratory behaviour" and, in Eastern Europe, as "orientational-investigatory activity."

Early demonstrations of the prevalence and strength of these activities in higher animals were rather embarrassing to then current motivation theories. Animals are, of course, most likely to explore and play when they have no emergencies to deal with, but there are times when these behaviours will even override what one would expect to be more urgent considerations. A hungry rat may spend time investigating a novel feature of the environment before settling down to eat (3). A bird may approach a strange and potentially threatening object at the risk of its life (4). Even human beings are reported to have played the lyre while Rome was burning and to have insisted on completing a game of bowls after an invading armada had been sighted.

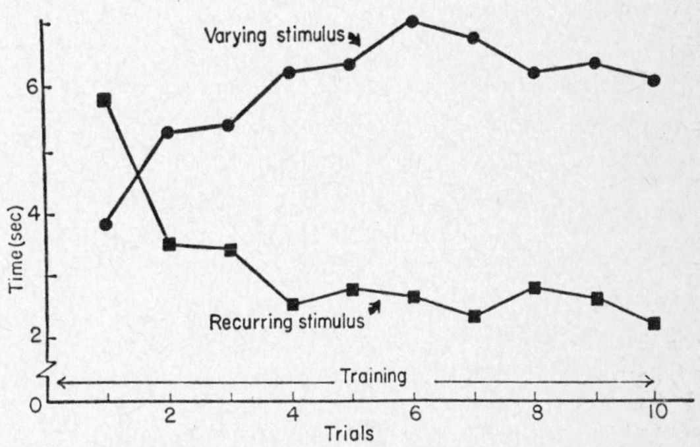

Fig. 1. Mean time spent by subjects fixating a novel (varying) and a familiar (recurring) pattern when the two were presented side by side for ten 10-second trials with 20-second intertrial intervals. [*Adapted from Berlyne (14)*]

Under the influence of Darwin's evolutionary theory and later of Cannon's concept of homeostasis, it had come to be widely believed during the 1930's and 1940's that the motivation of behaviour is bound up with clear-cut prerequisites of survival, such as eating, drinking, procreating, and avoiding bodily injury. Behaviour is set in motion, it was thought, either by biological dangers or by events associated (through contiguity or through similarity) with biological dangers. Similarly, the goals for which animals and human beings strive were commonly assumed to have inherent or learned connections with biological gratification or relief. These assumptions, in different forms, were shared by the early neobehaviourists, physiological psychologists, and psychoanalysts.

As knowledge accumulated about the conditions that govern exploratory behaviour and about how quickly it appears after birth, it seemed less and less likely that this behaviour could be a derivative of hunger, thirst, sexual appetite, pain, fear of pain, and

Reprinted, by permission, from *Science*, Vol. 153 (July 1, 1966), pp. 25-33.

the like, or that stimuli sought through exploration are welcomed because they have previously accompanied satisfaction of these drives. The facts about exploratory behaviour were especially hard to reconcile with the view once offered by Freud (5) and later espoused by neo-behaviourists (6) that behaviour is essentially directed toward minimizing stimulation and excitation, a view that anybody who has had to handle a child "with nothing to do" must have been tempted to question.

Being now compelled to recognize that higher animals put a great deal of effort into securing access to stimuli with no manifest ecological importance, we can discern two groups of reasons why this phenomenon may make biological sense. First, we know that spontaneous activity is constantly present within the central nervous system and that, during waking hours, the organs are ceaselessly bombarded with stimuli, all of which initiate excitatory processes within the brain. We also know that the brain is a highly intricate organ in which many processes can be initiated simultaneously and can interact to their mutual impediment. The only way in which the brain can perform its prime function of selecting adaptive responses is to allow one process to advance and complete itself while competing processes are held in check. To determine which process shall be granted priority, the brain depends on information about conditions inside and outside the organism, some of which enters through sense organs and some of which is stored after having been deposited by previous learning or by natural selection. The required information will often be lacking, in which case the brain will be unable to arbitrate between, or reconcile, the discrepant demands that are made on it. Reciprocal interference between processes going on within it and – if the organism is beset by an urgent call for action – conflict among incompatible response-tendencies may eliminate the effectiveness of behaviour. So, in such cases, it is clearly useful for an organism to secure access to stimulus patterns that contain the information from lack of which it is suffering.

The second group of reasons is quite different. It seems that the central nervous system of a higher animal is designed to cope with environments that produce a certain rate of influx of stimulation, information, and challenge to its capacities. It will naturally not perform at its best in an environment that overstresses or overloads it, but we also have evidence that prolonged subjection to an inordinately monotonous or unstimulating environment is detrimental to a variety of psychological functions (7, 8). How much excitement or challenge is optimal will fluctuate quite widely with personality, culture, psychophysiological state, and recent or remote experience. But we can understand why organisms may seek out stimulation that taxes the nervous system to the right extent, when naturally occurring stimuli are either too easy or too difficult to assimilate.

With accumulating research, there have been more and more indications that exploratory responses can be of two distinct classes, corresponding to these two distinct biological needs. On the one hand, when an animal is disturbed by a lack of information, and thus left a prey to uncertainty and conflict, it is likely to resort to what we may call *specific* exploratory responses. These supply or intensify stimulation from particular sources – sources that can supply the precise information that the animal misses. The condition of discomfort, due to inadequacy of information, that motivates specific exploration is what we call "curiosity." In other circumstances, an animal seeks out stimulation, regardless of source or content, that offers something like an optimum amount of novelty, surprisingness, complexity, change, or variety. For this kind of behaviour the term *diversive* exploration has been proposed. It is not preceded by receipt of partial information about the stimulus patterns at which it is aimed and thus seems to be motivated by factors quite different from curiosity.

Specific Exploration

One of the earliest discoveries coming out of Pavlov's work on "higher nervous activity" was the phenomenon that he called the "orientational" or "investigatory" reflex (9). A dog would respond to any unusual or unexpected happening by desisting from whatever activity it might otherwise have been engaged in and turning its eyes, head, and trunk toward the source of stimulation. This was an unconditioned or innate reflex, and yet it was subject to many of the processes to which conditioned reflexes are subject, including extinction and disinhibition. If the stimulus evoking it were repeated at short intervals, the orientational response would gradually disappear. It would come back if the stimulus recurred, say, a day later, but, after several recoveries and extinctions the power of a particular stimulus to evoke the response might be permanently weakened (1, chap. 4). It was thus shown that novelty, especially short-term novelty, is a potent factor governing this reaction.

The influence of novelty was amply confirmed when specific exploratory behaviour began to be studied in the West. It was found, for example, that a rat is more likely to walk up to and sniff at an object that it has not seen before than one to which it has been exposed during the last few minutes (10). When a rat is confined in a novel environment, the amount of wandering about that it does and the frequency with which it approaches a particular feature of the environment decline with time – that is, as the stimulus patterns that are present lose their novelty (11, 12). When the animal is put back into the situation after spending some time away from it, exploration will revive, but the revival will become less and less marked if the repeated exposures extend over several days.

Apart from the influence of novelty, the strength

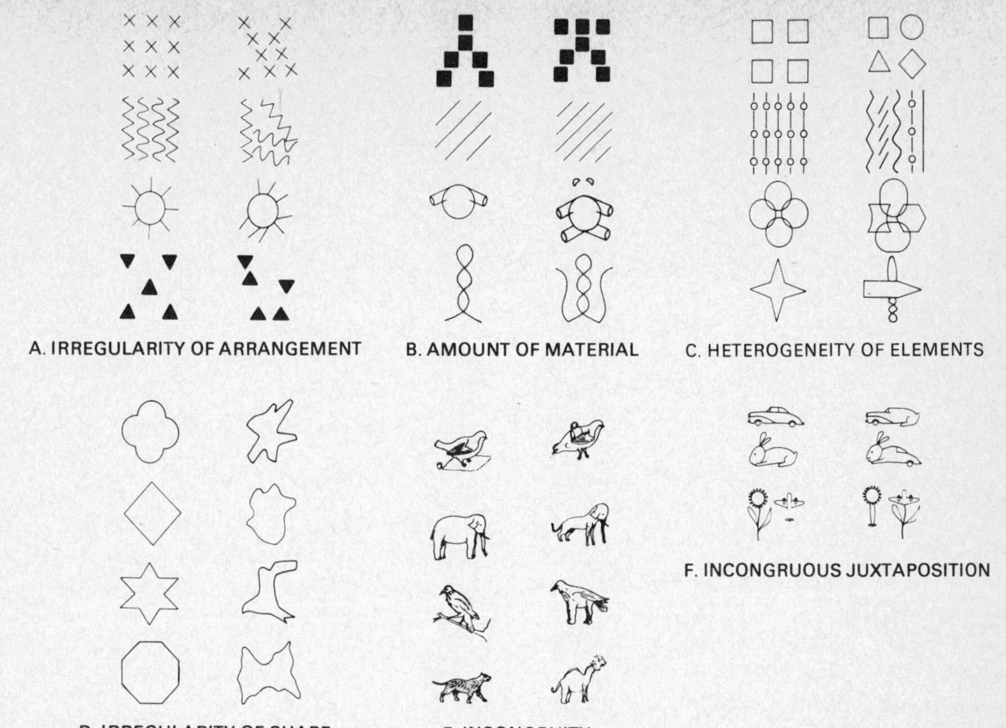

Fig. 2. Visual patterns, representing various "complexity" and "incongruity" variables, used in experiments on exploratory and related behaviour in human adults. [From Berlyne (16); some of the same patterns were used in experiments reported in 14, 15, 17, 18, 30, 31, and 39-41]

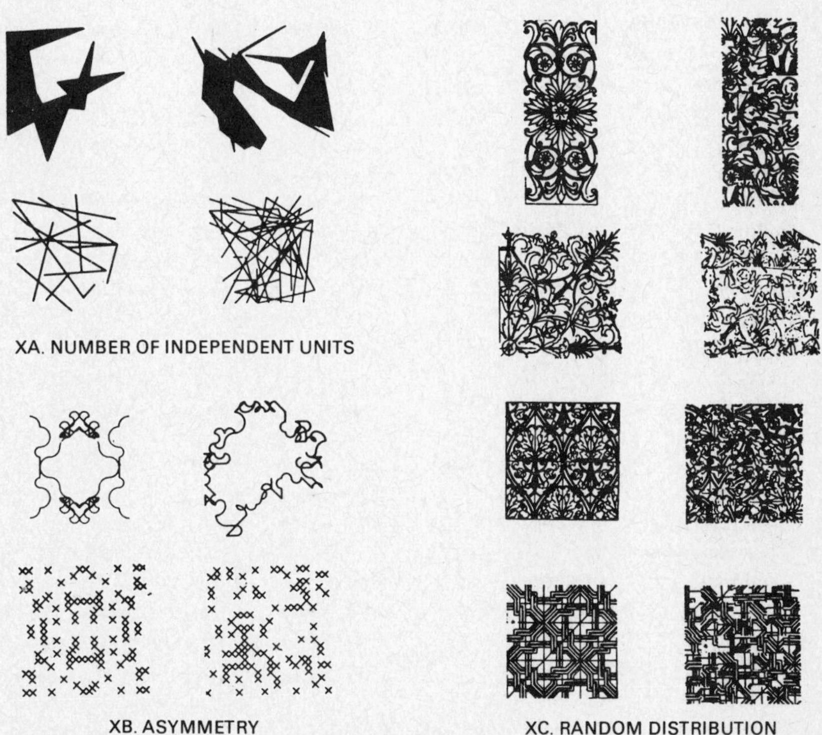

Fig. 3. Visual patterns, representing various "complexity" variables, of a higher order of complexity than those of Fig. 2. [These patterns were first published in Berlyne and Lawrence (15), but some have been used for experiments reported in 17, 18, 30, 31, and 39-41]

and direction of exploratory responses in animals have been shown to depend on stimulus properties of the kind usually denoted by words like *complexity*. More vigorous and prolonged exploration will generally be attracted by objects that offer more varied or more irregular stimulation (12, 13).

Similar variables have been found to govern specific exploration in the human adult. We have used a number of techniques to compare the power of different visual patterns to attract and sustain inspection when subjects are given no special reason to attend to them. We have allowed subjects access to a switch controlling a tachistoscope, by means of which they could give themselves as many successive brief (0.14-second) glimpses of a pattern as they wished before calling for the next pattern (14). We have presented successions of patterns in an automatic projector, letting subjects look at each pattern for as long as they wished before pressing the button that replaced it with the next one (15). We have presented patterns side by side on a screen and measured how much time the subject spent fixating each of them; this measurement was made either by having eye movements observed by an experimenter who did not know which patterns were being exposed (16) or by recording them with an eye-movement camera (17). The influence of novelty is shown by one experiment (16) in which we showed a series of pairs of animal pictures, the picture on one side (the left and the right sides for equal numbers of subjects) being the same on every trial and the picture on the other side being changed from one trial to the next. Observation of eye movements (see Fig. 1) revealed that, as trials succeeded one another, the subjects spent a lower and lower proportion of the time inspecting the recurrent pattern and more and more time looking at the changing patterns.

All the techniques just mentioned have been used to study effects on exploration time of several stimulus properties that, although distinct, exemplify the kind of variable we mean when we use words like *complexity, irregularity,* or *incongruity*. In each of the pairs of patterns shown in Fig. 2, the member on the right is the more "complex" or "irregular" one, but the actual property that distinguishes it from its neighbour varies from one category of pairs to another. We have regularly found that the subject spends more time looking at the "more complex" than at the "less complex" pattern of a pair. Since all these patterns are relatively simple, we have more recently added the patterns of Fig. 3 (15, 17, 18). These likewise comprise categories representing different "complexity" variables, but all of them contain notably more elements than the patterns in categories A through D of Fig. 2 and thus allow us to probe the upper reaches of the dimensions underlying judgements of "complexity." It has been demonstrated that the material in categories XA through XC (Fig. 3) is rated significantly more "complex" by adult subjects that the material in categories A through D (17). Experiments incorporating categories XA through XC have indicated that exploration time reaches a peak and declines as complexity becomes extreme. The point at which the peak is reached seems, however, to vary quite widely from individual to individual and from population to population.

An experiment (19) was carried out with 3- to 9-month-old babies, after casual observation of one infant suggested a strong predilection for looking at newsprint, maps, and the like. Spock (20) advises, in fact, that babies enjoy watching leaves and shadows. In the experiment, pairs of adjacent patterns were brought simultaneously down into the field of vision, and it was found that patterns B3 and D3 of Fig. 4 were more likely than others in the same series to attract the subject's gaze first. These patterns seem to be more "complex" than the others in the sense that they possess more internal contour. There seemed to be some inconsistency between this result and Hershenson's finding (21) that newborn infants are inclined to spend more time looking at a 2 by 2 checkerboard than at a 4 by 4 or 12 by 12 checkerboard – that is, more time looking at the least complex stimulus pattern.

The discrepancy has since been resolved by Brennan, Ames, and Moore (22), who have shown that the preferred degree of complexity goes up with age: 8-week-olds prefer to look at a checkerboard of intermediate grain (8 by 8), whereas 20-week-olds prefer a 24 by 24 checkerboard to less complex ones. These investigators have also demonstrated that this development is not simply a matter of increasing visual acuity. Eight-week-olds can distinguish 24 by 24 checkerboards from gray rectangles. Other experiments have ascertained that novelty (23), surprisingness (a disparity between a stimulus event and expectation) (24), and regularity or irregularity of form (25) are other stimulus characteristics influencing infantile exploration.

In recent years, measurement of exploratory behaviour has become a standard means of investigating not only motivational but also perceptual processes in subjects who are too young for traditional techniques, such as questioning and discrimination training. A difference in the power of two visual patterns to elicit exploration implies that the subject can tell them apart. By this means, it has become evident that some degree of visual form discrimination, presumably innate, exists before learning has had time to mould perception, a question that was formerly open to debate (26).

Table I – Mean numbers of responses in 15-minute session on training days

Reinforcing stimulus	Methamphetamine	Placebo	Mean
Familiar	9.0	4.8	6.8
Novel	3.9	11.7	8.2
Mean	6.6	8.2	

According to a theoretical view that suggests itself (1, 27), specific exploratory responses, whether unlearned or learned, are likely to result from an aversive condition or condition of heightened drive due to lack of information (subjective uncertainty). Such a condition, which may appropriately be called "perceptual curiosity," is apt to result from exposure to novel, surprising, highly complex, or ambiguous stimulus patterns.

At present, my associates and I are engaged in experiments designed to test the hypothesis that subjective uncertainty is aversive – that its termination will reinforce an instrumental response. Presentation of blurred pictures is our means of inducing uncertainty. Our preliminary results have provided some tentative confirmation for our expectations. The replacement of a blurred picture by a clear version of the same picture seems, in at least some circumstances, to be a more effective reward or reinforcer (as shown by the rate at which a key is pressed to secure it) than the replacement of a blurred picture by an unrelated clear picture or by another blurred picture. Furthermore, we have some hint that a clear picture is most rewarding when it replaces a picture with an intermediate degree of blurredness. This seems to be a degree at which some differentiation is beginning to emerge but no objects or detail can be recognized, so that there is maximum scope for competing hypotheses.

Collative Variables

The widespread attention that exploration and related forms of behaviour are now receiving, after decades of relative neglect, seems justified when one considers the prevalence of such behaviour in higher animal species. As psychologists are coming to recognize more and more, exploratory responses are indispensable adjuncts of many vital activities. When unlearned behaviour patterns or discrimination learning have invested an external stimulus object with a special significance, an animal must initiate a segment of behaviour by bringing its receptors into contact with the crucial cues that indicate what action is likely to have beneficial consequences. How sense organs are oriented must profoundly affect the form in which a stimulus pattern is perceived and represented in memory. But, as often happens with a new area of investigation, the examination of exploratory behaviour has raised questions of a much wider import and reopened some fundamental theoretical questions that at one time seemed settled.

What is explored, and how vigorously, depends on many factors inside and outside the organism. Properties of external stimuli with which psychologists have long been concerned have an undeniably potent influence. They include psychophysical properties, closely dependent on specific physicochemical variables (for example, brightness, loudness, colour), and ecological properties, dependent on association with noxious events or visceral gratifications. It was, however, not long before experiments on curiosity and specific exploration had demonstrated the psychological importance of a third group of stimulus properties, which evidently outweighed the others in controlling this kind of behaviour.

Fig. 4. Four sets of three visual patterns used in experiments with 3- to 9-month-old infants. The patterns of a set were presented in pairs, and the member of each pair that first attracted the subject's gaze was noted. The numeral under each pattern denotes the number of times out of 56 presentations (four with each of 14 subjects) that the pattern was fixated first.

These are the properties for which I have suggested the term *collative* (1, 27), since they depend on comparison or collation of stimulus elements, whether they be elements appearing simultaneously in different sectors of a stimulus field or elements that have been perceived at different times. They comprise the properties that we designate by words like *novelty, surprisingness, incongruity, complexity, variability,* and *puzzlingness.* Just as the psychophysical properties are derived from distributions of energy and the ecological properties connect stimuli with the factors that govern natural selection, thus making contact with the two great unifying concepts of 19th-century science, the collative properties have close connections with information, the unifying concept responsible for some revolutionary developments in 20th-century science.

The technical language of information theory does not suffice for an adequate description of the collative variables, but its concepts can help a great deal in specifying and measuring them. Provided that certain assumptions are fulfilled, how "novel", "surprising," "regular," or "orderly" a structure is, how numerous its elements are, and how interdependent, determine its information content, uncertainty (from an external observer's point of view) regarding an organism's reaction to it, and the organism's degree of subjective uncertainty regarding what will happen next or regarding the nature of elements that have not yet been inspected.

What all the collative variables have in common to give them the motivational effects that they apparently share is an interesting but still debatable question. One hypothesis for which supporting arguments can be found (1, 27) is that these effects all depend on *conflict* between incompatible neural, and ultimately motor, reactions that are simultaneously mobilized.

The motivational effects of collative stimulus properties are by no means confined to occasioning and directing exploratory responses. They include the factors making for "good" or "bad" form, which were shown by the Gestalt psychologists to govern many perceptual phenomena. They include the factors constituting "form," "composition," or "structure" in the visual and performing arts, in literature, in music, and in humour.

Instead of eliciting exploration – which means approach and sustained contact – novel, surprising, and strange objects may provoke terror and flight (28). Approach (for the sake of obtaining additional information or perhaps simply for the sake of relief through habituation) and escape are, after all, alternative ways of alleviating a disturbance due to a conflict-inducing sight or sound. Which will prevail seems to depend on many things, including how disturbing the stimulus pattern is, how agitated or relaxed a subject is, and what personality traits he possesses. Forms of behaviour that apparently represent vacillation between curiosity and fear in the face of something unusual have frequently been observed in animals and in human beings. Whether something is experienced as pleasurable, annoying, or vapid oftens turns in an extremely subtle way on how much novelty, variety, or unpredictability it affords. This is true even when some extrinsic source of motivation is at work, as in the culinary and erotic domains.

Arousal

Still further ramifications come into view as we pursue the relations between exploratory behaviour and arousal (1, 27). The concept of "arousal level" is an outgrowth of several developments in neurophysiology and psychology that have occurred during the last 15 years or so. It connotes a psychophysiological dimension, indicative of how "wide-awake," "alert," or "excited" an organism is at a particular time. Fluctuations in arousal are reflected by changes in the electrical activity of the brain, in electrical and thermal properties of the skin, in muscular tension, in the circulatory system, in the respiratory system, and in the diameter of the pupil, all of which can be recorded and precisely measured. A great deal has been learned, and more is coming to light, about the neural processes on which arousal depends, involving interactions among the brain-stem reticular formation, the hypothalamus, the diffuse thalamic system, and the cerebral cortex.

Few, if any, motivational aspects of behaviour have been untouched by fresh thinking inspired by the concept of "arousal." One particularly pregnant trend has been a progressive coalescence between the new concept of "arousal" and the concept of "drive," which has dominated discussion of motivation since the 1920's. If "arousal" can be identified with "drive" (and more refinement of both concepts is required before we can tell how far and in what sense it can be), the implications may be quite far-reaching. First, we shall have at our disposal more precise and direct techniques than we had before for measuring drive. Secondly, any factor that can be shown to raise or lower arousal will have to be included among the factors that induce and reduce drive, and thus among those that can motivate behaviour and give rise to changes in behaviour through learning.

The grounds for connecting exploratory responses with rises in arousal are twofold. First, a great deal of experimental work, (largely, but not entirely, carried out in the U.S.S.R.) has shown at least some forms of exploratory behaviour to be accompanied by pervasive psychophysiological changes, including several recognized indices of increased arousal (29). This work has led to a broadening of Pavlov's notion of an "orientational reflex" or orientation reaction. Pavlov used this term to denote the immediately visible bodily movements through which an animal focuses its sense organs on an unusual source of stimulation. It is now clear that these are accompanied by a whole network of processes, most of them not detectable without special amplifying and recording equipment, which seem to represent a mobilization of the animal's capacities to absorb information through its sense organs, process the information through its central nervous system, and act promptly and energetically.

Secondly, evidence is accumulating that the collative stimulus properties by which exploratory behaviour is so profoundly influenced are capable of increasing arousal. Several experimenters have shown that a stimulus gradually loses its power to evoke an orientation reaction – that is, to raise arousal – as it loses its novelty through repetition (1, chap. 4). In our own research, my associates and I have been measuring the effects of various collative stimulus properties on the galvanic skin response (15, 30) (a transient increase in conductance or in potential difference between two points on the palms or soles) and on the duration of electroencephalographic desynchronization (31) (the replacement of alpha waves by an irregular, low-amplitude, predominantly high-frequency pattern, indicative of an alerted cerebral cortex) as indices of arousal or components of the orientation reaction. We have been able to show that the magnitude of the galvanic skin response declines not only as one visual pattern is repeatedly exposed but also as different patterns succeed one another.

Table II – Mean numbers of responses in 15-minute session on test days

Reinforcing stimulus	Methamphetamine	Placebo	Mean
Familiar	13.9	4.8	9.1
Novel	6.5	10.7	8.8
Mean	10.4	7.8	

We have found the intensity of the orientation reaction to increase with surprisingness (when surprising and nonsurprising stimuli are equated for novelty) and with the complexity and incongruity variables embodied in the patterns of Figs. 2 and 3. We have also demonstrated that the mean amplitude of the galvanic skin response increases with degree of conflict, which, as explained earlier, is suspected of being the common underlying factor responsible for the motivational effects of the collative variables. At present we are investigating electroencephalographic effects of various "complexity" variables descriptive of auditory stimuli. It has already become clear that white noise evokes longer desynchronization than equally loud sine-wave tones or combinations of two or three such tones.

Epistemic Curiosity

Specific exploratory responses in human beings are, as often as not, "epistemic" responses as well as exploratory responses. The use of this term is proposed in order to indicate that they are aimed not only at obtaining access to information-bearing stimulation, capable of dispelling the uncertainties of the moment, but also at acquiring knowledge – that is, information stored in the form of ideational structures and giving rise to internal symbolic responses that can guide behaviour on future occasions. Bringing sense organs into contact with appropriate external events is, of course, not the only means of accumulating knowledge. Thinking can be another form of epistemic behaviour (32).

Extending the notion of perceptual curiosity suggested by studies of specific exploration, we may suppose that epistemic behaviour is motivated by "conceptual conflict," or conflict between mutually discrepant symbolic response-tendencies – thoughts, beliefs, attitudes, conceptions (32, 33). Conflicting elements or requirements often characterize the "problems" that start us off inquiring or experimenting or thinking (32, chap. 10). Several experimenters have recorded variations in arousal level while subjects are engaged in thinking, and these variations are influenced by degree of "difficulty," in senses that seem to involve degree of conceptual conflict (32, chap. 11).

Unfortunately, the motivational aspects of epistemic behaviour and of thinking in particular are only just beginning to receive study. We have made some preliminary investigations of the determinants of "epistemic curiosity" (as we may call a motivational condition favouring epistemic behaviour) by presenting human subjects with a series of questions and simply asking them to specify a certain number of questions whose answers they would most like to know (34).

In one such experiment, questions about invertebrate animals were used. According to verbal reports, the most curiosity was induced by questions about the more familiar animals, by questions that subjects found surprising, and by questions that attributed to species characteristics they seemed unlikely to possess. These findings confirmed predictions from hypotheses regarding conceptual conflict. It had been argued that more familiar concepts would produce greater conflict than less familiar ones, by producing more numerous and stronger divergent associations.

In two later experiments, subjects were presented with quotations, each followed by the name of two or three possible authors. Each author's name was coupled with a number, purporting to show how many teachers out of a group of 100, had guessed it to be the correct name. One experiment provided evidence that curiosity was greater when there were three than when there were two alternative authors, and another demonstrated the influence of the distribution of supposed teachers' guesses: the more even the distribution, the greater the curiosity. These two variables – number of alternatives and nearness to equiprobability – are identifiable as the two principal determinants of subjective uncertainty just as uncertainty in the information-theoretic sense is an increasing function of the two corresponding variables. Conceptual conflict is assumed to increase with subjective uncertainty.

Experiments in which other techniques were used have also confirmed the importance of such factors for epistemic curiosity (35). Novelty, surprise, and incongruity make children ask more questions and affect the content of their questions. Several investigators have found adult subjects more likely to seek symbolically expressed information as uncertainty and the gains and losses at stake increase, although there are signs that information-seeking may decline as these variables assume very high values.

Diversive Exploration

There have been many reports from animal studies of exploratory behaviour that seem to be aimed not at obtaining stimulation from a specific object or event about which there is a specific uncertainty but, rather, at obtaining stimulation from any source that can afford an optimum dosage of novelty, complexity, and other collative properties. For example, rats will, all other things being equal, tend to enter a maze arm that differs from the one they entered on the preceding trial or that has undergone some change since they were last in the maze (1, chap. 6; 36). Monkeys confined in a box will work hard, sometimes for as long as 19 hours at a stretch, at repeatedly opening a door so that they can see what is going on in the room outside (37). Human beings confined in a dark room with a minimum of stimulation will press buttons to make patterns of coloured spots of light appear, preferring those sequences of pattern that offer the most variety and unpredictability (38). These and similar forms of behaviour are classifiable, according to the proposed terminology, as "diversive" exploration, and it seems important to distinguish them at this stage of research from the specific exploratory responses that may be motivated by perceptual curiosity.

The advisability of drawing a distinction between specific and diversive exploration is supported by experiments with human subjects. When a subject is shown a pair of patterns from Figs. 2 or 3 and then asked to choose one of the two patterns for further viewing, which he is likely to choose depends on the duration of the initial exposure. If he has seen the two patterns briefly (for 1 second or less) before making his choice, he is more likely to want to see the *more* complex pattern again (39). Preliminary exposures of such brevity are presumably not long enough to allow him to see what the patterns are like and thus to relieve his curiosity. He chooses the more complex pattern, presumably because that is the one about which he has more residual curiosity. If, on the other hand, the preliminary exposures are long enough (3 seconds or more) to allow him to become adequately acquainted with the patterns, he is more likely to want another look at the *less* complex pattern (17, 39, 40). In this case, curiosity, having been largely eliminated by the initial exposures, must play a minor role. Factors akin to aesthetic taste will presumably have more influence. Experiments in which verbal scaling techniques are used have, in fact, suggested that patterns attracting more specific exploration when perceptual curiosity is at work tend to be rated more "interesting," whereas patterns attracting more diversive exploration when a subject has no cause to wonder what a pattern is like tend to be rated more "pleasing" (15, 17, 39, 41).

There might seem to be a close affinity between specific exploration and activities such as science, philosophy, and mathematics, with diversive exploration more closely akin to entertainment and the arts. But this distinction is not absolute. The importance of pleasing structure in science, mathematics, and philosophy has been noted too often to be overlooked, while curiosity – wondering what will come next, trying to make sense of a work, and so on – certainly plays a part in aesthetic appreciation.

Diversive exploratory behaviour is likely to be especially strong after an animal or a human subject has spent some hours in an environment that is highly monotonous or devoid of stimulation (38, 42). The desperate craving of a bored person for a change of any kind is attested by everyday experience and by experiments on "sensory deprivation" (7).

One phenomenon that has been much investigated during the last 10 years and was particularly surprising when it was first discovered is the reward value that stimulus changes of no specific biological significance (for example, light coming on or becoming momentarily brighter, the sound of a buzzer or a click) can have, as shown by the power of such changes to reinforce a bar-pressing response in mice and rats (43).

Some recent experiments in which my associates and I sought factors governing diversive exploration (44) have confirmed the importance that the interaction between collative stimulus properties and arousal level has for this behaviour also. The role of these variables in diversive exploration seems, however, to be somewhat different from their role in perceptual curiosity and specific exploration. Fortuitous circumstances compelled us to house some of the rats to be used for one experiment next to a room containing some extremely noisy printout counters. A quiet room became available later, and the remaining animals were housed in it. The experiment lasted for 8 days. On odd-numbered days (training days), each subject was placed in a Skinner box for a 30-minute pretraining period, during which no bar was present in the box. The pretraining period was immediately followed by a 15-minute training session, during which two bars protruded from the rear wall, and every time either was pressed, the illumination became brighter for 1 second or a buzzer sounded for 1 second. On even-numbered days (test days) there was a 15-minute test session during which the bars were present but no light change or buzzer sound occurred when one of the bars was pressed.

It turned out that, in animals maintained in the noisy quarters, a familiar stimulus (one that was presented every minute during pretraining periods) had a greater reward value than a novel stimulus (one not presented during pretraining periods), as evidenced by the rate of bar-pressing during both training sessions and test sessions. In animals maintained in the quiet room, on the other hand, novel stimuli were more rewarding than familiar stimuli.

These unexpected findings could be explained by making three assumptions: (1) that the rats subjected to noise between experimental sessions had a higher arousal level than the rats maintained in the quiet room; (2) that the reward value of a stimulus resulting from diversive exploration is an inverted U-shaped function of the degree to which the stimulus raises arousal; and (3) that the extent to which a stimulus raises arousal increases with its novelty and with the subject's initial arousal level. This explanation was corroborated by a subsequent experiment, in which injections of methamphetamine were used to raise arousal and a change in illumination served as reward. It was found, in accordance with predictions, that the drugged animals performed more responses with a familiar reinforcing stimulus, whereas control animals injected with saline solution performed more responses with a novel reinforcing stimulus (see Tables I and II).

A number of experiments (18, 45) have indicated that conditions conducive to abnormally high levels of arousal (for example, hunger, pain, fear, noise, exposure to an incomprehensible tape-recorded message) make rats and human beings less eager than usual to seek out novel or complex stimulation. The findings just cited seem relevant to this phenomenon, among others.

Conclusions

Under the impact of experimental findings on exploratory behaviour and cognate phenomena, motivation theory is undergoing some extensive remodeling. These findings have opened our eyes to the pervasive psychological importance of collative variables and arousal. We find ourselves forced to recognize that the disturbances that motivate behaviour can come not only from external irritants, visceral upheavals, and deprivation of vital substances, but also from clashes between processes going on in the central nervous system. Related to these additional sources of motivation, there must be a wide range of hitherto overlooked reinforcing conditions that can promote learning of new behaviour patterns. In opening up these new prospects, the study of curiosity, exploration, and epistemic behaviour merges with developments in several other areas of psychological research (1, 27, 32), including personality theory, ethology, child development, education, attitude change, social interaction, aesthetics, and humour.

References and Notes

1. BERLYNE, D. E. *Conflict, Arousal and Curiosity* (McGraw-Hill, New York, 1969).
2. WELKER, W. I. In *Functions of Varied Experience*. D. W. FISKE and S. R. MADDI, eds. (Dorsey, Homewood, Ill., 1961); FOWLER, H. *Curiosity and Exploratory Behaviour* (Macmillan, New York, 1965); VORONIN, L. G. *et al.*, eds., *Orientirovochny Refleks i Orientirovoch-no-Issledovatel'skaia Deiatel'nost* (Academy of Pedagogical Sciences, Moscow, 1958); BERLYNE, D. E., in *Handbook of Social Psychology*, 2. ed. LINDZEY, G., and ARONSON, E., eds. (Addison-Wesley, Cambridge, Mass., in press).
3. MAJORANA, A. *Riv. Psicol, 46*, No. 4, 1 (1950); CHANCE, M. R. A., and A. P. MEAD, *Behaviour, 8*, 174 (1955).
4. HINDE, R. A. *Proc. Roy. Soc. London, B142*, 306 (1954).
5. FREUD, S. *Intern. Z. Artztl. Psychoanal. 3*, 84 (1915).
6. MILLER, N. E., and J. DOLLARD. *Social Learning and Imitation* (Yale Univ. Press, New Haven, Conn., 1941).
7. BEXTON, W. A., W. HERON, T. H. SCOTT. *Can. J. Psychol. 8*, 70 (1954).
8. KUBZANSKI, P. in *The Manipulation of Human Behaviour*, A. D. BIDERMAN and H. ZIMMER, eds. (Wiley, New York, 1961).
9. PAVLOV, I. P. *Conditioned Reflexes* (Oxford Univ. Press, Oxford, 1927).
10. BERLYNE, D. E. *Brit. J. Psychol., 41*, 68 (1950).
11. MONTGOMERY, K. C. *J. Comp. Physiol. Psychol., 46*, 129 (1953).
12. BERLYNE, D. E. *ibid., 48*, 238 (1955).
13. WILLIAMS, C. D., and J. C. KUCHTA, *ibid., 50*, 509 (1957); WELKER, W. I., *ibid., 49*, 181 (1956).
14. BERLYNE, D. E. *J. Exp. Psychol., 53*, 399 (1957).
15. ——— and G. H. LAWRENCE. *J. Gen. Psychol., 71*, 21 (1964).
16. BERLYNE, D. E. *J. Exp. Psychol., 55*, 298 (1958).
17. DAY, H., thesis, University of Toronto, 1965.
18. BERLYNE, D. E., and J. L. LEWIS. *Can. J. Psychol., 17*, 398 (1963).
19. BERLYNE, D. E., *Brit. J. Psychol., 55*, 298 (1958).
20. SPOCK, B., *Baby and Child Care* (Pocket books, New York, 1946) p. 166.
21. HERSHENSON, M., *J. Comp. Physiol. Psychol., 58*, 270 (1964).
22. BRENNAN, W. M., AMES, E. W., MOORE, R. W., *Science, 151*, 354 (1966).
23. SAAYMAN, A., AMES, E. W., MOFFAT, A., *J. Exp. Child Psychol., 1*, 189 (1964); ZAPOROZHETS, A. V., in "European Research in Cognitive Development," P. H. MUSSEN, ed., *Monograph Soc. Res. Child Develop., 30*, No. 2, (1965).
24. CHARLESWORTH, W. R., paper read before the Society for Research in Child Development, 1965.
25. GRAEFE, O., *Psychol. Forsch., 27*, 177 (1963).
26. FRANTZ, R. L., *Science, 140*, 296 (1963).
27. BERLYNE, D. E., in *Psychology—a Study of a Science*, vol. 5, S. KOCH, ed. (McGraw-Hill, New York, 1963).
28. HEBB, D. O., *Psychol. Rev., 53*, 259 (1946); MONTGOMERY, K. C., *J. Comp. Physiol. Psychol., 48*, 254 (1955).
29. SOKOLOV, E. N., *Perception and the Conditioned Reflex* (Macmillan, New York, 1963).
30. BERLYNE, D. E., *J. Exp. Psychol., 62*, 476 (1961); ———, CRAW, M. A., SALAPATEK, P. H., LEWIS, J. L., *ibid., 66* 560 (1963).
31. BERLYNE, D. E., and McDONNELL, P., *Electroencephalog. Clin. Neurophysiol., 18*, 156 (1965).
32. BERLYNE, D. E., *Structure and Direction in Thinking* (Wiley, New York, 1965).
33. ———, *Brit. J. Psychol., 45*, 180 (1954).
34. ———, *ibid.*, p. 256; ———, *ibid., 53*, 27 (1962).
35. ——— and FROMMER, F. D., *Child Develop., 37*, 177 (1966); IRWIN, F., and SMITH, W. A. S.,

J. Exp. Psychol., 54, 229 (1957); BECKER, A. M., *ibid., 55,* 628 (1958); DRISCOLL, J. M., and LANZETTA, J. T., *Psychol, Rep., 14,* 975 (1964); HAWKINS, C. K., and LANZETTA, J. T., *ibid., 17,* 791 (1965).

36. GLANZER, M., *J. Exp. Psychol., 45,* 387 (1953); MONTGOMERY, K. C., *J. Comp. Physiol. Psychol., 45,* 287 (1952); DEMBER, W. N., *Amer. Scientist, 53,* 409 (1965).
37. BUTLER, R. A., and HARLOW, H. F., *J. Comp. Physiol. Psychol., 47,* 258 (1954).
38. JONES, A., WILKINSON, H. J., BRADEN, I., *J. Exp. Psychol., 62,* 126 (1961).
39. BERLYNE, D. E., *Can. J. Psychol., 17,* 274 (1963).
40. HOATS, D. L., MILLER, M. B., SPITZ, H. H., *Amer. J. Mental Deficiency, 68,* 386 (1963).
41. BERLYNE, D. E., and PECKNAN, S. *Can. J. Psychol.,* in press.
42. BUTLER, R. A. *J. Comp. Physiol. Psychol., 50,* 177 (1957); FOX, S. S., *ibid., 55,* 438 (1962).
43. GIRDNER, J. B. *Amer. Psychologist, 8,* 354 (1953); HURWITZ, H. M. B. *Brit. J. Animal Behaviour, 4,* 31 (1956); KISH, G. B. *J. Comp. Physiol. Psychol., 48,* 261 (1965); ROBERTS, C. L., MARX, M. H., COLLIER, C., *ibid., 51,* 575 1958).
44. BERLYNE, D. E., SALAPATEK, P. H., GELMAN, R. S., ZENER, S. L. *J. Comp. Physiol. Psychol., 58,* 148 (1964); ——— and KOENIG, I. D. V., *ibid., 60,* 275 (1965); ——— and HIROTA, T. T., *ibid.* in press.
45. CHAPMAN, R. M., and LEVY, N. *J. Comp. Physiol. Psychol., 50,* 233 (1957); THOMPSON, W. R., and HIGGINS, W. H. *Can. J. Psychol., 12,* 61 (1958); HAYWARD, H. C. J. *Personality, 30,* 63 (1962).
46. Research discussed in this article has been supported by grants from the Carnegie Trust for the Universities of Scotland, the Ford Foundation, the National Institute of Mental Health (U.S. Public Health Service), the National Research Council of Canada, and the Ontario Mental Health Foundation.

11 / Timing of Punishment as a Determinant of Response Inhibition[1]

Richard H. Walters and Lillian Demkow *University of Toronto*

At one time or another every child behaves in an undesirable manner and every parent has been faced with the decision of how to use punishment most effectively. Should punishment be delayed until, say, the father gets home, or should punishment be given immediately after the act? It is sometimes possible to adminster punishment just before the child has completed the act. Will punishment be most effective if it is given at that time or should it be delayed until the act has been completed? The experiment reported here seeks to ascertain when punishment is most effective in inhibiting undesirable actions.

Professor Walters was Chairman of the Department of Psychology, University of Waterloo, from 1963 until his death in 1967, at the age of 49 years. During the short span of his life he published more than 70 papers, co-authored two books, Adolescent Aggression *and* Social Learning and Personality, *and, at the time of his death, was working on three additional books.*

Mowrer (8, 9) has distinguished active avoidance learning from passive avoidance learning. In active avoidance learning, a formerly neutral *external* cue which has been paired a number of times with a noxious stimulus acquires the capacity to elicit an avoidance response . The cue, according to Mowrer, arouses a conditioned emotional response ("fear") which motivates the avoidance behaviour. In passive avoidance learning a similar process occurs, but the conditioned stimuli are in this case the cues *produced by the agent's own responses.*The punished agent learns not to commit a socially deviant act because proprioceptive and other response-produced cues acquire the capacity to arouse fear. Thus, in both active and passive avoidance learning, formerly neutral cues become capable of eliciting a conditioned emotional response, and the processes differ primarily in the nature of the stimuli that are conditioned.

Response inhibition, *learning not to perform* a socially deviant act, is an important aspect of socialization which merits more study in human subjects than it has so far received. According to Mowrer's paradigm, the execution of a deviant act involves a sequence of responses, each providing sensory feedback (response-produced cues). A painful stimulus (punishment) can be presented at various points in this sequence and so lead to the relatively direct association of a fear response with the response-produced cues occurring at the time of punishment. If the punishment occurs only on the completion of a deviant act, the fear will be most strongly associated with the stimuli accompanying the actual commission of the deviation and less strongly with the stimuli produced by the agent's preparatory responses. On the other hand, punishment occurring early in the sequence should result in a relatively strong association of the stimuli accompanying certain preparatory responses and the emotion of fear; in this latter case, even the initiation of a deviant act may be quickly forestalled. Since once an act is initiated, numerous not easily identifiable secondary reinforcers may serve to maintain and facilitate the response sequence, and thus counteract the inhibitory effect of fear, punishment administered early in a response sequence should more effectively prevent the actual commission of a deviant act than punishment administered only when the act has occurred.

A number of experimental studies (3, 4, 10) has provided evidence that delayed punishment is less effective than immediate punishment in inhibiting responses. Punishment administered at the termination of a response sequence is delayed in respect to neuromuscular responses occurring at the commencement of the sequence; the hypothesis that response inhibition should be more complete if punishment occurs early in a deviant sequence thus receives support from the results of studies of the effects of delay of punishment.

More direct support comes from a study by Black, Solomon, and Whiting, reported by Mowrer (9). Puppies who had been trained to avoid eating horsemeat by tapping them on the nose as they approached the tabooed food showed more "resistance to temptation," when food-deprived and offered

[1]This study was supported by a Canadian Mental Health grant, No. 605/5/293, and by a grant from the Ontario Society for Emotionally Disturbed Children. The authors wish to express their appreciation to the York Township Board of Education and to the Principal and staff of Humbercrest School for their cooperation in this study. John Zichmanis served as the observer during the training and testing of subjects.

Reprinted, by permission, from *Child Development*, 1963, *34*,207-214.

no alternative nutriment, than did puppies who had been tapped on the nose only after commencing to eat the tabooed meat. The Black, Solomon, and Whiting procedure provided the model for the experiment with children reported in this paper.

In North American society, much deviant behaviour is less readily tolerated in girls than in boys; consequently, the effects of this difference in severity of socialization should generalize to the experimental situation and be reflected in stronger "inner restraints" and greater response inhibition in girls. Generalization of this kind is probably responsible for sex differences found, for example, in studies of the incidence of aggressive responses in young children (7, 11).

The following hypotheses were advanced:

1. Children who are punished early in a sequence of deviant responses show greater response inhibition than children who are punished late in the sequence.
2. Girls will, in general, show greater response inhibition than boys.

Method

Subjects

Children in the kindergarten class of a metropolitan Toronto school served as *Subjects*. Boys and girls in this class were randomly assigned to one of two experimental conditions – punishment administered early in a deviant response sequence and punishment administered late in a response sequence. The final sample on which this report is based consisted of the 23 boys and 21 girls who completed the training session and who were subsequently available for testing. Some Subjects became too emotionally upset to complete the training session; others were absent through illness or other causes at the time they were scheduled for testing. The 44 Subjects ranged in age from 5 years, 4 months, to 6 years, 4 months, with a median age of exactly 6 years.

Experimental Arrangements

A transportable one-way vision booth was constructed for this experiment. Three panels, each 7 ft. high and 4 ft. wide, were cut from 3/4 in. plywood[2] Holes were cut in one panel to permit the insertion of two 1 ft. square sheets of one-way vision glass, one to the left of the panel and at standing height for the average observer and one to the right of the panel and at sitting height. Beneath one of the glass sheets was attached a small protruding shelf, on which a comb and brush could be placed. Hinges were fitted to the panels in such a way that the booth could be transported to the school in three pieces and then set up in the space allocated for the experiment. When the booth was erected, the glass panels appeared to be mirrors, one set at adult height and one at child height. The booth was placed against the wall of a classroom, facing a large window, in such a way that a child could be clearly observed without the observer being seen by the child. A large assortment of small toys – play money, stuffed animals, toy soldiers, rubber cars, metal insects, plastic dolls, and various games of skill – were attractively arranged on a table placed between the booth and the window. Two chairs were placed at the side of the table away from the booth, so that when the child was seated his movements and facial expression could be easily observed.

Two chairs were placed behind the screen, one for the observer and one holding a stopwatch and a buzzer-and-bell system used to give signals to E and to present aversive stimuli to the child.

Procedure

Training session. E went to the classroom, was introduced to S by the teacher, and then conducted S to the experimental room. S was seated at the table and told: "We are going to play a game, but before we begin, I have some work to do in the next room. Also, I have to get some other toys to play with, because the toys on this table belong to some other boys (girls).While you are waiting for me to come back, would you like to look through this book?"

S was presented with a 92-page book printed in Russian and containing no pictures. Pilot studies had shown that this task was particularly effective in establishing and maintaining boredom throughout the training session.

S was again told by E: "Now, remember, these toys are for other boys (girls). You just look through the book until I come back."

E's assistant (*O*), who was seated behind the screen, began to time the session, and *E* left the room. *O* watched *S* very carefully and administered punishment if *S* deviated. The punishment consisted of a loud unpleasant sound from the buzzer which a pilot study had shown to be a negative reinforcer. *S*s assigned to the late-punishment condition received the stimulus only after they had touched a toy. *O* recorded the times at which deviations occurred and made notes on *S*'s behaviour throughout the session. At the end of 30 minutes *O* sounded the bell to indicate to *E* that she should return to the room. On her return, *E* walked up to *S* and said: "I am very sorry, but we won't have time to play our game today. I'll take you back to your classroom now. You can come and see me tomorrow, and we'll have more time to play our game then." *E* then conducted *S* back to the classroom.

*Testing session.*On the following day, or as soon after as possible,*E* again brought *S* to the experimental room. *S* was seated at the table, but this time the book was not presented. Instead, *S* was told: "Today we're going to play the game that we didn't have time for yesterday. But first, I must go out of

[2]The senior author is indebted to Roger V. Burton for suggesting the use of a transportable one-way vision booth and for hints on its construction.

the room and get the things we need. You just sit here and wait until I come back."

E left the room, and *O* began the timing session as before. *O* recorded *S*'s behaviour and the time that elapsed before *S* deviated, if a deviation occurred before 10 minutes. During this session, he did not punish the commission of a deviant act. Two minutes after a deviation or at the end of 10 minutes, *O* rang the bell to summon *E* back into the room. On her re-entry, *E* sat down beside *S* and said: "I'm sorry, but there doesn't seem to be enough time left to play the game after all. But, because you have been sitting here waiting for me, I am going to give you one of the toys to take home. Which toy would you like to have?" *S* was presented with the toy he selected and was then taken back to his classroom.

Some *S*s did not deviate during the training session. These children were tested in the same way as the punished groups and thus constituted a no-punishment group who had been exposed to all the experimental conditions except the presentation of the aversive stimulus.

Results

Since a large number of *S*s did not deviate in the testing session, the only meaningful analysis of data consisted in comparing distributions of deviations among *S*s in the early-punishment and late-punishment groups. Because of the hypothesized difference between sexes, the effect of the experimental manipulations was separately tested for boys and girls. Expected cell frequencies were consequently small, and no over-all test of the significance of differences among distributions was possible. Consequently, Fisher's Exact Probability Test was used to test separately the significance of differences between any two distributions. When the sum of the probabilities of the cases more extreme than the observed case was less than .05 and the sum of probabilities of the observed case and of cases more extreme than the observed one was greater than .05, Tocher's modification of Fisher's Test, described by Siegel (10) was applied.

Table I – Distribution of deviant responses during testing for early-punished, late-punished, and not-punished groups of boys and girls

	Boys		Girls	
	Deviated	Did not Deviate	Deviated	Did Not Deviate
Early-Punishment	2	7	2	5
Late-Punishment	4	4	3	5
No-Punishment	5	1	1	5

Table I gives the distribution of deviant and non-deviant responses during the testing session for the early-punishment, late-punishment, and no-punishment groups of boys and girls. Comparison of the early-punishment and late-punishment boys yielded *p* values that justified the application of Tocher's procedure. On the basis of this procedure it was decided to reject the null hypothesis (Tocher's ratio =.0344; random number = .0115).

The difference between male and female *S*s who had not received punishment was significant at the .04 level. In contrast, sex differences were not apparent among *S*s who had received punishment.

Girls and boys were also compared with respect to the number of times they deviated during the training session. For each of the two punishment conditions, the median number of deviations for the combined groups of boys and girls was identified and a Fisher's Exact Probability Test was carried out on the basis of a median split (Table II). Tocher's modification of the Fisher Test was applied to the data for early-punishment *S*s and the null hypothesis rejected was rejected (Tocher's ratio = .2137; random number = .1188).

Table II – Sex differences in number of deviations during training

	Early-Punished		Late-Punished	
	Boys	Girls	Boys	Girls
Above median	6	2	4	3
Below median	3	5	4	5

Finally, since the incidence of punishments during the training session could have influenced responses during testing, all boys who received punishment (early or late) were grouped together for a median test of the relation between the number of punishments and the presence or absence of deviations during testing. A similar procedure was followed for girls. As Table III indicates, the number of punishments received bore little relation to the presence or absence of response inhibition.

Table III – Incidence of punishments during training received by subsequent deviators and nondeviators

	Boys		Girls	
	Deviators	Nondeviators	Deviators	Nondeviators
Above median	3	7	3	4
Below median	3	4	2	6

Discussion

The use of Tocher's modification of the Fisher Exact Probability Test resulted in the rejection of the null hypothesis in two cases in which it would have been accepted had the modification not been applied. Consequently, the conclusions of this study should be regarded as tentative only. There were indications, however, that early-punishment boys were more likely than late-punishment boys to refrain from deviating during the subsequent testing session and that girls were more likely to resist temptation than boys. The finding that boys who did not deviate during training were more likely to deviate during testing than were girls under comparable conditions suggests that verbal instructions not to deviate have a shorter-term effect on boys than on girls. This suggestion is perhaps supported by the finding that, under early-punishment conditions, boys were more likely to persist in deviating than were girls. However, after training with an aversive stimulus, sex differences disappeared.

The study revealed some interesting methodological problems in the study of response inhibition in children. A prolonged pilot study was necessary before conditions were found under which children would deviate. At first, *E* remained in the room during training and left for the testing period; under these conditions some children did not deviate during the testing period even when given a boring task lasting a whole hour, and it was consequently impossible for *E* to administer the punishment originally selected, a tap on the hand and a verbal rebuke. The task assigned to the children during training had to be made less and less interesting; neither the routine task of dropping a ball in one of two holes, using the discrimination apparatus employed by Gewirtz and Baer (5, 6) and Walters and Ray (15), nor the presentation of a book containing English prose was sufficiently devoid of interest to permit many deviant responses. As originally planned, the study was to include the appearance of another child, trained to play with the toys and to invite participation from *S* during the testing of those *S*s who did not spontaneously deviate in a 10-minute period. This plan was dropped primarily because of the amount of time the confederates would have been required to spend away from their classrooms. As Bandura, Ross, and Ross (1) have shown, a film or TV model is a more than adequate substitute for a real-life deviant; consequently, in a later study (14) motion pictures were used as a means of eliciting deviant acts.

Studies of the effects of timing of punishment on response inhibition have implications for current theorizing about child-training practices. Sears, Maccoby, and Levin (12), for example, present nonpermissiveness and punitiveness as alternative means of parental control of child behaviour. A nonpermissive parent is one who does not allow disapproved behaviour to occur, whereas a punitive parent allows the behaviour to occur but then administers punishment. Perhaps nonpermissiveness ("attempts to stop child immediately" (p.234), "aggression is frowned upon" (p.266)) is sometimes equivalent to the presentation of an aversive stimulus early in the disapproved sequence, whereas punitiveness is sometimes equivalent to the presentation of an aversive stimulus much later in the sequence. Sears, Maccoby and Levin report that mothers who are nonpermissive of aggression, but do not punish when it occurs, have nonaggressive children, while mothers who both permit and punish aggression have much more aggressive children. These findings would be expected on the basis of Mowrer's (8, 9) theory concerning response inhibition. However, the timing of punishment is only one of the factors that distinguish nonpermissiveness from punitiveness, as these are described by Sears, Maccoby, and Levin. A second factor, the performance of aggressive (socially deviant) acts by the parent model, also enters into the distinction. This factor should not be confounded with the first, since any kind of negative reinforcer (e.g., physical punishment, remonstration, restraint) can be presented at any stage of a deviant response. In other words, the effects of models and those of the timing, nature, and scheduling of punishments need careful and, as far as possible, separate analyses (2).

Summary

Forty-four kindergarten children, 23 boys and 21 girls, served as *S*s in a study designed to assess the effects of timing of punishment on strength of response inhibition. Early-punished children were presented with an aversive stimulus – a loud, unpleasant noise – as soon as they initiated a deviant response sequence; late-punished children were punished only after the deviation had occurred. A subsequent testing session suggested that early punishment had been somewhat more effective than late punishment in producing response inhibition in boys. There were also indications that response inhibition is more readily produced in girls than in boys.

References

1. Bandura, A., Ross, D., and Ross, S. A. Imitation of film-mediated aggressive models. *J. abnorm. soc. Psychol.*, 1963, in press.
2. Bandura, A., and Walters, R. H. *Social learning and personality development.* Holt, Rinehart, & Winston, 1963, in press.
3. Bixenstine, V. E. Secondary drive as a neutralizer of time in integrative problem solving. *J. Comp. Physiol. Psychol.*, 1956, *49*, 161-166.
4. Davitz, J. R., Mason, D. J., Mowrer, O. H., and Vier, P. Conditioning of fear: a function of delay of reinforcement. *Amer. J. Psychol.*, 1967, *70*, 69-74.
5. Gewirtz, J. L., and Baer, D. M. Deprivation and satiation of social reinforcers as drive conditions. *J. Abnorm. Soc. Psychol.*, 1958, *57*, 165-172.
6. Gewirtz, J. L., and Baer, D. M. The effect of social deprivation on behaviour for a social reinforcer. *J. Abnorm. Soc. Psychol.*, 1958, *56*, 49-56.
7. Jegard, S. F., and Walters, R. H. A study of some determinants of aggression in young children. *Child Develpm.*, 1960, *31*, 739-747.
8. Mowrer, O. H. *Learning theory and behaviour.* Wiley, 1960.
9. Mowrer, O. H. *Learning theory and the symbolic processes.* Wiley, 1960.
10. Mowrer, O. H., and Ullman, A. D. Time as a determinant of integrative learning. *Psychol. Rev.*, 1945, *52*, 62-90.

11. SEARS, P. S. Doll-play aggression in normal young children: influence of sex, age, sibling status, father's absence. *Psychol. Monogr.*, 1951, *65*, No. 323.
12. SEARS, R. R., MACCOBY, E. E., and LEVIN, H. *Patterns of child training*. Row, Peterson, 1956.
13. SIEGEL, S. *Nonparametric statistics for the behaviour sciences*. McGraw-Hill, 1956.
14. WALTERS, R. H., LEAT, M., and MEZEI, L. Inhibition and disinhibition of responses through empathetic learning. *Canad. J. Psychol.*, 1963, in press.
15. WALTERS, R. H., and RAY, E. Anxiety, social isolation, and reinforcer effectiveness. *J. Pers.*, 1960, *28*, 358-367.

12 / Emotional Development in Early Infancy

Katherine M. Banham Bridges *McGill University*

The human adult displays an exceedingly wide variety of emotions ranging from violent anger to tender love, but the newborn infant is not characterized by such diverse and subtle emotions. Early theorists had argued that emotions of fear, rage, and love were present at birth but Bridges' investigations led her to conclude that only general excitement was exhibited at birth. Through the careful use of naturalistic observation she traced the stages of emotional development and showed that global excitement gradually differentiates into specific emotions such as jealousy and disgust. Her observations also emphasized the role that maturation and learning play in emotional expression. The study is considered by most psychologists to be a classic in the area of emotional development.

The emotional behaviour of 62 infants in the Montreal Foundling and Baby Hospital was carefully observed and recorded daily over a period of three or four months. The circumstances attendant upon these reactions were noted, and the whole data was studied from the point of view of development from age to age. A summary of the findings will be presented in the following paragraphs. They will be seen to lend support to the writer's (2) (3) theory of the genesis of the emotions and to add further illuminating detail.

The babies under observation were in separate wards more or less according to age. In different rooms were infants under one month, one to three months, three to six months, six to nine months, nine to twelve months, and twelve to fifteen months. An older group of children between fifteen and twenty-four months of age played together in the nursery.

Table I shows the number of children at the different ages whose behaviour was observed for this study.

Development in the emotional behaviour of the young child comprises 3 main classes of change. From birth onward there is a gradual evolution of the emotions taking place. The earliest emotional reactions are very general and poorly organized responses to one or two general types of situation. As weeks and months go by the responses take on more definite form in relation to more specific situations. It seems to the writer, as already mentioned elsewhere, that in the course of genesis of the emotions there occurs a process of differentiation. Coincident with the partial isolation of certain responses is a combining of the simpler reactions within the unit responses and the formation of bonds of association between these emotional syndromes and detailed aspects of the provoking situations. In this manner slowly appear the well known emotions of anger, disgust, joy, love, and so forth. They are not present at birth in their mature form.

Table I

Age (months)	Number of Children
Under 1	3
1-3	16
3-6	23
6-9	18
9-12	11
12-15	20
15-18	8
18-21	5
21-24	6
Over 24	2

In addition to the progressive evolution of the emotions, there is, going on at the same time, a gradual change in the mode of response of each specific emotion. Muscles are developing, new skills are being learned. So that the anger, for instance, expressed by the eighteen-month-old differs in detail of form from the anger manifested by the ten-month-old baby. Fresh bonds of association are being made between emotional behaviour and the always slightly varying attendant circumstances. Different situations come to have emotional significance for the growing child and subsequently provoke emotional responses. Thus a gradual substitution takes place of the situations which prompt the emotions. In the language of the behaviourists, emotional responses become conditioned to fresh stimuli.

Excitement, The Original Emotion

After observing the behaviour of babies *under one month* of age, the writer felt more than ever convinced that the infant does not start life with 3 fully matured pattern reactions, such as have been men-

From *Child Development*, 1932, *3*, 324-341. Reprinted by permission of the author and the Society for Research in Child Development, Inc.

tioned by behaviourists and named fear, rage, and love. Unfortunately the writer was not able to observe the infants within a few hours of birth, but this fact in no way invalidates observations made on children two or three weeks old. Moreover, if the above named emotional responses are really the 3 great primary emotions from which all our adult emotions are derived, surely they may still be observed a month or more after birth. And, even if the process of conditioning begins before or immediately upon birth, one may expect the original emotion-producing stimuli to elicit their natural responses at least for two or three weeks after birth.

It was observed in the hospital that, on presentation of certain strong stimuli the infants became agitated, their arm and hand muscles tensed, their breath quickened, and their legs made jerky kicking movements. Their eyes opened, the upper lid arched, and they gazed into the distance. The stimuli producing such agitation or excitement were: bright sun directly in the infant's eyes, sudden picking up and putting down on the bed, pulling the child's arm through his dress sleeve, holding the arms tight to the sides, rapping the baby's knuckles, pressing the bottle nipple into the child's mouth, and the noisy clatter of a small tin basin thrown on to a metal table whence it fell to the radiator and the floor.

The loud sound startled only four of the one- and two-month-old babies, while six others lay practically undisturbed. None of the infants cried after hearing the noise. The same experiment was tried upon children of successive ages up to fifteen months. Under two or three months the reaction was one of sudden but rather mild general excitement as described above. Children of three or four months and older gave more of a jump and looked definitely in the direction of the sound. Afterwards they remained still with eyes and mouth open, and stared towards the source of the commotion. One baby of eight months stiffened and turned away on the second trial. The corners of his mouth turned down, his eyes moistened and he looked to the adult for sympathy and comfort. Another child of eleven months sat wide-eyed and still, the corners of his mouth drooping as if he were ready to burst into tears. The older children merely stood, or sat, alert and attentive without further sign of distress.

Lowering the babies suddenly into their cribs, and in some cases lifting them quickly, also startled and excited them. Sometimes they would cry following upon such a surprise. Rocking a quiet child would cause him to open his eyes attentively. But gently rocking a crying infant would often, though not always, cause him to reduce his activity, stop crying, and eventually become tranquil. Gentle handling, slow patting, wrapping in warm blankets, and nursing easily soothed an agitated or crying infant, making him relax and yawn and become sleepy.

Light pinching of the arm left the three- or four-week-old baby unmoved. Deeper pressure caused him to kick slightly, breathe faster and move his arms. A sharp flick on the hand produced similar agitation, but a second rap resulted in a sudden check to breathing followed by a prolonged cry and other signs of distress. The first exciting experience had been found disagreeable and the second rap produced unmistakable distress.

Time after time on waking suddenly from sleep the infants were observed to wave their arms jerkily, kick, open and close their eyes, flush slightly, and breathe quickly and irregularly. Some grunted, some cried spasmodically for a moment or two, while others cried loudly for several minutes. The combined stimulation of light, of sounds, of damp or restricting bed clothes, and the change from sleeping to waking breathing-rate seemed to produce a temporary agitation and often distress. Waking apparently requires emotional adjustment.

The hungry child before feeding would often show restless activity, waving, squirming, mouthing and crying at intervals. The infant who had been lying in one position for a long time and the tired child before falling asleep would also show emotional agitation. Their breath would come jerkily, uttering staccato cries of "cu-cu-cu-ah," and they would thrust out their arms and legs in irregular movements. At the moment the nipple was put into the hungry baby's mouth he again breathed quickly, occasionally cried, waved the free arm, and kicked in excited agitation.

The emotional reactions of the tiny infant are certainly not highly differentiated. The most common response to highly stimulating situations seems to be one of general agitation or excitement. It is a question which word most aptly describes the behaviour. The former perhaps conveys more the idea of general disturbance, although the two words are often used synonymously. This vague emotional response to a large variety of circumstances must surely be one of the original emotions, if not the only one.

A kind of general excitement over new and startling or other highly stimulating circumstances may be seen at any age. The behaviour manifestations vary from time to time, but the main characteristics of accelerated response, alertness, slight tension or restlessness remain as constant attributes. In the babies, excitement is frequently manifested in kicking movements. The month-old infants kick jerkily with both feet at random. In another month or so, the kicking becomes more regular, the legs being thrust out alternately. By five or six months the babies express their emotions in combined leg thrusts, kicking with one foot, and in swinging the legs from the hips. At fourteen months when the children can stand they will hold on to a support and "mark time" with their feet or stamp. Stamping, jumping and running express excited agitation at a still later age.

Two- and three-month-old babies may be seen to suck their thumbs or fingers rapidly in moments of stress. At seven months and over, children bite, pull and suck their garments, as well as their fingers. This behaviour seems to produce a gradual subsidence of the emotion. Body-rocking accompanied in many instances by rhythmic vocalizations is another expression of mixed emotion. Hungry, annoyed, excited or restless children will sit and rock for minutes on end. The five-month-old baby lies prone and pushes with his knees, or sways when lying dorsally. Seven-month-old infants support themselves on their arms and rock back and forth murmuring "mm-um, mm-um." After nine months they sit up and rock to and fro, or they kneel and bounce up and down holding on to the crib bars. Sometimes they sit and bump their backs against the side of the crib. This kind of behaviour was observed in the nursery up to eighteen months of age.

Rhythmical movements were observed not only to be the outcome of emotional excitement or tension, but they were seen to have a soothing and pacifying effect. These must be attempts at adjustment on the part of the organism to reduce tension and restore emotional equilibrium or tranquility. In the light of these observations, it can be easily understood how long walks, games, field sports, singing, dancing, and sea-voyages are found to be so universally health-giving and positively curative for "nervous wrecks."

Distress and its Derivatives

It is a moot question whether "distress" is an original emotion or whether it is a very early differentiated reaction to disagreeably painful and unsatisfying experiences. It may be that it is a part of the general emotional response of excitement which copes more satisfactorily with obnoxious stimuli. Tense muscles resist or remove pressure; activity warms a chilled body and reduces tension; and cries, at first reflex due to the rush of air in and out of the lungs, bring comfort and aid. These responses become differentiated from excitement, associated together and conditioned to the disagreeable stimuli as a result of experience. If such differentiation actually takes place, it must begin immediately after birth. For the two emotions of excitement and distress are already distinguishable in a three-weeks-old infant.

On the other hand, it is possible that there is a native emotional response to pain, particularly muscle pain. The sympathetic branch of the autonomic nervous system is predominantly active and the overt behaviour is definitely that of distress. Other stimuli, such as loud sounds and sudden falling merely produce startled excitement. Blanton (1) observed that the infant's cry of colic had a specially shrill character accompanied by rigidity of the abdominal walls. She also noted that infants during the first days of life cried from "(1) hunger; (2) in response to noxious stimuli (including rough handling, circumcision, lancing and care of boils, sores, etc.); and (3) possibly fatigue or lack of exercise." The writer has observed the same phenomena in three-weeks-old babies. But, hunger, rough handling, and fatigue were also noticed on many occasions to produce a restless excitement rather than specific distress.

It is not easy, in the case of the very young infant, to distinguish distress from general agitation. Perhaps the most characteristic marks of the former are greater muscle tension, interference with movement and with breathing, closing of the eyes, and loud rather high-pitched crying. In children of two months and over, the eyes become moist and tears may flow. The crying of the infant *under a month* or even six weeks often seems to be part of the general activity in excitement. Breath comes more or less regularly, the cry emerging on both intake and expiration of air. There are no tears, and the skin does not flush. Movement is free though rather jerky; and the mouth is held open in an elliptic, round, or square shape.

The cry of distress, recognizable in the *month-old* baby, is irregular. There are short intakes of breath and long cries on expiration. The eyes are "screwed up" tight, the face flushed, the fists often clenched, the arms tense, and the legs still or kicking spasmodically. The mouth is open and square in shape or, more usually kidney-shaped with the corners pulled down. The pitch of the cry is high and somewhat discordant, and sounds something like "ah, cu-ah, cu-ah, cu-aeh."

Cries of distress were heard from month-old babies in the hospital on the following occasions; on waking suddenly from sleep, struggling to breathe through nostrils blocked with mucous, when the ears were discharging, when lying awake before feeding time, lying on a wet diaper, when the child's buttocks were chafed, and when the fingers were rapped. The three main causes of distress at this age, therefore, seemed to be discomfort, pain, and hunger.

Crying from discomfort and on awakening usually developed slowly, and sounded like "cu-cu-cu-cah-ah-." The cry of pain came suddenly, often after a holding of the breath. The sound was a loud shrill prolonged "ă-ă-ă," and lowered in pitch slightly from the first emission. The cries of hunger were rather like those of discomfort. The former came perhaps more in intermittent waves, the intervening moments being taken up with mouthing or sucking movements. Occasionally the hungry child would utter a sharp loud cry, as if in pain, and then whine or moan for a time.

Two-month-old babies cry less of the total waking time; but slighter discomforting stimuli seem to cause distress more frequently than in the case of the younger infants. They are more disturbed by a wet diaper, by flatulence, and by tight clothing which restricts movement and makes breathing difficult. Their movements are freer and they tend to move their heads from side to side when they are distressed. While one-month-old babies kick irregularly with jerky movements, the two-month-old kicks his legs alternately and more regularly. He waves his arms up and down when agitated or distressed, as well as in spontaneous play. The sound or sight of an approaching person will not quiet his distress; but being picked up will do so, or being fed if he is hungry.

By *three months* of age a child will cry and show other signs of distress when placed in an unusual position or moved to a strange place; as, for instance, when lain temporarily at the foot of another child's bed. He will wave his arms laterally as well as up and down, and will kick more vigorously. The hospital baby has learned to associate feeding time with the presence of an adult; for, when he is hungry he shows some excitement at the close approach of a person. He stares at the person's face, waves, kicks, breathes faster, and opens his mouth. If no food is forthcoming, he becomes more tense and jerky in his movements and begins to cry. He is distressed at the delay in normal proceedings.

Should the adult remain tantalizingly near for some minutes without either picking up the child or feeding him, his cry increases in intensity, his eyes become moist with tears, he holds his breath longer, and utters a prolonged flat "ă-ă-ă" sound reminiscent of an older child's "paddy" or temper cry. The infant's motor responses were all set for being picked up and fed, and then he was thwarted and disappointed. His excitement changed into bitter distress with a semblance of angry vexation.

The slight change in vowel sound of the cry, the long holding of breath combined with more than usually vigorous leg thrusts and arm movements, seemed to suggest that the emotion of anger is beginning to evolve from general distress at about this age. Although for the most part the distress shown at discomfort differs almost imperceptibly from distress in response to disappointment, occasionally the latter includes, to a marked degree, those behaviour elements peculiar to the emotion of anger. The situations which evoke these demonstrations of temper in the tiny infant are a stop or check in the progressive satisfaction of a physical need. In the above instance the child's appetite was aroused but not satisfied. Lack of even the first sign of a need being satisfied merely produces vague distress.

A *four-month-old* baby shows distress at the same general sort of situation that troubles the younger child. He is, however, less frequently disturbed by bodily discomfort. He moves about sufficiently to relieve tired muscles and local pressures, and to eliminate gas from his stomach. He cries vigorously at delay in the feeding process and may show decided temper on such occasions. His arms then stiffen and tremble; he screws up his eyes, flushes, holds his breath and utters prolonged and irregular cries on expiration of breath; he kicks violently, pushes with his feet and looks at any adult, presumably to see the effect. He is getting very fond of attention at this age; and will show distress and often anger when a person leaves the room or ceases to pay attention and play with him.

At *five months*, the baby's interest in small objects, such as rattles, stuffed animals and, of course, his milk bottle, causes him to be distressed when these objects are removed. He may express his displeasure as formerly by crying, squirming, waving and kicking, but he may also be heard merely to call out in a protesting tone of voice, "ah aye," without the half-closing of the eyes and the accompanying tensions of crying.

By this age the child may show slight revulsion for certain foods, coughing, spluttering, frowning, and crying while he is being fed. Chopped vegetables and soup too thick in consistency were specially disliked by some babies in the hospital. Cereals, milk, and sweetish foods were almost always taken readily. It was noted that babies under three months often refused to drink sterile water. They just let it run out of their mouths without swallowing. There was no emotion involved in this reaction. Similarly, three- and four-month-old babies sometimes rejected their thin vegetable soup, but were not very disturbed about it. A genuine emotional revulsion did not appear till five months or later. Perhaps this is the beginning of the emotion of disgust. Revulsion at nauseating sights and smells, the adult form of disgust, apparently does not develop until two or more years of age.

Several of the babies in the hospital *between six and eighteen months* were observed to splutter and choke, and refuse to swallow spinach more than other vegetables. The mouthfuls that were rejected were usually, though not always, those containing large or stringy pieces of spinach. When the latter was chopped fine it was swallowed a little more easily; but only when it was mixed with other vegetables was it eaten without any protest. There must be factors other than consistency and size of morsel to account for this objection to spinach.

It seemed to the writer that some cans of spinach tasted more bitter than others and were less palatable on that account. In order to find how the children would react to a bitter taste, two teaspoonsful each of unsweetened grape-fruit juice were given to nine children in the nursery. Four of them pursed or curled their lips, 1 turned his head away, and 1 frowned. The others sat still and solemn, and kept tasting their lips attentively for some time. There were certainly individually different reactions to this bitter-sour, astringent taste. Several of the children definitely disliked it and none of them seemed to like it. It is possible then that there is a bitter taste to spinach which may in part account for children's aversion to it. Another factor, that of the dark green colour of spinach may influence older children's and adult's feeling reaction towards it. One two-year-old in the hospital on turning away and refusing to eat the vegetable was seen to point to it and say "dirty."

The *six-month-old* baby's attention is usually arrested by the presence of a stranger. His movements are inhibited and he watches the newcomer intently. He is not pleased and one could hardly say he is afraid. But he seems diffident and uncertain what to do, or utterly unable to move for a few moments. At seven months he reacts in the same way to the approach of a stranger, though the general inhibition of movement is greater and lasts longer. After a few moments or several seconds of tension he may begin to cry slowly, or burst suddenly into tears. The whole body is usually rigid and inactive. The eyes, previously wide open, close tight and the head bends. Should the stranger touch the child he will probably turn or draw away. Here is the emotion of fear already differentiated. Frightened distress results when the child through inhibition, ignorance, or inability finds himself unable to respond at all adequately to the situation.

At *seven months* of age an infant calls out protestingly when a familiar person ceases to attend to him, instead of crying distressfully like a four-month-old. He still cries and kicks angrily if some object in which he was deeply engrossed is taken from him. He does so also after being highly excited by a playful adult when the latter goes away or stops playing with him. He now makes prolonged attempts to get at objects out of reach. If he fails to attain his objective he may give up and cry in helpless distress, or he may just grunt in protestation.

A *nine-month-old* child will struggle longer and make more varied attempts to reach the object of his desire. Should he fail to do so after putting forth considerable effort he may become tense and red in the face with anger. He will kick and scream and look for assistance, while tears flow copiously. The cry at this age is becoming exceedingly loud, and tears flow more readily than at the earlier age. Prolonged crying at four or five months is accompanied by slight lacrimal secretion, but after six months of age tears often flow down the child's cheeks as he cries, especially after an adult's attention has been attracted.

Strangers are still quite terrifying to the nine-month-old baby. His movements are more completely arrested by the unfamiliar presence than those of the six-month-old. He will remain immovable for several minutes unless the newcomer approaches very close to him. In that case he will lie face down or bend his head and probably begin to cry. At ten months of age he may even be so frightened as to flop down suddenly on the bed and scream loudly. Then follows prolonged and tearful crying.

When children of *ten months* and over are hungry, uncomfortable, tired, or fretful and unwell, they will set up a whine or cry as the result of suggestion when another child cries. They do not, however, ordinarily imitate crying when they are occupied and happy. Under these circumstances they may call or babble in a pitch similar to that of the other child's cry. Small objects which can be manipulated interest them so intensely that they can be distracted from a distressing trouble fairly easily at this age. These objects need not necessarily be new so long as they are freshly presented.

Year-old babies often cry suddenly when they feel themselves falling, or when they lose their grip while climbing. If they miss the assistance of a helping hand they will also sit down and cry loudly. Sometimes their emotion is anger at the thwarting or failure of their endeavours. They scream, flush, and tremble in rage. At other times they sit motionless in fright and look for aid or comforting sympathy. When strangers approach the *twelve- or thirteen-month-old* baby he may hold his hand behind his ear in a withdrawing motion and stare apprehensively. He may actually hide his eyes behind his hands or look away so as not to see the awe-inspiring or annoying intruder.

At *fourteen months* or thereabouts we may see the real temper tantrum. At least, that is the age when it became noticeable in the hospital. If a child is not given his food or a coveted toy exactly when he wants it he may respond by throwing himself suddenly on the bed or floor. He then screams, holds his breath, trembles, turns red, kicks or thrusts his feet out together. Tears flow and he will wave away anything that is not the desired object. These outbursts may occur frequently for a few weeks, or only spasmodically for another year or eighteen months. The children under observation seemed to have their "off-days" when they were fretful and easily distressed or roused to anger. Such days were usually when they were incubating, or recovering from colds, when the hospital routine was disturbed, or after the children had been excited by parents' visits.

Distressful crying becomes less common as the months go by. Extreme hunger and weariness after a long day or great activity may be accompanied by whining and intermittent outbursts of tears. Anger is expressed more in protesting shouts, pushing and kicking, but less in tearful screaming. So long as adults are present, however, the interference and rough handling of another child may bring forth cries and tears. A *fifteen-month-old* may show his annoyance by hitting a child who has taken his toy or who is holding on to the thing he most wants. He may even bite him or pull his hair without a preliminary scream or shout.

The attention of familiar and interested adults is much sought by children of *fifteen to eighteen months*. If such attention is given to another child there may be signs of deep distress. The neglected one may stiffen, stand motionless, bend his head and burst into tears. Here is perhaps the beginning of jealousy, distress at the loss of, or failure to receive, expected attention and affection. Some children will show aggressive annoyance when another receives the attention they covet. They do this usually by hitting the envied child.

A *twenty-one-month-old* child will show less mistrust of strangers than will a younger infant. He may, however, run away and watch the newcomer for a time at a safe distance. After eighteen months he shows anger at adult interference by obstinate refusal to comply with their requests. He may shake his head and refuse either to be fed or to feed himself. At two he will play with his food, throwing it about instead of eating it, as a spite against some offending or scolding adult. Distress is shown chiefly at pain and acute discomfort, though the child will cry miserably at much less discomfort if a sympathetic adult is close at hand.

The children in the nursery group, *between fifteen and twenty-four months,* were more or less unconcerned when being undressed for the annual physical examination. This part of the procedure was familiar and not unpleasant. Several of the children cried and stiffened somewhat when placed on the table in the examining room. One or two continued to show distress throughout the examination. Others smiled cheerily at the attendant nurse or the doctor, until they felt sudden and unexpected local pressure. All of the children criéd at some time during the procedure. The most distressing events were when a flashlight was thrown into the eyes, and when the throat and ears were examined with the aid of the usual tongue-depressor and otoscope. The children had to be held firmly and their movements curbed during these operations.

It was patent to the observer that the children were undergoing rather different emotions according to their fast-developing individual idiosyncracies. Some were mainly startled and afraid, their movements were paralyzed. Some seemed to be just generally distressed at the unusual proceeding and the discomfort; while others were chiefly annoyed at the interference with their freedom. Several children showed signs of all three emotions. These individual differences probably have their foundation in variants in the physical constitutions of the children, both hereditary and acquired. They are certainly very much determined by the particular experiences the infants have gone through since their birth. A continuous study of behaviour week by week reveals the actual differentiation and consolidation of individual traits of temperament.

Two or three of the nursery children over fourteen months developed fears for specific objects or persons. Toy animals that squeaked frightened one or two, causing them to draw away, stare wide-eyed and perhaps cry. This squeak could hardly be called a "loud low sound" such as Watson (4) describes as one of the original fear-producing stimuli. The sound is, however, rather unusual and comes at first as a surprise to the babies. One child was afraid of a particular aggressive little boy. No doubt he had gone up and hit her unexpectedly some time when the nurses were not watching. One youngster showed fear of a dark grey dog with a rough fur, rather different from the soft teddy-bears and other stuffed animals in the nursery.

Parents often remark how their children may suddenly show fear of some surprisingly trivial and inoffensive object. The answer to this may be found in certain partial associations with disturbing events of the past. It may also be found in the particular mental set of the child's mind and body when he came in contact with the object. He may have become suddenly aware of its presence and perceived it as an unwelcome intruder upon an entirely different line of thought or action. Still another phenomenon may account for the peculiar fears and objections of children. Timid behaviour may be actually learned and preserved as a social asset, one of the numerous means of drawing attention.

The nursery child who cried and crawled away after touching the rough-haired, stuffed animal was flattered with the attention of all the adults in the room. A nurse brought the dog up to the child, smiling and saying "nice doggie." He looked up at her face, saw her kindly smile, then bent his head and began to whimper again. Another nurse laughed appreciatively as he put his hand to his eyes, and tried to coax him with a toy cat. He turned away quickly, cried out again, then looked up to see the effect on the adults. He was having a delightful time out of his apparent fear.

Delight and its Derivatives

Delight is much later in becoming differentiated from general excitement than distress. The baby under a month old is either excited or quiescent. Gentle stroking, swaying and patting soothe him and make him sleepy. When satisfied after a meal he is no longer exicted nor even distressed by hunger. And yet he is not positively delighted. He is just unemotionally content, and either tranquil or busy mouthing and staring at distant objects. When he is *over two weeks old* he will sometimes give a faint reflex smile upon light tapping at the corners of his mouth. This is hardly an emotional response.

One- and two-month-old babies cry and kick from hunger before they are fed, rather than show delight on presentation of the much desired food. They become calm, however, immediately when given their milk, but not at the mere approach of the adult who brings it. A two months infants will give fleeting smiles upon being nursed, patted, wrapped warmly, spoken to, tickled, or gently rocked. Perhaps this is the beginning of the emotion of delight.

By *three months* of age the emotion of delight is becoming more clearly differentiated from agitated excitement on the one hand and non-emotional quiescence or passivity on the other. The child kicks, opens his mouth, breathes faster, and tries to raise his head upon sight of his bottle. He gives little crooning sounds when being fed, nursed or rocked. He smiles when an adult comes near and talks to him; and he will even stop crying momentarily at the sound of a person's voice. He may also show delight in distant moving objects. One baby in the hospital, for instance, lay and watched the moving leaves of the creeper on the window for a minute or two at a time. Her eyes were wide and her mouth rounded and open. At times she would breathe fast, or inspire deeply, and utter murmurings of "uh-uh-uh." Her arms would wave up and down and her legs kick alternately.

The chief characteristics of delight are: free as against restrained movement; open eyes and expansion of the face in a smile as contrasted with the puckering of the forehead and closing of the eyes in distress; body movements or muscle tension of incipient approach rather than withdrawal; audible inspirations and quickened breathing; soft, lower pitched vocalizations than those of distress or excitement; more or less rhythmic arm and leg movements; prolonged attention to the object of interest; and cessation of crying. Although behaviour varies in detail from child to child at successive ages, delight is always recognizable from certain general types of response. Free and rhythmic movements, welcoming and approaching gestures, smiles and vocalizations of middle pitch are most common features.

A *four-month-old* baby laughs aloud when some person smiles and frolics with him. He smiles in response to another's smile and even when anyone approaches his crib, whether they be stranger or not. He spreads out his arms, lifts his chin, and tries to raise his body in approach to the attentive person. He takes active delight in his bath, kicking and splashing the water. Food, though sometimes welcomed eagerly, is often neglected for the more interesting attendant who talks and smiles at him.

At *five months* a child vocalizes his delight in sounds of "uh-uh-ung" in addition to waving, laughing, kicking and wriggling around. He shows special interest in small objects that he can handle and explore. Musical or noisy rattles are popular at this age. When hungry he kicks, breathes fast, and calls out eagerly at the first sign of the person who brings his food. His smiles are more transient, however, and his movements less vigorous on approach of a stranger.

By *six months* of age a child will reach towards a familiar person but will lie still and observe a stranger dubiously. He crows and coos frequently, taking pleasure in his own movements and sounds. In the hospital the babies of this age would watch each other through the bars of their cribs, sometimes laughing and kicking in response to the sight of the other's movements. They would swing their legs rhythmically when lying on their backs, or sway sideways when lying prone.

A *seven-month-old* baby is becoming increasingly interested in small objects and in the act of reaching and grasping those close at hand. He will even struggle to attain things somewhat out of his reach. When his efforts meet with success he often smiles, takes a deep breath and expresses his satisfaction in a sort of grunt. After a moment or two spent in examination and manipulation of the object, he goes exploring again with fresh vigour. Possibly this is the beginning of the emotion of elation, exhilarating pleasure in personal accomplishments. Resting periods after the delightful satisfaction of feeding or explorative activity, are often taken up with a rhythmical rocking back and forth, the child supporting himself on his hands and knees.

At *eight months* of age the child seems to take more delight than ever in self-initiated purposeful activity. He babbles and splutters and laughs to himself. Especially does he seem delighted with the noise he makes by banging spoons or other playthings on the table. Throwing things out of his crib is another favourite pastime. He waves, pats and coos, drawing in long breaths, when familiar adults swing him or talk to him. He will watch the person who nurses him attentively, exploring her, patting gently, and often smiling. Here are perhaps the earliest demonstrations of affection. The child will also pat and smile at his own mirror image. But his behaviour is rather more aggressive and inquisitive than really affectionate.

A *nine-month-old* baby is very popular with adults. He laughs frequently, bounces up and down and tries to mimic their playful actions. He pats other babies exploratively but does not show particular affection for them. Strange adults may frighten him at first. But, after studying them for some time in the distance he will smile responsively and join in play with them. By *ten months* of age the child is taking more interest in other babies. He will mimic their calls and even their laughter. The hospital babies of this age would pat and bang and laugh in imitation of each other.

An *eleven-month-old* baby takes great delight in laughter, not only his own but that of another. He will laugh in order to make another child laugh, then jump and vocalize and laugh again in response. At twelve months of age he will repeat any little action that causes laughter. He is becoming increasingly affectionate. He puts his arms around the familiar adult's neck, and strokes and pats her face. Sometimes he will actually bring his lips close to her face in an incipient kissing movement. He looks eagerly for attention; and may stand holding a support and changing weight from one foot to the other in rhythmic motion, as a solace when neglected.

Between *twelve and fifteen months* a child usually learns to walk with a little help. This performance, though often accompanied by panting and tense effort, causes great delight and even elation when a few steps have been accomplished. The child calls out, smiles and waves ecstatically (i.e. rapidly and jerkily). Without further encouragement from adults, he will then set out again with renewed fervour. When attentive adults are too enthusiastic in their appreciation, the little one may become positively tense with excitement. His efforts may consequently meet with less success, and then he cries in vexatious disappointment.

There is already a noticeable difference between the responsiveness of different *fifteen-month-old* children to demonstrated affection. Some children come readily to be nursed and petted, others require a little coaxing. One or two will kiss back when kissed, while others merely cling closely to the adult caressing them. At this age the children begin to show definite affection for each other. They take hands, sit close to one another, put their arms about one another's neck or shoulders, pat and smile at each other. Eighteen-month-olds will also jabber nonsense amicably together. Again, with regard to playmates as well as adults some children are more affectionate than others.

These variations in affection no doubt have a number of causal factors. They depend upon the child's physical constitution and his condition of health at the moment. Sick children may be very clinging and affectionate with adults, or, in some instances, refractory and irritable. They may be both by turns. Whether a child is affectionate or not also depends upon the nature of his dominant interest at the moment. Affection for a grown person depends upon the child's attitude towards adults in general; and that again is largely a matter of the amount of fondling or scolding the child has received. Affection for other children is considerably determined by the agreeable or exasperating nature if chance contacts.

Between *fifteen and twenty-one months* the children find increasing enjoyment in walking and running about. They chase each other laughingly and enjoy snatching one another's toys. They come back again and again to be lifted high or swung round. The nursery slide is very popular at this age. One or two of the hospital children pulled away and watched apprehensively in the distance after the first slide. A little encouragement from the nurses and the eager shouts of the other children soon overcame their fear, and they joined the sliding group again.

Gramophone music was listened to intently by almost all the nursery children. Some of them responded by swaying or nodding motions to time. The children at this age were beginning to find individual interests in things and to express their enjoyment each in their own peculiar way. Absorbed preoccupation, tight clasping, biting, and varied manipulation of the attractive object were common expressions of interest. Some children would knock one object against another in play, some would collect things, and others would find pleasure in throwing and scattering toys about. These variations in appreciative interest in things and activities may be the precursors of the more mature emotion of joy.

Most of the eighteen-month-olds in the hospital were anxious to attract attention. They called out or came running to greet an adult. They would smile and hold out their arms to a familiar nurse in expectation of being lifted. A stranger they would watch solemnly for a while. Then they would approach slowly, touch and explore her clothes, or hit and watch for the effect. The children seemed to recognize their nurses at this age, whether the latter appeared in uniform or not. Babies of seven to twelve months, however, would sometimes turn away in fear or hostility when the nurses approached them wearing outdoor clothes.

Slight preferences for certain nurses were noticed as early as six months, but definitely affectionate attachments were observed chiefly between the ages of twelve and twenty-four months. One or two youngsters of eighteen months showed preferences for certain playmates. A twin boy and girl seemed especially fond of each other. The children would be more responsive and playful with those they liked, more delighted at their approach and very anxious to keep them close. Some children were friendly with almost everybody including strange visitors. Others showed more specific and decided likes and dislikes. When a terrifying stranger was present, some times a child would show more than usual affection for his familiar nurse, but at other times he would be restrained and aloof from everybody. Similarly when a beloved parent was nursing a child on visiting day he might be hostile to anyone else; but more often he would smile agreeably at everybody including awe-inspiring strangers.

A specific "like" does not necessarily enhance a specific "dislike" by force of contrast, though this does sometimes happen. If the disliked object threatens the satisfaction or enjoyment of the object preferred then the dislike becomes stronger. Similarly a preferred object may be enjoyed with greater intensity in the presence of, or following upon, something disliked. It is a comforting relief from distress. This effect of contrast is perhaps what Freud terms "ambivalence." There are situations, however, where it has no noticeable effect. For instance, as cited above, a child made happy by one person may like everybody for the moment, regardless of previous attitudes towards them. A troubled child may be annoyed with everybody, even his favourite playmates. Strong emotions may thus have a decided "halo" effect.

Although children between *eighteen months and two years* of age tease and hit each other frequently, they show more affection for one another than younger infants. They not only pat and stroke fondly, but they will kiss and hug each other on occasion. The older children in the nursery group were seen to direct the younger ones' activities and point out their errors by gesture and exclamation. There was no evidence, however, of the parental affection and almost self-sacrificing care shown by four-year-olds for their much younger playmates.

Noisy activities delighted the eighteen- to twenty-four-month old youngsters. They took pleasure in tearing and pulling things to pieces and in lifting large but portable objects, such as their own chairs. They jabbered happily to each other at table. One child would repeatedly make strange noises to arouse the attention and laughter of another. With adults they would practice newly learned words and would seek to share their enjoyments. When the children received new toys in the hospital they would cling to them and guard them jealously from the other children. But they would hold them out for the nurses to share in their appreciation. Here is a mark of trusting friendship for their kindly guardians such as the children had not yet developed for one another. They would always rather share the other child's plaything than give up or share their own.

Affection, thus, begins as delight in being fondled and comforted by an elder. It becomes differentiated from general delight and manifested in tender caressing responses at about eight months of age. This earliest affection is essentially reciprocal in nature. Spontaneous affection for adults may be seen, however, by eleven or twelve months of age. Both reciprocal and spontaneous affection for other children make their appearance around fifteen months, but they are not as strong as affection for adults.

Specific affection for the grown-ups who give special attention may be manifested as early as demonstrative affection itself, i.e., eight or nine months. These preferences persist as long as the care and attention continue. Attachments between two children were not observed in the hospital till after fifteen months of age. They were usually very temporary, lasting only for a few hours or days. The behaviour of a child-friend is so much more erratic and less dependable than that of an adult. Friendships between eighteen- to twenty-four-month-old children would sometimes last, however, for several weeks. There seemed to be no preference in these attachments either for the same or the opposite sex. Little girls would become friends together, or little boys, or a boy and girl would show mutual affection for one another.

Summary and Conclusion

The emotional behaviour of young infants as observed in the Montreal Foundling and Baby Hospital seemed to lend support to the writer's theory of the genesis of the emotions. Emotional development was found to take place in three ways. The different emotions gradually evolved from the vague and undifferentiated emotion of excitement. The form of behaviour response in each specific emotion changed slowly with developing skills and habits. Different particular situations would arouse emotional response at succeeding age-levels, although these situations would always be of the same general type for the same emotions.

The one-month-old baby showed excitement in accelerated movement and breathing, upon any excessive stimulation. He exhibited distress by crying, reddening of the face and tense jerky movements at painful and other disagreeable stimulations. But he was more or less passive and quiescent when agreeably stimulated.

By three months of age the child was seen to exhibit delight in smiles, deep inspirations and somewhat rhythmic movements when his bodily needs were being satisfied. Between three and four months angry screaming and vigorous leg-thrusts, in response to delay in anticipated feeding, were observed. A few weeks later anger was aroused when an adult's playful attention was withdrawn.

Distress and delight came to be expressed more in specific vocalizations with increasing age. General body movements gave place to precise responses to details of a situation. A four-month-old baby would laugh aloud with delight and cry tearfully when distressed. A child of five months was seen to cough and reject foods of a certain taste and consistency in incipient disgust. He would reach towards objects that caused him delight. By six months of age he showed definite fear when a stranger approached. He remained motionless and rigid, his eyes wide and staring. It is possible that "non-institutional" children might show fear in response to other unusual or unexpected events a little earlier than this. There was little variation in the daily routine of the children under observation, and fear was a rare occurrence.

By seven months of age the child showed positive elation, and renewed his activity as a result of success in his own endeavours. At eight months he began to show reciprocal affection for adults, and by twelve months spontaneous affection. Delight was manifested in much laughter, bouncing up and down, and banging with the hand.

Between nine and twelve months of age the hospital babies would hide their heads, like ostriches, upon the approach of a relatively unfamiliar person. They would scream and become flushed with anger when their efforts or desires were thwarted; and they would cry out in fear and sit motionless after perceiving themselves falling.

It was observed that a child learns to kiss soon after twelve months of age, and by fifteen months he expresses his affection for other children. Anger over disappointment becomes more dramatic in its manifestation. The true temper-tantrum makes its appearance roughly about fourteen months of age. By eighteen months anger at adults is expressed in obstinate behaviour; and annoyance at interfering children is manifested in hitting, pulling and squealing.

Eighteen-month-olds would constantly seek the attention of adults, and take great delight in running about and making noises. One or two children of this age showed depressed, and others angry, jealousy when another child received the coveted attention. A few specific fears were noticed; and several children developed particular affectionate attachments.

Thus it seems that in the course of development, emotional behaviour becomes more and more specific, both as regards arousing stimuli and form of response. Distress, though more readily aroused, comes to find adequate expression in a variety of actions, and delight becomes sensitive appreciation and joy in numerous pursuits. The emotions evolve slowly, and the exact age of differentiation is difficult to determine.

A diagram showing the approximate ages of the appearance of the different emotions, as observed in the Montreal Foundling Hospital, is given in *Figure 1*. Study of a number of children in private homes might suggest a somewhat different age arrangement.

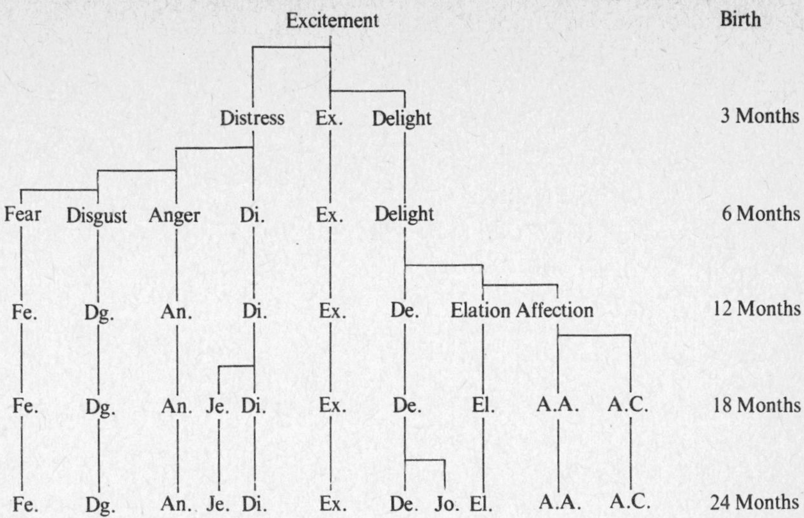

Fig. 1. Showing the approximate ages of differentiation of the various emotions during the first two years of life. Key: A.A.= Affection for adults, A.C.= Affection for children, An.= Anger, De.= Delight, Dg.= Disgust, Di.= Distress, El.= Elation, Ex. = Excitement, Fe.= Fear, Je.= Jealousy, Jo.= Joy.

Readers of the *Journal of Genetic Psychology* will note that a greater number of different emotions are attributed to the two year level than were suggested in a previously published diagram, (3) based on a study of nursery school children.

Emotional behaviour and development are very much determined by particular events and experiences and the routine of living. It is, therefore, to be expected that "institution babies" will show some deviations in their reactions from those of children at home. The former will probably exhibit fear of a larger number of things than other children, due to their very limited experience. On the other hand, they may show greater tolerance of interference, as a result of much practice in self-control in the nursery. They may also be more affectionate with other children, in consequence of the many happy play-hours spent together.

The daily round of feeding, washing, dressing and sleeping, however, has so many factors in common for all babies, that the observations made on the emotional development of a few hospital children, and the suggested inferences presented above, may have at least some general significance for infants brought up under other circumstances.

References

1. Blanton, Margaret Gray. The behaviour of the human infant during the first thirty days of life. *Psychol. Rev.*, 1917, *24*, 456-483.
2. Bridges, K. M. B. The social and emotional development of the pre-school child. London: Kegan Paul, 1931, p. 277.
3. ———. A genetic theory of emotions. *Journal of Genetic Psychol.*, 1930, *37*, p. 514-527.
4. Watson, J. B. Experimental studies on the growth of the emotions. *Ped. Sem.*, 1925, *32*, 2, pp. 328-348.

13 / On the Nature of Fear

D.O. HEBB *McGill University*

A large number of objects or situations can arouse fear in an individual. Some fears, such as fear of loud, unexpected noises, are probably innate while others, such as a child's fear of a hot stove, are classically conditioned habits. However, a fear of mutilated or dead bodies, despite the fact that it is prevalent in man and certain animals, does not readily fit into either the innate or learned category. Professor Hebb describes here the fear responses of chimpanzees and proposes a general theory to explain various kinds of fear.

In the course of an experiment dealing with individual differences of behaviour among chimpanzees, observations of fear were made which held an immediate interest. Besides extending the information concerning the causes of anthropoid fear which is provided by the work of Kohler (23), Jacobsen, Jacobsen and Yoshioka (17), Yerkes and Yerkes (42), Haslerud (10), McCulloch and Haslerud (31) and Hebb and Riesen (14), the new data brought up again the question of mechanism. Analysis of the behaviour leads, in the present discussion, to a review of the whole problem and an attempt to formulate an hypothesis of the causes and nature of fear.

Nature of the Data

Validity and reliability.
The validity of naming fear in chimpanzees, or recognizing something in animals which can be identified with fear in man, and the reliability of naming have been discussed elsewhere (13). There it was shown that the recognition of emotion in an animal is possible in the same way as in another human being. Fear named in an animal means either that there was actual avoidance of some object or place, or that the observer inferred from incidental behaviour ("associated signs") that avoidance was imminent and likely to appear with further stimulation. When such inferences are made with confidence by experienced observers, it appears that they are valid and reliable, the criterion being the animal's subsequent behaviour.

Definition of fear behaviour.
The symbol "W," for withdrawal, was recorded when the animal actually moved away from a test object in such a way as to show that he did not move by coincidence, but was responding to the test situation. The evidence was of several kinds: (1) when change of position of the test object produced a corresponding movement of the animal, maintaining his distance from it; (2) when the original movement was abrupt and coincided exactly with the appearance of the test object; (3) when there was coincident evidence of unusual excitation, such as erection of hair, screaming, threatening gestures directed at the test object, or continued orientation of gaze at the object, while moving directly away from it. On occasions one of these three forms of evidence alone, if exceptionally clear, might provide the basis for an entry of "W" in the record; usually, at least two were present before the entry was made. In many instances the experimenter was certain that an animal would be afraid to approach the test object, but did not record his opinion since the formal behavioural criteria were not met.

Experimental Method

The experimental procedures were part of a study of individual differences of emotionality and temperament, and not planned to meet the problem of defining the adequate stimulus to fear. Thus the range of test objects was limited, and the order in which they were presented does not permit an exact comparison of the excitatory value of each.

Test objects.
The test objects were representations of animals, from reptile to man, varying considerably in completeness and verisimilitude. They fall in three classes: picture, primate, and nonprimate objects. It was not expected that the pictures would induce fear – they were used for another purpose – but they were presented in the same way as the other objects and consequently are useful as control material.

Primate objects.
There were 9 objects representing primates. The responses to these are the main interest of the study.

1 An adult chimpanzee head, three-fifths life size, made of papier-mâché, and painted to appear reasonably lifelike.

From D. O. Hebb. On the nature of fear. *Psychol. Rev.*, 1946, *53*, 259-276. This research was conducted at the Yerkes Laboratories of Primate Biology.

2 An unclothed doll representing a human infant, one-half life size.
3 An infant chimpanzee's head and shoulders, nearly life size, modelled in wax and painted – about as lifelike as the adult chimpanzee head.
4 The cadaver of a chimpanzee infant, newborn, fixed in formalin.
5 A lifelike full-sized human head from a window-display dummy.
6 The skull of a 5-year-old chimpanzee, with movable jaw controlled by a string.
7 The roughly mounted skin of a spider monkey, with head and shoulders movable by means of string.
8 An unpainted plaster of Paris cast of the visage of an adult chimpanzee without the ears or the rest of the head, made from a death mask.
9 The cured and flexible hide of a 5-year-old chimpanzee, somewhat denuded of hair; the proportions of the skin about the head and face were distorted out of recognition, but the hands and feet were recognizable.

The pictures are not described in detail, since they are important here only as 14 emotionally unexciting objects, presented in the same way as the others.

Nonprimate objects varied greatly in verisimilitude, from a careful replica of a snake to a bug which was a rectangular block of wood on coiled-spring legs.

1 A dog's head and forequarters, of cloth, slipped over the hand and manipulated from inside with the fingers; this common toy is surprisingly lifelike in its movements.
2 A model of an imaginary white grub, 4 inches long, with long white legs.
3 A grub identical in proportions and color, one-third as large.
4 A rubber tube, ½ inch in diameter, 24 inches long, with a roughly carved wooden snake's head at one end; so mounted, with string inside the tube, that it could be given a snakelife movement without apparent external agency.
5 A rectangular wooden bug, 6 inches long. It was capable of an oscillating movement, since it was mounted on six coiled-wire legs, and had oscillating antennae.
6 A grasshopper, a mechanical toy with moving legs.
7 A similar turtle.
8 A rubber dog, 3 ½ inches high.
9 A brightly colored cloth dog, 7 inches high.
10 A painted wax replica of a coiled 24-inch snake.

Procedure.

Test objects were presented to the animals while they were in their own living cages. The animal or pair of animals was first brought to the front of the cage by an offer of a small amount of food. The hinged top and front of the presentation box (which was wheeled from cage to cage) was then lifted, exposing one test object to the chimpanzee. At the end of 15 seconds the test object was set in motion if it had movable parts; if not, it was moved forward about 6 inches nearer the animal. The presentation box was closed at the end of another 15 seconds; total exposure was thus 30 seconds. The box had three compartments, and three objects were shown in succession on each experimental period, once or twice a week. The objects were shown to all animals in the same order with the same time intervals.

Experimental Results

With a fixed order of presentation to all subjects, there is a probability that the serial position of a test object will affect the degree of response to it, either by negative adaptation or cumulative effect. There were marked indications that such effects occurred. Some animals apparently learned that the test objects, at first terrifying, would not move out of the presentation box; others began to show fear in the later trials before the box was opened at all.

The total number of animals making fear responses to any object, therefore, is not a wholly satisfactory index of its relative effectiveness in provoking fear. However, there is evidence that the amount of such error is limited. In each group of three objects one or more pictures were included. The number of avoidance responses was consistently low for these pictures, while remaining high for objects, such as dog or snake, known from the work of others (Yerkes, Haslerud) to be fear provoking. This means that transfer or generalization effects were limited. Also there was no sign of a steady increase or decrease of fear responses as the experiment progressed. The animals' responses were highly selective. Preliminary observations, and tests made after the completion of the experiment, also make it clear that such objects as a head without the body attached are in themselves capable of eliciting panic, and that the number of fear responses to human or chimpanzee head, recorded experimentally, is not due to an association of these test objects with the others.

Table I presents the number of fear responses to each test object, separating primate, pictorial and nonprimate objects. The table gives the order of presentation and also shows which three objects were grouped together for each test period. It is assumed, partly on the basis of evidence not presented here, that what particular pictures were used is irrelevant and that the number of animals avoiding the pictures is an index of the "spread" of fear from exciting to neutral objects. From a total of 30 animals the mean number making fear responses to each primate test object was 9.6; to pictures, 0.9; to nonprimate objects, 6.7. These scores, it must be remembered, are the number of actual overt withdrawals which met the criteria set up in advance for a definable fear response. They take no account of signs of fear which were peculiar to an individual animal. Also, they are the number of such responses made while animal and test object were separated by a stout wire

Table I – Number of animals (from a total of 30) making fear responses to primate test objects, pictures, and nonprimate objects

Test		Primate		Picture	Nonprimate	
Test	I	Adult ape head	7	0	dog head (M)*	10
	II	Doll	4	1	large grub	3
	III	Infant ape head	3	2	rubber tube (M)	3
	IV	Infant	1	1	wood-wire bug (M)	3
	V	–		0	mechanical grasshopper (M)	4
	VI	Human head	12	1	rubber dog	5
	VII	Skull (M)	24	0		
		Monkey (M)	16			
	VIII	–		4	small grub	2
	IX	Cast of ape visage	14	4	mechanical turtle (M)	8
	X	Ape hide	5	0	cloth dog	8
	XI	–		0		
				0		
				0		
				0	Cast of snake	21
Total			86	13		67
Mean			9.6	0.9		6.7

* (M) Indicates that the object was put in motion during the presentation period.

mesh. Tests in other circumstances show a higher percentage of avoidance, and show also that the relative effectiveness of two objects as causes of fear may vary somewhat according to the mode of presentation. In the conditions of the experiment, the following are the most effective stimuli, in descending order: *skull* (with moving jaw); painted wax *snake*; *monkey* (with moving head); plaster cast of *chimpanzee visage*; and *human head*. Least exciting are, in ascending order: chimpanzee infant; small wax grub; infant chimpanzee head; large wax grub; moving rubber tube (snake); and moving wood-and-wire bug.

Supplementary Observations

The chimpanzee's fear of toy animals and snakes is of course well known (23, 42). The data which are new and which were the occasion of this report are those showing that the chimpanzee is excited by, and avoids, parts of chimpanzee or human bodies. It was evident that such a conclusion had important implications, and that further observations would be desirable as a control of the data. Control observations, accordingly, were made after the formal experiment was completed. Their purpose was to discover whether some peculiarity of the actual experimental objects, or some detail of procedure, might have been the true cause of fear; or whether the behaviour falls into a more general class related to the common human avoidance of a mutilated face and of dead bodies.

Preliminary experiments had already shown that all the adult chimpanzees were excited at the first sight of a chimpanzee head modelled in clay and carried in the hand from cage to cage. A majority showed avoidance, which was outright panic in five or six of the thirty subjects. In the supplementary observations an unpainted plaster cast of the clay model, and also an actual head from a dead chimpanzee, produced definite avoidance.

With different presentations the results were essentially the same, although intensity of response varied, in part with adaptation to sight of so many similar objects. Avoidance was observed when a head was carried by hand; when it was exposed by removing a cloth or opening a box; and when the head was first put in the chimpanzee's cage and the animal admitted afterward. In another observation the head was placed behind a small ledge, so that the actual termination of the neck was not visible (although the chimpanzee "knew" from familiarity with the cage in which the test was made that there was no space large enough for a body beneath the head). The chimpanzee was then admitted from a detaining inner room from which none of the preparations could be seen. A marked fear response occurred immediately, before the lapse of enough time to make the unresponsiveness of the head abnormal. Thus lack of movement in the test object did not determine the fear, nor yet an actual perception of the termination of the neck.

A painted human eye and eyebrow (sawn from a plaster manikin's head) produced marked avoidance.

Finally, observations were made with anaesthetized chimpanzees as stimulus objects. Four adults were shown an anaesthetized infant, two years old, carried by two members of the staff. The infant was recovering from nembutal, and made some spontaneous movements of an arm and hand. Three of the four adults were very excited and one at least afraid, in spite of the fact that they had often seen young chimpanzees being carried by the staff. A more deeply anaesthetized adult was taken on a low, flat, two-wheeled barrow up the cages of nine of the adults. Definite fear was shown by six, aggression (possibly related to fear) by two others, and the remaining animal was almost certainly afraid but remained at a distance without showing definable avoidance.

The fear evoked by a detached face or head in the formal experiment, therefore, was not a product of some uncontrolled detail of procedure or of the construction of the test objects. Any of a number of related stimuli have the same effect, in a number of situations.

From the data is appears that *either* lack of responsiveness in a whole animal, *or* an evident lack of a body when the head or part of the head is seen, can determine the fear. The first conclusion depends on the observations with anaesthetized animals as stimuli. The second follows from the fact that avoidance of an isolated head was immediate and certainly was not delayed long enough for an unusual unresponsiveness, as such, to have become apparent before fear occurred.

Spontaneity of the Fear

The fears observed must also have been spontaneous,[1] and not conditioned by some association of the test objects with a more primitive source of fear such as pain. This is shown by the following considerations.

There are two ways in which fear of a detached head or an anaesthetized animal could be due to learning. Fear might occur (1) because the subjects recognized part of a whole which they had learned to fear in the past, or (2) because of an earlier association of a class of objects (detached heads, abnormally unresponsive chimpanzees) with a more primitive cause of fear.

1. The first explanation can be ruled out. The dummy human head represented an ordinary young man whom the adults of the colony might have teased or injured, as they often tend to do with strangers whose general appearance is similar to that of members of the laboratory staff, but whom they would not have feared. The cast of a face was a faithful replica of the chimpanzee Lita's, made from the death mask. She had died not long before the experiment began, and certainly would not have been a source of fear to any of the other chimpanzees with cage wire intervening, as in the conditions of the experiment. The anaesthetized infant in his normal state would not have been feared by an adult; and the anaesthetized adult who was used as a stimulus object was Don, who is dominated by almost all of the other adults of the colony. The test object which aroused fear therefore did not do so because it was recognized as part of a whole which in its normal completeness would have caused the response.

2. The second possibility to be examined is that an association had been formed earlier between the class of stimulus objects and some event such as pain, loud noise, or a fall. For animals born in the bush and captured when their mothers were killed this was a real possibility. But nine of the adolescent and adult subjects of the experiment were born and reared in captivity and definitely had no opportunity to make such associations. None of these had seen a detached human or chimpanzee head; a few of them had seen a dead chimpanzee, but no more primitive cause of fear would be associated with the sight. The nine animals who are known not to have such associations showed on the average rather more frequent and stronger avoidance than the remaining twenty-one animals.

These facts require the conclusion that the fears discussed are spontaneous. Further support for the conclusion is found in the behaviour of human beings.

Human Avoidance of Mutilated and Dead Bodies

Human emotional responses to the dead and to such things as the sight of a major operation or of a badly mutilated face cannot reasonably be attributed to conditioning. The responses tend to be strongest on the first experience which eliminates direct conditioning as an explanation and requires the supporting assumption of a preliminary verbal conditioning which forms the whole basis of the response. But if avoidance were so readily established, with no innate tendency toward fear of the conditioned stimulus itself, one could easily keep children from playing in dangerous places or train adults to drive automobiles carefully – by verbal instruction alone. This is the essence of Valentine's (39) brilliant criticism of Watsonian theory and my rejection of the explanation by conditioning rests upon his argument. What he did was to show how easy it is to condition fear of some things, how hard with others, and thus demonstrated the existence of emotional susceptibilities which are the basis of spontaneous and almost spontaneous fears.

Watson's (40) theory of fear has rightly had a profound effect upon psychological thought, and a radical departure from his ideas is not readily accepted. Yet the present situation is that the theory has been demolished, with no good substitute in sight. Jones and Jones' (22) experiment on the human fear of snakes constituted a strong and radical attack on Watson's theory. The evidence adduced by Valentine (39) reinforced the attack with evidence from a variety of fears. He has shown that there is a wide range of situations, not easily defined or classified, which have some tendency to evoke human fear. Finally, Hebb and Riesen (14) have shown the existence of a spontaneous fear of strangers in infant chimpanzees, where the customary appeal to the subject's unknown past experience is impossible and the explanation by conditioning ruled out.

Watson's work, consequently, provides no more

[1]The term "spontaneous" is used here to mean that the fear is not built up by association, as a learned response. The term is not synonymous with "innate" since there are definite factors of past experience involved. . . .

than a starting point in determining the causes of fear and gives no reason to reject the conclusion that human fear of dead or mutilated bodies is spontaneous. The conclusion is also not affected by the fact that an almost complete adaptation to such stimuli is possible, nor by the fact that some persons may not have an emotional disturbance at their first sight of an operation, autopsy, or dissection. It has sometimes been assumed that if a fear is not general it must have been learned by those who do have it: that an innate fear should be found in all persons. This argument of course is quite invalid in view of the existence of individual genetic differences, and it has been seen that some of the chimpanzee fears discussed in this paper are not found in all animals and yet cannot be ascribed to learning.

The evidence, therefore, is that both in man and in chimpanzee there occur spontaneous fears of mutilated and unresponsive bodies. The chimpanzee knows nothing of anaesthesia, has no abstract conception of death, and presumably may confuse a model of a head and the real thing. Considering the intellectual differences between the species and the extent to which man's behaviour is influenced by speech, one must say that human and chimpanzee fear susceptibilities, with dismembered or inert bodies as stimulus objects, are remarkably similar. In this fact there is further support for the idea that such fears are spontaneous and not associative or conditioned.

So that this conclusion will be seen in the proper perspective, the reader is reminded that the importance of learning is not minimized. There are essential factors of past experience in the fears which have been discussed; and the hypothesis which is to be presented lays a good deal of emphasis on learning as an element in the development of any fear.

Central Versus Sensory Factors Determining Fear

The first step in an analysis of fear is a better definition of the problem and of its relation to other psychological investigations.

It should be specified that the problem is not simply that of the subcortical motor integration of fear behaviour. The earlier studies of Bard (2) had the effect of concentrating attention on the hypothalamus, but it is now evident that more must be taken into account. The analysis by Lashley (24) and Masserman (32) has limited the emotional functions of the diencephalon to a motor integration. More recently, Bard (3) has described rage in a cat lacking *only* the hypothalamic region which he formerly considered to be essential to emotional activity. In view also of the marked differences of the stimuli which are effective in each case, and the absence of "after-discharge" in the decorticate preparation, it is evident that the processes of normal and decorticate emotions cannot be equated. Fear behaviour has been demonstrated by Bard in the decorticate cat, but only with auditory stimuli. An essential problem remains in understanding cortico-subcortical interaction and the important role of perception in the fear responses of the normal animal.

The evidence presented has shown that the chimpanzee's fear of a detached head is in some way related to the physical lack of an attached body or of movement or both. But our real interest is not in the physical properties of the stimulus object but in the way they act on the organism. The first question to be asked concerns the existence of a sensory control of the response: can one find any property of the sensory excitation which in itself determines the occurrence and form of the response?

The answer seems to be no. In the first place, the physical lack in the stimulus object cannot be equated with a sensory lack by saying that the sight of a head without the normally associated sight of a body causes fear, for the statement would not be true. When a chimpanzee sees a man's head only, without movement and with the rest of the man's body out of sight behind a door, he is not afraid. There are certainly sensory cues which distinguish the two situations (i.e., detached head *vs* attached head with body hidden) but I have not been able to find any generalization that distinguishes the purely sensory[2] event which causes fear from the one which does not. In the second place, it has been shown that the fears are spontaneous. If they were also sensorily determined, it would follow that there are innate connections from the sensory cells, excited in seeing any chimpanzee or human head, to the motor centres determining avoidance; or in a more gestalt formulation, that the dynamic properties of every such sensory excitation have an innately selective action on those particular motor centres. It would follow further that this sensori-motor relationship is consistently inhibited and nonfunctional throughout the animal's lifetime, no matter how many times he sees a human or chimpanzee head, unless by chance the head has been cut off from its owner. The improbability of such ideas is evident. They seem to be a product of the assumption (quite reasonable in itself) that the form of a response is fully determined by the sensory event that precipitates it: since a physical lack in the stimulus object cannot excite receptor cells, the assumption means that the part of the stimulus object which is present is an adequate excitant of fear, and since the whole object does not cause fear, that the part which is missing is normally an inhibitor or in some way prevents an innately determined response to the other part. Such reasoning will be found to lead rapidly to absurdities. Doubt is then cast on the original assumption, and the alternative conclusion is indicated that the determinant of certain strongly marked anthropoid fears is not any property of the sensory excitation alone

[2]"Sensory" in the present discussion is defined as referring to activity, in afferent structures, which is directly determined by environmental events; roughly, activity in the receptor organ and afferent tracts, up to and including the corresponding sensory projection area.

but may have to be sought in some interaction of sensory events with other cerebral processes.

This argument depends on the accuracy of the analysis which has been made of the stimulating conditions in which fear of dismembered or inert bodies is observed. Other interpretations are possible, but seem either to beg the question or to amount to the same thing. (One might say, for example, that it is strangeness or mysteriousness that produces fear of a decapitated head and of an inert chimpanzee being carried by human beings. Actually, reference to strangeness only strengthens the preceding argument, as we shall see in a moment.) Nevertheless, it would be unwise to depend too strongly on the evidence of behaviour into which so many complicating factors of experience may enter. Let us turn to fear of strangers (14) and of sudden noise (8). The theoretical interpretation suggested by fear of a dismembered body gains decisive support from these other observations and in turn makes their theoretical significance clearer.

The growing chimpanzee is persistently afraid of strange persons, objects and places, although the response is not always predictable in the individual case. Hebb and Riesen (14) have shown that the fear of strangers by chimpanzee infants is spontaneous and cannot be accounted for as a conditioned response. Also, a slight change of clothing may produce fear of a familiar attendant who was not feared before. To assume that the form of the response on seeing something strange is controlled alone by some property of the sensory event is to assume that *any* visual excitation is primarily a cause of fear and that other responses are substituted merely by repetition of the stimulation. Fear of strangers would mean that the visual excitation from any human or chimpanzee face (strange chimpanzees are feared as much as strange men) or any pattern of clothing is an innately adequate excitant of fear; for any pattern whatever may be strange, depending on accidents of experience. The idea seems absurd in itself, and is definitely contradicted by observations of the behaviour of an infant chimpanzee blindfolded from birth to the age of four months, when the avoidance of strangers by normal animals is beginning (Nissen).[3] In Senden's (35) comprehensive review of the literature on persons born blind and given their sight after infancy, there is no mention of fear aroused by the first visual form-perception; and Dennis (7) explicitly denies that fear occurs in these persons. Fear of a strange person is, therefore, not determined by a particular property of the sensory excitation, but by some discrepancy of the pattern from those which have been frequently experienced by the subject – by a complex relationship, that is, of the sensory event to preexistent cerebral processes.

A similar meaning lies in the fact noted by English (8) that a noise must be sudden to cause fear. When auditory intensity is built up gradually, the response is hard to elicit. The same is true of loss of support. An unexpected drop is the one that causes fear, not one for which preparation has been made verbally or by playful swinging of infant subjects. Jones (21) has shown that unexpectedness is an essential feature of a number of fear-provoking situations. In all such fears the major determinant cannot be the afferent excitation alone but involves a relationship of that excitation to concurrent cerebral activity.

These facts actually raise no new theoretical issue. Their effect is to sharpen the definition of a problem which has been formulated in various ways by other writers. That both sensory and central processes are involved in the control of behaviour and must be distinguished for theoretical purposes is implied by the concept of "operants" (Skinner, 37) and of "stimulus trace" (Hull, 16) no less than by the "expectancy" of Cowles and Nissen (6), Mowrer (34) and Hilgard and Marquis (15). It is the real problem of attention and of the selectivity of response to the several properties of a sensory event (Leeper, 27; Lashley, 26). The problem is made explicit by Hilgard and Marquis's "central process which seems relatively independent of afferent stimuli," Beach's (4) "central excitatory mechanism," and Morgan's (33) "central motive state." Every serious attempt in recent years to analyze the neural mechanisms of the more complex forms of behaviour has found the need of distinguishing, as more or less independent factors, sensory and central states of processes; in other words, of denying that the direction of transmission of a sensory excitation is determined by the properties of that excitation alone, even when the stable changes of learning have been taken into account. This is thoroughly consistent also with modern electro-physiology. All parts of the brain are continuously active and there are reasons for believing that the activity may be self-maintaining, and even self-initiating (1, 18, 29, 30, 41). An afferent excitation does *not* arouse inactive tissue, but modifies an activity already in existence. The conclusion, therefore, that there are nonsensory factors in the determination of certain fears agrees with existing theory.

It must be added that the conclusion is not necessarily trivial. Current opinion recognizes the necessity of postulating central determinants of behaviour but it has done so reluctantly, always with reference to single, rather narrow aspect of behavioural theory, and apparently without recognizing how generally the necessity has actually cropped up in psychological analysis. The preceding discussion may do no more than suggest a change of emphasis, but the change is one which, as I shall try to show, has a considerable effect on theory. Besides drawing attention to facts

[3]Personal communication from Dr. H. W Nissen. The experiment was not an investigation of emotional behaviour, and detailed records on this point were not kept. But it is known with certainty that there was no avoidance evoked by the chimpanzee's first visual perception of human beings.

of behaviour which are usually forgotten, it reveals some order in the facts and makes possible a coherent hypothesis of the nature of fear.

Development of an Hypothesis

Avoidance of strangers provides a possible starting point for a theory of the nature of fear. An essential feature of the stimulating conditions is the divergence of the object avoided from a familiar group of objects, while still having enough of their properties to fall within the same class. It is a most important fact that the fear or shyness does not develop at first vision, as the already cited data of Nissen, Senden (35), and Dennis (7) have shown. Common experience indicates also that the fear is minimized or absent if the growing infant has always been exposed to sight of a large number of persons. It is therefore dependent on the fact that certain perceptions have become habitual, a limited number of central neural reactions to the sight of human beings having been established with great specificity by repeated experience. The idea that there are such habits of perception was developed by Gibson (9) and further supported by later studies of the effect of set upon perception (5, 27, 43). A number of facts relating to the development of intelligence, and its changes with advancing age, have the same import (11, pp. 286, 289). From this point of view, it might be proposed that fear occurs when an object is seen which is like familiar objects in enough respects to arouse habitual processes of perception, but in other respects arouses incompatible processes.

Such a treatment of the fear of strangers would amount to an interference, incongruity, or conflict theory. It might subsume fear of mutilated bodies as well, by classifying them as strange objects, and could be extended to cover fears due to pain and sudden loud noise, which obviously tend to disrupt concurrent psychological processes. But farther than this such a conflict theory will not go. There might be some difficulty in applying it even to the fear of strange objects, when the strangeness is apparently due to incompleteness in a familiar object (as with the chimpanzee's fear of a detached head); and conflict cannot account for causes of fear such as darkness (39) in which a sensory deficit is the effective condition, or nutritional disturbance (38).

Moreover, a fundamental question would remain as to the meaning of "conflict," and why an incompatibility between two perceptions should produce the incoordinations of emotional behaviour. This is the crucial question, and in trying to answer it I believe we can find the possibility of a more comprehensive hypothesis, according to which conflict is only one of several ways in which a true source of fear occurs. If two perceptual processes, which cannot coexist, cannot even alternate without producing gross disturbances of behaviour (which is what the conflict notion implies), ordinary unemotional behaviour must depend on an essential temporal integration in cerebral processes, and fear may be a direct result of their disorganization. Let us ask what such ideas would involve.

It has already been seen that sensory and central processes contribute separately to the control of behaviour. For convenience, let us designate the specific pattern of cellular activity throughout the thalamocortical system, at any one moment, as a "phase". Behaviour is directly correlated with a phase sequence which is temporally organized (4), in part by the inherent properties of the system (the constitutional factor) and in part by the time relations of various afferent excitations in the past (the factor of experience). The spatial organization of each phase, the actual anatomical pattern of cells which are active at any moment, would be affected by the present afferent excitation also. Subjectively, the phase sequence would be identified with the train of thought and perception. Now each phase is determined by a neural interaction, between the preceding phase and the concurrent afferent excitations. Lorente De No's (29) discussion of the dynamics of neural action shows that two or more simultaneous neural events might reinforce each other's effects and contribute to a single, determinate pattern of subsequent cerebral activity; or on the contrary might be indeterminate, in the sense that slight changes of timing and intensity could lead to marked and sudden fluctuations of pattern. A phase sequence, that is, could be stable or unstable, and one can assume that vacillating, unpredictable, and incoordinated behaviour is the expression of unstable cerebral activity. Also, the effect of learning in general is to increase the predictability and co-ordination of behaviour. The element of learning in emotional behaviour will be discussed more specifically, but in the meantime we may speak of the cerebral processes controlling predictable, coordinated behaviour as "organized," and recognize the tendency of learning to establish and maintain cerebral organization.

Disorganization could occur in several ways, some of which may be called conflict. (1) A sensory event might disrupt the concurrent phase sequence. The event might be one whose facilitation has been integrated into other phase sequences, and disruptive only because it is "unexpected." If so the disruption would be brief, another well-organized phase sequence would be promptly established, and one would speak of the subject as having only been "startled." The disruption would be brief but it would occur; a well-organized phase could not be set up instantaneously, independent of facilitation from the preceding phase. On the other hand, the sensory event might fail to set up another organized sequence, and so initiate a prolonged disturbance; or might, like loud noise, and especially pain, tend persistently to break down cerebral organization. (2) Simultaneous sensory events might have facilitations which are enough unlike to make the following phase sequence unstable, even though each event separately might be capable of integration with the concurrent phase. Evidently (1) and (2) would be modes of conflict, one sensory-central, the other sensory-sensory.[4] But disorganization might also result (3) from the absence of a usually present sensory process. Cerebral organization involves learning. If a sensory activity A has always been present during adaptation to a sensory event B, facilitation from A would necessarily affect the final pattern of cellular activities which constitutes the adaptation to B, and might be essential to it. If so, B in the absence of A could again produce behavioural disturbance (if B without A occurs often enough, however, another adaptation would be established. Finally (4) metabolic and structural changes in the central nervous system could obviously be a source of disorganization, by changing the time relations between the activities of individual cells, apart from any unusual conflict or sensory deficiency.

Attention must now be turned to the way in which cerebral processes tend to maintain their organization, in order to round out the picture of fear behaviour. Whatever else may be true of it, avoidance certainly averts or minimizes disruptive stimulation. When we distinguish between the disruption and the processes tending to avert it, and assume that the degree of disruption may vary, we obtain the valuable result of seeing how a single mechanism of fear could on different occasions produce perfectly co-ordinated flight, a less co-ordinated avoidance accompanied by trembling and so on, startle, or the paralysis of terror: When cerebral disruption is extreme, it might presumably prevent any co-ordinated action, even flight.

It seems evident that the so-to-speak homeostatic processes which maintain the dynamic equilibrium of unemotional behaviour are to a great extent processes of learning, operating in either of two ways. On the one hand there is negative adaptation to strange objects, which implies that a sensory-central conflict may be banished by an effect of learning on the central organization alone. The sensory event remains the same, yet disturbance disappears. With still further exposure, the formerly strange object may become not merely tolerated but "liked" and "pleasant," which is to say that the originally disturbing sensory event now actively supports cerebral integration.

On the other hand, learning may contribute to this integration indirectly, by reinforcing a mode of behaviour (avoidance) which minimizes or removes the disturbing sensation. The inco-ordinations of emotional behaviour, its most characteristic feature, are unlearned; they are apt to be most marked on the first occasion on which they are aroused by any particular stimulus. But the co-ordinated element of the behaviour tends to become more prominent on repetition of the stimulus and to increase, while the unlearned inco-ordination is decreasing. It thus appears that the co-ordinated avoidance which occurs in fear behaviour of normal animals is mainly learned.

There is indeed a primitive innate avoidance (manifested, e.g., in the flexion reflex of Sherrington's (36) spinal animals, and the cowering of Bard's (3) decerabrate cats), but the avoidance which operates most efficiently to maintain co-ordinated effector activity is acquired. In the normal mammal at least, simple avoidance appears as a conditioned response to cues which in the past have preceded a disruptive stimulation. When a disruptive event is sudden and without warning the response is never an uncomplicated avoidance, a smooth and economical co-operation of effector organs, but involves startle, trembling, sweating, vocalization, and so on. The optimum toward which behaviour tends, with repetition of such disturbances, is a response (to premonitory cues) which completely averts the disturbing sensory event. At this final stage of learning, avoidance is fully effective in maintaining integrated cerebral action, and no emotional component is left in the behaviour. Thus avoidance without fear occurs. In the avoidance that does involve fear the learning process is not complete or premonitory cues have not been available, and the belated avoidance appears side by side with the excess of effector activity that justifies the inference of cerebral disorganization.

The reciprocal relationship of learning to the disruption of integrated behaviour is most simply illustrated by an adult's unemotional avoidance of a hot stove which as an infant he may once have feared. Another illustration is provided by observation of adult chimpanzees where the course of learning in a very unusual social situation could be followed from its beginning. The experimenter, disguised with a grotesque false face and a change of clothing, approached each animal's cage wearing heavy gloves and acted the part of a very aggressive individual, instead of the cautious role one ordinarily takes with the chimpanzee. The results suggested an interpretation similar to that of Bridges (cited by Jones, 21) who concluded that an infant's fear develops out of primitive undifferentiated excitement. The first response by a number of animals was a generalized excitement and marked autonomic activity. An animal might be "friendly" and viciously aggressive, almost in the same breath, or show erection of hair and scream and yet solicit petting. Attack, flight, and the friendly pattern alternated unpredictably. As the stimulus was repeated over a 5-week period, the autonomic activity decreased and one or other of the various patterns dominated. Eventually each animal's behaviour became predictable, but it appeared often to be a matter of chance whether the original disturbance would develop into fear, aggression or (less often) friendliness. When avoidance became dominant, the animal would move back out of reach

[4] Logically, another category of "central-central" conflict would be possible, which might have some meaning with regard to emotional disturbances and anxiety arising from a conflict of ideas or beliefs. Such a concept might be applied to fear of socialism or of catholics and emotional disturbances due to such purely intellectual ideas as those of Galileo or Darwin.

while the experimenter was still distant, with a marked decrease of the excessive effector activity. Learning was clearly involved. We shall also see that the possibility, suggested by this example, that the learning may take more than one form, has a bearing on the theoretical relation of fear to other emotional patterns.

The hypothesis implicitly developed in this discussion can now be made explicit. The immediate source of fear is a disruption of a co-ordination, principally acquired in the timing of cellular activities in the cerebrum. The disruption may be due to conflict, sensory deficit or constitutional change. With disruption there at once occur processes tending to restore the integration of cerebral activities; in fear these include either liminal or subliminal (13) activation of processes determining avoidance. Optimally, avoidance tends toward completely averting the cerebral disruption, and at this stage avoidance without fear would be said to occur.

Classification of Specific Fears

The value and limitations of the hypothesis will be clearer if we next see how it would be related to specific causes of fear.

1. *Fears due to "conflict."* Here may be included fears induced by pain, loud noise, dead or mutilated bodies, and strange persons and animals. Pain and loud noise appear to have a primitive disrupting action, not psychologically analyzable nor dependent on any previous experience. To this extent fear of such things is in a special class. It is also noteworthy that there is little adaptation to the repetition of pain and sudden intense noise except in very special conditions (28).

Fear of the strange and of dead and mutilated bodies is included under the heading of conflict on the assumption that strange objects arouse incompatible perceptual and intellectual processes. If it should be concluded however that the effective condition is a perceptual deficit, fear of the strange should be included in the following category (2). Finally, fear of snakes and certain small mammals may belong either in this or the following category. Although some basis for including them in the present category might be proposed it would be much too speculative, and it is best to let such fears stand for the present as not fully accounted for.

2. *Fears due to sensory deficit.* Loss of support, darkness and solitude, as causes of fear, have in common an absence of customary stimulation.

Proprioceptive and pressure stimulation due to maintained position in space is practically always present, and it is plausible to suppose that the afferent excitation from these sources would have an essential part in maintaining experientially organized, or habitual, modes of cerebral action. With loss of support, however, the proprioception accompanying maintenance of posture against gravity, and exteroception from the surfaces on which the body's weight rests, are decreased or abolished. Redistribution of blood pressure and changes of position of viscera would no doubt also lead to positive stimulation, but it seems unlikely that this is an effective cause of fear in the infant. In the adult, of course, such stimulation would have become conditioned by experience. (If it should be true that positive visceral stimulation is the main cause of fear in an infant dropped for the first time, the fear should be classed in the preceding category 1, as one of those aroused by an unaccustomed stimulation.)

Fears induced by darkness and solitude (39) do not occur with time relations such that the emotional excitation can be attributed to the positive visual activity of the "off-effect." The response appears to be genuine reaction to deficit (25), intelligible only on the assumption of the present discussion that a "response" need have no direct *sensory* excitant. The violent attempts of the growing chimpanzee to avoid isolation, even in full daylight, seem to require a quite similar interpretation. Kohler (23) has shown that the effective condition here is the social deprivation, as such. Just as a few patterns of postural stimulation are a practically constant feature of the afferent influx to the brain, and visual stimulation during waking hours, so social perceptions are frequent (though intermittent) and might be expected to become an integral element in the organization of cerebral action patterns. It is important to note that this would be a function of experience, and that no fear of darkness or of being alone should be expected in the subject who has only infrequently experienced anything else. Such a subject would develop a different cerebral organization, in which the perceptions referred to would play no essential part. It is also implied that in early infancy neither darkness nor isolation would have any emotional effect; and that as psychological development continues the patterns of cerebral action might, toward maturity, become so stable as to be relatively independent of any particular set of perceptions. Some adults, or most adults in a particular culture, might have no fear of darkness and isolation.

3. *Constitutional disturbances and maturation.* Spies *et al.*(38) have provided exceptionally clear evidence that the psychotic fears so frequently found in pellegra are, in some instances at least, directly due to nutritional disturbance (see also Jolliffe, 20). When the psychosis is acute (before irreversible neural damage has been done), fear of friends and relatives and of hallucinatory creatures may clear up dramatically upon administration of nicotinic acid. The patient regains insight rapidly, can recall his fears clearly, but also is puzzled at the lack of any incident that might have caused them. Controls made to exactly define the action of nicotinic acid rule out psychological influence as essential either to the mental illness or its cure. Such fears must be regarded as originating in a disturbance of the metabolism of the individual cell, changing (for example) the timing of its detonation cycle and thus its

relationship to the activity of other cells. In other words, metabolic changes would have disrupted the orderly sequence of cerebral events which is postulated here as the basis of normal unemotional behaviour.

It is also evident that endocrine factors might at times produce a similar effect, partly accounting for the increased shyness and emotional instability of adolescence. The gonadal hormones must be supposed to have a selective action on certain central neural cells (4, 25) changing their properties of excitability and thus disrupting to a greater or less degree the neural organizations into which those cells have entered. With the passage of time reorganization would occur and shyness would decrease.

I do not of course suggest that constitutional changes are the only cause of shyness, or even the main cause. In its most pronounced form it must be thought of simply as an avoidance of strangers; and the next most important factor, after the sight of a strange person, may well be the fact that as the child matures others begin to behave toward him in a different way, according to his age. The child is confronted by "strange" behaviour, and situations which are strange to him. Thus shyness can be treated mainly as avoidance of the strange. It is not impossible however that structural and endocrine changes may also play a part in the emotional instabilities of youth. One thinks of maturation as slow and gradual; but there is actually little evidence on this point, and spurts of growth might well make a significant modification of cerebral organizations established by earlier experience. In general terms, such an approach makes intelligible the sporadic appearance of the "imaginative, subjective, or anticipatory fears" classified as such by Jersild and Holmes (19). The fears referred to by Jersild and Holmes are markedly subject to maturation during a period of rapid and irregular growth, and when one observes them in the growing child it is characteristically hard to discover any sufficient cause in experience.

The Relationship of Fear to Rage and Other States

Fear and rage are notoriously related, and it is impossible to frame any statement of the causes of rage (12) which would not on some points comprise causes of fear as well. The question, whether there is in fact any definite distinction, has been raised elsewhere (13). The hypothesis developed here suggests a kinship between the two emotions which may be put as follows.

The fundamental source of either emotion is of the same kind, a disruption of co-ordinated cerebral activity. Flight and aggression are two different modes of reaction tending to restore the dynamic equilibrium, or stability, of cerebral processes. The question may be left open at present whether there are different kinds of disturbance, one kind leading to rage, the other to fear. It seems almost certain that such a difference exists between extremes, but with no clear dichotomy; for in some situations, as I have suggested above, it appears to be a matter of chance whether aggression or flight will dominate behaviour. Each of these modes of response tends to restore integrated cerebral action, one by modifying the disturbing source of stimulation, the other by removing the animal from it.

Fawning would be another mode of reaction which would tend to modify disruptive stimulation (by placating the source). It is evident also that the hypothesis of this paper opens a wide field of speculation concerning a number of socially and clinically familiar conditions, such as shame, grief, chronic depression and so on. To deal with these varied emotional disturbances the first step would be to classify the source of disturbance as modifiable by the subject's responses, or unmodifiable; and further to classify the modifiable according to the mode of overt reaction which would be effective. Thus shame or grief would arise from unmodifiable conditions; fear primarily from situations which are (or appear to the subject to be) modifiable by retreat; and so on. Finally, neurosis and some forms of psychosis would be regarded as a chronic condition of cerebral disorganization which according to the hypothesis might be initiated either by severe and prolonged conflict, or by a metabolic disturbance.

It would be idle at present to carry speculation farther, but it has been worthwhile observing that a theoretical relationship of fear to other emotional patterns is provided. If the proposed hypothesis is on the right track, the details of the relationship will become evident when more is known of the physiology of the cerebrum.

Conclusions

The conclusions of this paper may be put as follows:

1. Anthropoid fears of inert, mutilated, or dismembered bodies are spontaneous: that is to say, although experience of a certain kind is a prerequisite and learning is definitely involved, the avoidance of such objects is not built up by association with a more primitive cause of fear.

2. These and a number of other fears are evidently not determined by a sensory event alone, and the behaviour is not intelligible except on the assumption that its control is a joint product of sensory and "autonomous" central processes. Consequently no amount of analysis of the stimulating conditions alone can be expected to elucidate the nature of fear, or to lead to any useful generalization concerning its causes.

3. An adequate hypothesis of the nature of fear cannot be framed in psychological terms alone, but must utilize physiological concepts of cerebral action. No common psychological ground can be discovered for all the various causes of fear. What is there in common, for example, between the characteristically high level of the auditory and low level of visual

stimulation which induces fear in children? Or between fear of strangers, which decreases, and fear induced by pain, which tends to increase, with repetition?

The hypothesis developed here has made a considerable synthesis of formerly unrelated facts, although it remains vague on some crucial points. It proposes in brief that fear originates in the disruption of temporally and spatially organized cerebral activities; that fear is distinct from other emotions by the nature of the processes tending to restore cerebral equilibrium (that is, *via* flight); and classifies the sources of fear as involving (1) conflict, (2) sensory deficit, or (3) constitutional change. By distinguishing between processes which break down and those which restore physiological organization in the cerebrum, the variability of fear behaviour is accounted for.

The conceptions of neurophysiological action on which this is based were developed originally as an approach to other problems.... When this is done, and the neurophysiological implications are made explicit, it may appear that a basis has been laid at last for an adequate theory of emotion and motivation – something which is lacking in psychology at present.

References

1. ADRIAN, E. D. Electrical activity of the nervous system. *Arch. neurol. Psychiatr.*, 1934, *32*, 1125-1136.
2. BARD, P. On emotional expression after decortication with some remarks on certain theoretical views. *Psychol. Rev.*, 1934, *41*, 309-329.
3. BARD, P. Neural mechanisms in emotional and sexual behaviour. *Psychosom. Med.*, 1942, *4*, 171-172.
4. BEACH, F. A. Analysis of factors involved in the arousal, maintenance and manifestation of sexual excitement in male animals. *Psychosom. Med.*, 1942, *4*, 173-198.
5. CHARMICHAEL, L., HOGAN, H. P., and WALTER, A. A. An experimental study of the effect of language on the reproduction of visually perceived form. *J. exp. Psychol.*, 1932, *15*, 73-86.
6. COWLES, J. T., and NISSEN, H. W. Reward-expectancy in delayed responses of chimpanzees. *J. comp. Psychol.*, 1937, *24*, 345-358.
7. DENNIS, W. Congenital cataract and unlearned behaviour. *J. genet. Psychol.*, 1934, *44*, 340-350.
8. ENGLISH, H. B. Three cases of the "conditioned fear response." *J. abnorm. soc. Psychol.*, 1929, *24*, 221-225.
9. GIBSON, J. J. The reproduction of visually perceived forms. *J. exp. Psychol.*, 1929, *12*, 1-39.
10. HASLERUD, G. M. The effect of movement of stimulus objects upon avoidance reactions in chimpanzees. *J. comp. Psychol.*, 1938, *25*, 507-528.
11. HEBB, D. O. The effect of early and late brain injury on test scores, and the nature of normal adult intelligence. *Proc. Amer. phil. Soc.*, 1942, *85*, 275-292.
12. ———. The forms and conditions of chimpanzee anger. *Bull. Canad. psychol. Assoc.*, 1945, *5*, 32-35.
13. ———. Emotion in man and animal: an analysis of the intuitive processes of recognition. *Psychol. Rev.*, 1946, *53*, 88-106.
14. HEBB, D. O., and RIESEN, A. H. The genesis of irrational fears. *Bull. Canad. psychol. Assoc.*, 1943, *3*, 49-50.
15. HILGARD, E. R., and MARQUIS, D. G. *Conditioning and learning*. New York: Appleton-Century, 1940.
16. HULL, C. L. *Principles of behaviour: an introduction to behaviour theory*. New York: Appleton-Century, 1943.
17. JACOBSEN, C. F., JACOBSEN, M. M., and YOSHIOKA, J. G. Development of an infant chimpanzee during her first year. *Comp. Psychol., Monog.*, 1932, *9*, 1-94.
18. JASPER, H. H. Electrical signs of cortical activity. *Psychol. Bull.*, 1937, *34*, 411-481.
19. JERSILD, A. T., and HOLMES, F. B. *Children's fears*. New York: Teachers College Bureau of Publications, 1935.
20. JOLLIFFE, N. The neuropsychiatric manifestations of vitamin deficiencies. *J. Mt. Sinai Hosp.*, 1942, *8*, 658-667.
21. JONES, M. C. Emotional development. In C. MURCHISON (ed.), *A handbook of child psychology*. (2nd ed.) Worcester, Mass.: Clark Univ. Press, 1933. Pp. 271-302.
22. JONES, H. E., and JONES, M. C. A study of fear. *Childhood Educ.*, 1928, *5*, 136-143.
23. KOHLER, W. *The mentality of apes*. New York: Harcourt, Brace, 1925.
24. LASHLEY, K. S. The thalamus and emotion. *Psychol. Rev.*, 1938, *45*, 42-61.
25. ———. Experimental analysis of instinctive behaviour. *Psychol. Rev.*, 1938, *45*, 445-471.
26. ———. An examination of the "continuity theory" as applied to discrimination learning. *J. gen. Psychol.*, 1942, *26*, 241-265.
27. LEEPER, R. A study of a neglected portion of the field of learning: the development of sensory organization. *J. genet. Psychol.*, 1935, *46*, 41-75.
28. LIDDELL, H. S. Animal behaviour studies bearing on the problem of pain. *Psychosom. Med.*, 1944, *6*, 261-263.
29. LORENTE DE NO, R. Transmission of impulses through cranial motor nuclei. *J. Neurophysiol.*, 1939, *2*, 402-464.
30. ———. Cerebral cortex: architecture. In J. F. FULTON (ed.), *Physiology of the nervous system*. (2nd ed.) New York: Oxford Univ. Press, 1943. Pp. 274-301.
31. MCCULLOCH, T. L., and HASLERUD, G. M. Affective responses of an infant chimpanzee reared in isolation from its kind. *J. comp. Psychol.*, 1939, *28*, 437-445.
32. MASSERMAN, J. H. The hypothalamus in psychiatry. *Amer. J. Psychiatr.*, 1942, *98*, 633-637.
33. MORGAN, C. T. *Physiological psychology*. New York: McGraw-Hill, 1943.
34. MOWRER, O. H. Preparatory set (expectancy)—a determinant in motivation and learning. *Psychol. Rev.*, 1938, *45*, 61-91.
35. SENDEN, M. v. *Raum- und Gestaltauffassung bei operierten Blindgeborenen vor und nach der Operation*. Leipzig: Barth, 1932.
36. SHERRINGTON, C. S. *Integrative action of the nervous system*. New York: Scribner's, 1906.
37. SKINNER, B. F. *The behaviour of organisms: an experimental analysis*. New York: Appleton-Century, 1938.
38. SPIES, T. D., ARING, C. D., GELPERIN, J., and BEAN, W. B. The mental symptoms of pellagra:

their relief with nicotinic acid. *Amer. J. med. Sci.*, 1938, *196*, 461-475.

39. Valentine, C. W. The innate bases of fear. *J. genet. Psychol.*, 1930, *37*, 394-419.
40. Watson, J. B. *Behaviourism*. New York: Norton, 1924.
41. Weiss, P. Autonomous versus reflexogenous activity of the central nervous system. *Proc. Amer. phil. Soc.*, 1941, *84*, 53-64.
42. Yerkes, R. M., and Yerkes, A. W. Nature and conditions of avoidance (fear) response in chimpanzee. *J. comp. Psychol.*, 1936, *21*, 53-66.
43. Zangwill, O. L. A study of the significance of attitude in recognition. *Brit. J. Psychol.*, 1937, *28*, 12-17.

FOUR HUMAN LEARNING AND MEMORY

14 / Evidence Suggesting the Acquisition of a Simple Discrimination During Sleep [1]

Harold Weinberg *University of Saskatchewan*

The intriguing possibility has been raised that learning can occur during sleep and there are some experimental studies that appear to support such a possibility. Nevertheless, many remain skeptical because of problems of definition and methodology. How do we know that a person is really sleeping when the materials are presented? Is it sufficient to define sleep in terms of whether the person has his eyes closed and appears relaxed? This kind of criterion is unsatisfactory and it has been necessary to define sleep in terms of the electrical activity of the brain and other physiological measures.

The complexity of material is another variable which may affect learning during sleep. It may indeed be true that relatively simple learning, such as classical conditioning, may occur but the question remains whether learning which is heavily dependent upon the use of past learning occurs. As Professor Weinberg points out "Behaviour requiring attention to the relevant stimuli and responses – complex associations of language material, for example – may not be subject to the influence of training during sleep."

In recent years considerable attention has been directed toward the question of whether humans can learn during sleep. In their review of the sleep learning literature Simon and Emmons (1955) suggested that inadequate criteria of sleep were an important limitation of those studies purporting to show learning or discrimination during sleep. In most studies since then, electroencephalographic activity and, in particular, the presence of high amplitude ½ to 5 c.p.s. activity, has been accepted as the criterion for deep sleep. Although Dement and Keitman (1957) and others offer good evidence to support the use of this criterion, Dement himself has cautioned that the relation between the amount of low-frequency, high-amplitude activity and the auditory awakening threshold is often not substantiated (1958). This is particularly apparent during spindling when the K complex is most easily observed.

Several noteworthy studies have been done recently using slow, high-amplitude *EEG* activity as the criterion of sleep. Some of these suggest that little or no learning can occur during sleep (Simon and Emmons, 1955; Emmons and Simon, 1956) and others that both instrumental behaviour and discrimination may occur during sleep (Granada and Hammack, 1961; Beh and Barratt 1965).

Beh and Barratt used peripheral shock during sleep to elicit a K complex. The response (K complex) was apparently conditioned to a previously neutral tone by pairing the stimuli according to a Pavlovian paradigm. Habituation of the response to an unreinforced tone, 200 c.p.s. greater or less than the CS, demonstrated discrimination. In the Granada and Hammack study a subject could avoid peripheral shock by closing a hand switch at a rate of at least 3 per second. A fixed ratio schedule was programmed to another switch, which was taped to the subject's other hand, allowing "time out" periods that were contingent on the number of switch closures. The results suggest that, during all stages of sleep, subjects could display organized instrumental behaviour that was contingent on concomitant peripheral stimulation. It is not clear, however, to what extent this behaviour was learned during sleep, since the sequence of scheduled events occurred throughout the session and was not contingent on a predetermined level of sleep.

The Simon and Emmons studies dealt with substantive language material. In the first study questions and answers were presented auditorily at five-minute intervals throughout the sleep period. The percentage of retention, measured by tests of recognition given the next morning, was positively related to the amount of alpha present during periods when the material was presented. There was little or no recall of material presented during 4-6 c.p.s. activity. The second study used a paradigm which allowed for repetition of a list of one-syllable nouns. The words were presented only during periods when alpha was

[1]Supported by a National Science Foundation Grant NSF-G 21832.

Reprinted, by permission, from the *Canadian Journal of Psychology*, 1966, *20*, 1-11.

absent from the *EEG*. These subjects failed significantly to select more correct words from a list of 50 than did an untrained control group.

Thus, although it may be true, as Oswald, Taylor, and Treisman suggest (1960), that cortical alerting (K complexes) or behavioral arousal may occur during presentation of substantive language material (the subject's own or a preselected name), the Simon and Emmons studies suggest that meaningful language material cannot be acquired during sleep.

Method

Subjects

Five male high school seniors were paid seven dollars per night and a ten-dollar bonus for completing the experiment. Each accumulated fee was paid at the end of the experiment; however, monetary rewards earned during the night were paid each morning. These rewards are described below.

Apparatus

A photocrystal plethysmograph was used to measure vasomotor activity. It consisted of a cadmium selenide photocrystal (Clairex Elx-103) embedded in one side of a ring which was of adjustable diameter. In the opposite side of the ring a small 10-volt light bulb, powered with a 6-V. DC source, was aimed at the photocrystal. Changes in the amount of light transmitted through the finger were measured with an Esterline Angus recording milliameter.

A Grass model III-C *EEG* instrument and type E-1 Grass silver disc electrodes were used for recording. Electrodes were placed over both occipital poles and bilaterally in the region of the external canthus. Digital muscle potentials were recorded with an electrode placed on the volar surface of the forearm approximately 8 cm. above the wrists. Monopolar recording techniques were used; the indifferent electrode was placed on the right ear lobe and the ground electrode on the left ear lobe. Heart rate and forearm muscle potentials were obtained by recording between the forearm and indifferent electrodes. All electrodes, with the exception of the occipital, were affixed to the skin with surgical tape. The electrolyte used was Sanborn Redux electrode paste. The method of fixing the occipital electrodes was somewhat unique. A small amount of Burgess conductive wax was melted at about 80°C. When sufficiently cool the wax was pressed into the hair over the occipital poles. Redux paste was applied to the scalp under the wax and the disc electrodes were pressed into the wax. The electrodes and wax were then protected and anchored with tape.

The manual response was defined by closure of a microswitch taped to S's right thumb. The switch was closed by pressing the index finger against the thumb.

The stimulus for vasoconstriction consisted of five 100-V. capacitor-discharged (3 uF) spikes delivered to the first and second fingers of the left hand at approximately 0.5-sec. intervals. A Heathkit fixed-frequency sound generator was the source of a pure tone which was delivered through an 8-in. speaker located approximately one meter behind the head of the sleeping S.

Ss slept in an air-conditioned room of relatively constant temperature (approx. 72° F.). Standard single beds with double innerspring mattresses were used. Ss and all apparatus in the immediate proximity, with the exception of the speaker, were located within a shielded room 8 x 8 x 6 constructed of fine mesh bronze.

Procedure

Ss were pretested for one or two nights to determine their vasomotor responsiveness to shock and tone and to estimate their general adaptability to the experimental conditions. If selected, they were given the following instructions:

"During the course of the night several tones will be presented. Two tones are used, a high tone and a low tone. When one of the tones is presented (S is told which one) your task is to press the hand switch within 15 sec. after the onset of this tone. Each time you are able to do this you will receive 25 cents. If you fail to make the response within 15 sec. you will be awakened by a loud bell which will continue to sound until you turn it off by pressing the same hand switch. Thus you may avoid being awakened by pressing the hand switch within 15 sec. after the onset of this tone. If the other tone is presented (S is told which one) you are to avoid pressing the switch. If you avoid pressing the switch when this tone is presented you will receive 25 cents. If you press the switch to this tone you will not receive the reward for that presentation."

Two tones were used in the experiment, 500 and 1500 c.p.s. Four *Ss* were assigned 1500 c.p.s. and one S (Burns) was assigned 500 c.p.s. as the positive tone (tone which signaled switch closure). An approximation of the absolute auditory threshold for 1500 c.p.s. was made for all Ss. The loudness of 1500 c.p.s. was then increased by 10 db. and Ss were required to match the loudness of the 500 c.p.s. tone with that of the 1500 c.p.s.

Determination of the shock intensity which reliably elicited vasoconstriction was made by delivering successive 100-V. shocks (of the kind mentioned above) to the first and second fingers of the left hand during wakefulness. A response was defined as vasoconstriction if it exceeded five times the magnitude of baseline fluctuations in the 10-sec. period preceeding the stimulus. In all cases Ss reported the stimulus to be painful.

Conditioning: After the electrodes were applied Ss were allowed one or two hr. before any stimuli were presented. The *EEG* was aperiodically sampled during the night; if subjects showed stage C, D, or E activity five 100-V. shocks were delivered at approximately ½-sec. intervals. If Ss responded with vasoconstriction, or if *EEG* or behavioural arousal occurred, the procedure was repeated at a later time during the night. If there was no vasomotor response, and also no behavioural or EEG arousal, one of two randomly selected tones was presented. The contingencies described in the instructions followed presentation of the tones. Ss were presented, on the average, one tone an hour throughout the night and returned 2-4 times a week for a period of 1-3 months.

Results

Three of the five subjects showed clear indications of a discrimination which developed during the training procedure and two appeared to have discriminated from the beginning.

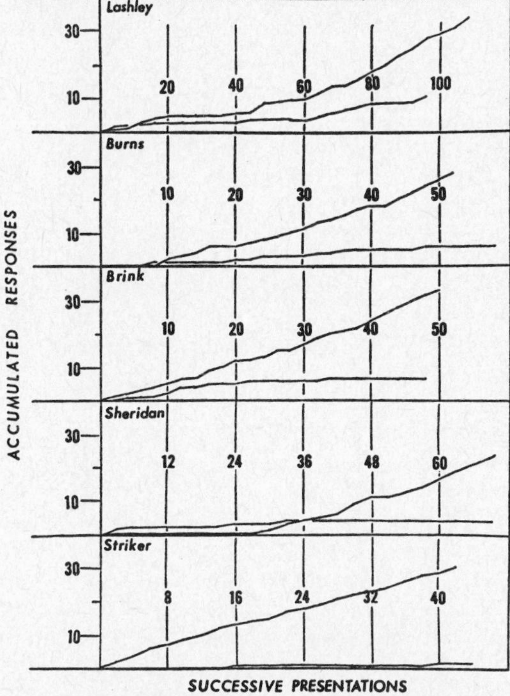

Fig. 1. Cumulative response curves for each of 5 Ss. The upper curves represent responses to positive tones, the lower curves responses to negative tones.

Figure 1 shows the accumulated switch closures plotted against presentations. Table I summarizes the frequencies of switch closures (A) and the frequencies of failures of the response (B) which occurred under the positive stimulus conditions (+s; tone which signaled the response) and negative stimulus conditions (-s; tone which signaled no response). It can be seen that in the cases of Lashley, Burns, and Sheridan there is an increase in the frequency of switch closures to the positive tone (500 c.p.s. for Burns, 1500 c.p.s. for others) but a somewhat smaller increase under the negative conditions. Table I (cols. 3 and 4) shows that, if presentations which occurred in the first half of the total sequence are compared with those which occurred in the last half, an increase in the proportion of correct to incorrect responses is significant under positive but not under negative tone conditions. This is also reflected by columns 1 and 2 which show that, for these three subjects, the differences in the proportion of responses to the positive and negative stimuli were not significant for the first half but were significant for the second half of the total sequence of successive presentations. The remaining two subjects, Brink and Striker, showed a significantly greater tendency to respond to the positive tone during both the first and the second half; neither showed significant changes in frequency of switch closure during the positive or the negative tone conditions. Thus, it appears that Brink and Striker discriminated from the beginning and showed no change as a function of training. It should be mentioned, however, that, for one of these two subjects (Brink) the change in frequency of responses under the positive tone condition does approach significance when the first third is compared with the latter two-thirds.

TABLE I

MANUAL RESPONSES OCCURRING UNDER POSITIVE AND NEGATIVE STIMULUS CONDITIONS*

Subject		1st ½ trials		2nd ½ trials		+ stimulus		− stimulus		all trials	
		+s	−s	+s	−s	1st ½	2nd ½	1st ½	2nd ½	+s	−s
	A	10	4	24	7	10	24	4	7	34	11
Lashley				x		xx				xx	
	B	44	43	30	40	44	30	43	40	74	83
	A	9	3	19	3	9	19	3	3	28	6
Burns				xx		xx				xx	
	B	17	26	7	26	17	7	26	26	24	52
	A	15	6	19	1	15	19	6	1	34	7
Brink		x		xx						xx	
	B	11	18	6	23	11	6	18	23	17	41
	A	4	4	20	0	4	20	4	0	24	4
Sheridan				xx		x				x	
	B	31	31	15	35	31	15	31	35	46	66
	A	16	1	15	1	16	15	1	1	31	2
Striker		x		x						xx	
	B	5	21	6	21	5	6	21	21	11	42

+s, positive stimulus;-s, negative stimulus. A, frequency of switch closures; B, frequency of failures of switch closures. *, significant chi-square at .05 level (significant interaction between value of stimulus and occurrence of switch closure);, significant chi-square at .01 level.*

Figures 2-4 are examples of *EEG* and vasomotor activity associated with the conditioning procedure. Figure 2 shows the occurrence of a positive tone, with subsequent failure of the avoidance response, and demonstrates the nature of the *EEG* changes that may accompany the positive but not the negative tone. The change in *EEG* activity appears to be one of increased high amplitude synchronization rather than blocking, return to alpha, or K complexes. This change was not apparent, however, in all records taken during the occurrence of the positive tone; nor was it particularly characteristic of presentations during which there was an avoidance response. Figure 3 shows the occasion of an avoidance response without

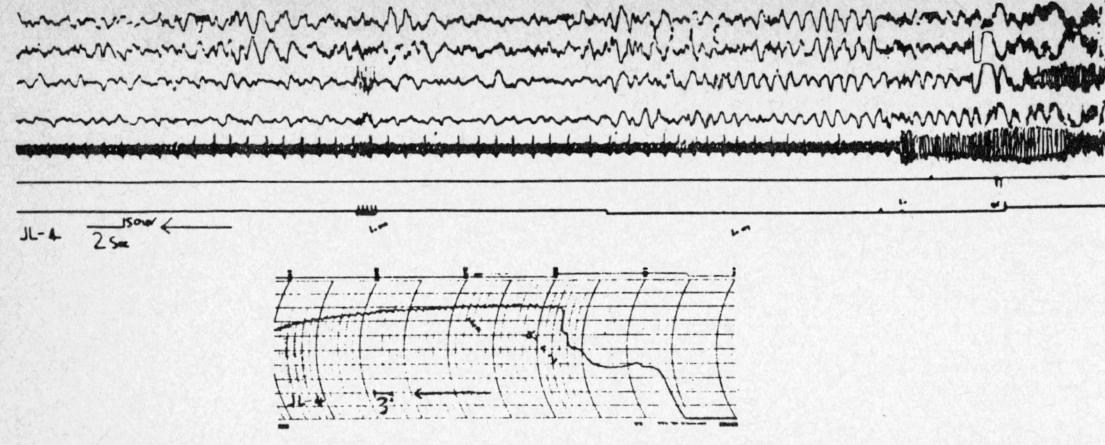

Fig. 2. The upper recordings are EEG and the lower vasomotor. Trial No. 425 (Lashley). EEG line: 1, right occipital; 2, left occipital; 3, right temporal; 4, left temporal; 5, heart rate and muscle potentials; 6, manual response marker; 7, shock and tone marker (shock can be seen marked by five spikes followed by onset and offset tone). Vasomotor record: Shock and tone indicated on top line. Shift in base line due to vasoconstriction. Arrows in both records indicate direction in which paper is moving.

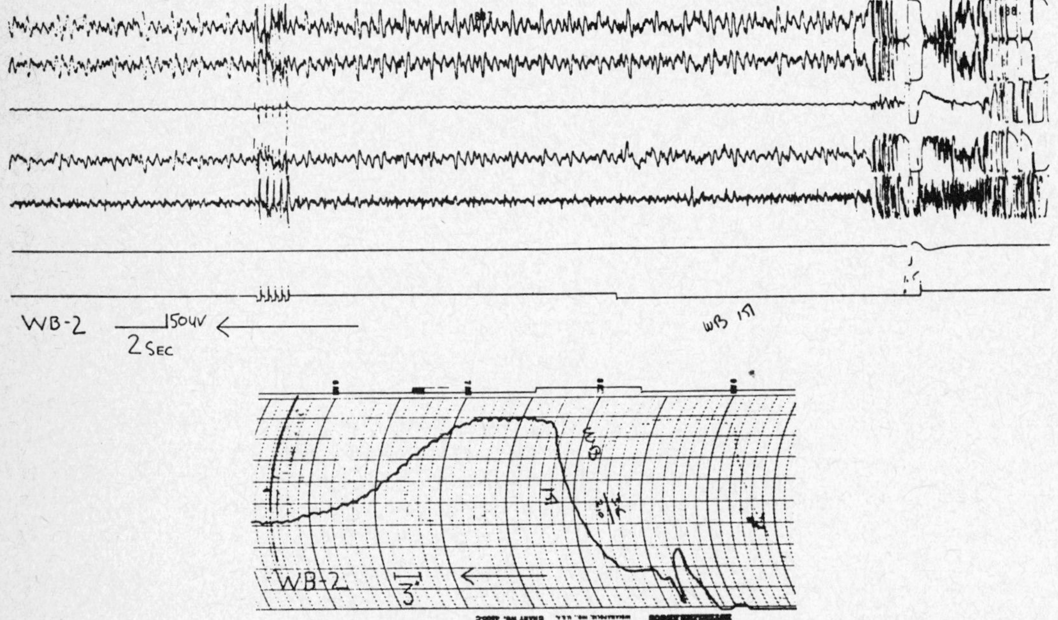

Fig. 3. Information on Figure 3 is arranged in the same order as is shown in Figure 2. This figure shows an avoidance response to a positive tone with no apparent EEG response to the tone.

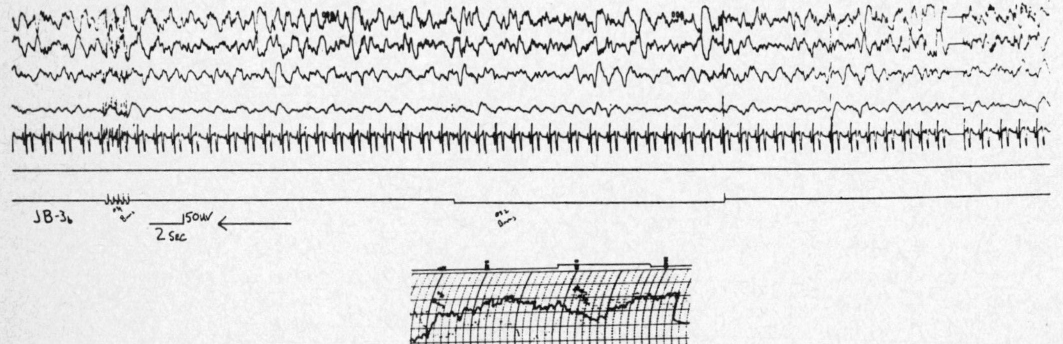

Fig. 4. Information arranged in same order as is shown in Figure 2. This figure shows the presentation of a negative tone. There is no arousal response to the negative tone and no sign of muscular activity.

obvious *EEG* changes occurring during the tone. Figure 4 shows the occurrence of shock and subsequent vasomotor activity. From these data it appears that the vasomotor system may be responsive to peripheral stimulation when, in the *EEG*, there is no apparent indication of a K complex or of other signs of arousal. Figure 4 shows the presentation of a negative tone. Although there are some signs of spindling during the presence of the negative tone, there is no arousal or alerting response in the *EEG* and so signs of muscular activity during or after the offset of the stimulus. It thus appears that the negative tone has no arousal properties.

Discussion

These data, together with other observations of instrumental and conditioned behaviour occurring during sleep, suggest that instrumental behaviour may be acquired during sleep.

Muscle potentials occurring during switch closure blocked the *EEG*; however, the records taken after peripheral shock and during tone presentations indicate that the subjects were asleep at the time of discrimination. *EEG* responses to the positive tone which occasionally occurred were not characteristic of either K complexes or general arousal. During presentation of the negative tone, when switch closure did not occur, there were no signs of alerting or arousal before, during, or after presentation of the tone. The observation of Granada and Hammack (1960) suggested that switch closure responses, of a type more complex than those used in this experiment, could readily occur without awakening the subject. Thus, since there is no reason to believe that arousal is necessary for the performance of the response and the *EEG* observations indicate the subjects were asleep during the tone presentation the data suggest acquisition during sleep. Although the data are not sufficient to determine whether arousal was a concomitant of performance, it should be pointed out that, since no arousal occurred during presentation of the negative tone, any differential arousal response with respect to the two stimuli also constitutes a discrimination.

The absence of a K complex during occurence of peripheral shock and tone (positive or negative) is not surprising. Presentation of both tones occurred only after vasomotor unresponiveness and clear signs of slow activity. K complexes are notably absent during delta activity and the absence of them in these data adds further support to the assertion that the subjects were in deep sleep during the discrimination.

The use of vasomotor unresponsiveness as an additional criterion of sleep is also of interest. Although increases in skin resistance have been observed during sleep, it is unlikely that these changes account for vasomotor unresponsiveness. The vasomotor response, initiated under the conditions employed in this experiment, was to the initial capacitor discharge rather than to subsequent voltage decay (which was in this case instantaneous). Since the instantaneous amplitude of the voltage spike and current transfer are very closely related to the initial capacitors load and relatively independent of the skin resistance through which the current is discharged, changes in skin resistance have little influence over the stimulus. The fact that the vasomotor system may be responsive to peripheral stimulation during sleep is itself interesting. However, the observation that, even when the vasomotor system is unresponsive to a peripheral unconditioned stimulus, organized complex behavior may occur and be contingent on peripheral stimulation is also important.

That learning has occurred during the course of training is demonstrated by the gradual increase in the number of correct responses to the positive tone. Few errors to the negative tone for two subjects who showed early discrimination (Brink and Striker) contributed to the observed significance of differences between positive and negative tones for these subjects. Oswald (1960) observed alerting responses in the EEG that were a function of prior instructions. The instructions in this experiment and the resultant set which was established, together with the simplicity of the response, could have contributed to the acquisition of the response. The observation of good performance from the beginning, for these two subjects, suggests that this may have occurred.

However, three of the five subjects showed significant changes in the proportion of correct to incorrect responses as a function of training. This suggests a more gradual acquisition and demonstrates most clearly, not only discrimination, but also the acquisition of that discrimination.

These findings, when considered together with other observations of learning and performance during sleep, suggest that responses which may be learned without awareness during the awake state may also be learned during sleep. Behaviour requiring attention to the relevant stimuli and responses – complex associations of language material, for example – may not be subject to the influence of training during sleep. Another important prerequisite for acquisition during sleep may be the opportunity to practice. The difficulty in teaching paired auditory associates presented during sleep may be partially accounted for by the absence of any opportunity for the subject to practice the response to be learned.

Abstract

A manual response, defined by switch closure, was rewarded with $.25 if it occurred within 15 sec. after the onset of a *correct* or if it failed to occur in the presence of an *incorrect* tone. Failure to respond to the *correct* tone occasioned the onset of a loud bell which awakened S. Tones of equal loudness were randomly presented only during sleep. The criteria of sleep were: (1) *EEG* activity and (2) vasomotor and *EEG* unresponsiveness to peripheral shock. Of the five Ss used three showed gradual acquisition of the discrimination during sleep and two discriminated within the first 10 trials.

Résumé

Une réponse manuelle (fermeture d'un circuit) rapporte $0.25 au dormeur quand il la donne en deçà de 15 sec. après le début d'un son "positif" ou quand il ne la donne pas en présence d'un son "négatif". Le dormeur est éveillé par une cloche bruyante quand il ne réussit pas à répondre au son "positif". Les deux sons présentés (au hasard) sont d'égale force, mais le sujet doit répondre seulement au plus haut ou au plus bas. Les critères du sommeil sont les suivants: (1) activité de l'EEG; (2) absence de réponse vasomotrice et d'EEG à un choc périphérique. Les résultats montrent que, des cinq dormeurs soumis à l'expérience, trois parviennent peu à peu à faire la discrimination voulue et deux y parviennent en deçà des 10 premiers essais.

References

BEH, H. C., and BARRATT, P. E. H. Discrimination and conditioning during sleep as indicated by the electroencephalogram. *Science,* 1965, *147,* 1470.

DEMENT, W., and KLEITMAN, N. Cyclic variations in EEG during sleep and their relation to eye movements, body mobility and dreaming. *EEG clin. Neurophysiol.,* 1957, *9,* 673-90.

DEMENT, W. The occurrence of low voltage, fast electroencephalogram patterns during behavioural sleep in the cat. *EEG clin. Neurophysiol.,* 1958, *10,* 291-6 .

EMMONS, W. H., and SIMON, C. W. The non-recall of material presented during sleep. *Amer. J. Psychol.,* 1956, *69,* 76-81.

GRANADA, A. M., and HAMMACK, J. T. Operant behaviour during sleep. *Science,* 1961, *133,* 1485.

OSWALD, I., TAYLOR, A. M., and TREISMAN, M. Discriminative responses to stimulation during human sleep. *Brain,* 1960, *83,* 440.

SIMON, C. W., and EMMONS, W. H. Learning during sleep? *Psychol. Bull.,* 1955, *52,* 328-43.

———. Responses to material presented during various levels of sleep. *J. exp. Psychol.,* 1956, *51,* 89-97.

———. EEG, consciousness and sleep. *Science,* 1956, *124,* 1066.

15 / Two-Stage Paired-Associate Learning and Eye Movements

P.D. McCormack and E.J. Haltrecht *Carleton University*

An observer will often spend more time attending to certain elements in a task than to others. When the task involves vision, a good indication of his attention can be provided by measuring eye movements. In this study the authors describe the results of an experiment in which eye movements were recorded during a learning task. The theoretical implications of the results are discussed.

In experiments on verbal paired-associate learning, subjects are required to associate pairs of items, usually nonsense syllables, such that the presence of the first or stimulus member comes to elicit the second or response member. A number of investigators (1) regard the learning of such lists as a two-stage process, subjects consolidating the responses during the first or "response-learning" phase and then connecting them to the appropriate stimuli during the second or "hook-up" stage. We evaluated this notion by examining the eye movements of subjects throughout the course of their learning paired-associates, concentrating on the proportion of time each subject spent fixating the stimulus and the response when the two were presented together. If subjects scanned the response out of proportion to the stimulus during the early learning trials, the two-stage concept would be supported.

Twenty male students of introductory psychology were used as subjects. As each entered the laboratory he was placed in a dental chair, the various attachments of which facilitated the recording of eye movements, and was given standard instructions for paired-associate learning. We told him that he would be required to learn a list consisting of seven pairs of nonsense syllables. Each syllable had a Nobel (2) m' value within the range 1.80 to 1.93. For each syllable-pair, we exposed the stimulus alone and then with the response by projecting slides onto a green-surfaced chalkboard 1.37 m in front of the subject. We told him that when the stimulus was presented by itself he had 2 seconds in which to anticipate the response and when the two appeared together, the stimulus on the left and the response on the right, he would discover whether he was correct or incorrect. The list was given in each of four different random orders (trials) to prevent serial learning, and we inserted two blank slides at the end of each trial to provide a 4-second intertrial interval. The subject was given a 1-minute test at the end of every four trials and the session was terminated after 24 trials, or before that if he successfully anticipated the seven responses in any of the four orders.

Reprinted, by permission, from *Science*, Vol. 148, (June 25, 1965), pp. 1749-1750. Copyright 1965 by the American Association for the Advancement of Science.

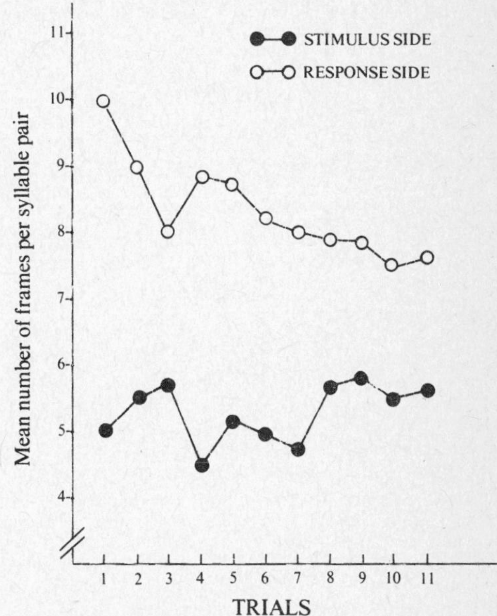

Fig. 1. Mean number of frames of stimulus and response as a function of trials.

We recorded eye movements continuously throughout the duration of the task by means of an eye-marker camera (3), mounted on the head, which consisted of a 2- by 8-mm motion picture unit and a periscope that transmitted a spot of light reflected from the cornea to a moving film. The developed film shows the paired-associate slides, and superimposed upon each, a bright circular spot indicating the position of actual fixation. We analyzed the data frame by frame, by examining the stimulus-response slides through a film viewer. This method of analysis was highly dependable, the between and within experimenter-reliability coefficients being 0.98 for a film of 24 trials, selected at random.

Sixteen of the 20 subjects reached the criterion of an errorless trial, the fastest doing so on the 11th trial. We have summarized the main findings in Fig. 1. The first 11 trials for all subjects are shown along the abscissa, while the ordinate represents the average number of frames per syllable-pair for those slides where the stimulus and response appeared together. The open circles represent response frames, the closed circles stimulus frames. For any given trial, total frames of stimulus and response may be calculated by adding the ordinate values for the open and closed circles. The difference between this value and 21 represents frames involving fixations of the central portion of the display. The two functions shown in Fig. 1 are not perfect mirror images of one another and this is reflected by a – 0.43 correlation between stimulus and response frames.

We examined the findings shown in Fig. 1 by means of analysis-of-variance techniques and discovered that the two trend lines depart reliably from being parallel ($p < .001$), with time on stimulus remaining constant over trials and time on response becoming systematically shorter as learning progresses. This last trend has a chance expectancy of less than one in one thousand, an orthogonal polynomial comparison revealing no dependable nonlinear components. We obtained the same results by examining time on stimulus and response as a function of the first three of the four quarters of learning for those 16 subjects who reached the errorless-trial criterion. (We omitted the data for the fourth quarter because of their unreliability.) All 16 subjects showed less time on the response during the third quarter than during the first. Again, time on stimulus remained essentially invariant throughout the session.

In view of the fact that each subject saw the stimulus twice as often as the response, it is not surprising that the latter was scanned out of porportion to the former throughout the duration of the task. Nor were we surprised to discover less total time on stimulus and response during the latter stages of learning. This resulted from a tendency to fixate the central portion of the display, or even to look away, once a syllable pair had been learned. The phenomenon of most interest, however, that of the systematically decreasing ratio of response- to stimulus-time with trials, is clearly consistent with the two-stage hypothesis. This phenomenon reflects the transition from the response consolidation to the stimulus hook-up phase.

We also analyzed scanning behaviour before and after the learning of each of the seven pairs and found what could be interpreted as additional support for the two-stage theory. Although there were no differences in time on the stimulus, all 20 subjects showed less time on the response after the pairs had been learned than before. The difference on the response side and lack of it on the stimulus side of the display is presumably due to a disproportionate amount of time on the response during stage one, even though the data presented before learning reflect both stages.

We were unable to reveal any reliable differences in scanning behaviour between slow and fast learners, nor were we able to demonstrate any systematic changes in patterns of viewing the stimulus-response slides as learning progressed. Most subjects looked right-left-right and maintained this pattern throughout the duration of the session.

Abstract

Eye movements of 20 male students were photographed continuously throughout the course of their learning verbal paired-associates. As learning progressed, proportionately less and less time was spent scanning the response when the stimulus and response were presented together. These findings are interpreted as supporting a two-stage theory of verbal learning.

References

1. Mandler, G. *Psychol. Rev., 61,* 235 (1954); Postman, L. *in Verbal Learning and Verbal Behaviour,* C. N. Cofer, ed. (McGraw-Hill, New York, 1961), pp. 152-197; Underwood, B. J., and Schulz, R. W., *Meaningfulness and Verbal Learning* (Lippincott, Chicago, 1960), pp. 92-94.
2. Noble, C. E. *Psychol. Rep., 8,* 487 (1961).
3. Mackworth, N. H., and Thomas, E. L. *J. Opt. Soc. Amer., 52,* 713 (1962).

4. This research was supported by a grant-in-aid from the Associate Committee on Experimental Psychology of the National Research Council of Canada (grant APA-78) and by the Carleton University Arts Research and Publication Fund.

16 / Vividness of Words and Learning to Learn in Free-Recall Learning[1]

Endel Tulving, John A. McNulty, and Marcia Ozier *University of Toronto*

Words have several dimensions each of which may facilitate the rate at which they can be learned and retained. These dimensions include, among others, frequency of usage, meaningfulness, abstractness, and vividness. This study explores the manner in which vividness of the stimuli affected learning and the subsequent recall of those stimuli.

It has been thought for a long time that the vividness of an experience is an important determinant of the ease with which the experience can be remembered. In the laboratory, investigations of this problem have usually taken the form of testing the recall for verbal materials varying in vividness. Haagen (1949) had subjects rate pairs of adjectives for several attributes, including vividness of connotation. Miller and Dost (1964) used Haagen's lists of high, medium, and low vivid adjectives in a memory task and found that recognition of previously seen words was a function of their vividness. Bowers (1931) found positive correlations between rated imagery of words and their frequency of recall by groups of subjects, and in another paper (Bowers, 1932) reported very reliable ratings of "distinctness of visual images" for single letters and groups of letters. These scattered experiments suggest that vividness of verbal units can be assessed experimentally and that it is related to retention of these units. The present experiment was designed to explore the relation between vividness and free-recall learning of English nouns.

The study consisted of two parts. In the first, vividness (V) of a set of 82 nouns was measured by a rating-scale procedure. The same set of words was also rated for meaningfulness (M). Rated meaningfulness of nonsense syllables has been shown to be closely related to meaningfulness measured by other kinds of scaling methods (Noble, Stockwell, and Pryer, 1957), and to such variables as judged speed of learning, familiarity, and pronunciability (Underwood and Schulz, 1960).

In the second part of the study, word lists at a fixed level of M and frequency of occurrence, but varying in V, were used to determine the relation between V and free-recall learning. The design of the experiment also permitted an evaluation of learning to learn effects in free-recall learning, a topic on which there exists conflicting evidence (Dallett, 1963; Murdock, 1960).

Measurement of Vividness

Method

A sample of 82 two-syllable nouns, 5 to 7 letters in length, was selected from among the words in the Thorndike-Lorge word book (1944) whose *G* count was between 15 and 19. These words were listed in a haphazard order and mimeographed on two sheets of paper. The two sheets (A and B), together with a face sheet containing instructions, were stapled into three-page booklets used in obtaining ratings of V and M. In half the booklets the sheets were in the order AB, in the other half they were in the order BA.

In the instructions for rating vividness, vividness was defined as "the ease with which you can picture something in your mind." The raters were to indicate how vivid each word was by indicating the position of the word on a seven-point scale on which the rating of 1 corresponded to "no image" and 7 corresponded to "extreme vividness." The instructions for rating meaningfulness were similar to those on vividness. The raters were asked to indicate on a seven-point scale "how meaningful" each word was to them. On the scale, 1 corresponded to "meaningless" and 7 to "extreme meaningfulness." In rating of both V and M, the raters were asked to use the full range of the scale and to treat each word independently.

The ratings were obtained from a total of 200 Ss, consisting of 100 psychology undergraduates (Group 1) and 100 premedical students (Group 2). In each of these groups, 50 Ss rated the 82 words for V (Groups 1V and 2V), and 50 Ss rated the words for M (Groups 1M and 2M).

[1]This study was first reported to the Canadian Psychological Association at Montreal, June, 1961. It has been supported by the National Research Council of Canada, Grant No. APA-39, and the National Science Foundation, Grant No. GB-810. It was prepared for publication while the senior author held a National Research Council of Canada Senior Research Fellowship at the Institute of Human Learning, University of California, Berkeley.

Reprinted, by permission, from *Canadian Journal of Psychology*, 1965. *19*, 242-252.

Results

The rating procedure yielded 100 ratings of V and 100 ratings of M for each of the 82 words. The V score of a given word was defined as the mean of the V ratings from a given sample of raters, and the M score as the mean of the M ratings.[2] In Table I are shown mean V scores and mean M scores for all 82 words and their standard deviations for separate groups of 50 raters as well as the total sample of raters. The important fact in Table I concerns the variability of V and M scores. The variance is greater for V than for M. The F test for the testing of the differences between the two variances based on data from two groups of 100 Ss yields an $F(81 \& 81df) = 4.03, p < .001$.

The variability of M scores in the sample of 82 words is relatively small presumably because of the restricted range of Thorndike-Lorge frequencies of these words. To the extent that frequency and meaningfulness are correlated, restriction of the range of frequencies is expected to reduce the variability of M scores. The restriction of the frequency range seems to have much less effect on V, however. The observation that the variance of V scores is approximately four times greater than the variance of M scores can be regarded as evidence for the absence of a strong relation between V and M.

Table I – Means and variances of V and M scores for 82 words based on data from four groups of 50 raters

Raters	Variable rated V		Variable rated M	
Group 1	Mean	= 4.23	Mean	= 4.48
	Var	= 1.12	Var	= .247
Group 2	Mean	= 4.27	Mean	= 4.31
	Var	= 1.23	Var	= .347
Mean	Mean	= 4.25	Mean	= 4.39
	Var	= 1.19	Var	= .295

More important than the over-all means and variances of the V and M scores, however, is the evidence pertaining to their reliability and their intercorrelation across the sample of 82 words. The product-moment correlation coefficient between two sets of 82 V scores, one from Group IV and the other from Group 2V, was 0.941. When the Spearman-Brown correction formula was applied to this statistic, the reliability coefficient of V was estimated as 0.970. The product-moment correlation coefficient between two sets of M scores, one from Group 1M and the other from Group 2M, was found to be .818. The application of the Spearman-Brown formula yielded an estimate of the reliability coefficient of 0.900. The lower coefficient of reliability for M than for V is attributable to the smaller variance of M scores than V scores, as shown in Table I. We can estimate what the reliability coefficient of M scores would be if their variance were the same as that of V scores. When the appropriate correction is applied (Guilford, 1942, p. 281), the coefficient of reliability of M becomes 0.975, closely resembling that of V. The product-moment correlation between V and M scores was found to be 0.420 for Groups 1V and 1M, and 0.541 for Groups 2V and 2M. Although these statistics are significantly different from zero, their magnitude indicates that V and M are only partly related and that each of the two variables taps underlying processes not tapped by the other.

In view of the high reliability of V an M scores and the fact that the variance of one accounts for only a part of the variance of the other, it seemed justifiable to construct word lists varying in V, but holding constant M, and to investigate ease of free-recall learning for such lists.

Vividness and Learning to Learn in Free-Recall Learning

Design

Three lists of 16 words used in this experiment differed in V of their constituent words, but were approximately equal in rated M as well as in Thorndike-Lorge frequency. Twenty-four Ss learned all three lists, each for eight study and recall trials. The order of lists was completely counterbalanced. Performance over successive trials was examined as a function of V and stage of practice. Subjective organization scores (Tulving, 1962) were also calculated and related to the two independent variables and to performance scores.

Method

Lists. From among the 82 words for which both V and M scores were available three lists of 16 words were selected. These lists are shown in Table II. Table II also gives the V and M scores for each word, based on samples of 100 raters. In each list the words were first arranged into a random word order and then seven other word orders were systematically constructed such that no word occurred in a given serial position, preceded any other word, or followed any other word more than once in the total set of eight orders. The sequence of word orders on eight trials was different for each S learning a given list.

Counterbalancing of lists. With three lists (high, medium, and low) there are six possible orders in which they can be given to Ss: HML, HLM, MHL, MLH, LHM, LMH. Each of these list orders was given to four randomly determined Ss. This counter-

[2] The complete list of 82 words and their V and M scores can be obtained from the senior author.

Table II – Experimental lists

High V			Medium V			Low V		
Word	V	M	Word	V	M	Word	V	M
Apron	5.17	4.00	Abode	4.13	4.06	Buyer	2.94	3.93
Balloon	5.63	4.03	Bucket	4.50	3.88	Crisis	2.10	5.23
Bunny	5.23	3.93	Builder	4.00	4.28	Entry	2.08	3.71
Butler	5.79	3.79	Cargo	4.57	4.03	Founder	1.85	3.92
Cabbage	5.32	4.06	Fiber	3.96	3.50	Output	1.50	3.77
Camel	5.79	3.88	Hamlet	4.83	4.03	Patron	2.70	3.50
Chorus	5.63	4.43	Handful	4.36	3.43	Renown	1.33	3.94
Cigar	6.53	4.41	Madame	4.61	4.27	Routine	1.28	4.64
Circus	6.08	4.54	Pebble	4.76	4.15	Rover	2.11	3.30
Comet	5.81	3.96	Porter	4.64	3.79	Rumour	2.20	4.57
Granny	5.00	4.17	Pudding	4.61	4.05	Session	2.86	3.83
Jungle	6.00	4.36	Summit	4.77	4.46	Surplus	1.83	4.43
Lantern	5.43	4.32	Thicket	4.54	3.75	Tariff	1.50	3.61
Rainbow	6.13	4.94	Trainer	4.25	4.19	Topic	1.50	4.03
Runner	5.64	4.61	Veteran	4.07	4.40	Treason	1.50	4.70
Satin	5.42	3.62	Voter	4.32	5.15	Vigour	2.70	4.44
Mean	5.66	4.19	Mean	4.43	4.09	Mean	2.00	4.10

balancing of lists means that each of the three lists (H, M, and L) was learned by an equal number of Ss at each of three stages of practice (first, second, or third list).

Subjects. The Ss were 24 female second-year general arts students at the University of Toronto who had not participated in any other verbal learning experiments and were naive with respect to the nature and the purpose of the present experiment.

Procedure. All Ss were tested in individual sessions. Each S was told that she would be learning three lists of English words, one after another; that she would be given eight trials of practice on each list; that the words would be in a different order from trial to trial; and that her task was to recall as many words as possible from a given list after each trial, but that the order in which she recalled the words did not matter. The words were presented on a memory drum at the rate of one sec. per word. At the end of the input phase of each trial S was given 60 sec. to record her recall on a sheet of paper. The intertrial interval was approximately five sec. The *E* collected the recall sheet from S after each trial. When eight trials on a given list were concluded, the S was given two min. of rest before starting on the next list.

Results

The three learning curves associated with three levels of V are shown in Fig. 1. There is a clear separation between HV and LV curves over all eight trials indicating that HV words are recalled more readily than LV words. The recall of MV words falls between that of HV and LV words on most trials.

The three learning curves associated with three stages of practice are shown in Fig. 2. These curves are remarkably similar to the three curves shown in Fig. 1, with the curve of the first list comparable to the curve of the LV list, the second to MV, and the third to HV. This close correspondence is reflected in the mean recall scores over all eight trials: 12.03, 12.64, and 13.19 for the LV, MV, and HV lists, respectively, and 12.04, 12.77, and 13.05 for the first, second, and third lists, respectively. Thus variations in V in the present experiment had approximately the same effect on recall as did variations in stage of practice.

The arcsin transformed recall scores were evaluated statistically by an analysis of variance based on the cross-over design (Cochran and Cox, 1957). This analysis showed that the main effects associated with trials, V, and stage of practice were all significant at better than the .001 level, and that none of the interactions was significant.

In evaluating the recall data from the present experiment, possible "ceiling effects" must be kept in mind. In learning the HV list, 14 subjects out of 24 reached a criterion of two successive perfect trials during the total of eight trials given to all subjects, while only four subjects did so in learning the LV list. Recall performance on the HV list, therefore, is probably artifactually attenuated because of limited list length. The same consideration applies to learning to learn effects. Only five subjects reached the two-trial criterion in learning the first list, while 12 did so in learning the third list.

A subjective organization (SO, Lag 0) score, based on the order of recalled words on successive

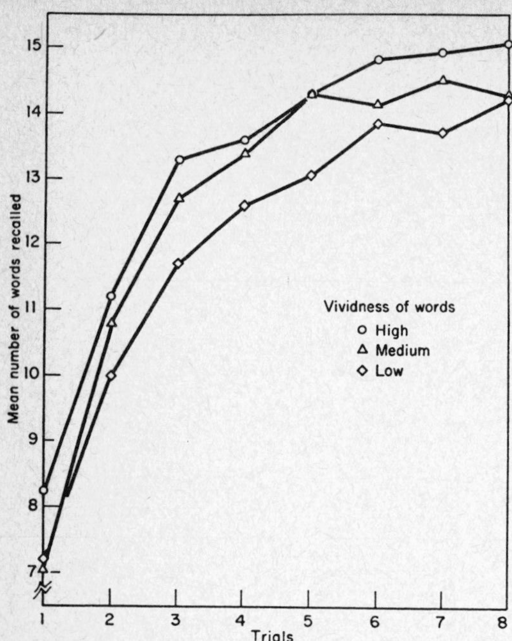

Fig. 1. Mean number of words recalled as a function of trials for three lists differing in word vividness.

trials, was also calculated for each subject learning a given list (viz. Tulving, 1962). Each score was based on the data from the total block of eight trials. Thus each subject had three SO scores, one for each of the three lists. The mean SO scores were .219, .277, and .264 for the LV, MV, and HV lists, respectively, and .208, .263, and .289 for the first, second, and third lists, respectively. Analysis of variance showed that the differences associated with stage of practice, F (2,44) = 6.82, and with V, F (2,44) = 3.80, were both significant, p values being .01 and .05 respectively.

Finally, we computed Spearman rank-order correlation coefficients (rho) between mean recall scores and SO scores for the 24 subjects. Rho was .42, .86, and .76 in the LV, MV, and HV lists, respectively, and .50, .78, and .73 in the first, second, and third lists, respectively. All these correlation coefficients are significant at the .01 level, with the exception of a rho of .42 in the LV list, which is significant at the .05 level. Thus, there is evidence for a tendency for subjects' recall scores to parallel SO scores, this tendency being somewhat stronger in the case of MV and HV lists than in the LV list, and stronger in the second and third lists than in the first.

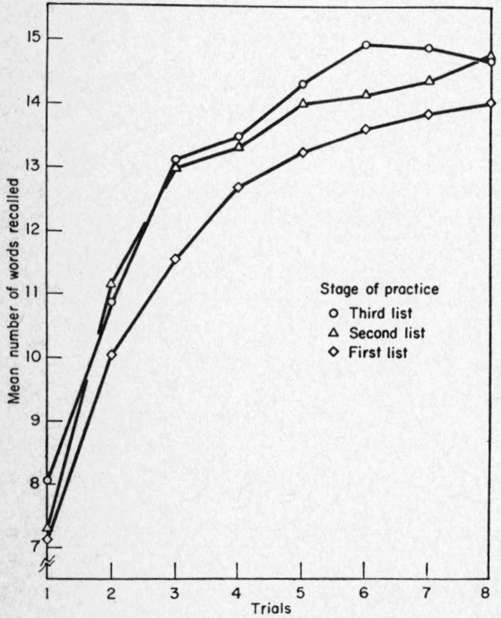

Fig. 2. Mean number of words recalled as a function of trials for lists at three stages of practice.

Conclusions and Discussion

The following conclusions seem to be justifiable on the basis of the findings of this study: (1) It is possible to obtain reliable ratings of vividness and meaningfulness of words from groups of raters. (2) Vividness and meaningfulness are only partly related to each other. (3) Vividness is directly related to the ease with which words equated for frequency and meaningfulness are learned in the free-recall situation. (4) More vivid words are not only learned more readily than less vivid words but their recall is also organized to a somewhat greater extent. (5) Learning to learn effects occur in the course of learning of three successive lists. (6) Increasing efficiency of performance over successive lists is accompanied by an increase in the degree of subjective organization.

That reliable ratings of vividness of words can be obtained is hardly surprising, despite the fact that apart from its operational definition the concept may appear vague to some. Both Haagen (1949) and Bowers (1931, 1932) have reported similar data for other types of verbal units. What is perhaps more interesting is the relatively weak relation between M and V. It is interesting, because there have been very few reports in the literature about characterisitcs of materials which can be measured reliably, which are related to ease of learning or recall, and which at the same time are relatively independent of the cluster of interrelated variables such as familiarity, frequency, and meaningfulness (Underwood and Schulz, 1960). Haagen (1949) did report even lower correlations between vividness of pairs of adjectives on the one hand and their similarity of meaning and closeness of associative connection on the other hand, but there has been little experimental work done with his materials on the problem of vividness. The study of Miller's and Dost's (1964), mentioned earlier, is the only one of which we are aware. The present data on the role of vividness in recall are in good agreement with those of Miller's and Dost's.

It is not immediately obvious from the present study why more vivid words are learned more easily in the free-recall learning situation. But the fact that the recall of more vivid words was also organized by subjects to a greater extent than that of less vivid words is compatible with the hypothesis that vividness or picturability is an important component of meaning of words that affects the ease with which words can be grouped into higher-order memory units (Miller, 1956; Tulving, 1964). Even though the number of units that the subject can retrieve from the storage at any given time is limited at some fixed value, the number of words recalled varies directly with the average size of the units (cf. Tulving and Patkau, 1962). The higher word-recall in the HV list than in the LV list can thus be regarded as reflecting the existence of larger memory units in the HV list than in the LV list.

The main weakness of that part of the present experiment that deals with the relation between V and learning – a weakness shared by all other published experiments investigating the relation between some characteristics of the material and ease of learning or recall – lies in the fact that the data reveal only a correlation between vividness and learning. Although we held constant word frequency and rated meaningfulness, and although it appears reasonable that as a consequence other variables related to meaningfulness and frequency may also have been minimized, it is still possible the V was confounded with other variables.

One such variable, for instance, may have been abstractness (or concreteness) of words. Gorman (1961) used a two-point rating scale to assess a large number of words on an abstract-concrete dimension. She found short-term recognition to be better for concrete than for abstract words. In the sample of 82 words used in the present study, there were 30 that overlapped with Gorman's sample. Of these seven were abstract, as defined by Gorman, and 23 were concrete. On our V scale, the seven abstract words had the mean V score of 2.93 (SD = 1.12) and the mean V score of the 23 concrete words was 4.81 (SD = 1.01), a highly reliable difference. Thus it appears that V may be correlated with the abstractness-concreteness of words.

Another type of variable that might correlate with vividness is associative relatedness of words. This variable, measured in a number of ways, has also been shown to be related to the recallability of verbal materials (Marshall and Cofer, 1963). Quite possibly our three lists differed from one another with respect to this variable, but in absence of available free-association data for the words that we used, the relation between vividness and associative relatedness could not be assessed.

The reliable finding of learning to learn (LTL) effect in the present experiment corroborates Dallett's (1963) findings for a free-recall task in which multiple recall tests on the same list were given, but it appears to contradict Murdock's (1960) conclusion that neither LTL nor warm-up occurs in multitrial free-recall learning. Since SO scores in the present experiment also increased over successive stages of practice, it may be that LTL effects occur only in situations in which subjects can learn how to organize the materials to be recalled. Murdock (1960) used a procedure in his experiments which may have minimized learning of subjective organization. Subjects in his experiments were given recall sheets provided with spaces for words beginning with different letters, and they were asked to write their recalled words in corresponding spaces on the recall sheets. This requirement may have induced subjects to adopt different strategies of memorizing than grouping of words according to various aspects of their meaning as it occurs in subjective organization (Tulving, 1962). To the extent that subjective organization may play only a minor role in one trial recall, the failure to demonstrate LTL effects in free-recall studies in which only one recall trial is given (e.g., Dallett, 1963) also seems to be consistent with the view that LTL may depend on interlist improvement in subjective organization.

Abstract

Eighty-two words of approximately equal frequency-of-occurence value were rated for vividness (V) and meaningfulenss (M) by two independent groups of 100 raters. From this set of words three lists of 16 words each were then constructed. The lists varied in V, but were equal in M. They were used as learning materials in an experiment that was designed (1) to investigate the relation between V and free recall, and (2) to demonstrate learning to learn effects. The results showed that Ss learned lists of higher V more readily than the list of low V, and subsequent lists more readily than the first. Subjective organization (SO) scores were related to both vividness and learning to learn effects.

Résumé

Deux groupes indépendants de 100 juges chacun évaluent le niveau de vividité (V) et d'intelligibilité (M) de 82 mots de fréquence d'usage approximativement égal. Trois sous-listes de 16 mots sont formées à partir de cet ensemble de mots. Ces listes varient quant à V, mais sont égales quant à M. Elles constituent le matériel d'apprentissage d'une expérience visant (1) à chercher la relation entre V et le simple rappel et (2) à illustrer des effets d'apprentissage à apprendre. Les résultats montrent que les listes à vividité élevée s'apprennent mieux que les listes à vividité inférieure, et que la première liste s'apprend plus difficilement que les suivantes. Mise en relation de cotes d'organisation subjective (SO) avec le niveau de vididité et avec les effets d'apprentissage à apprendre.

References

BOWERS, H. Memory and mental imagery. *Brit. J. Psychol.*, 1931, *21*, 271-82.

———. Factors influencing visual imagery for letter groups. *Amer. J. Psychol.*, 1932, *44*, 775-9.

COCHRAN, W. G., and COX, GERTRUDE M. *Experimental designs*. Second edition. New York: Wiley, 1957.

DALLETT, K. M. Practice effects in free and ordered recall. *J. exp. Phychol.*, 1963, *66*, 65-71.

GORMAN, ALOYSIA M. Recognition memory for nouns as a function of abstractness and frequency. *J. exp. Psychol.*, 1961, *61*, 23-9.

GUILFORD, J. P. *Fundamental statistics in psychology and education*. New York: McGraw-Hill, 1942.

HAAGEN, C. H. Synonymity, vividness, familiarity, and associative value ratings of 400 pairs of common adjectives. *J. Psychol.*, 1949, *27*, 453-63.

MARSHALL, G. R., and COFER, C. N. Associative indices as measures of word relatedness: a summary and comparison of ten methods. *J. verb. Learn. verb. Behav.*, 1963, *1*, 408-21.

MILLER, G. A. Human memory and the storage of information. *IRE Trans. Inform. Theory*, 1956, *2*, 129-37.

MILLER, MARILYN E., and DOST, JOYCE A. Stimulus vividness and anxiety level in intentional incidental learning. *Psychol. Rep.*, 1964, *14*, 819-25.

MURDOCK, B. B., Jr. The immediate retention of unrelated words. *J. exp. Psychol.*, 1960, *60*, 222-34.

NOBLE, C. E., STOCKWELL, F. E., and PRYER, M. W. Meaningfulness (*m'*) and association value (*a*) in paired-associate syllable learning. *Psychol. Rep.*, 1957, *3*, 441-52.

THORNDIKE, E. L., and LORGE, I. *The teacher's word book of 30,000 words*. New York: Teachers College, Columbia University, 1944.

TULVING, E. Subjective organization in free recall of "unrelated" words. *Psychol. Rev.*, 1962, *69*, 344-54.

——— Intratrial and intertrial retention: notes towards a theory of free recall verbal learning. *Psychol. Rev.*, 1964, *71*, 219-37.

TULVING, E., and PATKAU, JEANNETTE E. Concurrent effects of contextual constraint and word frequency on immediate recall and learning of verbal material. *Canad. J. Psychol.*, 1962, *16*, 83-95.

UNDERWOOD, B. J., and SCHULZ, R. W. *Meaningfulness and verbal learning*. Chicago: Lippincott, 1960.

17 / Availability Versus Accessibility of Information in Memory for Words[1]

Endel Tulving and Zena Pearlstone *University of Toronto*

Contemporary information-processing models of memory emphasize the fact that failure to recall may be due to either a complete loss of memory trace or to the fact that the individual simply cannot retrieve the information. The authors present evidence to show that recall can be enhanced by providing cues which aid the retrieval process.

If a person is shown a long list of familiar words and is then asked to recall the list, he can recall some words, but not all of them. It can be assumed that the person learns each single word at the time of its presentation, in the sense that the probability of recall of the word rises from a value near zero immediately before the presentation to a value near unity immediately after the presentation. The failure to recall some of the words, therefore, reflects intratrial forgetting (Tulving, 1964).

Intratrial forgetting is a descriptive label that carries no implications as to the fate of the memory traces associated with nonrecalled words. It may be attributable to the decay of traces as a consequence of passage of time between the presentation and attempted recall of an item (Brown, 1958), or to the displacement of some of the items stored earlier by subsequently presented items (Waugh and Norman, 1965). In either case, failure to recall a certain item would be interpreted to mean that the trace of the item is no longer available in the memory storage at the time of recall. It is also possible, however, that intratrial forgetting represents a failure to "find" otherwise intact traces in the storage. According to an information processing model of memory described by Feigenbaum (1961), for instance, forgetting occurs not because information in storage is destroyed, but because learned material becomes "inaccessible in a large and growing association network." Thus, to interpret intratrial forgetting, it is useful to draw a distinction between what information or what traces are *available* in the memory storage and what are *accessible*. This distinction parallels the distinction between retention and recall, or the distinction between trace storage and trace utilization (Melton, 1963).

The present paper is concerned with a conceptual and experimental analysis of nonrecall of learned items in terms of such a distinction between availability and accessibility. It describes an experiment whose primary purpose was to explore the hypothesis that a substantial part of nonrecall of familiar words under typical experimental conditions is attributable to inaccessibility of otherwise intact memory traces.

Experimental demonstrations of the distinction between availability and accessibility of information require that critical experimental treatments be administered at the time of the recall test, rather than at some earlier stage in the sequence of events involved in any memory task. Only if conditions of the experiment are held constant until the beginning of the recall period can differences in observed recall scores be attributed to differences in accessibility. While scattered examples exist in the literature of experiments satisfying these requirements (e.g., Fox, Blick, and Bilodeau, 1964; Peterson and Peterson, 1962, Exp. IV), there have been no systematic attempts to distinguish between availability and accessibility of mnemonic information. Experiments in which various "measures of retention," such as unaided recall and recognition, have been compared (e.g., Luh, 1922; Postman and Rau, 1957) lend support to the proposition that unaided recall does not tap all of the information that is available about previously learned material, but the interpretation of data in these experiments with respect to the distinction between availability and accessibility is complicated. Unaided recall requires the *S* to reproduce the whole item, while in recognition the correct item is given to the *S* and his task is to decide whether or not it occurred in the list. To distinguish between availability and accessibility of information that is sufficient for *reproduction* of a given item, comparisons between recognition and recall are only partly relevant and other methods must be used.

The experiment described in this paper uses one such other method. Categorized word lists were pre-

[1]This research was supported by the National Science Foundation, under grant GB-810. It was prepared for publication during the senior author's tenure of a National Research Council of Canada Senior Research Fellowship at the Institute of Human Learning, University of California, at Berkeley. We are grateful to the Director and the Board of Education of the Township of Scarborough and to the Forest Hill Collegiate Institute and its Principal, who permitted us to test many students as subjects in their schools. We are also grateful to many teachers in the high schools in Scarborough and Forest Hill, who kindly made class time available for the experiment. Our special thanks goes to Dr. Howard Russell and Mr. Vernon Trott for their generous assistance.

Reprinted, by permission, from *Journal of Verbal Learning and Verbal Behaviour*, 1966, 5, 381-391. The section entitled "Interpretation of Findings on Word-Recall," pp. 387-389, was deleted.

sented to *S*s for learning, and recall of words was tested in the presence or absence of category names as retrieval cues. It was expected that a large proportion of words not accessible for recall under the unaided conditions would become accessible as a consequence of experimental presentation of such retrieval cues, thus indicating that sufficient information was available in the storage for the reproduction of these words, but that this information was not accessible. The results of the experiment thus were expected to clarify the nature of intratrial forgetting as defined earlier. As the results turned out, they also illuminated the retrieval processes involved in a memory task such as the one used in the experiment, and had several interesting implications for other types of experiment.

Method

Design

Categorized word lists, consisting of (a) *category names*, and (b) *words* representing instances of categories, were presented to *S*s once. Immediately after the presentation, two recall tests were given in succession. The *S*s were instructed to try to remember as many *words* as possible.

Three independent variables were manipulated: (a) list length–L (12, 24, and 48 words), (b) number of words or items per category–IPC (1, 2, and 4 words), and (c) conditions of recall in the first recall test–cued recall (CR) and noncued recall (NCR). The second recall test was always given under the conditions of CR.

All possible combinations of L and IPC were used to yield nine lists. Lists are designated in terms of the values of these two variables. For instance, List 24-2 refers to a 24-word list in which there are two items per each of 12 categories.

All combinations of nine lists and two conditions of recall in the first recall test were used to yield 18 experimental conditions. Experimental conditions are designated in terms of the list and recall condition. For instance, condition 12-4 CR refers to List 12-4 recalled under the conditions of cued recall. Thus, the design of the experiment was 3 X 3 X 2 factorial. With respect to the first recall test the independent variables were L, IPC, and recall condition; with respect to the second recall test they were L, IPC, and recall condition of the first test. Since the second recall test was always given under identical conditions (CR), experimental groups can be uniquely defined in terms of list characteristics and recall condition of the first test. For instance, Group 48-1 NCR designates the sample of *S*s who learned List 48-1 and who were first tested under the conditions of noncued recall.

Subjects and Experimental Groups

The *S*s were high-school students of both sexes from Grades 10 to 12 from a number of different schools in two school systems in the Metropolitan Toronto area.

A total of 948 *S*s were tested in the experiment. Data from 19 *S*s had to be discarded because of incompleteness of recall protocols. The data discussed in this report are thus based on the records from 929 *S*s. The age of *S*s ranged from 14 to 21 years, with a great majority (94%) of *S*s being between 15 and 18 years of age.

The *S*s were tested in groups during a regular class period. Each of nine lists was learned by *S*s in four classes. Within each class, all *S*s were presented with identical material under identical conditions, but half the *S*s were tested first under the conditions of CR while the other half was tested first under the conditions of NCR. The second recall test of the material, as mentioned earlier, occurred under the conditions of CR for all *S*s.

The sizes of the 18 experimental groups, each composed of *S*s from four different school classes, ranged from 48 to 56.

Lists

A practice list, consisting of 24 common adjectives, was administered under the typical single-trial free-recall conditions to all *S*s prior to the presentation of the experimental list.

Two different sets of nine experimental lists were constructed with the aid of the Connecticut word associations norms (Cohen, Bousfield, and Whitmarsh, 1957) and with the aid of norms from a small pilot study patterned after the procedure used by Cohen *et al.* (1957). Two groups of *S*s under each of the 18 experimental conditions learned a list from the first set, while the other two groups learned a corresponding list from the second set.

Corresponding lists in the two sets contained identical categories but different words. The words in List 48-1 represented 48 different categories, 40 taken from the Connecticut norms and eight from the pilot study. Twenty-four categories were selected randomly for Lists 24-1 and 48-2. The 12 categories represented in Lists 12-1 and 48-4 in turn were selected randomly from those occurring in Lists 24-1 and 48-2, respectively. The same general procedure was followed in the selection of categories for other lists.

Words in a given category of a list in which IPC=4 were, in the first set, usually the second, fourth, sixth, and eighth ranking words in the norms, and in the second set, the third, fifth, seventh, and ninth ranking words in the norms, but some deviations from this general rule occurred. Words for categories containing two items or one item were selected randomly from such sets of four words.

The order of categories in a list and the order of words within categories were determined randomly. All the words within a category occurred in immediately adjacent positions. The lists presented to *S*s thus consisted of a number of category names, each category name being followed by one, two, or four items appropriate to the category. For instance, List 12-2 in the first set was as follows: four-footed animals – *cow, rat*; weapons – *bomb, cannon*; crimes – *treason, theft*; forms of entertainment – *radio, music*; substances for flavouring food – *cinnamon, pepper*; professions – *engineer, lawyer*.

Procedure

The *S*s recorded their recall in specially prepared recall booklets that were distributed at the beginning of the experimental session. Instructions about *S*s' task, and about the use of recall booklets, as well as all lists were presented to *S*s by means of a high-fidelity tape-recorder. The *S*s were first informed that they were going to take "a test to find out how people remember words," and that although *E* was not interested in how well each of them did individually, they should do their best in the test. The standard free-recall instructions were then given for the practice list, followed by the presentation of the practice list, at the rate of 2 sec. per word. Two min. were given for recall.

The instructions for the second part of the test, the experimental list, informed *S*s that they would next hear and try to memorize a list of nouns, or "names of various things," pairs of nouns (in case of IPC = 2), or groups of four nouns (in case of IPC = 4), and that each word (or pair of words or group of four) would be "preceded by another word or phrase that describes the word (words) to be remembered, but which in itself does not have to be remembered." Next, an illustrative list of the kind that *S*s in a particular group had to learn was given as part of the instructions. This short list contained five categories (country in Europe, boy's name, city in U.S., name of a river, and statesman of our day), each category being accompanied by one, two, or four names, depending on the IPC of the experimental list. The illustrative list was read and the *S*s reminded that "we want you to remember only the word (words) that followed each descriptive phrase, or category." These words that *S*s had just heard, but not the category names, were then read again and referred to as the part of the list *S*s would have to remember. The *S*s were then told the number of words, number of categories, and number of words per category in the list they were going to learn.

Apart from the general instructions to recall as many words as possible, no information was given to *S*s exactly what the conditions of the recall test were going to be nor were they told that there would be different recall conditions for different *S*s in the same group.

The duration of presentation of the list varied for different lists according to the formula: T = 3 NoC + L, where T is the total duration of presentation in seconds, NoC is the number of categories (L/IPC), and L is list length. The amount of time given for recall also varied for different lists, depending on L. The *S*s had 1, 2, or 4 min. to recall lists of 12, 24, or 48 words, respectively.

For the condition of NCR, the recall booklets contained L consecutively numbered lines. For the condition of CR, the recall booklet listed all category names that had occurred in the list, in the same order as in the input list, and each category name was followed by one, two, or four lines, depending on IPC.

At the end of the first recall test of the experimental list, all *S*s recalled all the words they could remember a second time under the conditions of CR.

Results

The mean number of correctly recalled words on the practice list for the total sample of 929 *S*s was 9.48 (*SD* = 2.27). The breakdown of these recall scores in terms of the 18 experimental groups showed the means to range from 8.81 to 10.06. A one-way analysis of variance of these data yielded an *F*(17, 911) of 2.53 which is unexplainably significant at the .01 level. Since the median correlation coefficient between practice and experimental list recall was only + .228 for the nine CR groups and + .284 for the nine NCR groups, possible differences in ability among the groups suggested by differences in practice-list scores probably had only a minor effect on the evaluation of the effects of experimental treatments.

Recall of Words

The first analysis of the data was concerned with the number of words recalled under various experimental conditions. The stability of these data was tested in the following manner. In each of the 18 experimental groups, the *S*s were randomly divided into two subgroups, the mean recall score on the first recall test computed for each subgroup, and an intraclass correlation coefficient (McNemar, 1962) between the 18 resulting pairs of means calculated. This coefficient turned out to be .997, indicating a high degree of stability of the mean recall scores for various experimental groups.

First Recall Test. Mean number of words recalled in the first recall test of the experimental lists is shown by filled (CR) and unfilled (NCR) circles in Fig. 1 as a function of L and IPC. An overall analysis of variance of the number of words recalled in the first recall test showed all three main effects and all three double interactions to be significant at better than the .001 level. The triple interaction among R, L, and IPC was not significant.

Recall of words was higher under the condition of cued recall for all nine lists. The smallest numerical difference between CR and NCR was found for List 12-4. This was not significant by *t*-test ($t = 1.88$), but all other differences were significant at better than the .01 level. As can be seen from Fig. 1, the superiority of CR over NCR was an increasing function of list length and a decreasing function of IPC. The largest difference (19.8 items, or 126%) was found for List 48-1.

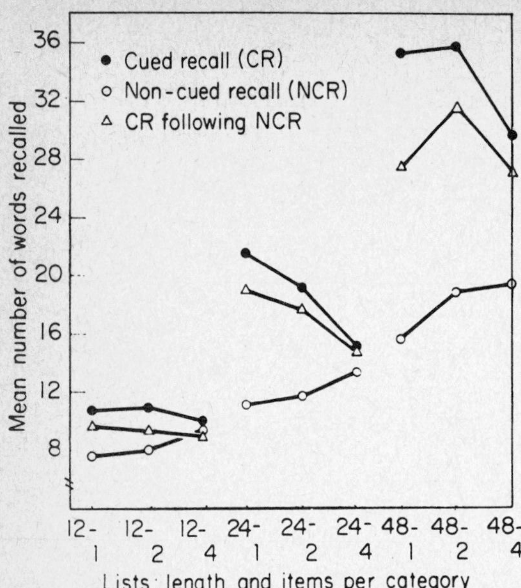

Fig. 1. Mean number of words recalled in the first recall test (circles) and the second recall test (triangles) as a function of list length and number of items per category.

When we consider CR and NCR separately, we find in Fig. 1 that NCR increases with IPC at all three levels of list length, but under the conditions of CR the effect of IPC depends on L. the inverse relation between CR and IPC is quite clear for the 24-word list and is also obvious when we compare recall for IPC = 1 with that for IPC = 4 for the other two lists, but there was no decrease in cued recall from IPC = 1 to IPC = 2 for the 12-word and 48-word lists. All six possible comparisons of mean recall scores between IPC = 1 and IPC = 4 yielded significant differences when tested by means of *t*-tests, five being significant at the .001 level and one (CR for the 12-word list) at the .05 level.

Second Recall Test. The second recall test was administered to all *S*s under the conditions of cued recall, where category names were available on recall sheets. For *S*s in all nine CR groups the mean number of words recalled on the second test was practically identical with the mean number of words recalled on the first test. The overall mean word-recall in all nine groups on the first test was 21.17, and on the second test 21.20. Thus there was neither any forgetting nor "reminiscence" from the first to the second test.

The mean recall scores on the second test for the NCR groups are shown by triangles in Fig. 1. These means were significantly higher than the means on the first test for all lists except List 12-4. But for none of the nine lists did the mean second test recall score in the NCR groups equal that of the CR groups, as can be seen in Fig. 1.

The second recall test was included in the design, and the data from the second test are included in this report, primarily in order to illustrate that subsequent presentation of category names as retrieval cues in the NCR groups would result in an increase in the number of retrieved words. More detailed analyses of these data, however, are not warranted, since no safe assumptions can be made about availability of information in the memory storage after different treatments in the first recall test. For this reason, data from the second recall test will be ignored in the rest of this paper.

Error Data and Guessing Bias. Errors of recall were classified into three categories: repetitions of list words, noncategorical intrusions, and categorical intrusions. Errors falling into the first two classes were few in number. On the first recall test, for instance, a total of 24 repetitions and a total of 73 noncategorical intrusions were found in all 929 recall protocols.

Categorical intrusions are extralist intrusions that are members of one of the categories used in a given list. Mean numbers of such intrusions are shown in Table I. Three observations are of interest. First, the frequency of categorical intrusions tended to increase with IPC at all levels of L. Second, the frequency of intrusions increased with L at all levels of IPC. Third, the number of intrusions for a given list was always greater for CR than NCR, with the exception of List 12-4. . . .

Table I – Mean number of categorical intrusions in the first recall test of experimental lists

List Length (L)	First recall	Items per category (IPC) 1	2	4
12	CR	.66	.59	.77
	NCR	.21	.31	1.23
24	CR	.91	2.12	2.58
	NCR	.22	.92	1.23
48	CR	4.22	3.87	5.52
	NCR	1.59	1.29	2.92

Category and Words-Within-Category Recall

The analysis of word-recall data in an experiment such as the present one can be regarded as a first-level analysis only. It indicates the gross effects of the variables manipulated, but it does not provide much insight into the underlying relations. Some such insight, however, can be obtained from an analysis of the data in terms of two further response measures.

The first of these is referred to as category recall. This is defined in terms of the number of categories from which *at least one word* is recalled. The measure has been used earlier by Cohen (1963). We designate this measure as R_c. In lists where IPC = 1, R_c is identical with the number of words

Table II – Mean number of categories recalled (R_C) in the first recall test of experimental lists

List length (L)	Recall condition	Items per category (IPC)		
12	CR	(10.70	5.88	2.98
	NCR	(7.70)	4.42	2.92
24	CR	(21.70)	11.16	5.79
	NCR	(11.18)	6.84	4.87
48	CR	(35.35)	20.49	11.36
	NCR	(15.57)	10.52	7.29

Table III – Mean number of words recalled per category recalled ($R_{W/C}$) in the first recall test of experimental lists

List length (L)	Recall condition	Items per category (IPC) 1	2	4
12	CR	(1.00)	1.86	3.35
	NCR	(1.00)	1.84	3.19
24	CR	(1.00)	1.73	2.61
	NCR	(1.00)	1.73	2.75
48	CR	(1.00)	1.75	2.61
	NCR	(1.00)	1.79	2.65

recalled (R_w), but in lists where IPC > 1, the two measures do not necessarily covary and usually yield different values.

The second measure is word-within-category recall, or words recalled per category recalled. It is defined in terms of the ratio of the number of words recalled to the number of categories recalled. This measure has been referred to as "mean word recall per category" by Cohen (1966). We designate this measure as $R_{w/c}$. In lists where IPC = 1, $R_{w/c}$ is always 1.00 by definition, given that *S* recalls at least one word from the list, but for higher levels of IPC, $R_{w/c}$ can assume all values between 1.00 and IPC.

The word-recall score (R_w) is a simple multiplicative function of category recall score (R_c) and words-within-category recall score ($R_{w/c}$), i.e., $R_w = R_c \cdot R_{w/c}$. The word-recall data that we considered in the two preceding sections thus reflected the effects of the independent variables on both of the two components of R_w. We will now examine the data from the first recall test with respect to the two components of R_w. Table II shows mean R_c scores for all experimental conditions. It can be seen that R_c varies systematically with all three independent variables. It is less under the NCR conditions than under the CR conditions for all lists, but the magnitude of this difference depends on both L and IPC. At a given level of IPC the difference is an increasing function of L, and at a given level of L it is a decreasing function of IPC. In Table II, the values of R_c for lists in which IPC=1 are in parentheses to remind the reader that they are identical with the corresponding R_w values.

The mean recall scores of words recalled per category recalled ($R_{w/c}$) are shown in Table III. Again the scores for lists where IPC=1 are included for the sake of completeness, although they are always unity by the definition of the $R_{w/c}$ measure.

Table III shows that while $R_{w/c}$ is systematically related to IPC, it seems to be independent of recall conditions and also independent of list length for lists of 24 and 48 words. When $R_{w/c}$ scores are averaged over all six lists for which IPC > 1, the overall means are identical at 2.32 for both CR and NCR. None of the differences in $R_{w/c}$ between CR and NCR for the six lists approaches significance by *t*-tests. And when the data are averaged over both recall conditions and IPC levels of 2 and 4, the mean $R_{w/c}$ for 24-word lists is 2.21 and the mean for the 48-word lists is 2.18 . . . .

Discussion

The most important finding of this experiment was higher recall under the conditions of cued recall than under the conditions of noncued recall. Since the experimental treatment administered to the *S*s in the two recall conditions was the same, both the amount of information and the organization of this information in the memory storage at the beginning of the recall test must have been identical for the CR and NCR groups. The superiority of cued recall over noncued recall thus suggests that specific information about many words must be available in the storage, in a form sufficient for the reproduction of words, even when this information is not accessible under a given set of recall conditions.

Intratrial forgetting, defined in terms of nonrecall of words learned in the input phase of a trial, thus does not necessarily reflect the loss of relevant information from the storage, but only its inaccessibility. Accessibility of the information clearly depends on its availability, but it also depends on retrieval cues. While the present findings do not rule out the possibility that some information stored in memory in the course of presentation of a list decays over intratrial retention intervals or is erased by other incoming information, they do make clear that inferences about what is available in memory cannot be made on the basis of what is accessible.

Retrieval cues obviously constitute an extremely important factor in determining the level of recall. The presence of a single experimentally manipulated retrieval cue, the category name, resulted in large increments in the number of recalled words, particularly for longer lists. It is entirely within the realm of possibility that additional and more powerful retrieval cues would produce an even greater facilitation of recall. Experimental work on memory has largely ignored recall conditions as an important source of variance in recall. Melton (1963) has discussed three broad theoretical problems concerned with retrieval and utilization of traces, but only one of these – dependence of the retrieval on the completeness of reinstatement at the time of recall of the stimulating situation present at the time of input – involves the analytical separation of conditions affecting storage and those related to retrieval, and very little experimental work has been done on this problem.

The analysis of recall data in the present experiment in terms of the logically definable components of word recall, namely category recall and words-within-category recall, showed that category recall was greater under the conditions of CR than NCR and that it increased directly with the length of the list, while words-within-category recall was independent of recall conditions and remained invariant when list length increased from 24 to 48. The latter finding confirms the data reported by Cohen (1966) who found that mean word recall per category was constant for lists of 35, 53, and 70 words.

The fact that variations in recall conditions and list length have an effect on only one component of the word recall measure, but not on the other, suggests that the two components represent two independent processes of recall. One of these has to do with the accessibility of higher-order memory units into which material has been organized, while the other is concerned with the accessibility of individual items comprising the higher-order units. Accessibility of higher-order units depends on appropriate retrieval cues and on the total number of stored higher-order units (or list length), while accessibility of items within higher-order units is largely independent of these variables.

In the present experiment, and in other experiments with categorized word lists the words to be memorized were organized into higher-order units by the *E*. This organization apparently determined the arrangement of words in the storage and their retrieval not only for *S*s working under the CR conditions, but also for those working under the NCR conditions. When two or more words from a given category were recalled by the NCR subjects, almost invariably these words occurred in immediate succession.

Even when the *E* does not impose any particular organization on the material the *S* has to memorize, by selecting words for inclusion in lists randomly and by presenting them without any additional descriptive labels, *S*s can and do organize the words into larger units (Tulving, 1962, 1964). Some of these subjective units (S-units) consist of words from meaningful conceptual categories, but others seem to be based on other principles – associative grouping, structural characteristics, and similarity of sound patterns – and still others appear to be determined idiosyncratically. It has been suggested previously (Tulving, 1964) that the functional significance of S-units, whatever their nature, lies in the increased accessibility of individual items constituting a unit. We do not yet know much about the mechanism underlying the retrieval of a single unit of information, be it an individual word or a larger S-unit, but it appears that if an individual list-item has been stored as a part of a larger unit it does become more accessible for retrieval when other items in the same unit are accessible. Thus organization of material, whether suggested by the *E* or imposed by the *S*, seems to affect recall performance primarily by making the desired information more accessible in an otherwise limited biological retrieval system. It need not have any effect on the availability of the information in the storage.

Abstract

The *S*s learned, on a single trial, lists of words belonging to explicitly designated conceptual categories. Lists varied in terms of length (12, 24, and 48 words) and number of words per category (1, 2, and 4). Immediate recall was tested either in presence or absence of category names as retrieval cues. Cued recall was higher than noncued recall, the difference varying directly with list length and inversely with number of items per category. This finding was interpreted as indicating that sufficiently intact memory traces of many words not recalled under the noncued recall conditions were available in the memory storage, but not accessible for retrieval. Further analysis of the data in terms of recall of categories and recall of words within recalled categories suggested two independent retrieval processes, one concerned with the accessibility of higher-order memory units, the other with accessibility of items within higher-order units.

References

BROWN, J. Some tests of the decay theory of immediate memory. *Quart. J. exp. Psychol.*, 1958, *10*, 12-21.

COHEN, B. H. Recall of categorized word lists. *J. exp. Psychol.*, 1963, *66*, 227-234.

COHEN, B. H. Some-or-none characteristics of coding behaviour. *J. verb. Learn. verb. Behav.*, 1966, *5*, 182-187.

COHEN, B. H., BOUSFIELD, W. A., and WHITMARSH, G. A. Cultural norms for verbal items in 43 categories. Tech. Rep. No. 22, Nonr-631(00), 1957, University of Connecticut.

FEIGENBAUM, E. A. The simulation of verbal learning behaviour. *Proc. West. Joint Computer Conf.*, 1961, *19*, 121-132.

FOX, P. W., BLICK, K. A., and BILODEAU, E. A. Stimulation and prediction of verbal recall and misrecall. *J. exp. Psychol.*, 1964, *68*, 321-322.

LUH, C. W. The conditions of retention. *Psychol. Monogr.*, 1922, *31, No.* 142.

MCNEMAR, Q. *Psychological Statistics* (3rd Ed.). New York: Wiley, 1962.

MELTON, A. W. Implications of short-term memory

for a general theory of memory. *J. verb. Learn. verb. Behav.*, 1963, *2,* 1-21.

PETERSON, L. R., and PETERSON, M. J. Minimal paired-associate learning. *J. exp. Phychol.*, 1962, *63,* 521-527.

POSTMAN, L., and RAU, L. Retention as a function of the method of measurement. *Univ. Calif. Publ. Psychol.*, 1957, *8,* 271-396.

TULVING, E. Subjective organization in free recall of "unrelated" words. *Psychol. Rev.*, 1962, *69,* 344-354.

———. Intratrial and intertrial retention: Notes towards a theory of free recall verbal learning. *Psychol. Rev.*, 1964, *71,* 219-237.

WAUGH, N. C., and NORMAN, D. A. Primary memory. *Psychol. Rev.*, 1965, *72,* 89-104.

18 / Forgetting of Verbal Paired Associates After Low Degrees of Learning[1]

Willard N. Runquist and Ronald A. Snyder *University of Alberta*

It has been repeatedly demonstrated that retention of material improves with an increase in practice. However, the present study shows that under certain specific conditions retention becomes worse as practice increases. This finding may be significant for understanding the processes involved in memory.

Among the subsidiary findings of a recently published study (Joinson and Runquist, 1968) was a demonstration of less forgetting of a verbal paired-associate list after one acquisition trial than after three trials. Forgetting decreased as expected after nine trials. These data, and others (Runquist, 1957) indicate a possible non-monotonic relation between degree of learning and forgetting which may have been ignored due to the fact that most studies investigating this relationship (Krueger, 1929; Underwood and Keppel, 1963) have used only relatively high degrees of learning.

The experiments reported in this paper are concerned with long term forgetting following variations in amount of practice with low levels of acquisition. In the first experiment, different groups of *S*s were given 1, 2, 3, 4, or 6 trials on a paired-associate verbal list and asked to recall the pairs after 1 week. In the second experiment, individual items within the list were repeated 1, 3, 5, or 7 times during learning with recall again required after 1 week.

Experiment I

Method

Although the experiments will be reported separately, there are certain common aspects which will be described here.

The lists used in both studies consisted of eight pairs with low association value trigrams (less than 25% according to Archer, 1960) as stimulus terms and common two syllable nouns as response terms. There were no repeated consonants among the stimuli, but vowels were repeated unsystematically, i.e., not used an equal number of times. Three equivalent lists were used in each experiment for greater generality.

All learning was by the anticipation method at a 2:2-second rate. Dunning Animatic filmstrip projectors were used to present materials. The *S* sat in a booth facing an 8-inch square translucent screen. Neither *E* nor the projector were visible.

A paced recall test was given 1 week after learning. Stimuli were presented for 2 seconds followed by a 2-second blank on the screen. Three trials were given on each stimulus, with the order of presentation being different on each trial. Correct response terms were not presented. Wherever the list was presented in "trial" form, a 4-second inter-trial interval was used.

The *S*s in both experiments were Introductory Psychology students who served as part of a course requirement. All were naive to verbal learning experiments. They were assigned to groups or conditions in order of appearance at the laboratory according to a scheme which randomized the order of conditions within blocks containing each condition. All *S*s were run by trained undergraduate *E*'s.

Procedure and Design. Five groups of 24 *S*s were tested in Experiment 1. Each *S* received one study trial and either 1, 2, 3, 4, or 6 anticipation trials followed by the 1-week recall test. Each of the three lists was learned by eight *S*s and was presented in four different unsystematic orders during learning. None of the three recall orders was the same as any learning order.

Results

Estimates of immediate recall were made by single entry probability analysis (Underwood, 1964) which has been shown to provide reasonably valid estimates of terminal acquisition level (Runquist and Joinson, 1968). Generally, this procedure uses the number of correct anticipations on each item to predict the performance on an immediate recall test for each *S*. His score on the first (or any subsequent) recall trial may be subtracted from his predicted score to yield a forgetting score for each *S* in terms of number of items lost (absolute loss), or this loss score may be divided by the predicted value and multiplied by 100 to give a percentage loss. Predictions were made by using data only from the particular group to which *S*s belonged.

None of the comparisons involving lists produced significant main effects or interactions; hence, lists were combined in all analyses presented here. The

[1]This work was supported by Grant APB-88 from the National Research Council of Canada and Grant GB-6166 from the National Science Foundation. Data were collected by the junior author, Marva Swenson, and Tom Gray.

mean estimated immediate recall scores for the five groups were 3.02, 4.11, 4.80, 5.11, and 5.18 items, showing the effects of increasing practice. The mean absolute loss is shown in Figure 1 plotted as a function of estimated final performance in acquisition. Also shown on the graph are results from the Joinson and Runquist (1968) experiment which used only one of the lists from the present experiment, but otherwise was run under identical conditions. Only data from the first recall trial are presented here for comparison with the earlier study.

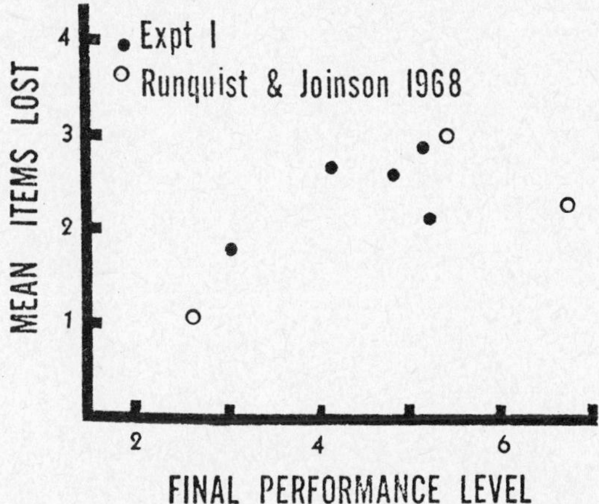

Fig. 1. Mean absolute forgetting as a function of terminal acquisition performance in experiment 1.

The continuity between the two sets of data is striking. Generally, the absolute forgetting scores in the present experiment fall between those from the Joinson and Runquist study, which is not surprising since the estimates of final performance also fall between values previously obtained. There is one discrepant point in that forgetting after six trials is somewhat less than that obtained previously after attaining nearly the same performance level during learning. This six-trial group shows better retention than the group which received four trials while showing nearly equal predicted values, suggesting that either the mean for immediate recall may be underestimated, or that this group is slightly inferior to the other groups in ability. Inspection of performance during anticipation trials of acquisition suggested that the latter might be the case.

The most interesting aspect of the results, however, is the *increase* in forgetting with increasing practice. Although an overall analysis of variance failed to produce evidence of significant variation in mean loss, $F(4, 105) = 1.65$, $p > .10$, a trend test resulted in a significant quadratic component, $F(1, 105) = 4.55$, $p < .05$, and a t test between the means of the one and two trial groups indicated a reliable increase in number of items forgotten $t(46) = 2.06$, $p < .05$. These results, when considered alone with the results of the earlier study provide considerable evidence for an initial increase in forgetting with increasing practice. If it is then argued that further practice must eventually result in less forgetting, as most data show, a non-monotonic function necessary ensues.

It may be argued, however, that absolute loss is an inappropriate measure of forgetting at low degrees of learning since *S*s who fail to recall a single item are limited in the size of the loss score by the fact that predicted immediate recall scores are low. In essence, the maximum amount of forgetting possible under these circumstances is less for lower degrees of learning. This argument may be countered in part by analyzing data from *S*s who can recall at least one item. The mean loss scores, with the number of *S*s in parentheses were 1.21 (15), 2.18(14), 1.64(16), 2.36(20), 2.01(20) for the 1, 2, 3, 4, and 6 trial groups, respectively. Clearly, the results do not change if *S*s showing total forgetting are eliminated.

Nevertheless, percentage forgotten presumably avoids the bias and is often considered to be a more appropriate measure of forgetting when comparing groups having different terminal acquisition performance levels. In this experiment, the mean percentage loss scores were 63, 69, 54, 53, and 46%, for the 1, 2, 3, 4, and 6 trial groups, respectively, thus reflecting a more monotonic relationship. Indeed, analysis of variance on these values showed only a significant linear decrease, $F(1, 105) = p < .05$, despite the slight increase between one and two trial groups. This measure also contains a source of bias, however, in that *S*s who fail to recall a single item all receive a score of 100% irrespective of the predicted immediate recall score. It could be argued that since failure to recall any items is more serious if the predicted recall is higher, the failure to weight the loss by this factor favours better recall at higher degrees of learning. This argument is somewhat vindicated by again considering only *S*s who recalled at least one item. The percentage forgotten was 27, 47, 31, 43, and 35% for the groups having 1, 2, 3, 4, and 6 trials, respectively. Clearly, the amount of forgetting is least in the group having the fewest practice trials.

Since the practice of differentially eliminating *S*s does produce bias, all of these results must be considered tentative. Consequently, the conclusion to be drawn from these data depends upon which measure is considered. In terms of absolute loss, the relationship between number of trials and amount forgotten is non-monotonic with maximum forgetting occurring between two and four trials. If percentage forgotten is considered, the relationship is essentially a monotonic decreasing function, although in both the present study and the earlier study there was little differential loss until at least three trials had been given.

The data from the second and third recall trials will not be presented. Generally, all groups showed improved recall performance with successive recalls except the group having only one trial. The total amount of improvement was small, being on the order of one-half item. Nevertheless, the total effect was to reduce the superiority of the one-trial group.

Discussion

Regardless of differences in the two measures of forgetting, it is still apparent that the group which received only one anticipation trial recalled at least as much of what they had learned as the group which received two trials, despite the fact that the latter group was superior in immediate recall. This, then, provides an exception to the usually accepted generalization that better learning yields better retention.

Whether this represents a basic relation between response strength and forgetting is debatable, however. Items learned on the first trial are the "easy" items, and might be expected to be less readily forgotten. With further practice, *S*s begin to acquire more difficult items which may be less resistant to forgetting. Item analyses have continually denied this interpretation (Joinson and Runquist, 1968), and yet there is still some question as to whether the relationship is due in some way to differential distribution of item strengths within a list.

The second experiment was designed to investigate the relationship between degree of learning and forgetting by *manipulating* the strength of individual items within the list at the end of learning. If item "difficulty" is the major factor involved, then the relationship obtained above should not hold.

Experiment II

The presentation of the eight pairs for this experiment was arranged so that after the first study trial, two items were presented once, two items three times, two items five times and two items seven times. For a given list, four different assignments of items to the four conditions were used in four different arrangements of the list so that across all *S*s each item participated in each condition equally. An equal number of *S*s learned each arrangement. Items were presented as an unbroken sequence. The order of appearance of items in conditions was identical for all *S*s. If A and B represent items presented once, C and D items presented three times, E and F items presented five times, and G and H items presented seven times, the order of presentation was CAHEFBDGHECDGFHEGCHGEHFGDHFGCBHEFGDHEAFG. Two main groups of 24 *S*s were tested. Group I had a recall test immediately following acquisition, while Group D had recall after 1 week. Within each group, eight *S*s each learned one of the three different lists used in Experiment I and two *S*s in each of these subgroups used each item x condition arrangement described above. All other procedures were identical to those in Experiment I.

Results

Table I reports the major findings of Experiment II. Shown are the mean correct on the immediate recall test for each set of items, and the mean correct on the delayed test for those items. Clearly, the experiment was not very successful in manipulating intra-list item response strength as there is little difference in the mean immediate recall for items given 3, 5, or 7 repetitions. After 1 week, there is considerable loss for all items, but it is also apparent that the loss was less for items receiving one trial as opposed to the remaining items. The analysis of variance, however, failed to provide support for the reliability of this result as the interaction $F(3, 138) < 1.00$. Both recall interval, $F(1, 46) = 21.60$, $p < .01$, and number of repetitions, $F(3, 138) = 5.45$, $p < .01$, produced significant main effects.

Table I – Mean items recalled within each set

	Retention interval	
Repetitions	Immediate	Delayed
1	.87	.33
3	1.36	.58
5	1.29	.50
7	1.33	.59

Although these results appear to be essentially negative, it should be pointed out that the test lacks considerable power due to the fact that mean immediate recall did not differ for three of the four sets of items. Consequently, further analyses were performed using recall data from the delayed group only, and making comparisons of forgetting of items within those *S*s.

Estimates of immediate recall for the different sets of items for each *S* in the delayed recall group were made by determining the probability of correct immediate recall given 0 to *n* correct anticipations on each item for the immediate recall group. The predicted immediate recall score for each set of two items in the delayed recall group was obtained by summing the probabilities assigned to the two items based on the number of correct anticipations for those two items. Forgetting scores were then obtained by subtracing the obtained recall score (0, 1, or 2) from these predicted values.

Mean absolute loss (number of items) was .46, .78, .69, and .72 for items given 1, 3, 5, and 7 trials, respectively, corresponding fairly closely with the between groups comparison. Again it should be noted that forgetting was less for items given only one anticipation trial. Furthermore, a Friedman's chi-square test (Siegel, 1961) on the ranked forgetting scores within *S*s showed that differences in ranks were reliable across *S*s, chi-square $(3) = 25.15$, $p < .001$, with most of the effect resulting from consistently lower score for items with fewest presentations. In short, the relationships shown in Experiment I and in the previously reported experiment (Joinson and Runquist, 1968) seem to be confirmed at least in part when individual item strength rather than overall "list" strength is manipulated.

Discussion

There are now three types of demonstrations that poorly learned items are better recalled than items which are somewhat better learned. In two studies, the present one and Joinson and Runquist (1968), a list given one trial resulted in better retention than a list given two or three trials. In an earlier study (Runquist, 1957) items which were correctly anticipated the fewest number of times during learning showed less absolute loss than items which were correctly anticipated more often. The final type of experiment is represented by Experiment II of the present paper, in which items presented fewer times during learning were retained better than items presented more frequently. The empirical facts, then, seem well established. It only remains to account for the results theoretically.

The methodological argument that absolute loss is a biased measure does not seem to provide an adequate solution. Generally, while the increase in forgetting with increases in "degree of learning" may not be obtained when forgetting is measured in terms of percentage forgotten, there is still no evidence of a decrease. Moreover, both measures involve different biases and it is not clear which one should be considered more important.

Joinson and Runquist (1968) offered an explanation for the results involving manipulations of trials on the list as a whole. They hypothesized that the items acquired with further practice interfered with items learned on earlier trials. Thus, the latter items would be better retained if these additional trials were not given since the additional interference would not be produced.

Unfortunately, this explanation cannot apply to the results of the other two types of experiments, since in these studies comparisons are not made at different stages of practice but are made among items within individual *S*s at the same stage of practice. Nevertheless, similar processes may be operating to reduce forgetting in the weak items. It seems likely that some kind of organizational process produces functional isolation of these weak items and increases their resistance to forgetting. Organization is a well-known facet of free recall learning (Tulving, 1968) and has also been shown to be extremely important in paired associate acquisition (Battig, 1968; Runquist, 1965, 1966). Hence, the operation of these principles in retention is not unlikely.

The basic principle is that a small number of "weak" items are somehow isolated or psychologically form a discriminable subset of items and hence are protected from being interfered with by the other items both during acquisition and at recall. In the case where item strength is defined in terms of correct responses to criterion, the item characteristics which produce greater difficulty may provide this differentiation. In the case where strength is manipulated by varying repetitions of individual items, differentiation may be made on the basis of sheer frequency or on the basis of the fact that in the present Experiment II items presented only once in addition to the initial study exposure appeared only toward the end of the learning session. In both cases, it is possible that items were differentiated according to strength, or according to when they are learned.

The results of several experiments (Battig, 1965, 1966; Battig and Miller, 1965; Battig, Allen, and Jensen, 1965; Runquist, 1965) have been interpreted as demonstrating categorization on the basis of these variables, so that such an explanation is certainly reasonable. Nevertheless, the present experiments were designed only to determine the empirical relationship between practice and forgetting so that a definitive explanation for the phenomena must await more analytic research. It is possible, however, that despite the similarity in the results, experiments involving manipulations of practice varying the number of trials on the entire list and those involving differential practice or performance on individual items incorporate different processes.

Abstract

Two experiments investigated retention of verbal associates over 1 week. In one experiment, lists were given 1, 2, 3, 4, or 6 anticipation trials. Forgetting was less for the list given 1 trial than for the others. In the second experiment, different items were given 1, 3, 5, or 7 repetitions. Forgetting was less for items given 1 repetition than for the others. Results were interpreted in terms of heightened resistance to interference by weak items.

References

ARCHER, E. J. A re-evaluation of the meaningfulness of all possible CVC trigrams. *Psychological Monographs,* 1960, *73,* (Whole No. 497).

BATTIG, W. F. Further evidence that strongest free recall items are not recalled first. *Psychological Reports,* 1965, *17,* 745-746.

———. Evidence for coding processes in "rote" paired associate learning. *Journal of Verbal Learning and Verbal Behaviour,* 1966, *5,* 172-181.

———. Paired associate learning. In T. R. DIXON and D. L. HORTON (eds.), *Verbal Behaviour and General Behaviour Theory*. Englewood Cliffs, N.J., Prentice-Hall, 1968.

BATTIG, W. F., and MILLER, S. M. Classification of learning of items grouped on the basis of degree of prior learning. *Psychological Reports,* 1965, *17,* 807-814.

BATTIG, W. F., ALLEN, M., and JENSEN, A. R. Priority of free recall of newly learned items. *Journal of Verbal Learning and Verbal Behaviour,* 1965, *4,* 175-179.

JOINSON, P. A., and RUNQUIST, W. N. Effects on intralist stimulus similarity and degree of learning on forgetting. *Journal of Verbal Learning and Verbal Behaviour,* 1968, *7,* 554-559.

KRUEGER, W. C. F. The effect of overlearning on retention. *Journal of Experimental Psychology,* 1929, *12,* 71-78.

RUNQUIST, W. N. Retention of verbal associates as a function of strength. *Journal of Experimental Psychology,* 1957, *54,* 369-375.

———. Order of presentation and number of items as factors in paired associate verbal learning. *Journal of Verbal Learning and Verbal Behaviour,* 1965, *4,* 535-540.

———. Intralist interference as a function of list length and interstimulus similarity. *Journal of Verbal Learning and Verbal Behaviour,* 1966, *5,* 7-13.

RUNQUIST, W. N., and JOINSON, P. A. Predictions of terminal acquisition performance for individual subjects. *Journal of Verbal Learning and Verbal Behaviour,* 1968, *7,* 98-105.

SIEGEL, S. *Nonparametric statistics.* New York: McGraw-Hill, 1961.

TULVING, E. Theoretical issues in free recall. In T. R. DIXON and D. L. HORTON (eds.), *Verbal Behaviour and General Behaviour Theory.* Englewood Cliffs, N.J., Prentice-Hall, 1968.

UNDERWOOD, B. J. Degree of learning and the measurement of forgetting. *Journal of Verbal Learning and Verbal Behaviour,* 1964, *3,* 112-129.

UNDERWOOD, B. J., and KEPPEL, G. Retention as a function of degree of learning and letter sequence interference. *Psychological Monographs,* 1963, *77,* (Whole No. 567).

19 / Memory Storage and Aging[1]

David Schonfield and Betty-Anne Robertson *University of Calgary*

Elderly people frequently tell a story and a short time later repeat the story without any apparent awareness of their original statement. Such a phenomenon indicates that they have a memory deficit. The precise nature of this deficit is not well understood. In the following experiment, memory was assessed in subjects of different ages. The authors concluded that "Voluntary recall, which involves retrieval, shows a loss with age, whereas recognition, which does not require retrieval, shows no such deterioration."

Of learning's three stages – acquisition, retention, and remembering (Woodworth, 1938) – it is the last, that of remembering, which is necessarily the dependent variable from which conclusions are drawn concerning the influence of independent variables operating at any of the three stages. If a loss at the remembering stage is demonstrated, it can be interpreted as due to imperfect acquisition, interference in retention, or deficient recollection. When remembering is tested in a situation where acquisition is likely to have been imperfect, or where there are good grounds for assuming interference, there is no need for an additional hypothesis of special impediments operating at the remembering stage itself. The well-established deficits of older subjects in the remembering of a variety of materials have generally been interpreted in just such a manner. Both Jerome (1959) and Welford (1958) in their recent surveys concluded that older people learn more slowly and are perhaps more liable to interference than the young, but that experiments provide no indication of a special incapacity among the aged in the remembering of acquired information or skills.

The evidence that increasing age results in deficiencies in acquisition and retention does not exclude, however, the possibility that there are additional problems for older people at the remembering stage. In fact, the results of several investigations can be interpreted as suggestive of an age-linked impairment in remembering. The well-known difficulty of older groups in the performance of paced tasks (Canestrari, 1963) indicates their need for additional time in retrieving from storage. The proneness of the aged to errors of omission rather than commission (Korchin and Basowitz, 1957) shows a similar difficulty in retrieving from storage. Broadbent and Heron's (1962) demonstration that older subjects show a disproportionate loss in tasks which involve a shift of attention could be considered an example of the difficulty in reinstating a previous memory into the focus of attention. The same explanation could cover Talland's (1959) experiments with the aged on change of set. These investigations thus point to a particular kind of impairment at the remembering stage. Retrieving from storage would seem to constitute a special difficulty for older groups.

The implication of the previous discussion is that a test of memory which does not require retrieval from storage will show less of a loss with age than a test which involves retrieval. The psychological difference between a voluntary recall method and a recognition method of testing memory seems to fit the distinction between the presence and absence of the requirement of retrieving from storage. As Deese (1963) says, "In recall a subject must produce a set of responses, whereas in recognition the set of responses is produced for him." The prediction would be, therefore, that the aged would have far superior scores on a recognition than on a voluntary recall test, since the act of recognition demands the matching of a stimulus to a stored trace, but does not involve retrieval as such. Of course, recognizing a symbol among a set as the one previously presented almost invariably results in higher scores than requiring a subject to recall a symbol voluntarily. The prediction here is that among older groups the difference between recognition and recall scores will be greater than among younger groups. Further, by comparing the recall scores of both older and younger subjects with their own recognition scores the methodological problem of equating acquisition in different age groups is obviated.

Method

Subjects

Ss used in this study were 134-persons aged between 20 and 75 years with a minimum of 20 *S*s in each decade between 20 and 60 and over 60 years of age. Approximately half of the *S*s were male and half female, but there were more males below 40 and more females over 40 years old. The *S*s in the younger age groups were, or had been, attending

[1]This research was supported by Grant No. APA-89 from the National Research Council.

Reprinted, by permission, from *Canadian Journal of Psychology*, 1966, *20*, 228-236.

university. Older age groups consisted of professional people, wives of professionals, and parents or grandparents of university students.

Material
Two lists – A and B – each of 24 monosyllabic or bisyllabic nouns or adjectives constituted the memory tasks.The words were chosen on the basis of frequency on the Thorndike-Lorge count. Each list contained 8 words of high frequency (100 per million), 8 of medium frequency (50 per million), and 8 of low frequency (1 per million). The lists were matched for the number of words beginning with the same letter; thus 4 words beginning with the letter "b" were in one list and 4 beginning with "c" were in the other. Consecutive words began with different letters.

The two recognition lists consisted of the 24 words from lists A or B each within a group of 4 other words. These additional words were chosen from those given by Palermo and Jenkins (1964) or Russell and Jenkins (1954) as having high (over 100) medium (35-99), low (2-34), and zero association value with the original learning word.

Procedure
The instructions to the *S* were as follows: "I am going to show you a list of words one at a time. As soon as the word appears on the screen I want you to say the word aloud once. Try to remember as many words as you can. Do not worry if you forget some of them since no one has remembered all the words."

The words in a list were presented consecutively on a screen, each for 4 sec., by means of a Kodak Carousel projector. Letters were 2 in. high and the *S* sat 2 ft. from the screen. Immediately after *S* had pronounced the last word on the list he was either instructed to say as many of the words as he could recall in any order he wished, or was given the recognition list and told to underline the one word in any group of 5 which he had previously seen on the screen. The recognition and recall tests were untimed.

*S*s were tested individually for recognition on one list and recall on the other. Approximately half of the *S*s in each group performed the recognition task first, the others the recall task first. Similarly, approximately half the *S*s were presented with list A for recognition and with list B for recall, while the remainder had the recognition test on list B and recall test on list A.

In order to provide information on the effect of recall on recognition of the same list and the effect of recognition on the recall of the same list, *S*s were given a subsidiary recognition test on list A immediately after their recall of list A. Similarly, after recognition on list A they were given a subsidiary recall test on list A.The same procedure was adopted after recall or recognition of list B.

Results

Table I shows the mean recognition scores and voluntary recall scores for lists A and B. It can be seen that the recognition means for the two lists are almost identical, as are the voluntary recall means. The slightly lower recognition score on list A is balanced by the slightly lower voluntary recall score for list B. The differences are obviously due to chance factors and not significant statistically. It can, therefore, be concluded that the attempt to equalize the level of learning difficulty of the two lists was successful.

Table I – Mean recognition and recall scores by list

	Recognition	Recall
List A	$\bar{X}$ = 19.58	$\bar{X}$ = 11.11
	σ = 2.82	σ = 3.10
List B	$\bar{X}$ = 20.06	$\bar{X}$ = 10.80
	σ = 2.48	σ = 3.30
	t = 1.04	t = .55
	$p >$ .10	$p >$ .10

Table II – Mean recognition and recall scores by order of presentation

	Recognition	Recall
First	$\bar{X}$ = 19.87	$\bar{X}$ = 11.10
	σ = 2.57	σ = 3.55
Second	$\bar{X}$ = 19.76	$\bar{X}$ = 10.78
	σ = 2.78	σ = 3.66
	t = .23	t = .52
	$p >$ .10	$p >$ .10

Table II compares the mean recognition score when recognition precedes and when it follows voluntary recall on the alternate list; the mean recall scores of subjects tested prior to recognition on the alternate list is also compared to the mean on recall following alternate list recognition. The results show that the two recognition scores are almost identical as are the two recall scores. Neither positive nor negative transfer occurs between the first and second memory tests whether recall or whether recognition comes first. It seems, therefore, justifiable to combine all of the recognition results – whether from list A or B and whether recognition precedes or follows recall. This also applies to the combination of all the voluntary recall results.

Table III gives the mean recognition and voluntary recall scores by age groups. The results show little difference between age groups on recognition scores, but demonstrate a steady decline with age on the voluntary recall scores. The difference between recognition and recall scores shown in the final column has a rho correlation with age groups of +1.00. The Pearson product-moment correlation between recognition-minus-recall scores and age is +.66, which is significant at beyond the .001 level.

Table III – Mean recognition, recall, and recognition minus recall scores by age

Age range	N	Recognition	Recall	Recognition minus recall
20-29	36	20.01	13.78	6.42
30-39	23	19.48	12.30	7.17
40-49	32	19.53	10.01	9.47
50-59	21	19.90	9.57	10.24
60+	22	20.09	7.50	12.59

Table IV – Recognition before and after recall on the same list and recall before and after recognition on the same list

	List A	List B
	Recognition	
Before recall	$\bar{X} = 19.58$	$\bar{X} = 20.06$
After recall	$\bar{X} = 19.40$	$\bar{X} = 19.64$
	$t = 0.32$	$t = 0.93$
	$p > 0.10$	$p > 0.10$
	Recall	
Before recognition	$\bar{X} = 11.11$	$\bar{X} = 10.80$
After recognition	$\bar{X} = 9.19$	$\bar{X} = 10.72$
	$t = 2.78$	$t = 0.12$
	$p < 0.01$	$p > 0.10$

The results of the subsidiary experiment are given in Table IV. This table compares recognition scores before and after recall on the *same* list, as well as recall scores before and after recognition on the *same* list. The figures show that recognition is not aided by prior recall on the same list, and, surprisingly, recall may be hindered by recognition on the same list.

Discussion

The prediction that the difference between recognition and recall scores is greater in older than younger subjects is clearly supported by the experimental results. There is no apparent deterioration with age in recognition, whereas on voluntary recall there is a loss of almost 50 per cent between the scores of this group of younger and older people. The subjects performing this experiment were admittedly of superior intelligence level, but there is no obvious reason why the conclusions cannot be generalized to other intelligence levels. There is some evidence (Gilbert, 1935) that differences between age groups of high general ability are less than differences at lower levels. It might, therefore, be expected that recognition scores of those at lower intelligence levels would show some loss, although the relative superiority of recognition compared to recall should be maintained. Gilbert (1935), who included recall and recognition types of tests in her battery, found a greater loss in recall than in recognition, but some loss in both.

It is difficult to envisage how these findings can be explained on the basis of age differences operating at either the acquisition or retention stage of learning. Any such differences in these two stages should manifest themselves to some degree in the recognition scores as much as in the recall scores. The fact that the recognition scores show no loss with age, although surprising, indicates that the results must be explained by factors operating at the time of remembering.

It might be suggested that the 24 words in a list provide a spurious upper limit for recognition scores in the younger groups. Were this true the recognition scores for the young would not portray their real potential in recognition, while the parallel scores for older groups might show their top capacity. The choice of 24 words in each list was based on a pilot study where no one managed to recognize 24 words. Unfortunately, the maximum recognition score of 24 was reached by 9 of the 134 subjects participating in the present experiment. However, these 9 were evenly distributed among age groups – 2 in each decade under 60 and one older than 60 years of age. Consequently, the increase with age in recognition-minus-recall scores cannot be attributed to the inability of the young, as opposed to the old, to reach their ceiling score.

The findings are, therefore, interpreted as supporting the hypothesis that aging causes special difficulties in retrieving memories from storage. Voluntary recall, which involves retrieval, shows a loss with age, whereas recognition, which does not require the retrieval, shows no such deterioration. It is worth emphasizing that the original prediction was not that recognition would show no loss; it was that recognition scores would not deteriorate to the same extent as recall scores. A repetition of the present experiment which showed some drop in older subjects' recognition scores would not necessarily constitute evidence against the present hypothesis.

The tripartite division of the learning process into acquisition, retention, and remembering might be thought to imply that retrieval is confined to the third stage – that of remembering. However, stages of learning are not paralleled by the psychological mechanisms involved. The acquisition stage of learning normally involves not only an acquisition mechanism, but also a retrieval mechanism. In most learning situations new learning has to be continuously placed in and brought out of storage. A difficulty of older people in retrieving from storage might, therefore, be the main cause of their inefficiency during this so-called acquisition stage. This suggestion is not quite the same as that of other investigators who consider that limitations in immediate memory are the primary cause of learning deficiencies among the aged. The immediate memory span, in fact, shows little if any deterioration with age (Gilbert, 1941; Bromley, 1958). It is, therefore, increased liability of short-term memory to interference which is usually hypothesized as the cause of special age-linked deterioration in acquisition. The suggestion derived from the present experiment is rather more specific and does not involve interference of the usual proactive or retroactive varieties. The special consequences of interference among the aged do not result from information having to be placed in storage, or from effects taking place during storage. It is the problem of reclamation that constitutes the difficulty.

Inglis (1965), on the basis of his experiments with dichotic stimulation, has emphasized another facet of immediate memory as a cause of poorer acquisition among older persons. He and his colleagues (Inglis and Caird, 1963; Inglis and Mackay, 1963) have demonstrated that there is no significant loss with age in the recall of first half-spans but reproduction of the second half-span by older subjects shows progressively greater difficulty. Inglis (1965) interprets his findings as due to an increase in the rate of trace decay as well as increased sensitivity to interference. However, since Broadbent's (1958) distinction between S and P systems is rejected by Inglis, there is no easy explanation for the absence of loss in digits recalled first when similar decay and interference should be operating. According to Inglis' suggested analysis, when 3 digits are presented to each ear, individual digits of the half-span recalled first are held in storage for 3 seconds, while digits recalled last are held for 6 seconds. The greater number of errors in the recall of the final half-span is thus said to be due to the fact that this material is in a holding system for twice as long as material recalled first. By the same argument, however, the first half-span of a 12-digit series presented dichotically should show the same loss as the second half-span of a 6-digit series. But Inglis (1965) emphasized that age differences were found in the second and not in the first half-spans.

In the present experiment the difficulty of the aged in retrieval is detected by a loss or absence of response, but this should not be considered the only way in which such a difficulty might manifest itself. The production of a correct response with a considerably longer latency might be thought of as an alternative manifestation of the difficulty of access to storage. Disproportionate loss of speed, according to the present formulation, should not be expected when there is a prior set for just one response. In such a situation the subject is unlikely to have to retrieve anything from storage, the response being already present at the focus of attention. However, repeated access to storage is required when the subject must execute a series of different responses, and in these cases exaggerated slowness by the aged would be anticipated. The experimental evidence, which shows a relatively small increase with age in simple reaction time (Welford, 1959) but a disproportionate increase in serial and choice reaction times (Singleton, 1955; Goldfarb, 1941), is in accordance with this formulation.

There would appear to be two main strategies which older people utilize in order to overcome their difficulty in retrieval. The first is to prepare for future action by having the necessary information at the focus of attention before the need for it arises. This could be achieved through prior rehearsal. The characteristic care and caution of the aged, observed in many experimental investigations (Welford, 1958), would permit such rehearsal and might be thought of as the organism's attempt to adjust to future retrieval problems. A second strategy employed in endeavouring to reduce the time required for access to storage is to increase the number of stimulus cues which lead to a particular stored item. The tendency of older people to utilize extra cues – visual, auditory, and kinesthetic – has been noticed in a number of investigations (Welford, 1958). The anecdotal evidence that the aged can recall with ease material acquired early in life may be due in part to an accretion of such stimulus cues. If the difficulty in retrieval can be considered as the result of increased "noise" in the aging nervous system (Gregory, 1957) the extra cues serve the function of adding to the signal to noise ratio. Although not specifically concerned with age differences, Miller, Galanter, and Pribram (1960) put forward essentially the same argument. They state that plans for remembering often involve an increase in the number of associations and these serve the function of overcoming the problem of retrieval.

Abstract

Recall and recognition tests were administered to *S*s aged between 20 and 75 years. The results showed no deterioration with age in recognition scores and a consistent drop in recall scores. The age disparity is interpreted as due to the requirement of retrieval from storage in recall tests and the absence of this requirement in recognition tests.

Résumé

Administration de tests de rappel et de récognition à des sujets âgés de 20 à 75 ans. La récognition ne se détériore pas avec l'âge, mais le rappel diminue de façon consistante. L'interprétation de cette disparité fait intervenir la nécessité de puiser dans un réservoir de souvenirs, nécessité présente dans les tests de rappel, mais absente dans les tests de récognition.

References

BROADBENT, D. E. *Perception and communication.* London, Pergamon, 1958.

BROADBENT, D. E., and HERON, A. Effects of a subsidiary task on performance involving immediate memory by younger and older men. *Brit. J. Psychol.*, 1962, *53*, 189-98.

BROMLEY, D. B. Some effects of age on short-term learning and remembering. *J. Gerontol.*, 1958, *13*, 398-406.

CANESTRARI, R. E. Paced and self paced learning in young and elderly adults. *J. Gerontol.*, 1963, *18*, 165-8.

DEESE, J. Comments on Professor Murdock's paper. In C. N. COFER and B. S. MUSGRAVE, eds., *Verbal behaviour and learning*. New York, McGraw-Hill, 1963.

GILBERT, JEANNE G. Mental efficiency in senescence. *Arch. Psychol.*, No. 188, 1935.

———. Memory losses in senescence. *J. abnorm. soc. Phychol.*, 1941, *36*, 73-86.

GOLDFARB, W. An investigation of reaction time in older adults and its relationship to certain observed mental test patterns. *Teachers' Colleges Contribution to Education,* No. 831, New York, Columbia Univ., 1941.

GREGORY, R. L. Increase in "neurological noise" as a factor in ageing. In *Proc. 4th Cong. Internat. Ass. Gerontol.* (Merano), 1957, *1*, 314-24.

INGLIS, J. Immediate memory, age and brain function. In A. T. WELFORD and J. E. BIRREN, eds., *Behaviour, aging and the nervous system.* Illinois, Thomas, 1965.

INGLIS, J., and CAIRD, W. K. Age differences in successive responses to simultaneous stimulation. *Canad. J. Psychol.*, 1963, *17*, 98-105.

INGLIS, J., and MACKAY, H. A. The effects of age on a short-term auditory storage process. Paper read at the *Sixth International Congress of Gerontology,* Copenhagen, 1963.

JEROME, E. Age and learning—experimental studies. In J. E. BIRREN, ed., *Handbook of aging and the individual.* Chicago, Univ. Chicago Press, 1959.

KORCHIN, S. J., and BASOWITZ, H. Age differences in verbal learning. *J. abnorm. soc. Psychol.*, 1957, *54,* 64-9.

MILLER, G. A., GALANTER, T., and PRIBRAM, K. H. *Plans and the structure of behaviour*. New York, Henry Holt, 1960.

PALERMO, D. S., and JENKINS, J. J. *Word association norms grade school through college.* Minneapolis, Univ. Minnesota Press, 1964.

RUSSELL, W. A., and JENKINS, J. J. The complete Minnesota norms for responses to 100 words from the Kent-Rosanoff word association test. Studies on the role of language behaviour. *Tech. Rep. No. 11, August, 1954.* Minneapolis, Univ. Minnesota Press.

SINGLETON, W. T. Age and performance timing on simple skills. In R. E. TURNBRIDGE, ed., *Old age in the modern world.* London, Livingstone, 1955.

TALLAND, G. A. Age and the effect of anticipatory set on accuracy of perception. *J. Gerontol.*, 1959, *14,* 202-7.

WELFORD, A. T. *Aging and human skill.* London, Oxford Univ. Press, 1958.

———. Psychomotor performance. In J. E. BIRREN, ed., *Handbook of aging and the individual.* Chicago, Univ. Chicago Press, 1959.

WOODWORTH, R. S. *Experimental psychology*. New York, Henry Holt, 1938.

FIVE
LANGUAGE AND THINKING

20 / Early Development in Spoken Language of the Dionne Quintuplets[1]

W.E. Blatz, M.I. Fletcher, and M. Mason *St. George's School for Child Study, University of Toronto*

On May 28, 1934, an event occurred which caught the imagination of the entire world. Five identical quintuplets (females) were born to a French-Canadian family living in Callander, Ontario, a small community 200 miles north of Toronto. Although 57 cases of previous quintuplets had been recorded in history, none of them had survived past the age of one year. The survival of the five sisters, therefore, became a matter of vital importance, a situation which was complicated by their premature birth (at seven months), the primitive facilities for their care, and the inaccessibility of their remote location. In addition, the world-wide publicity generated by their birth soon precipitated an avalanche of curious visitors, representatives of news media, promoters who wished to exhibit the quintuplets for a fee, and some rumours and threats of kidnapping, all of which interfered with their care.

Plans were therefore laid for the construction of a hospital-residence unit, to be located across the road from the family home (the Dionne home was too small since they already had five older children), to which the quintuplets were transferred at the age of four months. They lived here for many years under the care of Dr. William Dafoe, who delivered the babies, and two nurses, their home surrounded by two high wire fences and under the constant guard of policemen. Eventually, the five sisters were given court-appointed guardians and, through an Act of Parliament, their future material welfare was guaranteed. (Emilie died in 1954; Annette and Cecile were married in 1957; Marie was married in 1958 and died in 1970; and Yvonne joined a convent in 1964 but left two years later to become a teacher of handicrafts to children.)

When it became evident that the five sisters would survive, requests were received from scientists in various parts of the world for permission to examine and study them. Never before in the history of human genetics had five identical children been born into circumstances which permitted their growth and development to be investigated under controlled conditions. In view of the unique contribution which such a study could make to science, Dr. W. E. Blatz, a medical doctor and a professor of child psychology at the University of Toronto, was appointed to direct a team of Canadian scientists who embarked upon the study of the physical, mental, language, social, and self-discipline development of the quintuplets from the age of 10 months to 3 years. The chief contribution of this research to scientific knowledge was the demonstration that the quintuplets, in spite of a common heredity, showed considerable variation in their behaviour, abilities, and personality.

Reprinted, by permission, from *University of Toronto Studies, Child Development Series.* No. 16, 1937.

This article, written by Dr. Blatz and two of his associates, describes the development of spoken language in the Dionne quintuplets and compares it with the language development of single children and twins. Dr. Blatz, who was the director of the University of Toronto's Institute of Child Study for many years, died in 1964. He was the author of numerous books on child psychology, the best known of which are The Five Sisters *(1938) and* Understanding the Young Child *(1944).*

The acquisition of language has always been considered a prognostic sign of the subsequent intellectual development of the individual although it is not an infallible sign, pro or con. This function is so important that any delay or distortion or absence handicaps the individual not only psychologically but economically and socially.

In this study, although special emphasis is placed upon the vocal aspect of language, i.e., speech, the term language is employed in the title because the whole matter of "communication" is under scrutiny.

At the age of 12 months it was apparent that the Quintuplets were slow in vocal language development. The understanding of spoken language and language responses occupy, in intelligence testing, more and more prominent a place with increasing age so that a low score is inevitable under circumstances of delay in this function. For this reason, arrangements were made immediately to keep records of vocalization so that the whole developmental process could be studied.

Although some excellent studies have appeared upon the early speech sounds of children, there still seems to be some difference of opinion as to the earliest sounds enunciated and the age at which the various sounds appear. Foulke and Stinchfield[2] in a study of four children state that six articulate sounds appeared before the seventh month. Taine[3] pointed out that vowels alone were noticed up to three and a half months but that all sounds were noted by the twelfth month. Moore[4] claims that all sounds were uttered by the fourth month. Fenton[5] reports all English sounds, except *f* and *v*, during the first year but Hall[6] says all but *l*, *f*, and *s* before the 25th month. Kenyères[7] places two years as the limit for all French sounds. Pollock[8] noted that all sounds but *l*, final *t* and *p* have appeared before the 19th month. Tracy[9] claims that syllables are sounded before the sixth month.

A great deal of the difference of opinion arises from the difficulty in recording sounds. The English phonetic equivalents are applicable to spoken English and account for all *English* words but for French some new symbols are added, and for Russian and so on. Furthermore anyone who has listened to a child vocalizing knows that sounds are heard which perhaps have appeared in *no* articulate language. It is quite apparent that of the infinite gradation and tone (vowels), and variety of interruptions of sounds (consonants), that an infant uses, only a very few are selected for use in spoken language. Language is capable of infinite variation in complexity but the more complex it is the more difficult it is to acquire. The simple phonetic system of the Hawaiians which has fourteen consonants and all long vowels is an example of an early language system. The average man would rather add new meanings to words already laden with meaning than invent a new phonetic response pattern. Witness the use of and the variety of meanings that are added to "oh yeah". To be sure the inflection changes but the phonetics remain constant; all of which leads us back to the conclusion that the recording of sounds is difficult and that undoubtedly many of the articulations of the children in this study were omitted. However, the English and French sounds were certainly recorded and since we were concerned here with the development of the language of the Quintuplets as compared with single children, and not with the general theme of the origin of language, the data were probably equally reliable, as concerned the five children and the control group (see below) and hence comparable.

Method

Beginning at the 12th month, observations of speech sounds were made and recorded. The staff in charge of the children, all of whom spoke English and

[1]Acknowledgement is made to Mrs. J. Denison who drew the charts; to Miss A.L. Harris and Miss H.Shepherd who assisted with the tabulation; to Miss M. Poppleton and Miss J.Gillies, who edited the text and the tables; and also to Miss Alison Ewart of the University of Toronto Press.

[2] Foulke, Katharine and Stinchfield, Sara M. The Speech Development of Four Infants under Two Years of Age. *Ped. Sem. & J. Genet, Psychol.*, 1929, *36* 140-71.

[3]Taine, M. The Acquisition of Language by Children, *Mind*, 1877, *2*, 252-9.

[4]Moore, Kathleen Carter. The Mental Development of A Child. *Psychol. Monog.*, 1895-7 *1*, no. 3, 150.

[5]Fenton, Jessie Chase. *A Practical Psychology of Babyhood: The Mental Development and Mental Hygiene of the First Two Years of Life.* Boston, Houghton Mifflin, 1925, pp. xvi, 348.

[6]Hall, Mrs. Winfield S. The First Five Hundred Days of a Child's Life. *V. Child Study Monthly*, 1896-7, *2*, 586-608. *20*, 191-218.

[7]Kenyeres E. Les premiers mots de l'enfant et l'apparition des espèces de mots dans son langage. *Arch. de psychol.*, 1927, *20*, 191-218.

[8]Pollock, F. An Infant's Progress in Language. *Mind*, 1878, *3*, 392-401.

[9]Tracy, Frederick.*The Psychology of Childhood*. 3d ed. Boston, D.C. Heath, 1895, pp. xiii, 170 (pp. 114-51).

French, kept a record of every new sound which they heard the child utter. In order to be able to identify the sound later, because transcription of sounds is a difficult art, a word was placed beside the symbol in brackets to indicate the value of the vowels or consonants recorded. No special time was set aside for speech recording since the variety of sounds, rather than their frequency of use, was being considered.

In this manner the development of new sounds, syllables, and words was recorded. Three members of staff (and at regular times the authors) all kept records and as these records were filed away there were a great number of duplicates, but it was felt that by this means a more accurate picture of the developing pattern was obtained.

These data were then transcribed to a chart divided into vertical columns, one for each month, and the sounds were entered as spelled, and below each sound was placed its vocal equivalent. It was thus easy to see at a glance what sound was uttered, whether vowel or combination, and in which month it was first recorded. Later the combination of vowels and consonants into syllables appeared, and finally words. The development of sentence construction and use is left for a later study.

Data collected by observing a control group of 17 children (13 single, 4 twins) are included in this study as comparable material. These children attended St. George's Nursery School and the language development was recorded in the manner above by the parents who had been instructed by a member of the staff. There are included only the data on the first 12 months which were missing in the Quintuplet records. Since the data collected on the Quintuplets are more reliable, the later development of the control group was not included.

Order of appearance of vowels

Control Group			*Quintuplets*		
	Earliest	Latest		Earliest	Latest
true	1st month	6th month	car	12th month	13th month
bush			about		
sit			true		
hat			hat		
late			lie		
car			note		
get			sit		
but			get		
lie			free		
note			bush		
about			law		
free			late		
law	3rd month	13th month.	but	13th month	22nd month

Order of appearance of consonants

Control Group			*Quintuplets*		
	Earliest	Latest		Earliest	Latest
go	1st month	10th month	yet	12th month	15th month
me			row		
be			hay		
do			do		
no			me		
hay			no		
row			be		
lay			key		
we			pie		
key			go		
tea			lay		
no*se*			tea		
jay			th		
fee			we		
yet			see		
th			ch		
see			no*se*		
ng			jay		
vie			sh		
sh			vie		
pie			fee		
ch			ng		(had not
wh	9th month	13th month	wh	39th month	appeared)

Results

First Appearance of Sounds

As has been noted by most authors, vowels appeared before consonants.

Wellman[10] gives the following as the easier vowels to pronounce – fr*ee*, *a*bout, tr*ue*, and tr*y*. The Quintuplets approximate this order of ease of pronunciation by order of appearance, more closely than the control. The correlation in rank order of month of appearance of the sound, between the Quintuplets and the control group, is + .30. Since the early development of the Quintuplets was not included, the correlation is low. But there is also the consideration that these children were learning French and the control group English. The vowel sounds are quite different in the two; thus the *a* sound in *a*bout is second in order of appearance in the Quintuplets and eleventh in the control, while the *u* sound in b*u*sh was second in the control[11] and tenth in the Quintuplets. The *a* sound in l*a*te is much earlier in the control group.

To see whether the difference in the spoken language which the children heard was a factor in determining the order of appearance of sounds, the consonants were also arranged in order of appearance.

The rank correlation between the Quintuplets and controls of the appearance of the consonants is + .67. But if the three sounds *y*, *p*, and *g* are eliminated the rank correlation would be + .90. *Y* appeared earliest in the Quintuplets as a sound, *ya ya ya* in crying, and does not appear until much later in an articulated syllable. In the control group this crying sound is never reported as *ya* in the first 12 months. *G* appears as the first consonant sound in the control group and tenth in the Quintuplets and *p* appears in the twenty-eighth rank in the controls and eighth in the Quintuplets.

[10]Wellman, Beth, L.; Case, Ida Mae; Mengert, Ida Garder; Bradbury, Dorothy E. *Speech Sounds of Young Children*. Published by the University, Iowa City, 1931.

[11]Blanton, Margaret Gray. The Behaviour of the Human Infant during the First Thirty Days of Life. *Psychol. Rev.*, 1917, *24*, 456-83, – also reports the *u* in b*u*sh as an early sound in English children.

The order of ease in accuracy of pronunciation of consonants as given by Wellman is *t, p, b, m, n, f, p, d, h, w, g, k*. These all appear in the first half of the rank order except *f* and *p* for the control and *f* and *w* for the Quintuplets.[12]

Since consonant sounds are more common to languages than vowel sounds, one would expect the correlation between the Quintuplets and controls to be higher than with the vowels. This may indicate that the order of appearance of a sound is a function of the sounds heard, rather than the ease with which they are produced.

Speed of Acquisition

The order of appearance of sounds seems to be vowels, syllables, words, and then sentences. Starting at an early age the child duplicates a sound or syllable two to seven times, *e.g., da da da da,* and this persists till well after words begin to be used. This is not strictly a "language" habit but more a practice in vocalizing comparable to finger excersises in music. Graph 1 shows the cumulative record of the five children in the use of syllables. Starting at the 12th month, when from 8 to 23 different syllables were employed by each child, the new syllables were added to the previous number every month so that at any time the number of syllables used or having been used by each child is represented by the distance of the point on the curve above the ordinate. There is a slow gradual increase in the number of syllables used by all children up to about the 22nd month, after which there is an acceleration which is maintained. Also, although the rank order of the children is not widely separated at first, the divergence increases so that at 36 months Yvonne is definitely at the top, Annette in second place, Emilie third, and Cecile and Marie equal. This final rank order of the children is comparable to the mental rating[13] but the separation between the five is much more marked.

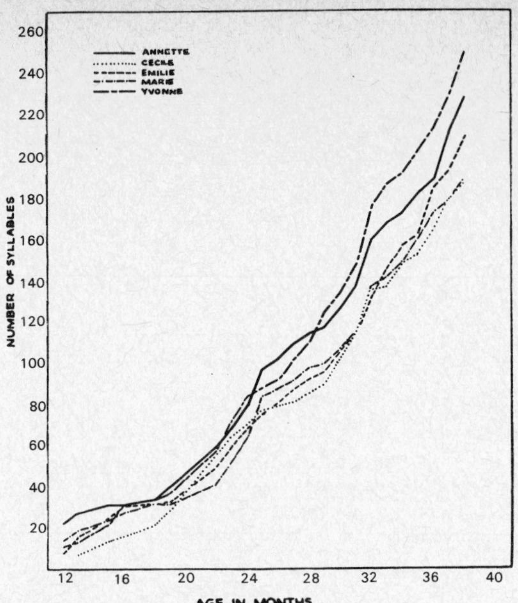

Graph 1. Progress in syllablization.

Compared with the control group the children are retarded in the use of syllables because at the 12th month they are at the point in the development curve reached by the single child control group at five to six months. But if the four twins' score for syllables is observed (Graph 3), the Quintuplets are at the eight to nine month level (especially Yvonne). Although there are only four twins in the control group, their rate of progress in the appearance of vowels, as well as frequency in the use of syllables, is reliably lower than in the record of the single children.

Words

Words appear later than single or duplicated syllables. Bateman[14] states that the first words appear at the 10th month. These words are usually reduplications, *e.g., mama, dada, papa, bébé.* He states further that 74.28% of his group (35 children) began articulate speech before the end of the first year. O'Shea[15] confirms this statement. Drummond[16] says that specific sounds are uttered at the 15th month; by this is meant that deliberate communication of meaning is intended. McCarthy[17] implies

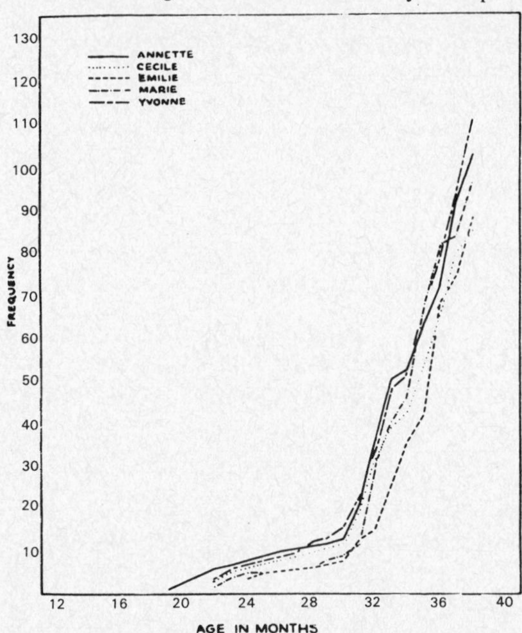

Graph 2. Accumulative record of new words used by Dionne quintuplets.

[12] Both Fenton and Hall (*op. cit.*) state that the "f" sound is late in appearing.

[13] Blatz, W. E. and Millichamp, D.A. *The Mental Growth of the Dionne Quintuplets.* Univ. of Toronto Studies, Child Development Series, no. 12; Univ. of Toronto Press, 1937.

[14] Bateman, W.G. Papers on Language Development. I. The First Word. *Ped. Sem.*, 1917, *24*, 391-8.

[15] O'Shea, M.V. *Linguistic Development and Education.* New York, Macmillan Co., 1907.

[16] Drummond, Margaret. Notes on Speech Development. *I. Child Study,* 1916, *9*, 83-6.

[17] McCarthy, Dorothea A. *The Language Development of the Preschool Child.* Minneapolis, Univ. of Minnesota Press, 1930. Monograph Series, no. 4.

that between the 18th and 54th month the child becomes interested in the meaning of sentences.

The first five words used by the Quintuplets were – *papa, mama, tantan, dotteur* (docteur), *tit-tat*.

The first five words used by the control group were – *dada, mama, tata, bye-bye, mum*. It is reasonable to suppose that there are not, strictly speaking, "meaningful" words at this age but merely automatized reduplicated syllables fixed by the attention which the adult pays to them. Note *dotteur* in the Quintuplets which did not appear at all in the control group. This word was pronounced and emphasized by the fact that Dr. Dafoe has been the "father-substitute" owing to his more than daily visits to his five charges.

At the 19th month Annette began to use words and by the 22nd month all were using a few. There is a slow increase in the number of words used or articulated till about the 32nd month when the acceleration increases remarkably, until by the 38th month the curve is ascending almost vertically. Note that the increased acceleration in the use of words is much later than the acceleration in the use of syllables, 22nd-32nd month. There is a ten-month lag which indicates that the mere joining of syllables is not the mechanism by which words are formed. Meanings must be added. The child must have something to say before he *says* it. He *can* say it prior to this.

The same lag in the use of words is shown in Graph 3. This graph does not show the acceleration period in either curve because it apparently does not appear until the second year, but the slopes of the two curves are quite disparate, showing, as above, that the progress in using words is a different mechanism from the simple enunciation of syllables. Note the delay in the twins as compared with the single children.

An analysis of the words used by the Quintuplets shows some curious relationships.

(a) The words were arranged according to initial sounds and of the 185 words used 106 began with 5 of the letters *p, b, d, m, t,* in this order; of these *b* and *d* ranked first in order of first appearance (see above), *m* second, *t* sixth, and *p* eighth. With the control group, of the 47 different words, *d, b, p, t, g* accounted for 30 in this order; *g* was the first consonant in order of appearance, *b* third, *d* fourth, *t* eleventh, *p* twenty-first.

In order to determine whether any one child was initiating the language habits, since imitation of environmental sounds is so important, the number of times that a child spoke a word one month ahead of the others, was calculated.

Annette	Emilie	Yvonne
12	8	6
Cecile	Marie	
5	6	

In addition there were words which were used by one child only and did not appear in any other child's record.

Annette	Emilie	Yvonne
17	15	24
Cecile	Marie	
10	16	

Obviously some of these *only* words may have been left out of the records of one or other of the children but there is no reason to suppose that one child was more or less favoured than another. Annette serves as the imitatee twice as often as the other four. This corresponds to her rank in social contacts. She is most aggressive, shows most initiated *to* contacts, and is watched most.[18] Yvonne has the most "unique" words. But Yvonne's position is due to a spurt in the last two months, for it may be seen from Graph 2 that Annette has actually given leadership in use of words throughout the early months.

Single Children vs. Twin Births

There is a wide variation among all children in the date at which they begin talking. There is also a difference of opinion among authors as to the distinction between controlled vocalization and reflex crying, and syllables and reduplicated syllables and words, and word sentences and syntax, *etc.*, so that the literature is not clear on the influence of multiple births on talking.

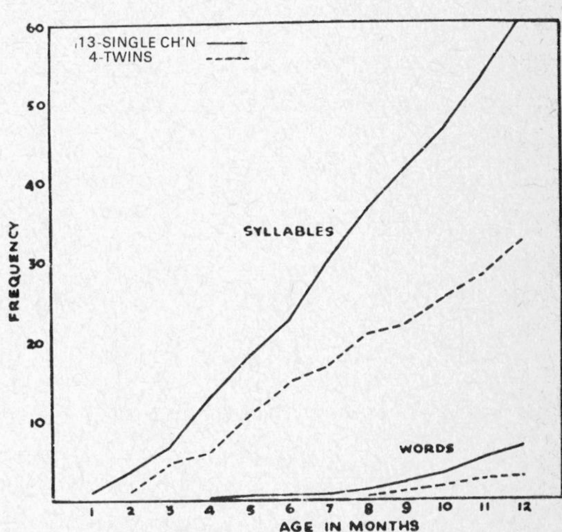

Graph. 3. Development in use of syllables and words – control group.

Day,[19] in her excellent paper on a comparison of twins and single children, observed 80 pairs of twins and 160 single children and gives the following re-

[18]Blatz, W. E., Millichamp, D.A., and Charles, M.W. *The Early Social Development of the Dionne Quintuplets.* Univ. of Toronto Studies, Child Development Series, no. 13; Univ. of Toronto Press, 1937.

[19]Day, Ella J. The Development of Language in Twins. *Child Development, 3,* 1932.

sults on the number of words used at the ages indicated:

C.A.	Single	Twins
24 (mos.)	66	55
36	170	114
48	216	146
60	...	158

Thus the twins are retarded as late as the fifth year in this respect.

The data on the control group in this paper are not extensive but the records are relatively reliable and comparable. The records of the twins (2 pairs) and the single children (13), all of the same age and all above 100 I.Q., show (Graph 3) that the twins are definitely retarded in the use of syllables and words not only in beginning but in actual progress of development. To test whether *all* the twins were slow in speech as compared with the 13 single children, the age of each child at the appearance of each sound was compared with the average age, and recorded as early or late.

	13 Singles		4 Twins	
	Early	Late	Early	Late
Consonants	139	160	22	70
Vowels	101	68	26	26

Thus the twins showed a retarded rate of *initiating* the sounds also. The five Quintuplets are, of course, much more delayed in speech than the twins observed in the study by Day, who reports a delay of about 2 to 4 months at 24 months. The twins of this study are about three months retarded in syllables and about six months in words as compared with the single children.

Compared with the single children in the control group, the Quintuplets are about 6 to 8 months retarded for syllables and in words about 16 to 18 months. Taking Day's norm of 66 words at 24 months for single children, it is seen that the Quintuplets did not reach this level till 32 to 33 months, showing a retardation of 16 to 18 months.

One may conclude that if twins are retarded because of their early contemporary social life then Quintuplets should show this same effect, only more pronounced. The *need* for communication may be satisfied other than by spoken and articulate speech. Gestures and grunts are sufficient for the needs of young children. When the need for adult communication arises then the speech must be more articulate. This may explain why the words lag behind syllables even after the process of word articulation has begun. The mechanism is ready but there is no need for it to function. The gestures of the Quintuplets are remarkably expressive and hence we may conclude that their retardation in speech is due to (a) the care which they received in which most demands were met before the need for asking arose, and (b) their intercommunication among themselves which was sufficiently skilled without the use of language.

For whatever reason, the Quintuplets show a marked delay in "talking". That it was delay rather than retardation is indicated by the slope of the progress in development after a slow beginning.[20]

The Quintuplets are now being taught English since they live in a bilingual environment and the progress of the development of English and French will be observed.[21]

Summary

The Quintuplets were slow in starting to use syllables and words, as compared with the control group of 13 single children.

Two sets of twins who were observed have a position between these two groups above.

The suggestion is made that the speech development of the Quintuplets is slow by reason of the same factors that cause twins to talk later than single children, but magnified by the fact that there are five.

---

[20] *Cf.* Wellmann, B.L. *et al.* (*op. cit.*): "With C.A. constant the correlation, between M.A. and the ability to pronounce, is .24±.08; the correlation, between C.A. and the ability to give the proper pronunciation, is .80±.03; thus the C.A. of the child is a more important function than mental development." One may conclude that the Quintuplets, because of the lack of stimulation and hence practice, and their lesser need for language are delayed rather than retarded.

[21] *Cf.* McCarthy, D.A. (*op. cit.*): "bilingualism does not seem to be a serious handicap in linguistic development."

21 / Verbal Satiation and Changes in the Intensity of Meaning[1]

Wallace E. Lambert and Leon A. Jakabovits *McGill University*

If a word such as "apple" is repeated continuously, that word begins to lose its meaning. In this experiment, a method of measuring loss of meaning (semantic satiation) is investigated. The results indicate that semantic satiation can be measured reliably and that the loss of meaning is not due to fatiguing of the peripheral muscular mechanisms involved in speech.

Several investigators have demonstrated that *S*s experience a change or loss of meaning for words which have been continuously repeated or fixated for a certain period of time (Basette and Warne, 1919; Mason, 1941; Smith and Raygor, 1956; Wertheimer and Gillis, 1956). For instance, Basette and Warne (1919) reported that the meanings of familiar nouns which were repeated aloud "dissipated" for their *S*s within 3 or 4 sec. More recently, it was found that if *S*s fixated a word exposed on a screen for 20 sec., their first association to the word is uncommon as measured by the Kent-Rosanoff Word Association Test (Smith and Raygor, 1956). The lapse or radical change of the meaning of a word as a result of its continued repetition is known as verbal satiation. Before the full implication of this concept for theories of learning and meaning can be determined, it is necessary to develop a method for reliably measuring the extent of meaning change which can be attributed to the satiation experience. The purpose of the present study is to extend the significance of the concept of verbal satiation by introducing a more comprehensive method of measuring the phenomenon and thereby relating it to a contemporary theory of meaning.

Osgood, Suci, and Tannenbaum (1957) have proposed an objective and reliable instrument for the measurement of certain aspects of connotative meaning. This instrument, the "semantic differential," consists of a series of scales each representing a 7-point, bipolar dimension. The meaning of a word, such as "father," is given by its position on an evaluative factor (its degree of goodness or badness), on an activity factor, and on a potency factor. The theory underlying this method assumes that the meaning of a word has a place in a multidimensional semantic space. A word without meaning would rest at the point of origin for all dimensions. Each scale has three degrees of polarity (see Jenkins, 1959) which describe the appropriate placement of the word along the scale. The middle position indicates lack of applicability of the word to either polar adjective, or "meaninglessness" on one dimension. A semantic profile is illustrated in Table I.

Table I – Illustration of a semantic profile

	Father							
Good	X		Y					Bad
Strong				Y	X			Weak
Passive					Y	X		Active
	3	2	1	0	1	2	3	

Note. – *S* rates the concept "father" by indicating on each scale the position considered most appropriate. The polarity score in the present example is 6 for the X ratings and 2 for the Y ratings. The polarity-difference score for this example using one concept and three scales is -4, indicating that the second ratings (Ys) moved 4 scale units closer to the zero point.

In the present studies, the semantic differential is used as a method of indexing changes in meaning induced by means of verbal repetition of words. The study was carried out in several independent steps and the present report describes two separate experiments.

Experiment I

If *S* is requested to indicate the placement of a word on a semantic dimension immediately after continuous repetition of the word, his responses should fall on the zero point of the dimension of a total lapse of meaning has occurred. The semantic differential permits one to assess decreases of meaning short of total lapses. Thus, if under normal conditions *S* considers the word "father" and assigns it to Position 1 on an evaluative dimension ("extremely good") and then, after continuous repetition of the word (father) assigns it to Position 3 ("slightly good"), we will

[1]This research was supported in part by the Canadian Defence Research Board Grant D77-9401-10. We are particularly grateful to C.E. Osgood for his assistance and advice in the planning as well as the presentation of this study. R.C. Gardner and D.O. Hebb helped us by their suggestions and criticisms.

infer, when consideration is given to various controls, that the connotative meaning of the concept "father" has decreased (by about two-thirds) on this dimension.

Procedure
Three groups of college students were tested individually under several different conditions. As each *S* (with the exception of those in the retest control group, see below) came to the experimental room, he was asked to fill out a booklet in which he rated five words (child, me, rich, truth, family), each one on nine semantic scales (three scales for each of the three most prominent factors determined by Osgood et al., 1957). Then each *S*, depending on the condition to which he was assigned, followed a procedure outlined below. Each of the five words and each scale was printed on a separate 5 X 3-in. card. The cards were placed in a Kardex folder so that *E* could expose them in a predetermined order.

Experimental satiation. – For each of the 22 *S*s in this group, a word was first exposed for about 1 sec. and *S* was asked to say the word aloud for 15 sec. at a rate of 2-3 repetitions per second. Then *E* immediately exposed a scale and *S* made his rating by pointing to one of the positions on the 7-point dimension. This was done for all words on all scales, a total of 45 responses per *S*. The order of presentation maximized the separation of the reoccurence of each word and each scale. The initial and final ratings were subsequently compared.

Silence control. – The same procedure was used with 19 other *S*s with the exception of one change: the *S*s did not repeat aloud the words during the 15-sec. interval which elapsed between the time of exposure of the word and the semantic rating. They were initially instructed to "sit and wait" until a dimension was presented. No reference to "thinking about" the word presented was made in the instructions.

Different-word control. – The same 19 *S*s participating in the previous phase also took part in this second control condition. Four additional words (war, death, teacher, athlete) were added to the booklet which was completed at the beginning of the experimental session. Using the same general procedure, the *S*s repeated aloud a particular word during the time interval, but were then presented with a different word to rate. For example, the word "key" was exposed (the words used for repetition in this case were: key, moon, shoe, and book) and *S* repeated it aloud for 15 sec.; then the word "war" was exposed, read out loud by *S* who immediately gave a semantic rating on "war." This control condition was introduced to determine what effect the act of repeating words aloud had upon the stability of the ratings. Whereas the previous condition is a "unfilled-interval" control, the present condition is a "filled-interval" control.

Retest Control. – The 22 *S*s in this group did not fill out a booklet at the start of the experiment. In this case, ratings were taken immediately after the exposure of the words, with no repetition or interval interposed. Furthermore, after the first 45 ratings were obtained, the same complete series was repeated, and the ratings for the two series were compared.

Results
Mean polarity-difference scores were computed for each *S*. These represent the changes in degree of polarization (see Table I) from the first testing under normal conditions and the second testing under experimental or control conditions. The changes are presented as average changes per word summed over all scales (in this case, nine). Thus, one *S* with a mean polarity-difference score of -3.6 had a total polarity score for the first testing of 102 (based on 45 ratings, 5 words on 9 scales) compared to 84 for the second testing under the satiation condition. The difference between these two totals, or 18, is 3.6 scale unit changes per word. A minus sign indicates a change from a higher to a lower score, i.e., a decrease in the intensity of association between the word and the bipolar adjective. Values of zero would indicate no change and positive scores would indicate an increase in intensity of connotative meaning.

Table II shows that the decrease in the intensity of meaning occuring under the experimental satiation condition was significantly greater than zero. Tests of significance between the experimental and control conditions on meaning change are presented in Table III. The differences between the experimental and each of the three control conditions are significant, while none of the differences among the control conditions reaches significance. We conclude, therefore, that the decrease of meaning (verbal satiation) obtained with the experimental treatment is attributable to the continuous repetition of the word just before semantic ratings were made, and not to either of three other possible features of the experiment, namely, the unreliability of the measuring instrument, the 15-sec. interval period, or the interpolated task of repetition.

Table II – Average change in polarity per word over the sum of 9 scales: Exp. I

Condition	*Change in Polarity*			
	N	Mean	*SD*	*t*
Satiation	22	−2.85	2.93	4.45*
Silence control	19	0.03	1.41	0.09
Diff.-word control	19	−0.66	1.91	1.46
Retest control	22	−0.21	0.73	1.31

* Significantly different from zero beyond the .01 level.

Table III – *H* Tests of significance between conditions: Exp. I

Condition	Silence Control	Diff.-Word Control	Retest Control
Satiation	12.83	6.56	11.10
Silence control	–	0.92	0.69
Diff.-word control	–	–	0.03

Note – If $H > 6.63, P \leqslant .01$; if $H < 3.84, P > .05$.

Examination of the data reveals that verbal repetition of a word may lead to small decreases of meaning as well as total lapses. In fact, when we calculate scores which each *S* would have obtained had there occurred a total loss of meaning, the obtained scores represent only 21% of those values that would have been obtained had there occurred a total loss of meaning as measured by the semantic differential. It is left for further studies to determine what amount of repetition would yield maximum satiation effects.

The results are consistent with Osgood's (1953, p. 410 ff.) interpretation of meaning. In this framework, the meaning of a symbol (or sign) is some replica of the actual reactions elicited by the environmental event which serves as a referent for the sign. These mediating reactions should follow the same principles as any other response. During verbal repetition, the mediating reactions are repeatedly and rapidly elicited. Under such circumstances we would expect that a form of reactive inhibition would be generated which would temporarily decrease the availability of the mediators. Since Osgood's semantic differential is designed to index the strength as well as the kind of mediating reactions elicited by a sign, the development of inhibition during verbal repetition should be exhibited as a decrease in the extremeness of the ratings on the semantic differential, as indeed the present experiment has demonstrated.

The second experiment to be described was meant to replicate the above findings and to study further the nature of mediating reactions. One might argue that the changes in intensity of meaning noted above may be due in large part to the muscular components of the act of continuous verbal repetition. The following study bears directly on this point.

Experiment II

For Osgood, the mediation process is the meaning of a symbol. He leaves the question open as to the possible locus (loci) of the mediational responses. They may be peripheral ("muscular or glandular reactions") (Osgood, 1953, p. 697) or central ("purely neural responses") (Osgood, 1957, p. 7). In this study, we presume that the mediation process that transmits significance to a symbol is inhibited by the continual verbal repetition of that symbol. The fact that the satiation effect was noted only for the experimental *S*s, those who continuously repeated a symbol before it was rated, suggests that the mediation process may in large part be dependent on muscular reactions. In order to test the comparative importance of peripheral and central components of mediation processes, one might compare the behaviour of the experimental *S*s described above with another group of *S*s who would be directed to "think about the word presented" but not to repeat it aloud. Should such a group display the satiation effect, however, one could still argue that they actually had said the words subvocally and no conclusive evidence would be given either the central or peripheral possibilities.

We attempted to circumvent this ambiguity by using another procedure which indirectly tests the comparative influence of peripheral responses and a central cognitive process on verbal satiation. We assume that saying aloud a meaningful word involves both muscular-glandular activity as well as some more central cognitive response as the meaningful nature of the symbol is registered. On the other hand, saying aloud a meaningless word with low association value involves peripheral muscular response accompanied by diversified cognitive acitvity, such as searching for possible significance in the word or associations with the sound or form of the word, etc. In the case of the meaningful word, there is a relation between the peripheral and cognitive activities which is mediated by the meaning of the symbol. We argue that the cognitive acitvity is only distantly or not identifiably related to the peripheral in the case of the saying aloud of a meaningless word. The muscular reactions brought into play in the continual repetition of the words "canoe" and "nuka" (with the accent on the first syllable) are identical. (This assertion is supported by the fact that a listener cannot determine whether *S* is repeating "canoe" or "nuka", once the sequence of repetition is underway. The fact that the original peripheral feedback of the sequence "nu-ka-nu-ka" is different from that of the sequence "ca-noe-ca-noe" does not invalidate the present argument since the rest of the two sequences are essentially identical, and hence both should have the same effect on the peripheral responses.) The representational mediating processes which are elicited in the two situations, however, must be quite different since only one is a meaningful English word. The peripheral theory maintains that motor responses are both necessary and sufficient for thinking. Thus, the continuous repetition of "nuka" and "canoe", involving identical muscular reactions, should have a similar satiation effect on the meaning of "canoe." For Osgood, whether the mediators are peripheral or central, they are *not* of the same form as the overt verbal response, since their character depends entirely upon the total reactions made to the thing signified and not the mediated verbalization. Since thinking of "ca-noe-ca-noe" and of "nu-ka-nu-ka" involve different cortical processes, repetition of "nuka" should not lead to satiation of "canoe."

Procedure

Twenty-three *S*s (male and female public school teachers enrolled in a summer school) were tested under three different conditions. These are described below.

Satiation. – The procedure was identical with that used in the experimental satiation condition in Experiment I, except that words and scales have been changed. The purpose of this condition was to attempt to reproduce the results obtained previously as well as to serve as a comparison condition to the other two conditions described below.

Peripheral control. – The "centrality" hypothesis was tested by requiring *S*s to repeat the words "grony" (accent on second syllable)) and "nuka" before semantic ratings of the words "negro" and "canoe," respectively. The procedure was thus identical with the Different-Word Control in Experiment I. At the end of the experiment each *S* was asked whether he had "caught on" to the fact that "grony" and "nuka" were actually "negro" and "canoe" repeated backwards.

Nonsense control. – The effect of the repetition of a nonsense word on semantic ratings was determined by having *S*s repeat "troga" and "blatu" before ratings of "house" and "soldier."

There were six words used in all (two words for each condition) and eight scales, six of these representing the three standard factors, and two scales representing a Familiarity factor (meaningful-meaningless; comprehensible-incomprehensible). The ratings given for the last factor were separately analyzed and will be discussed below.

Each *S* took part in three testings. The first was an assessment of *S*'s meaning of words under normal conditions. The words and scales were individually exposed in the Kardex folder and responses were recorded by *E* (no booklets were used in this experiment). The second testing consisted of the three conditions described above. The third testing, identical with the first, was given a rest period of 5 min. to determine whether the satiation effect dissipates with time.

Results

The polarity-difference scores in Table IV are averages for the group and represent mean changes of polarity per word on all six scales (absolute values cannot be compared with those in Table II since a different number of scales was used in Experiments I and II). Entries under the Exp. column are differences in polarity scores between the first and second testing, whereas entries under the Dissipation column are differences in polarity scores between first and third testings. It can be seen that the only significant changes in meaning took place under the Satiation condition. The possibility exists that the failure to obtain a satiation effect in the Peripheral Control and Nonsense Control conditions was due to the fact that the initial polarity of the particular words used under these conditions was already low, and hence could not decrease further. We therefore have calculated the mean initial polarity per word over the sum of six scales, as measured during the first testing, of all three conditions. These were as follows: 8.89 for the Satiation condition, 8.76 for the Peripheral Control and 9.17 for the Nonsense Control. None of these means was significantly different from another when a signed rank test was applied. It is evident, then, that differences in initial polarity of the ratings cannot account for the obtained results.

Table V shows that there is no significant difference between the Exp. and Dissipation scores under

Table IV – Average change in polarity per word over the sum of 6 scales: Exp.II ($N = 23$)

Condition	Experimental			Dissipation		
	Mean	*SD*	*t*	Mean	*SD*	*t*
Satiation	-1.95	2.06	4.43*	-1.76	2.11	3.91*
Peripheral control	0.19	1.37	0.65	-0.02	1.17	0.08
Nonsense control	-0.06	1.22	0.23	0.45	2.05	1.02

* Significantly different from zero at the .01 level.

Table V – *H* Tests of significance between conditions: Exp. II

Condition	Satiation, Exp.	Peripheral Control, Exp.	Nonsense Control, Dissip.
Satiation, Exp.	–	13.78	–
Satiation, Dissip.	0.21	–	10.14
Peripheral control, Dissip.	–	0.71	0.75
Nonsense control, Exp.	11.96	0.81	1.35

Note. – If $H > 6.63, P \leqslant .01$; if $H < 3.84, P > .05$.

the Satiation condition, suggesting that the loss of meaning as a result of repetition persisted after a 5-min. rest (the mean dissipation score for the group obtained by subtracting the Exp. from the Dissipation scores is 0.19 ($t = 0.35$). The other differences in Table V are in harmony with a centrality hypothesis of meaning.

All but one of the 23 *S*s reported that they became aware of the fact that "grony" and "nuka" were actually "negro" and "canoe" repeated backwards. It appears from *S*s' reports that repetition of "grony," even though it involves the same muscular reactions, was not the same task as repetition of "negro." As one *S* put it, "When I was repeating 'grony' I was trying not to think of 'negro.' But when I was repeating 'father' I kept on thinking of 'father.'" Translating this into our terminology, we can say that, given instructions to repeat "grony," the mediating processes identified with "negro" were not consistently and reliably elicited. In view of these findings, we contend that in order to satiate the meaning of a symbol through continuous repetition one must consistently call into play some particular cognitive activity which is related to the symbol.

Discussion

The continuous repetition of words reduces the intensity of their connotative meanings. The effect appears to be reliable and to persist for at least a period of 5 min. The effect also appears to depend on a consistent reactivation of some type of cognitive activity which is related to the word repeated. We conceptualize this phenomenon as a type of "semantic satiation" and consider the findings as support for a central interpretation of representational mediation processes.

The results show that by dint of continuous verbal repetition of words the semantic ratings *S*s made moved closer to the point of meaninglessness on the scales. It is not clear from the above results whether the satiation effect is restricted solely to the words which are repeated or if the effect is generalized, affecting the intensity of meaning of both the words and the bipolar adjectives, as well as the task of making a judgment. The finding of a decrease in intensity of meaning across the standard semantic scales is not inconsistent with the notion of a generalized satiation effect; if the bipolar adjectives were also satiated, they would have contributed to the decrease in the degree of association between the repeated words and the adjectives. If it could be shown, however, that *S*s were also able to perceive increases in intensity of meaning on certain scales at the time of rating, we could argue that the inhibition effect is primarily restricted to the words which are repeated. As a test, we presented *S*s in Experiment II with two additional scales: "meaningful-meaningless" and "comprehensible-incomprehensible" and all words were rated along these scales as on the standard scales. These two scales should elicit a movement of ratings toward the "meaningless" and "incomprehensible" poles following the satiation treatment. Scores were assigned to *S*s for the amount of movement of ratings, comparing the first testing under normal conditions with the experimental and control condition testings, towards or away from the "meaningless" and "incomprehensible" poles. It was found that there was an average movement in the predicted direction of 1.43 scale units for the group under the satiation condition, a change which is reliably different from zero ($t = 3.25$, $P < .02$). No reliable change was noted for the other two control conditions ($t = 0.02$ for the satiation and peripheral control conditions and $t = 0.15$ for the satiation and nonsense control conditions).

One last point should be made about an alternative interpretation of our results; namely, that *S*s "caught on" to the fact that repetition of a word renders it less meaningful and consciously "played along" with *E* by making neutral judgements. There are several arguments against such an interpretation. Firstly, in the discussion which followed the experiment, *S*s were asked whether they thought that they had changed their judgements as the experiment went on and whether repetition influenced their ratings. The typical answers were "maybe" or "slightly," but the reason given for the change was "... because I forgot which judgement I had made previously." (In a current experiment using the same procedure, the question period at the end of the experiment was standardized and *S*s' answers were recorded. Only 1 out of 31 *S*s stated that repetition rendered the word more "meaningless." The typical answers were again "slight changes because I forgot what I had done before," or "... because I thought of something else.") Secondly, had *S*s wanted to please *E* by making neutral judgements, it is difficult to understand why they did not go all the way and give neutral ratings all the time. Thirdly, the dissipation scores in Experiment II exhibit the satiation effect on the words used under the Satiation condition only. Since the ratings of these words were mixed with those of the other conditions, it is improbable that *S*s could remember which were the satiation words and which were not. (In the current study mentioned above, only 3 *S*s could recall the words used for each condition.)

Summary

The phenomenon of verbal satiation – the decrease in the meaning of symbols – was studied by having college *S*s continuously repeat a word and then rate the word along scales of the semantic differential. Changes in semantic ratings, comparing normal and satiation conditions, indicate that there is a reliable movement of ratings toward the meaningless points of scales. Control group comparisons suggest that this movement is not due to the unreliability of the measuring instrument, to the time interval involved in repetition, nor to the activity of repetition per se. The phenomenon is conceptualized as a cognitive form of reactive inhibition and is related to Osgood's theory of representational mediation processes.

A second experiment sheds light on the nature of mediation processes, presenting evidence that they depend more on central than peripheral-muscular activities. In order to satiate the meaning of a symbol through continuous repetition, some particular cognitive activity which is related to the symbol must consistently be called into play. Further findings suggest that the satiation effect is not generalized but stems primarily from changes in the symbol which is continuously repeated.

References

BASETTE, M. F., and WARNE, C. J. On the lapse of verbal meaning with repetition. *Amer. J. Psychol.*, 1919, *30*, 415-418.

JENKINS, J. J. Degree of polarization and scores on the principal factors for concepts in the semantic atlas study. Studies of Verbal Behaviour, Rep. 1, Univer. Minnesota, 1959. (Mimeo.).

MASON, M. Changes in the galvanic skin response accompanying reports of changes in meaning during oral repetition. *J. gen. Psychol.*, 1941, *25*, 353-401.

OSGOOD, C. E. *Method and theory in experimental psychology*. New York: Oxford Univer. Press, 1953.

OSGOOD, C. E., SUCI, G. J., and TANNENBAUM, P. H. *The measurement of meaning*. Urbana: Univer. Illinois Press, 1957.

SMITH, D. E. P., and RAYGER, A. L. Verbal satiation and personality. *J. abnorm. soc. Psychol.*, 1956, *52*, 323-326.

WERTHEIMER, M., and GILLIS, W. M. Some determinants of the rate of lapse of verbal meaning. Paper read at Rocky Mountain Psychol. Assoc., Moran, Wyoming, 1956. (Mimeo.)

22 / The Effect of Word Abstractness and Pleasantness on Pupil Size During an Imagery Task[1]

Allan Paivio and Herb M. Simpson *University of Western Ontario*

The occurrence of pupillary changes during mental effort has been known since about 1900 but virtually no experimental interest was shown in this phenomenon until 1964 when Professor Eckhard Hess, of the University of Chicago, reported a correlation between the difficulty of arithmetic problems and the pupillary reactions they evoke. The following article is an example of the type of subsequent research which has been done on the relationship between pupillary changes and cognitive activity.

Another important finding is that pupil size can be influenced by the interest value of visual stimuli. This fact, it is important to note, has recently been put to some practical use by the advertising industry in the design of new products.

It is generally recognized that psychological factors are potent determinants of pupil size (Berrien and Huntington, 1943; Lowenstein and Loewenfeld, 1962; Sokolov, 1963). Hess and his co-workers found, specifically, that pupillary reactions are affected by the interest value of visual stimuli (Hess and Polt, 1960; Hess, Seltzer, and Shlien, 1965), difficulty of mental arithmetic problems (Hess and Polt, 1964), and pleasantness of stimuli (Hess, 1965). The present study investigated changes in pupil size when S attempts to generate "mental images" of objects or events suggested by stimulus words that vary in concreteness and pleasantness. Previous related research has indicated that concrete nouns elicit images more readily than do abstract nouns, presumably because of the more frequent association of concrete nouns with objective referents (e.g., Paivio, 1965; Paivio, in press). In view of the sensitivity of the pupillary reaction to cognitive activity, it was reasoned that the apparent difference in the image-evoking capacity of concrete and abstract terms should be reflected in differential pupillary reactions to the two classes of words. Hess's report that unpleasant stimuli evoked pupillary constriction whereas pleasant stimuli resulted in dilation suggested further that the pleasantness-unpleasantness of the words might have an effect.

Method

The stimuli were 12 nouns, six of which are relatively concrete and six abstract, as rated by the Es. The concrete nouns exceed the abstract in their capacity to evoke imagery, according to ratings obtained from 32 university students following Paivio's 1965) procedure, and half of each class are relatively pleasant and half unpleasant in meaning as judged by the same Ss using a 7-point pleasant-unpleasant scale. The concrete words were candy, honeycomb, pudding, blister, lice, mucous; the abstract words were charm, love, warmth, agony, disease, sadness.

In general, the procedure was to present each word visually to S, who was asked to imagine an object or event related to the word and to press a key when an image occurred. The words, on 35-mm negative slides, were projected on a ground glass screen at the back of a box-like compartment. S was seated at the front of the compartment, his head positioned in a head holder to standardize the distance between his eye and the screen at 60 cm. A motor-driven Bolex 16-mm movie camera was used to photograph S's right eye at a rate of 2 frames per sec. through an opening just below the screen. The camera was enclosed in a partially sound-insulated casing to reduce the sound of the camera shutter, and masking was also provided by continuous white noise fed through earphones. An interval timer controlled the inter-stimulus intervals and stimulus durations, and started a clock which recorded the key press used to indicate image arousal. A small light in the base of the lens of the camera went on during the inter-stimulus interval to identify the intervals by overexposing that portion of the movie film. Illumination during projection, provided by the projector and a 30-cm fluorescent tube, was such that pupil size (as assessed using pilot Ss) was "moderate" on the average, allowing for either dilation or constriction to occur. Eastman Kodak Tri-X reversal movie film (165 ASA) was used. To determine pupil size, the film was examined frame by frame using a 10 x 15-cm film editor, and the diameter of the pupil thus magnified was measured with a millimeter ruler.

Experiment 1 involved 14 adult Ss (8 males and 6

[1] This research was partially supported by grants from the National Research Council of Canada (Grant APA-87) and the University of Western Ontario Research Fund.

Reprinted, by permission, from *Psychonomic Science*, 1966, *5*, 55-56.

females) who were presented the words one at a time, following exposure to four practice words. Two different, random orders of presentation were used. The exposure duration to each word was 10 sec., resulting in 20 photographic frames per word. Six Ss in a control group were exposed to four blank slides equated in brightness with the word slides. Experiment II, involving 20 adult Ss (8 males and 12 females), employed essentially the same procedure with one major change: each word slide was preceded by a 10 sec. presentation of a blank slide of equal brightness, so that an appropriate within-S control was available for each word.

Results

In both experiments, pupil size was averaged over all words of a type (e.g., concrete-pleasant) as well as for the respective control conditions. The effects of pleasantness-unpleasantness were nonsignificant in both experiments (the crucial Fs from the analyses of variance were less than 1.00), and Fig. 1 (A and B) shows the function over time, i.e., photographic frames, only for concrete and abstract words and the control conditions. Average pupil size differed somewhat in the two experiments because a lower level of illumination was used in the second. Otherwise, the pattern of results was highly similar in both. The figure shows an initial pupillary constriction (the light reflex) to the presentation of a slide. The reaction to words is dilation followed by gradual reconstriction, and the dilation is apparently greater to

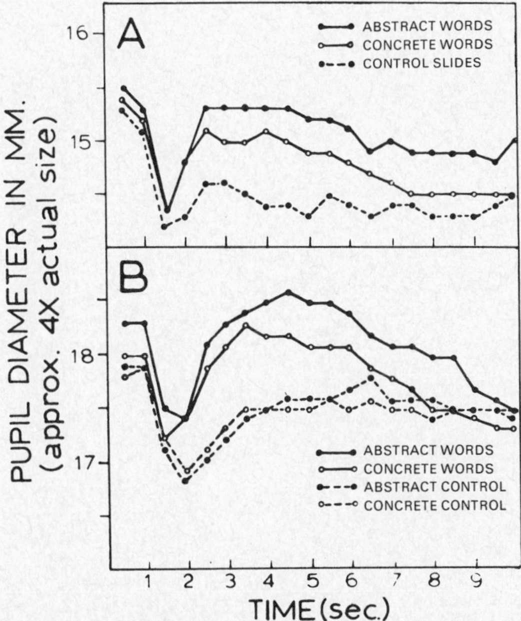

Fig. 1. Mean pupil size in two experiments for Ss viewing abstract and concrete words under imagery instructions, and when viewing blank control slides; Experiment I (A) involved a separate control group. Experiment II (B) involved within-S control conditions.

abstract than to concrete words. The curves for control conditions are flatter than those for words. These data were evaluated by analyses of variance for repeated measures.

Experiment I

The data from the 20 frames for the experimental group were collapsed into four equal time blocks, and analyzed with pleasantness, concreteness, and blocks as factors. Since the six control Ss were not part of the factorial design, their data were excluded from the analysis. The results showed that the blocks effect was significant ($F=5.18$, $df=3/39$, $p<.001$), and that the concrete-abstract difference approached significance ($F=4.24$, $df=1/13$, $p<.10$).

Experiment II

The data were again collapsed into four equal time blocks, and analyzed with stimulus conditions (words vs. blank slides), concreteness, pleasantness, and blocks as variables. The resulting main effects indicate a significant change over time blocks ($F=10.26$, $df=3/57$, $p<.001$), and that dilation was greater to words than to control slides ($F=47.11$, $df=1/19$, $p<.001$). The interaction of stimulus conditions by blocks ($F=10.30$, $df=3/57$, $p<.001$) indicated that the curves differed for words and control stimuli over time. Since the design included a within-S control condition, any effect of a word attribute would appear only as an interaction of that attribute and word vs. no word conditions. The interaction of stimulus conditions by concreteness was significant ($F=4.98$, $df=1/19$, $p<.05$), indicating that dilation was greater to abstract than to concrete words.

Discussion

The similarity in the results of the two experiments (Figure 1A and B) and the statistical analysis of the second reliably demonstrate that a S's pupils dilate when he attempts to generate mental images to stimulus words, and that the dilation is greater to abstract than to concrete words. This is not to say that the effect is necessarily due to a central neural process related specifically to imagery. Instead, it can be explained more parsimoniously as a general arousal effect, occurring when the task is cognitively more difficult (cf. Hess and Polt, 1964). So interpreted, the present findings provide physiological support for rating scale and reaction time data (e.g., Paivio, in press), which also have indicated that it is more difficult to generate images to abstract than to concrete words.

The failure to find a pleasant-unpleasant effect differs from Hess's findings for nonverbal visual stimuli. In addition to the difference in stimuli, however, the tasks used in the studies are different and it is possible that the imagery task may have inhibited any constriction that might have otherwise occurred to the unpleasant words.

Abstract

Findings from two studies demonstrate that a S's pupils dilate when he attempts to generate mental images to words. Dilation, which may reflect the cognitive difficulty of the imagery task, was greater to abstract than to concrete words, but did not vary with word pleasantness-unpleasantness.

References

BERRIEN, F. K., and HUNTINGTON, G. H. An exploratory study of pupillary responses during deception. *J. exp. Psychol.*, 1943, *32*, 443-449.

HESS, E. H. Attitude and pupil size. *Scient. American*, 1965, *212*, 46-54.

HESS, E. H., and POLT, J. M. Pupil size as related to interest value of visual stimuli. *Science*, 1960, *132*, 349-350.

HESS, E. H., and POLT, J. M. Pupil size in relation to mental acivity during simple problem solving. *Science*, 1964, *143*, 1190-1192.

HESS, E. H., SELTZER, A. L., and SHLIEN, J. M. Pupil response of hetero- and homosexual males to pictures of men and women: a pilot study. *J. abnorm. Psychol.*, 1965, *70* 165-168.

LOWENSTEIN, O., and LOEWENFELD, I. E. The pupil. In H. DAVSON (ed.), *The eye*. Vol. III. New York: Academic Press, 1962. Pp. 231-267.

PAIVIO, A. Abstractness, imagery, and meaningfulness in paired-associate learning. *J. verbal. Learn. verbal Behav.*, 1965, *4*, 32-38.

———. Latency of verbal associations and imagery to noun stimuli as a function of abstractness and generality. *Canad. J. Psychol.*, in press.

SOKOLOV, E. N. *Perception and the conditioned reflex*. New York: Macmillan, 1963.

23 / Postdecision Dissonance at Post Time[1]

Robert E. Knox and James A. Inkster *University of British Columbia*

Individuals often behave in ways which are not consistent with their beliefs, or they may hold beliefs which contradict each other. The theory of cognitive dissonance, proposed by Leon Festinger, contends that such inconsistency causes the individual to behave in ways which will reduce inconsistency or dissonance. For example, a heavy smoker who is confronted with evidence that smoking causes cancer may act in one of two ways. He may believe the evidence and quit smoking or he may continue smoking and belittle or reject the evidence. In either case, he seeks to reduce the inconsistency between his beliefs and his behaviour.

The theory of cognitive dissonance provides an explanation of many kinds of behaviour and the study reported here explores the changes that occur in a person's opinion once he commits himself to a particular course of action – placing a bet at the race track.

In the last decade there have been numerous laboratory experiments conducted to test various implications of Festinger's (1957) theory of cognitive dissonance. In spite of sometimes serious methodological faults (cf. Chapanis and Chapanis, 1964), the laboratory evidence as a whole has tended to support Festinger's notions. Confidence in the theory, as Brehm and Cohen (1962) have previously suggested, can now be further strengthened by extending empirical tests from lifelike to real-life situations. The present study investigates the effects of postdecision dissonance on bettors in their natural habitat, the race track.

Festinger (1957) had originally contended that due to the lingering cognitions about the favourable characteristics of the rejected alternative(s), dissonance was an inevitable consequence of a decision. Subsequently, however, Festinger (1964) accepted the qualification that in order for dissonance to occur, the decision must also have the effect of committing the person. A favorite technique for reducing postdecisional dissonance, according to the theory, is to change cognitions in such a manner as to increase the attractiveness of the chosen alternative relative to the unchosen alternative(s). At the race track a bettor becomes financially committed to his decision when he purchases a pari-mutuel ticket on a particular horse. Once this occurs, postdecisional processes should operate to reduce dissonance by increasing the attractiveness of the chosen horse relative to the unchosen horses in the race. These processes would be reflected by the bettor's expression of greater confidence in his having picked a winner after his bet had been made than before.

In order to test this notion, one need only go to a race track, acquire a prebet and postbet sample, and ask members of each how confident they are that they have selected the winning horse in the forthcoming race. The two samples should be independent since the same subjects in a before-after design could contravene the observed effects of dissonance reduction by carrying over consistent responses in the brief interval between pre- and postmeasurements. In essence, this was the approach employed in the two natural experiments reported here. More formally, the experimental hypothesis in both experiments was that bettors would be more confident of their selected horse just after betting $2 than just before betting.

Experiment I

Subjects

Subjects were 141 bettors at the Exhibition Park Race Track in Vancouver, British Columbia. Sixty-nine of these subjects, the prebet group, were interviewed less than 30 seconds *before* making a $2 Win bet. Seventy-two subjects, the postbet group, were interviewed a few seconds after making a $2 Win bet. Fifty-one subjects, interviewed before the fourth and fifth races, were obtained in the exclusive Clubhouse section. Data from the remaining 90 bettors were collected prior to the second, third, sixth, and

[1]This study was supported by a grant from the Faculty of Graduate Studies, University of British Columbia. The cooperation of the British Columbia Jockey Club and the management of the Delta Raceways Limited is gratefully acknowledged. The authors also gratefully acknowledge the assistance of Herbert Kee, Ronald Douglas, and Warren Thorngate during the data-collection phases of these studies.

seventh races at various betting locations in the General Admission or grandstand area.

No formal rituals were performed to guarantee random sampling, but instead, every person approaching or leaving a $2 Win window at a time when the experimenters were not already engaged in an interview was contacted. Of those contacted, approximately 15% refused to co-operate further because they could not speak English, refused to talk to "race touts," never discussed their racing information with strangers, or because of some unexpressed other reason. The final sample consisted of white, Negro, and Oriental men and women ranging in estimated age from the early twenties to late sixties and ranging in style from ladies in fur to shabby old men. The final sample was felt to be reasonably representative of the Vancouver racetrack crowd.

Procedure

The two experimenters were stationed in the immediate vicinity of the "Sellers" window during the 25-minute betting interval between races. For any given race, one experimenter intercepted bettors as they approached a $2 Win window and the other experimenter intercepted different bettors as they left these windows. Prebet and postbet interview roles were alternated with each race between the two experimenters.

The introductory appeal to subjects and instructions for their ratings were as follows:

I beg your pardon. I am a member of a University of British Columbia research team studying risk-taking behaviour. Are you about to place a $2 Win bet? (Have you just made a $2 Win bet?) Have we already talked to you today? I wonder if you would mind looking at this card and telling me what chance you think the horse you are going to bet on (have just bet on) has of winning this race. The scale goes from 1, a slight chance, to 7, an excellent chance. Just tell me the number from 1 to 7 that best describes the chance that you think your horse has of winning. Never mind now what the tote board or professional handicappers say; what chance do you think your horse has?

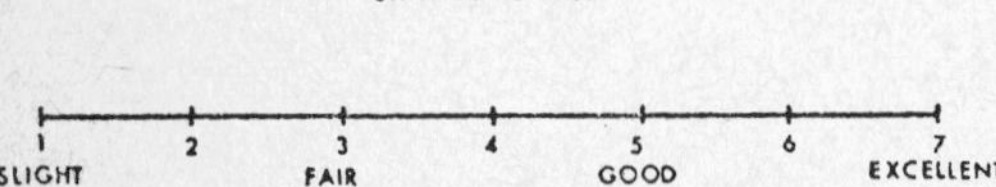

Fig. 1. The rating scale shown to subjects in the study.

It was, of course, sometimes necessary to give some of the subjects further explanation of the task or to elaborate further on the cover story for the study.

The scale, reproduced here in Figure 1, was prepared on 8½ x 11-inch posterboard. The subjects responded verbally with a number or, in some cases, with the corresponding descriptive word from the scale.

After each prebet rating the experimenter visually confirmed that his subject proceeded directly to a $2 Win window. In the few instances that subjects did wander elsewhere, their data were discarded. No effort was made to collect data in the 3 frantic minutes of betting just prior to post time.

Results

Since no stronger than ordinal properties may be safely assumed for the rating scale, nonparametric statistics were employed in the analysis. Several χ^2 approximations of the Kolmogorov-Smirnov test (Siegel, 1956) were first performed to test for distributional differences between the ratings collected by the two experimenters. For prebet ratings (χ^2 .274, $df = 2$, $p > .80$) and for the combined pre- and postbet ratings ($\chi^2 = 2.16$, $df = 2$, $p > .30$) the differences in the two distributions may be considered negligible according to these tests. Distributional differences on postbet ratings ($\chi^2 = 3.14$, $df = 2$, $p > .20$) were greater but still did not meet even the .20 probability level.[2] On the basis of these tests the two experimenters were assumed to have collected sufficiently comparable ratings to justify pooling of their data for the subsequent test of the major hypothesis of the study.

The median for the 69 subjects in the prebet group was 3.48. In qualitative terms they gave their horse little better than a "fair" chance of winning its race. The median for the 72 subjects in the postbet group, on the other hand, was 4.81. They gave their horse close to a "good" chance in the race. The median test for the data summarized in Table I produced a χ^2 of 8.70, ($df = 1$), significant beyond the .01 level.

These results, in accord with our predictions from dissonance theory, might also have arisen, however, had a substantial number of bettors simply made last-minute switches from relative long shots to favourites in these races. Although this possibility was not pursued with the above sample as subjects, two follow-up inquiries on another day at the same race track indicated that the "switch to favourites" explanation was unlikely. The first of these inquiries involved 38 $2 bettors who were contacted prior to the first race and merely asked if they ever changed their mind about which horse to bet on in the last minute or so before actually reaching a Sellers window. Nine of the 38 indicated that they sometimes changed, but among the 9 occasional changers a clear tendency to switch to long shots rather than to favourites was reported. Additional evidence against a "switch to favourites" explanation was obtained from a sample of 46 bettors for whom the prebet procedure of Experiment I was repeated. Each of these bettors was then contacted by a second inter-

[2]The χ^2 approximation for Kolmogorov-Smirnov is designed for one-tailed tests, whereas the hypothesis tested here is nondirectional. However, since the differences were insignificant by a one-tailed test, they would necessarily be insignificant by the two-tailed test.

viewer just as he was leaving the $2 Win window and asked if he had changed to a different horse since talking to the first interviewer. All 46 responded that they had not changed horses in midinterviews.

In order to investigate the robustness of the findings in Experiment I a second study was undertaken which was like the first study in its essentials but employed different experimenters, a different response scale, and a different population of subjects. It also provided for a test of the "switch to favourites" explanation among subjects in a postbet group.

Table I – Division of subjects with respect to the overall median for the prebet and postbet groups: experiment I

	Prebet group	Postbet group
Above the *Mdn*	25	45
Below the *Mdn*	44	27

Experiment II

Subjects and Procedure

Ninety-four subjects were interviewed at the Patterson Park Harness Raceway in Ladner, British Columbia. Forty-eight of these subjects, the prebet group, were interviewed prior to the first six races as they approached one of the track's four $2 Win windows. This contact was usually completed just a few seconds before the subject actually reached the window to make his bet, but occasionally, when the betting lines were long, up to ¾ minute elapsed between interview and bet. Forty-six subjects, the postbet group, were interviewed a few seconds after leaving one of the $2 Win windows. As in Experiment I, all persons approaching or leaving a $2 Win window at a time when the experimenters were not already engaged were contacted. Of those contacted, fewer than 10% refused to co-operate, thus producing a heterogeneous and, presumably, representative sample of $2 Win bettors.

The overall design was the same as in the first study. Two experimenters, different from those who interviewed bettors in Experiment I, were located in the immediate area of the Sellers windows. One of these experimenters would intercept bettors as they approached a $2 Win window and the other intercepted different bettors as they left a $2 Win window. The prebet and postbet interview roles were alternated between the two experimenters as in the first study.

After a brief introductory preamble, the experimenter established whether a bettor was about to make a $2 Win bet (or had just made such a bet) and whether he had been previously interviewed. The experimenters proceeded only with those $2 bettors who had not already provided data. These subjects were then asked to indicate on a 23-centimeter scale how confident they felt that they had picked the winning horse. The mimeographed response scales were labeled with the words "No confidence" at the extreme left and "Complete confidence" at the extreme right. Although no other labels were printed on the scale, the experimenters made explicit that mild confidence would fall in the middle of the scale and ". . . the more confident that a person felt, the further along he should put his mark on the scale." When subjects indicated understanding they were handed a pencil and a mimeographed scale and directed to ". . . just draw a line across the point in the scale that best corresponds to your own confidence." All bettors in the postbet sample were also asked if they changed their mind about which horse to bet on while waiting in line or while on the way to the window.

Within the limits permitted by extremely crowded conditions, the prebet experimenter visually confirmed that subjects in his sample proceeded to a $2 Win window. Data collection was suspended during the last minute before post time.

Confidence scores for each subject were determined by laying a ruler along the 23-centimeter scale and measuring his response to the nearest millimeter.

Table II – Division of subjects with respect to the overall median for the prebet and postbet groups: experiment II

	Prebet group	Postbet group
Above the *Mdn*	19	28
Below the *Mdn*	29	18

Results

On the strength of insignificant Kolmogorov-Smirnov tests for distributional differences between ratings collected by the two experimenters, data from the two experimenters were combined to test the major hypothesis of the study. The median rating for the 48 subjects in the prebet group was 14.60, and for the postbet group it was 19.30. The median test for these data, summarized in Table II, produced a χ^2 of 4.26 ($df = 1$), significant at less than the .05 level.

Since data in Experiment II might reasonably be assumed to satisfy interval scale assumptions, a t test between pre- and postbet means was also performed. The difference between the prebet mean of 14.73 and the postbet mean of 17.47 was also significant ($t = 2.31, p < .05$).

No subject in the postbet sample indicated that he had changed horses while waiting in line or, if there were no line, just before reaching the window.

Discussion

These studies have examined the effects of real life postdecisional dissonance in the uncontrived setting of a race track. The data furnished by two relatively heterogeneous samples of bettors strongly support our hypothesis derived from Festinger's theory. The reaction of one bettor in Experiment I well illustrates the overall effect observed in the data. This particular bettor had been a subject in the prebet sample and had then proceeded to the pari-mutuel window to place his bet. Following that transaction, he approached the postbet experimenter and volunteered the following:

Are you working with that other fellow there? (indicating the prebet experimenter who was by then engaged in another interview). Well, I just told him that my horse had a fair chance of winning. Will you have him change that to a good chance? No, by God, make that an excellent chance.

It might reasonably be conjectured that, at least until the finish of the race, this bettor felt more comfortable about his decision to wager on a horse with an excellent chance than he could have felt about a decision to wager on a horse with only a fair chance. In the human race, dissonance had won again.

The results also bear upon the issue of rapidity of onset of dissonance-reducing processes discussed by Festinger (1964). On the basis of an experiment by Davidson described in that work, Festinger argued that predecisional cognitive familiarity with the characteristics of alternatives facilitated the onset of dissonance reduction. It is reasonable to assume that most bettors in the present studies were informed, to some extent, about the virtues and liabilities of all the horses in a race before making a $2 commitment on one. Since never more than 30 seconds elapsed between the time of commitment at the window and confrontation with the rating task, the present results are consistent with the notion that the effects of dissonance reduction can, indeed, be observed very soon after a commitment is made to one alternative, providing that some information about the unchosen alternatives is already possessed. Furthermore, the exceedingly short time span here suggests that the cognitive re-evaluation process could hardly have been very explicit or as deliberate as conscious rationalization.

Finally, these studies, like the earlier Ehrlich, Guttman, Schonbach, and Mills (1957) study which showed that recent new car buyers preferred to read automobile advertisements that were consonant with their purchase, demonstrate that meaningful tests of dissonance theory can be made in the context of real life situations. Insofar as real life studies are unaffected by contrived circumstances, improbable events, and credibility gaps, they may offer stronger and less contentious support for dissonance theory than their laboratory counterparts. It is also clear that such studies will help to define the range of applicability of the theory in natural settings.

Abstract

2 experiments were conducted to investigate postdecisional dissonance reduction processes following a commitment to bet on a horse in the natural and uncontrived setting of a race track. In the 1st study, 69 $2 Win bettors rated the chance that the horse they had selected would win the forthcoming race and 72 other bettors provided ratings immediately, after making a $2 Win bet. On the 7-point rating scale employed, prebet subjects gave a median rating of 3.48, which corresponded to a "fair chance of winning"; postbet subjects gave a median rating of 4.81, which corresponded to a "good chance of winning." This difference was significant beyond the .01 level. The general findings were replicated in a 2nd study in which harness-race patrons rated how confident they felt about their selected horse either just before or just after betting. Results from both studies provide support for Festinger's theory in a real life setting and indicate that dissonance-reducing processes may occur very rapidly following commitment to a decision.

References

Brehm, J. W., and Cohen, A. R. *Explorations in cognitive dissonance.* New York: Wiley, 1962.

Chapanis, N. P., and Chapanis, A. Cognitive dissonance: Five years later. *Psychological Bulletin, 61,* 1-22.

Ehrlich, D., Guttman, I., Schonbach, P., and Mills, J. Postdecision exposure to relevant information. *Journal of Abnormal and Social Psychology,* 1957, *54,* 98-102.

Festinger, L. *A theory of cognitive dissonance.* Evanston, Ill. Row, Peterson, 1957.

———. *Conflict, decision, and dissonance.* Stanford, Calif.: Stanford University Press, 1964.

Siegel, S. *Nonparametric statistics for the behavioural sciences.* New York: McGraw-Hill, 1956.

24 / An Approach to the Measurement of Creative Thinking

B.M. Springbett, J.G. Dark, and J. Clake *University of Manitoba*

The twentieth century has seen the development of highly sophisticated tests of intelligence, aptitudes, interests, and achievement. However, progress in the development of tests predicting creativity has not been rapid. One of the major drawbacks has been that the creative process itself is not well understood. In the following article, the authors attempt to clarify the processes involved in the creative act and present a unique way of measuring creativity.

It has long been recognized that thinking and problem-solving involve unconscious[1] processes (2). On the basis of arguments offered later, we should like to suggest that "creative" thinking differs from conventional problem-solving only because it involves a greater sensitivity to such unconscious processes. Hence a test which will measure creative thinking must show some relation to tests of reasoning, intelligence, and so forth, and yet, at the same time, it must measure a degree of sensitivity to unconscious processes greater than that required by such tests of reasoning.

One solution to this problem of measuring the contribution of unconscious processes is offered here in the form of what we call the Lines Test. Evidence of its empirical validity is offered in terms of correlations with four criterion tests of reasoning and intelligence. In addition, a claim is made for "face" validity, but with no implication that this removes the need for an empirical demonstration that the test measures creative ability.

The discussion of creative thinking and the analysis of conventional tests of reasoning which follow are intended to provide a rationale for the Lines Test, and to define the requirements it must meet. The point of view expressed here could be accommodated by a number of formal theories of thinking, such as those of Hebb (1), Osgood (5), and Malzburg (3).

The Nature of Creative Thinking

The unconscious aspects of creative thinking are suggested by the fact that the end-product, the solution, is open to introspection but the processes leading up to it are not. A logical validation of the solution can frequently be worked out, but it is doubtful whether this logical chain can be identified with the processes responsible for the solution. This is indicated by the fact that the logical validation is often difficult to construct, and that once the logical relations are clear the solution frequently carries new meanings and implications.

Another characteristic of creative thought is that the solution is both new and valid. It creates new meanings in the phenomenal world and so re-structures it.

If creative thought is to be identified both with the newness and the validity of its product, a dual set of determinants is implied. The loose work of dream and phantasy produces much that is new, but the products possess little validity. The application of a set of conventional rules to a set of data produces valid results, but little that is new in the creative sense. Creativity requires the flexibility of phantasy to seek out what is new, but the result must be tied to the conventional to secure validity.

For example, in the application of mathematics to chemistry there are a number of possible approaches, all equally promising from a mathematical viewpoint; but only some of these prove to be valid for chemistry. The conditions of freedom lie within the complex, conventional mathematical field. The creative act employs this freedom to seek out the mathematically conventional line which has valid linkages with what is conventional within the framework of chemistry. The greater the improbability of such linkages the more creative do we consider the act. The improbability appears as a function of dissimilarity between the newly discovered and previously known linkages.

Creative thinking is the process by which such improbable linkages are discovered; and, if we accept Hebb's[2] view of consciousness, it follows that creative thinking is a function of the relative strengths of conscious and unconscious processes.

The assumption is that consciousness is no more and no less than a fully activated, well-organized neural pattern. When we are confronted with a problem, and with the relevant data, a wide range of such

[1]This term is used with reluctance. The "content" to which it refers is akin to the Freudian pre-conscious. See below.

Reprinted, by permission, from *Canadian Journal of Psychology*, 1957,*11*, 9-20.

[2]The development here may not fit Hebb's views in all respects. Osgood (5, p. 40) suggests a similar point of view. A philosophical system which accomodates this position in considerable detail is that presented in S. Alexander's *Space, Time, and Deity* (London: Macmillan, 1920).

organizations is available, but some will have higher probabilities of being activated than others. Those with the highest probability are the ones most highly organized with respect to the particular problem and data: in short, the best learned organizations. These will also be, for a given individual, the most conventional and commonplace modes of organizing the data. Thus the initial conscious reaction has a high probability of being conventional, valid, but not new.

Other neural organizations, with lower probabilities of being engaged, may be thought of as being partially activated. These may modify the patterning of the fully activated (conscious) organizations and produce deviations from the usual conscious content. Such interactions may enhance or detract from the possibility of a solution at the conscious level. Solutions found under these conditions would be novel ones, though still closely tied to the conventional.

Since, by our definition, the creative act requires the discovery of improbable relations, it follows that a creative solution is to be found through the engagement of the partially activated (unconscious) organizations.

When the well-organized patterns fail to produce a solution, the probabilities of the partially activated organizations becoming fully activated, in relation to the data, will increase. This will be due to inhibitory factors operating in the well-organized patterns, together with recruitment of strength in the partially activated ones. The latter may arise from simple summation effects of partial activation, but other factors are likely to play a part. The probabilities of the partially active becoming conscious might be expected to vary with changes in the sequence in which the data are viewed, with reformulations of the problem, with leaving the problem and returning to it, and so on.

If we accept the above rough description of problem-solving, the creative thinker will be one in whom there is a sensitive interplay among the possibly available organizations. The conventional problem-solver will be dominated by one set of such organizations, namely, those learned specifically in relation to the type of problem confronting him.

Conventional Tests

Conventional tests of reasoning, intelligence, and the like, all demand the creative type of interaction in some degree. However, they afford no means of assessing the contribution of unconscious factors to the solution, nor do they offer a situation which demands a high degree of sensitivity to such interaction, that is, they fail to provide optimum conditions for the creative act to occur.

The most formidable barrier to creative thought in the majority of conventional tests is that the principle under which the problems are to be solved is given, in the instructions, or through practice questions. Only with this sort of information can the subject meet the conditions of the test. The creative thinker, in contrast, must discover the principle, the nature of the organization, under which the solution is possible.

A second defect lies in the sequence in which the elements of a specific problem are presented. Verbal problems are put into logical form. Matrices of various sorts are found in orderly progression so that, although there is a hidden principle, its discovery is, in a sense, imposed on the subject. Or, if the elements have a disorderly array, as in the jumbled sentence, rules of grammar and habits of speech automatically provide the basis for an orderly and conventional arrangement. On the other hand, the creative act must discover, in a disorderly array, the principle which will make it meaningful and orderly.

Finally, in the conventional tests all the data of a specific problem are perceptually present. The words, figures, or other information are all before the subject, so that they can be immediately checked if memory is doubted or difficulty arises. In the creative situation the various elements are usually simultaneously present only in ideational form.

This line of reasoning points to the following as the requirements of a test of creative thinking: (a) The elements of the problem must permit organization (possess relations), but the directions given in the test must yield no hint that such organization exists; (b) the elements of the problem must be capable of being presented in such a way that the eduction of relations is difficult; (c) the various elements must be presented separately, so that they can be simultaneously present to the subject only ideationally; (d) the test must yield some measure of the interaction of conscious and unconscious processes.

The Lines Test

After a number of attempts to meet the foregoing requirements in a test of thinking, a solution of the problem finally presented itself in the form of a test of immediate memory. This is described below, and followed by a discussion of how it meets the above requirements.

Figure 1(a) shows three figures, each of which is drawn with nine straight lines. Since names can be attached to these figures (box, prism, chair), they are called meaningful figures (M). Figure 1(b) shows three figures, each of nine lines, which have symmetry but are difficult to name. These are gestalt figures (G). Figure 1(c) shows three nonsense figures (N) without symmetry or meaning, each consisting of nine lines.

In the test situation the subject is shown the nine lines of one figure, for example, the box. These are presented one at a time, each line being drawn on a 4 X 4 grid. When the nine lines have been presented in succession he is asked to draw all of the lines he can remember on a single 4 X 4 grid. If he is entirely successful he will, of course, reproduce the box on his answer sheet. Each of the nine figures is

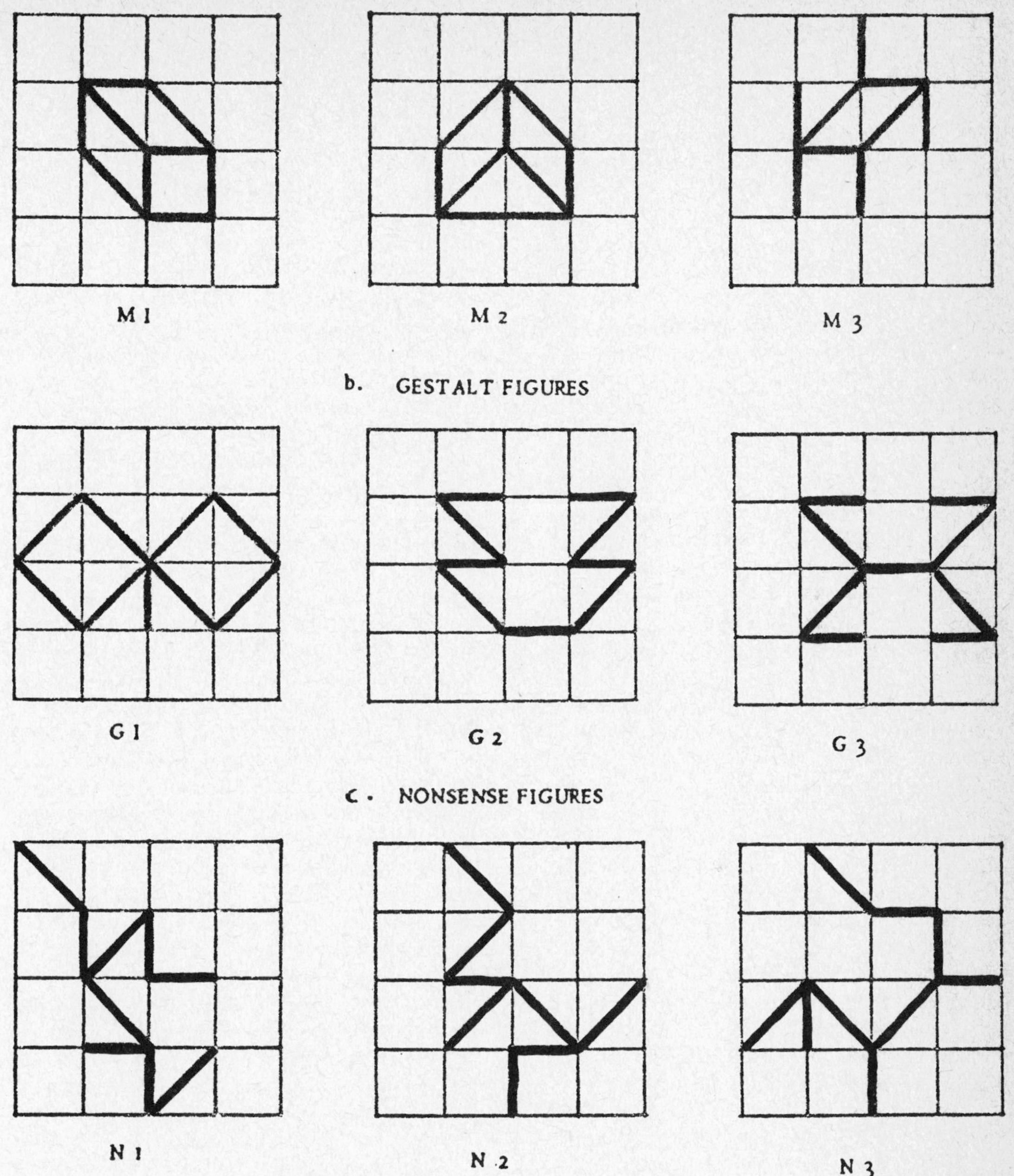

Fig. 1. Figures used in experiments I and II.

similarly presented, and he is asked to reproduce the component lines of each from memory.

With respect to the meaningful figures it is clear that (a) the nine lines have meaningful organization, but no hint has been given to the subject that such an organization exists; (b) the nine lines can be presented in a sequence which will make the eduction of relations, relevant to the over-all organization, difficult: (c) since the lines are presented singly, they can be simultaneously present to the subject only ideationally; (d) if the subject fails to reproduce all nine lines we may infer that he is unconscious of the over-all organization.

If the subject's performance on the meaningful figures, though not perfect, is superior to that on the nonsense figures, this may be attributed to the organization in the former of which the subject is not aware. If performance on the meaningful figures is superior to that on the gestalt figures, this will guard against the criticism that the meaningful figures were better remembered than those of the nonsense figures because the subject became aware of sub-organizations such as squares, triangles, etc. On these grounds the test appears capable of measuring the interaction of conscious and unconscious processes, and this, we suggest, is the essential problem in measuring creative thinking.

The conscious organization by which the subject will achieve rote memory of the lines is related to the spatial framework in which each line is presented. The role of the unconscious organization is viewed as follows: it is assumed that the nine lines of a meaningful figure, separately presented, will partially activate the neural organization normally involved in perceiving such a figure; when the subject attempts to recall these lines they will be better remembered by virtue of their membership in this organization, provided the subject is not dominated by his conscious processes but is sensitive to those which are unconscious.

Since, on the whole, such interaction will aid recall, the demand will be, for group results, that the meaningful figures be better remembered than the gestalt or nonsense, and the gestalt better than the nonsense.

If sensitivity to such interaction is required to a high degree in creative thinking and to a lesser degree in reasoning and problem-solving, scores on the Lines Test should show the following relationships with scores on tests of reasoning and intelligence: scores on the meaningful and gestalt figures should show significant correlations with such tests, because they possess conventional organizations which provide the basis of the postulated interaction. The scores on the nonsense figures, being wholly dependent on conscious processes (and possessing the character of rote memory), should not show significant correlations with the scores of such tests.

The nature or patterning of the predicted correlations may be understood better by considering the structure of the variance presumed to be present in the scores of each class of figures. The chief sources of variance in the meaningful figures will be (a) rote memory, (b) an unconscious spatial component, (c) an unconscious verbal component. For the gestalt figures (a) and (b) will apply; for the nonsense figures (a) only.

These sources of variance may be separated by using difference scores; for example, meaningful minus nonsense should leave the variance of the unconscious spatial and verbal components, and so forth.

Experiments: General Procedure

In the experiments reported below, the lines in each of the nine figures shown in Figure 1 were presented one at a time, each line being drawn on a 4 X 4 grid. Each line was exposed for two seconds with no time interval between exposures. After viewing the nine separately presented lines of a figure, the subject was asked to reproduce all he could remember on a single 4 X 4 grid.

In order to check on procedures and the general promise of the test, a pilot study involving nine subjects was carried out. The results were encouraging, and on the basis of this experience the following experiments were designed.

Experiment I

The aims of this experiment were (a) to provide a check on the results of the pilot study; (b) to demonstrate that the subjects were not conscious of the over-all organization of the test figures.

Method and Procedure

In order to support the claim that the differences in mean scores obtained on M, G, and N figures are due to the operation of unconscious factors it is necessary to control the variable "difficulty of line sequence." It is possible that, in selecting a given line sequence for presentation, a more difficult sequence might be selected for the N figures than for the M figures. If this were the case, the observed differences in means would reflect difficulty of sequential order.

Systematic exploration of all possible orders of presentation would be so formidable a task that the following assumptions were made as to what would constitute easy and difficult sequences. It was assumed that an "easy" sequence would be one in which each line presented would be in contact with the preceding one at some point..[3] A "difficult" sequence would be one in which successively presented lines would be as widely separated as possible, while a sequence of "intermediate" difficulty would be obtained by a mixture of the "easy" and "difficult."

Results in the pilot study showed the necessity of counterbalancing for series effects. In order that these effects would fall equally on each of the three orders of line sequences and each of the three classes of figures (M, G, and N), nine groups of subjects were required. Four subjects (university students) were assigned to each group, making 36 in all. Each group was tested on all nine figures, (presented in a different order to each group), but a different order of line sequence was used for each group. Thus the mean score for each class of figures, based on 36 subjects, is derived from data counterbalanced for series effects, with respect to both line sequence and class of figure.

Results

(a) The mean scores for M, G, and N figures, respectively, are: 17.75, 15.48, 12.57. The pattern of results is consistent with the hypothesis. M scores are significantly higher than G scores ($t = 2.225$, $p < .05$) and N scores ($t = 6.17$, $p < .001$). G scores are significantly higher than N scores ($t = 3.009$, $p < .01$).

(b) Did the subjects become aware of the organi-

[3]This is not strictly achieved in Fig. 1c (1). One break in the consecutive sequence is unavoidable.

zation of M and G figures? Each subject performed on three figures of each class, making a total of 108 attempted reproductions of each class. Out of these totals of 108, there were only 8 perfect reproductions of the M figures, 9 of the G figures, and none of the N figures. Even assuming that these perfect reproductions resulted from being aware of the "meaning" of the lines before they were drawn, they are not numerous enough to account for the results shown in (a) above.

Experiment II

Group results in Experiment I supported the hypothesis that the operation of unconscious factors would produce differences in M, G, and N scores. The question remained whether these M, G, and N scores were differentially related with performance in reasoning and problem-solving. Demonstration of this relation, it was argued in the Introduction, would constitute one stage in the validation of the Lines Test as a measure of creative thinking. An answer to the question was sought in the form of product-moment correlations between scores on the Lines Test and on four criterion tests.

Methods and Procedures

For this experiment a specific line sequence was selected for each of the nine test figures. This selection was based on the results of Experiment I and was such that no M figure had a mean score smaller than any G or N figure, and no G figure had a mean score smaller than any N figure.[4]

Four criterion tests were chosen: (1) the *Mooney Closure Test* (4), because it seemed to involve, at the perceptual level, processes similar to those assumed to be operating in the Lines Test; (2) the *D.A.T. Spatial Relations Test,* chosen as a check on the assumed unconscious spatial component in the Lines Test; (3) the *D.A.T. Abstract Reasoning Test,* as an example of a test based on matrices like those discussed in the Introduction; (4) the *Otis Intelligence Test* (higher form) as a test of general verbal intelligence.

The subjects were 53 male office workers.

Results

Results are shown in Table I. To aid in their interpretation, the presumed sources of variance for each of the scores derived from the Lines Test may be repeated – M: rote memory, unconscious spatial and verbal components; G: rote memory, unconscious spatial component; N: rote memory; M – N: unconscious spatial and verbal component; G – N: unconscious spatial component; M – G: unconscious verbal component; M – G plus N: rote memory, unconscious verbal component.

Table I – Product-moment correlations obtained in experiment II between various scores on the lines test and the 4 criterion tests

Test	1	2	3	8	9	10	11
1. M		.63**	.41**	.36**	.43**	.57**	.29*
2. G			.37**	.33*	.33*	.58**	.26
3. N				.17	.22	.22	.17
4. M–N				.20	.28*	.42**	.23
5. G–N				.19	.16	.45**	.06
6. M–G				.06	.03	–.06	.17
7. M–G plus N				.17	.29*	.21	.25
8. Mooney					.33*	.03	.09
9. Space relations						.43**	.25
10. Abstract reasoning							.53**
11. Otis I.Q.							

*Significant at 5% level.
**significant at 1% level.

Table I shows that the correlations between criterion tests and M, G, and N scores are consistently in line with the hypothesis. M scores are significantly correlated with all criterion test scores; G scores are significantly correlated with all but one (the correlation between G scores and Otis scores falls slightly below the 5 per cent level of significance). N scores are not significantly related to any of the criterion test scores.

The various difference scores produce few significant correlations with criterion tests. However, the over-all pattern of results suggests that the postulated sources of variance are operating. Effects of the unconscious verbal component do not show up strongly, but wherever this factor is presumed to be present (M, M – N, M – G) there are on the average higher correlations with the verbal criterion test (Otis) than when it is absent (G, N, G – N). The scores where the unconscious spatial component is presumed to be present (M, G, M – N, G – N) show higher correlations with the *D.A.T. Spatial Relations Test* than do those in which this factor is absent (N, M – G). It is of interest to note also that the highest correlations are obtained with the *D.A.T. Abstract Reasoning Test.* Matrices tests are the closest in principle to the Lines Test since they contain a "hidden principle," but one which, because of the orderly sequence of the matrix, is relatively easy to discover.

The basic results as they concern M, G, and N scores, together with the more detailed evidence related to the postulated sources of variance, fit with some degree of comfort into the general hypothetical framework of this investigation.

Discussion

At a factual level, the results show that, in a task of rote memory, the presence of a meaningful organization of which the subject is unaware produces results significantly related to his performance on tasks involving reasoning and problem-solving. When the organization is absent these relations do not appear. It has already been argued that the demonstration of

[4]This does not bias the outcome of the experiment. The absolute levels of scores are of no consequence; our only concern is the covariance between scores on the Lines Test and the criterion tests. (Hindsight, however, acknowledges little merit in the logic underlying this selection, and better results could probably be secured by using the most difficult sequence in each class of figures.)

these relationships is one stage in the validation of the Lines Test. Negative results would have destroyed any claim that it could measure creative thinking.

Although final validation must rest on empirical evidence involving admittedly "creative" subjects, there are grounds for expecting such a test to be successful. In the criterion tests, especially in the matrices test, there is obviously a hidden principle; as already stated, however, this principle is relatively easy to discover. It is equally evident that the hidden principle in the Lines Test is very difficult to discover under the test conditions. We would argue that it is precisely the difficulty of discovering the hidden principle which distinguishes creative thinking from reasoning and problem-solving. An analogy may clarify this point.

Darwin's discovery of the principle of evolution would be generally accepted as a creative achievement. Comparing the data as he had to deal with them and as they would be presented in a matrices test, we have an apt parallel with the comparison between the Lines Test and the matrices test.

What Darwin had to discover was that a temporal sequence which applied to rock formations also applied to fossils.[5] This was difficult because the rock formations were nowhere in complete order and were often jumbled together, fossils were of relatively rare occurrence, and they were discovered at different times and places. A further factor in making his discovery "improbable" lay in the general acceptance of the story of Genesis.

If geological formations were regularly found neatly stacked in correct temporal order, with a fossil visibly implanted in each layer, one cannot believe that the common temporal sequence would long have evaded discovery, or that its discovery would have been regarded (even in spite Genesis) as a particularly creative act. In other words, it seems to be the relative difficulty of discovering the hidden principle which underlies the accepted distinction between creative thinking and simple reasoning.

The material in the Lines Test is presented to the subject in the jumbled order and temporal separation which characterized Darwin's data, and the subject's acceptance of the task as one of "rote memory" may perhaps be equated with the effect of the story of Genesis. It is on the basis of this apparent "face validity" that we expect the test to survive empirical validation.

That no such validation can yet be presented is owing to the necessity of adapting the test to various types of content. Since creative thinking typically occurs in those fields in which the thinker is well learned, different forms of the test will be required to investigate creativity in different fields. For example, to investigate literary creativity, the test must be of such a nature as to engage (produce interaction between) verbal organizations. In its present form, while the presumed spatial component gave convincing results, the presumed verbal component failed to produce significant correlations with the verbal criterion test. The verbal aspects of the meaningful figures were perhaps not sufficiently conspicuous.

Another form of the test, possessing unmistakable verbal organization, has been prepared, and is found to correlate substantially with verbal intelligence. Direct validation is being planned, and a third, "art," form is also being constructed.

Regardless of the outcome of the validation studies, the present results seem worth communicating, since they suggest ways in which some of the problems involved in thinking and problem-solving may be reformulated and investigated.

[5]This is not intended to slight the tremendously difficult task of working out all the logical implications.

Summary

The assumptions are made that: (a) reasoning, problem-solving, and creative thinking all involve finding a principle, or mode of organization, which holds the key to the solution; (b) creative thinking may be distinguished by the greater degree of difficulty in finding this principle. The difficulty lies in the fact that in the creative act a principle, already well established in relation to certain data, must be related to markedly different data. The process which "discovers" this relationship is conceived of as an interaction between conscious and unconscious processes.

A test of immediate memory, the Lines Test, is offered as an approach to measuring this interaction. Items designed to elicit such interaction correlated significantly with tests of reasoning and intelligence. Items designed as controls did not.

References

1. HEBB, D. O. *The organization of behaviour*. New York: Wiley, 1949.
2. HUMPHREY, G. *Thinking*. New York: Wiley, 1951.
3. MALZBURG, I. Thinking: From a behavioristic point of view. *Psychol. Rev.*, 1955, *62*, 275-286.
4. MOONEY, C. M., and FERGUSON, G. A. A new closure test. *Canad. J. Psychol.*, 1952, *5*, 129-133.
5. OSGOOD, C. E. *Method and theory in experimental psychology*. New York: Oxford Univer. Press, 1953.

SIX
ATTENTION AND PERCEPTION

25 / An Electromyographic Study of Attentive Listening

Harvey Wallerstein *Allan Memorial Institute of Psychiatry and McGill University*

This study by the late Dr. Wallerstein describes some interesting changes in muscular activity which occur during sustained attention to two types of verbal material: listening to a recorded detective story and a philosophical essay.

Courts (3) has reviewed some studies of muscle tension changes during mental arithmetic and memorization tasks. An increase of tension from rest to mental activity was reported by most investigators. The increases seemed to involve multiple factors such as degree of difficulty, distraction, and practice.

Recently, experiments have been concerned less with tension changes from rest to activity than with changes during the course of a given task. Smith (7) reported a continuous increase of tension in the active arm during mirror drawing. He interpreted this rising gradient as associated with increasing organization of central neural events underlying progress through the task; active arm potentials being a motor index of these central events. This gradient was confirmed in a similar experiment by Bartoshuk (1), who found in addition very regular increases in the passive arm, as well as rising (though less regular) gradients in the chin (2).

The question whether these rising gradients of muscle tension would occur during tasks requiring no overt movements, e.g., during listening activity, has not been fully answered. Thus far, there has been one pertinent study, which has proved both equivocal and provocative. Smith, Malmo, and Shagass (8) requested subjects to listen to a six-minute recorded article, with instructions to remember. Since the purpose was to induce stress, the playback was made difficult to hear in spots, by lowering the volume over a number of short, random intervals.

Under these conditions, recordings from the chin and forehead muscles reached peak amplitude at the fourth minute and then declined. Left and right forearm muscle potentials rose and declined more quickly and sharply. Comments of the subjects suggested a lack of sustained interest in the presentation, rather than concern over its poor quality. The authors suggested that the rise and fall of the curves for the facial muscles may have been associated with the presence and decline of attentive listening. This interpretation, although reasonable, was possibly complicated by other factors such as disturbance and difficulty.

Would continuous attentive listening, with such factors minimized, produce rising gradients of muscle tension? The present experiment was designed to answer this question. In addition, a study was made of (a) listening to materials differing in ease of comprehension; (b) repetition of the materials – with particular reference to their influence on muscle tension.

Method

Materials. A situation was arranged in which a subject was to listen to some recorded material. An adjustable hospital bed with foam rubber mattress was provided. Two selections were used: a detective story and a philosophical essay. The story "Coroner's Inquest" was written in dialogue form, and was therefore recorded by two voices.[2] An excerpt from Emmanuel Kant's *Critique of Pure Reason* was recorded by the person who played the major part in the story.[3] Both selections were 10 minutes long. Each was presented three times. A magictape recorder (Utah Electronics) was used for original recording and playback. A questionnaire concerning the subject's attention and feelings was devised, to be filled out when the session ended.

Subjects. Nineteen male subjects heard the detective story. Of these, 15 were university students, three were *RCAF* personnel, and one was a university graduate. Sixteen male individuals listened to the essay; this group consisted of 15 university students and one *RCAF* man. All the *RCAF* recruits had some secondary school training. The group who heard the story ranged in age from 18 to 31 years (mean, 20.9).

[1]This research was performed under Contract No. DA-49-007-MD-70 between the U.S. Department of the Army, Office of the Surgeon General, and McGill University. The present report is based on a thesis submitted to McGill University, in partial fulfilment of the requirements for the degree of Doctor of Philosophy. Grateful acknowledgment is made of the interest and support of Dr. Robert B. Malmo in the execution of this research, and to Dr. Tom J. Boag for assistance during its preliminary stages.

Reprinted, by permission, from ***Canadian Journal of Psychology***, 1954, *8*, 228-238.

[2]Marc Connelly, "Coroner's Inquest." In the Ellery Queen edition, *To the Queen's Taste*, pp. 472-477. Boston: Little, Brown, 1946.

[3]Emmanuel Kant. Critique of Pure Reason. In C. J. Friederich (ed.), ***The Philosophy of Kant***, pp. 24-27. New York: Modern Library, 1949. Sections I and II.

Recording apparatus. Muscular tension was measured in terms of electromyographic potentials between bi-polar electrodes, continuously amplified and recorded on an Edin ink-writing electromyograph. An ink-writing integrator designed by J. F. Davis (4), averaged these potentials over half-second intervals.

Recordings were taken from forehead, chin, and both forearm extensors. All lead placements were standard (4).

Procedure. Preparation for recording and the experiment proper took place in one room of a double-room suite, the other being reserved for the recording equipment. The subject was informed of the experiment's purpose: to investigate the electrical activity of his muscles while he listened to some recorded material. After making him comfortable on an adjustable bed,[4] the experimenter (the present writer) told the subject about the kind of material he was to hear – detective story or philosophical essay – its approximate length, and that a rest period would precede and follow its presentation. This was not a test of intelligence, memory, or the like. The subject was merely to lie quietly, relax and listen, as he would to a radio program. He would be asked to close his eyes when the test commenced, to reduce distraction and eyeblink artifacts. The experimenter would stay in the same room to run the playback machine, and to keep a record of the subject's movements; the latter should be minimal. Formal instructions to this effect would be given when the test proper began.

When the subject indicated that he understood the instructions, he was asked to close his eyes. Electromyographic (*EMG*) recording then commenced. Formal instructions were played on the tape. A one-minute rest interval preceded the story or essay; and two minutes of rest followed it. This procedure was run through three times with intermissions of approximately five minutes.

After the third repetition, the leads were removed and the subject was seated at a table. He then formally rated his own attention and feelings during the three presentations on a questionnaire. Finally, he was asked to write a brief summary of what he had heard. The experimenter did not press the subject to recall as much as possible; he was just to put down what easily came to mind.

Treatment of data. The primary (*EMG*) record was used only to gain general impressions and to determine artifacts. All quantitative measurements were made on the integrator records. A 20-second sample (in mm.) was taken from the middle of each successive minute, and these measures converted to microvolts by reference to standard calibration curves. Thus from each subject were obtained, for each of the three presentations and for every channel: one microvolt value for the pre-rest, 10 values for the 10-minute presentation, and two values for the post-rest period.

[4] Five subjects reclined in a leather-cushioned armchair.

Results

Frontalis. For both types of material and for all three hearings, tension rose significantly from first to last minute of listening.[5] The increases were consistent and regular from minute to minute (Figures 1 and 2). The curves show an increase from pre-rest to initial minute of listening, small but significant in every case ($P = .05$). When the story was heard, a significant drop from last minute of listening to first minute of post-rest occurred after all three presentations (Figure 1). Such was not the case for the essay; indeed, the curves after the second and third essay hearings show practically no change (Figure 2).

The increases from first to last minute of listening were of larger magnitude for the story than for the essay. Though the differences did not reach significance, those for the second hearing are suggestive ($P = .10$).

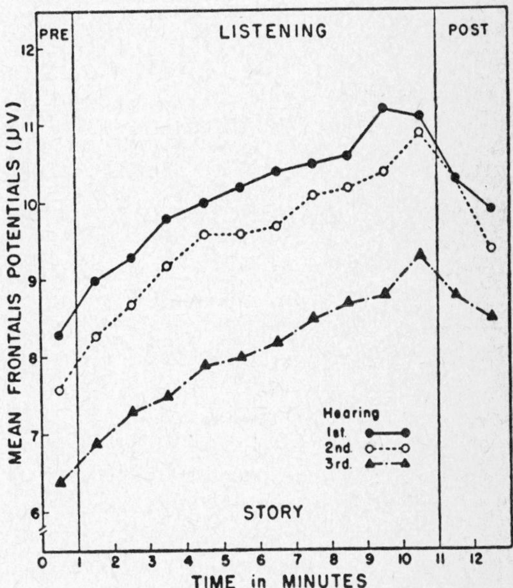

Fig. 1. Effect of listening to a detective story on ***frontalis*** *tension. Approximately five minutes intervened between each presentation.*

Both the essay and the story groups showed an orderly and significant fall in pre-rest tension from first to third hearings (Figures 1 and 2). It is pertinent to note here that the rising gradients failed to decrease from first to third hearings; in fact, the rise from first to last minute of listening to the essay showed an orderly (though not significant) increase in successive hearings.

[5] Since electrical activity as measured by electromyography parallels tension as measured by pull on a strain gauge (6), the present writer uses the terms *muscle potentials* and *muscle tension* interchangeably.

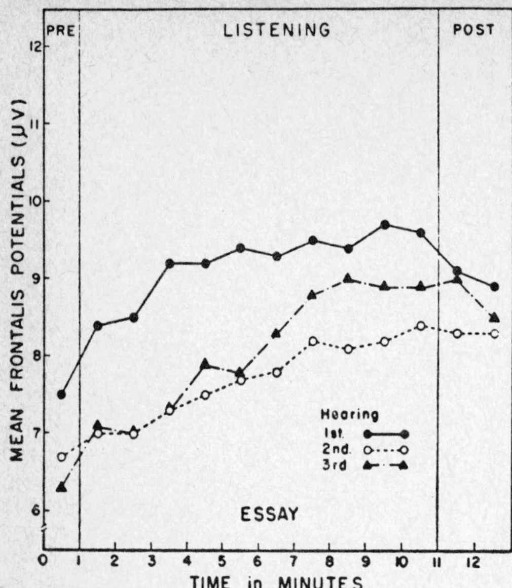

Fig. 2. Effect of listening to a philosophical essay on ***frontalis*** *tension. Approximately five minutes intervened between each presentation.*

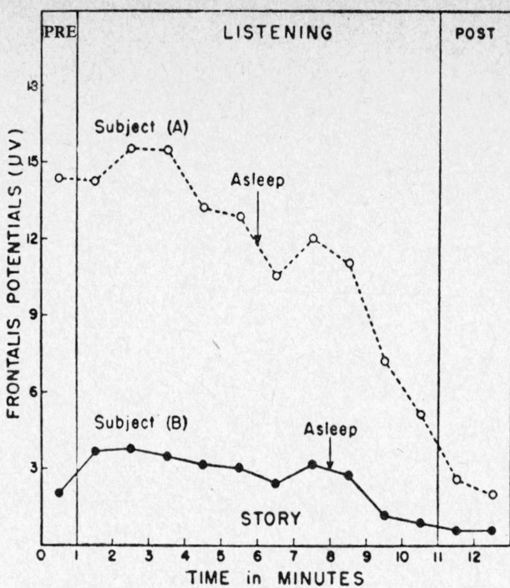

Fig. 3. Changes of ***frontalis*** *tension in two subjects who fell asleep, during the third hearing of a detective story.*

Two subjects fell asleep during the third presentation of the story. Their tension changes are illustrated in Figure 3. Note the fairly regular fall of tension beginning some time before the approximate onset of sleep. No other subjects showed a fall of such magnitude during listening.

Chin. A rise from first to last minute of listening to the story occurred during each presentation. This rise was close to significance for the first hearing ($P = .10$), and reached significance during the second and third hearings. Listening to the essay, on the other hand, produced only slight and insignificant changes from beginning to end, except for the third presentation, where a substantial and significant increase was obtained. When corresponding hearings of essay and story were directly compared, a significant difference was found for the second presentation: chin tension rose more when listening to the story ($P = .05$).

Curves from the chin changed less regularly from one minute to the next than those from *frontalis.* This is probably owing to the fact that the chin leads recorded from a complex of muscles which take part in speech, facial expression, and swallowing.

Pre-rest tension fell from first to third hearings for both story and essay groups. The fall for the essay group was significant. Again, as with *frontalis,* the rising gradients during listening failed to decrease with successive presentations. Instead, the story gave an orderly increase from first to third presentation; the essay group, as already stated, rose significantly within the last hearing only.

Right and left extensors. Inspection of the electromyographic records gave the following overall impressions:

(a) Low tension (under three microvolts) present at the start and persisting to the end of the record.

(b) Sharp increases of muscle tension lasting anywhere from one second to a minute or more, then falling just as abruptly back to a low background.

(c) Appreciable individual differences in the number, magnitude, and duration of these tension bursts.

Since these bursts might have resulted from slight arm movements, as in small shifts of position on the bed, the decision was made to analyse a hearing, for any subject, only if it showed minimal burst activity.

Figure 4 shows the minute-to-minute potential

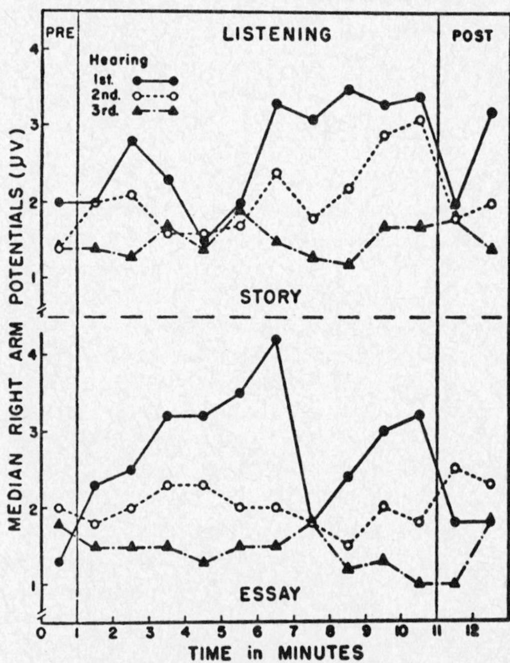

Fig. 4. Effects of listening to a detective story and philosophical essay on right extensor muscle tension. Approximately five minutes intervened between each presentation.

changes from the right extensor. Skewed distributions demanded the use of medians rather than means as estimates of central tendency. For the same reason, significance of differences was tested by a non-parametric technique for paired replicates (10). Almost no significant differences of any kind appeared. An important exception was the rise from pre-rest to initial minute of the first essay presentation. Left extensor, like right, gave essentially negative results.

In summary, the available EMG evidence presents the following picture. Rising gradients occur in *frontalis* and chin from beginning to end of listening. The magnitude of the gradients is larger when the subject is listening to the story, especially for the first two hearings. Such gradients do not appear in right and left extensors.

Retrospective data from the questionnaire. Twenty-four subjects reported being most sleepy on the third playing of the material, whereas only five were most sleepy during the second, and three during the first presentation. The probability of such an answer pattern occurring by chance is less than 1 in 1000 ($\chi^2 = 25.1$ with two degrees of freedom). Also, this decrease in alertness (or increase in sleepiness) was orderly; a majority of subjects estimating themselves less alert during the second hearing, and still less during the third hearing. Both the story and essay group followed this pattern.

The material listened to did, however, involve other dimensions of thought, such as interest, attention, anticipation. Table I indicates that, in the later hearings, such responses were more frequently reported for the essay than for the story. In other words, it required more hearings to produce maximum attention and interest in the essay than it did in the story.

Average number of words written in recall was 150 for the story and only 65 for the essay, this difference being significant ($P = .001$).

Table I – Subjective comparisons of successive hearings along some dimensions of thought

(Particular hearings compared are those splitting the reports most closely into equal groups.)

	Story	Essay
Number of subjects more interested		
in 1st hearing than in 2nd	12	3
in 2nd hearing than in 1st	5	12
Story vs. Essay $\chi^2 = 8.19$; $P = .01$		
Number of subjects more attentive		
in 1st hearing than in 2nd	13	3
in 2nd hearing than in 1st	5	10
Story vs. Essay $\chi^2 = 7.30$; $P = .01$		
Number of subjects thinking ahead more		
in 2nd hearing than in 3rd	14	5
in 3rd hearing than in 2nd	5	8
Story vs. Essay $\chi^2 = 3.97$; $P = .05$		

Discussion

Attention and Organization

The occurrence, during non-stressful hearing of organized material, of regularly rising gradients of tension in *frontalis*, and similar (though less regular) increases in chin, would appear to reflect a state of continued attention. An attempt to clarify this view leads to consideration of two general questions: attention under varying degrees of difficulty, and the problem of organization.

Attention and difficulty during listening. Let us regard the present findings in the light of results previously obtained by Smith and his co-workers (in this issue of *Canada. J. Psychol.*, p. 221). On presentation of poorly recorded and rather dull material, which the subjects were instructed to remember, significant changes occurred in muscles of right and left arms. Both extensors rose abruptly, reached their peak in two or three minutes, and then declined. Our investigation, on the other hand, showed almost no such extensor changes during listening. It seems, therefore, that in a comfortably placed subject, increased arm tension with onset of verbal material might reflect application to a dull and difficult task. Such a conclusion is further supported by the single arm change, from pre-rest to listening, found in our study: a significant increase of right extensor potentials with first presentation of the essay. No increase occurs for the second and third presentations, where the essay is presumably easier to grasp, and where most subjects report greater interest.

From chin and *frontalis,* Smith and his co-workers obtained a rising gradient to the fourth minute of listening, then a fall to the end of their six-minute article. Their interpretation was that the subjects attended for a few minutes, this attention being reflected in continuously rising muscle potentials. After the fourth minute, the individuals became bored and tension fell. This view was supported by some retrospective reports of boredom and sleepiness setting in before the article ended. *Frontalis* and chin curves in the present study showed a rise throughout listening, and our subjects failed to report a loss of interest during the record. Again one might say that continuous attention is reflected in rising gradients in particular muscles. But why should this be the case?

It may be that sustained thought *per se*, i.e., attention alone, would lead to increasing muscular activity. Such an occurrence might conceivably take place if a person were deliberately persisting along certain lines of thought, despite increasing difficulty, distraction, or boredom. The gradients would thus represent compensatory effort for decreasing efficiency in carrying through a task. Though such a possibility cannot be entirely ruled out, its likelihood is questionable. Distraction in the present study was minimal, and bored subjects were not forced to listen; witness the two individuals who fell asleep. As for difficulty, one might expect listening to the story to yield gradients of smaller magnitude; in fact, these were larger. Further, the size of the *frontalis* gradients showed an orderly (albeit small) increase from first to last hearing of the essay. Finally, only the last presentation yielded a significant gradient on the chin when the essay was listened to. It would appear that ease, rather than difficulty, is a positive factor here. Greater familiarity with and comprehension of the material seems to make for larger increases of tension during the course of listening (all this, admittedly, within the narrow range of our experiment; three successive hearings may not have allowed for extreme familiarity to develop). Now, terms like comprehension bring us to grips with the organizing functions of the thought process. To face this aspect more directly, a distinction between hearing and listening is in order.

Increase of organization during listening. The term *hearing* implies passive reception of the incoming auditory stimuli; the term *listening,* active integration of these stimuli. In our experiment, these stimuli, already organized into a familiar language structure, constitute items of information. The present thesis holds that these items did not merely impinge on the subject's auditory mechanisms, but were actively selected and organized by him. The individual's attention involved a set to understand, that is, to integrate the information. As the record played on and the number of items increased, the extent of the subject's organization also increased. Rising gradients of tension from *frontalis* and chin muscles may thus reflect growth of psychological organization.

To account for the correspondence between psychological organization and muscular tension, we shall turn briefly to the neuropsychological theory recently propounded by Hebb (**5**). Through learning (especially learning during early life) numbers of central neurons interconnect to form distinct groupings (assemblies) more or less permanent. A single assembly may denote a simple item in physical space – a triangle, for example. These simple items become organized into larger units, through sequential action of a number of assemblies firing in proper phase. A phase sequence might underlie a patterned mosaic, composed of simpler assembly units like triangles, circles, and squares. Now for our present thesis, the discrete stimuli are not geometrical forms, but word symbols. Word items referring to simple objects or events correspond to cell-assemblies. Patterns of such items, i.e., higher-order structures like sentences and paragraphs, involve higher-order neuronal action, namely, phase sequences. Through reverberation (self-stimulation) these units may maintain a course independent of sensory stimulation and motor response. This process is, of course, not completely independent. Central and sensory processes may reinforce each other or come into conflict. Similarly, central and motor components interact, leading to central facilitation or inhibition of muscular and overt action. A directed system, involving a degree of central independence in congruence with a degree of central-peripheral interaction, may constitute the thought process. Increasing organization of such a system may constitute growth of the thought process.

Returning to our experiment, it seems that *frontalis* tension constitutes a motor aspect of the phase sequence. It reflects reinforcement of the sequence with onset of listening, further recruitment of subsumed assemblies during listening, and decline of organization with end of listening. Chin muscle activity supported this picture, whereas muscles of the forearms proved negative. It may well be that during thinking muscles of facial expression and speech are particularly prone to direct central facilitation.

One finding of interest here is the failure of tension to fall significantly after the essay is heard. The poorer memory scores and smaller gradients suggest that the essay was not as well understood as the story. When an interested subject does not fully comprehend the material listened to, he may continue thinking about it after it has ended; whereas more fully understood material may fail to occupy his attention to the same degree. Neuropsychologically, the more fully organized phase sequence "short-circuits" more rapidly (**5**, pp. 227 ff.).

Wakefulness

One more pattern of findings, suggesting some independence between degree of wakefulness and other aspects of thought, merits consideration. The results have shown an orderly decrease in pre-rest level of *frontalis* tension from first to third hearings. *Frontalis* tension gradients during listening failed, however, to show a similar decrease. Also, retrospective reports indicated an increase of sleepiness from one hearing to the next. These same reports, however, did not show a similar decrease of interest, attention, and anticipation.

It may therefore be that changes in the pre-rest level of *frontalis* activity reflect changes in wakefulness; that the differences in magnitude of the rising gradients reflect changes of attention and anticipation during listening; and that within the major limits of our experiment these two states are independent. Not within the entire limits, however; as indicated by the two subjects who failed to keep awake, and their decline in *frontalis* tension prior to actual onset of sleep. Falls of *frontalis* potentials preceding sleep have previously been reported by Travis and Kennedy (**9**), whose subjects also showed poorer reaction time performance with decreasing *frontalis* activity. It may be that attention and anticipation are more intimately bound to alertness when a subject is nearing sleep, and less so when he is wide awake.

At present, however, this distinction between waking level and the more directive aspects of thought is only tentative, and awaits the test of further research.

Summary

In an experiment designed to investigate muscular activity during sustained attention, two groups of subjects were requested to listen to three successive presentations of a recorded detective story and philosophical essay.

Results showed rising gradients of tension from

forehead and chin throughout the course of listening. Listening to the story tended to produce increases of greater magnitude than did listening to the essay. Forearm muscles failed to show any clear variations during listening.

The rising gradients of muscle tension may be associated with increasing comprehension or organization of incoming verbal material – organization which may take place during attentive listening.

References

1. BARTOSHUK, A. K. An electromyographic study of goal-directed activity. Unpublished master's dissertation, McGill Univer., 1951.
2. BARTOSHUK, A. K. An electromyographic study of goal-directed activity. Paper read at Canadian Psychological Association, Kingston, May, 1953.
3. COURTS, F. A. Muscular tension and performance. *Psychol. Bull.*, 1942, *39*, 347-369.
4. DAVIS, J. F. *Manual of surface electromyography*. Montreal: Laboratory for Psychological Studies, Allan Memorial Institute, 1952 (mimeo.)
5. HEBB, D. O. *Organization of behaviour*. New York: Wiley, 1949.
6. INMAN, V. T., RALSTON, H. J., SAUNDERS, J. B., FEINSTEIN, B., and WRIGHT, E. W. Relation of human electromyogram to muscular tension. *J. Electroenceph. clin. Neurophysio.*, 1952, *4*, 187-194.
7. SMITH, A. A. An electromyographic study of tension in interrupted and completed tasks. *J. exp. Psychol.*, 1953, *46*, 32-36.
8. SMITH, A. A., MALMO, R. B., and SHAGASS, C. An electromyographic study of listening and and talking. *Canad. J. Psychol.*, 1954, *8*, 219-227. (Abstracted in *Amer. Psychol.*, 1953, *8*, 437-438.)
9. TRAVIS, R. C., and KENNEDY, J. L. Prediction and automatic control of alertness. *J. comp. physiol. Psychol.*, 1947, *40*, 457-461.
10. WILCOXON, F. *Some rapid approximate statistical procedures*. Stamford, Connecticut: American Cyanamid Company, 1949.

26 / Towards a Theory of Vigilance[1]

C.H. Baker *Defence Research Medical Laboratories, Toronto*

Many tasks in our modern technological society require continuous monitoring of a repetitive signal. A common observation is that the efficiency of an observer decreases as the vigilance period is prolonged. The reason for this decrement is not entirely clear and Dr. Baker describes here an expectancy theory to explain the decrement.

Little is known about the stability of perceptual performance as a function of time. One area which has excited considerable interest in recent years, however, concerns changes in perceptual performance in time under conditions where weak and randomly occurring signals, serially presented, must be observed and responded to. The best known, and among the earliest experiments in this field, have been reported by Mackworth (18, 19, 20, 21, 22).

Mackworth devised a Clock Test having a single rotating hand on a plain dial. Once each second the hand jumped forward 3.6 degrees to a new position, 100 jumps completing a revolution. Occasionally, however, the hand jumped double the usual distance and subjects responded to these double jumps, or "signals," by pressing a button. The interesting feature of these studies was that, as time progressed, fewer and fewer signals were detected. Typical data (22) showed that in four successive half-hour periods, the percentages of signals escaping detection were, respectively, 16, 26, 27, and 28. Such a decrement in performance with time has been demonstrated by more than twenty-five investigators working independently (see 1,3,16,17, and 25 as representative). The decrement has been shown to occur in the absence of any change in the sensory threshold (15, 25, 26) and is thus considered to be central in origin.

Theory

In a study of the effect of signal frequency Jenkins (16) found that, "the probability that an observer will detect a particular signal depends much more upon the prevailing or mean signal rate than upon the length of time that has elapsed since the preceding signal was detected." In examining these two possibilities Deese (12) advanced an expectancy hypothesis to account for the general level of performance during a vigilance task. It states that "the probability of detection – is determined by a large and rather indeterminant number of signals preceding the signal in question – the observer – continuously performing a kind of averaging of previous input in order to extrapolate the results to future behaviour of the search field," and so, "expectancy should be low immediately after a signal, should increase as the mean intersignal interval is approached, and finally should become quite high as the intersignal interval grows beyond the mean."

This hypothesis implies that the observer would be "eternally hanging on an expectant limb" after a series of signals terminated, and consequently has been expanded (6) to read, "as the interval grows still longer expectancy again falls to a low level." It should be noted that the term "expectancy," as used in this paper, does not necessarily imply any conscious formulations on the part of the observer. The degree to which he is aware of such expectancies is unknown.

The work of Mowrer (23) serves admirably to illustrate the expanded hypothesis. In order to "obtain an *objective* record of the course of expectancy," he used a simple reaction time technique, subjects responding to a tone which appeared "at an unvarying interval of 12 seconds." Occasional "test trials" were inserted, these consisting of intervals of as small as 3 to as large as 24 seconds. "As the test interval approached the standard interval the reaction time became progressively shorter (with rising expectancy) until, at the 12-second test interval – which was, of course, the same as the standard interval – the obtained reaction time was "normal".... As the test intervals varied beyond 12 seconds, up to 24 seconds, the average reaction time again increased but not to the same heights it had reached on the shorter test trials" ... (23). Mowrer's study has been repeated (4) using series of 20 unvarying intervals of 10 seconds, followed by a twenty-first "unexpected" interval of 2, 5, 20, 25, and 30 seconds, on separate trials.

In Figure 1 the data from this study are plotted in terms of the percentage increase in time to respond to a twenty-first signal inserted after the five "unexpected" intervals. For signals at 202 and 205 seconds the mean response time was longer (43 and 37 per cent respectively), than the mean of the preceding series. This difference is significant at the 1 per cent level although the apparent downward trend of the three "late" signals is not.

[1]Defence Research Medical Laboratories Project no. 234, DRML Report no. 234-3, PCC no. D77-94-20-42, H.R. no. 165.

Reprinted, by permission, from *Canadian Journal of Psychology*, 1959, *13*, 35-42.

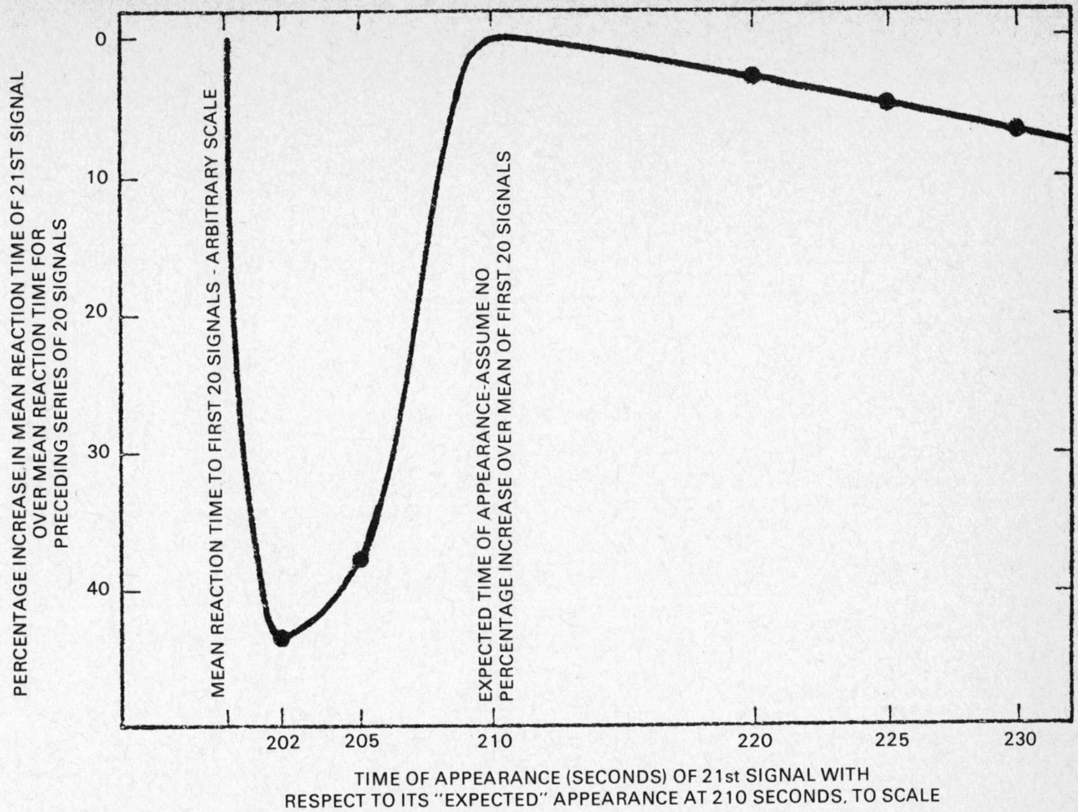

Fig. 1. Showing the mean percentage increase in reaction time to a 21st signal appearing at shorter and longer intervals than that employed in the preceding regular series N = 12.

Figure 1 is interpreted as the shape of the expectancy function – expectancy drops to a low level shortly after each signal, mounts rapidly as the next signal is expected, and then tends to taper off if the expectancy is not confirmed. Experiments employing regular intervals of two minutes, followed by "unexpected" intervals, have yielded similar results.

Supporting Data

In addition to explaining the decrement in performance often found in vigilance tasks, a satisfactory model must also explain the effects of at least six factors which are known to retard or accelerate the decrement. These factors are given below, each followed by a brief description of how the position outlined above can account for their known effects.

(1) *Rate of signal appearance.* A greater percentage of signals is detected, or signals are responded to more quickly, as signal frequency increase (8, 10, 11, 16, 24).

This follows for two reasons: (i) observers have a larger sample of data upon which to base expectancies, and (ii) it has been shown (28) that observers can estimate short intervals with greater precision than longer intervals. It should be noted that we are not concerned here with the oft-found decrement in performance, but with the over-all level, that is, with the proportion of signals detected during a complete session.

(2) *Inter-signal interval.* The more regular the temporal interval between signals, the more signal detections (4,6).

Here we are concerned with the decrement in detection performance in time. The accuracy of perception of the temporal structure of a series of signals must be a function of the degree of regularity of the series, and the more accurate the perception the more probable the confirmation of expectancy. For signals occurring with less apparent regularity, confirmation of expectancy is less probable. Lack of confirmation lowers the apparent signal frequency, with the consequent lowering of the over-all level of performance. This lowering of the over-all level of performance proceeds in successive steps in time. These steps are invariably masked when the results from individual subjects are pooled, and appear as a smooth decrement.

At some point in time the observer abandons his efforts to build expectancies. This occurs when the apparent frequency is so low that the intervals are too long to permit extrapolation with any precision. The probability of signal detection is now determined solely by chance events, that is, he is looking at the right place at the right time. Such chance events, being independent, result in a consistent probability of detection as time progresses, that is, in performance which shows no further decrement, as typified, for example, in Mackworth's studies (22).

The above explanations of the effects of signal frequency and interval regularity are basic to the expectancy position. Expectancy is a function of signal frequency and interval regularity. It follows that any condition which reduces either frequency or regularity, or both, will result in a lower over-all level of performance or a greater decrement in time, or both.

(3) *Signal magnitude*. Signals of large magnitude (size, duration, intensity) escape detection less frequently than those of smaller magnitude (1, 16, 22).

Such signals make confirmation of expectancy more probable, simply because the greater the magnitude the greater the probability of perception.

(4) *Knowledge of results*. Knowledge of results during a vigilance session prevents a decrement in performance from occurring (22).

Explanation of this effect is based upon the proposition that knowledge of results serves to establish perception of the true sequential nature of the series and so to increase the probability of expectancy confirmation, that is, knowledge of results, in this particular context, is synonymous with feedback. In other words, telling an observer, "yes, that was right," or, "you missed one there," tells him, in effect, that there is a signal *now*, and nothing more. We would not, therefore, expect knowledge of results to be a potent factor until the task had proceeded for some time, and indeed Mackworth found "a clear advantage in favour of the men who were supplied with knowledge of results, except during the first half-hour" (22).

The proposition that knowledge of results in a vigilance situation serves simply as feedback by revealing the true temporal nature of the series has recently been tested (4). Three experimental conditions were compared. In one, the "no information" condition, no information was given when a signal was detected or missed. In the second, knowledge of results was given: a small display was illuminated for one second above the main display, to read "correct," "missed," or "false," as appropriate. In the third or "feedback" condition a missed signal was repeated a second, a third, or an even greater number of times, at intervals of five seconds until it was responded to, but the observer was *credited with a miss even though he eventually responded*. The Mackworth intervals mentioned above were employed in this study as they are known to produce a decrement when no information is supplied. Seventy-five paid female subjects were employed, twenty-five being randomly assigned to each condition. (The procedure of testing each subject under each condition was avoided because of the possibility of order effects.)

The data are shown in Figure 2. The decrement in the "no information" condition is significant at the 0.02 level of confidence. As hypothesized, there is no significant decrement in the "knowledge" or "feedback" conditions. The general superiority of the "feedback" group is attributed to chance differences between the groups.

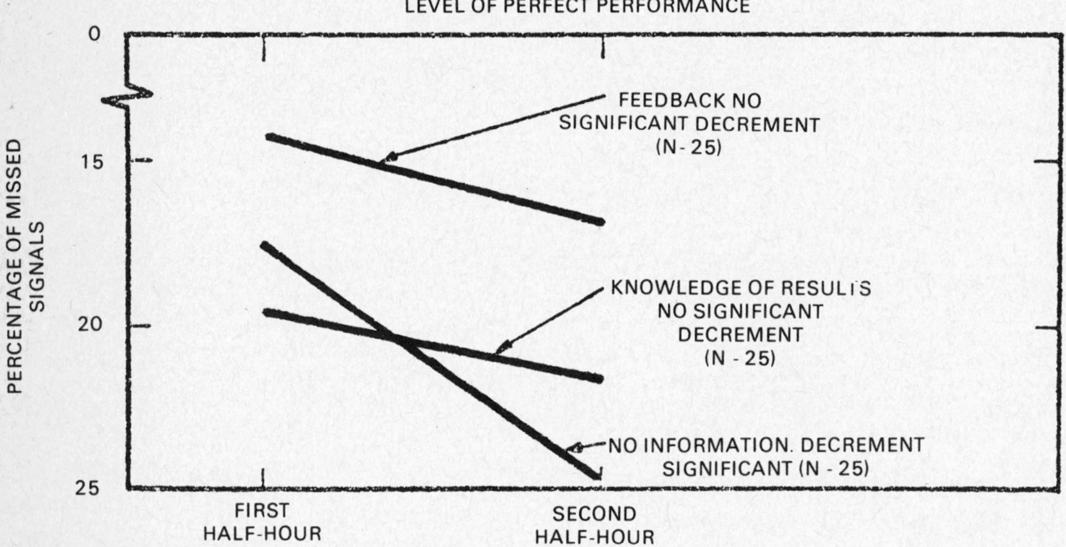

Fig. 2. Showing the percentage of signals missed under each of three experimental conditions during the first and second half-hour periods.

(5) *Environmental factors*. Significantly more signals are detected at 79°F. than at 70° or 90° when subjects are dressed in shorts (20, 22). High ambient noise levels also impair performance (9).

The explanation of these effects is simply that any distraction which competes for attention with the vigilance task will lower the apparent signal frequency and consequently result in a deteriorated performance.

(6) *Knowledge of signal location*. When signals

appear at locations which cannot be predicted, performance is generally poorer than when the location is known, that is, when visual search is not involved (15). This follows because under the condition of uncertainty of signal location an expectancy may be "correct," but the signal may appear at a location not being scanned at that moment. Such unconfirmed expectancies will serve to lower the apparent signal frequency. Supporting data have been reported (7, 15, 26).

Discussion

An attempt has been made here to examine an expectancy hypothesis of vigilance proposed by Deese (16), expand it, illustrate it, and present some supporting data.

Two merits of the position outlined here are worth emphasizing. First, in vigilance experiments performance never becomes nil, that is, the curve of performance always becomes asymptotic with the time base and never intersects it. The expectancy position can account for this phenomenon. Second, it has been shown that knowledge of results can assume new meaning. Knowledge of results is typically (and vaguely) considered as a motivating factor – something akin to the use of incentives (the individual approach), or to the use of authority or peer figures (the social approach), in inducing high and sustained levels of performance. But the mode of operation of such knowledge in a vigilance task has been shown to differ fundamentally from this general concept: here "knowledge of results" provides nothing more than *knowledge* of the true nature of the temporal structure of a series in order that observers can make accurate temporal extrapolations.

This approach has avoided what is an obvious and possibly a most important factor in determining the efficiency of perceptual performance in time-motivation. Fraser has shown (14), for instance, that performance is superior on a vigilance task if the experimenter sits quietly behind the observer, rather than outside the room, presumably because the experimenter is an authority figure in this particular situation. Worth mentioning, too, is our understanding that at sea officers of the watch make many more sightings than do members of the watch. (In passing we can note the findings (2, 20, 25) that there is no relation between intellectual ability and performance on a vigilance task.) Data, however, are few.

The theoretical position outlined above, however, should be true at any level of motivation on the part of the observer and even in the case of a changing level of motivation. The performance of even the most highly motivated observer must in time decline if the situation is such as to produce a decrement – small, brief, infrequent signals, irregularly spaced, with no feedback concerning performance. On the other hand, the least motivated subject could turn in an acceptable performance if signals were large, prolonged, frequent, fairly regularly spaced in time, with feedback proved.

In closing it is worth pointing out that in the experiments described here the measure of performance has been the percentage of signals escaping detection. Many other measures have been reported. Considerable emphasis has been placed upon the "effective threshold" technique, which consists basically of increasing signal magnitude in steps until it *is* reported, that is, apparent signal frequency and input frequency are the same (13). In view of the data reported above concerning the effects of feedback it appears that use of the "effective threshold" technique will generate data which are not descriptive of the actual situation.

References

1. ADAMS, J. A. Vigilance in the detection of low-intensity visual stimuli. *J. exp. Psychol.*, 1956, *52*, 204-208.
2. BAKAN, P. Personal communication.
3. ———. Discrimination decrement as a function of time in a prolonged vigil. *J. exp. Phychol.*, 1955, *50*, 387-390.
4. BAKER, C. H. Three minor studies of vigilance. Defence Research Board of Canada. *DRML Rep.* No 234-2, 1958.
5. ———. Attention to visual displays during a vigilance task. I. Biasing attention. *Brit. J. Psychol.*, 1958, *49* (in press).
6. ———. Attention to visual displays during a vigilance task. II. Maintaining the level of vigilance. *Brit. J. Psychol.*, 1959, *49* (in press).
7. BAKER, C. H., and BOYES, G. E. Increasing probability of target detection with a mirror-image display. 1958 (in press).
8. BOWEN, H. M., and WOODHEAD, M. M. Vigilance. The effect of frequency of signals. *Med. Res. Council, A.P.U. Memorandum Rep.*, 1956.
9. BROADBENT, D. E. The twenty dials and twenty lights test under noise conditions. *Med. Res. Council, A.P.U.* 160/51, 1951.
10. BROWNE, R. C. The day and night performance of teleprint switchboard operators. *J. occup. Psychol.*, 1949, *23*, 121-125.
11. DEESE, J., and ORMOND, E. Studies of detectability during continuous visual search. *U.S.A.F., W.A.D.C. Tech. Rep.* 53-8, 1953.
12. DEESE, J. Some problems in the theory of vigilance. *Psychol. Rev.*, 1955, *62*, 359-368.
13. ELLIOTT, E. Auditory vigilance tasks. *The Advancement of Science*, 1957, *53*, 393-399.
14. FRASER, D. C. The relation of an environmental variable to performance in a prolonged visual task. *Quart. J. exp. Psychol.*, 1953, *5*, 31-32.
15. GARVEY, W. D., and HENSON, J. B. Effect of length of observing time on earth satellite visibility. *U.S. Naval Res. Lab. Rep.* 5094, 1958.
16. JENKINS, H. M. Performance on a visual monitoring task as a function of the rate at which signals occur. M.I.T., Lincoln Laboratory, *Tech. Rep.* 47, 1953.
17. JERISON, H. J. Performance on a simple vigilance task in noise and quiet. *J. acoust. Soc. Amer.*, 1957, *29*, 1163-1165.

18. MACKWORTH, N. H. Notes on the clock test: A new approach to the study of prolonged visual perception to find the optimum length of watch for radar operators. *Med. Res. Council, A.P.U.* I, 1944.
19. ———. Faulty perception caused by blank spells without signals during experiments on prolonged visual search. *Med. Res. Council, A.P.U.* 17/45, F.P.R.C. 586(a), 1945.
20. ———. Effects of heat and high humidity on prolonged visual search as measured by the clock test. *Med. Res. Council, A.P.U.* 33/46, F.P.R.C. 586(c), 1946.
21. ———. The breakdown of vigilance during prolonged visual search. *Quart. J. Exp. Psychol.*, 1948, *1*, 6-21.
22. ———. Researches on the measurement of human performance. *Med. Res. Council Report*, No. 268. London: H.M. Stationery Office, 1950.
23. MOWRER, O. H. Preparatory set (expectancy): Some methods of measurement. *Psychol. Monogr.*, 1940, *52*, No. 2 (Whole No. 233).
24. POLLOCK, I., and KNAFF, P. R. Effect of rate of target presentation on target detection probability. *Amer. Psychol.*, 1958, *13*, 414 (Abstract).
25. SOLANDT, D. Y., and PARTRIDGE, R. C. Research on auditory problems presented by naval operations. *J. Canad. med. Services*, 1946, *3*, 323-329.
26. WALLIS, D. Auditory and visual search problems. *Memorandum Rep.*, Dept. of the Senior Psychologist, Admiralty, 1957.
27. WILKINSON, R. T. Recent Research on the effects of lack of sleep. *Med. Res. Council, R.N.P.R.C.*, OES 269, 1955.
28. WOODROW, H. Time perception. In STEVENS, S. S. (ed.), *Handbook of experimental psychology*. New York: Wiley, 1951, 1224-1236.

27 / Behavioural and EEG Changes During and After 14 Days of Perceptual Deprivation and Confinement[1]

John P. Zubek *University of Manitoba*

The importance of this paper lies in its demonstration that a varied and patterned sensory environment is essential to the maintenance of normal human behaviour. If a person is required to live for many days in a monotonous, non-changing sensory and perceptual environment, his physiological and psychological processes may operate in extraordinary ways. The study of man under extreme conditions can contribute much to our understanding of the ordinary functioning of the organism.

A relatively recent development in experimental psychology has been the study of the effects upon human behaviour of a severe reduction in the level and variability of visual, auditory, and tactual-kinesthetic stimulation. The experimental attempts to achieve such a non-changing sensory environment are often referred to by such terms as stimulus deprivation, sensory or perceptual deprivation, or sensory and perceptual isolation. Whatever the terminology, this condition can produce marked behavioural and physiological changes.

Although interest in this field has had a long history (see Brownfield, 1965 for a description of the experiences of solitary sailors, Arctic and Antarctic explorers, prison inmates, mystics in seclusion, etc) the first experimental work on it began in 1951 at McGill University under the direction of Professor D. O. Hebb (Bexton, Heron and Scott, 1954). Its purpose was to further our understanding of the mechanisms underlying "brainwashing" (a term first employed during the Korean War) and of the lapses of attention noted under monotonous environmental conditions, such as watching a radar screen for a prolonged period of time. The results of this research were quite startling and unexpected. The subjects, who were paid to do nothing except lie alone in a semi-soundproofed chamber for several days, wear translucent goggles and listen to a constant masking sound of low intensity, reported a variety of unusual subjective phenomena, e.g., vivid and highly structured hallucinations, delusions, and gross changes in the appearance of the perceptual environment upon emerging from isolation. In addition to these introspective reports, objective test data were obtained which indicated an increased susceptibility to propaganda material, impairments in cognitive and perceptual functioning, and a progressive slowing of occipital alpha frequencies with increasing duration of isolation.

These dramatic results, together with four other post-World War II developments, soon excited world-wide scientific interest in the effects of sensory isolation and confinement. The first source of interest came from the highly publicized "confessions" extracted by communist interrogators (e.g., the Cardinal Mindzenty case). What little information was available suggested that the results were obtained by techniques which often employed solitary confinement and the deliberate impoverishment of the prisoner's perceptual environment (Brownfield, 1965). Drugs and physical torture were apparently not used. The second development was the arrival of the space age in October, 1957. The crew of a space vehicle will not only have to live in very restricted quarters under relatively monotonous conditions but also, more importantly, they will be subjected to prolonged separation from their accustomed environment. Other technological advances, as reflected in increased use of submarines, isolated radar and meteorological stations, and of automated equipment in general, also provided considerable impetus to the initiation and development of research programs dealing with reactions to restricted sensory and social environments.

A third major source of interest originated in certain advances in neurophysiology, particularly the discovery of the reticular activating system which is important in producing a general state of "arousal" or alertness in the organism. Since this alerting action appeared to be dependent upon the organism's exposure to a constantly changing sensory input, behavioural experiments employing conditions of either constant, non-varying sensory stimuli, or a lack of sensory stimuli were required as possible tests of these neurophysiological findings. Finally, certain developments within academic psychology were instrumental in directing attention to this topic. One of these was in the area of motivation, in which attempts were made to show that animals have an active need for experience, i.e., they possess an ex-

This article is largely based on material which has been reported in *Science,* 1963, *139*, 490-492 and *Psychonomic Science,* 1964, *1*, 57-58. The research program has been supported by Grant 9425-08, Defence Research Board, Canada, and Grant APA-290, National Research Council, Canada.

ploratory drive or curiosity (Fiske and Maddi, 1961, pp. 175-226). A study of human reactions to an impoverished environment might clarify the mechanisms underlying this need for experience, change, or novelty. Another development within psychology came from studies of early sensory deprivation in animals. The experiments of Austin Riesen, D. O. Hebb, and their associates had shown that laboratory animals reared under various types of isolation subsequently exhibited strikingly abnormal behaviour (Beach and Jaynes, 1954; Fiske and Maddi, 1961, pp. 57-105). These findings suggested the possibility of extending this research to humans, but, because of ethical considerations, only adults and relatively short periods of isolation could safely be employed. As a consequence of the converging influence of these various developments, experimental studies similar to those at McGill University were initiated in numerous institutions not only in North America but also in such countries as England, The Netherlands, Italy, Czechoslovakia, South Africa, Australia, and Japan, resulting, at the present time, in well over 1,000 publications. (See Zubek, 1969 for a review of this literature.)

The research program on sensory isolation and confinement at the University of Manitoba was initiated in 1959 under a research grant from the Defence Research Board of Canada. It differs from that at other laboratories in two main respects. First, it is concerned with much longer isolation durations (7 to 14 days) and, second, an appraisal is made of a wide range of reactions involving various behavioural, physiological, and biochemical measures. In general, the research at other laboratories has employed a maximum duration of four days (usually a day or less) and has been directed at obtaining information of a restricted nature, e.g., appraisal of intellectual functioning or a determination of emotional and motivational effects. Since the inception of the Manitoba research program 11 years ago, approximately 300 experimental subjects have been isolated under conditions of either constant darkness and silence (sensory deprivation) or constant, unpatterned light and white noise (perceptual deprivation) and for durations ranging from 1 to 14 days. The remainder of this paper will be devoted to a description of the effects which occur during and after the exposure of a group of university students to 14 days of perceptual deprivation, the longest duration employed so far in the experimental literature.

Problem

For several years researchers at the University of Manitoba have been studying the behavioural effects of 7-day periods of perceptual deprivation (Zubek et al., 1960, 1961, 1962). Recently, it was decided to extend the period to 2 weeks. It was considered important to obtain, first, some data on the electrical activity of the brain during isolation, particularly during the second week, as well as data for some days after termination of isolation.

Although there is a voluminous literature on the effects of sensory and perceptual deprivation, data on electroencephalographic (EEG) changes are almost non-existent (Kubzansky, 1961). In one of the McGill studies (Heron 1957), EEG tracings from six subjects who completed 4 days of perceptual deprivation revealed a progressive decrease in occipital lobe alpha frequencies with increasing duration of isolation; i.e., more slow activity was evident after 4 days than after 2, in all six subjects. Tracings taken 3½ hours after isolation still showed some signs of abnormality. EEG records taken in some of the Manitoba studies also revealed a decrease in occipital alpha frequencies after 7 days of perceptual deprivation, a decrease still present 3 to 4 hours later. Finally, we have data on one subject isolated for 10 days. In this case, the EEG activity was still abnormal 7 days after the end of isolation. It is of interest that this subject experienced a severe and long-lasting motivational loss (Zubek et al., 1961). In the light of these meagre but provocative findings, further research seemed warranted.

Method

Isolation Chamber

A cross-sectional view of the isolation chamber is shown in Figure 1. It consists of a translucent plexiglas dome measuring 7 ft. in height, 9 ft. in diameter, and 7½ ft. at the base, with a floor surface area of approximately 45 sq. ft. It is surrounded on five sides by a system of fluorescent and incandescent lights by means of which the inside of the dome can be flooded with diffuse light of any intensity or wave-length. Toilet facilities, a food chamber, a two-way intercom system and an air-conditioning unit are all built into the floor of the dome making it unneccessary for *S* to leave the chamber for any purpose during the isolation period. The only piece of furniture in the dome is a mattress on which *S* lies. Entrance to the dome is through a trapdoor in the floor which also serves as a food chamber. The plexiglas dome and its external lighting system are housed inside a semi-soundproofed chamber measuring 14 ft. X 14 ft. X 14 ft.

Subjects

The *S*s were 15 male university students (mean age = 23.6 years) who volunteered to spend 14 days in the University of Manitoba isolation chamber. None of them had participated in any prior isolation experiment. The remuneration was $300 for the successful completion of the 14-day period. Because of the long duration involved, the experiment was conducted during the summer vacation period.

Procedure

A group of 15 male *S*s were placed individually in the isolation chamber, under a condition of constant, unpatterned light and white noise (a hissing sound), for a prescribed period of 14 days. Of the 15 *S*s, five failed to endure the full duration; all terminated

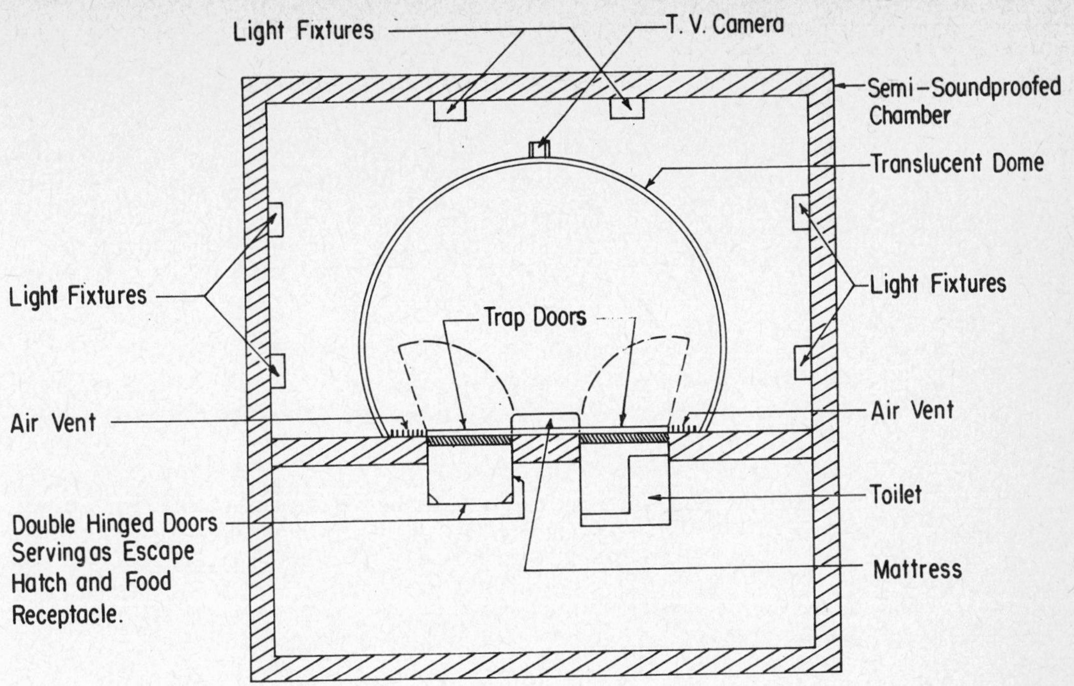

Fig. 1. The isolation chamber.

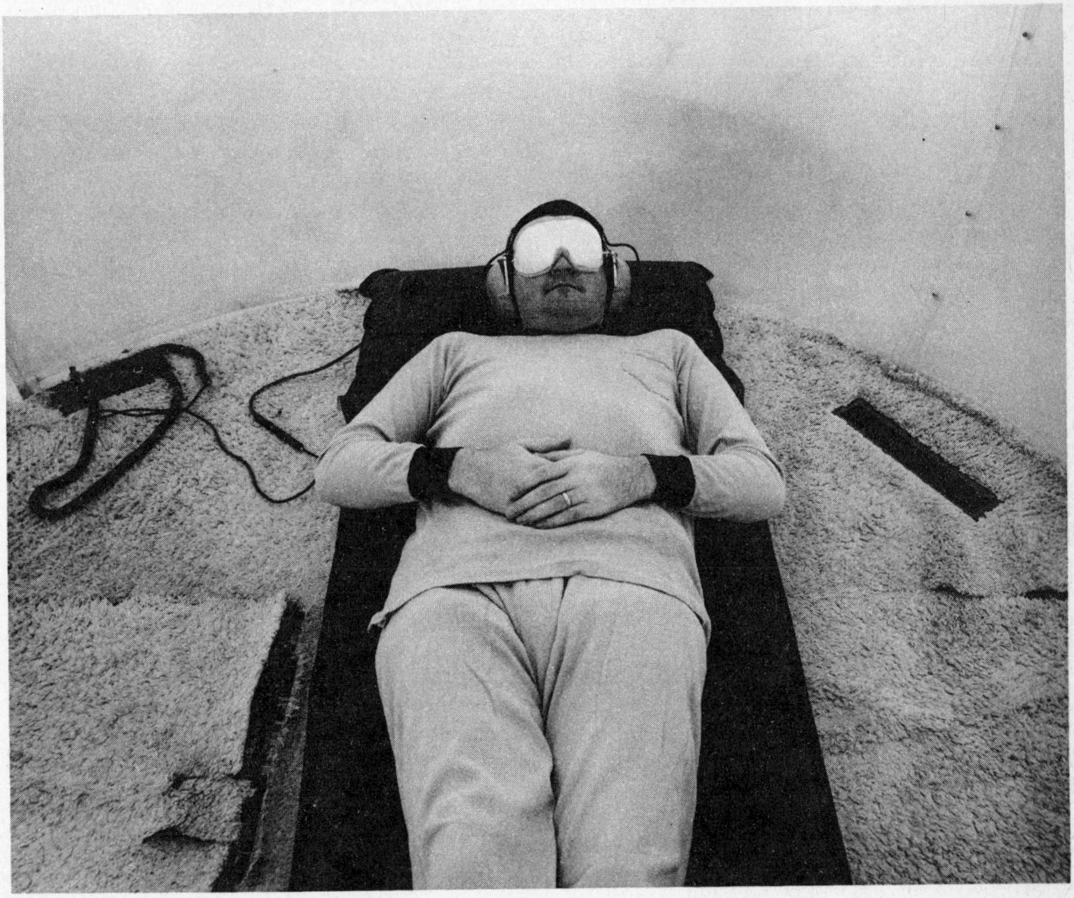

Fig. 2. A subject in the chamber.

isolation within the first 4 days. The *S*s wore translucent goggles which permitted light (20 ft-ca) but excluded all pattern vision (see Fig. 2). Each *S* also wore a pair of special gloves to minimize tactual stimulation, and a set of earmuffs through which white noise, somewhat above the threshold of hearing, was constantly presented. He was not permitted to sing, hum, or engage in any other vocal activity. He was allowed to move about the chamber but not to exercise. Each *S* was monitored throughout the isolation period by a communication system and a closed-circuit TV system which revealed satisfactory adherence to the experimental instructions. Conversation over the two-way intercom system was kept to a bare minimum; it occurred on the rare occasion when *S* did not adhere to certain restrictions, such as those against singing or exercising. At least one experimenter was on duty at all times. The food, which was available on a 24-hour basis in the food locker, consisted of a variety of sandwiches, fruit juices, coffee, tea, and milk. Each *S* was informed, beforehand, that he could terminate the experiment at any time if he so desired – at a reduced rate of payment.

Measures

EEG activity. EEG records were taken on an Offner type T, eight channel machine before isolation, and then during isolation at intervals of 7, 10, and 14 days. At these specified times the electroencephalographer entered the chamber and attached a set of electrodes to the *S*'s skull. The entire intrusion lasted approximately 30 minutes. During this interval the white noise was shut off, but *S* continued to wear the translucent goggles. Follow-up records were also taken at intervals of 1, 2, 7, and 10 days after the termination of the 14-day isolation period. The EEG tracings were taken at the same time of the day (10 A.M.) at each test session. Sixteen Ediswan monopad electrodes were applied to the head in International Federation 10/20 positions and two S.L.E. suction electrodes to the ears. Average, bipolar, and monopolar recordings were taken.

In order to obtain a quantitative measure of EEG changes, two types of analyses were performed. In the first, the period count technique (Engel et al., 1944) was used to determine the occipital alpha frequency of each *S*. Mean values were calculated from 300, 1-second samples of artifact-free occipital lobe tracings where sufficient countable wave activity of alpha frequency was available. In several cases, a somewhat smaller sample had to be employed. The second method involved a frequency spectrum analysis. This consists of determining the percentage of time that a particular frequency (e.g., 8, 9, or 10, waves per second) appears in the occipital lobe tracings during the total 300-second period.

Depth perception. This was measured by the Howard-Dohlman apparatus. The measure of depth perception was the mean of four binocular trials where half of the trials started with the movable rod in front of the standard and the other half with it in the back. Scores were recorded in terms of the mean separation, in cm., of the variable rod from the standard (taken as zero).

Size constancy. A black equilateral triangle, of variable height, was presented at 15 ft. *S* was required to adjust the height of this triangle until it looked the same in size as the near one, the standard triangle. This triangle was 20 cm. high and was maintained at a distance of 4 ft. Four trials were given.

The measures of depth perception and size constancy were administered before and after the 14-day deprivation period. For comparative purposes, a group of 15 control *S*s also received these two tests, 14 days apart. These two behavioural tests were administered in order to determine whether prolonged deprivation periods would disrupt these basic perceptual processes; previous research had indicated no effect after 7 days.

Results and Discussion

Figure 3 shows the changes in the EEG frequency spectrum for subject A at various intervals during the 14-day isolation period. It can be seen that there is a progressive shift in the spectrum toward the lower end of the frequency scale as isolation duration increases. After isolation, as Figure 4 indicates, this spectrum gradually shifts back to the higher frequencies. However, at the end of 7 days the frequency pattern is still unlike that for the pre-isolation period. Table I shows the mean occipital alpha frequencies of each of the 10 subjects at various time during and after the 14-day isolation period. One finding which clearly emerges is the presence of a progressive decrease in mean alpha frequency with increasing duration of deprivation. Furthermore, the mean decrease during the second week (1.11 cps) is approximately twice as great as that during the first (0.52 cps). Table I also indicates a progressive increase in mean frequency following termination of isolation. However, even after 10 days there are still some indications of EEG abnormality. Although these physiological changes, in general, are quite large they would undoubtedly have been even greater if restrictions had been placed on the subject's motor activity (Zubek and Wilgosh, 1963), e.g., if they had been required to lie quietly on the mattress, the usual procedure in sensory and perceptual deprivation experiments.

Perhaps the most important finding is the existence of large individual differences. As Table I indicates, the decrease in alpha frequency, at the end of the 14-day period, varies from 0.26 cps (which is in the range of normal day-to-day variations) to 3.56 cps, a decrease of considerable magnitude. This suggests, therefore, that certain individuals can withstand conditions of reduced sensory and social stimulation much better than others. Similar results have also been observed in prison situations. Hinkle (1961), for example, has reported that "under prison isolation, as this has been carried out by Russian and

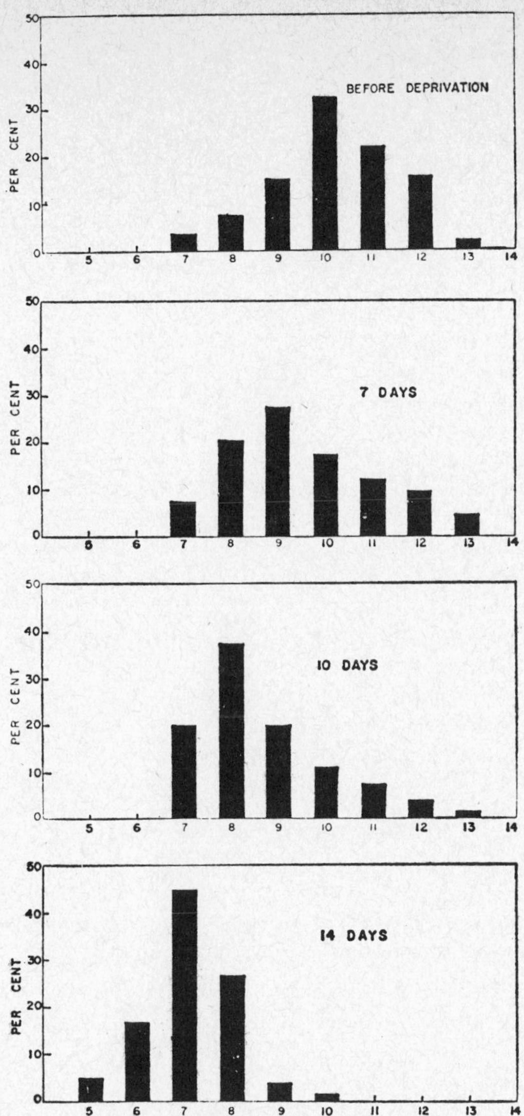

Fig. 3. Frequency spectrum for subject A before perceptual deprivation and at 7, 10, and 14 days after the beginning of deprivation. The ordinate shows the percentage of time that waves of various frequencies appear in the occipital lobe tracings during a 300-second period.

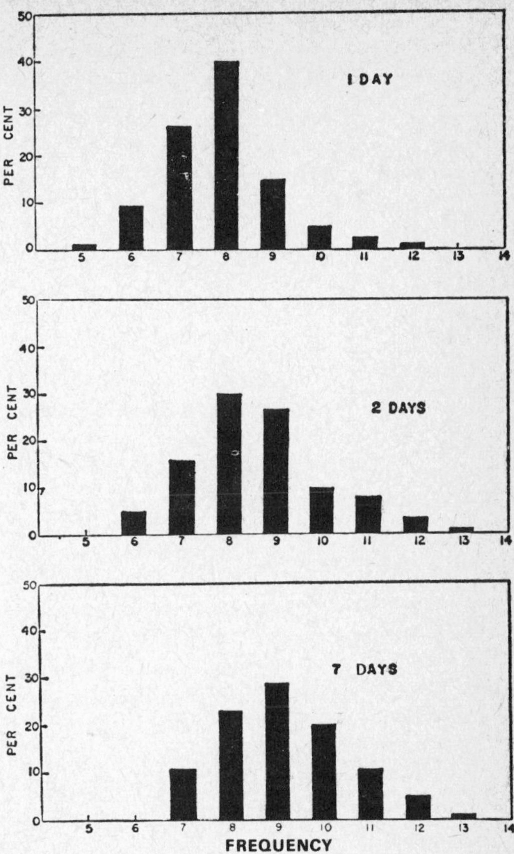

Fig. 4. Frequency spectrum for subject A at 1, 2, and 7 days after the completion of 2 weeks of perceptual deprivation.

Eastern European state police, most prisoners developed symptoms of disorganization within three to six weeks; but some have been known to endure this for many months, and some have succumbed within days." Large individual differences also exist in the capacity to withstand the effects of sleep deprivation. Some people can endure 100 hours with their functions largely intact whereas others become disorganized and ineffective after only 48 hours of sleep deprivation (Hinkle, 1961).

Depth perception and size constancy were not impaired, a finding in agreement with our earlier 7-day experiments (Zubek et al., 1961, 1962). This suggests that certain basic perceptual processes are not affected by even prolonged durations of reduced sensory stimulation.

Since volunteers who have experienced perceptual deprivation and confinement for 14 days are rare, some mention will be made of their subjective reactions. Data on these were obtained after isolation by means of a short questionnaire, an interview, and diaries. Various precautions were taken to minimize the factor of suggestion. Eight of the 10 subjects reported marked intellectual deficits during isolation – inability to concentrate, difficulty in organizing their thoughts, and reduced motivation for thinking and reasoning. These deficits, contrary to what the EEG data suggest, did not appear to be accentuated during the second week of confinement. This discrepancy, however, may be due to the unreliability of retrospective reports.

Hallucinatory-like experiences, of a visual nature, were infrequent and when reported were almost invariably of a simple, unstructured variety, e.g., "a black dot racing across my field of vision," "flickering pinpoints of light," and "cloud-like formations in front of my eyes." These generally lasted from 10 to 20 seconds and tended to be most frequent toward the end of the experimental period. (Since this information was based on retrospective reports, it is possible that the subjects may have forgotten some of their experiences early in the experiment.) Frequent references were made to repetitive auditory events

Table I – Mean occipital alpha frequencies at various intervals during and after 14 days of perceptual deprivation

Subject	During Deprivation				After Deprivation			
	Day 0	Day 7	Day 10	Day 14	Day 1	Day 2	Day 7	Day 10
A	10.10	9.16	8.60	7.15	7.89	8.62	9.57	----*
B	13.03	12.65	11.40	10.44	11.04	11.34	12.50	----*
C	11.56	----*	10.14	8.00	10.21	----*	11.01	----*
D	11.27	10.13	9.87	9.08	9.61	9.83	10.14	10.68
E	9.67	9.27	8.75	8.39	8.57	8.97	9.18	9.46
F	11.51	11.04	10.93	9.96	10.35	10.54	10.36	10.94
G	10.66	10.06	10.02	9.72	10.01	10.30	10.45	10.50
H	10.92	10.65	10.63	10.66	10.75	10.67	10.67	10.65
I	10.65	10.70	10.56	10.16	9.91	10.04	10.38	10.61
J	10.46	10.50	10.42	9.90	10.11	10.32	10.47	10.44
Mean	10.98	10.46	10.13	9.35	9.84	10.07	10.47	10.47

* No EEG records were taken at this time period

throughout the entire 14-day period – birds chirping or singing, waves splashing, water dripping, and so on. These experiences, however, are believed to have been auditory illusions rather than hallucinations, since the subjects were not convinced of their reality and regarded them largely as distortions of the continually present white noise.

Upon emerging from isolation, none of the subjects reported any "profound and prolonged disturbances of visual perception" of the type mentioned in one of the McGill 6-day studies (Heron, Doane and Scott, 1956) – for example, warping and curving of lines, walls moving in and out, and gross changes in the size and shape of objects – effects which in some instances were present 24 hours later, as reported in the McGill study. Various objects were seen as much brighter and more vivid in colour than usual, but they did not seem changed in size, shape, or movement. Although this infrequent occurrence of hallucinations and absence of post-confinement perceptual distortions is at variance with the McGill findings, the results are in agreement with those of the more recent 7-day deprivation experiments. In our earlier studies (Zubek et al., 1961, 1962) and in the studies of Ruff and Levy (1959), hallucinations and post-isolation perceptual distortions were rare. Furthermore, Cameron et al. (1961) also reported similar negative results in one subject exposed to two weeks of perceptual deprivation. The reasons for these conflicting results remain to be determined.

Certain dramatic and prolonged psychological changes were observed, but they were of a motivational rather than a perceptual nature. After the termination of isolation, most of the subjects reported (in their diaries) pronounced motivational changes, e.g., "an inability to get started doing anything," a "loathing to do any work requiring even the slightest degree of physical or mental exertion," and "a don't-give-a-damn attitude toward everything." These types of effects persisted from less than a day to 8 days (mean = 3½ days). As might be expected, some relation existed between the magnitude of the subject's alpha frequency decrease and the duration of their motivational losses (Rho = 0.67). Finally, one volunteer (Subject D, Table I) reported a strong craving to go back into isolation shortly after his release – *even without financial renumeration*. Such a reaction has been observed in our laboratory only once before – after 10 days of darkenss and silence. This phenomenon may, therefore, only occur after very long periods of deprivation. It is of interest to note that some long-term prison inmates as well as Polar explorers and inhabitants have also reported a similar phenomenon – a strong desire to return to their former isolated environment. Whether these two sets of observations are related remains an interesting speculation.

Although this study is based on a relatively small sample of subjects, the results are remarkably consistent. They indicate that a prolonged period of perceptual deprivation and confinement can produce, in most cases, a considerable disturbance of brain-wave activity, with effects still discernable 10 days later. In the light of these results, one can only wonder about the possible physiological and psychological state of prisoners of war and others who, in the past, have been isolated for months or even years.

References

BEACH, F. A., and JAYNES, J. Effects of early experience upon the behaviour of animals. *Psychol. Bull.*, 1954, *51*, 239-263.

BEXTON, W. H., HERON, W., and SCOTT, T. H. Effects of decreased variation in the sensory environment. *Canad. J. Psychol.*, 1954, *8*, 70-76.

BROWNFIELD, C. A. *Isolation: Clinical and experimental approaches*. New York: Random House, 1965.

CAMERON, D. E., LEVY, L., BAN, T., and RUBENSTEIN, L. Sensory deprivation: Effects upon the functioning human in space systems. In B. E. FLAHERTY (ed.), *Psychophysiological aspects of space flight*. New York: Columbia University Press, 1961. Pp. 225-237.

ENGEL, G. L., ROMANO, J. FERRIS, E. B., WEBB, J. P., and STEVENS, C. D. A simple method of determining frequency spectrums in the electroencephalogram. *Arch. Neurol. Psychiat.*, 1944, *51*, 134-146.

FISKE, D. W., and MADDI, S. R. *Functions of varied experience*. Homewood, Ill.: Dorsey, 1961.

HERON, W. The pathology of boredom. *Sci. American*, 1957, *196*, 52-56.

Heron, W., Doane, B. K., and Scott, T. H. Visual disturbances after prolonged perceptual isolation. *Canad. J. Psychol.*, 1956, *10*, 13-18

Hinkle, L. E. The physiological state of the interrogation subject as it affects brain function. In A. D. Biderman and H. Zimmer (eds.), *The manipulation of human behaviour*. New York: Wiley, 1961. Pp. 19-50.

Kubzansky, P. E. The effects of reduced environmental stimulation on human behaviour: A review. In A. D. Biderman and H. Zimmer (eds.), *The manipulation of human behaviour*. New York: Wiley, 1961. Pp. 51-95.

Ruff, G. E., and Levy, E. Z. Psychiatric research in space medicine. *Amer. J. Psychiat.*, 1959, *115*, 793-797.

Zubek, J. P. (ed.), *Sensory deprivation: Fifteen years of research*. New York: Appleton-Century-Crofts, 1969.

Zubek, J. P., and Wilgosh, L. Prolonged immobilization of the body: Changes in performance and in the electroencephalogram. *Science*, 1963, *140*, 306-308.

Zubek, J. P., Sansom, W., and Prysiazniuk, A. W. Intellectual changes during prolonged perceptual isolation (darkness and silence). *Canad. J. Psychol.*, 1960, *14*, 233-243.

Zubek, J. P., Pushkar, D., Sansom, W., and Gowing, J. Perceptual changes after prolonged sensory isolation (darkness and silence). *Canad. J. Psychol.*, 1961, *15*, 83-100.

Zubek, J. P., Aftanas, M., Hasek, J., Sansom, W., Schludermann, E., Wilgosh, L., and Winocur, G. Intellectual and perceptual changes during prolonged perceptual deprivation: Low illumination and noise level. *Percept. mot. Skills*, 1962, *15*, 171-198.

28 / Visual Perception Approached by the Method of Stabilized Images

R. M. Pritchard, W. Heron, and D.O. Hebb *McGill University*

This paper presents evidence that small eye movements are essential for the maintenance of normal visual perception. When the image of a single line is stabilized on the retina by a focusing device, the line is seen only intermittently; more complex stimulus objects, on the other hand, appear to be fragmented. This phenomenon, together with the others described in this article, has an important bearing on two theoretical approaches to perception: the Gestalt theory of Köhler and Koffka, and Professor Hebb's theory of cell assemblies.

The present paper reports some preliminary experiments on the Ditchburn-Riggs effect which is obtained with stabilized images. Our results are such as to show that the original discovery, made independently by Ditchburn and Riggs and their collaborators about 1952, has opened a new and valuable avenue of approach to the analysis of visual perception.

In normal visual fixation, the image that falls on the retina is never really stable; "physiological nystagmus," the continuous tremor of the normal eye at rest, causes a slight but constant variation in the rods and cones that are excited. It is now known that the variation plays a vital role in perception, for it was shown by Ditchburn and Ginsborg (1952) and Riggs, Ratliff, Cornsweet and Cornsweet (1953) that stabilizing the image (experimentally eliminating variability of retinal excitation) leads rapidly to the disappearance of the visual object, followed by intermittent reappearance.

In their experiments, the target was projected on a screen after being reflected from a small mirror attached to a contact lens worn by the observer. Thus each slight involuntary movement of the "fixated" eye would produce a movement of the target. By having the subject observe through a complex optical system, it was possible to make the two movements correspond exactly: the angular extent and direction of the eye movement were matched by the movement of the target, cancelling out the normal tremor of the eye and producing a stabilized retinal image. In these conditions the line of demarcation between the two halves of a 1 degree field, separately lighted so as to give intensity ratios of up to 3:1, disappears intermittently for 2 to 3 sec., at intervals of about 1 min. (Ditchburn and Ginsborg, 1952). Similarly, within a few seconds of stabilized viewing, a thin black line crossing a bright 1 degree field fades out; coarser lines are seen for longer periods, but still intermittently, the length of time the line remains visible being a direct function of its thickness (Riggs *et al.*, 1953).

Later papers using this technique dealt with other aspects of the phenomenon, still with simple targets. Experimentally controlled movement of the image on the retina, as might be expected, restores the object to view, as does intermittent instead of continuous illumination (Cornsweet, 1956; Ditchburn and Fender, 1955; Ditchburn, Fender and Mayne, 1959; Krauskopf, 1956). Krauskopf also showed that narrow bars need a higher intensity (higher contrast ratio) than broad bars to be seen 50 per cent of the time; Fender (1956) and Clowes (1959), using coloured targets, showed that stabilization affects discrimination of hue as well as saturation and brightness.

Achieving stabilization by reflecting the image off the contact lens, however, has some limitations. The field that can be used is small, mainly because torsional movement is not controlled. The next step in the development of method was to attach the complete optical system to the eyball itself (Ditchburn and Pritchard, 1956; MacKay, 1957; Yarbus, 1957). Since the optical system produces an apparently distant target, which is viewed with a relaxed eye, gross fluctuations of accommodation due to muscular fatigue could be ruled out as an explanation of fading. More important, larger and more complex figures could be used.

Ditchburn and Pritchard (1956) used interference fringes produced by a small calcite crystal between two polaroid sheets, and fastened by a stalk to a contact lens, to get a concentric ring pattern which covered a wide field and was in focus for a fully relaxed normal eye. With this method, it was found that the visual object is present for a very small fraction of the viewing time. Moreoever, several observations of great interest were made (Pritchard, 1958; Pritchard and Vowles, 1960). It was found, in brief, that stimulation of other senses could affect the

[1]We wish to acknowledge invaluable assistance from Myron R. Haugen, Klear Vision Contact Lens Specialists of Canada Ltd., and from Fred J. Kader, McGill University. This study was primarily supported by the Defence Research Board (9401-11), with aid also from the National Research Council of Canada (AP17) and the U.S. Public Health Service (M-2455).

Reprinted, by permission, from *Canadian Journal of Psychology*, 1960, *14*, 67-77.

amount of time that the target was seen, and that when the subject's attention was directed to a particular part of the target, this part would usually remain in view longer. Also, it was shown that parts of interference fringes might appear and disappear independently of each other. It is these results which lead directly to the experiments which we now report.

Method

In the present investigation the method used to compensate for retinal-image motion produced by the involuntary eye movements is that described by Pritchard (1960). It consists, essentially, of a collimator device (i.e., one producing parallel rays of light), carried on a contact lens, as illustrated in Figure 1. The target to be viewed is maintained in the focal plane of a high-power glass lens and illuminated by a miniature surgical bulb attached to a diffusing screen. It is seen against a circular patch of light subtending 5 degrees, while the rest of the diffuser is blackened to shield the eye from stray light. The assembly of lens, target, and light source is mounted by a ball-socket joint to a stalk carried on a contact lens, corrected for the subject's visual defects, if any. The lens is tight fitting and thus follows small eye movements accurately (Ratliff and Riggs, 1950; Riggs, Armington, and Ratliff, 1954). The target is easily changed by unscrewing the top of the collimator assembly and replacing one small circular target by another. When the top is screwed down again, the new target is immediately secured in the focal plane of the high-power lens and no additional focusing is necessary.

The targets are produced by photographing India ink drawings on white cards, or drawings in white ink on black cards. Then, 5 mm. discs of the negative

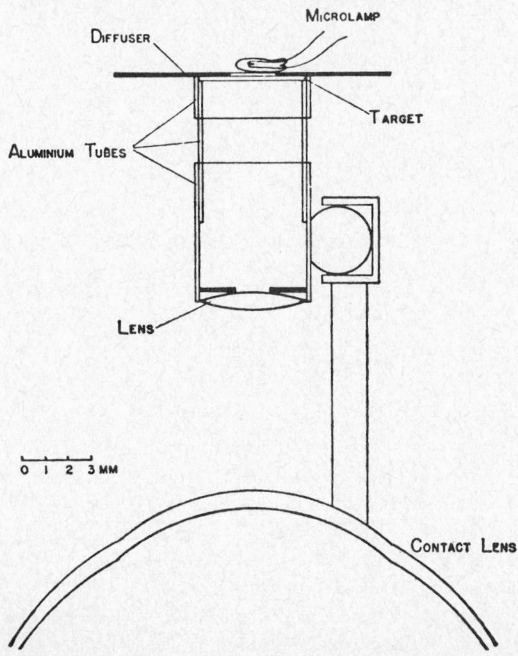

Fig. 1. The apparatus used to produce stabilized images.

are viewed by the subject through the collimating lens and consequently are seen as if located at infinity. They are in focus, therefore, for the normal relaxed eye.

In the present study all the targets were presented within a central 2 degree field, in view of the earlier finding (Pritchard, 1958) of a marked difference between perception within this central region and more peripheral regions. All observations were monocular, the other eye being occluded. The luminance of the brightest parts of the target was maintained at approximately 25 millilamberts, with the experiment room in darkness during the viewing period.

The subject lay on a couch with his head supported, in a partly sound-proofed room or, in some of the observations, in an ordinary room at times when irregular auditory stimuli were at a minimum (cf. Pritchard and Vowles, 1960). The target was then put in position by the experimenter, and a continuous recording was made of the subject's report. Control observations were also made, in which the subject viewed the same targets through the contact lens and collimator system, but without attaching one to the other, so that the image was not stabilized.

It is important to note that the subject must first be habituated to the viewing conditions, and for this reason reports obtained during the first three sessions, of approximately an hour each, were not recorded. For some subjects it is desirable at first to use a local anaesthetic to minimize sensations from the contact lens, which tend to produce frequent blinking and jerky movements of the eyeball, causing a slight slipping of the contact lens and loss of stabilization. But further, the visual phenomena themselves are so striking at first that the subject inevitably tries to look at the object that has suddenly vanished or equally suddenly popped into vision after having vanished, again destroying stabilization. Only when he has adapted to the phenomena themselves, enough to be able to observe passively, does he begin to obtain the full range of phenomena. When adaptation was achieved, in the present experiment, the subject observed and reported on some fifty different visual objects.

The Phenomena

The phenomena of perception with stabilized images and complex targets seem at first to have a bewildering variety, mostly without precedent in the subject's previous experience, but signs of order begin to appear with continued observation. The phenomena described here are from the reports of four experienced observers; unless otherwise stated, each phenomenon has been independently confirmed at least once, a second observer simply being asked to look at a new figure without being told what the preceding observer had found of interest in it.

When the figure is first presented, it remains intact for a length of time which depends on its complexity. With a single line as target, the line fades and disappears, leaving the more dimly illuminated field only. Eventually this disappears also, replaced by a "rich" or intense black patch. Subsequently it regenerates. A more complex target may behave similarly or it may instead lose one or more of its parts, in ways that will be described.

The time of the first disappearance varies, perhaps because of different levels of attention in the observer or because of variations in the level of unfamiliar auditory stimulation (Pritchard and Vowles, 1960), But disappearance is quicker with simpler figures. Also, it has been possible to determine that a simpler figure such as a line is visible for about 10 per cent of viewing time, while a more complex figure such as an unconnected set of curlicues or a facial profile (Figures 2, 3) retains at least one of its parts for as much as 80 per cent of the time. Such a comparison can be made directly by presenting two figures simultaneously (e.g., Figure 3); or the comparison may be quantified with repeated separate presentations, during which the observer presses a key whenever the figure is visible (Kader, 1960).

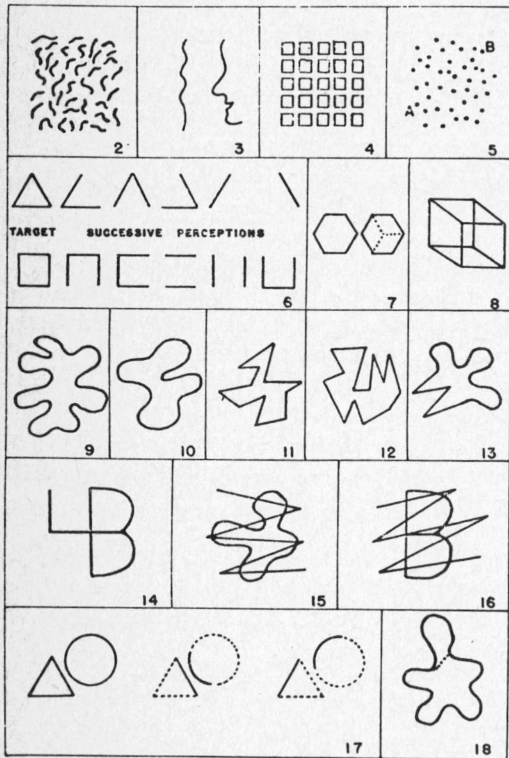

Figs. 2-18. Examples of visual stimuli used (Figures 6, 7, 17, and 18 also show successive perceptions).

The greater time during which a more complex figure is present cannot be explained by assuming a random fluctuation of threshold in the different parts of the field. One might conclude, on such an assumption, that one or other part of the more complex figure remains visible only because the figure covers more of the field, and therefore is more likely to involve an area in which the visual threshold is, for the moment, lower than elsewhere. But, chaotic as the activity of the figure may seem at first, it still obeys some rules which relate to the form of the figure itself. It is these that we are now concerned with.

The "rules" may be summarized as follows. A meaningful diagram is visible longer than a meaningless one: an effect possibly related to the fact that attending to a diagram keeps it visible longer (Pritchard and Vowles, 1960). A straight line tends to act as a unit (i.e., to appear or disappear as a whole) even though it extends across the whole 2 degree field; if the line breaks up, the break is likely to occur at the point of intersection with another line. The several lines of a triangle, square, etc., act independently, with the exception that the activity of parallel lines in a figure is correlated. Jagged diagrams are more active, less stable than rounded ones: a "good" figure (Koffka, 1935), is more likely to act as a complete unit than a "poor" figure, and there are occasional observations of completion or regularization of a figure. Finally, there are clearly marked field effects, in which the presence of a figure in one part of the field modifies the activity of parts of a neighbouring figure.

These results are illustrated in Figure 3 to 18. Figure 3 shows two curves which are similar except that one is a recognizable profile of a face. When they are seen with the apparent fixation point midway between them, the left curve, without meaning, fades faster and is absent more frequently than the right. Figure 14 combines three meaningful symbols: a "4," a "B" and a "3." Fading of the parts of this complex does not occur at random; almost all the time, when any part of the figure is present, it includes one or more of the symbols, complete. Similarly in Figure 16: the meaningless superimposed lines, over the letter "B," act independently of it, and fade more frequently.

Figures 4 and 5 are configurations which behave in such a way as to emphasize the importance of linear organization. This may be horizontal, vertical, or diagonal, but the horizontal is usually predominant. In Figure 4, whole rows of squares may disappear together, leaving one row intact; in Figure 5, a more or less random collection of dots, there is a strong tendency for the dots to organize themselves, so that a line of dots such as that running from A to B may take on unity and repeatedly remain in the field when the others have disappeared. For one observer, one of the rows of Figure 4 at times acquired a further unity which is hard to describe: the squares within the row remained fully distinct visually, but the row became one thing, separate from the other parts of the figure. Possibly this was one of the three-dimensional depth effects discussed below, but the observer could not be certain on the point.

With the diagrams of Figures 6, 7, and 8, the independence of separate straight lines making up a more complex figure is very striking. Figure 6 shows two series of events which might occur with triangle and square respectly. Lines act as units. It is very seldom that an incomplete one is observed, except where a slight trace may occasionally remain at an intersection with another line. None of our data supports the assumption made elsewhere (Hebb, 1949) that it is the angle or corner that is a perceptual element. In these figures, again, the influence of parallel lines on one another is evident since opposite sides of square or hexagon (at the left in Figure 7) remain together too frequently for this to be explained as coincidence, whereas with the square it is rare for two adjacent sides only to remain. This parallel-line effect is most striking with the Necker cube; in addition, when the cube is seen in three dimensions (as it always is with the stabilized image), surfaces which are separate but in parallel planes act frequently together. The front and back of the cube may remain in sight, for example, while the other edges (the lines which connect the square which constitute front and back faces) have disappeared. The parallel-line effect is not invariable, of course, and still less the parallel-surface effect: in addition to complete inversion of the cube (which occurs with the stabilized image as with normal vision) there may be a partial inversion, the same surfaces being seen at right angles to each other.

Our emphasis has been on the independent action of parts of a complex figure, but the figure can also – less frequently – act as a whole, appearing and disappearing as a single unit. The probability that it will do so is principally determined by its shape. A circle, or a diagram such as those of Figures 9 and 10, is relatively stable and quiet, whereas another, as in Figures 11 and 12, is quite unstable and likely to produce an effect of violent motion, as the separate parts appear and disappear in rapid succession. In general, the pattern composed of rounded curves is less active than a jagged one, and more likely to act as a whole. The difference between smoothness and jaggedness appears dramatically in a single pattern such as that of Figure 13, in which the angular parts are likely to be active and unpredictable and the rounded parts to form a more stable unit or part figure. This effect is clearly related to the "good" figure of Gestalt psychology, but it must be said that even the circle, the good figure *par excellence*, frequently acts as though composed of separate perceptual elements (see discussion of Figure 17, below). We have in fact found no other extended figure than an uninterrupted straight line which reliably acts as a unit.

The behaviour of wholes is further illustrated by the diagrams of Figures 14, 15, and 16. We have already reported that Figure 14, containing three symbolic patterns, tends to break down in such a way as to leave one or more of the symbols intact. Here an effect of meaning and past experience is evident: similarly in Figure 16, where the "B" tends to remain for longer periods than the hatching lines, and even when they are present, the "B" is seen in a separate plane nearer the observer, as a separate entity. The diagram of Figure 15, however, shows that the effect can occur with a figure which lacks both meaning and goodness of form: the closed loop also tends to act as a whole though it is quite irregular.

Figure 17 illustrated a field effect which has been observed repeatedly. There is a marked influence of one of the two figures on the other, seen in two ways. First, the parts of the triangle and the circle which are nearest to each other frequently remain visible while the other parts disappear (Figure 17, first example) and second, less frequently, a side of the triangle which remains is accompanied by an arc of the circle which is "parallel" to it (Figure 17, second and third examples). This, with the tendency of parallel lines to act together which was mentioned earlier, seems clearly to show the existence of an influence of a visual object which extends well beyond the actual area of stimulation.

The final illustration, Figure 18, concerns a completion phenomenon which occurs in several ways, including the special case of closure. When a diagram such as that of Figure 9 or Figure 10 loses one of its limbs, we have obtained several reports of a transient closure which is diagrammed in Figure 18. This appears to be a clear case of production of a better figure, and to it we may add the report of one observer that a slightly irregular hexagon became definitely regular. (On the other hand, a circle or other regular figure may be temporarily distorted, with an equally definite change of shape (one observer). The effect is similar to the perceptual distortions reported by subjects who have just come out of "isolation" (Heron, Doane and Scott, 1956).) A second example of completion is found in the hallucinatory addition of an eye to the profile of Figure 3 (one observer, but confirmed by a second observer with another profile figure).

Thirdly, a case which is perhaps equivocal as an instance of completion, but is of considerable interest and one which also bring us to our final topic, of depth effects. With the hexagon as presented in Figure 7, left, we have obtained reports of a "strong cube impression," the hexagon being perceived as the outline of a cube in three dimensions. The cube, also, is seen to reverse as the Necker cube does. The diagram at the right of Figure 7 shows how this may occur; the dotted lines do *not* appear in vision, but the figure acts in other respects as if they were present. In this sense, at least, there is completion.

Depth effects are ubiquitous. When the hexagon just referred to is seen as a two-dimensional figure instead of a cube, it is still clearly in a different plane from that of the background: nearly always above the surface, or closer to the observer. The effect is the same whether the figure is brighter than the ground or darker. The squares of Figure 4 have the appearance of a waffle iron, as protrusions from the surface (or, for one observer, occasionally as depressions); a row of circles of about the same dimensions looks like a row of craters of small volcanoes. The tridimensionality of the Necker cube is much more definite than with ordinary vision; with prolonged viewing it may deteriorate from the appearance of regular cube, but is still definitely in three dimensions, the interior connecting lines appearing like wires strung over and under each other.

Comment

The phenomena that have been described bear directly on two theoretical approaches to perception: Gestalt theory (Kohler, 1929; Koffka, 1935), and the theory of cell assemblies (Hebb, 1949; Milner, 1957) or trace systems (Lashley, 1958). On the one hand, Gestalt ideas concerning the phenomena of perception find further new support; on the other, an independent action of parts even of good figures demonstrates that an exclusively holistic treatment of the percept is not sufficient, so that the explanatory conceptions of Gestalt theory require modification. We believe that the data offer support to both approaches, and qualify them to a greater or less extent; it is too soon to go into detailed analysis, but we may say in general that the holistic ideas become more compatible with analytical ones than was evident previously.

The Gestalt closure that has been described (Figure 18) is most clear-cut and unambiguous, comparable only to what has been observed in cases of hemianopia (Fuchs, 1920; Lashley, 1941). There is clear evidence of the functional meaning of the conception of the "good" figure; of the functioning of the whole as a perceptual entity, distinct from part functions; and of groups as entities, and of similarity and contiguity as determinants of grouping. Finally, we have found evidence of marked field effects.

But with this we have found an extraordinary action of parts, independent of the whole. In the conditions of the experiment, this action tends to predominate over the whole in a way that never occurs in normal vision. The phenomena described, we believe, make inevitable the conclusion that perceptual elements (as distinct from sensory elements: Hebb, 1949) exist in their own right. In conformity with Gestalt ideas, these are organized entities, and the conclusion to be drawn here, perhaps, is not that Gestalt emphasis on organized wholes is erroneous but rather (a) that the wholes in question are often simpler ones than are usually discussed – that is, straight lines or short segments of curves – and (b) that the more complex wholes, such as square or circle, are synthesis of simpler ones though they may also function as genuine single entities. The earlier literature treated perception-by-parts and perception of wholes in antithetical, mutually exclusive ideas. In retrospect, one seems that such a theoretical opposition is quite unnecessary, logically; and our data show that both conceptions are valid and complement one another.

The action of parts that has been described is also a very considerable confirmation of the theory of cell assemblies, in its main lines. As we have said above, the data show a need for revision, no support being provided for the idea that an angle or an intersection of lines is a perceptual element. Revision or development of the theory becomes necessary in other respects; for example, to account for the unexpected influence of contiguity as such, seen with Figure 17 (see above). In general terms, however, the phenomena confirm the earlier analysis (Hebb, 1949) to a very surprising extent.

Today there are further data to support this approach. Apart from the present experiment, we may cite the auditory "holding" demonstrated by Broadbent (1956), and the phenomena of serial order in visual perception (Miskin and Forgays, 1952; Orbach, 1952; Heron, 1957; Kimura, 1959; and Bryden, 1960). All are intelligible in terms of a semiautonomous activity of closed systems in perception but unintelligible when perception is regarded as a simple input system, and the concept of cell assembly or trace system becomes less remotely speculative than it may have seemed at first, and closer to the realities of behaviour. Further experiments of the kind we have reported, with the use of stabilized images, should make it possible to specify in more detail the properties of these closed systems and so provide a new understanding of the perceptual process.

References

BROADBENT, D. E. Successive responses to simultaneous stimuli. *Quart. J. exp. Psychol.*, 1956, *8*, 145-152.

BRYDEN, M. P. Tachistoscopic recognition of non-alphabetical material. *Canad. J. Psychol.*, 1960, *4*, 74-82.

CLOWES, M. B. Eye movements and the discrimination of brightness and colour. Unpublished doctoral dissertation, Univ. of Reading, 1959.

CORNSWEET, T. N. Determination of the stimuli for involuntary drifts and saccadic eye movements. *J. opt. Soc. Amer.*, 1956, *46*, 987-993.

DITCHBURN, R. W., and FENDER, D. H. The stabilised retinal image. *Opt. Acta*, 1955, *2*, 128-133.

DITCHBURN, R. W., FENDER, D. H., and MAYNE, S. Vision with controlled movements of the retinal image. *J. Physiol.*, 1959, *145*, 98-107.

DITCHBURN, R. W., and GINSBORG, B. L. Vision with a stabilised retinal image. *Nature, Lond.*, 1952, *170*, 36-37.

DITCHBURN, R. W., and PRITCHARD, R. M. Stabilised interference fringes on the retina. *Nature, Lond.*, 1956, *177*, 434.

FENDER, D. H. The function of eye movements in the visual process. Unpublished doctoral dissertation, Univ. of Reading, 1956.

FUCHS, W. Untersuchungen über das Sehen der Hemianopiker und Hemiambliopiker, II. In A. GELB and K. GOLDSTEIN (eds.), *Psychologische Analysen hirnpathologischer Fälle*. Leipzig: Barth, 1920.

HEBB, D. O. *The organization of behaviour*. New York: Wiley, 1949.

HERON, W. Perception as a function of retinal locus and attention. *Amer. J. Psychol.*, 1957, *70*, 38-48.

HERON, W., DOANE, B. K., and SCOTT, T. H. Visual disturbances after prolonged perceptual isolation. *Canad. J. Psychol.*, 1956, *10*, 13-18.

KADER, F. J. Target complexity and visibility in stabilised images. Unpublished B.A. honours thesis, McGill Univ., 1960.

KIMURA, DOREEN. The effect of letter position on recognition. *Canad. J. Psychol.*, 1959, *13*, 1-10.

KOFFKA, K. *Principles of Gestalt psychology*. New York: Harcourt, Brace, 1935.

KÖHLER, W. *Gestalt psychology*. New York: Liveright, 1929.

KRAUSKOPF, J. Effect of retinal image motion on contrast thresholds for maintained vision. *J. opt. Soc. Amer.*, 1957, *47*, 740-744.

LASHLEY, K. S. Patterns of cerebral integration indicated by the scotomas of migraine. *Arch. Neurol. Psychiat., Chicago*, 1941, *46*, 331-339.

———. Cerebral organization and behaviour. *Res. Publ. Ass. nerv. ment. Dis.*, 1958, *35*, 1-18.

MACKAY, D. M. Some further visual phenomena associated with regular patterned stimulation. *Nature, Lond.*, 1957, *180*, 1145-1146.

MILNER, P. M. The cell assembly: Mark II. *Psychol. Rev.*, 1957, *64*, 242-252.

MISHKIN, M., and FORGAYS, D. G. Word recognition as a function of retinal locus. *J. exp. Psychol.*, 1952, *43*, 43-48.

ORBACH, J. Retinal locus as a factor in the recognition of visually perceived words. *Amer. J. Psychol.*, 1952, *65*, 555-562.

PRITCHARD, R. M. Studies of visual perception with a stabilised retinal image. Unpublished doctoral dissertation, Univ. of Reading, 1958.

———. Visual illusions viewed as stabilised retinal images. *Quart. J. exp. Psychol.*, 1958, *10*, 77-81.

———. A collimator stabilising system. *Quart. J. exp. Psychol.*, in press, 1960.

PRITCHARD, R. M., and VOWLES, D. The effects of auditory stimulation on the perception of the stabilised retinal image. In press, 1960.

RATLIFF, F., and RIGGS, L. A. Involuntary motions of the eye during monocular fixation. *J. exp. Psychol.*, 1950, *40*, 687-701.

RIGGS, L. A., ARMINGTON, J. C., and RATLIFF, F. Motions of the retinal image during fixation. *J. opt. Soc. Amer.*, 1954, *44*, 315-321.

RIGGS, L. A., RATLIFF, F., CORNSWEET, J. C., and CORNSWEET, T. N. The disappearance of steadily fixated test-objects. *J. opt. Soc. Amer.*, 1953, *43*, 495-501.

YARBUS, A. L. *Biofizika*, 1957, *2*, 703.

29 / An Assimilation Theory of Geometric Illusions

A. W. Pressey *University of Manitoba*

Using two postulates as bases, one concerning assimilation and one concerning attentive fields, the author explains several common illusions.

It is well established that our perception of an object may be altered if that object is located in a different context. The object may change in colour, size, shape, direction, or position depending upon the object and the nature of the context. Such perceptual distortions are called "illusions." The most obvious example of a distortion that occurs in nature is the moon illusion. When the moon is located at the horizon it appears much larger than when it is at the zenith.

At about the middle of the nineteenth century it was shown that, not only real objects, but drawings of objects also displayed distortions. Many illusory patterns were discovered and investigated. Some of these illusions are shown below. In the Müller-Lyer figure (Fig. 1) a standard line appears shorter if its ends are bounded by ingoing obliques (arrowheads). On the other hand, outgoing obliques (arrowfeathers) produce an apparent elongation of the standard line. In a modified version of the Müller-Lyer figure (Fig. 2) a line is bisected by a dot and an arrowhead is placed at one end and an arrowfeather at the other. In this case the dot appears displaced towards the arrowhead. In the Sander parallelogram (Fig. 3) the oblique line within the large parallelogram appears longer than the oblique line within the small parallelogram. The Oppel illusion is an illusion of filled and unfilled space. In Fig. 4 the distance AB appears longer than the distance BC.

Another illusion of size is provided by the Delboeuf configuration. Here a circle which is surrounded by a larger circle appears larger than one which surrounds a smaller circle. The Titchener Circles illusion appears to be similar to the Delboeuf pattern yet it yields an opposite effect. The circle surrounded by larger circles appears smaller than the one which is surrounded by smaller circles. In the Ponzo illusion two lines of equal size are located within a large acute angle and in this case the line near the apex appears larger than the line below it. The final example of an illusion of size is the inverted-T pattern. A vertical line appears longer than a horizontal line of equal size.

The most striking examples of distortion are provided by illusions of direction and shape. In the Poggendorff illusion two portions of a single oblique line are interrupted by two separate parallel lines but the obliques do not appear collinear. In the Zöllner and Hering figures parallel lines are distorted by various hatchings. Finally, in Fig. 12 a square is distorted by the intersecting oblique lines.

Theories of Illusions

What causes the geometric illusions? Many explanations have been proposed but none of these has proved to be entirely satisfactory. The major theories of illusions have been reviewed recently by Gregory (1966) and Over (1968).

1. *The eye movement theory.*
   The basic idea expressed in this theory is that the extent of eye movements influences the perception of length. Thus, in the arrowfeather portion of the Müller-Lyer illusion the outgoing obliques draw the eye past the end of the standard line which results in an overestimation of the standard. On the other hand, the arrowheads arrest the eye movements so that they stop short of the ends of the line. This results in an underestimation of the standard lines.
   The major difficulty with eye movement theory is that it would predict no illusion in situations in which eye movements are prevented. Optically stabilizing the target on the retina (see Pritchard, Heron and Hebb, 1960) should destroy the illusions; yet it is not weakened.
2. *The limited acuity theory.*
   This theory argues that it is the failure of the eye to resolve contours which produces illusions. For example, in the Müller-Lyer figure, the ends of the standard line are not perceived clearly because the obliques that join it form a continuous contour. This theory is inadequate because, in the Müller-Lyer figure, for example, the obliques can be moved slightly away from the ends of the standard line thus perceptually clarifying those ends. Nevertheless, the illusion still occurs. A second weakness of limited acuity theory is that it is difficult to apply it to illusions such as the Delboeuf.
3. *The confusion theory.*
   This theory states that the context in which a figure is embedded "confuses" the perceptual system. It can hardly be argued that this is a theory since no predictions can be made in regard to the conditions which will confuse the perceptual systems and those which will not.

4 *The empathy theory.*
   The idea expressed here is that certain figures trigger off emotional states which distort our intellectual judgements. Thus, the outgoing fins of the Müller-Lyer illusion yield a feeling of expansion and hence lead to an overestimation

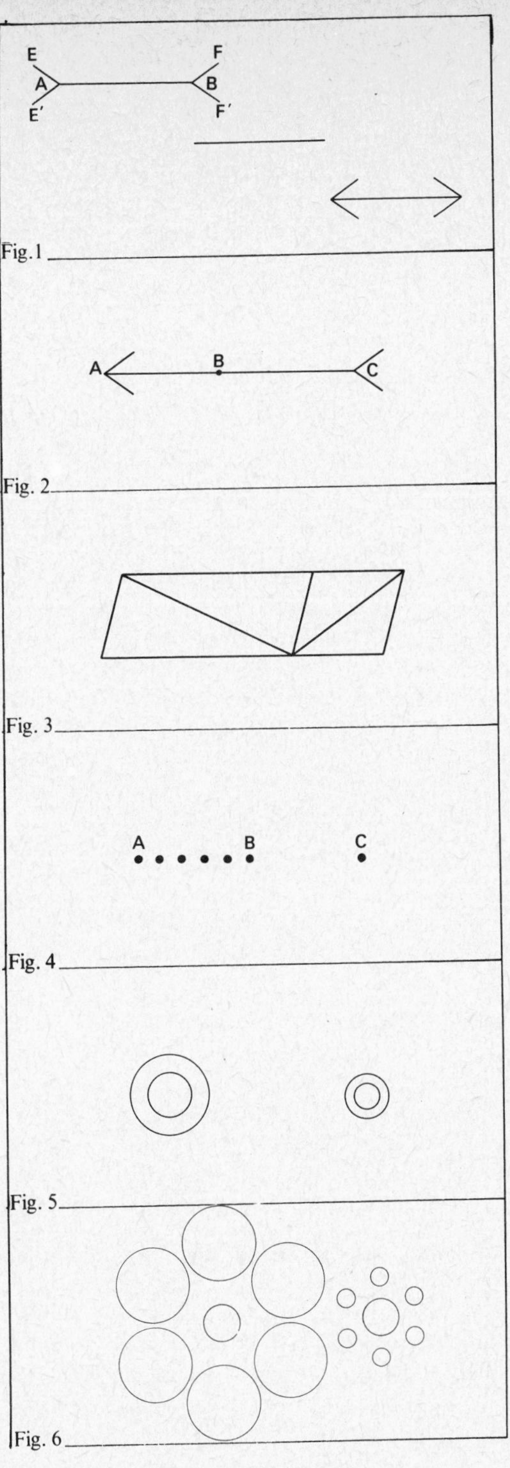

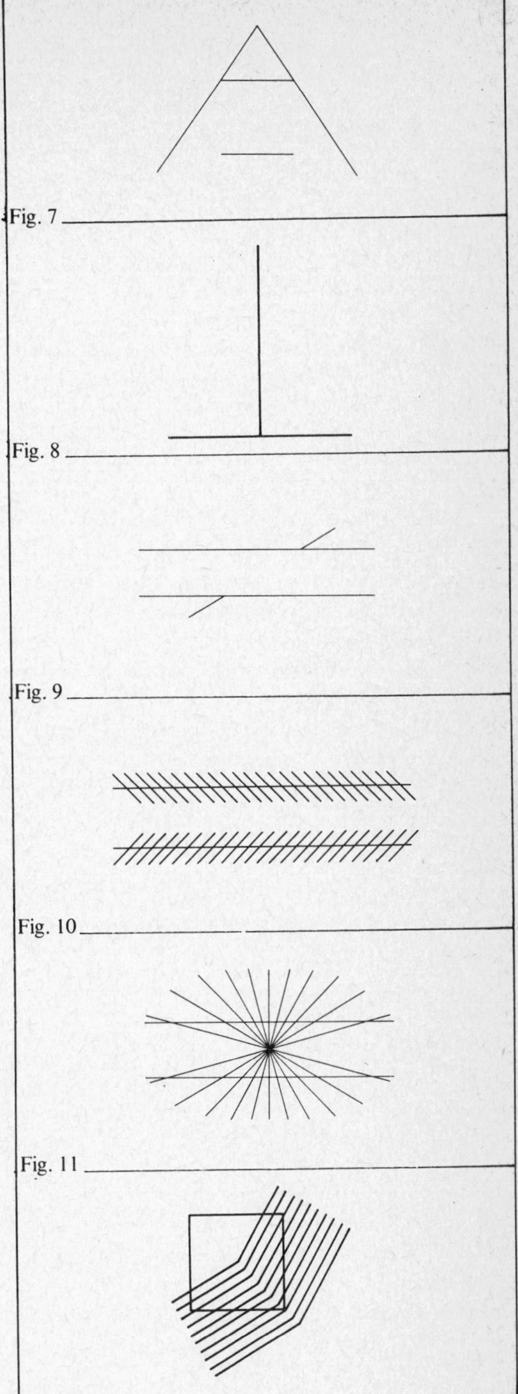

Fig. 1. The Müller-Lyer illusion.

Fig. 2. A modified Müller-Lyer illusion.

Fig. 3. The Sander parallelogram.

Fig. 4. The filled-space illusion.

Fig. 5. The Delboeuf illusion.

Fig. 6. The Titchener circles.

Fig. 7. The Ponzo illusion.

Fig. 8. The horizontal-vertical illusion.

Fig. 9. The Poggendorff illusion.

Fig. 10. The Zöllner illusion.

Fig. 11. The Hering illusion.

Fig. 12. A distorted square.

of the standard length. The ingoing fins, on the other hand, result in a feeling of constriction which produces an underestimation of the standard length. It is difficult to see how this theory would explain the modification of the Müller-Lyer illusion shown in Fig. 2 or the Poggendorff illusion.

5. *The "good-figure" theory.*
   According to this viewpoint, the distance between elements which "belong together" appears shorter than the distance between elements which do not belong together. Thus, the arrowheads of the Müller-Lyer figure appear to belong together, (and form a "good" figure) with the result that the apparent distance between the arrowheads is reduced. This theory is too vague to yield satisfactory predictions.
6. *The perspective theory.*
   This theory has been, and still is, the most popular explanation of geometric illusions. The basic idea is that certain contexts suggest depth features which alter apparent size. For example, Gregory (1963) has argued that "The parts of the figure corresponding to distant objects are expanded and the parts corresponding to nearer objects are reduced. Thus ... in the Ponzo figure the upper horizontal line would be further away and also expanded in the flat illusion figure." Research on this theory is continuing.

The Assimilation Theory

The term "assimilation" refers to the idea that, in a group of entities, the extremes take on the properties (or become more like) the average of the entities. Assimilation has had a long history of use as an explanatory construct in psychology. For example, in social psychology the phenomenon of acculturation is the process whereby the individuals of one culture alter their behaviour to conform, at least in part, to the modal culture. An Englishman, living in Paris, becomes assimilated into the French culture.

Assimilation has also been used to explain certain phenomena in memory. In one study (Carmichael et al., 1932) the stimulus shown in Fig. 13 was presented along with either the word "bottle" or the word "stirrup." As indicated in Fig. 13, the type of figure that was later reproduced differed markedly depending upon the word that was associated with it. The reproductions indicated that memory for the form assimilated to (became more like) the verbal label.

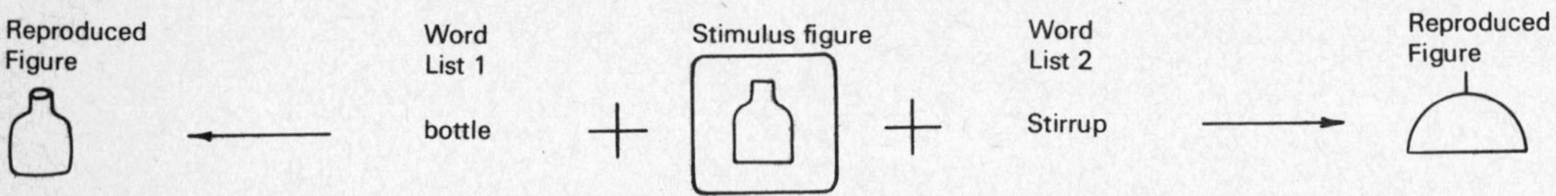

Fig. 13. The effects of assimilation in recall (adapted from Carmichael, Hogan and Walters, 1932).

A simple way to demonstrate assimilation in judgements is to ask observers (*O*s) to reproduce a series of time intervals of, say, 5, 10, 15, and 20 sec. It will be observed that the 5-sec. interval will be *overestimated* and the 20-sec. interval will be *underestimated*. In both cases the extremes become more like the average of the intervals. This principle can be stated as the major postulate of assimilation theory.

Postulate 1.
Whenever judgements are made of a series of entities, the smaller magnitudes in that series will be overestimated and the larger magnitudes will be underestimated.

The Müller-Lyer illusion
The first postulate is sufficient to provide an explanation of the Müller-Lyer illusion. Consider first the arrowfeather portion shown in Fig. 1. It can be argued that, when *O* is asked to judge AB he also inadvertently judges a series of lengths defined by the obliques EAE′ and FBF′. This idea is clarified in Fig. 14A. In this figure CD is the shortest line in the series and, according to Postulate 1, it should be overestimated. In Fig. 14B, which is the arrowhead portion of the Müller-Lyer illusion, the standard line EF is the longest line in the series and therefore it should be *underestimated*. In other words, in each form of the Müller-Lyer figure, the standard line assimilates with the series of lines which the obliques define and, consequently, that standard line either elongates or shrinks.

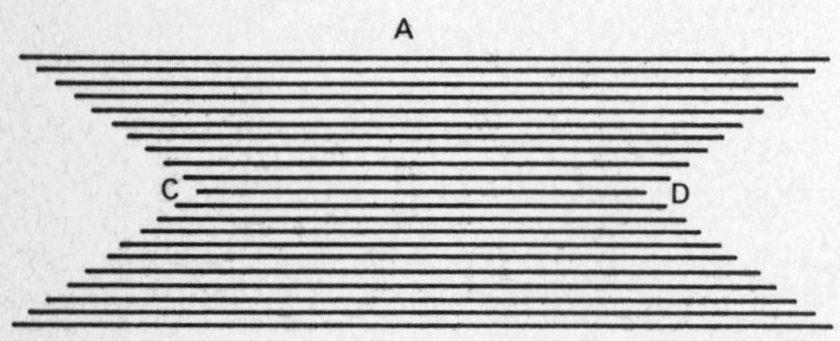

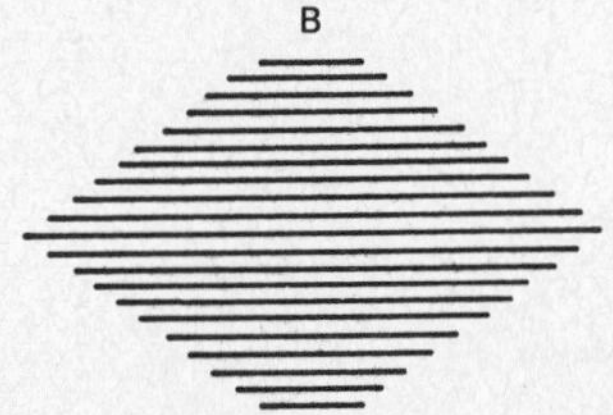

Fig. 14.

A Modified Müller-Lyer Illusion.

In Fig. 2 a target is shown in which the apparent midpoint of a standard line appears shifted towards the arrowhead. An explanation of this illusion is as follows: When an *O* judges AB, the arrowhead forces him to make judgements, not only of AB, but also an indefinite number of lengths defined by the arrowhead. Similarly, when he judges BC, that judgement is embedded in a series of magnitudes defined by the arrowfeathers. The implicit lengths are illustrated in Fig. 15 which shows that AB is the longest line in the series and thus will be underestimated. On the other hand, BC is the shortest line in the series and will be overestimated. Consequently, in order for AC to appear bisected, B would have to be moved toward the arrowfeather.

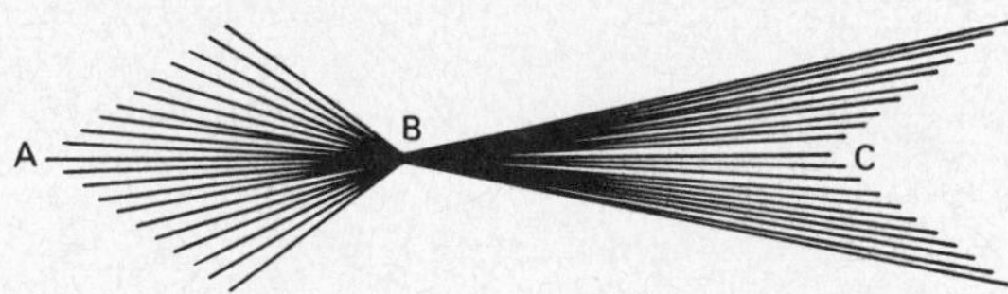

Fig. 15.

The Sander Parallelogram

Fig. 15 illustrates that there is a close link between the modified Müller-Lyer illusion and the Sander parallelogram. A simplified version of Fig. 15 is shown in Fig. 16 in which AB is equal to BC but

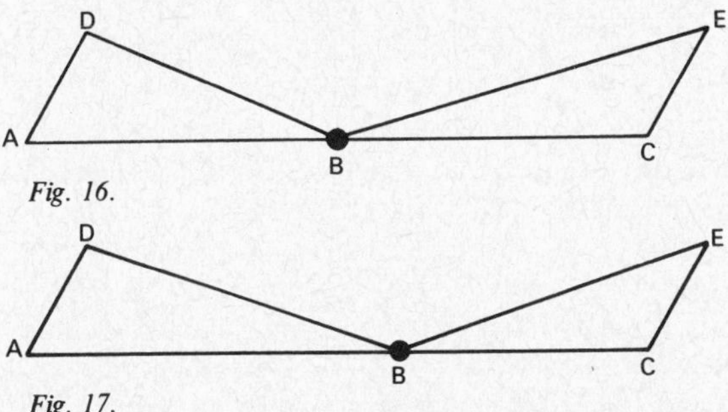

Fig. 16.

Fig. 17.

DB is shorter than BE. Now suppose that the point B is shifted towards C so that DB = BE as shown in Fig. 17. This figure is a simplified version of the target shown in Fig. 3. In this case, DB assimilates with a series of longer lines (the extreme of which is AB) and therefore appears elongated. BE, on the other hand, assimilates with a series of shorter lines (the extreme of which is BC) and thus appears shorter.

The Attentive Field Postulate.

An important modification of the Müller-Lyer illusion is shown in Fig. 18 in which the distance AB appears shorter than the distance BC. This configuration is important because it leads to an extension of assimilation theory. As it stands, assimilation theory is ambiguous about what should occur in Fig. 18 because, logically, the context can be formed by either AD and AE (which would yield shorter lines)

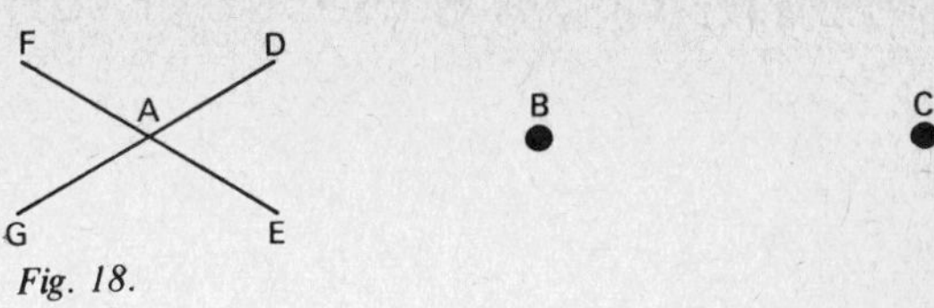

Fig. 18.

or AF and AG (which would yield longer lines). However, since AB appears to shrink it must be the arrowhead which forms the effective context. And the reason for this may be due to attentional factors. Consider a non-illusory target such as Fig. 19 in

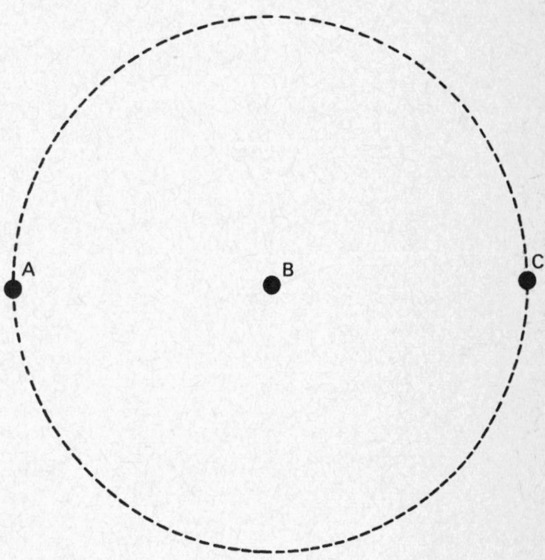

Fig. 19.

which the *O* compares AB and BC. In his comparison he will probably focus his attention primarily in the region bounded by the points A and C. A rough approximation of his attentive field might be as shown by the dotted line. Now, if Fig. 19 is superimposed on Fig. 18, it will be seen that the arrowheads fall within the attentive field and the arrowfeathers fall outside that field. As such, it is highly likely that it is the arrowheads which form the context within which AB is embedded.

On the basis of Fig. 18, a second major postulate of assimilation theory is proposed.

Postulate 2.

Other things being equal, a context which falls within the attentive field will be more effective than a context outside that field.

There is one major problem with Postulate 2 and that is how to specify the boundaries of the attentive field. This is difficult to accomplish precisely but two methods which might give rough approximations do suggest themselves. The first is an empirical one and the second is a logical one. Empirically, eye movements might be measured under the assumption that what one looks at is that to which he is attending. The second method is to logically analyze what response is required of the observer and assume that his attention will be focused primarily on the elements that are to be judged. This procedure of approximating the attentive field has been adopted here. Two points, corresponding to the most distant edges of the elements to be judged, are joined and this line defines the diameter of a circle. Elements within that circle are said to be within the attentive field. One example of this method of approximating the attentive field has already been given in Fig. 19. A second example is given in Fig. 20, and, if it is granted that the attentive field is roughly as defined, then an explanation of the Ponzo illusion readily follows.

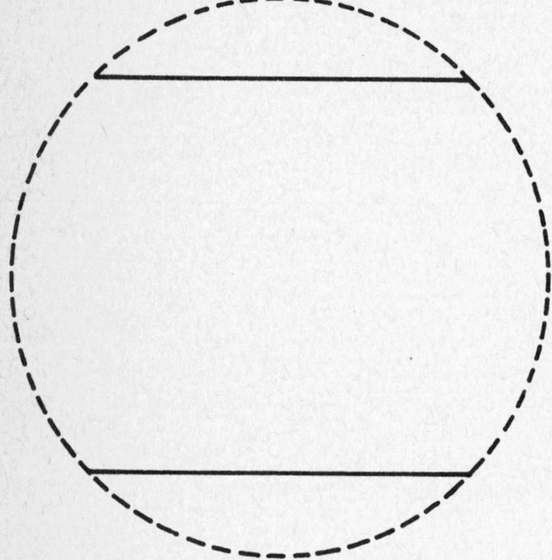

Fig. 20.

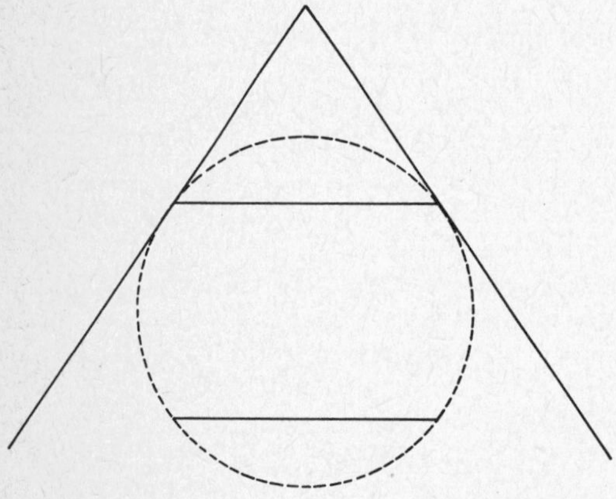

Fig. 21.

The Ponzo Illusion.
In Fig. 21 an acute angle is superimposed on Fig. 20 to produce the Ponzo illusion and, as can be seen, certain parts of the oblique contours fall within the attentive field and the remainder fall outside that field. The contours which fall within the attentive field and hence provide the most effective context are shown in Fig. 22. But Fig. 22 is nothing more than an incomplete form of a Müller-Lyer illusion with the same explanation being given. That is, the standard horizontal line assimilates with longer horizontal lines which the arrowfeathers define with the result that the standard line appears elongated. The bottom horizontal line, on the other hand, does not have effective contours in the attentive field and, as a result, it is judged veridically. Therefore, when the top and bottom lines are compared the former appears longer.

Fig. 22.

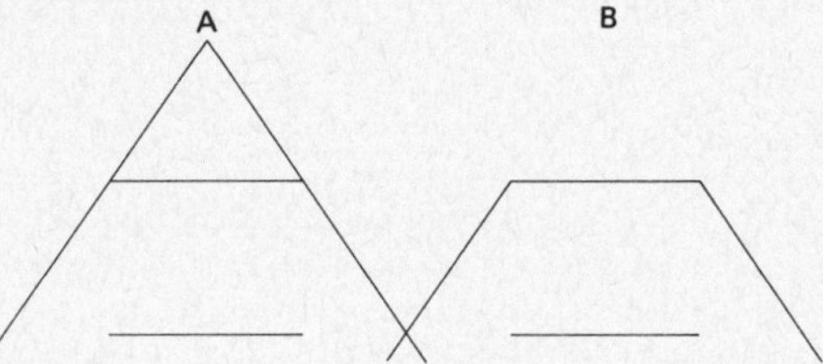

Fig. 23.

The targets shown in Fig. 23 are particularly critical because perspective theory and assimilation theory make different predictions about which target should yield the larger illusion. It appears that perspective theory would have to predict that the target with the "full" acute angle (A) would yield a stronger illusion than the one with an incomplete angle (B). This is because the full angle appears to be a better perspective cue to depth. Assimilation theory, on the other hand, predicts just the opposite effect. This is because the converging lines directly above the upper horizontal line, although outside the attentive field, still have *some* effect on the length of the standard line. This can be demonstrated by constructing a pattern as shown in Fig. 24. Here converging lines are located above the upper standard line. In this case, the upper line appears *shorter* than the lower line although the illusion is not very striking. The shortening effect is due to the assimilation of the standard line to the shorter lines formed by the converging obliques. It is obvious, therefore, that if converging obliques are added above the upper standard line they will subtract from the effect of the diverging obliques below that line. The net result is that the strongest illusion should be produced by the target shown in Fig. 23B and, as has been verified by many *O*s in our laboratory, this is indeed the case.

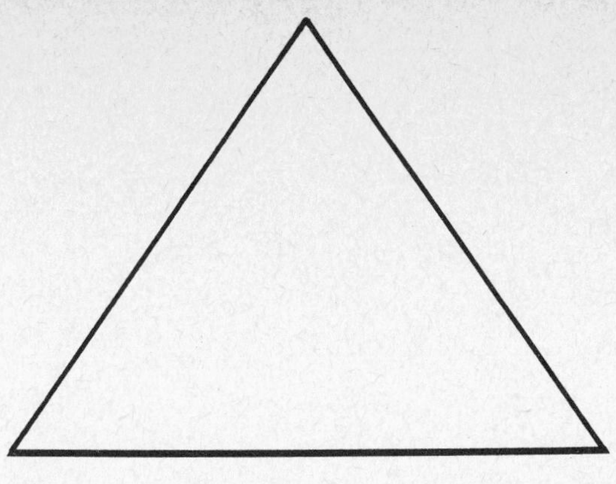

Fig. 24.

From the above analysis of the Ponzo illusion, a new illusory figure is predicted. In Fig. 25 two triangles are placed one above the other. When the two baselines are compared the upper baseline looks longer than the lower one. The reason for this is evident if the attentive field is drawn as in Fig. 20. The converging obliques of the lower triangle fall within the attentive field and hence are highly effective in shrinking the baseline. On the other hand, the ingoing obliques of the upper triangle fall outside the attentive field and hence are less effective in shrinking the standard line. Therefore, when the two standards are compared, the upper one appears longer than the lower one.

Fig. 25.

The Poggendorff Illusion

Unlike the Muller-Lyer or the Ponzo illusions which are illusions of size, the Poggendorff illusion is one of direction. The *O* is asked to extend an oblique line until it appears to join the farthest horizontal line. (See Fig. 1). This projected line deviates systematically from the point of objective continuation.

By introducing a slight modification of the assimilation postulate, an explanation of the Poggendorff illusion is possible. In order to simplify the explanation a partial illusion which contains no acute angles is employed. In this configuration, shown in Fig. 26, the oblique (AB) appears to point above the dot (C) which is the objective continuation of AB. This partial illusion has been shown to correlate substantially with the full illusion (Pressey and Sweeney, 1969).

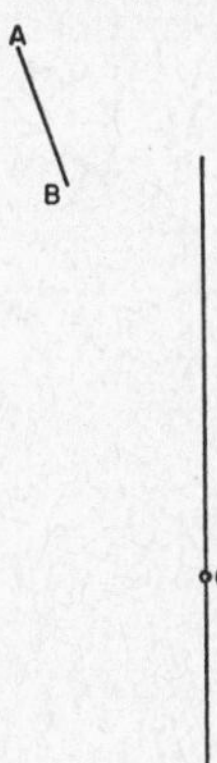

Fig. 26.

In order to determine what the most effective contextual contours are, a hypothetical field of attention is drawn as shown in Fig. 27. It is immediately obvious that the dominant contextual contour is that portion of the vertical line which is directly above the point of objective continuation as shown in Fig. 28. Now, when an *O* is asked to subjectively extend the oblique line, he extends a *series of lines* as shown in Fig. 29. This series consists of lines that are *shorter* than the line of objective continuation. The choice of a line, therefore, will assimilate to the mean of the series; and one will select a line which is shorter than the line of objective continuation. But if a shorter line is selected, this means that the oblique will appear to point above the point of objective continuation which is precisely what occurs in the Poggendorff illusion.

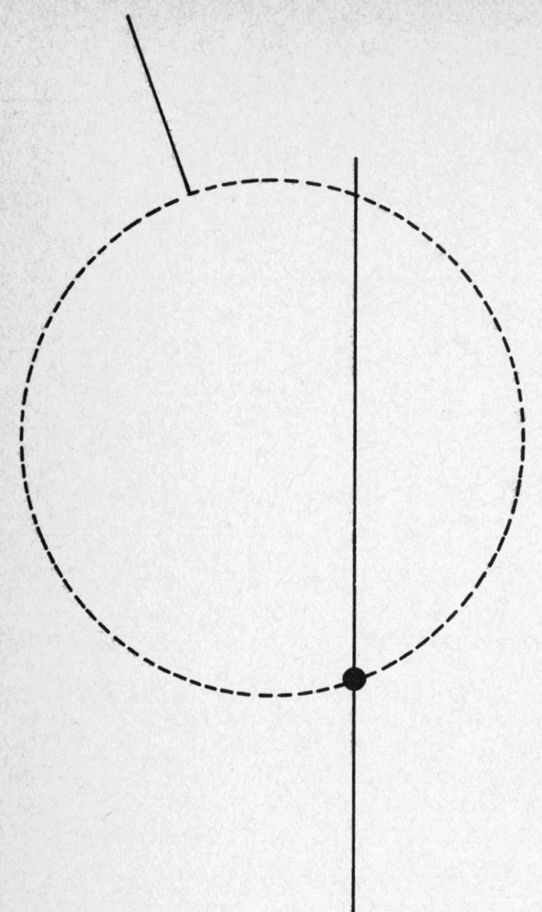

Fig. 27.

Fig. 28.

Fig. 29.

A Reversed Poggendorff Illusion

It follows from the above analysis that if one eliminated the portion of the vertical line which forms the effective context (see Fig. 27) and retained only the portion below the point of objective continuation, as shown in Fig. 30, the illusion should reverse. The *O* would project a series of lines, but in this case, he cannot project shorter lines because there is no contour present to form such lines. The only contour available is one which will form a series of lines that are *longer* than the line of objective continuation as shown in Fig. 31.The *O* will therefore select a longer line with the result that the oblique line will appear to point below the point of objective continuation. The strength of the reversed illusion, however, should be greatly diminished as compared to the classical illusion because the context is relatively outside the attentive field. There is some empirical evidence to support the prediction of a reversed illusion. Restle

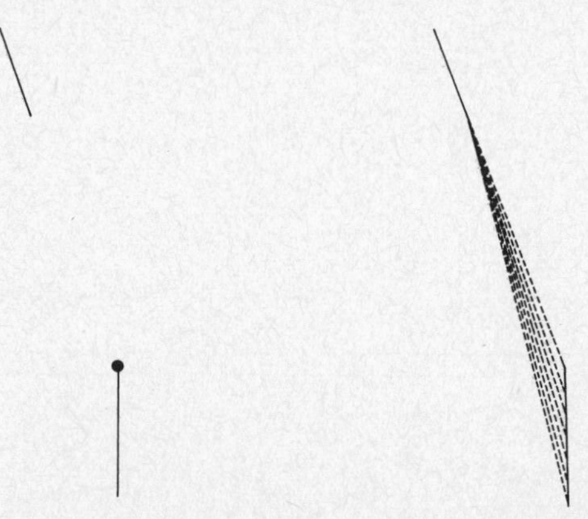

Fig. 30.

Fig. 31.

(1969) found a reversal in a target such as that shown in Fig. 32. This target is, of course, simply a more complex version of Fig. 30.

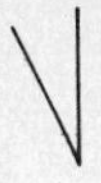

Fig. 32.

Another prediction which follows from assimilation theory is: if Fig. 30 was altered in such a fashion that longer lines were accentuated, then the reversed illusion should become very pronounced. In Fig. 33, the oblique line is joined to the bottom of the vertical line, and as predicted, that oblique appears to point below the dot which is the point of objective continuation.

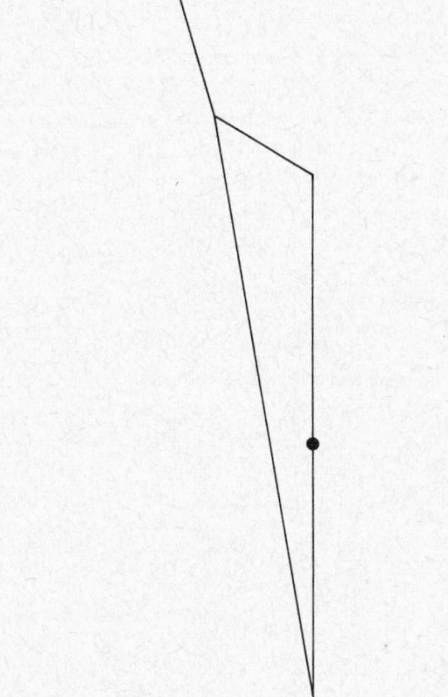

Fig. 33.

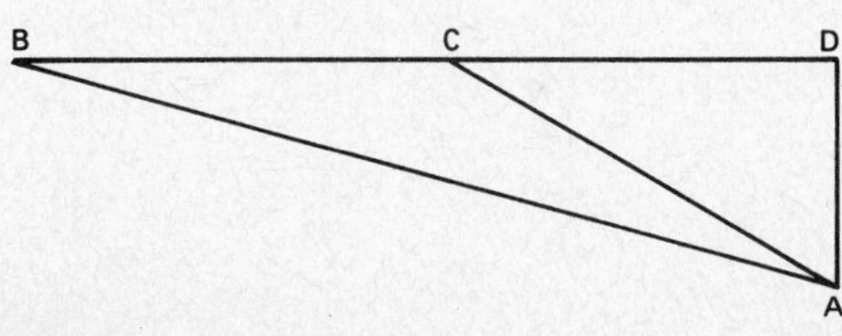

Fig. 34.

The Hering Illusion

In the Hering illusion (Fig. 11) two parallel lines appear bowed if they are located in a context of radiating lines. Postulate 1 is sufficient to provide an explanation of this illusion. Consider a simplified version as shown in Fig. 34. The lines AB, AC, AD form a series of lines in which AB is the longest and AD is the shortest line. AB will therefore appear shorter than it really is and AD will appear longer than it really is. Therefore, subjectively AB, AC, and AD will appear as shown in Fig. 35 which results in an apparent bowing of the horizontal line.

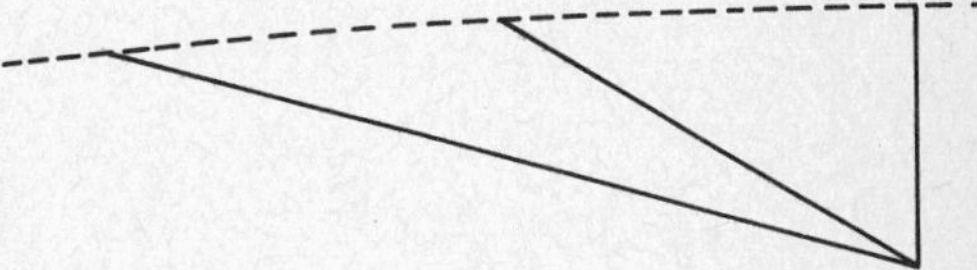

Fig. 35.

Conclusion

By a systematic application of an assimilation postulate and an attentive field postulate, an explanation of many geometric illusions is provided. In principle, it appears that assimilation theory could be extended to include other illusions such as the Delboeuf and the filled-unfilled space illusions. Nevertheless, there are some configurations which are exceptions. For example, in the Titchener Circles (Fig. 6) the central circle which is surrounded by the large circle should appear larger if that central circle assimilates to the circles which form the context. However, the central circle appears smaller than it really is. This means that factors other than assimilation must be operating. Future research could focus on isolating all the factors which are operating in geometric illusions.

References

CARMICHAEL, L., HOGAN, H. P., and WALTER, A. A. An experimental study of the effect of language on the production of visually perceived form. *Journal of Experimental Psychology*, 1932, *15*, 73-86.

GREGORY, R. L. Distortion of visual space as inappropriate constancy scaling. *Nature*, 1963, *199*, 678-680.

———. *Eye and brain: the psychology of seeing.* New York: McGraw-Hill, 1966.

OVER, R. Explanations of geometrical illusions. *Psychological Bulletin*, 1968, *70*, 545-562.

PRESSEY, A. W., and SWEENEY, O. A variation of the Poggendorff illusion. *Perceptual and Motor Skills*, 1969, *28*, 883-886.

PRITCHARD, R. M., HERON, W., and HEBB, D. O. Visual perception approached by the method of stabilized images. *Canadian Journal of Psychology*, 1960, *14*, 67-77.

RESTLE, F. Illusion of Bent Lines. *Perception and Psychophysics*, 1969, *5*, 273-274.

30 / The Perceptual Redintegration of Words Which Differ in Connotative Meaning [1]

P.L. Newbigging *McMaster University*

A stimulus may be exposed for such a short period of time that it will not be recognized. But, as length of exposure increases, the chance that the word will be recognized also increases. An accurate measure of length of exposure necessary for a stimulus to be "just recognized" can be obtained by means of a tachistoscope. Here Professor Newbigging demonstrates that words which have a "bad" connotation take longer to be recognized than words which are "good" or neutral.

There has been considerable experimental interest in connotative meaning as a determinant of recognition threshold for words. In different experiments, connotative meaning has been varied in terms of the emotional significance of words (e.g., McGinnies, 1949) word value (e.g., Solomon and Howes, 1951; Postman and Schneider, 1951; Johnson, Thomson, and Frincke, 1960), and "goodness" or "badness" as defined by rating on the good-bad scale of the Semantic Differential (Johnson, Thomson, and Frincke, 1960). Some authors have attempted to explain the effect of connotative meaning in terms of frequency. Solomon and Howes (1951), for example, argue that values operate to produce idiosyncratic variations in word frequency. A subject high in aesthetic value, the argument goes, is likely to read material containing words relevant to his dominant value area and therefore these words have a higher frequency for him than for the general population. The predictably lower recognition threshold for these words as compared with words of equal population frequency and relevant to other value areas is explained in terms of this idiosyncratic frequency and not in terms of connotative meaning. In a recent experiment, however, Johnson, Thomson, and Frincke (1960) have shown that when frequency is held constant, connotative meaning acts as a determinant of the threshold.

The question remains: how does connotative meaning have its effect on the threshold? The terms "perceptual sensitivity" and "perceptual defence" have been variously used as descriptive labels for the observed effects. Johnson, Thomson, and Frincke (1960) favour the following explanation: "It may be that the differential reinforcement of various stimuli causes those stimuli (as well as those responses) that have most frequently led to reinforcement in the past to be more readily observable or available in the present." They go on to say that because of the reinforcement history of a word "the stimulus qualities of rewarding or reinforcing words would be such that less information is needed before the word is correctly recognized than would be the case for words which were presented with equal frequency but were not equally reinforcing. Something that might be called perceptual sensitivity might then be said to exist." (p.341).

The essential point of this argument would appear to be that because of past reinforcement a smaller fragment of a reinforcing word (defined as rated toward the "good" end of the good-bad scale on the Semantic Differential) would elicit the correct response than would be required for a non-reinforcing or negatively reinforcing word (defined as rated toward the "bad" end of the good-bad scale on the Semantic Differential).

In a recent experiment, Newbigging (1961) showed that words occurring frequently in the written language according to the Thorndike-Lorge count are redintegrated from smaller recognized fragments, as judged from the similarity of the response preceding correct recognition of the stimulus word, than is the case for infrequently occurring stimulus words. The purpose of the present experiment is to apply the method of analysis used in that experiment to pre-recognition responses to words varying in connotative meaning, specifically, varying in ratings on the good-bad scale of the Semantic Differential. If the interpretation of the effect of connotative meaning proposed by Johnson, Thomson, and Frincke is correct, that is, that more information is required for the recognition of "bad" as compared with "good" words, pre-recognition responses to "bad" words should be more similar to the stimulus word than is true for "good" words. This would indicate that with "bad" words, a larger fragment of the word, or cue, is necessary for the correct redintegration of the word.

[1]The research for this paper was supported in part by the Defence Research Board of Canada under Grant no. 9401-13. My thanks are due to Miss Janet Hay for experimental assistance.

Reprinted, by permission, from *Canadian Journal of Psychology*, 1961, *15*, 133-141.

Method

Subjects

Ss were 9 male and 9 female volunteers from a local teachers' college. They ranged in age from 19 to 25 (to nearest birthday) with a mean age of 20.6.

Apparatus

The list of eighteen words given in Table I was used. The words were selected from the list published by Jenkins, Russell, and Suci (1958) so as to constitute three groups of six according to good-bad rating: one group rated at the "good" end of the scale, one group rated near the middle of the scale, and a third group rated at the "bad" end of the scale. So far as possible the three lists were equated according to length and frequency of occurrence.

Each word was typed in élite capital letters on a plain white card. The words were presented for recognition in a Gerbrand's tachistoscope. A Hunter KlocKounter was connected in the circuit with the timer of the tachistoscope so that both were started simultaneously. S stopped the KlocKounter by releasing a telegraph key.

Procedure

S was instructed as follows: "I am going to present some words to you one at a time. If you look in the eye-piece of the box you will see two lines. The words I shall show you will appear directly between the lines. Each word will be presented for a very short period of time and you may not be able to tell what the word is at first. However, after each presentation I want you to make a guess as to what the word was. Remember, even if you do not recognize the word I still want you to tell me what you think it was. Each word will be presented to you several times until you have correctly recognized it. I will inform you when you are correct and then I will show you another word. I shall say 'ready' before each word is flashed. When I say 'ready' I want you to hold down the key and watch between the two lines. After the word is flashed and you are ready to say what you think the word was, release the key. Remember, hold the key down when I say 'ready' and release it when you are ready to say the word you think was flashed."

It will be noted from these instructions that S was required to respond with a word to every presentation. The presentation of the experimental list was preceded by three practice words (McMASTER, TEACHER, HAMILTON) to familiarize S with the task. The experimental list was then presented in a different random order for each S. For every word the first exposure was for 20 millisec. and successive exposures were increased by 10 millisec. until correct recognition occurred. E recorded the response word and the response time for each exposure.

Table I – Stimulus words

	Number of letters	Frequency	Rating on good-bad scale
Graceful	8	19*	1.90**
Harmonious	10	6	1.83
Lovable	7	3	1.77
Patriot	7	17	1.90
Radiant	7	13	1.87
Symphony	8	6	1.87
	7.83	10.67	1.86
Boulder	7	5	4.17
Frosty	6	8	3.73
Politician	10	25	3.90
Socialism	9	4	4.57
Somber	6	7	3.63
Spanking	8	9	3.67
	7.67	9.67	3.94
Crooked	7	18	5.93
Discomfort	10	6	6.10
Mosquito	8	8	6.17
Putrid	6	1	6.37
Sickness	8	25	6.30
Stagnant	8	4	6.27
	7.83	10.33	6.19

* Frequency of occurrence according to the Thorndike-Lorge general count.

**Ratings reported by Jenkins, Russell, and Suci (1958).

Results

Thresholds

The threshold data are presented as a function of the good-bad scale ratings of the stimulus words in Figure 1. A Friedman two-way analysis of variance by ranks was performed on the threshold data yielding a $\chi^2_r = 8.08$ ($p < .02$). Subsequent comparisons of pairs of lists using the Wilcoxon matched-pairs signed-ranks test showed the thresholds of "bad" words to be significantly higher than either "good" or "neutral" words, but thresholds, of these latter two lists are not significantly different from each other. (For "good" and "neutral" words $T = 65.5$ (N.S.); for "good and "bad" words $T = 28.5$ ($p < .01$); and for "neutral" and "bad" words $T = 16.5$ ($p < .005$).) Since these lists did not differ significantly, the data for "good" and "neutral" words were pooled to simplify subsequent analyses.

Response Similarity

Two indices of the similarity between the subject's response word and the stimulus word were computed. The first, termed letter similarity, was obtained by counting up the number of letters in the response word that were the same as those in the stimulus word and adding to this total one point for each correct pair of letters which were adjacent and in the right order. Thus, the response word SYMPATHY given to the stimulus word SYMPHONY would be scored 9, or 60 per cent similar, since the maximum number of points in the example is 15. While the index is imperfect, it nevertheless permits desired comparisons between response words given to the different lists of stimulus words.

The data for letter similarity of "good" and "neutral" and for "bad" stimulus words for four critical responses are plotted as a function of expo-

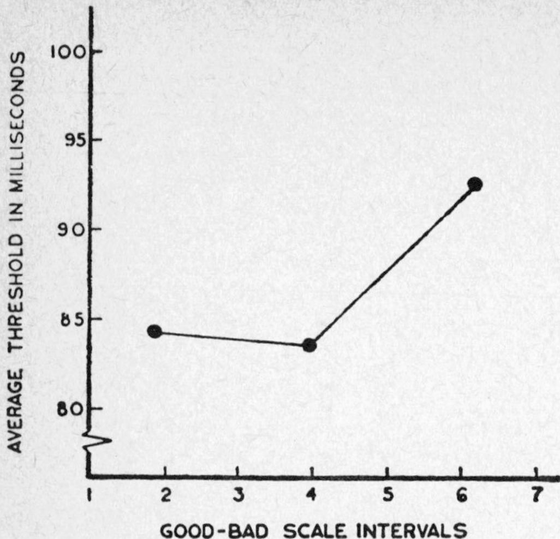

Fig. 1. Average threshold in milliseconds plotted as a function of the rating on a good-bad scale of the stimulus words.

sure time in Figure 2. The plot had to be restricted to four points on each curve in order to include every subject in each point. It will be noted from the figure that letter similarity for the response immediately preceding correct recognition (RT – 1) and the response before that one (RT – 2) does not appear to be different for "good" and "neutral" as compared with "bad" words. The slight differences observed were tested for significance using the Wilcoxon matched-pairs signed-ranks test with the following results: RT – 1 ($T = 96$, N.S.), RT – 2 ($T = 46$, N.S.). This lack of significant differences in letter similarity is of particular interest because the RT– 1

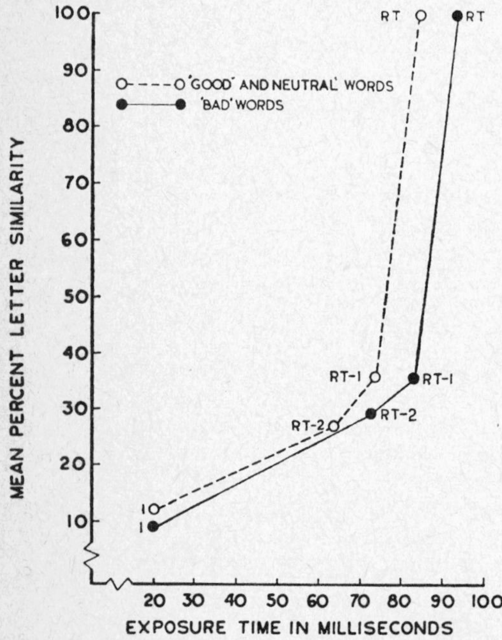

Fig. 2. Mean per cent letter similarity of four critical response words plotted as a function of the exposure time in milliseconds.

and the RT – 2 responses for "good" and "neutral" words are significantly different from the corresponding responses for "bad" words in terms of exposure time. The conclusion to be drawn is that "bad" words must be exposed for a significantly longer time than "good" and "neutral" words for the same-sized fragment (as measured by letter similarity) to be recognized.

The data for similarity of length of response words to "good" and "neutral" and "bad" words for four critical responses are plotted as a function of exposure time in Figure 3. The curves in this figure are essentially similar in shape to those for letter similarity. Tested by the Wilcoxon matched-pairs signed-ranks test neither RT – 1 nor RT – 2 for "good" and "neutral" words are significantly different in length from the corresponding responses for "bad" words (T = 39, N.S., and T = 43.5, N.S., respectively). While these responses do not differ significantly in terms of similarity of length, they do differ significantly in terms of exposure time. This is the same result as was obtained for letter similarity.

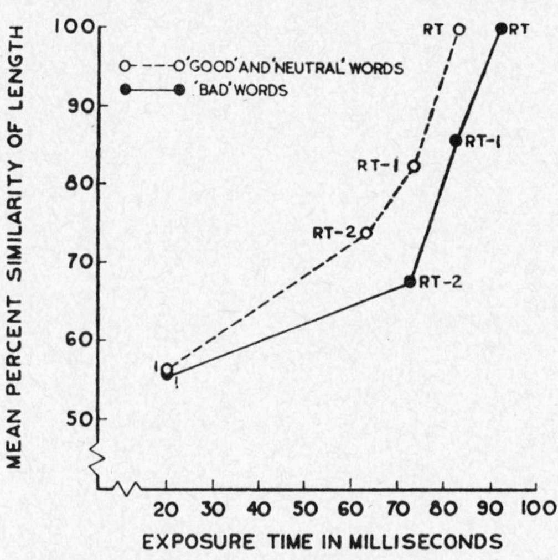

Fig. 3. Mean per cent similarity of length of four critical response words plotted as a function of the exposure time in milliseconds.

Response Time

The response time reported is the time elapsing from the onset of the stimulus to the beginning of the subject's response. These data for four critical responses to "good" and "neutral" and "bad" stimulus words are plotted as a function of exposure time in Figure 4. It is evident from Figure 4 that response time is directly related to exposure time for all responses up to correct recognition (RT) for which response, response time drops precipitously. Comparing response times for "good" and "neutral" with those for "bad" words, times for the latter are obviously much longer. To determine if the differences are significant the Wilcoxon matched-pairs signed-ranks test was used with the following results: RT ($T = 7$, $p < .01$); RT – 1 ($T = 38.5$, $p < .025$); RT – 2 ($T = 67$, N.S.).

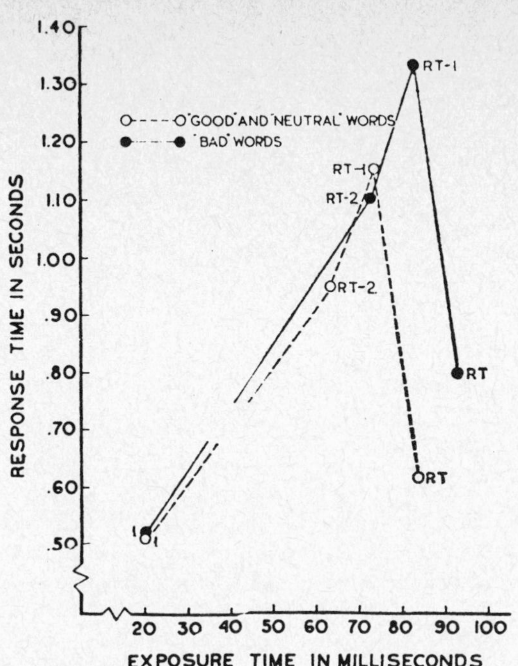

Fig. 4. Response time in seconds of four critical response words plotted as a function of the exposure time in milliseconds.

Discussion

The results of this experiment confirm the finding reported by Johnson, Thomson, and Frincke (1960) that words rated towards the "good" end of the good-bad scale of the Semantic Differential have a lower recognition theshold than do words rated towards the "bad" end.[2] They do not, however, support these authors' interpretation of how connotative meaning has its effect on the threshold. According to their interpretation, less information (that is, a smaller fragment or cue) would be required for the correct redintegration of "good" as compared with "bad" stimulus words. Of critical importance to this interpretation is the finding that, according to both indices of similarity employed (letter similarity and similarity of length), there is no significant difference in similarity between the response words given immediately prior (RT − 1) to the recognition of "good" and "neutral" as compared with "bad" stimulus words. These words, then, are redintegrated from the same size fragment. It would appear that connotative meaning affects the threshold in a different manner from word frequency since in a previous paper (Newbigging, 1961) it was shown that a larger fragment of an infrequent stimulus word was required for correct redintegration than was the case for a frequent stimulus word. Since it was also shown that a longer exposure time was required for recognition of the larger fragment, the higher threshold of infrequent words was entirely explained.

Two findings in the present experiment would seem to require the postulation of an inhibitory or perceptual defence mechanism. These are, first, that a significantly longer exposure time is required for the recognition of the same size fragment (as measured by the two indices of response similarity) of "bad" as compared with "good" and "neutral" stimulus words, and, second, that the response time for the response preceding the recognition of "bad" words (that is, RT − 1) is significantly longer than that for "good" words and "neutral" words. Consistent with this is the additional finding that the correct verbal response at recognition (RT) has a longer latency for "bad" as compared with "good" and "neutral" words. It would appear necessary, then, to conclude that in some way the recognition of fragments of "bad" words is inhibited as is the verbal response incorporating the recognized fragment.

It is possible only to speculate about how this perceptual defence or inhibitory process operates and the following is offered in that vein. Essentially what is proposed is a two-process theory. First, it is postulated that experienced stimulus words leave a trace whose strength is a simple function of the number of times the word has been experienced. The strength of the trace may be inferred from the size of the word fragment required to elicit the correct verbal response. The effect of word frequency on the recognition threshold may be explained entirely in terms of the trace hypothesis if this line of reasoning is accepted, since it has been shown (Newbigging, 1961) that a larger fragment of infrequent as compared with frequent stimulus words is required to elicit the correct verbal response. Where frequency is controlled, however, as in the present experiment, and connotative meaning is the variable, the trace hypothesis alone will not account for the results obtained since the word traces in all connotative meaning classes will be of the same strength. It is proposed that a second process that operates in an inhibitory manner on the trace is involved. Presumably certain letter combinations involved in "bad" words become conditioned to some emotional response that has an inhibitory effect. McGinnies' (1949) finding of a greater PGR response prior to the recognition of "taboo" as compared with non-taboo words suggests such a process. The finding in the present experiment, that it requires a significantly longer exposure time for the recognition of the same size fragment of a "bad" as compared with a "neutral" or "good" word suggests that this inhibitory process operates on perception as well as on the motor response, as is suggested by the significantly longer response times for "bad" words even prior to their correct recognition.

Summary

Eighteen words varying in connotative meaning as

[2] Of some interest is the failure to find a significant difference in the thresholds of "good" as compared with "neutral" words. On the basis of a mechanism of perceptual sensitivity it would have been predicted that "good" words would have a lower threshold. The slight difference observed is opposite to that prediction.

defined by rating on the good-bad scale of the Semantic Differential were exposed for recognition in a Gerbrand's tachistoscope to each of 18 Ss. The main findings were: (1) that "bad" words had a significantly higher threshold than "good" and "neutral" words; (2) that "bad" and "good" and "neutral" words were correctly redintegrated from the same size fragment, as measured by two indexes of similarity of pre-recognition responses to the stimulus word, but that a significantly longer exposure time was required for the recognition of the fragment of the "bad" words; (3) response times for the response preceding recognition and for the correct response was significantly longer for "bad" as compared with "good" and "neutral" stimulus words.

These results are interpreted in terms of a perceptual defence mechanism.

References

JENKINS, J. J., RUSSELL, W. A., and SUCI, G. J. An atlas of semantic profiles of 360 words. *Amer. J. Psychol.*, 1958, *71*, 688-99.

JOHNSON, R. C., THOMSON, C. W., and FRINCKE, G. Word values, word frequency and visual duration thresholds. *Psychol. Rev.*, 1960, *67*, 332-42.

MCGINNIES, E. M. Emotionality and perceptual defence. *Psychol. Rev.*, 1949, *56*, 244-51.

NEWBIGGING, P. L. The perceptual redintegration of frequent and infrequent words. *Canad. J. Psychol.*, 1961, *15*, 123-32.

POSTMAN, L., and SCHNEIDER, B. H. Personal values, visual recognition and recall. *Psychol. Rev.*, 1951, *58*, 271-84.

SOLOMON, R. L., and HOWES, D. H. Word frequency, word value, and visual duration thresholds. *Psychol. Rev.*, 1951, *58*, 256-70.

THORNDIKE, E. L., and LORGE, I. *The teacher's word book of 30,000 words*. New York: Columbia University, 1944.

31 / Pain

Ronald Melzack *McGill University*

Professor Melzack, one of the world's foremost experts on pain, reviews the psychological and physiological aspects of pain perception, the various theories that have been proposed, and finally concludes the topic with a description of his own "gate control theory" of pain.

The relief of pain and suffering has been a continuing human endeavour since the dawn of recorded history (see Keele, 1957). Yet despite centuries of observation and study, we are only beginning to achieve an understanding of the subtleties and complexities of pain. Even though pharmacologists have provided effective "painkillers," we know little about where and how these drugs act. Surgical procedures that are usually effective in relieving pain can sometimes produce dismal failures, often enough to convince us that we are far from understanding the neurological mechanisms that subserve pain perception.

Part of the difficulty of understanding pain mechanisms lies in the divergent empirical approaches to the problem. Sensory physiologists, anatomists, and psychologists (see Ruch and Fulton, 1960, pp. 300-368) have studied pain as a sensory phenomenon and have tended to neglect its motivating aspects. Learning theorists (Miller, 1951; Bindra, 1959) have dealt with pain primarily as a drive producer and negative reinforcing agent but have generally ignored the other facets of the problem. Finally, medical clinicians, such as anaesthetists (Beecher, 1959) and surgeons (White and Sweet, 1955), have regarded pain as indicative of tissue pathology that has to be treated and abolished and have often had to postulate hypothetical neural mechanisms to account for the complex phenomena they observe. These three approaches are so different that it is not surprising that "pain" has never been satisfactorily defined (Beecher, 1959).

The major obstacle to understanding pain, however, has been the perpetuation of a number of theories that have had a powerful influence on the field. The persistence of these theories has resulted in heated controversies that have endured since the beginning of this century. Consequently, one of the most difficult tasks in this field is to separate fact from theory. For this reason the psychological and clinical phenomena of pain, which must be accounted for by any satisfactory theory, will be described before any physiological theories and experiments are discussed.

Psychological Aspects of Pain Perception

The obvious biological significance of pain has led to the general belief that it must always occur after injury and that the intensity of pain perceived is proportional to the amount and extent of the damage. The positive aspect of pain is universally recognized: it warns us that something biologically harmful is happening. Reports (Sternbach, 1963) of people who are born without the ability to feel pain provide convincing testimony to its value. Such a person sustains extensive burns and bruises during childhood and learns only with difficulty to avoid inflicting severe wounds on himself. Nevertheless, there is convincing evidence that pain, in higher species at least, is not simply a function of the amount of bodily damage alone. Rather, the amount and quality of pain perceived are also determined by past experience and attention, by the ability to understand the cause of the pain and to grasp its consequences. This fact, supported by a large body of evidence, presents a challenge to pain theorists.

Cultural factors.

Cultural values are known to play an essential role in the way a person perceives and responds to pain. In Western culture, for example, childbirth is considered by many to be one of the worst pains a human being can experience. Yet the practice of couvade (Kroeber, [1923] 1948, pp. 542-543) in cultures throughout the world indicates the extent to which culture contributes to the intensity of pain. In some of these cultures a woman who is going to have a baby continues to work until the child is about to be born. Her husband then gets into bed and groans as though he were in great pain while she bears the child. In more extreme cases, the husband stays in bed with the baby to recover from the terrible ordeal and the mother returns almost immediately to her household work. Dick-Read (1944) has stressed the great extent to which culturally determined fear enhances the amount of pain felt during labour and birth and points out how difficult it is to dispel such fear.

Role of anxiety.

The effect of anxiety on the intensity of perceived pain is further demonstrated by studies on the effectiveness of placebos. Beecher found that severe pains (such as postsurgical pain) can be relieved in about 35 per cent of patients by giving them a placebo, such as sugar or saline solution, in place of morphine or other analgesic drugs. As Beecher has pointed out, only about 75 per cent of patients experiencing severe pain are satisfactorily relieved even when given large doses of morphine; the placebo effect thus accounts for about 50 per cent of the drug effectiveness (1959, p. 169). This is no way implies that people who are helped by a placebo do not have real pain; no one will deny the reality of postsurgical pain. Rather it illustrates the powerful contribution of anxiety to pain perception, since the physician may often relieve pain significantly by prescribing placebos to lower the patient's anxiety as well as by treating the wounded areas of the body. Similarly, experiments by Hall and Stirde (1954) have shown that the anticipation of pain raises the level of anxiety and, consequently, the intensity of perceived pain. Experiments by Hill and his associates (1952*a*; 1952*b*) have shown that a given level of electric shock or burning heat is perceived as significantly more painful when anxiety is experimentally induced than it is after anxiety has been dispelled. These studies also show that morphine diminishes pain if the anxiety level is high but has no demonstrable effect under conditions of low anxiety.

Role of attention.
Attention to stimulation also contributes to pain intensity. It is frequently noted that contestants in a fight or in the heat of a game can receive severe wounds without being aware that they have been hurt. Indeed, almost any situation that attracts a sufficient degree of excited, prolonged attention may provide the conditions for other stimulation to go by unnoticed, including wounds that would cause considerable suffering under normal circumstances. Hypnosis, a trance state in which attention is focused intensely on a person or an object, is perhaps the best-known condition in which people can be cut or burned without their reporting any perception of the event (Barber, 1959). Failure in attention may also account for the fact that dogs raised in sensory isolation in specially constructed cages from infancy to maturity (Melzack and Scott, 1957) show a frequent failure to respond to normally painful stimulation, such as a flaming match or pinprick, after they are released from their cages. Since these dogs exhibit a remarkably high level of excitement, it is reasonable to suppose (Melzack and Burns, 1963) that they fail to attend selectively to these noxious stimuli when they are presented in an unfamiliar environment in which all stimuli are equally attention-demanding.

Role of meaning.
Finally, there is striking evidence to show that the meaning associated with a pain-producing situation is extremely important in determining the degree and quality of pain that are perceived. Beecher observed soldiers who were severely wounded in battle and found that only one out of three claimed that he had enough pain to require morphine. Most of the soldiers denied having pain from their wounds or had so little that they did not want medication to relieve it. In contrast, four out of five hospitalized civilians who had surgical incisions matching the wounds received by the soldiers claimed that they were in severe pain and demanded a morphine injection. Beecher concluded that in the wounded soldier, the response to injury was relief, thankfulness for his escape alive from the battlefield, even euphoria (his wound was a good thing); to the civilian, his major surgery, even though essential, was a depressing, calamitous event; there is no simple direct relationship between the wound per se and the pain experienced (1959, p. 165).

The importance of the meaning associated with a pain-producing situation is made especially clear in conditioning experiments by Pavlov (1923). He found that if electric shocks administered to a dog's paw are followed consistently by the presentation of food, they eventually fail to elicit signs of pain and produce an entirely different response: the dog salivates, wags its tail, and turns toward the food dish. Masserman (1950) has carried these experiments still further. After cats had been taught to respond to electric shock as a signal for feeding, they were trained to administer the shock to themselves by walking up to a switch and closing it.

Medical Aspects of Pain

Theories of pain are satisfactory only to the extent that they are able to account for all of the relevant phenomena. There are many forms of pathological or clinical pain that present bizarre features that are difficult to explain; yet they must fit into the framework of pain theory. Two pain syndromes, *phantom-limb pain* and *causalgia*, have been studied in detail and represent the most terrible of human pain experiences.

Phantom-limb pain.
The presence of a painless phantom limb is reported by the majority of amputees almost immediately after amputation. About 30 per cent, however, have the misfortune to develop pains in the phantom limb, and in about 5 per cent the pain is severe. These pains may be occasional or continuous, but they are felt in definite parts of the phantom limb (Livingston, 1943; Feinstein et al., 1954). The pain tends to decrease and eventually disappear in most amputees. There are a few, however, in whom the pain increases in severity over the years and may even spread to other regions of the body, so that merely touching these new "trigger zones" will provoke spasms of severe pain in the phantom limb (Cronholm, 1951). Unfortunately, the conventional surgical procedures for controlling pain usually fail

to bring permanent relief; thus, these patients may undergo a series of such operations without any decrease in the severity of the pain (Livingston, 1943). Phenomena such as these defy explanation in terms of our present physiological knowledge. Attempts have been made to label these unfortunate people as "neurotic" (see Kolb, 1954), but there is convincing evidence that argues against such an explanation for all cases (Livingston, 1943).

There are a number of features of phantom-limb pain that provide clues toward understanding the mechanisms underlying it.

Peripheral factors. It is known (Livingston, 1943) that the neuromas (small nodules of regenerating nerve tissue) in the stumps of amputated patients contribute to phanton-limb pain, since pressure on them can trigger bouts of unbearable pain. Yet excision of neuromas or reamputation at a higher level usually fails to relieve pain for more than a few weeks or months (Livingston, 1943; Cronholm, 1951). Indeed there is almost unanimity of opinion that peripheral operations are likely to fail and that other procedures should be sought.

Role of sympathetic nervous system. The sympathetic nervous system also plays an important role, because cutting or temporarily anaesthetizing the sympathetic ganglia entering the spinal cord (Livingston, 1943) is capable of dramatically removing the pain for variable periods of time. Yet it is clearly not the sole cause of phantom-limb pain because pain often returns after the sympathetic ganglia are surgically removed. The contribution that the autonomic nervous system as a whole makes to phantom-limb pain is clear, moreover, from observations (Henderson and Smyth, 1948) that pain is triggered in many patients at the start of urination or defecation. Similar sudden increases of pain may be triggered by sexual excitement and orgasm (Kolb, 1954).

Emotional factors. Phentom-limb pain is greatly enhanced by emotional factors. Seeing a disturbing movie (Kolb, 1954), having an argument with wife or husband (Livingston, 1943), and other emotionally disturbing situations are capable of initiating or increasing the intensity of phantom-limb pain.

Role of sensory input. Either increasing or decreasing the sensory input from the stump or related areas is capable of providing relief from phantom-limb pain. Feinstein, Luce, and Langton (1954) have demonstrated that injection of the vertebral tissues of amputees with 6 per cent salt solution produces severe pain at the site of injection, which then radiates into the phantom limb. After this initial onset of pain, there is usually a decrease of the phantom-limb pain. Occasionally the pain vanishes completely following a single injection. Similarly dramatic results may occur after an injection of anaesthetic procaine into the vertebral tissues in the attempt to decrease sensory input from these regions. Comparable findings are reported when stimulation is increased or decreased at the peripheral level. Injection of the tender neuromas of the stump with procaine solution often brings about sudden and dramatic relief for variable periods of time. On the other hand, stimulation of the stump, by massage or by hitting it with a small rubber mallet, often produces the only possible relief from phantom-limb pain in a large number of patients (Russell and Spalding, 1950).

Spread of pain and trigger sites. Finally, there is the spread of pain and of trigger sites beyond the segments directly involved in the limb. Thus Cronholm (1951) found that touching the small of the back or the forehead may induce spasms of pain in a phantom leg. These trigger zones spread in unusual, seemingly random patterns and are not related in any apparent way to the segmental distribution of the somatic afferent nerves.

Causalgia.

Causalgia is a severe, unremitting, burning pain that occurs in about 2 per cent of people who have sustained a peripheral-nerve injury. The pain is felt in the affected limb but may spread to other parts of the body. It exhibits many of the features of phantom-limb pain as well as other even more bizarre characteristics. Surgical procedures have only limited success in the treatment of causalgic pain. Section of the peripheral nerve at a higher level, amputation of the limb, and cutting the dorsal sensory roots that enter the spinal cord have all produced as many failures as successes. Indeed, operations have been performed for causalgic pain at nearly every possible site in the pathway from the peripheral receptors to the sensory cortex, and at every level the story is the same: some encouraging results but a disheartening tendency for the pain to return (see Livingston, 1943).

Nonspecific triggering stimuli. A further remarkable feature of causalgia is that a variety of stimuli that can hardly be called "adequate pain stimuli" can produce increases in pain. Sudden noises, the sound of airplanes, the scraping of a shoe on the floor, emotional disturbances, almost any stimulus that elicits a startle response, touching the damaged leg or arm or even blowing lightly on it are all capable of making the pain worse (Livingston, 1943).

Sympathetic nervous system in causalgia. The involvement of the sympathetic nervous system in causalgia, as in phantom-limb pain, is obvious. The skin becomes dry and cool, and sweat may drip from a single finger (Livingston, 1943). Moreover, injection of anaesthetic procaine into the sympathetic ganglia may dramatically abolish the pain for variable periods of time. But the fact that pain may return after surgical removal of sympathetic ganglia (Livingston, 1943) indicates that sympathetic-nervous-system activity is not the primary cause of the pain.

Role of sensory input in causalgia. Similarly, an abnormal sensory input from the site of the nerve lesion is clearly implicated as an important cause of causalgic pain. Procaine blocks proximal or distal to the lesion may abolish pain for hours or days, and on rare occasions it never returns. Livingston (1943) reports, moreoever, that the pain can be abolished if the patient is trained to tolerate sensory stimulation of the affected limb and is encouraged to use it normally. But the frequent failure of peripheral-nerve surgery to abolish pain indicates that more is involved than simply an irritating peripheral lesion.

Psychophysiology of Pain

The psychological and clinical phenomena of pain that have been described above must be taken into account in any satisfactory theory of pain. Since physiological evidence on the sensory mechanisms of pain is intimately bound up with the theories in vogue at the time, it is necessary to consider the physiology in terms of theoretical orientation.

Orthodox specificity theory.
The orthodox theory of pain, still the most widely held, was first proposed by Max von Frey in 1895 (see Melzack and Wall, 1962) and was subsequently extended in a vast literature on pain mechanisms (see Bishop, 1946; White and Sweet, 1955). Von Frey's theory, also known as specificity theory, proposed that there are specific pain receptors (the free nerve endings) which, when stimulated, give rise to pain and only to pain. Following this idea, physiologists proposed that pain is carried by peripheral-nerve fibres of particular diameter (the A delta and C fibres) a distinct spinal-cord system (the spinothalamic tract), and a particular projection area in the thalamus, which is presumed to be the seat of pain sensation. Specificity theory has been the subject of heated debate and controversy since it was first proposed, and an attempt has recently been made (Melzack and Wall, 1962) to analyze the features of this theory that make it both attractive and repugnant.

Von Frey's specificity theory has three underlying assumptions. The first is physiological: the theory assumes that each receptor in the skin has a specific irritability, that is, a lowest threshold for some particular stimulus energy. There is convincing evidence to indicate that this assumption is valid, and it has been restated by Sherrington (1906) as the law of the adequate stimulus. The second assumption concerns the morphological receptor that is associated with pain experience. It is now certain (Weddell, 1955) that the free nerve endings transmit information not only about pain but also about warmth, cold, touch, itch, tickle, and the myriad other experiences that derive from cutaneous stimulation. The third assumption of specificity theory is psychological: it assumes a one-to-one relation between skin receptor and psychological experience.

Inadequacy of specificity theory. It is the assumption of a one-to-one relation between skin receptor and psychological experience that has led to attempts at outright rejection of von Frey's theory. The theory implies a direct transmission system in which there is an invariant, one-to-one relationship between stimulus intensity, peripheral receptor, central-nervous-system pathway, and intensity of pain perceived. Almost all of the psychological and clinical phenomena described above argue against this simple one-to-one relationship. The fact that a light puff of air on the skin, emotional disturbance, or arousal of the autonomic nervous system can elicit bouts of excruciating causalgic and phanton-limb pain indicates that there is more to pain mechanisms than a straight-through system from specific peripheral receptors to a pain center in the brain.

Pattern theory.
Alternative theories have been proposed to replace specificity theory. Their history dates back to the time of von Frey's theory, and each is characterized by complex physiological mechanisms that are postulated to account for the complex psychological and clinical phenomena of pain. Collectively, these alternative theories may be brought together under a single conceptual name: pattern theory. It proposes essentially that information at the skin is coded in the form of nerve-impulse patterns, which provide the basis of our sensory perceptions. These patterns, moreover, can undergo modification during their transmission centrally, that is, the quality and intensity of pain can be modulated by events in the central nervous system, such as memories, emotions, and attention. The most recent formulation of a pattern theory for cutaneous perceptions (Melzack and Wall, 1962) proposes that skin receptors have specialized physiological properties for the transmission of particular kinds and ranges of stimuli into patterns of nerve impulses, rather than modality-specific information, and that every discriminably different somesthetic perception is produced by a unique pattern of nerve impulses.

The concept of patterning of nerve impulses, together with three recently discovered features of the skin sensory system, provides the basis for a new theory of pain (Melzack and Wall, 1965). First, there is now abundant physiological and anatomical evidence of efferent fibre systems that run from the brain down to the afferent pathways and are capable of modifying or inhibiting the afferent pattern in the course of its transmission centrally (see Livingston, 1959). Second, the dorsal-column and dorsolateral systems of the spinal cord have properties (see Melzack and Wall, 1965) indicating that their function may well be that of arousing the central processes subserving memories of prior experience, attention, and so forth, which are then able to act downward on the afferent impulse patterns.

The third line of evidence derives from the recent work of Wall (1962), which shows that a sensory input arriving at the spinal cord has two effects. First, it transmits information from the peripheral nerve to spinal-cord cells whose fibres go to the brain, and, second, it influences the properties of the *substantia gelatinosa*, a diffusely interconnected band of tissue lying throughout the length of the spinal cord in the dorsal horn. Mendell and Wall (1964) have shown that the *substantia gelatinosa* can both inhibit and facilitate the transmission of the coded sensory information from peripheral fibre to central cell. They point out that there is a continuous tonic input from the periphery to the *substantia gelatinosa*, so that continual inhibitory control is exerted over the transmission of nerve impulses across the synapses from peripheral fibres to central cells.

This tonic inhibition can be increased or decreased by the size of the fibre stimulated. Thus the largest A fibres increase the tonic inhibitory effect of the *substantia gelatinosa*, while the small-diameter C fibres decrease the inhibitory influence, that is, actually facilitate the transmission of information in such a way that there is a greater likelihood of all inputs, from the peripheral and autonomic nervous systems, as well as from the brain, summating and thereby producing the characteristic pattern of high-frequency bursts of impulses that signals pain. The *substantia gelatinosa*, moreover, is a functionally continuous unit, so that different parts of the body are connected in a way that permits the spread of trigger zones observed in phantom-limb and causalgic pain.

Gate control theory.
These three features of the skin sensory system provide the basic for a gate control theory of pain (Melzack and Wall, 1965). The theory proposes that (1) the *substantia gelatinosa* functions as a gate control system that modulates the amount of input transmitted from the peripheral fibres to the dorsal horn transmission (T) cells; (2) the dorsal column and dorsolateral systems of the spinal cord act as a central control trigger, which activates selective brain processes that influence the modulating properties of the gate control system; and (3) the T cells activate neural mechanisms that constitute the action system responsible for both response and perception.

Figure 1 provides a schematic diagram of the gate control theory, showing the large-diameter and small-diameter peripheral fibres and their projections to the *substantia gelatinosa* (SG) and T cells in the dorsal horn. The inhibitory effect exerted by the *substantia gelatinosa* on the afferent fibre terminals is shown to be increased by activity in the large fibres and decreased by activity in the small fibres. The central control trigger is represented by the heavy line running from the large-fibre system to the central control mechanisms; these mechanisms, in turn, project back to the gate control system. The T cells project to the entry cells of the action system. Excitation is represented by +; inhibition by -.

The theory proposes that pain phenomena are determined by interactions among these three systems. For example, a marked loss of the large peripheral-nerve fibres, which may occur after traumatic peripheral-nerve lesions or in some of the neuropathies (Greenfield, 1958), such as postherpetic neuralgia

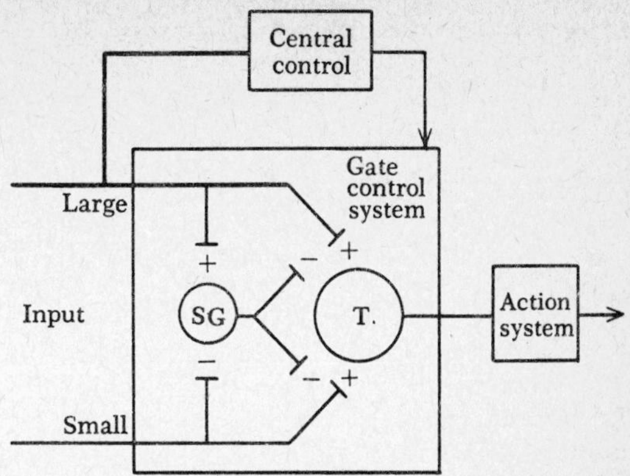

Fig. 1. Schematic diagram of the gate control theory.
From Melzack and Wall, 1965. Copyright © 1965 by the American Association for the Advancement of Science.

(Noordenbos, 1959), would decrease the normal presynaptic inhibition of the input by the gate control system. Thus, the input arriving over the remaining large and small fibres is transmitted through the unechecked, open gate produced by the small-fibre input. This, together with the opportunity for summation of inputs into the *substantia gelatinosa* from other parts of the body and from the brain, provides the basis for the triggering of pain by a variety of stimuli that are normally not noxious.

Affect and Motivation

Pain has generally been considered primarily a sensory experience somewhat similar to sight or hearing. In one important respect, however, pain differs from vision and hearing: it has a unique, distinctly unpleasant quality that wells up in consciousness and obliterates anything we may have been thinking or doing at the time. It becomes overwhelming and demands immediate attention. Besides its sensory component, then, pain also has a strong emotional *quale* that drives (or motivates) the organism into doing something about it. Ensuing responses are such as to stop the pain quickly by whatever course of action is possible.

Introspectionist psychologists at the turn of the century made a sharp distinction between the sensory and the affective dimensions of the pain experience. Titchener (1909) was convinced that there is a continuum of *feeling* in conscious experience, distinctly different from sensation, that ranges through all degrees of pleasantness and unpleasantness. These two dimensions, the sensory quality and the affective *quale*, are brought clearly into focus by clinical studies on prefrontal lobotomy (Freeman and Watts, 1942), a neurosurgical operation for intense pain in which the connections between the prefrontal lobes and the rest of the brain are severed. Typically, these patients report after the operation that they still have pain but that it no longer bothers them; they simply no longer care about the pain and often forget it is there. It is certain that the operation does not stop pain perception entirely, since the sensory component is still present. The predominant effect of the operation seems to be on the affective colouring of the total pain experience; the terribly unpleasant quality of the pain has been abolished.

Brain areas involved. Recent experiments suggest that there are portions of the brain that are particularly concerned with the motivating aspects of behaviour. Miller (1957) has recently found subcortical areas in the brain that produce vigorous escape reactions, cries, and other emotional behaviour characteristic of pain perception when they are stimulated electrically. It seems possible that the activities in these areas provide the neural substrate for the affective, "driving" component of pain perception.

Toward a Definition of Pain

In recent years the evidence on pain has moved in the direction of recognizing the plasticity and modifiability of events occurring in the central nervous system. In the lower part of the brain at least, the patterns of nerve impulses evoked by noxious stimulation travel over multiple pathways going to widespread regions of the brain and not along a single path going into a "pain centre." The psychological evidence lends strong support to the consideration of pain as a perception determined by the unique past history of the individual, by the meaning the stimulus has to him, by his "state of mind" at the moment, as well as by the sensory nerve patterns evoked by a physical cause. In this way, pain becomes a function of the whole individual, including even his thoughts and hopes for the future.

Pain, then, refers to a category of complex experiences, not to a kind of stimulation. Clearly, there are many varieties and qualities of experience that are simply categorized under the broad heading of pain because they defy more subtle verbal description. There are the pains of a scalded hand, a stomach ulcer, a sprained ankle; there are headaches and toothaches. But there is also the heartache of the scorned lover, the pain of losing a dear friend. It may be argued that the pain of bereavement is very different from the pain that follows surgery. But the pain of a coronary occlusion is just as uniquely different from the pain of a scalded hand.

Why is it so difficult to achieve a satisfactory definition of pain? The answer appears to be that pain is not a single, specific experience that can be analyzed and manipulated. It may be agreed that pain, like vision and hearing, is a complex perceptual experience. But the numerous, diverse causes of pain prevent the specification of a particular kind of environmental energy as the specific stimulus for pain, in the way that light can be specified as the adequate stimulus for vision, and air pressure waves for hearing. Pain is a category of experiences, signifying a multitude of different unique events having different causes and characterized by different qualities varying alone a number of sensory and affective dimensions.

References

BARBER, THEODORE X. (1959). Toward a Theory of Pain: Relief of Chronic Pain by Prefrontal Leucotomy, Opiates, Placebos, and Hypnosis. *Psychological Bulletin, 56,* 430-460.

BEECHER, HENRY K. (1959). *Measurement of Subjective Responses: Quantitative Effects of Drugs.* New York: Oxford Univ. Press.

BINDRA, DALBIR (1959). *Motivations: A Systematic Reinterpretation.* New York: Ronald.

BISHOP, GEORGE H. (1946). Neural Mechanisms of Cutaneous Sense. *Physiological Reviews, 26,* 77-102.

CRONHOLM, B. (1951). Phantom Limbs in Amputees: Study of Changes in Integration to Referred Sensations. *Acta psychiatrica et neurologica scandinavica, 72,* (Supplement), 1-310.

DICK-READ, GRANTLY ([1944] 1959). *Childbirth Without Fear.* 2nd ed., rev. New York: Harper. A paperback edition was published in 1962 by Dell.

FEINSTEIN, BERTRAM, LUCE, JAMES C., and LANGTON, JOHN N. K. (1954). The Influence of Phantom Limbs. Pages 79-138 in National Research Council, Advisory Committee on Artificial Limbs. *Human Limbs and Their Substitutes.* New York: McGraw-Hill.

FREEMAN, WALTER, and WATTS, JAMES W. ([1942] 1950). *Psychosurgery in the Treatment of Mental Disorders and Intractable Pain.* 2nd ed. Springfield, Ill.: Thomas.

GREENFIELD, JOSEPH G. ([1958] 1963). *Greenfield's Neuropathology,* by W. BLACKWOOD et al. 2nd ed. London: Arnold.

HALL, K. R. L., and STRIDE, E. (1954). The Varying Response to Pain in Psychiatric Disorders: A Study in Abnormal Psychology. *British Journal of Medical Psychology, 27,* 48-60

HENDERSON, W. R., and SMYTH, G. E. (1948). Phantom Limbs. *Journal of Neurology, Neurosurgery and Psychiatry, 11,* 88-112.

HILL, HARRIS E. et al. (1952*a*). Effects of Anxiety and Morphine on Discrimination of Intensities of Painful Stimuli. *Journal of Clinical Investigation, 31,* 473-480.

HILL, HARRIS E. et al. (1952*b*). Studies on Anxiety Associated With Anticipation of Pain: I. Effects of Morphine. *Archives of Neurology and Psychiatry, 67,* 612-619.

KEELE, KENNETH D. (1957). *Anatomies of Pain.* Oxford: Thomas.

KOLB, LAWRENCE C. (1954). *The Painful Phantom: Psychology, Physiology and Treatment.* Springfield, Ill.: Thomas.

KROEBER, ALFRED L. ([1923] 1948). *Anthropology: Race, Language, Culture, Psychology, Prehistory.* New ed., rev. New York: Harcourt. First published as *Anthropology.*

LIVINGSTON, W. K. (1943). *Pain Mechanisms.* New York: Macmillan.

LIVINGSTONE, ROBERT B. (1959). Central Control of Receptors and Sensory Transmission Systems. Volume 1, section 1, pages 741-760 in *Handbook of Physiology.* Washington: American Physiological Society.

MASSERMAN, JULES H. (1950). A Biodynamic Psychoanalytic Approach to the Problems of Feeling and Emotion. Pages 40-75 in International Symposium on Feelings and Emotions, Second, Moose Heart, Illinois, 1948, *Feelings and Emotions.* New York: McGraw-Hill.

MELZACK, RONALD, and BURNS, S. K. (1963). Neuropsychological Effects of Early Sensory Restriction. México, Universidad Nacional de, Instituto de Estudios Médicos y Biológicos, *Boletín, 21,* 407-425.

MELZACK, RONALD, and SCOTT, T. H. (1957). The Effects of Early Experience on the Response to Pain. *Journal of Comparative and Physiological Psychology, 50,* 155-161.

MELZACK, RONALD, and WALL, PATRICK D. (1962). On the Nature of Cutaneous Sensory Mechanisms. *Brain, 85,* 331-356.

MELZACK, RONALD, and WALL, PATRICK D. (1965). Pain Mechanisms: A New Theory. *Science, 150,* 971-979.

MENDELL, L. M., and WALL, PATRICK D. (1964). Presynaptic Hyperpolarization: A Role for Fine Afferent Fibres. *Journal of Physiology, 172,* 274-294.

MILLER, NEAL E. (1951). Learnable Drives and Rewards. Pages 435-472 in S. S. STEVENS (ed.), *Handbook of Experimental Psychology.* New York: Wiley.

MILLER, NEAL E. (1957). Experiments on Motivation. *Science, 126,* 1271-1278.

NOORDENBOS, W. (1959). *Pain.* Amsterdam: Elsevier.

PAVLOV, IVAN P. ([1923] 1928). *Lectures on Conditioned Reflexes: Twenty-five Years of Objective Study of Higher Nervous Activity (Behaviour) of Animals.* New York: International Publishers. First published as *Dvadtsatiletnii opyt ob'jektivnogo izucheniia vysshei nervnoi deiatel'nosti (povedeniia) zhivotnykh.*

RUCH, THEODOR C., and FULTON, JOHN F. (eds.) (1960). *Medical Physiology and Biophysics.* 18th ed. of Howell's *Textbook of Physiology.* Philadelphia: Saunders.

RUSSELL, W. R., and SPALDING, J. M. K. (1950). Treatment of Painful Amputation Stumps. *British Medical Journal, 2,* 68-73

SHERRINGTON, CHARLES S. ([1906] 1948). *The Integrative Action of the Nervous System.* 2nd ed. New Haven: Yale Univ. Press.

STERNBACH, RICHARD A. (1963). Congenital Insensitivity to Pain. *Psychological Bulletin, 60,* 252-264.

TITCHENER, EDWARD B. ([1909] 1910). *A Textbook of Psychology.* New York: Macmillan.

WALL, P. D. (1962). The Origin of the Spinal Cord Slow Potential. *Journal of Physiology, 164,* 508-526.

WEDDELL, G. (1955). Somesthesis and the Chemical Senses. *Annual Review of Psychology, 6,* 119-136.

WEISS, PAUL, EDDS, MCV., and CAVANAUGH, MARGARET. (1945). The Effect of Terminal Connections on the Caliber of Nerve Fibres. *Anatomical Record, 92,* 215-233.

WHITE, JAMES C., and SWEET, WILLIAM H. (1955). *Pain: Its Mechanism and Neurosurgical Control.* Springfield, Ill.: Thomas.

32 / Changes in Olfactory and Gustatory Sensitivity after Prolonged Visual Deprivation [1]

W. Schutte and John P. Zubek *University of Manitoba*

One problem which has long interested experimental psychologists is the determination of intersensory effects, i.e., what is the effect of stimulating or not stimulating one sense modality upon the functioning of other sense modalities? In this experiment, the authors have demonstrated that an absence of visual stimulation (darkness) for a prolonged period of time produces an improvement in olfactory and taste sensitivity. This facilitatory effect is believed to be mediated by a central control mechanism, the reticular activating system.

Various investigators have reported that subjects who are deprived of visual, auditory, tactile-kinesthetic, and social stimulation, for periods ranging from one to seven days, show a significant increase in tactual acuity (Doane, Mahatoo, Heron and Scott, 1959; Nagatsuka and Maruyama, 1963; Nagatsuka and Suzuki, 1964; Zubek, 1964), in pain sensitivity (Vernon and McGill, 1961), and in taste sensitivity (Nagatsuka, 1965). Recently, however, three studies from the Manitoba labotratory have indicated that a reduction in sensory stimulation from several modalities is not essential for the production of some of these facilitatory effects. They can be produced by visual deprivation alone (Zubek, Flye, and Aftanas, 1964; Zubek, Flye, and Willows, 1964; Duda and Zubek, 1965). Subjects who were visually deprived for a week but who otherwise were exposed to a normal and varied sensory environment showed a significant increase not only in tactual acuity and in pain sensitivity but also in auditory discrimination (auditory flutter fusion frequency). This effect of visual deprivation was uniform with all, or almost all, of the experimental subjects showing the phenomena. Furthermore, these facilitatory effects were long-lasting, persisting for several days after restoration of normal visual stimulation.

The purpose of this experiment is to determine whether visual deprivation alone can produce a similar increase in gustatory and olfactory sensitivity. If this should occur, it will suggest that prolonged visual deprivation may produce a general enhancement of sensory functioning. It will also provide experimental support for certain aspects of Schultz's (1965) sensoristatic model of the nervous system according to which the reticular activating system acts as a "homeostat" or regulator of the overall level of sensory functioning.

Procedure

Twelve male university students, each wearing a black mask, were placed in groups of two in an ordinary room for one week. Apart from the exposure to constant darkness, their environment was quite normal. No gloves were worn and no restrictions were placed on their motor activity or on conversation with one another or with the *E*s. Furthermore, a radio was available in the room at all times. It was frequently in use. Measures of olfactory and taste sensitivity were taken before and immediately after the week of darkness as well as at intervals of 1, 2, and 5 days after the termination of visual deprivation. A group of 12 control *S*s were tested at the same time intervals and at the same time of the day as the experimentals.

Determination of Olfactory Sensitivity

Olfactory sensitivity (recognition threshold for benzene) was determined by placing S inside a glass enclosed chamber, 5 ft. x 3 ft. x 5 ft., which was equipped with an air conditioner capable of filtering dust and ambient odours from the air while maintaining a constant temperature of approximately 25°C and 50 per cent humidity. Both the air conditioner and chamber were constructed of materials with low rates of odour absorption, i.e., glass, aluminium, stainless steel, and silicone rubber. Air pressure in the chamber was slightly higher than that of the outside air in order to minimize contamination by unfiltered air. The odorous substance, benzene (thiophene-free reagent grade), was delivered to *S* by a silicone rubber tube from an olfactometer located outside of the chamber. The silicone tube was connected to a nylon nosepiece shaped to make a tight

[1]This research was supported by the National Research Council, Canada (APT-106) and by the Defence Research Board, Canada (No. 9425-08). The authors wish to express their appreciation to Messrs. L. Bayer, K. Denheyer, D. Dickson, K. Fuerst, D. Oleson, and S. Milstein for experimental assistance and to Dr. E. Bock of the Dept. of Chemistry for aid in the calculation of the olfactory thresholds.

Reprinted, by permission, from *Canadian Journal of Psychology*, 1967, *21*, 337-345.

seal with one nostril. The nosepiece was sterilized in ethanol before use by each *S*.

The olfactometer was similar in construction to one developed by Jones (1954). This instrument provides a close control over the duration, volume, pressure, and temperature of the stimulus and permits stimulus specification in molar terms. Basically it consists of a 50-c.c. syringe which may be filled with different proportions of pure air and a certain dilution of the odorous substance from evaporation bottles immersed in a constant temperature bath maintained at 26.1°C. The odorous substance is mixed with odourless mineral oil to reduce its volatility. The syringe, a three-way stopcock, and the nosepiece are clamped into holders on the main body of the apparatus and connected to the evaporation bottles by means of a short length of silicone rubber tubing. When clamped in position, the plunger of the syringe makes contact with a rack, which is driven by two reversible constant speed motors in tandem, controlled by a switch. The length of travel of the rack was determined by the positioning of two microswitches at an interval which allowed a 40-c.c. displacement in the syringe. The 40-c.c. odorous blast was delivered in 1.8 sec. According to Jones (1954), these magnitudes are such as to minimize quantity of stimulus blast as a determiner of threshold.

Thresholds are determined by metering various amounts of odorous air into the syringe by proper adjustment of the three-way stopcock and then filling the syringe with pure air provided by a three-bottle chain containing silica gel, activated charcoal, and silica gel, in that order. This method provides a fine control of concentration and, since a knowledge of the vapour pressure of benzene, its molecular weight, the molecular weight of the mineral oil, the temperature, and barometric pressure permit calculation of the concentration of the benzene in the evaporation bottles, the stimulus concentration in the syringe can also be stated in molecular terms.[2]

The method of limits, with ascending series only, was used to determine the threshold of sensitivity to benzene. The threshold was for recognition which was found to be easier to judge than the absolute threshold. *S* was initially presented with an odorous concentration below threshold with successive presentations increased systematically in steps of 1 c.c. of odorous air while the quantity of pure air was decreased successively by 1 c.c. The threshold was taken as the average of the three ascending determinations. The pre-experimental recognition threshold for the 24 *S*s was 0.97×10^{-4}, a value somewhat lower than that reported by Jones (1954) using four *S*s (1.5×10^{-4}).

Determination of Gustatory Sensitivity

In the determination of gustatory sensitivity, the test stimuli consisted of 21 different concentrations of sucrose (sweet) ranging from 0.006% mole of sucrose per mole of distilled water to 2.000%, 20 for NaCl (salt) ranging from 0.005% to 2.000%, 22 for HCl (sour) ranging from 0.000006% to 0.0270%, and 23 for quinine sulphate (bitter) ranging from 0.000003% to 0.0020%. Each concentration in the series was a multiple of 0.75 of the preceding concentration. The test solutions were maintained at a temperature of 25°C ± .025°C.

The procedure was similar to that employed by Nagatsuka (1965) in a study on the effect of perceptual deprivation on taste sensitivity. *S* was blindfolded and rinsed out his mouth with distilled water maintained at the same temperature as the test solutions. Following rinsing, the test solution was presented in 4-c.c. doses by spoon, swirled in the mouth for 15 sec., and then spewed out. Immediately after spewing, *S* was required to report the presence or absence of the specific taste quality being appraised. If the report was negative, the procedure was repeated with successively higher concentrations until a positive report was obtained. Three ascending trials were given on each of the four taste solutions. At the beginning of each series the *S*s were told which taste quality to look for, whether sweet, salty, sour, or bitter. A short rest interval (three min.) was interspersed between the different trials of a particular series. The mouth was thoroughly rinsed before the next taste substance was used.

Results

Figure 1 summarizes the results on olfactory sensitivity. A *t* test for correlated measures indicated that the experimental subjects showed a significant increase in sensitivity immediately after the one-week period ($p < .05$), an effect which was seen in 11 of the 12 subjects. The controls, on the other hand, showed no significant change over the same interval; one-half of the group showed an increase in threshold and the other half, a decrease. Furthermore, no significant difference between the two groups was present on the pre-test measure of sensitivity. None of the changes on "post days 1, 2, and 5" was significant indicating that the increase in olfactory sensitivity was only present immediately after the termination of visual deprivation. It is interesting to note, however, a suggestion of an oscillatory phenomenon in the experimental subjects, that is, an "overswing" to decreased olfactory sensitivity two days after the termination of visual deprivation (see Figure 1).

Figure 2 summarizes the results on taste sensitivity for salty and sweet solutions. A statistical analysis revealed a significant increase in sensitivity to both salty and sweet immediately after visual deprivation ($ps < .02$) and on "post day 1" ($ps < .05$). In both cases, all experimental subjects but one showed this increase. On the other hand, the control subjects showed no significant pre/post diffences in sensitivity to either salty or sweet. Nor did they differ signifi-

[2] Since Jones (1954) does not provide the necessary formulae required to calculate olfactory thresholds in molecular terms, these can be obtained from the authors.

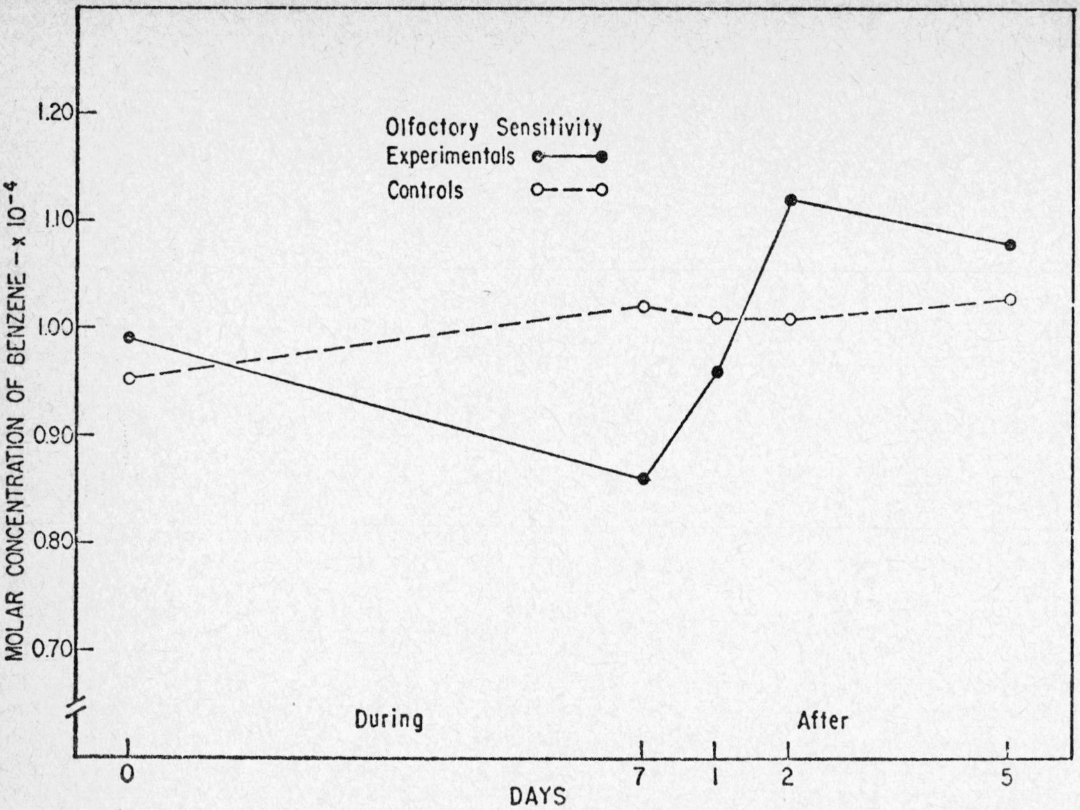

Fig. 1. Changes in olfactory sensitivity (benzene) before and after 7 days of visual deprivation, or of a control condition, and 1, 2, and 5 days later. Note the suggestion of an "overswing" to decreased olfactory sensitivity in the experimental subjects on "post day 2."

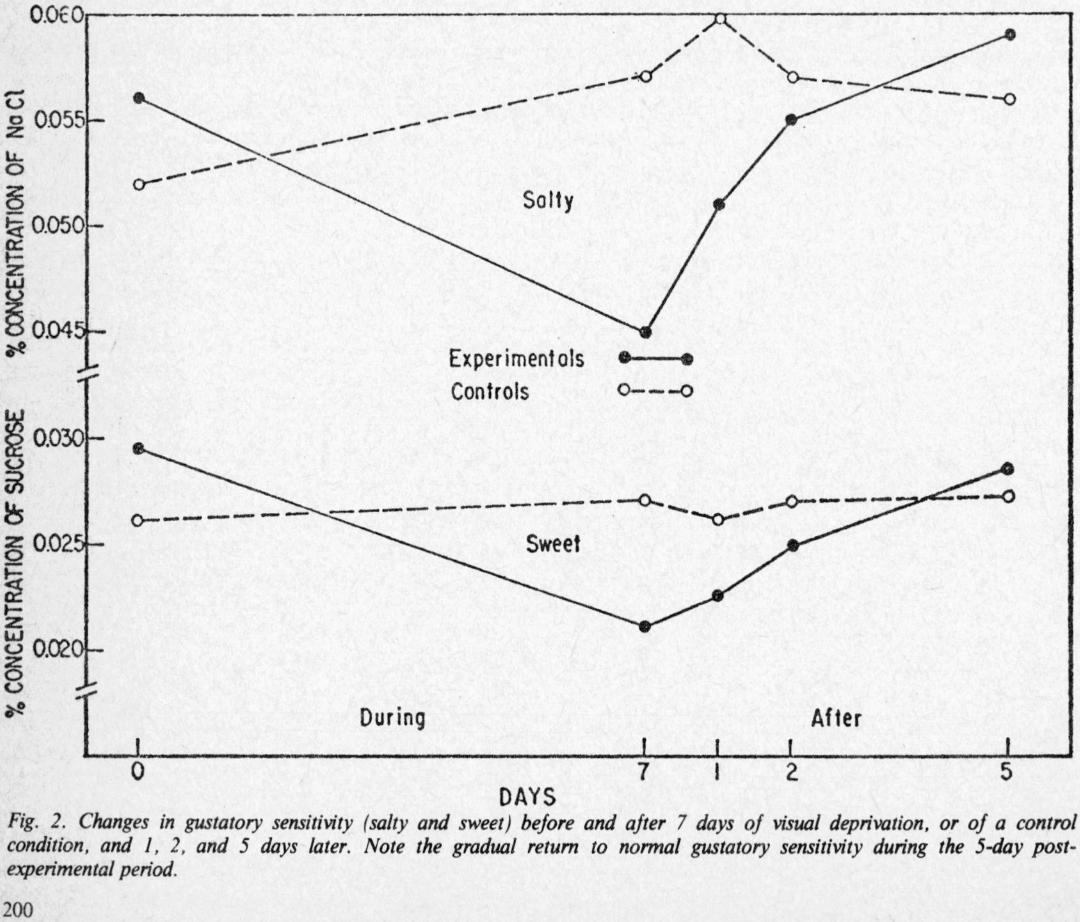

Fig. 2. Changes in gustatory sensitivity (salty and sweet) before and after 7 days of visual deprivation, or of a control condition, and 1, 2, and 5 days later. Note the gradual return to normal gustatory sensitivity during the 5-day post-experimental period.

cantly from the experimentals on the two pre-test measures of taste sensitivity.

The results on sensitivity to sour showed a pattern similar to that observed with salty and sweet, that is, an increase in taste sensitivity immediately after visual deprivation with a gradual return to normal sensitivity during the subsequent five-day period. However, none of the pre/post differences for either the experimental or the control group was statistically significant. Despite this, the presence of a strong trend is indicated by the fact that 11 of the 12 experimental subjects showed a lower threshold immediately after visual deprivation whereas only 7 of the 12 control subjects exhibited the same change over a one-week period. Finally, on sensitivity to bitter there were again no statistically significant pre/post differences in either group. However, in contrast to sour, no trend toward increased taste sensitivity immediately after visual deprivation was evident. Further support for the lack of a trend is indicated by an essentially similar individual performance by the two groups of subjects. Nine of the 12 experimental and 8 of the 12 control subjects showed a lower threshold at the end of the one-week period.

Discussion

This experiment has demonstrated that not only cutaneous and auditory sensitivity but also olfactory sensitivity is increased significantly after a week of visual deprivation. This facilitatory phenomenon, however, is only evident immediately after visual deprivation. It does not persist for several days as was found to be the case in our earlier research on cutaneous and auditory sensitivity. Another important finding was the suggestion of an "overswing" to decreased olfactory sensitivity two days after the termination of the experimental condition. Although this unusual reversal was not statistically significant, it appears to be similar in nature to an oscillatory phenomenon recently reported by Glazer and Zenhausern (1966). In this study, measures of pain sensitivity and auditory sensitivity were taken before and immediately after five minutes of sensory deprivation (darkness and silence) and subsequently at one-minute intervals for four minutes. The results revealed an initial lowering of pain and auditory thresholds (increased sensitivity) immediately after deprivation, an "overswing" to raised thresholds two minutes later, and then a return to the normal pre-deprivation levels at the end of four minutes. The presence of these oscillatory changes was interpreted as indicating a temporary disturbance of some homeostatic regulatory mechanism such as the reticular activating system. In view of these results it is surprising that no indication of an oscillatory pattern was seen in either our earlier research on cutaneous and auditory sensitivity or in the present experiment on gustatory sensitivity (see Figure 2). Two possible explanations may be offered. First, oscillatory changes on these latter modalities may only occur under a condition of both visual and auditory deprivation and not under visual deprivation alone. Second, the temporal course of these oscillatory changes may extend over a period of many days. Since a one-week deprivation period is being employed it is possible that the "overswing," if it does occur, may only be evident several days after our fifth post-experimental follow-up period.

The measures of gustatory sensitivity yielded a differential pattern of results. Sensitivity to NaCl (salty) and sucrose (sweet) was increased significantly after visual deprivation with the after-effects persisting for one day after restoration of normal visual stimulation. Sensitivity to HCl (sour) and quinine (bitter), on the other hand, was not affected significantly although a marked trend toward increased sensitivity to sour was evident immediately after visual deprivation. These differential results, it is important to note, appear to be related to the per cent concentration of the four taste substances that were employed. Quinine and HCl, which subjects can normally detect at very low concentrations, produced negative results whereas NaCl and sucrose, to which subjects are much less sensitive, resulted in a significant increase in sensitivity. Further evidence in support of the possible importance of this variable is provided by a rank-ordering of the four taste solutions according to concentration and the magnitude of the post-deprivation change. The greatest sensory change was shown by NaCl followed by sucrose, HCl, and quinine, in descending order, a rank order corresponding to the descending concentrations of the four taste substances. In view of this correspondence it is possible that increased sensitivity to both sour and bitter may have occurred if other taste substances, to which subjects are less sensitive, had been substituted for HCl and quinine.

The failure to demonstrate even a trend toward increased sensitivity to bitter is puzzling since the Japanese investigator, Nagatsuka, reported (1965) that subjects exposed to one day of visual *and* auditory deprivation showed a 36 per cent increase in sensitivity to bitter (quinine) and sweet (sucrose). Unfortunately, sour and salty substances were not employed. One possible explanation of this difference may be that increased sensitivity to bitter only occurs after visual-auditory deprivation and not after visual deprivation alone. A more likely explanation, however, may lie in the difference in the duration of the two experiments. Some evidence for the importance of duration has been provided by Doane *et al.* (1959) who observed a greater increase in tactual acuity after two days than after three days of perceptual deprivation. Vernon, McGill, Gulick, and Candland (1961) also reported that two days of sensory deprivation produced a greater deficit than did three days on colour perception, mirror drawing, and on a rotary-pursuit task. Since in both studies a recovery of function, with increasing duration, is indicated it is possible that a significant increase in sensitivity to both bitter and sour could have been demonstrated in the present experiment if measures had been taken after one or two days rather than at the end of the one-week period when most of the effects may have dissipated. Regardless of the reason for this apparent discrepancy in results, it is clear that future research in this area should be directed at the temporal course of sensory changes occurring at various intervals of a prolonged duration. If this were to be done, some of the apparently contradictory results derived from short-term and long-term deprivation studies might be resolved. Furthermore, this type of research might throw further light on why only certain primary taste qualities appear to be affected by a prolonged period of visual deprivation.

These intersensory facilitatory effects produced by visual deprivation provide some experimental support for the sensoristatic model of the nervous system recently formulated by Schultz (1965). According to Schultz, sensoristasis is a condition in which the organism strives to maintain an optimal range of sensory variation, a range which is capable of shifting to some degree as a function of several variables. The monitor serving to maintain the sensoristatic balance is the reticular activating system which Lindsley (1961) conceives of as serving as a sort of "homeostat" or regulator adjusting "input-output" relations. One of the predictions which Schultz derives from his model is that "when stimulus variation is restricted, central regulation of threshold sensitivities will function to lower sensory thresholds. Thus, the organism becomes increasingly sensitized to stimulation in an attempt to restore the balance" (p. 32). Our demonstration of an increase in olfactory, gustatory, cutaneous, and auditory sensitivity following prolonged visual deprivation appears to support this theoretical prediction. Schultz's model would also predict that auditory deprivation alone should likewise produce lower thresholds in the non-auditory modalities. An experimental test of this prediction will shortly be undertaken at the Manitoba laboratory.

Abstract

*S*s who were placed in darkness for a week but who otherwise were exposed to a normal and varied sensory environment showed a significant increase in olfactory sensitivity (benzene). The measures of gustatory thresholds yielded a differential pattern of results. Sensitivity to NaCl (salty) and sucrose (sweet) was increased significantly with the after-effects persisting for one day after restoration of normal visual stimulation. On the other hand, sensitivity to HCl (sour) and quinine (bitter) was not affected significantly. The results were interpreted as providing experimental support for a sensoristatic model recently formulated by Schultz (1965).

Résumé

On observe une augmentation significative de la sensibilité olfactive (benzène) chez des sujets d'abord tenus dans l'obscurité pendant une semaine, mais par ailleurs exposés à des conditions d'environnement sensoriel normales et variées. La mesure des seuils gustatifs montre une constellation de résultats variés. La sensibilité au NaCl et au sucrose augmente de façon significative, les effets consécutifs persistant pendant une journée après le rétablissement de la stimulation visuelle normale. Par ailleurs, la sensibilité au HCl et à le quinine n'est affectée de façon significative. L'interprétation voit dans ces résultats une confirmation expérimentale du modèle sensori-statique récemment formulé par Schultz. (1965)

References

DOANE, B. K., MAHATOO, W., HERON, W., and SCOTT, T. H. Changes in perceptual function after isolation. *Canad. J. Psychol.*, 1959, *13*, 210-14.

DUDA, P., and ZUBEK, J. P. Auditory sensitivity after prolonged visual deprivation. *Psychon. Sci.*, 1965, *3*, 359-60.

GLAZER, S., and ZENHAUSERN, R. The effects of short-term sensory deprivation on auditory and pain thresholds. Paper presented at the annual meeting of the Eastern Psychological Association, April, 1966.

JONES, F. N. An olfactometer permitting stimulus specification in molar terms. *Amer. J. Psychol.*, 1954, *67*, 147-51.

LINDSLEY, D. B. Common factors in sensory deprivation, sensory distortion, and sensory overload. In P. SOLOMON *et al.*, eds., *Sensory deprivation*, pp. 174-94. Cambridge: Harvard Univer. Press, 1961.

NAGATSUKA, Y. Studies on sensory deprivation. III, Part 2: Effects of sensory deprivation upon perceptual functions. *Tohoku psychol. Folia*, 1965, *23*, 53-9.

NAGATSUKA, Y., and MARUYAMA, K. Studies on sensory deprivation. I, Part 2: Effects of sensory deprivation upon perceptual and motor functions. *Tohoku psychol. Folia*, 1963, *22*, 5-13

NAGATSUKA, Y., and SUZUKI, Y. Studies on sensory deprivation. II, Part 2: Effects of sensory deprivation upon perceptual and motor functions. *Tohoku psychol. Folia*, 1964, *22*, 64-8.

VERNON, J., and MCGILL, T. E. Sensory deprivation and pain thresholds. *Science*, 1961, *133*, 330-1.

VERNON, J., MCGILL, T. E., GULIK, W. L., and CANDLAND, D. K. The effect of human isolation upon some perceptual and motor skills. In P. SOLOMON *et al.*, eds., *Sensory deprivation*, pp. 41-57. Cambridge: Harvard Univer. Press, 1961.

SCHULTZ, D. P. *Sensory restriction*. New York: Academic Press, 1965.

ZUBEK, J. P. Behavioural changes after prolonged perceptual deprivation (no intrusions). *Percept. mot. Skills*, 1964, *18*, 413-20.

ZUBEK, J. P., FLYE, J., and AFTANAS, M. Cutaneous sensitivity after prolonged visual deprivation. *Science*, 1964, *144*, 1591-3.

ZUBEK, J. P., FLYE, J., and WILLOWS, D. Changes in cutaneous sensitivity after prolonged exposure to unpatterned light. *Psychon. Sci.*, 1964, *1*, 283-4

SEVEN
INTELLIGENCE AND APTITUDES

33 / On Learning and Human Ability [1]

George A. Ferguson *McGill University*

Professor Ferguson presents a theory which attempts to integrate our conceptions of learning with those of intellectual abilities. He contends that the term "ability" refers simply to performance at some crude limit of learning. Although biological factors are not excluded, Ferguson emphasizes the environmental contributions to the development of abilities. He points out that the differences in performance on standard intelligence tests of various cultural groups can be explained by the different opportunities that are provided for practising particular skills.

Professor Ferguson is a Fellow of the Royal Society of Canada and the author of the widely used textbook, Statistical Analysis in Psychology and Education, *now in its third edition.*

My purpose is to present a generalized theory which draws together within a single conceptual framework the study of human learning and the study of human ability. Those concerned with the description and classification of man's abilities have usually adopted an individual difference approach. They have paid scant attention to problems of learning. The experimentalists, engrossed in the study of learning, have for various theoretical and practical reasons shown little interest in individual differences. They seem unaware that they too are students of man's abilities. This divergence between two fields of psychological endeavour has led to a constriction of thought and an experimental fastidiousness inimical to a bold attack on the problem of understanding human behaviour.

At present no systematic theory, capable of generating fruitful hypotheses about behaviour, lies behind the study of human ability. Current approaches are largely empirical. Psychological test theory and factor theory, evolved as they were for the study of human ability, are largely technologies which do not presume to answer psychological questions *per se*, although they may aid in the answering of such questions once raised. The pioneers of factor analysis, Spearman (16), Thomson (17), and others, proposed theories of brain functioning, and resorted to factor analysis as a means of testing deductions from those theories. Few attempts are made today to correlate the descriptive parameters of behaviour identified by factorial methods with any structural or dynamic properties of a brain model. Many factorists, although accepting this as a legitimate problem, regard its exploration as beyond their province and possibly premature. Earlier factorists thought otherwise. Many physiological psychologists on the other hand still concern themselves with rather vague and global concepts of intelligence, and seem unaware that these concepts are regarded as obsolete by many students of human ability. The concept of intelligence, however it be framed, is no longer a useful scientific concept except as subsuming some defined set of clearly distinguishable abilities.

If the study of human ability lacks theoretical buttressing, the study of human learning most certainly does not. The physical bases of memory have been the subject of much speculation at least since the time of Rene Descartes. One of the postulates of a recent theory proposed by Hebb (10) is identical in form with the postulate of Descartes. The extent and persistence of this class of theorizing are apparent in a recent extensive review by Bronislaw Gomulicki (8). One recent line of speculation in this area has been advanced by the cyberneticists and by those concerned with the development of electronic calculators and related devices. Analogies have been drawn between the principles which govern the functioning of machines that "learn" and "remember" and the principles which govern the functioning of the human brain.

In the field of human learning there is clearly a plenitude of diverse theoretical constructs, together with an extensive accumulation of experimental data. In the field of human ability, although we suffer from a paucity of systematic theoretical constructs, we have an extensive technology, much data based on the study of individual differences, and formal ways of thinking about problems which are, I believe, foreign to many who work in the learning field. It follows that, if we can logically incorporate the two fields in a single conceptual framework, some mutual enrichment may occur.

Ability and Overlearning

"Ability" is defined operationally by the performance of an individual in a specified situation. Thus L.

[1]D.R.B.Project No. D 77-94-01-01.

Reprinted, by permission, from *Canadian Journal of Psychology*, 1954, *8*, 95-112.

L. Thurstone (18) states that "an ability is a trait which is defined by what an individual can do." It follows, as Thurstone points out, that "there are as many abilities as there are enumerable things that individuals can do." Factor analysis, a classificatory technique, undertakes a parsimonious description of the multitudinous array of abilities in terms of a relatively small number of categories. It is clear that the term "ability," in addition to its operational meaning, may be assigned a formal postulational meaning within a framework of theory.

"Learning," as conventionally used in experimental psychology, refers generally to changes, with repetition, in "ability" to perform a specified task, the changes being regarded as functionally dependent on, or in part assignable to, repetition. Other assignable causes of change, such as fatigue, sensory adaptation, artifacts of measurement, and the like, are presumed to be controlled. This commonly accepted statement of what is meant by learning is inadequate and leads to logical pitfalls. It will, however, serve my immediate purpose. Note that I have introduced the term "ability" into the definition of learning. It is seldom used in connection with learning experiments, although indices of performance used in such experiments are clearly measures of the ability of the subject at various stages in the learning process. Conventional learning curves are simply descriptions of changes in ability with repetition.

If we regard the term "ability" as defined by an individual's performance, we may identify two broad classes of ability: a class which is more or less invariant with respect to repetition or its cessation, and a class which is not. Thus some of the things which individuals can do appear to have a fairly high degree of permanence, showing little change, either in the presence or in the absence of repetition. Other things individuals can do may exhibit gross improvement with repetition, or gross impairment following a period in which no repetition occurs.

The typical learning curve shows that in most learning situations a level of performance is attained with repetition beyond which no further improvement is observed. Moreover, in certain learning situations, particularly those demanding a high degree of overlearning, the subject when tested may exhibit no impairment in performance even after lengthy periods of time without repetition. It seems that in most learning situations the ability of the subject reaches a crude limit[2] beyond which no systematic improvement is likely to occur with repetition. Of course in some cases rapid improvement may occur following a "plateau" in learning.

While the term "ability" may be used generally to refer to performance on any type of task, whether or not it varies with repetition, many psychologists conventionally use the term, in the case of adults, to refer to performance which does not vary much over lengthy periods of time. Likewise it is assumed that the abilities of children are reasonably stable over short time intervals, although they may show systematic improvement with age. For example, in Thurstone's classification of mental abilities (19), reasoning ability, number ability, perceptual ability, spatial ability, and the like, are presumed, in the adult subject, to be reasonably stable attributes of behaviour over lengthy periods and, in the child, to have considerable stability at any given age level. It is not presumed that an individual's reasoning ability will be markedly changed by solving large numbers of verbal analogies or number series items, or that his spatial ability will show pronounced improvement with practice on paper form-board items or other spatial tasks. Although some improvement with practice will occur in many subjects, we do not expect such improvement to be gross.

These observations bring us to the first hypothesis of this discussion, namely, that in the adult subject in our culture, those more or less stable attributes of behaviour which we ordinarily speak of as abilities, and which are defined in terms of performance on psychological tests, refer to performance at a crude limit of learning. This is regarded as applying to all attributes in the Thurstone classification and to whatever is subsumed under the term "intelligence." The hypothesis implies that these abilities are overlearned acquisitions, and that the stability which characterizes them is the result of overlearning. It assigns to learning a central role in the study of human ability, and opens the way for the study of ability and learning within the same conceptual framework. It is proposed that any theory which implies that individual differences in ability are individual differences at some crude limit of performance reached by overlearning be referred to as a *limits of learning* theory of human ability.

The role of learning in human ability is well illustrated by number ability. Number ability is defined by the performance of individuals on certain simple arithmetical tasks involving addition, subtraction, multiplication, and division. Tests of number ability are usually highly speeded. In our culture the majority of educated adults are fairly facile at tasks entailing ordinary arithmetical operations. Arithmetical facility has for many individuals been so reinforced by innumerable repetitions over prolonged periods of time that a crude limit of learning has been attained. Although some might show improvement with systematic practice, this would probably not be great. It seems plausible, therefore, that in many adults individual differences in number ability refer to individual differences at some crude limit of performance.

The role of learning in perception is a controversial subject. Much evidence supporting the view that perception involves a prolonged period of learning

[2] The term "limit" is used here in a very loose and imprecise sense to refer to a level beyond which no very gross and systematic change seems likely to occur. The term is not used in the rigorous sense in which it is understood in elementary mathematics or in the stochastic sense of probability theory.

has been marshalled by Hebb in *The Organization of Behaviour* (10). This evidence strongly suggests that various perceptual abilities represent performance at the limits of learning in perception. In the normal child the limits of learning in many perceptual tasks may be reached at a fairly early age.

The role of learning in reasoning – that is, in the type of ability required for the solution of number series items, verbal analogies, and so on – is far from obvious. But numerous arguments can be advanced to support the view that reasoning ability involves a prolonged period of learning.

The view that "ability" has reference to performance at some crude limit of learning is not new. It is implicit in the theories of Hebb (10) although not formulated by him in the above manner. In much of the work carried out in the animal laboratories at McGill the "intelligence" of the rat or dog is defined in terms of performance on a maze test following a lengthy learning period. The animal performs in the test situation until his performance reaches a crude stability, or until a limit of performance is very roughly approximated, and this limit serves to define his "intelligence."

Gross individual differences in ability do exist. These differences are a complex result of the interaction of the biological propensities of the organism and the learning which occurs at particular stages of life. This topic has been discussed by Hebb (10). His distinction between early and late learning is relevant here. It appears that the state of an organism at any given time and its ability to respond to any immediate situation is a complex function, not only of its biological properties and previous learning, but also of the stage in life at which learning of various types has occurred. This implies that the stage of development at which learning of a particular class has occurred is one factor in determining the limit of overlearning at the adult stage. Thus, as Hebb observes, early learning or its lack may have a permanent and generalized effect in the adult.

Many of the abilities which psychologists have studied increase with age. Intelligence as defined by such tests as the Stanford-Binet increases until about the age of 17, when a limit of performance is reached. In our culture children are exposed to an environment that demands rapid learning of many things. They proceed as rapidly through the school system as their abilities at any stage will allow. It is probable that many children at any particular age are functioning fairly close to the limit of their potentiality with regard to certain classes of activity. It follows that some of the abilities measured by psychologists are, for many children, indices of performance at a crude limit of learning for the age in question. However, if a child's environment is restricted with respect to certain activities he may function well below the limit of his potentiality in those activities at varying ages, and a permanent impairment at the adult stage may result. Presumably children reared in different environments, which demand different types of learning at different ages, develop different patterns of ability.

Transfer

"Transfer" is frequently used in a general sense to refer to the effects of changes, resulting from repetition, in ability to perform a specified task, on the ability to perform either the same task under altered conditions or a different task. This is the meaning usually assigned to the term "transfer" for laboratory experimentation. An implicit condition is that the prior task is in some respect different from the subsequent task. When the two tasks are presumed on the basis of superficial inspection to be similar, the term "learning," and not "transfer," is used to refer to the changes in ability that occur. It seems therefore, that transfer is the general phenomenon and "learning" is a particular *formal* case which may never occur either in laboratory experimentation or in real life situations. The notion of learning implies the identity of a sequence of learning situations.[3] The fact that learning is a particular formal case of the general phenomenon of transfer has been recognized by Cook (6) who writes:

There is no separate problem of transfer of training. Or conversely, all learning (unless there exists a limiting case in which successive trials are identical on all counts) involves the problem posited in the transfer of training experiments: What identities and differences in successive trials affect what sort of learning?

With the possible exception of some learning which occurs very early in life, all learning occurs within the context of experience. We bring to bear on the learning of any task a mass of prior experience which may either facilitate or inhibit learning of that task. On this point McGeoch (12) writes:

---

[3]The inability of students of learning to deal appropriately with the problem of the identity of and difference between tasks has led to logical difficulties in our concepts of learning and transfer. To my mind these concepts require some revision. To say that an individual is repeating the same task, or that one task is different from another, demands a precise statement of what is meant by "same" and "different." The referents of these terms in current thinking on learning are largely phenomenological; that is, they have to do with our immediate experience upon inspection of the tasks in question. Two ways out of this difficulty suggest themselves. First, the terms "same" and "different" are always with respect to some property or properties. In view of this, it may be possible to define operationally properties with respect to which tasks may differ, and to study the relationship of such differences to differences in transfer effects. Attempts have been made to do this. Second, "same" and "different" may be defined in terms of correlation. If the correlation of the performance of a group of individuals on two tasks, or on successive trials of what experientially is the same task, is roughly in unity, error being taken into account, then the tasks may be said to be the same. If the correlation departs from unity then the tasks may be said to be in some degree different. We may be prepared to go beyond a strict operational statement of this kind and speak of tasks on successive trials as involving the same or different functions. This essentially is the rationale of factor analysis. This second approach in effect defines the stimulus in terms of the responses of the subjects.

After small amounts of learning early in the life of the individual every instance of learning is a function of the already learned organization of the subject; that is, all learning is influenced by transfer .... The learning of complex, abstract, meaningful materials and the solution of problems by means of ideas (reasoning) are to a great extent a function of transfer. Where the subject "sees into" the fundamental relations of a problem or has insight, transfer seems to be a major contributing condition. It is, likewise, a basic factor in originality, the original and creative person having, among other things, unusual sensitivity to the applicability of the already known to new problem situations. Perceiving, at whatever complex level, is probably never free of its influence, and there is no complex psychological event which is not a function of it.

Hebb (10) in discussing this same point writes:

If the learning we know and can study, in the mature animal, is heavily loaded with transfer effects, what are the properties of the original learning from which those effects come? How can it be possible even to consider making a theory of learning in general from the data of maturity alone? There must be a serious risk that what seems to be learning is really half transfer. We cannot assume that we know what learning transfers and what does not: for our knowledge of the extent of transfer is also derived from behaviour at maturity, and the transfer from infant experiences may be much greater and more generalized.

If all adult learning is heavily loaded with transfer, what is the nature of the prior learning which transfers to the learning of new tasks, and how does it affect the learning of such new tasks? Two hypotheses are put forward.

The first is that, in many adult learning situations, the most important variables exerting transfer effects on subsequent learning are the "abilities" – the prior acquisitions that have attained their limit of performance. This hypothesis has long been widely accepted and is deeply entrenched in our thinking. It is commonplace to say that "bright" children learn more quickly in school than "dull" children, where brightness and dullness are defined in terms of performance on an ability test. The validation of tests against training criteria implies that the abilities of man are significant variables in the learning process. Such a loose statement as "Intelligence is learning ability" reflects the important role frequently assigned to intelligence in learning situations. There are two reasons for emphasizing this hypothesis. First, it is formulated within a new theoretical framework which alters substantially our way of thinking about the role of human abilities in learning. Second, the role of human ability in human learning has always been a matter of major practical concern to the applied psychologist. Indeed, it may be the most important problem in the applied field. And yet this problem has received little attention from the theoreticians or the laboratory experimentalists. Experiments on transfer carried out under laboratory conditions are so distantly removed from learning as it occurs in real life situations that they provide few answers of the slightest usefulness in the field of applied psychology. Questions of what prior learned acquisitions, or abilities, transfer to what learning, and how, and under what conditions, remain largely unanswered.

The second hypothesis concerns the way in which overlearned acquisitions, or abilities, affect subsequent learning. It is that such abilities exert their effect differentially in any learning situation; that different abilities exert different effects at different stages of learning, and that the abilities which transfer and produce their effect at one stage of learning may be different from those which transfer and produce their effects at another stage. This means that individual differences in abilities which may be functionally related to individual differences in performance in the early stages of learning a task, may not be functionally related, or may be related in a different way, to performance in the later stages. An implication of this hypothesis is that an individual might posses the abilities to perform a given activity with a high degree of proficiency, but might lack the abilities to learn to perform the task under certain specified conditions of learning. Likewise an individual might possess the ability to improve rapidly in the early stages of learning, but might lack the abilities necessary to attain high proficiency at the stage of high habituation or overlearning. The learning of many motor activities probably belongs to this class.

This hypothesis, if experimentally confirmed, will have important educational implications. It implies, for example, that a slow learner under given learning conditions may have a capacity for ultimate performance in excess of the fast learner under the same training conditions. In the test validation field, where tests are frequently validated against the training criteria, it becomes important to consider the stage of training to which the criterion relates, since tests with an acceptable degree of validity at one stage of training may have little or no validity at another stage.

A prior overlearned acquisition, an ability, may not only facilitate the learning of a new task but may also inhibit it. Thus we may consider both positive and negative transfer effects, and the simultaneous operation of such effects. Although the terms positive and negative transfer are used to refer to net effect of the operation of a variety of variables, experiments could readily be designed to separate out the positive and negative effects of different abilities on the same learning situations.

Experimental Design

The experimental investigation of these hypotheses involves an individual difference approach. There have been a number of such approaches in the learning field (14, 20, 22, 23), but this line of attack has been relatively unpopular, owing to the practical difficulties of finding appropriate learning tasks which will provide reliable measures of performance and permit the collection of data on substantial numbers of subjects.

The type of experiment suggested by the hypotheses in this paper may be illustrated as follows. Say that we are concerned with the transfer of certain overlearned acquisitions, or abilities, to the learning of a motor task, that a number of learning periods are allowed, and that a measure of performance, or score, is obtained for each learning period for each subject. We may select and administer to our subjects a number of tests of abilities which *a priori* considerations have led us to believe may transfer either positively or negatively to the learning of the motor task. For any group of subjects the intercorrelations between all the variables may be calculated. The relationship between performance at various stages of learning is described by the correlation between scores on the learning task. The correlations between the ability tests and scores on the learning task are measures of the extent of transfer of the abilities to the learning situation at various stages of learning. The results obtained from such an experiment can probably best be handled by factorial methods, treating the tests of ability as criterion variables.

Experiments of this design will permit observation of the differential transfer of abilities at different stages of learning. The design may also be readily extended to cover forgetting, and the differential effects of transfer through a cycle of learning and forgetting. Further, the design permits the differentiation of the simultaneous operation of positive and negative transfer effects.

Culture and Human Ability

Extensive investigations have been carried out on the effects of various cultural factors on "intelligence," as defined by the standard intelligence tests. The general conclusion is that a variety of cultural variables are related to "intelligence" as so defined. Since this is so, the view is held by many investigators that existing intelligence tests when used in selection, classification, and the like are "unfair" to certain sections of the population. This has resulted in attempts to develop types of test material which are more or less invariant with respect to certain cultural factors. Examples of this are the "Culture Free Tests" developed by R. B. Cattell (**4**, **5**). A recent extensive investigation by Eells, Davis, *et al.* (**7**) attempted to isolate groups of test items which showed relatively small or negligible differences between individuals in various socio-economic groups.

Many investigators concerned with this class of problem regard "intelligence" as a basic underlying biological attribute. Methods of measuring it are, however, affected by cultural factors. How, then, can inferences be drawn regarding differences in cultural or racial groups in "intelligence" viewed as a biological attribute? There is no obvious answer to this question. One way out is to accept the hypothesis (incapable, of course, of any experimental test by existing methods) that no difference exists between cultural and racial groups in "intelligence," and that where such differences are found they are the result of cultural factors. If this hypothesis is accepted the next step is obvious.

Tests must be constructed which are invariant with respect to certain controllable cultural factors, and so are "better" measures of the basic biological variable called "intelligence." As Turnbull (**21**) has recently pointed out in criticizing this line of argument, a "fair" or "good" test is one which shows no differences. Thus, as Turnbull remarks, the process has gone full circle. The hypothesis is accepted that no differences exist between cultural groups in biological intelligence. Tests are constructed by the careful selection of items which show no differences between groups. These are then used as evidence that there *is* no real difference.

The position described above has been widely adopted, although its logical ramifications have seldom been explicitly stated. Its basic weakness lies in a naive concept of "intelligence," which leads to an experimental impasse avoidable only by the acceptance of an unverificable hypothesis. Thus the existing position held by many investigators is logically untenable, and hence cannot lead to profitable research.

The theory presented in this paper enables us to regard these problems in a different light, and to formulate them in more meaningful terms. It states that the more or less stable attributes of behaviour, commonly referred to as abilities, represent performance at crude limits of learning, and that such limits are determined by the biological propensities of the individual and by cultural factors which prescribe what shall be learned and at what age. Therefore, questions raised about the role of cultural factors in human ability are essentially questions about the relationship between learning and human ability.

The obvious inference from this line of argument is that individuals reared in different cultures will develop different patterns of ability. It is substantiated by a mass of anthropological evidence. It must be so. It cannot be argued that, if no differences between cultural groups on a particular test are found, we are measuring a biological capacity in which no differences exist between groups. Nor, conversely, can it be argued that where differences are found they are the result of biological differences. Such arguments are ruled out of court in the above theoretical position. The initial problem becomes one of describing the patterns of ability which are characteristic of individuals reared in different cultural environments. The initial problem is not one of demonstrating that intercultural differences exist with respect to a particular ability, or that they do not, or of drawing inferences from such findings one way or another.

I regard the inferences drawn from many of the extensive investigations on racial differences in "intelligence" as essentially invalid. Many of these studies sought differences in "intelligence," biologically regarded, between racial groups; race being a biological concept. Hypotheses pertaining to this problem are unverifiable in terms of the present theory. Racial groups may exhibit different patterns of ability, as defined by performance on particular tests, but to argue from these data for or against the existence of biological differences is not meaningful.

In Canada during the war the Armed Services attempted to develop parallel tests for French- and English-speaking personnel. The hypothesis underlying the development of such tests was that no differences in the pattern of abilities existed (or should exist) between these groups, an hypothesis which was politically expedient regardless of its scientific validity. This resulted in statistical manipulation to ensure that the French and English forms, when applied to samples of the respective populations, gave the same means and variances. A practicable approach to this problem, which avoids such difficulties, is to develop tests, possibly quite different, for French and for English, and to validate them separately in French and English situations. If similar non-language tests are developed for French and for English, and these then show pronounced differences in the patterns of ability between French and English, the problem is not one of obscuring these differences by statistical manipulation, but of ascertaining the best use to which these differences can be put in the selection and classification of personnel.

As for isolated, underprivileged, and restricted,[4] cultural communities, the initial problem is again one of developing tests for describing adequately the abilities of the members of such communities. These tests should conform to the usual criteria of reliability, discriminatory capacity, and the like. In the Newfoundland outports, for example, many individuals display excellent skill in boat building, navigation, and fishing. On tests of the abstract thinking type developed for use in urbanized cultures, the members of such communities make low scores. The tests discriminate poorly. The abilities that develop among the members of such communities, and upon which their survival depends, are probably quite different from those that our urbanized culture fosters. The first step is to discover adequate ways and means for describing these abilities. Once this is done, an attack can be made on other problems.

Age and Ability

There is a substantial body of experimental data on the relationship between test performance and age in different cultural groups, but it has not been adequately interpreted or carefully assessed in relation to a theory of mental ability. The theory proposed in this paper permits an interpretation of these data and leads to certain hypotheses which, if substantiated, may be of some practical consequence in the development of tests for different cultural groups.

Take the studies by Gordon (**9**)[5] on canal-boat and gypsy children in England. The canal-boat children received a very limited education. The average school attendance was estimated at only 5 per cent of that in the ordinary elementary schools. Each family led a relatively isolated existence and had little contact with other canal-boat families. In a sample of 76 children the average IQ (Stanford-Binet) was 69.6. Notable was the sharp decline in IQ with age. The correlation between IQ and age was -.755. The four- to six-year group had an average IQ of 90, whereas the oldest group averaged 60. In children of the same family a consistent drop from the youngest to the oldest was observed. The mental ages of children within a single family were similar, although chronological ages differed.

In the case of gypsy children the mean IQ in a sample of 82 was 74.5, and the correlation between age and IQ was −.430. The school attendance of the gypsy children was about 35 per cent of possible school days. Although IQ was negatively correlated with age, it was positively correlated with school attendance. The increment of mental with chronological age was far below that which generally obtains.

Similar results have been found in studies of mountain children made by Hirsch (**11**), Asher (**3**), Sherman and Key (**15**), and others. Studies on Eskimo children carried out by Anderson and Eells (**2**) report the same findings. The Mean IQ on the Stanford-Binet at the 8-year age level was 99.6 and at the 18-year age level 66.8. On the Goodenough scale for "drawing a man" the corresponding average IQ's were 100.0 and 87.2. Similar observations were made by Porteous (**13**) in applying the Porteous Maze Test to Australian aborigines. Yerkes (**24**) reported a similar result with respect to different socio-economic groups, the increment of score with age being less for a low-status than for a high-status group. This finding, however, does not seem to have been clearly substantiated by later work.

Unequivocal interpretation of the above findings is

[4]Implicit in the use of such terms as "restricted," "underprivileged," and the like to refer to cultural groups is the evaluation that because many cultures are different from our own they are in some vague sense "not as good." Even some of our better scientific thinkers seem incapable of observing a difference between cultures without implying a value judgement. Such terms have meaning only in relation to some particular criterion variable. If that variable is the availability of medical services or the number of refrigerators per 1,000 population, then these terms may be assigned a precise meaning in relation to such variables. If, however, the criterion variable is a phenomenological one, such as "happiness," then the terms are probably meaningless, because propositions relating to the relative "happiness" of peoples in different cultures are unverifiable. Some observers infer that the Eskimos in Baffin Island are a very "happy" people, whereas others seem prepared to contend that the inhabitants of Manhattan Island are not. That Baffin Islanders are "happier" than Manhattan Islanders still remains an unverifiable proposition.

[5]My account of Gordon's work is taken from Anastasi and Foley (1). I do not have access to the original sources.

not possible since the tests used at different age levels were somewhat different; but it seems reasonable to conclude that for any particular test the change in performance with age may vary markedly from one cultural group to another. In one the increment of test performance with age may be substantial, in another negligible. This must be mainly due to the demands of the cultural environment, which dictate what shall be learned and at what age.

If we accept this as the most plausible view, the inference may be drawn that those abilities that are of importance in a particular cultural environment, and that may be expected to correlate with performance in the important activities which the culture demands, are those which show a pronounced increment with age.[6] It is possible, that the abilities which the ordinary intelligence test defines are fairly independent of the types of activity which make for success in, say, a canal-boat culture, provided possibly that some minimal level is attained. It is possible that other abilities, if they could be defined, might show a marked increment with age, and be expected to correlate with the important classes of activity which make for survival in that culture.

The usual tests of intelligence correlate with a wide variety of classes of activity in our "more privileged" Western cultures. Such tests show substantial increase in performance with age until about the age of 17. We may speculate that tests which show a small age increment may correlate only with very specialized types of performance, and be of restricted usefulness.

If this line of inference could be substantiated, we would have available a criterion for the selection of tests which were likely to prove useful in a particular cultural environment. We would select those types of test material which had a high correlation with age and discard those which had a low one. Age would then be a general criterion for the validation of tests correlating with performance on important classes of activity demanded by a particular culture.

Culture and Factor Theory

There are implications for factor analysis in the theory proposed in this paper. The following observations are speculative and call for more elaboration and refinement than can be afforded here.

The hypothesis of differential transfer which has been proposed implies that the factors or underlying parameters which transfer, and either facilitate or inhibit performance of a task, are not invariant with respect to the stage of learning at which the task is performed. Although a task may appear on superficial inspection to be the "same" at different stages of learning, operationally – in terms of factorial content – it may be different. Further, since the level of performance of a particular class of task may differ markedly from one culture to another, depending on the cultural dictum concerning what is learned and when, it follows that the factorial composition of tests may differ markedly from one culture to another. This simply means that, through learning, individuals in diverse cultures may bring different abilities to bear on the solution of an identical problem. Factorial invariance presumably applies only within the framework of a clearly defined cultural group, and has no broad cross-cultural implications. Were it technically feasible to construct a battery of tests which could be appropriately administered to a random sample of adult subjects both in Toronto and in the Newfoundland outports, I have no doubt that we should find marked differences between the two groups in the factorial composition of many of the tests used. What we know about factors has reference to our own highly urbanized culture, which fosters the acquisition of certain verbal and reasoning abilities; our knowledge should not be presumed to extend beyond this.

The Problem of a General Factor

Spearman (16) strove to show that a general intellective factor operated in the performance of many mental tasks. Thurstone's (19) attempt to disprove Spearman's theory was not conclusive, since most of the factors in his classificatory system are correlated factors. The concept of a general factor is still with us. In the light of present knowledge this concept derives from the fact that many abilities, identified factorially in some loosely defined domain of intellectual activity, are not independent of one another. As currently regarded, it does not imply that all the innumerable identifiable abilities within that domain are correlated. Limitations on the generality of a general factor are not clearly prescribed.

A scrutiny of the general factor problem suggests that we must consider two aspects of it. We must account not only for the fact that many abilities are in some degree positively correlated with one another, but also for the fact that they are in some degree differentiated from one another. A theory which accounts for one aspect of the problem does not necessarily account for the other. Thus a theoretical explanation may account for abilities being correlated, but it may not, if pressed to its ultimate conclusion, account for their not being perfectly correlated, or there not being one ability only. The theory of human ability proposed in this paper can account very simply for the former aspect of the problem. To account for the latter aspect is more difficult.

[6]This hypothesis assumes a direct relationship between the abilities that a particular form of education fosters in the child and the demands that the culture imposes at the adult level. In the history of education many cases of incongruity exist between education and the changing demands of a culture. Probably only in the most stable culture is a really high degree of congruence attained. Incongruity may enrich a culture, may destroy it, or may produce other effects. For example, if we impose our rather urbanized system of education, with its great emphasis on verbal abilities, on isolated Newfoundland communities, either these communities may be greatly enriched or extensive migration may occur. The latter alternative is more probable.

Let us accept the general proposition that all learning, with the exception of some which occurs very early in life, occurs in a context of prior experience. This means that an individual will learn more readily activities which are facilitated by prior acquisitions, and will learn less readily those activities which are not facilitated or are perhaps inhibited by prior learning. Since in the adult many abilities are regarded as over-learned acquisitions, it follows that in the development of distinctive abilities those abilities will tend to develop which are facilitated and not inhibited by each other. It follows, therefore, that the positive correlation between abilities, which gives rise to the notion of a general factor, can be accounted for in the present theory by the operation of positive transfer. Although this is undoubtedly an oversimplification, it does provide a simple and plausible explanation.

Can we account for the fact that many abilities, while correlated, are none the less clearly differentiated? In approaching this problem we may observe that any attempt to explain learning and the formation of abilities by transfer alone leads to an obvious absurdity, since it cannot explain how early learning can occur at all. To escape this difficulty I propose a two-factor theory of learning. This theory states that much learning, excluding some very early learning, involves not only transfer components which are common to prior learning and the learning of a new task, but also components which are specific to the new task. In terms of the factorial model, this means that variation in performance at various stages of a task can be accounted for in part by the variation in prior acquisitions, and in part by specific abilities that emerge and are formed during the process of learning the task itself. I should anticipate that, as the learning of certain classes of tasks continues through a series of stages, the variance attributable to general transfer components may decrease, whereas the variance attributable to abilities specific to the task itself, or common only to the task, will increase. Further, it seems reasonable that variation in early learning can be accounted for much less by transfer than by other processes, since there are fewer prior acquisitions to transfer. In the adult, learning may be accounted for largely in terms of transfer and to a much lesser extent in terms of other processes.

In sum, it seems to me that what happens is this. Some early learning must occur which is independent of prior learned acquisitions. As the individual grows, learning is facilitated more and more by prior acquisitions. It is probable that transfer effects become continuously and increasingly more important with age. In the learning of a particular task, transfer effects are probably greater at the earlier than at the later stages of learning. Thus, as the learning of a particular task continues, the ability to perform it becomes gradually differentiated from, although not necessarily independent of, other abilities which facilitate its differentiation. Learning is clearly a process by which the abilities of man are differentiated from one another, but the process of differentiation is aided and abetted by the abilities which the individual already possesses.

In conclusion, therefore, we may account for a component general to many abilities in terms of the operation of positive transfer, and for the differentiation of abilities in terms of the learning process itself, which, according to the theory presented here, operates in such a way as to facilitate differentiation.

Summary

In an attempt to draw together crudely within the same scheme the study of learning and the study of human ability I have advanced the following views. Different environments result in the overlearning of certain patterns of behaviour, which, because they are overlearned, become more or less invariant with respect to repetition or cessation. A crude limit of performance is reached. What is spoken of as an ability, in conventional psychological usage, has reference to performance at some crude limit of learning. This applies to the abilities of the Thurstone system and to whatever is subsumed under the term "intelligence." Differences in ability are the results of the complex interaction of the biological propensities of the organism, prior learning, and the age at which prior learning occurs. The role of human ability in subsequent learning, for example, intelligence in relation to scholastic performance, can be viewed as a problem in transfer; the question is in what way prior overlearned acquisitions – the abilities – affect subsequent learning. Abilities may transfer differentially in any learning situation; that is, the abilities which transfer and produce their effects at one stage of learning may be different from those which transfer and produce their effects at a later stage of the same task. An individual may possess the necessary ability to perform a task adequately, but may lack the ability to learn to perform the task under particular learning conditions. The investigation of problems emerging from these lines of argument involves an individual difference approach and use of the methods of factorial analysis. The implications of the theory for problems of the role of cultural factors in human ability are elaborated. The line of theory developed leads to the inference that those abilities which are of importance in a particular culture, and which may be expected to correlate with performance in the important activities demanded for survival in the culture, are those which show a pronounced increment with age. This provides a basis for test validation of a certain type. The implications of the theory of human ability for factor theory are considered. The inference is drawn that ostensibly similar tests may have different factorial compositions in different cultures and in different strata of the same culture. The problem of a general factor is examined. A two-factor theory of learning is proposed. The correlation among abilities is explained in terms of positive transfer, and their differentiation by the development of abilities specific to particular learning situations.

References

1. ANASTASI, ANNE., and FOLEY, J. P. *Differential psychology*. New York: Macmillan, 1949.
2. ANDERSON, H. D., and EELLS, W. C. *Alaska natives: a survey of their sociological and educational status*. Stanford, Calif.: Stanford University Press, 1935.
3. ASHER, E. J. The inadequacy of current intelligence tests for testing Kentucky Mountain children. *J. genetic Psychol.*, 1935, *46*, 480-486.
4. CATTELL, R. B. A culture-free intelligence test. *J. educ. Phychol.*, 1940, *31*, 161-179.
5. ———. A culture-free intelligence test: Evaluation of cultural influences on test performance. *J. educ. Psychol.*, 1941, *32*, 81-100.
6. COOK, T. W. Repetition and learning: I. Stimulus and response. *Psychol. Rev.*, 1944, *51*, 25-36.
7. EELLS, KENNETH, DAVIS, ALLISON, *et al. Intelligence and cultural differences*. Chicago: Univ. of Chicago Press, 1951.
8. GOMULICKI, R. BRONISLAW. The development and present status of the trace theory of memory. *British J. Psychol. Monogr. Suppl.*, 1953, *29*.
9. GORDON, H. *Mental and scholastic tests among retarded children*. Educ. Pamphlet No. 44. London: Board of Education, 1923.
10. HEBB, D. O. *The organization of behaviour*. New York: Wiley, 1949.
11. HIRSCH, N. D. M. An experimental study of East Kentucky Mountaineers. *Genet. Psychol. Monogr.*, 1928, *3*, 183-244.
12. MCGEOCH, JOHN A. *The psychology of human learning*. New York: Longmans Green, 1946.
13. PORTEOUS, S. D. *The psychology of a primitive people*. New York: Longmans Green, 1931.
14. SIMRALL, D. Intelligence and the ability to learn. *J. Psychol.*, 1947, *23*, 27-43.
15. SHERMAN, M., and KEY, C. B. The intelligence of isolated mountain children. *Child Develpm.*, 1932, *3*, 279-290.
16. SPEARMAN, C. *The abilities of man: their nature and measurement*. London: Macmillan, 1927.
17. THOMSON, G. H. *The factorial analysis of human ability*. (2nd ed.) London: Univ. of London Press, 1946.
18. THURSTONE, L. L. *Multiple factor analysis*. Chicago: Univ. of Chicago Press, 1947.
19. ———. *Primary mental abilities*. Chicago: Univ. of Chicago Press, 1938.
20. TILTON, J. W. Intelligence test scores as indicative of ability to learn. *Educ. psychol. Measmt.*, 1949, *9*, 291-296.
21. TURNBULL, W. W. Socio-economic status and predictive test scores. *Canad. J. Psychol.*, 1951, *5*, 145-149.
22. WOODROW, H. Interrelations of measures of learning. *J. Psychol.*, 1940, *10*, 49-73.
23. ———. The ability to learn. *Psychol. Rev.*, 1946, *53*, 147-158.
24. YERKES, ROBERT M., and ANDERSON, HELEN M. The importance of social status as indicated by the results of the point-scale method of measuring mental capacity. *J. educ. Phychol.*, 1915, 137-150.

34 / Intelligence in a Restricted Environment[1]

A. Burnett, H.D. Beach, and A.M. Sullivan *Hospital for Mental and Nervous Diseases, St. John's Nfld.*

In the past fifty years much evidence has been gathered to show that individuals living in an impoverished environment score lower on intelligence tests than individuals from a stimulating environment. The following study describes the performance of inhabitants of isolated communities in Newfoundland on standard intelligence tests. Attention is drawn to the fact that deficits are present in certain kinds of abilities but not in others. These data are generally consistent with the emphasis that Ferguson (article 33) has placed on the role of learning in the development of abilitites.

The studies reported in this paper were carried out in a number of isolated outports in Newfoundland. The objectives were to assess the adequacy of different measures of intelligence for this population and to relate the findings to the environmental and social conditions in which the people live.

Anastasi (1958) has reviewed a large number of studies which indicate that measured intelligence is related to many factors. Education is apparently one of the more important factors, as shown by a positive relationship between amount of education and intelligence test scores, in both correlational and longitudinal studies. Type of occupation and socio-economic class have also been related to intelligence as measured. Urban and rural groups generally have been found to differ on their test scores, with rural subjects getting the lower scores. Furthermore, amount of test experience has exhibited a positive relationship with test scores. Whereas the general consistency of such findings is impressive, the relative contribution of any factor remains undetermined. Few if any "natural" settings provide conditions in which one factor operates in isolation from others. Wheeler (1942) found the median IQ of West Tennessee mountain children sampled in 1948 to be 11 points higher than that of a like sample in 1930. However, economic, social and educational conditions were observed to have improved in the interval. Perhaps because the presumed independent variables are usually confounded in this manner, authors often suggest another factor as contributing to intelligence test scores, namely, intellectual stimulation in home and community – which may be little more than an abstraction from the more easily measured variables of education, economic status and so on.

Intelligence test results on subjects from areas with poor education, low economic standards, etc., typically exhibit three characteristics. First, scores on verbal problems are usually particularly low, while scores on performance problems are not quite so depressed. This differential has been attributed to lack of education and other forms of stimulation which are assumed to promote the development of abstract thinking. Secondly, scores are especially low on tests which involve speed. Apparently the standard instructions are inadequate to induce subjects to perform quickly and/or the subjects have not learned to peform the requisite responses with alacrity. Thirdly, items dealing with material which is commonplace in a given area are handled best by the local subjects, for example, the Mare-and-Foal Test by farm children subjects. Such findings, together with variability from setting to setting in the relative difficulty of individual items, suggest the importance of particular environmental conditions as determinants of skills and other responses indicative of knowledge.

Ferguson (1954) proposed a theoretical frame of reference to account for the above types of findings with intelligence tests. He proposed that those abilities will be developed to a crude limit of learning which are perceived as important in a given culture and which presumably correlate with the activities demanded for survival in that culture. Thus, when two cultures differ in the activities which they value and encourage, the result will be two different patterns of abilities. If an intelligence test, that is, a test of abilities, is standardized on the members of one culture, it may be inappropriate as a measure of intelligence within another culture, giving lower total scores and lacking discriminatory power.

Ferguson did not attempt to formulate the manner in which the learning processes would be shaped

---

[1]Portions of this paper were read at the annual meeting of the Canadian Psychological Association in June 1956 and June 1957. Sullivan's study constituted his research for the M.A. at Dalhousie University. This series of studies was made possible by the interest, generous assistance and co-operation of the Newfoundland Department of Health and Department of Education.

Reprinted, by permission, from *Canadian Psychologist*, 1963, *4*, 126-136.

and determined by such variables as motivation, exposure to stimuli, practice and reinforcement. However, it was clearly implied that intelligence tests measure what the subject has learned to date, and that this will be a general function of the demands of the cultural and physical environment. Presumably these demands would be reflected in the value placed on particular occupations, on socio-economic levels, and on education. From this point of view, it is not surprising that intelligence is correlated with such social variables in our urban-industrial society. However, when the possibilities in terms of such variables are restricted, as they are in rural and isolated areas, and when the valued and environmentally prescribed skills are towards the lower end of the scale for these variables, one would expect people from such regions to make below "normal" scores on intelligence tests standardized on largely urban samples.

The outports of Newfoundland were observed to have many of the conditions which theory and other studies indicated are associated with poor and atypical performance on the usual intelligence test: relative isolation, limited education, poor economic conditions, lack of intellectual stimulation, and primary occupations requiring the performance skills of fishing, mining and lumbering. In a first study, Burnett (1955) confirmed the general relationship with the finding that the average IQ of 2,000 outport children was 80.5 on the Otis Intermediate Group Test of Intelligence. It thus became of practical importance for psychological work in education and mental health to determine the level of functioning of outport subjects on tests to be used in the setting. At the same time, it was opportune to try to relate measured abilities to the conditions prevailing in the outports.

The Wechsler-Bellevue Study

Burnett and Beach carried out a study to determine the scores on the Wechsler-Bellevue Intelligence Scale, Form I (Wechsler 1944) of adults residing in outports. Fifty adult volunteers took the test in Outport I, an outport that was judged to be less isolated than are many in the province. The test was also given to 45 outpatients at the local Cottage Hospital in Outport II, a more isolated outport. In administering the test, a few alterations were made, as suggested by the authors' experience in the setting. For example, "Who is the President of the United States?" was changed to "Who is the Premier of Newfoundland?"

The results on these two samples are shown in Table I. For comparison, the mean scores from Wechsler's standardization subgroup aged 30-34 are also shown. The age range for Outport I Ss was 17-73 and for Outport II Ss 20-60. The subjects from Outport I, the ostensibly less isolated community, received higher mean scores on all subtests and higher IQ's than did subjects from Outport II. Their mean education, grade 6.3, was also higher than that of Outport II (M = 5.6). Nevertheless, all of Outport I's mean scores, except Object Assembly, were lower than the norms. As expected, the Performance IQ was significantly higher than the Verbal IQ (Outport I: p. = .003), and Performance subtests also appeared to discriminate better (Performance range = 52, S.D. = 12.02; Verbal range = 47, S.D. = 9.40). Among these subtests, Picture Arrangement received the lowest scores, but it apparently discriminated as well as most other subtests (S.D. = 2.38). Contrary to expectation, the Digit Symbol subtest mean was not lower than the means of other subtests in either Outport sample, and the deterioration index was only 3 per cent in Outport I and 6 per cent in Outport II.

Although performance abilities measured higher than verbal abilities, there was no evidence that performance abilities are overlearned, because even in the "better" sample of Outport I, the Performance

Table I – Wechsler-Bellevue intelligence scale (Form 1) mean scores on two output samples of normal adults, with Wechsler's standardization group for comparison.

Test	Wechsler		Outport I		Outport II	
	Mean	S.D.	Mean	S.D.	Mean	S.D.
Information	9.8	3.12	7.1	2.19	5.1	2.70
Comprehension	9.7	3.15	8.2	1.72	6.1	3.25
Digit Span	9.0	3.31	7.6	2.59	5.3	2.86
Arithmetic	9.2	3.41	7.6	3.88	5.4	4.36
Similarities	9.5	2.76	6.9	2.04	4.9	2.85
Vocabulary	-	-	6.9	1.41	5.7	2.02
Picture Arrangement	9.2	3.28	5.9	2.38	4.7	3.00
Picture Completion	9.6	3.30	8.2	2.25	6.0	3.29
Block Design	9.7	3.30	8.4	2.67	7.7	2.90
Object Assembly	9.7	2.86	10.4	2.41	10.0	2.14
Digit Symbol	9.2	3.31	8.1	3.17	7.0	3.02
Subtest Mean	9.3	-	7.8	-	6.2	-
Verbal IQ	98.8	16.01	90.5	9.40	78.5	14.83
Performance IQ	100.0	15.78	95.2	12.02	89.7	13.32
Full Scale IQ	99.6	15.60	91.7	10.72	82.5	14.18
Age	30-34 (range)		34 (mean)		35 (mean)	
Education	-		6.3	2.77	5.6	3.5
N	111		50		45	

IQ was significantly lower than the norm of 100 (p = .003). This indicates either that performance abilities are not emphasized as much in outport as in urban cultures or that the performance subtests of the Wechsler scale do not measure the skills that are cultivated in outports. The latter interpretation is supported by an examination of individual subtest scores. One subtest, Object Assembly, rated "normal" scores. Indeed both outport samples earned somewhat higher than average means on this subtest. This finding would seem to be comparable to rural subjects' excellence of performance on the Mare-and-Foal Test (Anastasi, 1958). The task in the Object Assembly subtest is to fit together the parts of familiar objects. This is ostensibly an emphasized skill in outports where the tradition is that they build their own houses, boats and fish traps.

The Block Design subtest rated the next highest scores in both outport samples. That the scores of this subtest were not as high as those of Object Assembly is attributed to the speed factor involved in the former. While there are time credits in both tests, Block Design is unique in that no credit is given for partially completed designs and failure on consecutive items rules out a try on later items, which features do not obtain for Object Assembly. Moreover, it is possible to make an average score on the latter without earning any time credits. These differences suggest the inference that speed is not a cultivated ability in the samples studied. This tends to be confirmed by casual observation: life in the outports is not fast and competitive. However, it is likely that this problem is more complicated, for the people *do* act with speed and precision in a crisis involving their own craft. One interpretation is that test instructions do not mobilize a speed motive as do sudden storms or squalls, because of lack of experience with speed instructions and the reinforcement contingencies which are common in urban settings. A second possibility is that the novelty of the test situation and material made the subjects unusually anxious and cautious.

The Picture Arrangement subtest received lower scores than any other in both outports. This finding is consistent with a factor-analytic study (Burnett, 1955) in which a "cultural sophistication" factor was isolated with high loadings on Picture Arrangement, Block Design, the subject's or his father's travel experience, and occupations other than that of fisherman. It would seem that the isolation and occupational restriction that characterize outports minimizes the kind of experience and learning that underlies adequate performance on the Picture Arrangement subtest.

In summary, this investigation indicated that, whereas the Wechsler-Bellevue scale discriminates fairly well among outport subjects, it gives below "normal" intelligence quotients, especially on the verbal part of the test. Subtest scores are variable in terms of Wechsler's norms, and special experience or lack of it seems to be the associated factor. The obvious factors of lack of education and years since leaving school were not controlled and hence their contribution to the test measures could not be evaluated.

In the second study in this series Sullivan (1958) compared two urban and one outport samples of high school subjects on the Wechsler-Bellevue Intelligence Scale (Form I) and the Raven Progressive Matrices (1938 edition, 1956 revised edition). Each group contained 25 subjects, males and females, who were just finishing grade IX or beginning grade X. One urban group was from schools in a large urban centre in Newfoundland, and the other from schools in a large urban centre in Nova Scotia. The outport sample came from several coastal communities. The Wechsler-Bellevue was administered in the standard manner, while the Progressive Matrices was administered with no time limit. This study had three main objectives:

1) to determine if lack of education and years since schooling might have contributed to the low Wechsler scores in previous samples;
2) to compare outport and urban subjects on a type of material that is presumably as novel for one group as it is for the other (Progressive Matrices);
3) to compare outport subjects' speed of problem solving with that of urban groups.

The Wechsler-Bellevue scores of the two urban groups were very similar, with no significant differences by subtest of IQ (Table II). The IQ's were "average" at 103. The outport group's means scores on all subtests but Arithmetic, Digit Span and Object Assembly were significantly below the urban groups' scores. The Full Scale IQ was 85.6. This finding makes it clear that equivalent education, as defined by grades, does not necessarily make for the same level of achievement in the abilities measured by the Wechsler-Bellevue. Hence, the lack of schooling in the outport adults sampled by Burnett and Beach cannot be held responsible for their below-average Wechsler-Bellevue IQ's. It should be noted, that outport student's scores on Arithmetic and Digit Span were not lower than those for the urban students. Further and continuing education may have developed these two abilities beyond the levels attained by adults in the study by Burnett and Beach. Nevertheless, certain performance abilities still rate highest: Object Assembly and Block Design. Picture Arrangement, though still quite low, was higher than it was for outport adults and it did not get the lowest scores. Amont the outport students the lowest subtest scores were on Vocabulary (6.6) and Information (5.6). Apparently a higher education (grade 9 for the outport students in contrast to grades 5 to 6 for the outport adults) did not increase knowledge of general information and vocabulary as measured by the Wechsler. And achievement in these areas was markedly below that for the urban students.

At least two factors may be suggested to account for the underdevelopment of the students' verbal

Table II – Comparison of two urban and one outport groups of high school students on the progressive matrices, and on subtests and IQ's of the Wechsler-Bellevue (Form 1)

Test	N.S. Urban		Nfld. Urban		Nfld. Outport	
	Mean	S.D.	Mean	S.D.	Mean	S.D.
Information	10.56	2.04	10.44	1.98	5.64**	2.03
Comprehension	10.28	1.93	10.28	2.99	6.60**	3.11
Digit Span	8.48	2.65	8.52	2.04	7.88	2.30
Arithmetic	9.20	2.66	10.04	2.51	8.64	3.29
Similarities	9.40	2.39	9.64	2.10	6.96**	2.52
Vocabulary	8.76	1.77	9.36	1.52	6.56**	1.39
Picture Arrangement	10.12	2.43	11.24	2.10	7.32**	3.35
Picture Competion	10.02	2.84	10.12	2.42	8.12*	3.09
Block Design	10.44	2.88	10.52	2.08	9.20*	2.42
Object Assembly	10.48	2.45	10.36	1.02	10.00	2.50
Digit Symbol	9.48	1.96	9.96	1.97	7.88**	1.53
Verbal IQ	103.20	10.51	103.12	10.06	85.88**	13.02
Performance IQ	102.92	12.47	103.12	8.66	88.52**	12.98
Full Scale IQ	103.44	11.85	103.88	8.77	85.60**	13.32
Matrices Total	37.7	12.29	42.4	8.45	40.6	8.42
Matrices Time (Min.)	19.4	10.02	33.6	18.10	45.4	16.04
Age (years-months)	15.1		15.10		16.3	

* significantly lower than mean for Nfld. Urban at .05 level
** significantly lower than mean for Nfld. Urban at .01 level

skills. First, a restricted experience with words and general information in the pre-school years of childhood, and secondly, a lack of cultural emphasis on such skills. These skills were probably not immediately and obviously relevant to everyday life and goals in the outport. Hence there would not be a social context of motivation and reinforcement necessary to facilitate their acquisition. It would seem that formal education, assuming it involved the usual training with words and information, was severely handicapped by the cultural climate. Moreover, if concepts serve a mediating and integrating function that facilitates new learning (Dollard and Miller, 1950; Mowrer, 1954; Razran, 1955), deficient verbal-conceptual skills would impose serious limitations on future trainability.

The three groups of students obtained similar mean scores on the Raven Progressive Matrices (Table II), and these were comparable to the 50th percentile score of 40 which Raven (1952, 1956) established for English subjects of the same age level. Thus, urban students do no better than their outport fellows when the problem material is presumably equally novel for both groups. This finding also suggests that the outport subjects have no less intellectual potential than urban or mainland groups.

The time consumed in doing the Progressive Matrices differed greatly for the three groups: Nova Scotia urban mean = 19.4 minutes, Newfoundland urban mean = 33.6 minutes, and Newfoundland ourport mean = 45.4 minutes. The instructions for the test are: "Now carry on at your own pace. You can have as much time as you like. There is no need to hurry." Both Newfoundland groups worked more slowly than did the Nova Scotia group, suggesting that the habit of rapid work in the absence of explicit instructions has not been cultivated. This was especially true for the outport students. It was also observed that they took about twice as long to do the verbal part of the Wechsler-Bellevue. These results support the hypothesis that outport subjects' intelligence test performance may be lower than that of urban groups because the speed habit is not cultivated in their society.

This investigation, then, indicated that lack of formal education does not account for the low intelligence scores of outport subjects. It provided evidence that outport people have the same intellectual potential as do urban dwellers. It substantiated the hypothesis of a lack of speed factor in outport subjects' test performance, and supported previous findings of particular performance skills or lack thereof.

The final study in this series was carried out by Beach as one aspect of an investigation of the relationship between psychological tests and EEG waves. The Progressive Matrices test was administered twice to 19 aids and attendants in the Provincial Newfoundland Mental Hospital, with a test-retest interval of from three weeks to one year. These subjects had all been raised and educated in outports. Their mean education was comparable to that of Sullivan's outport group, grade 9.9, thus providing an opportunity to check Sullivan's findings.

The results of this study are shown in Table III. The attendants from outports received a mean Progressive Matrices score on first testing of 32.2, which is significantly below the mean of 40.6 which Sullivan's student group earned ($p = .01$). Sullivan's student group showed more variability of scores than did the attendant group (F ratio = 5.583; $p = .01$)

The attendants' scores on retest increased significantly ($p = .02$) to a level which was not significantly below that for Sullivan's student group ($t = 1.508$, p. = ns). The attendants' mean time taken to complete the test on first administration was significantly below that for Sullivan's students ($p = .01$), and the attendants' time decreased further on retesting (p. = .02).

Table III – Comparison of progressive matrices scores and times of output students with those of hospital attendants from outports

	Nfld. Attendants (N=19)				Nfld. Students (N=25)	
	1st testing		2nd testing		One testing	
	Mean	S.D.	Mean	S.D.	Mean	S.D.
Matrices score	32.2[2]	8.77	36.0	11.39	40.6	8.42
"A" test of change[1]		.191	(P.=.02)			
Matrices time (min.)	31.0[3]	6.87	26.3[3]	8.55	45.4	16.04
"A" test of change		.178	(P=.02)			

[1] See McGuigan (1960)

[2] Significantly lower than mean for Nfld. students (t = 3.158, p. = .01)

[3] Significantly lower than mean for Nfld. students (for the mean of 31: t = 3.891, p. = .01)

The discrepancies between the scores of Sullivan's students and those of the attendants on first testing were unexpected. It cannot be attributed to the amount of formal schooling, for the groups were equivalent on this variable. Nor were there any obvious grounds for attributing it to differences in the outport backgrounds from which the subjects came. The factors which differed for the two groups were:
(1) age – Sullivan's group was 16.2 years old on the average while the attendants were 20.5;
(2) the fact that Sullivan's outport students were still attending school while the attendants had been out of school for about 4 years and were now working in a mental hospital;
(3) the student group was living in outports while the attendant group was living in an urban setting; and
(4) the test was administered individually to the students in an office in their school, while it was administered to the attendants in groups of one to four in the psychologist's office.

The age difference between the groups, in itself, would hardly account for the difference in Progressive Matrices scores. However, any one or more of the other three differences could be responsible. In examining these possiblitites note will be taken of the fact that the attendants did the test much faster than the students (p = .01).

It is suggested that one or both of two general factors contributed to the attendants' initially lower test scores: test anxiety, and their evident speed motivation. These subjects had been away from school for about four years, that is, away from testing situations. In such circumstances testing could presumably cause more anxiety than it provoked in high school students. It is also conceivable that they perceived psychological tests as instruments for diagnosing mental illness and hence felt unusually threatened by the situation, and the small group testing situation may have made them more self-conscious and uneasy than the examiner-subject situation which obtained for the students. Thus there were several possible instigators of anxiety for the attendants. And it is amply demonstrated that test anxiety has an important influence on performance (Sarason *et al.* 1960).

Two observations suggest the speed motivation factor. First, the attendants did the test much faster than did the students; and secondly, although they increased their speed on the second testing, they also improved their scores significantly, to the point that that the scores no longer differed significantly from those of the students. It is suggested that these attendants, in their move from outport to urban setting and work situation, were trying to adopt some of the behaviour patterns and goals of their new culture. One of the goals they sought to attain was speed. However, they had had little practice in doing tests quickly, with the consequence that they made many errors. On the second administration they had the benefit of a rehearsal and their test scores improved. Thus, the presence of speed motivation, in itself an important finding as it indicates acculturation, could well have had a negative influence on problem solving proficiency as measured by the first administration of the Progressive Matrices.

Discussion

The findings in this series of studies reaffirm the principle that behaviour as measured at any given time is a complex function of kinds and amounts of past experience or practice and of the conditions of measurement. What is called intelligence is no exception to the rule. It only seems to involve special problems when it is treated as a substantive potential "thing" rather than as a particular kind of behaviour, and when it is forgotten that measures of intelligence are influenced by the same host of extraneous variables that affect any experimental comparison of groups.

Newfoundland outport adults scored considerably below the American normative group on the Wechsler-Bellevue Intelligence Scale (Form I). This kind of finding is fairly common among rural subjects and other groups living in an environment and subculture which do not have the same socio-economic, educational, and variety-of-experience amenities as do more urban settings (Anastasi, 1958). The outport subjects did better on the performance part of the Wechsler than on the verbal, and their scores were slightly above the normative groups on Object Assembly, and lowest on Picture Arrangement. These differential results would seem to be a valid reflection of their experience and of the skills which are valued and practised in their cultures.

Outports are small coastal communities which exist in relative isolation from one another and from the rest of the world. Travel is largely by boat and even this is precluded for several months of the year. Life in these areas has been a constant struggle for survival in the face of a hard and unpredictable environment. The necessary skills included woodcraft, boatbuilding, seamanship and housekeeping. These skills were passed on from father to son and from mother to daughter. Formal education was limited: it was the custom for boys as young as nine years to leave school and join their fathers fishing. The quality of the schooling was not always the best since facilities and trained teachers were difficult to obtain. In addition, it is likely that motivation to learn at school was low because school learning offered little that was functionally relevant to their struggle for survival. Even business relations were not such as to stimulate much learning: in many instances the people turned their fish catch over to the local merchant who in turn supplied their "store needs" by a system of credits.

In recent years there have been considerable advances in transportation and communication so that isolation is not nearly so marked. Radios are to be found in almost every home. Nevertheless, life has not changed radically in most of the outports. Radio listening tends to be restricted to the local news, personal messages and western music. Interpersonal relationships have remained uncomplicated and informal, with little evidence of competitive striving to achieve.

Within this cultural context it is not surprising that a greater amount of formal education did not result in a general increase in scores on the Wechsler scale. Available opportunities, rewards and local social attitudes were not such as to reinforce the practice and generalization of school learning outside the classroom. Moreover, the slower pace of life, without striving, had not developed the motive and generalized practice of speed. However, when given all the time they wished, grade 10 students achieved scores on the Progressive Matrices equivalent to the United Kingdom normative group. This test does not involve verbal material but presents problems in analysing, relating and abstracting from two-dimensional formal designs. The test problems are essentially spatial in nature. It is possible that these two features of the Matrices test, absence of verbal material and its spatial nature, were important conditions of the outport students' success with it. Spatial orientation, in the woods and on the sea, is an important ability in the Newfoundlanders' environment.

When the outport student with a good education moves to an urban setting and takes a job, he could be expected to try to adopt some of the ways and goals of his new peers. The group of attendant subjects had come from outports. They did the Progressive Matrices much faster than outport students still in school, but their success scores were considerably lower. It was suggested that their attempted speed represented one facet of their acculturation in the urban setting. However, unpractised in the handling of such tasks with speed, and probably affected by more than usual test anxiety, their errors were high. On retest their scores increased so as to be not significantly lower than those of the high school students.

The findings on the Progressive Matrices test indicate that the "intelligence" of outport people is normal. Nevertheless many of their abilities as measured by the Wechsler scale are lower than the normative and other urban groups. This is especially true for verbal-conceptual abilities. Apparently such abilities have not been emphasized, practised and reinforced within their culture. An important question is: assuming that the trend is toward improvement of education and socio-economic conditions, and that the more urban standards of achievement will constitute the dominant frame of reference for success in the society at large, then what behaviour that is relevant to the dominant frame of reference will tests such as the Wechsler and Matrices predict, and how well? To be more specific: will they predict trainability in the skills valued by the wider society.

The problem of measuring abilities and predicting trainability in different areas reduces to the problem of transfer of training (Anastasi, 1958; Cook, 1956; Ferguson, 1954). The concept of intelligence confuses the issues and should probably be put aside. Evidence and theory would suggest that a present ability or skill is the base on which related skills are acquired. If the current ability is limited, then presumably the individual would have to be given more time and or special training to reach the same level of achievement as one who started from a better base. What methods might accelerate the acquisition of an adequate baseline of ability? Or, to go back one step, what factors might be altered in the outport community to promote the acquisition of those abilities which are important as a basis for trainability and success in the wider society? Reliable answers to such questions would have considerable import for theory and practice.

References

ANASTASI, ANNE. *Differential psychology*. (3rd ed.) New York: MacMillan, 1958.

BURNETT, A. Assessment of intelligence in a restricted environment. Unpublished Ph.D. thesis, McGill Univ., 1955.

COOK, T. W. Transfer and ability. *Bull. Maritime psychol. Ass.*, 1956, *5*, 6-11

DOLLARD, J., and MILLER, N. E. *Personality and psychotherapy*. New York: McGraw-Hill, 1950.

FERGUSON, G. A. On learning and human ability. *Canad. J. Psychol.*, 1954, *8*, 95-112.

MCGUIGAN, F. J. *Experimental psychology: a methodological approach*. New York: Prentice-Hall, 1960.

Mowrer, O. H. The psychologist looks at language. *Amer. Psychol.*, 1954, *9*, 660-694.

Raven, J. C. *Human nature, its development, variations and assessment.* London: Lewis, 1952.

———. *Guide to using the Progressive Matrices.* London: Lewis, 1956.

Razran, G. A note on second-order conditioning—and secondary reinforcement. *Psychol. Rev.*, 1955, *62*, 327-332.

Sarason, S. B., *et al. Anxiety in elementary school children: a research report.* New York: Wiley, 1960.

Sullivan, A. M. *A comparison of the Performance on the Wechsler-Bellevue and Progressive Matrices Test of Subjects from Three Different Geographical Areas.* Unpublished M.A. thesis, Dalhousie Univ., 1958.

Wechsler, D. *The measurement of adult intelligence.* (3rd ed.) Baltimore: Williams and Williams, 1944.

Wheeler, L. R. A comparative study of the intelligence of East Tennessee mountain children. *J. educ. Psychol.*, 1942, *33*, 321-334.

35 / The Scholastic Aptitude of the Indian Children Of The Caradoc Reserve[1]

G.H. Turner and D.J. Penfold *University of Western Ontario*

The Canadian Indian suffers from many of the handicaps that the Negro faces in the United States. Indians form a minority group which has suffered from discrimination, inferior schooling, lack of opportunity for advancement, and generally, a lower economic status. The authors point out that these conditions, along with a lower aspiration level on the part of the Indian, have resulted in a deficit in certain skills which are highly important for adequate scholastic achievement. The investigations of Sydiaha and Rempel (article 42) and Burnett, Beach, and Sullivan (article 34) are particularly relevant to the issues raised here.

The purpose of this study was to assess the scholastic aptitude of the Indian children on the Caradoc Reserve, Muncey, Ontario. By the term "scholastic aptitude" is meant the capacity to attain the general educational standards of white school children, a capacity which is by no means restricted to intellectual capacity.

The Caradoc Reserve is situated on the Thames River in the southern part of Middlesex County. Approximately five hundred Chippewas and one hundred and fifty Munceys occupy the west bank and approximately one thousand Oneidas live on the east bank.

The Oneidas speak their native language in addition to English. In most cases Oneida is the preferred language, and consequently a significant number of Oneida children begin school with a scant knowledge of English. With the Chippewas and the Munceys, on the other hand, English is the predominant language. Only a few of the older members of the tribe speak their native tongue, the younger generations being familiar with comparatively few words. The religious faith of the people is almost entirely Protestant, the exception being a small but influential group of Oneidas practising the "Longhouse" religion.

There are five junior schools, two with two rooms, three with one room, providing instruction up to grade 8. In addition, there is one four-room senior school, opened in January, 1949, which provides instruction for grades 7 to 10, with instruction in some subjects beyond the grade 10 level. There is also room devoted to those pupils who have not yet reached grade 7 but who are above thirteen years of age. For those who have the desire and qualifications to complete their education to the grade 13 level in white schools (in Strathroy, St. Thomas, or London), there is a grant of one hundred dollars per annum.

With perhaps one exception, all of the schools now functioning seem to be, in construction and furnishing, as good as or better than the neighbouring rural white schools. All except two are centrally heated and provided with electric lighting.

The schools are operated by the Indian Affairs Branch, Department of Citizenship and Immigration, but the curricula are essentially those laid down by the Ontario Department of Education. They are inspected twice a year by the provincial inspectors of East and West Middlesex. All schools are under the immediate supervision of the Supervising-Principal, who is responsible to the resident Indian Superintendent, the official representative of the Indian Affairs Branch.

While E. E. M. Joblin, the present Supervising-Principal, made an extensive study of achievement and the factors promoting it (2) in 1947, there has been no systematic attempt to assess the scholastic aptitude of children on this Reserve since 1928 when Jamieson (1) compared the I.Q.'s of the pupils of the Mount Elgin Residential School with those of pupils in Indian schools in other communities.

Method

In Parts A and B of this study, the following general procedure was followed. Indian children were compared on group tests of intelligence with white children drawn from the surrounding rural districts (Byron and Delaware). It was felt that the sociophysical environment of the Indian children would have more factors in common with that of the surrounding rural white children than with the urban

[1]This investigation was supported by a grant from the Associate Committee on Applied Psychology of the National Research Council of Canada.
The material for this paper has been drawn from the M.A. thesis of D. J. Penfold, University of Western Ontario, 1951, which was supervised and planned by the senior author with the helpful advice of Dr. J. A. Long, Department of Educational Research, University of Toronto.

Reprinted, by permission, from *Canadian Journal of Psychology*, 1952, *6*, 31-44.

white children in America and England upon whom the tests were standardized.

In Part C, the *Wechsler Intelligence Scale for Children* (hereafter referred to by the letters WISC), was administered individually to a sample of Indian children in order to compare their verbal and non-verbal performance.

Part A: Otis and Henmon-Nelson Group Testing
Two group tests were selected for the first part of the study:

(A) The *Otis Quick-Scoring Mental Ability Test*, Alpha Form A, grades 1-4, Non-Verbal Section.

(B) The *Henmon-Nelson Test of Mental Ability*, Form A, grades 3-8.

Each test consists of 90 items; both are time-limited (20 minutes for the Otis and 30 minutes for the Henmon-Nelson). The Henmon-Nelson is a verbal test while the Otis is non-verbal.

During the first three months of 1950 these tests were administered to 240 Indian school children and to a control population of 215 white children from six schools in Delaware Township and one school in the village of Byron. In the schools visited all available pupils were tested.

Part B: Progressive Matrices Group Testing
To provide a scale that might be regarded as more culture-free than either the Otis or the Henmon-Nelson tests, and which would provide a greater age range than the Otis test, the *Progressive Matrices* (1947), Sets A, AB, and B were selected. The 1947 form of the test was designed to secure a greater dispersion of scores in the lower age groups than was provided by the 1938 form. The 1947 form is printed in colour and might hold promise of greater interest for the Indian children than other "school type" tests.

The Progressive Matrices is a power (unspeeded) test of 36 items and it can be administered to individuals or to groups. However, considerable individual attention must be given to the pupils of the lower grades, since the subject is required to fill in a form using numbers up to six (six numbered choices per item). In order that the examiner could more closely supervise the administration of the test, no more than five grade 1 pupils, and no more than eleven of the others, were tested at a time.

The test was administered during the fall and winter of 1950-51 to all pupils of ages 6 to 13 available in the Indian and white schools used in Part A. These numbered 205 Indian and 215 white pupils. Thus in Parts A and B the schools were the same but the populations of cases were slightly different.

Part C: Wechsler Individual Testing
In order to control motivation more closely and to obtain more detailed information concerning the abilities of Indian children to handle various kinds of test material, it was felt desirable to employ an individual intelligence test. For this purpose the *Wechsler Intelligence Scale for Children* was chosen. It is divided into Verbal and Performance scales, each consisting of five sub-tests.

Some changes in three of the items of the Verbal scale were thought to be desirable, since they placed the Canadian school children at a disadvantage with American school children.

1. *General Information*. Item 17 "What is celebrated on the Fourth of July?" changed to "What is celebrated on the 24th of May?"

Answer: Queen Victoria's Birthday.

2. *General Information*. Item 24 "How far is it from New York to Chicago?" changed to "How far is it from Toronto to Montreal?"

Answer: Any answer from 300 to 400 miles.

3. *General Comprehension*. Item 13 "Why do we elect (or need to have) senators and congressmen?" changed to "Why do we elect (or need to have) Members of Parliament?"

Scoring criteria were the same as for the original items.

Three age groups, 7, 10, and 14, were chosen as a sample. These age groups were selected as being the most representative of the age range of the test (4, p. 13) and of the Caradoc population.

The WISC was administered to the ten-year-old group during June 1950, and to the seven- and fourteen-year-old groups during the fall of 1950 and the winter of 1950-51. Some rechecking of the ten-year-old group was done during the latter period.

The following comprise the samples from the three age groups: (a) in the seven-year-old group, 31 cases; (b) in the ten-year-old group, 25 cases; (c) in the fourteen-year-old group, 26 cases; total, 82 cases.

All tests, both individual and group, were administered and scored by Penfold.

Results

Part A: Otis and Henmon-Nelson Group Testing

1. Indian children in grades 1-4 who took the Otis test obtained I.Q.'s which were, on the average, significantly lower (10 points) and slightly less variable than those obtained by the control group of white subjects.

For Indian and white respectively the data were as follows: number of cases, 132 and 128; mean I.Q., 91.2 and 101.2; S.D., 14.5 and 17.5; and a statistically significant difference between means of 10.0 in favour of white.

2. Indian children in grades 5-8 who took the Henmon-Nelson test likewise obtained I.Q.'s which were, on the aveage, significantly lower (20 points) and slightly less variable than those obtained by the control group of white subjects.

For Indian and white respectively the data were as follows: number of cases, 93 and 86; mean I.Q., 81.5 and 101.7; S.D., 15.5 and 18.0; and a statisti-

Table I – Otis and Henmon-Nelson median I.Q.'s, median raw scores, and median chronological ages in months, of Indian and white school children in each of the grades 1-8

Test	School Grade	Indian				White				Differences		
		N	I.Q.	Raw Score	C.A.	N	I.Q.	Raw Score	C.A.	I.Q.	Raw Score	C.A.
Henmon-Nelson	8	21	71.2	48.0	183.5	24	102.2	74.0	165.0	-31.0	-26.0	18.5
	7	18	86.0	55.5	163.5	14	96.0	65.0	153.0	-10.0	- 9.5	10.5
	6	21	82.8	49.3	162.5	24	100.0	58.2	144.0	-17.2	- 8.9	18.5
	5	33	85.0	40.8	143.5	24	98.1	48.0	129.5	-13.1	- 7.2	14.0
Otis	4	28	95.5	63.8	132.5	28	90.5	59.5	117.5	5.0	4.3	15.0
	3	30	89.5	55.3	118.5	28	93.2	53.0	105.0	- 3.7	2.3	13.5
	2	41	90.0	46.0	101.8	34	107.0	49.5	94.8	-17.0	- 3.5	7.0
	1	48	83.8	24.1	88.5	39	107.0	38.8	81.6	-23.2	-14.7	6.9

cally significant difference between means of 20.2 in favour of white.

3. At every *grade* level from 1-8, the average *age* of the Indian children was higher than that of the white controls. These mean differences ranged from 6.9 months to 18.5 months. It should be noted that the age difference tends to increase with increase in grade level.

4. The Indian subjects obtained median Otis and Henmon-Nelson I.Q.'s which were lower than those of the whites at every grade level, except grade 4. The differences were larger and more consistent on the Henmon-Nelson than on the Otis Test (Table I).

5. Grades 3 and 4 excepted, median *raw scores* on the Otis and Henmon-Nelson were lower for Indian than for white children at every *grade* level. On the Otis test the Indian children, relative to the white children, did better with increase in grade level, while in the Henmon-Nelson test, the process was reversed (Table I).

6. At every *age* level from 6-16, the median Otis and Henmon-Nelson I.Q. of the Indian children was lower than that for the white controls, and these differences were quite substantial at most of the age levels. However, it should be remembered that, for any given age, the average school grade level was appreciably lower for the Indian children (Table II).

Table II – Median Otis and Henmon-Nelson I.Q.'s of Indian and white children in each of the age groups 6-16

Age	Indian N	Indian Median I.Q.	White N	White Median I.Q.
16	21	67.0		
15				
14	18	78.5		
13	20	84.0	29	96.3
12	24	89.0	25	94.3
11	25	88.0	22	99.0
10	28	90.0	20	102.5
9	26	90.0	28	93.5
8	31	91.0	33	105.5
7	29	92.0	28	102.5
6	18	84.0	30	108.5
	240		215	

Table III – Means and standard deviations of progressive matrices scores at each age group from 6-13

Age	Indian N	Indian Mean	Indian S.D.	White N	White Mean	White S.D.	Differences Mean	Differences "t" ratio
13	11	28.9	3.8	15	29.7	4.2	0.9	0.69
12	20	26.8	4.3	25	29.7	3.6	2.9	2.42**
11	14	25.1	5.0	23	28.9	5.6	3.8	2.11**
10	33	22.9	5.4	24	26.8	4.7	3.9	2.78*
9	30	22.5	5.8	32	26.3	4.3	3.8	2.92*
8	43	19.1	5.8	35	21.6	6.1	2.5	1.78
7	35	18.8	5.2	39	20.6	5.3	1.8	1.50
6	19	13.9	6.3	22	14.0	11.1	0.1	0.004
	205			215				

*Significant at the 5 per cent level. **Significant at the 1 per cent level.

7. There was a slight tendency for I.Q. to drop with age. This tendency was most marked among Indian children over the age of twelve (Table II).

8. The median Otis I.Q.'s of the Indian children were found to be approximately the same for the Oneida as for the Muncey and Chippewa Bands. The numbers of cases were 103 and 44 respectively, and the corresponding median I.Q.'s were 88.9 and 87.5.

9. Six months previous to the administration of these tests the Otis test was administered to Indian children by E. E. M. Joblin, the Supervising-Principal of the Caradoc schools. Eighty-one cases of those tested by Joblin were among those tested by Penfold.

The product-moment (Pearson) coefficient of correlation was found to be .62.

Part B: Progressive Matrices Group Testing

1. On the Progressive Matrices test, white children did significantly better than Indian children at each of the age groups 9-12 inclusive (Table III).

2. Differences between Indian and white children in Progressive Matrices mean scores increased with age to age group 10, and then decreased with age to age group 13 (Table III).

3. While no significant difference in the means between Indian and white children was obtained for any grade, there was an obtained difference at all grade levels, except grade 1, in favour of the white children (Table IV).

4. The lack of cases in grade 8 and the small number of cases in grade 7 was a reflection of the high chronological age per grade (Table IV).

Table IV – Means and standard deviations of progressive matrices scores in each of grades 1-8

	Indian				White				Differences		
Grade	N	Median C.A.*	Mean	S.D.	N	Median C.A.	mean	S.D.	Median C.A.	Mean	"t"
8	..	....	....	...	12	12.1	33.3	3.1	...	...	...
7	7	13.4	29.7	3.0	15	12.7	30.1	2.3	0.7	0.4	0.3
6	18	12.2	27.9	3.9	27	11.9	29.7	3.7	0.3	1.8	1.6
5	21	11.6	25.1	4.7	26	10.7	26.6	5.8	0.9	1.5	1.3
4	22	10.1	23.9	5.7	27	9.6	25.5	4.0	0.5	1.6	1.1
3	42	9.6	22.6	5.4	35	8.1	24.1	5.6	1.5	1.5	1.5
2	43	8.3	18.8	3.1	43	7.8	20.3	5.4	0.5	1.3	1.6
1	52	7.4	16.8	5.7	30	6.1	15.3	8.9	1.3	–1.5	0.8
	205				215						

*In years to the nearest tenth.

Part C: Wechsler Individual Testing

1. The Indian children of ages 14, 7, and all ages combined obtained significantly lower I.Q.'s on the Verbal scale of the WISC than on the Performance scale.

2. The ten-year-old group obtained a lower mean I.Q. (6.6 points) on the Verbal scale, as opposed to the Performance scale, but the difference was not statistically significant (Table V).

3. Average I.Q.'s were obtained by the Indian children on the Performance scale of the WISC (Table V).

Table V – I.Q.'s obtained by Indian children on performance and verbal scales of the WISC, by age groups

		Performance		Verbal		Differences	
Age Group	N	Mean	S.D.	Mean	S.D.	Mean	"t"
14	26	98.3	13.8	84.2	11.1	14.1	3.99*
10	25	96.4	14.0	89.7	14.8	6.6	1.37
7	31	95.7	10.8	83.5	12.7	12.1	4.0*
Total	82	96.7	13.3	85.6	14.1	11.1	5.1*

*Significant at the 1 per cent level.

4. Indian children obtained consistently lower mean scores on Vocabulary than on any other test (Table VI).

5. Generally, low mean scores were obtained on General Information and General Comprehension (Table VI).

6. The ten-year-old group obtained slightly higher mean scores than the other two groups on all verbal tests (Table VI).

7. All age groups obtained lower than average mean scores on Picture Arrangement and Coding, and higher than average scores on Picture Completion (Table VI).

A Comparison of Some Henmon-Nelson and WISC I.Q.'s

Among those tested on the Henmon-Nelson test were 28 Indian children who were also tested on the WISC. These children were divided arbitrarily into two groups – group A, consisting of 13 children who obtained I.Q.'s above 90 on the Henmon-Nelson with a mean I.Q. of 102.1, and group B, consisting of 15 children who obtained I.Q.'s below 90 on the Henmon-Nelson with a mean I.Q. of 82.1.

Mean I.Q.'s obtained on the WISC were: (a) by group A, 104.0 on the Performance scale, and 101.4 on the Verbal scale with a difference of 2.6; (b) by

Table VI – Mean scaled scores obtained by Indians on tests of the verbal and performance scales of the WISC

N	Age		Verbal					Performance				
			Information	Comprehension	Arithmetic	Similarities	Vocabulary	Picture Completion	Picture Arrangement	Block Design	Object Assembly	Coding
26	14	Mean	7.5	7.3	8.7	8.5	5.5	10.7	9.4	10.3	9.8	8.5
		S.D.	2.0	4.2	2.8	2.1	2.8	3.1	2.2	2.5	3.5	3.2
25*	10	Mean	8.8	8.7	9.5	8.8	6.0	11.6	7.8	9.5	9.6	8.6*
		S.D.	3.0	3.2	3.2	2.5	2.5	3.6	3.3	2.7	2.4	2.9
31	7	Mean	6.9	7.4	8.7	8.1	5.8	10.2	8.3	9.6	9.2	9.7
		S.D.	2.8	2.8	2.1	3.0	3.2	2.4	2.5	2.4	3.0	3.0
Total 82*		Mean	7.7	7.8	8.8	8.5	5.8	10.8	8.5	9.8	9.5	9.1*
		S.D.	2.8	3.5	2.7	3.0	2.6	2.9	2.8	2.4	2.5	3.0

*One case fewer in "Coding."

group B, 97.6 on the Performance scale, and 82.3 on the Verbal scale, with a difference of 15.3.

For the entire group of 28 children, the mean I.Q.'s were: (a) for the Henmon-Nelson, 93.0; (b) for the Performance scale of the WISC, 100.6; (c) for the Verbal scale of the WISC, 91.1.

Summary of Findings.

1. The Indian children did as well as average white children on the Performance scale of the WISC.

2. The Indian children did less well than white children on the Verbal scale of the WISC and on the three group tests which were employed. For Indian children, average I.Q.'s on the Henmon-Nelson (verbal) test were lower than average I.Q.'s on the Otis (non-verbal) test.

3. The inferior performance of the Indian children on the WISC was most marked on the Vocabulary test, and to a lesser extent on the General Information and General Comprehension tests.

4. The inferiority of Indian children on the group tests applied at all *age* and *grade* levels with a few minor exceptions.

5. For any given grade, the age of the Indian children was, on the avearage, greater by six months or more. It follows that, at any age level, Indian children were, on the average, at a lower grade level.

Discussion

The Indian children did as well as the white on the Performance scale of the WISC and thereby provided their own argument for racial equality. But even had the Indian children obtained lower scores than the white on *all* of the tests used the inference would be the same, namely that differences in scholastic aptitude between Indian and white school children are most reasonably to be accounted for in terms of environmental differences which obviously exist between the two groups. Having reviewed the evidences for race differences between American Indian and white children, Klineberg states that "the conclusion is inescapable that, given equal opportunities, the American Indian children perform as well as any other" (3, p. 465).

There is no question but that this particular group of Indian children are labouring under many handicaps, some of which are obvious, others by no means readily apparent but probably no less important. In addition to numerous visits, Penfold spent four months of full-time residence in the community during which he supplemented his impressions by many informal, unsystematic but recorded interviews of Indian and white residents on the general subject of education. And it is from this background that many of the less obvious factors emerged. These impressions are included in the following list of handicaps under which the Indian children seemed to be labouring.

1. Lack of Confidence in Their Ability to Compete with Whites in Occupations Requiring Higher Levels of Education and Responsibility

(a) There seems to be a reluctance to accept the kind of responsibility that would ordinarily be accepted by their white counterparts.

(b) On their casual contacts with whites they seem to be characteristically withdrawn and suspicious.

(c) They seem to be inordinately sensitive to the discrimination to which they are subjected.

(d) A number of adolescents and parents have the feeling that further education would be useless as they probably would not obtain appropriate employment.

Lack of confidence may be inferred from the above. The reasons for lack of confidence may be found in a long history of social failure, absence of distinguished band members, further emphasized by discrimination by whites. In addition, some Indian adolescents have left the Reserve to continue their education elsewhere, and have not made a success of it. Such incidents appear to have had a damaging effect on the educational morale of the Indian people.

An interesting fact came to light during the scoring of the Coding test of the WISC. Out of the entire 82 cases, only three errors were found. This, in addition to the extremely long time taken to answer items of the General Information, General Comprehension, Similarities, and Vocabulary tests of the WISC, suggests that the Indian children are in greater fear of making a mistake than white children. This suggestion is further supported by the opinions of the teachers.

2. Lack of a Tradition of Education

Formal education has not been as fully accepted by the Caradoc Indian community as it has by the average Canadian white community. It is the opinion of most of the white personnel (and of the Indians) that there is a tendency among the people to take the short-term view, that is a tendency to look for quick returns for their efforts. Such a trait is not conducive to a high level of motivation. Little effective interest is shown by most parents towards the schools. Meetings of the Oneida T.P. Club (teacher-parent) are poorly attended. The Munceys and the Chippewas possess no club of this nature, although there was an abortive attempt to form one.

3. Lower Socio-Economic Level of the Indian People

Even a cursory inspection of the Caradoc Reserve and its environs would probably convince any observer that the socio-economic level of the Indian people is much lower than that of the white people in the districts from which the control children were drawn. As was indicated earlier, their occupations are not, over a long period of time, highly remunerative.

4. Reduced Attendance

Lack of confidence in their ability to compete with whites and lack of a tradition of education are perhaps reflected in low percentage attendance records of the schools. Much of the absenteeism has not been due to physical illness, but for reasons unacceptable in the average white community (drawing water, chopping wood, "helping mother," etc.) (2, p. 75). The school programme is never in *full* operation in the fall until the frost ends the tobacco and fruit harvests (usually about mid-October). Many of the older children work in the harvests, and often entire families leave the Reserve during this time – the children, in many cases, remaining out of school. Consequently, the school year is effectively shortened, since much of the work has to be repeated. This results in less time available for drills, individual attention, and remedial work in a situation where they are badly needed. The effect of this is shown in part by the "piling up" of pupils in the lower grades. Retardation in school achievement is shown by the progressive increase in the age differential by grade and by the progressive increase in the raw score differential from grade 5 on, shown in Table I.

5. Test Motivation

While there is no reason to believe that the scores obtained by the white controls are not reasonably valid reflections of their abilities, such is not the case with respect to the Indian children. In addition to greater difficulty in establishing rapport, the low test-retest correlation of the Otis test leaves serious doubt that the Indian children take the tests on equal terms with the white children with respect to strength of motivation. And while average scores were obtained by the Indian children on the Performance scale of the WISC, the individual attention and continuous presence of the examiner may have helped to keep the attention of the subjects on the task at hand.

6. Language

Even in homes in which English predominates, it is highly questionable if it would compare favourably with the English used in the homes of the white children in vocabulary, grammar, or any other respect (2, p. 79). The comparison of Henmon-Nelson and WISC I.Q.'s is a further indication that the verbal factor in intelligence tests handicaps the Indian children.

7. School System

That the improved school system now in effect on the Reserve may be reducing the disparity between the Indian children and the children of the average white community, is suggested by the narrower disparity between the Performance and Verbal scales of the WISC shown by the ten-year-old group. The present school system has been in effect only since 1946, and this age group is the only one tested with the WISC whose entire school life has come under the present system for any length of time. The present system, by relieving the teachers in the junior schools of grades 7 and 8, allows more time for extra instruction.

Conclusions

1. *As a group,* and age for age, the Indian children of the Caradoc Reserve have a significantly lower scholastic aptitude than a comparable group of white children and they cannot therefore be expected to equal the scholastic achievements of the white group at the present time.

2. Their abilities do, however, cover much the same range and the more capable Indian children are superior to the majority of white children.

3. The differences in scholastic aptitude between the groups of Indian and white children are not attributable to race but rather to environmental differences. Some of the environmental factors which may be pertinent are language, socio-economic sta-

tus, traditional attitudes, and other cultural characteristics.

References

1. JAMIESON, E. The Mental Capacity of Southern Ontario Indians. (Unpublished D.Paed. Thesis, University of Toronto, 1938).
2. JOBLIN, E. E. M. *The Education of the Indians of Western Ontario.* (Toronto: Department of Educational Research, University of Toronto, Bulletin No. 13, 1947).
3. KLINEBERG, O. Race Differences: The Present Position of the Problem. *International Social Science Bulletin, 4,* 465, 1950.
4. WECHSLER, D. *Manual for the Wechsler Intelligence Scale for Children.* New York: The Psychological Corporation, 1949.

36 / Psychometric Intelligence and Spatial Imagery in Two Northwest Indian and Two White Groups of Children[1]

W.H. Gaddes, Audrey McKenzie, and Roger Barnsley *University of Victoria*

This investigation is concerned with spatial abilities of the Saanich and Kwakiutl Indian children of British Columbia. Because the art work of these tribes exhibits highly sophisticated spatial design, it was hypothesized that the spatial abilities of these Indian children might be superior to that of white children. The results do not support this view.

Introduction

Any hypothesis proposing cross-cultural aptitudes implies a theory of innate abilities or culturally determined behaviour, or both. Most current research evidence supports the idea that both native and learned aspects of perception are present, but their relationship is extremely complex and not completely clear (20). Both innate factors (8, 10) and learned factors (4, 13, 17) are involved.

The present study, which compares the visual-spatial abilities of North American Northwest Indian children and white children, attempts to probe this relationship. In doing this the question was raised by Dr. S. D. Porteus as to whether the cultural art forms familiar to the Coast Indians might not give them an advantage in performance on mazes and other spatial tests. In the planning and executing of these forms, it seemed evident that spatial relationships are involved in the art work of the Northwest Indians, and also, though to a lesser degree, in maze threading.

While it seems likely that the cultural art of the Northwest Indians may in individual cases influence success in maze performance, this would likely affect only those who were themselves artists. Nevertheless, Indian Ss would be familiar with such standards of execution. How much this would affect the comparative test levels of white children it is impossible to determine. However, the situation calls for a brief reference to Indian art.

According to anthropologists, the Northwest Coast Indians had already developed a highly sophisticated art style by the time of the first visits by European explorers (6, p. 7). Captain James Cook collected many pieces of Nootka *objets d'art* in a visit he made to Vancouver Island in 1778, several of which are in the British Museum (see Inverarity (11, Plates 85 and 102)). Other pieces were collected by Captain George Dixon in 1787 and these, which included the first Haida pieces to be seen by Europeans, are also in the British Museum (9, pp. 3-4). Their carvings show that the Northwest Coast Indians by the eighteenth century had already reached a superior knowledge of design and a fine ability in the graphic and plastic arts, and that their culture was already established. While anthropological study has indicated a European influence on the native art of this region (6, p. 40) and an eventual deterioration of their culture, one can assume that basic aptitudes underlying their artistic imagery may still be evident in their descendants. Although relatively few of the current generation of Indians of this area are continuing an active interest in producing their cultural art forms, those with that interest seem to provide assurance that the native aptitude and excellence of skill still persist (1, 9).

In the present study, Saanich Indian children of the Coast Salish group living on southern Vancouver Island, and a group of Kwakiutl children living in an isolated community on the British Columbia coast near the northern tip of Vancouver Island, were

---

[1] This research was supported by a University of Victoria Faculty Research Grant.

Thanks are due to the following persons for helping to make this study possible: Mr. J. F. Boys, Commissioner of Indian Affairs, Vancouver; Mr. Ray Hall, Department of Indian Affairs, Vancouver; Mr. E. V. Janzen, District Superintendent of Indian Schools, Nanaimo; Mr. A. D. Jones, District Superintendent, School District No. 65, Cowichan; and the teachers of all the schools where the tests were carried out.

Dr. Stanley D. Porteus, Professor Emeritus of the University of Hawaii, has been a constant help. The authors are indebted to him for the original proposal of this study, for his editorial criticisms, and for supplying the mazes used in the study.

Drs. Barbara and Robert Lane, Department of Anthropology and Sociology, University of Victoria, have been unusually helpful in planning the field work and reading critically the whole text.

Dr. Richard M. May, Department of Psychology, University of Victoria, and Dr. and Mrs. G. A. Forsyth, Department of Psychology, University of New Hampshire, have made valuable suggestions about the research design and the implications of perceptual styles in a study of this type.

---

studied.[2] The Kwakiutl, while described by some as a tribe (9, p. 2), differed from the Salish in possessing a culture more markedly ceremonial. The art of the Salish, too, is less exact in terms of draftsmanship, but it is equally concerned with spatial design. Holm (9, p. 20) groups the two-dimensional graphic art styles of the Haida, Bella Bella, Tsimchian, and Tlingit, and states that it is "impossible to differentiate with certainty, on the basis of style alone, two-dimensional design of these four northern tribes.... It cannot be doubted that there are tribal variations, but on the basis of present knowledge they are not apparent." He also compares the Kwakiutl, Nootka, and Salish, pointing out some similarities of "fresh naturalism" (9, p. 20) between them and Eskimo paintings and the work of the Tlingit tribe further north. While recognizing different art styles of the Kwakiutl and Salish, a study of Salish two- and three-dimensional designs (6, p. 74; 11, Plates 60, 61, 62, 240, 241 and 242; 18, p. 198) reveals a serious concern with and competent handling of spacing, grouping, and balance, basically similar to Kwakiutl art forms. While it would have been desirable to have had two Indian groups from similar cultures, the spatial designs of both of these groups appear similar enough to infer that the spatial aptitudes of children of these two groups are reasonably equated for study purposes.

To attempt to compare the perception of different cultural groups, it is necessary to use test instruments as free as possible from cultural influences. It has been proposed By Kidd and Rivoire (12) that certain simple, definite, and basic spatial designs are culture-free. They claim that such forms "tend to be little influenced by idiosyncratic patterns of culture-specific norms and values" (12, p. 109). All tests used in this study, except the Goodenough Draw-A-Man Test, agreed with this criterion. It was introduced as a different type of test, possibly culture-free to provide a measure of intelligence.

Method

Subjects

The subjects were 124 elementary school children, 69 males and 55 females, ranging in ages from 6 years 2 months to 14 years 1 month, and enrolled in grades I to VII. The study was based on four groups. Group 1 consisted of 33 white children ($\bar{X}$ age = 9-9) from a rural, below average socioeconomic region. Group 2 was made up of 35 white children ($\bar{X}$ age = 9-1) from an urban, below average socioeconomic area. Group 3 included 30 Indian children ($\bar{X}$ age = 10-0) of a Vancouver Island Salish band residing close to urban development. Group 4 consisted of 26 Indian children ($\bar{X}$ age = 9.7) of the Kwakiutl tribe, living in an isolated community on the west coast of British Columbia. Thus, in group 4, there may have been a minimum of direct white culture influence. The Ss in groups 1, 2, and 3 were randomly selected from the 6, 9, and 12-year-old age populations from within their respective schools. The Ss in group 4 comprised the total enrollment of the school in their small isolated community.

Design

The dependent variables were the Wechsler Intelligence Scale for Children scale score on the Block Design Subtest (19), intelligence quotient as indicated by the Cattell Culture Fair short form (2, 3), intelligence quotient as measured by the Goodenough Draw-A-Man task (5), and the Porteus Maze Test quotient (16). The independent variable in the investigation included two racial groups, Northwest Indian and Canadian white children.

A simple, one-factor analysis of variance was carried out on all four dependent variables. Four analyses of covariance were performed using the Block Design scale score and Porteus Maze Test quotient as criterion variables. The Draw-A-Man and Culture Fair intelligence quotients were covariates for both criterion variables. The level of significance adopted for the rejection of the null hypotheses of no difference was the .05 level of significance.

Procedure

The Block Design Test, Porteus Maze Test, Goodenough Draw-A-Man Test, and the Classification subtest of the Cattell Culture Fair Test, Scale One, were individually administered to all *S*s by three *E*s. Individual testing was carried out in small rooms adjacent to the classrooms. All test rooms were relatively free from noise and disturbances. The Cattell Culture Fair Test, Scale Two, and the remaining sections of the Cattell Culture Fair Test, Scale One, were group-administered to *S*s in their classrooms. All tests were administered and scored according to standardized procedures.

Results

Analyses of variance performed on the data yielded significant *F* values for the Cattell Culture Fair intelligence quotients ($F = 6.84$, $df = 3/120$, $p < .01$), Porteus Maze Test quotients ($F = 3.02$, $df = 3/120$, $p < .05$), and WISC Block Design Scale scores ($F = 2.78$, $df = 3/120$, $p < .05$). No differences were found between the groups on the Goodenough Draw-A-Man intelligence quotients ($F = 0.64$, $df = 3/120$, n.s.).

Comparison of group means by the Scheffe procedure yielded no significant results for the scores of either the WISC Block Design Scale scores or the Porteus Maze Test quotient. However, on the Cattell Culture Fair intelligence quotients, differences were

[2]All tests were administered by Mrs. Audrey McKenzie, Mrs. Vicki Barnsley, and Mr. Roger Barnsley. Only Mr. and Mrs. Barnsley flew to the isolated Indian community as there was overnight accommodation for only two persons.

observed between rural white and semi-acculturated Indian children ($F = 10.45$, $df = 1/120$, $p < .05$), rural white and isolated Indian children ($F = 13.00$, $df = 1/120$, $p < .01$), and urban white and isolated Indian children ($F = 10.29$, $df = 1/120$, $p < .05$). The comparison between urban white and semi-acculturated Indians was not significant at the .05 level ($F = 7.92$, $df = 1/120$, $p < .10$).

Four analyses of covariance which were performed yielded nonsignificant results, hence no *post hoc* comparisons were made on the adjusted group means.

The means of the four groups on all of the tests, and also the means of the Block Design Scale scores and Porteus Maze Test quotients adjusted by covariance, may be found in Table I.

Table I – Group means and means adjusted by covariance for all measures

Group	N	Cattell Culture Fair	Goodenough Draw-A-Man	Block Design Scale score	Block Design Adj. by Draw-A-Man	Block Design Adj. by Culture Fair	Porteus Maze Test Test quotient	Porteus Maze Test Adj. by Draw-A-Man	Porteus Maze Test Adj. by Culture Fair
1	33	98.3	102.4	10.4	10.3	9.8	124.0	123.7	122.4
2	35	95.7	103.7	9.7	9.5	9.3	126.0	125.2	124.9
3	30	80.2	100.2	9.3	9.4	9.8	118.2	118.7	119.6
4	26	77.3	99.1	8.4	8.7	9.1	115.1	116.0	117.0

Note: Group 1=Rural white children, Group 2=Urban white children, Group 3=Semiacculturated Indian children, and Group 4=Isolated Indian children.

Discussion

Four groups of children, rural white, urban white, semi-acculturated Indians, and isolated Indians, were tested on four tests designed to be culture-free. In all but the isolated Indian group, age subgroups were 6, 9, and 12 years. In the isolated group, Group 4, all 26 children in the rural school, regardless of age, were tested.

Analyses of covariance were made with the Porteus Maze Test and the Goodenough and Cattell Tests as covariates, and with the WISC Blocks subtest and the same two tests as covariates. None of these measures showed any significant differences and hence provided no statistical support to the hypothesis that North American Indian children possess better spatial imagery as measured by the WISC Block Design Test and the Porteus Maze Test.

As it is difficult to ascertain the validity of the intelligence measures (i.e., Cattell Culture Fair and Goodenough Draw-A-Man) for the Indian children, it cannot be known just how much of the effects of intelligence were covaried out of the criterion variables. Indeed, the overall significance noted in the Cattell Culture Fair Test suggests several possibilities: (a) if we can accept the results as they stand, the conclusion might be drawn that this test is not culture-free and hence is invalid for this study, or (b) the test may be valid and the reported between-group differences may be due to sampling errors, or (c) the test may be a valid instrument for distinguishing between the groups on the basis of their unique perceptual habits or styles, and this may be partially unrelated to their intelligence. This latter possibility has some interesting implications. A scrutiny of the art of the Northwest Indians reveals an emphasis on facial features, whether animal, human, or mythical. The Cattell Test does not show this emphasis; hence the Indian children may have lost points on the Cattell and gained on the Goodenough Test regardless of either intelligence or spatial imagery. This may account for the closer clustering of the group measures on the Goodenough Test. In other words, the particular perceptual habits of the groups may be masking the attempted measure of relative spatial imagery. Harris (7, p. 133), in reporting the usefulness of the Goodenough Test in testing Eskimo children, has advised against cross-cultural comparisons because of the varieties of conceptual experiences and training of children in different cultures.

The weaknesses of cross-cultural comparisons using culture-bound criteria have been attacked by anthropologists at a descriptive level for some time (15). Lane (14) has described the contradiction of values of Indian children attending Canadian schools. It seems certain that these sociological imbalances interfere with the test performances of Indian children on tests designed for American children. Even so, the Indian children in our samples did reasonably well on the Cattell Test when we consider the impact of sociological stresses. If we could obtain tests completely culture-free, which would provide really valid measures of intelligence of Indian children, it seems likely that Porteus' original suggestion regarding spatial superiority might have been confirmed.

Subjective impressions of the testers support this last possibility and the belief that neither the Cattell, the Porteus, nor the Wechsler Blocks Tests are culture-free. Several white children in both urban and rural groups, even though of low socioeconomic grouping, remarked that they had had puzzle books with problems similar to the Cattell and the Porteus Mazes. They also reported having owned block sets with which to compose mosaic designs. The teachers of the Indian children reported that none of them owned either puzzle books or blocks. The equally competent performance by the Indian children suggests a possibly mildly superior spatial ability when compared with white children.

Summary

A total of 68 white children and 56 Indian children between the ages of 6 and 14 years were tested on four tests which were largely culture-free. Analyses of covariance showed no superiority nor inferiority of spatial imagery of the Indian children when compared with white children matched broadly for age, sex, intelligence, and socioeconomic status. Sociological theories suggest that genuinely culture-free intelligence tests might have revealed a slight spatial superiority on the part of the Indian children.

References

1. BOAS, F. *Primitive Art*. Cambridge, Mass.: Harvard Univ. Press, 1927.
2. CATTELL, R. B. A culture-free intelligence test, I, *J. Educ. Psychol.*, 1940, *31*, 161-179.
3. CATTELL, R. B., and CATTELL, A. K. S. *Handbook for the Individual or Group, Culture Fair Intelligence Test, Scales 1 and 2*. Champaign, Ill.: Inst. Personal. & Ability Testing, 1960, 1962.
4. GIBSON, J. J. *The Perception of the Visual World*. New York: Houghton, 1950.
5. GOODENOUGH, F. L. Measurement of Intelligence by Drawings. Yonkers-on-Hudson: World Book Co., 1926.
6. GUNTHER, E. Northwest Coast Indian Art, An Exhibit at the Seattle World's Fair Fine Arts Pavilion, April 21-October 21, 1962. Seattle, Wash.: Washington State Museum, Univ. Washington.
7. HARRIS, D. B. *Children's Drawings as Measures of Intellectual Maturity*. New York: Harcourt, Brace & World, 1963.
8. HEBB, D. O. *The Organization of Behaviour*. New York: Wiley, 1949.
9. HOLM, B. *Northwest Coast Indian Art, An Analysis of Form*. Seattle, Wash.: Univ. Washington Press, 1965.
10. HUBEL, D. H., and WIESEL, T. N. Receptive fields, binoculars interaction and functional architecture in the cat's visual cortex. *J. Physiol.*, 1962, *160*, 106-154.
11. INVERARITY, R. B. *Art of the Northwest Coast Indians*. Berkeley, Calif.: Univ. California Press, 1950.
12. KIDD, A. H., and RIVOIRE, J. L. The culture-fair aspects of the development of spatial perception. *J. Genet. Psychol.*, 1965, *106*, 101-111.
13. KOHLER, I. Experiments with goggles. *Sci. Amer.*, 1962 (May), *206*, 61-72.
14. LANE, B. The education of Indian children. *The B.C. School Trustee*, 1965, *21*, 7-10.
15. LEVI-STRAUSS, C. *The Savage Mind*, Chicago, Ill.: Univ. Chicago Press, 1962.
16. PORTEUS, S. D. *The Maze Test and Clinical Psychology*. Palo Alto, Calif.: Pacific Books, 1959.
17. STRATTON, G. M. Vision without inversion of the retinal image. *Psychol. Rev.*, 1897, *4*, 341-360.
18. UNDERHILL, R. *Indians of the Pacific Northwest*. Washington, D.C.: Educ. Div. U.S. Office Indian Affairs, 1944.
19. WECHSLER, D. *Wechsler Intelligence Scale for Children*. New York: Psychol. Corp., 1949.
20. WEINTRAUB, D. J., and WALKER, E. L. *Perception*. Belmont, Calif.: Brooks Cole, 1966.

EIGHT
PERSONALITY AND ADJUSTMENT

37 / The Case Study: Its Place in Personality Research

Dalbir Bindra *McGill University*

Successful investigations of personality begin with a careful observation of behaviour in its natural setting. The case study has proved to be particularly valuable in suggesting various avenues of research.

Professor Bindra is the author of Motivation: A Systematic Reinterpretation, ***1959 and co-editor, with Jane Stewart, of*** Motivation, ***1966.***

For better or for worse, the term personality research or personality study has come to denote at least two areas of psychological research. First, the term is used to refer to any study which describes and interprets the behaviour of a particular individual, John Doe, chimp Alpha, or dog Jack. In reports of this type the author attempts to describe the unique configuration of psychological factors (variables) in terms of which the behaviour of his particular subject can be understood. The second denotation of personality study refers to the investigation and general study of the variables along which characteristically human behaviour can be meaningfully described and studied. In studies of this kind certain specified variables, such as self-esteem involvement (2), "need" (3), and emotionality(5), are isolated experimentally or statistically and effects of their variations on behaviour are described. Such investigations of *variables* of human behaviour are quite different in nature from the detailed studies of particular *individuals* which are likewise implied by the term personality study.

This ambiguity is partly to blame for the lack of an explicit statement or a close examination of the relation between these two areas of research. In the present paper the term "personality study" is used to refer only to the general study of variables determining behaviour that is characteristic of and more or less peculiar to man; intensive studies of particular individuals are consistently referred to here as "case studies."

Overcoming the ambiguity in this way, the present paper discusses the place of case studies in personality research. More specifically, these pages contain an examination of the following proposition: Case studies are essentially naturalistic observations, and as such their contribution to personality research lies only in that they may generate accurate descriptions, and suggest new variables, problems, and hypotheses, all of which can be utilized in planning and conducting controlled investigations aimed at finding relations among the variables of behaviour. It might be well to begin the discussion with some remarks on the role of the naturalistic method in psychological research generally.

Reprinted, by permission, from *Canadian Journal of Psychology*, 1952, *6*, 11-17.

Naturalistic Method in Psychology

MacLeod (4), using the word "phenomenological" instead of "naturalistic," has defined this method as an "attempt to view phenomena in their entirety and without prejudice, to distinguish the essential from the nonessential, to let the phenomena themselves dictate the conceptual frameword and further course of the inquiry" (4, p. 210). This naturalistic method can be contrasted with methods that utilize some form of control. While naturalistic studies are aimed at description of phemonema and *delineation* of significant variables, the controlled investigations are concerned with *isolation* and *manipulation* of variables, and description of relations among those variables.

Whereas a collection of naturalistic observations by itself is admittedly of no scientific value, we must not overlook the important use to which such observations may be put when they are made within the framework of controlled investigations. Take, for example, a psychologist engaged in a simple experimental study. Before he decides to vary a particular factor and to observe some specified (dependent) variables, he already has some assurance that these variables are significant enough to work with. This assurance comes sometimes from a belief in the importance of certain systematic theories, and at other times from uncontrolled, but nevertheless unbiased and systematic, naturalistic observations of the type MacLeod recommends. The investigator must also have fairly reliable knowledge about many factors with which he is not directly concerned in his experiment. For instance, in an experiment on the effect of the palatability of the food incentive on maze learning in the white rat, the experimenter needs to know the life span of the white rat, its eating habits, its preference for various foods, its reactions to new situations, and so on. Such "extra" or backgound knowledge, a necessary prerequisite for controlled studies, is usually provided by naturalistic observations. When, at last, the experimenter faces the task of interpreting his results he often finds that he is unable to account fully for the results in terms of his independent variable alone, and that he has to give consideration to *other* variables, the significance of which was made apparent to him by "incidental" naturalistic observations during the course of collecting data. Not infrequently the investigator proceeds to another investigation based on a hypothesis or "lead" suggested by such observations.

It is evident that the background knowledge and "leads" gained from more or less systematic naturalistic observations may make an important contribution at all stages of research. But we must remember that these naturalistic observations are useful only to the extent that they are incorporated in statistically or experimentally controlled investigations of variables.

Case Study and Personality Research

Bearing in mind the general significance of naturalistic observations, we can proceed to discuss the place of case studies in psychological research. I wish to make two points: (1) Case studies are naturalistic in nature, and like other naturalistic explorations can be useful in psychological research. (2) In personality research, where the psychologist is dealing with complex forms of behaviour, and often with variables that cannot be readily manipulated, case studies may become especially useful and, at times, even indispensable. The first of these two points can be disposed of easily.

1. *The nature of case studies*. Even though psychologists, like other scientists, are (or should be) concerned with the study of general variables, it is the individual subjects from whom psychological data must necessarily be obtained. The difference between case studies and (psychological) investigations of variables, then, lies not in the peculiarity of the source of data, but in the way the data are treated. In general psychological investigations, certain specified and limited observations are made, and the observations made on any one individual are combined with *similar* observations on the same subject, or on others, in order to arrive at a general relation between the variables under investigation. In a case study, on the other hand, observations made on any one individual are combined with a *variety* of other observations on the same person in order to understand his characteristic behaviour. This goal is achieved by naturalistic observations. The clinical or research psychologist interested in the study of an individual observes his client or subject in a variety of standardized and "life" situations. An attempt is made to let the observations suggest the important features and variables of the subject's behaviour.

Unless one considers the understanding of the behaviour of *an* individual a scientific ideal, it is not possible to attribute any scientific value to a case study in and of itself. A case study is valuable to psychology only when it is compared with many other case studies, and statistical methods (for example, multiple correlation) are employed to uncover the relations among significant variables of behaviour.

2. *Case studies and personality research*. Personality research is concerned with the study of the variables that are significant in determining behaviour which more or less characterizes man. In undertaking research in this area psychologists have often found case studies to be extremely useful, and occasionally indispensable. An important question arises: Why have case studies been found more useful in personality research than in other types of psychological investigations? While "personality psychologists" (for example, 6) have made extensive use of case studies in their work, they have not explicitly stated the reasons why they do so. To answer this question a little digression is necessary.

There are many degrees of "completeness" with which an individual can be studied: on the one extreme, we can observe one or two characteristics (skin colour, submissiveness, education, etc.) of an individual, and on the other extreme we have the time-consuming and detailed observations of an individual that are usually implied by the term case study. In a controlled investigation it is always necessary to observe *some* characteristics of each individual subject (for example, age, sex) in addition to the responses (dependent variables) in which the investigator is primarily interested. The important question is how many of these "extra" observations have to be made on each individual subject. I shall illustrate my point.

In an experiment on dogs the investigator might notice that the strain of dogs is somehow related to the dependent variable. If the experimenter is not interested in strain as such, he will correct for this factor by separating in his experiment, or in his statistics, dogs of different strains. This he can do easily, either by observing some external characterisitcs known to be associated with different strains, or by finding out the genealogy of each dog from the laboratory records. If instead of strain, the investigator noticed that "shyness" or emotionality of the dogs is a significant uncontrolled variable, he will have to engage in a more time-consuming study of the individual dogs in order to determine and correct for differences in emotionality. Finally, if the experimenter suspects that some of his results are the function of uncontrolled past experiences or specific learning, he will have to undertake an even more thorough study of each dog before he is able to control that factor. Thus the study of the individual has a specific role in controlling extraneous factors. The degree of detail to which each subject has to be studied depends on the nature of the uncontrolled extraneous factors. Controlling, and correcting for, learning factors involves a more thorough study of each subject than does controlling of externally obvious or easily recognizable factors such as strain or emotionality.

Let us now return to the question asked two paragraphs above: Why should case studies be any more useful in personality research than in other types of psychological investigations? There seem to be two reasons which may make it desirable or even necessary to conduct fairly detailed observations on each subject (perhaps detailed enough to be called case studies) as a preliminary to controlled investigations of the variables determining characteristically human behaviour.

First, it is generally accepted that as we go higher up in the scale of evolution, learning factors become progressively more important in determining behaviour. And we have already seen that controlling and correcting for differences in past learning entails a more intensive study of each individual subject. It follows that as we go from rat to man, observations on each individual subject will have to become progressively more detailed. Of course, if one is investigating visual acuity, or some such function in which differential-learning factors are of minimal importance, or are easily controlled or corrected for, it is possible to proceed with the investigation without an intensive study of each individual. But if the investigator is studying behaviour which involves complex motivational variables, for example, self-esteem, projection, and so on, he will have to undertake a comprehensive study of each subject's habitual behaviour before he is able to proceed with any controlled study, or else he will have to work with a prohibitively large sample of subjects in the hope of "cancelling out" the effects of numerous uncontrolled factors.

The second reason is as follows: In animal studies, after an uncontrolled factor has been identified by the investigator, it is usually possible to manipulate that factor in subsequent investigations by, for example, selecting animals of a particular strain, by raising all animals in similar environments, giving them the same pre-experimental training, and so on. In the case of studies utilizing human subjects, on the other hand, such developmental controls are rarely possible, so that the investigator has to *correct for* uncontrolled factors by studying each subject with respect to each uncontrolled variable and then applying some form of statistical control. If these uncontrolled variables happen to be complex motivational ones, as is usually the case in studies of human behaviour, the investigator may be forced to undertake a fairly detailed case study of each subject. Alper's study (2) is a case in point.

Alper set out to investigate the effect of self-esteem involvement on selective recall of completed and incompleted tasks. She studied this variable experimentally by making the subjects recall under two conditions, one designed to threaten self-esteem, and the other designed not to do so. To obtain the relation between selective recall and self-esteem involvement, Alper had to take into account the fact that subjects were varyingly susceptible to self-esteem involvement. She could correct for this factor only if she knew something about the susceptibility of *each subject* to self-esteem involvement. A meaningful index of this susceptibility of "pride" is not easy to obtain without undertaking a fairly detailed study of the individual. Fortunately, Alper was able to get pride ratings on her subjects from her colleagues at the Harvard Psychological Clinic who were engaged in personality studies of these subjects at the time. These judgements of pride were based on systematic observations of the subjects over a long period of time by a large number of psychologists. With these case studies serving to correct for differences in pride, Alper was aided in achieving her goal of describing the relation between self-esteem involvement and selective recall.

The fact that case studies may have a fairly specific role to play in the study of characteristically human behaviour should not be taken to mean that case studies by themselves necessarily have any value for personality research. Rather these studies become scientifically valuable only when the information contained therein is utilized in the study of significant variables. In and of itself, a case study is nothing more than a story.

Summary and Conclusion

The aims of case study and personality research are not the same. A case study is primarily concerned with an *individual,* while personality research seeks to discover relations among *variables* significant in determining characteristically human behaviour.

Case studies are of scientific value only in so far as they may suggest significant variables for consideration in experimentally or statistically controlled investigations. In this respect case studies are similar to naturalistic observations that provide the groundwork for *any* controlled investigation. Even in an investigation on rats the psychologist is likely to study each individual animal at least to the extent of observing its strain, timidity, "sophistication," etc. These observations on each rat may not be extensive or detailed enough to be called case study, but in principle their significance is no more, or less, than that of detailed case studies in personality research. In both cases observations on individual subjects are utilized in isolating and controlling significant variables, and studying the relations among them.

Perhaps the contribution of personalistic psychologists (for example, Allport, 1) lies in that they explicitly pointed out the importance of making fairly extensive observations on each subject (case study) in the study of variables determining characteristically human behaviour (personality research) – a point that has always been well-recognized, and acted upon, in animal research. But in attempting to make the case study an end in itself, and by defining personality study as the study of the individual rather than of variables, personalistic psychologists overstated their case.

References

1. ALLPORT, G. W. *Personality, A Psychological Interpretation*. New York: Henry Holt, 1937.
2. ALPER, T. G. Memory for Completed and Incompleted Tasks as a Function of Personality: An Analysis of Group Data. *Journal of Abnormal Social Psychology*, 1946, *41*, 403-20.
3. MACKINNON, D. W., and HENLE, M. *Experimental Studies in Psychodynamics*. Cambridge, Mass.: Harvard University Press, 1948.
4. MACLEOD, R. B. The Phenomenological Approach to Social Psychology. *Psychological Review*, 1947, *54*, 193-210.
5. MCGINNIES, E. Emotionality and Perceptual Defense. *Psychological Review*, 1949, *56*, 244-51.
6. MURRAY, H. A., and collaborators. *Explorations in Personality*. New York: Oxford University Press, 1938.

38 / Sex Differences in Field Dependence for the Eskimo

Russell MacArthur *University of Alberta*

One of the major difficulties faced by students of personality is the complexity of human behaviour. The English language contains nearly 18,000 words which describe personality characteristics and, obviously, a satisfactory science cannot be based on so many constructs. In order to simplify their task, psychologists have postulated dimensions of personality (such as introversion-extraversion) along which individuals are assumed to vary.

One dimension which has received a good deal of attention in recent years is that of field dependence-independence. It is argued that certain individuals are characterized by analytic perceptual-cognitive styles and thus capable of efficiently using relevant information. Others are said to be global in their approach and highly susceptible to interfering field effects. Thus, for example, in a problem-solving situation a field-independent individual would be less affected by irrelevant (hence incorrect) cues for the solution of a problem whereas the field-dependent person would be less capable of overcoming the field of irrelevant cues and therefore would encounter more difficulty in solving the problem.

Many indices of field dependence have been developed but the most widely used is an Embedded Figures Test which consists of items similar to the example shown below. The task is to locate the simple figure in the complex one on the left. Its correct location is sketched in on the right. One prevalent finding has been that women tend to be more field dependent than men. In this study Professor MacArthur sought to determine whether this sex difference occurs in a Canadian Eskimo sample.

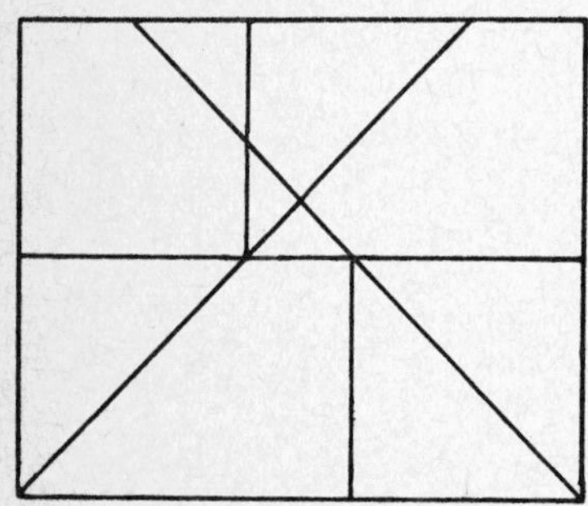

Complicated figure

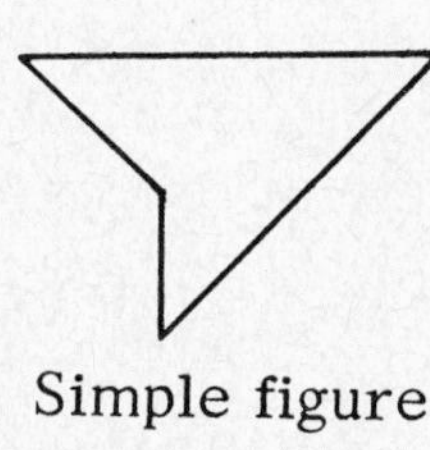

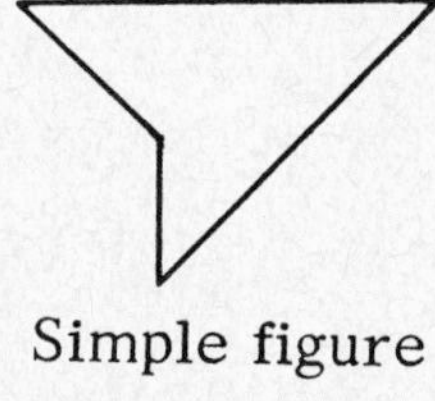

Simple figure

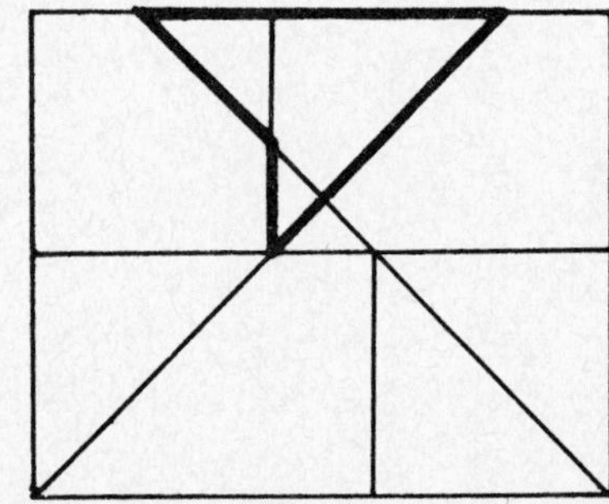

Simple figure sketched in

Witkin (1966) reported clear-cut and pervasive sex differences in field-dependence in numerous studies in the United States, England, Holland, France, Italy, Israel, Hong Kong, and Sierra Leone, women tending consistently to be more field-dependent than men. With such pervasiveness he found it tempting to think of these sex differences as dictated by biological factors, but he also considered that the cause may lie in the encouragement of a more dependent role for women in many cultures.

Berry (1966) found similar sex differences in his Temne and Scottish samples, but for his samples of Eastern Eskimo from Baffin Island there were no significant differences between male and female scores in field-dependence. Berry saw this as consistent with the fact that "Eskimo women and children are in no way treated as dependent in the society; very loose controls are exercised over wives and chil-

Reprinted from the *International Journal of Psychology – Journal International de Psychologie,* 1967, *2,* 139-140, by permission of the IUPS and DUNOD, Publisher, Paris.

dren." An embedded figures test has been one of the main measures of field-dependence used.

In connection with other studies, we administered Vernon's Embedded Figures Test to two samples of Western Eskimo pupils at Inuvik and Tuktoyaktuk, about 1,800 miles from Berry's Frobisher Bay samples. Near-zero point-biserial correlations between sex and Embedded Figures were found, as shown in Table I.

While reliability checks on Embedded Figures were not made for these samples, the correlations between this test and Raven's Standard Progressive Matrices were .70 and .63 for the respective samples, suggesting reasonable reliabilities. This replication of Berry's findings for the Eskimo adds evidence suggesting that observed sex differences in field-dependence in other cultures may be shaped largely by social or other environmental influences.

Table I – Correlations of sex and embedded figures[1]

	Age	Boys N	Girls N	Point-biserial r with sex	
				Prog. Mat.	Emb. Fig.
Sample 1	9 – 12 yrs.	60	27	.18	–.01
Sample 2	12 ½ – 15 ½ yrs	38	42	–.08	.05

[1] High scores are male and field-independent

Résumé

Bien que dans de nombreuses cultures, des différences selon le sexe aient été trouvées dans la dépendance vis-à-vis du champ, Berry n'en trouve aucune chez des Esquimaux de l'Est. Une réplique de son étude sur des Esquimaux de l'Ouest confirme l'hypothèse que ces différences, telles qu'on les observe dans d'autres cultures, peuvent être dues largement à l'influence de l'environement.

References

BERRY, J. W. Temne and Eskimo perceptual skills. *International Journal of Psychology,* 1966, *1,* 207-229.

WITKIN, H. A. Cultural influences in the development of cognitive style. In *Cross-cultural studies in mental development.* Symposium 36. XVIIIth International Congress of Psychology, Moscow, 1966. Pp. 95-109.

39 / Salivation as a Physiological Indicator of Introversion

Edgar Howarth and Nicholas F. Skinner *University of Alberta*

The most widely used method of measuring personality is by means of an inventory in which a person answers true or false to a direct question, such as, "I am a happy-go-lucky individual." The difficulty with this method is that the person might deliberately give false answers to convey an impression of good or, in some cases, poor adjustment. The search for a device which is not subject to deliberate falsification continues and it has been speculated that direct physiological measures might be useful indicators of personality styles. The following experiment explores the relationship between salivation in response to lemon juice and introversion as measured by a questionnaire.

Introduction

Several studies recently carried out in England have supported the hypothesis (3, 4, 5) that the characteristically greater effector output of introverts is a manifestation of a state of higher cortical facilitation. Corcoran (1) found the salivary output of introverts to be significantly greater than that of extroverts in response to stimulation of the tongue with four drops of pure lemon juice; no significant relationship was produced by citric acid, even though this stimulant effectively promoted salivation. Eysenck and Eysenck (4, 5) found high negative correlations between extraversion and salivation in response to the introduction of lemon juice onto the tongue. The correlation was not significant when a commercial substitute ("Jif") was used in place of lemon juice (5); in addition, there was no correlation of salivation with neuroticism. A tentative interpretation of a reversal of effect produced by having *S*s swallow pure lemon juice (4) was proposed in terms of the earlier appearance of Pavlov's transmarginal inhibition in individuals (introverts) with "weak nervous systems."

These results suggest the possibility of a purely physiological measure of personality. In view of the potential utility of such a measure – for example, in neutralizing the inherent fakeability of most current personality inventories and the high degree of "psychological test sophistication" of North Americans (especially students) – the present study constituted an attempt to extend its absolute and cross-cultural generality.

Method

Subjects

Fifteen introverts and 10 extraverts from an Introductory Psychology class were chosen on the basis of their scores on the Eysenck Personality Inventory (2), as summarized in Table I. Scores ranged from 4 to 8 for the introverts and 17 to 20 for the extraverts, while no significant differences in neuroticism were evident; *E* was unaware of the scores achieved until the completion of the study.

Table I – Extraversion (E) and neuroticism (N) scores on the Eysenck personality inventory (E.P.I.)

Subjects		Mean	SD
Introverts (N=15)	E	6.20	1.02
	N	10.20	4.31
Extraverts (N=10)	E	18.30	.90
	N	9.70	3.71

Procedure

Following an experimental technique devised by Corcoran (1) and modified by Eysenck and Eysenck (3) *S* was instructed to incline his chin a few degrees above the horizontal, open his mouth, and curl up the tip of his tongue slightly so that a small well or pocket was formed on its upper surface. A standard cotton wool dental swab, weighed (in thousandths of a gram) on a Mettler electric balance[1] just prior to testing (Weight 1), was then positioned by means of a pair of tweezers on the sublingual salivary gland of *S*. Immediately following this four drops of fresh, pure lemon juice from a medicine dropper were placed in the well of the tongue; after 20 seconds the swab was removed and immediately reweighed (Weight 2). Since Eysenck and Eysenck (4) had shown that it was unnecessary to establish the salivation rate without any stimulation, the difference

Reprinted, by persmission, from *Journal of Psychology*, 1969, *73*, 123-228. Copyright by The Journal Press.

[1]The cooperation of Dr. W. A. Ayer, Department of Chemistry, University of Alberta, for the loan of a Mettler electric balance, and Dr. R. Stuart for a supply of dental swabs, is gratefully acknowledged.

Weight 2-Weight 1 represented the amount of salivation in response to stimulation by the lemon juice.

Results

The data were straightforward and may be summarized as follows:

1. On the average, introverts salivated .133 gm (SD = .070), extraverts salivated .090 gm (SD = .051); the difference between means (.043 gm) was significant (t = 1.732, df = 23, $p < .05$, one-tailed test) and in the same direction as earlier studies.

2. The difference in mean amount of salivation (.009 gm) between men (N = 10) and women (N = 15) was not significant.

3. The difference between introverts and extraverts in terms of the distributions of individual amounts of salivation about the median salivation level (.091 gm) was significant ($\chi^2 = 4.20$, df = 1, $p < .05$), as shown in Table II.

Table II – Distribution of Ss about median level of salivation

Subjects	Introverts	Extraverts
Above median level of salivation (.091 gm)	9	2
Below median level of salivation (.091 gm)	6	8

4. The product-moment correlations between salivation, extraversion, and neuroticism are given in Table III. Correlations were calculated on (a) the full data matrix, and (b) a reduced data matrix which used only those *S*s having less than the mean neuroticism (N) score (i.e., N = 11); the full matrix contained 25 *S*s, the reduced matrix contained 19 *S*s. None of the correlations of salivation with neuroticism, or extraversion with neuroticism, reached significance, while the correlations between salivation and extraversion were significant at $p < .05$ (full data matrix) and $p < .01$ (reduced data matrix) levels respectively.

Discussion

In the sense that the data show (a) introverted *S*s to have a greater salivary response than extraverted *S*s to stimulation of the tongue with pure lemon juice, and (b) this difference to be unrelated to neuroticism or sex, they substantiate previous research. However, while the average amounts of salivation reported by Corcoran (1) and Eysenck and Eysenck (5) were approximately .700 gm and .450 gm respectively, mean salivation recorded in the present experiment was only .115 gm. If this fact is taken together with the markedly lower correlations between salivation and extraversion found in the present study as compared with previous studies – as summarized in Table IV – earlier work is thus seen to be supported in direction but not in degree.

Table III – Product-moment correlations between salivation, extraversion, and neuroticism

Variables	Full data matrix	Reduced data matrix
Salivation-Extraversion	–.34	–.46
Salivation-Neuroticism	–.24	–.14
Extraversion-Neuroticism	–.01	+.15

As has been pointed out (5), technique of administration of the salivation test must be rigorously followed, and the possibility exists (since details of technique are somewhat lacking in the literature) that the discovered differences in the amount of salivation between the present study and previous studies may be due merely to procedural inconsistencies. It is the suggestion here, however, that an explanation of the differences could lie to some extent in the nature of the groups tested. Although Corcoran (1) did not specify the source or background of his *S*s, Eysenck and Eysenck (5) used working men and housewives; on the other hand, the present work involved first-year university students. Thus, while the correlations between salivation and neuroticism did not quite reach significance, it is possible that the comparatively lower level of salivation of the students may have been due partially to apprehension about the experimental situation causing a relatively "dry-mouthed" condition (although in this regard, the lower ambient humidity level of the experimental environment in the present study as compared to the generally higher level obtaining in England, where all previously reported work has been carried out, also may have been a relevant variable).

Table IV – The relationship between salivation and extraversion

Study	Personality measure	Number of subjects	Procedure	Correlation obtained
Corcoran (1)	Heron Scale (6)	(1) 11	(1) 4 drops, 20 secs.	(1) Kendall's *tau* = .62
		(2) 12	(2) 2 drops, 10 secs.	(2) Spearman's *rho* = .70
Eysenck & Eysenck (3)	E.P.I.	93	4 drops, 20 secs.	r_{ES} = –.70 (men) r_{ES} = –.60 (women)
Eysenck & Eysenck (5)	E.P.I.	(1) 100	(1) 4 drops, 20 secs.	(1) r_{ES} = –.73 (men) r_{ES} = –.74 (women)
		(2) 24	(2) 4 drops, 20 secs.	(2) r_{ES} = –.60
		(3a) 27	(3a) 4 drops, ("Jif"), 20 secs.	(3a) r_{ES} = –.02
		(3b) 20	(3b) 6 drops ("Jif"), 30 secs.	(3b) r_{ES} = –.12
Howarth & Skinner	E.P.I.	(1) 25	(1) 4 drops, 20 secs.	(1) r_{ES} = –.34
		(2) 19	(2) 4 drops, 20 secs.	(2) r_{ES} = –.46

Conclusions

While previous research has identified the salivary response to lemon juice as a pure measure of introversion, in the light of the present study such a conclusion must be regarded with caution, and can only be tentatively accepted until a number of further conditions have been satisfied: (a) Standardization of, and rigorous adherence to, salivation test administration procedures; (b) Parametric manipulation of all aspects of the test – for example, position of the swab in relation to the sublingual and parotid salivary glands, quantity of lemon juice used, site of application to the tongue, elapsed time between application and measurement of salivation; (c) Validation and generalization of results across heterogeneous samples; (d) Improvement of introversion-extraversion devices to facilitate screening of spurious extraverts (and spurious nonneurotics) from test samples; (e) Biochemical investigations to determine the specific constituent(s) of lemon juice responsible for the observed experimental effects.

Summary

The increment in salivation in response to four drops of pure lemon juice dropped on the tongue was measured in 15 introverts and 10 extraverts. Although the introverts salivated significantly more than the extraverts (while there was no correlation between salivation and neuroticism), the mean salivation levels of both groups were markedly lower than those previously reported in the literature. On the basis of these results, it was suggested that acceptance of the salivary response to lemon juice as a pure measure of personality may be premature.

References

1. Corcoran, D. W. J. The relation between introversion and salivation. *Amer. J. Psychol.*, 1964, *77*, 298-300.
2. Eysenck, H. J., and Eysenck, S. B. G. *The Eysenck Personality Inventory*. London, England: Univ. London Press, 1965.
3. ———. On the unitary nature of extraversion. *Acta Psychologica*, 1967, *26*, 383-390.
4. ———. Physiological reactivity to sensory stimulation as a measure of personality. *Psychol. Rep.*, 1967, *20*, 45-46.
5. Eysenck, S. B. G., and Eysenck, H. J. Salivary response to lemon juice as a measure of introversion. *Percept. & Motor Skills*, 1967, *24*, 1047-1053.
6. Heron, A. A two-part personality measure for use as a research criterion. *Brit. J. Psychol.*, 1956, *47*, 243-251.

40 / Enhancement of Punitiveness by Visual and Audiovisual Displays[1]

Richard H. Walters and Edward Llewellyn Thomas *University of Toronto, Ontario Hospital, New Toronto*

The advent of television has markedly changed our society and in most cases this change has been advantageous. But many have expressed concern over the emphasis on, and vivid description of, violence on television. Does depicted violence affect the viewer in ways which lead him to become more aggressive in his everyday behaviour? Two conflicting points of view about the effects of viewing violence have been proposed. One is that overt aggression decreases because the individual identifies himself with a violent scene and implicitly acts out (and thus becomes "purged" of) his hostilities. The second viewpoint is that aggressive behaviour is enhanced following the viewing of violence. The following experiment assessed the likelihood that a person will become more punitive after watching a film in which violence is depicted. The authors also sought to determine whether punitiveness was related to age and sex of the viewer.

Studies in which children or adolescents have been exposed to film-mediated aggressive models (Bandura, 1962; Lövaas, 1961; Mussen and Rutherford, 1961; Siegel, 1959) have uniformly indicated that *vicarious* participation in aggressive activity increases, rather than decreases, the frequency and intensity of aggressive responses. In contrast, Feshbach (1961), in a careful study with college students, claims to have provided evidence that vicarious participation in film-mediated aggression has a cathartic effect on subjects who have been previously angered. Fifty-two students were subjected to "unwarranted and extremely critical remarks" (Insult group), while another fifty-two students (non-insult group) were given standard test instructions. Half the Insult and half the Non-insult subjects then witnessed a film clip of a prize fight, the remainder of the subjects in both groups saw a "neutral" movie depicting the effects of the spread of rumours in a factory. Subjects in the Insult group who saw the fight gave fewer aggressive responses to a word-association test (Gellerman, 1960) and to a questionnaire (Feshbach, 1955) than did the insulted subjects who saw the "neutral" movie. There was no significant difference between the two subgroups of non-insulted subjects. As Feshbach points out, the relatively low level of aggression of the Insult subjects who saw the prize fight could be due to the arousal of revulsion or guilt stimulated by the fight theme, an explanation of apparent cathartic effects which has been favoured by Berkowitz (1958,1962). Moreover, one may question the "neutrality" of a film depicting the effects of the spread of rumours. Indeed, for college students, socially disruptive rumour and gossip may represent highly aggressive responses. Inappropriateness of stimulus material may account also for Feshbach's failure to confirm his hypothesis that Non-insult subjects exposed to the prize fight would show a greater increase in aggression than Non-insult subjects exposed to the rumour movie.

In other catharsis studies experimental subjects have been *themselves* permitted to express aggression in fantasy, play, or real life and then tested for aggression in the same or a different stimulus situation. Again, studies in which children have served as subjects (Feshbach, 1956; Kenny, 1952) have failed to support the catharsis hypothesis, while findings from studies with adults (for example, Feshbach, 1955; Rosenbaum and de Charms, 1960; Thibaut and Coules, 1952) have been open, generally speaking, to alternative interpretations (Buss, 1961; Berkowitz, 1958, 1962; Rosenbaum and de Charms, 1960).

The discrepancy in findings yielded by the child and the adult studies and the conflicting results from experiments based on adult subjects may be partly attributable to variations in criterion measures. The child studies have without exception employed measures of overt aggression. In contrast, the adult

[1]This study was supported by the Department of Health, the Government of Ontario, and by grants to the senior author from the National Research Council of Canada (APA-47) and the (Canadian) National Health Grants Program (Public Health Grant 605/5/293). The authors are especially grateful to Dr. H. E. Moorhouse, Superintendent of the Ontario Hospital, New Toronto, and to Dr. D. R. Gunn, Director of Clinical Research, for their sponsorship of this study.

Reprinted, by permission, from *Canadian Journal of Psychology*, 1963, *17*, 244-255.

studies have generally relied on questionnaire responses, self-ratings, and ambiguous measures obtained from ratings of the experiment and the experimenter, all of which are subject to response sets which may seriously affect results.

This paper reports results from a three-phase study of the influence of film-mediated aggressive models in which the primary measure of aggression was behavioural, while questionnaires provided only supplementary data. The aggressive film sequence was the knife-fight scene from the motion picture, *Rebel Without a Cause.*[2] The control movie was an educational film depicting adolescents engaged in art work.[3] This latter stimulus differed from Feshbach's (1961) supposedly neutral movie in that it displayed constructive co-operative activities.

Some of the data obtained from the first phase of the study have already been reported by Walters, Llewellyn Thomas, and Acker (1962). For comparison, these data are included in the present paper. With only minor variations, the same procedures were used throughout all phases of the study. Consequently, only the procedure used in the second phase is reported in detail.

The following hypothesis was advanced: Subjects who watch an aggressive movie sequence depicting physical aggression will subsequently display more physically aggressive responses, delivered in the form of punitive electric shocks, than subjects who watch a movie sequence depicting constructive activities.

Method

Subjects (Ss)

In the first phase of the study 28 hospital attendants, with a median age of 34 years, were randomly assigned in equal number to the experimental and control conditions. *S*s were unpaid, but were permitted to participate during work hours. In the second phase, 24 Grade 9 and Grade 10 boys, with a median age of 15 years, 3 months, served as *S*s. All were paid volunteers who attended a single high school in the vicinity of the hospital at which they were tested.[4] *S*s were randomly assigned to the experimental and control conditions, with 12 *S*s in each group. In Phase III, *S*s were 32 females, with a median age of 20 years, from a hostel for working girls. All were unpaid volunteers.[5]

Confederates (Cs)

When hospital attendants served as *S*s, *C*s were University of Toronto students who were brought to the hospital for a half-day each. It was not possible to use a single confederate throughout this phase of the study, since his continued presence at the hospital would have caused *S*s to become suspicious of his role. In Phase II, *C* was a Grade 10 boy, who attended a different high school from *S*s, and was consequently unknown to them. In Phase III, *C*s were undergraduate students who were assigned to an equal number of experimental and control *S*s in a 2 x 2 factorial design. Half the experimental and half the control *S*s administered shock to a male *C*, while the remaining *S*s administered shock to a female *C*.

Apparatus

The equipment[6] was a modified version of a "conditioning" apparatus described by Buss (1961). It consisted of three panels: *S*'s panel, *C*'s panel, and *E*'s. *S*, who served as "*E*'s assistant," was provided with a panel which contained four switches controlling stimulus lights on *C*'s panel, a rotary switch for selecting shock intensities with settings from zero to ten, a red and green signal light operated from *E*'s panel, a pair of electrodes, and a spring-loaded toggle-switch which *S* depressed to administer shocks to *C* and raised to signal that *C* had made a correct response.

E's panel contained stimulus keys to activate the green and red lights on *S*'s panel, four lights which registered *S*'s selection of light switches, a row of eleven lights to indicate the intensity of shock chosen by *S*, and an outlet to a Standard Electric Timer for recording the duration, in 1/10-sec. intervals, of the shock administered.

C's panel was a dummy "unit" with no electrical connections to the other units. In order to deceive *S*, dead cables which appeared to provide such connections were led across the laboratory floor.

Tables holding the panels were arranged in such a way that *E* could observe *S* and *C*, both of whom faced away from *E*. *C* was seated behind a buttress 15 ft. to the rear of *S* so that he was not visible to *S* during testing.

Procedure (Phase II)

E first met *S* in the laboratory and explained to him that he and another subject (in fact, *E*'s confederate) would be required to watch a scene in a film and then, after a lapse of a few minutes, to answer some questions concerning the events they had witnessed. The experiment was presented as a test for memory for witnessed events which would provide comparative data concerning the attention and memory of persons of different ages.

The experimenter then explained that he was also collecting some data on the effects of punishment on learning and would need an assistant to help operate the equipment used for this purpose, a service which *S* was requested to perform. The "assistance" pro-

[2] Warner Bros. Pictures Distributing Co. kindly provided this film on extended loan.

[3] Provided on extended loan by the Toronto Metropolitan Film Library.

[4] The authors wish to express their appreciation to the New Toronto Board of Education and to the Principal and Guidance Officer of New Toronto High School for their co-operation in this phase of the study. Thanks are due also to C. W. Acker, who served as experimenter, and to John Ziegler, of Alderwood Collegiate, who acted as confederate.

[5] Appreciation is expressed to the President and members of Georgina House for their co-operation in this phase of the study, and to Norma Bowen and Jeannette Cochrane, who served jointly as experimenters.

[6] Photograph provided in Bandura and Walters, 1963.

vided by *S* was ostensibly to administer punishment, in the form of electric shocks, for errors made by *C* in the learning task.

After *S* had consented to act as an assistant, he was shown how to operate the equipment and was given a few shocks, not exceeding the level of 4, to familiarize him with the pain levels corresponding to sample settings on the dial. He was told that shock intensities became increasingly more painful as shock levels were increased from zero to ten.

S was then given a program of settings for the signal switches on his panel, each setting consisting of a pairing of two of the numbers 1 through 4. He was told that on each trial he must depress two of the four stimulus keys in the order indicated by his program and that these would light up two of the lights on the "subject's" (i.e., *C*'s) panel. He was informed that if the "subject" responded correctly, the green panel would go on and that he should signal to the "subject" that he was correct by raising the spring-loaded toggle-switch. However, if the red light came on, indicating that the "subject" had made an incorrect response, he was told to punish him by selecting one of the shock intensities and depressing the switch. A few practice trials were given to familiarize *S* with the equipment.

At this point *E* remarked that "the other fellow" should have arrived by this time and telephoned to "ask if he were there." The telephone call was, in fact, taken by *C*, who was waiting in *E*'s office and for whom it was a signal to come to the laboratory.

On his arrival *C* was also told, in front of *S*, that this was a study of memory for events in a movie but that, during the break between the movie and the recall test, *E* wished to gather additional data concerning the effects of punishment on learning. *C*'s consent to serve as a "subject" was then obtained.

E explained that he wished to have the interval between the showing of the movie and the recall test rather precise and that therefore he would like *S* and *C* to have a "practice run" on the learning equipment before seeing the movie to ensure that there would be no undue hold-ups on the later series of trials. *S* was given a program of 30 settings to present to *C*. The latter was seated at the "receiving" end of the punishment equipment with an electrode strap placed around his wrist. During this "practice" session, which supplied the *pre-test* measures, *S* was required to punish *C* 15 times, that is, *E* illuminated the red button on fifteen occasions. Since *E* had surreptitiously removed one of the electrodes from the strap, *C* in fact received no shocks.

Immediately after the "trial" run, experimental *S*s and *C* were shown the knife-fight scene, while control *S*s and *C* were shown the art scene.

The *post-test* series of trials on the learning task followed. Another program of 30 settings was handed to *S* and again he was required to punish *C* 15 times during the run.

Modification of Procedure for Adult Ss

Except for minor changes in the wording of instructions to make them appropriate to the ages of *S*s and *C*s, the procedures used in Phases I and II of the study were identical. Phase III of the study was conducted at the University of Toronto in two adjoining rooms, separated by a one-way vision mirror. The movie sequences were shown in the observation room, where *E*'s panel was located. The "conditioning" procedure was conducted in the adjoining room with *S* and *C* separated by a partition. The movie sequences were the same as in the other phases, except that *no sound was used,* that is, *the displays were purely visual in character.* The procedure was otherwise, except for minor necessary changes in instructions, identical with that used in Phases I and II.

Measures

The average of the shock-level settings selected by each *S* was obtained for both the pre-test and the post-test series of trials. The effects of exposure to film-mediated aggression was assessed primarily from pre-test–to–post-test changes in this behavioural index of punitiveness.

The Buss-Durkee Hostility-Aggression Inventory (Buss & Durkee, 1957) was utilized as a supplementary measure. The hospital attendants and young females were given this inventory immediately after the post-test session of the conditioning task. In the case of the adolescents it proved possible to administer the inventory about ten days before the experimental session and again after completion of the conditioning task.

All three sets of subjects were also required to fill out, at the very end of the testing session, a multiple-choice questionnaire concerning the film they had watched. This questionnaire was administered only to preserve the impression that the study was primarily one of memory for events; no analysis of the data was attempted.

Results

Shock-Level Data

Table I gives group means and *SD*s for pre-test shock levels and for changes (post-test minus pre-test) in the shock-level index of punitiveness.

Results for adult male subjects. As reported elsewhere (Walters, Llewellyn Thomas, and Acker, 1962), experimental and control male adults did not differ significantly in respect to pre-test shock levels ($p > .05$). There was a significant difference ($t = 2.37$; $p < .05$) between the two groups for the index of change in punitiveness, with experimental subjects showing a quite marked mean increase in punitiveness and control subjects a slight mean decrease.

Results for adolescent subjects. Adolescent experimental and control subjects did not differ in respect to pre-test shock levels ($p > .05$). Both adolescent groups showed a pre-test-to-post-test increase in shock level, with experimental subjects showing a greater increase than controls ($t = 2.04$; $p = .05$,

Table I – Means and *SD*s of pre-test shock levels and pre-test-to-post-test changes in shock level of experimental and control Ss

Groups	Pre-test Mean	Pre-test SD	Changes Mean	Changes SD
Male adult				
Experimental (N=14)	4.34	1.63	0.58	0.62
Control (N=14)	5.03	1.33	–0.14	0.88
Adolescent				
Experimental (N=12)	4.76	1.76	0.94	0.72
Control (N=12)	3.45	1.83	0.38	0.55
Female adult				
Female confederate				
Experimental (N=8)	2.42	1.05	0.62	0.74
Control (N=8)	3.30	1.75	–0.08	0.67
Male confederate				
Experimental (N=8)	3.28	1.35	0.78	0.50
Control (N=8)	3.92	1.36	0.12	0.67

approx.). A supplementary *t*-test was performed in order to ascertain whether the control group's scores had increased significantly beyond zero. The obtained value for *t* was 2.18, which for 11 df is again significant approximately at the .05 level.

Comparison of adult male and adolescent subjects. Although the conditions for testing adult and adolescent males were somewhat different, in that the adults delivered shocks to students who were generally somewhat younger than themselves while the adolescents delivered shocks to a confederate of approximately their own age, it was decided to compare these adult and adolescent subjects in respect to initial selection of shock levels and in a 2 X 2 analysis of variance of changes in shock level. The pre-test shock-level means of adult and adolescent subjects were compared by means of a *t*-test, which showed that the difference between the two groups was not significant ($p > .05$). The results of the analysis of variance of changes in shock level are given in Table II. Before carrying out this analysis, sums and sums of squares were adjusted to allow for the unequal number of subjects in the adult and adolescent groups, using a method described by Ferguson (1959, p. 259). As Table II indicates, when the results of both the experimental and control groups were taken into account, adolescents showed a significantly greater increase in shock level than did adults ($p < .05$). The significance of the difference between the combined experimental and combined control groups was $< .005$. The interaction effect was not significant.

Results for female subjects. Analysis of pre-test data collected for adult female subjects in Phase III

Table II – Analysis of variance of changes in shock level for male adult and adolescent Ss

Source	Sums of squares	df	Mean square	*F*	*p*
Conditions	5.217	1	5.217	9.54	<.005
Age group	2.512	1	2.512	4.39	<.05
Interaction	0.078	1	0.078	<1	
Error	26.272	48	0.547		

of the experiment involved comparison of experimental and control subjects in a 2 X 2 analysis of variance, which at the same time permitted an examination of the influence of the sex of the confederate on initial selection of shock levels. This analysis yielded no significant main or interaction effect ($p >$ .05 in each case).

Table III shows the results of the analysis of variance of pre-test-to-post-test changes in mean shock level for the adult female subjects. Subjects who watched the aggressive film sequence showed a significant increase in punitiveness ($p < .01$). The sex of the confederate did not influence results and there was no interaction effect.

Inventory Data

The Buss-Durkee inventory was administered to the adults, male and female, only at the end of the testing session. Table IV summarizes the results for the adult male subjects. On all four of the scales with high loadings on Buss's aggression factor, the experimental group scored significantly higher than the control group. In contrast, results for female subjects were all non-significant. Pre-test-to-post-test change scores were available for adolescent subjects.

Table III – Analysis of variance of changes in shock level for female adult Ss

Source	Sums of squares	df	Mean square	*F*	*p*
Conditions	3.920	1	3.920	8.03	<.01
Sex of confederate	0.349	1	0.349	<1	
Interaction	0.019	1	0.019	<1	
Error	13.670	28	0.488		

Table IV – Summary of results of *t*-tests of significance of differences between experimental and control male adult Ss on the Buss-Durkee inventory

	Group means			
	Experimental	Control	t	p
Inventory measures				
1. Assault	4.50	2.00	2.71	<.02
2. Indirect	4.93	2.57	3.15	<.01
3. Irritability	3.50	1.36	2.97	<.01
4. Negativism	2.57	1.43	1.78	ns
5. Resentment	1.71	2.36	1.15	ns
6. Suspicion	3.57	3.36	0.24	ns
7. Verbal	8.29	4.29	4.93	<.001
8. Guilt	4.21	3.64	0.70	ns
Over-all index (sum 1-7)	29.07	17.36	3.42	<.005

N=14 in each group.

There was no significant difference in change scores for experimental and control subjects on any of the individual scales. On the total aggression-hostility index, obtained by combining scores on Scales 1 through 7, experimental subjects showed a mean increase of 2.83, while the controls' mean increase was only 1.42. This difference, however, was not great enough to reach an acceptable level of significance ($t = 1.58$; $p > .05$).

Discussion

The results of this study in general lend considerable support to the hypothesis that subjects exposed to an aggressive movie sequence show a significant increment in aggressive pain-producing responses in comparison to a control group who watch a movie showing constructive activities. This finding is consistent with those obtained from studies in which children have served as subjects.

In the third phase of the study the auditory components of the stimuli were omitted and at the same time subjects were of a different sex from the aggressive model presented on film. Nevertheless, the results for the behavioural index were similar to those obtained for male subjects with the audiovisual display. A direct comparison of the effects of aggressive audiovisual, auditory, and visual stimuli on both male and female subjects is clearly indicated. It would also be of interest to investigate the influence of aggressive material which is presented in other media, for example, in still pictures or in print.

In contrast to the behavioural measure of punitiveness, the inventory data failed to provide consistent findings. Buss has pointed out that the pattern of results obtained with the male adults might have been expected, since only the aggression scales should be influenced by situational factors.[7] Possibly the inventory was not suitable for use with the adolescents, whose scores tended to be very high even on the first administration. The negative findings for the adult females cannot, however, be attributed to the unsuitability of the instrument. One problem with the inventory is that it is quite evidently asking questions concerning socially disapproved hostility and aggression in a variety of contexts, all different from the one provided by the experiment. In contrast, the administration of shocks was sanctioned in the experimental setting and had no apparent relation to the presentation of the filmed material.

When both experimental and control scores were taken into account, the adolescent subjects were found to have increased shock levels during testing to a greater extent than the adults. This finding is not too surprising, in view of the fact that inhibition of aggression is a gradual process that probably, for most individuals, continues into young adult life. Indeed, a significant interaction between the experimental treatments and the age of subjects might have been expected. *Rebel Without a Cause* portrayed adolescents engaged in aggressive activities; consequently, greater "identification" on the part of the adolescent subjects could have led to a greater pre-test-to-post-test increment in punitiveness (Maccoby and Wilson, 1957). However, the over-all findings suggest that neither sex nor age similarity between observer and model is necessary in order to produce an increment in punitive pain-producing responses.

The *control* group of adolescents showed a significant increment of aggression from pre-test to post-test. Two explanations suggest themselves. In the first place, as the adolescent confederate observed, the control movie may have been boring and therefore frustrating for the adolescent subjects. It is more likely, however, that most adolescents were initially somewhat timid of using shock, but tended to increase the shock level under conditions in which no serious consequences to the confederate were observed. Support for the latter interpretation is provided by the experimenter's observation that nearly every individual adolescent record sheet showed a pattern of gradually ascending shock level even during the pre-test trials.

The study thus suggests two ways in which disinhibition of aggression may occur. In the first place, mere observation of an aggressive model who is not punished for his aggression may lead to the lessening of inhibitions on the expression of aggression. Secondly, for some groups of subjects, aggression may

[7]Personal communication.

increase, even in the absence of anger, positive reinforcement, or the example set by a model, if no untoward social consequences of their previous aggression are apparent. It is probably only the continual expectation of retaliation by the recipient or by other members of society that prevents many individuals from more freely expressing aggression.

The authors were astonished at the shock-levels selected by some adolescents who, even near the commencement of the pre-test period, gave long shocks at levels between 8 and 10. The sample shocks provided at the commencement of the session clearly indicated that such levels, even if only briefly administered, were very painful. A few adolescents even made remarks, such as "I bet I made that fellow jump," which reflected enjoyment with the task of administering pain.

Perhaps such responses are to be expected from adolescent males who live in a society in which they are constantly exposed to aggressive sports, such as boxing, and to T.V. and motion-picture scenes of violence, warfare, and destruction. Schramm, Lyle, and Parker (1961) noted that Grade 10 students who were fantasy-oriented (high T.V. users, low users of print) scored significantly higher on a self-report measure of antisocial aggression (Sears, 1961) than did reality-oriented Grade 10 children (low T.V. users, high users of print). Under the influence of the catharsis hypothesis these authors interpret their findings as indicating that frustrated (high-fantasy) children "tend to try to work out some of their aggression vicariously through television fantasy (p. 121). In this instance, as with most field study findings, it is impossible to determine the direction of the cause-effect relationship if such a relationship is indeed involved. Indeed, it is just as reasonable to interpret the finding of Schramm, *et al.* as indicating that high T.V.-viewing predisposes an adolescent to express antisocial aggression. While it is quite evident that all children are not similarly influenced by T.V. scenes of violence (Himmelweit, Oppenheim, and Vince, 1958; Maccoby, 1955; Schramm, Lyle, and Parker, 1961), the bulk of evidence from controlled experimental studies suggests that the immediate effect of audiovisually presented violence is to increase the social aggression of the viewers.

It is possible, of course, that T.V.- or film-viewers who are emotionally disturbed either through temporary or long-term situational factors will be more adversely influenced by the presentation of violence than viewers who are not thus aroused. The field studies of television (Himmelweit, *et al.*, 1958; Schramm, *et al.*, 1961) certainly seem to indicate that, contrary to Feshbach's (1955, 1961) contention, the angry or hostile viewer is more likely than the non-angry viewer to behave aggressively as a result of viewing T.V. or filmed aggression. Moreover, previous studies by Walters and his collaborators (McNulty and Walters, 1961; Walters, Marshall, and Shooter, 1960) suggest that the influence of social models may be enhanced when observers are in an emotionally aroused state. While further studies of the manner in which "personality" and situational factors modify viewers' reactions to televised and filmed violence are undoubtedly necessary, mounting evidence against the catharsis hypothesis must raise questions concerning the social wisdom of the sponsors of such productions.

Summary

Male hospital attendants, high school boys, and young female adults served as *S*s in a study of the influence of film-mediated aggressive models. In the first phase, 14 attendants watched an adolescent knife-fight scene from the motion picture, *Rebel Without a Cause*. A control group of 14 attendants watched a film sequence showing adolescents engaged in constructive activities.

Exposure to the film occurred between pre-test and post-test trials of a "conditioning" experiment. During these trials *S* was required to administer shock to a confederate of the experimenter for "errors" in a learning task.

In the second phase, the procedures were repeated with 24 adolescent *S*s, 12 in each group. In the third phase, 16 young women from a hostel for working girls watched the aggressive sequence, in this case without the accompanying sound, while another 16 watched the film sequence depicting constructive activities. Half the female experimental *S*s and half the female control *S*s administered shocks to a female confederate; for the remaining *S*s, the confederate was a male.

A behavioural index of changes in punitiveness was based on differences between the pre-test and post-test shock levels selected by *S*s. Findings based on this index yielded consistent support for the hypothesis that *S*s exposed to aggressive film-mediated models show an increase in aggressive pain-producing responses. In contrast, the experimental procedures did not consistently influence *S*s' responses to an aggression-hostility inventory.

References

BANDURA, A. Social learning through imitation. In M. R. JONES (ed.), *Nebraska symposium on motivation.* Lincoln: University of Nebraska Press, 1962, pp. 211-69.

BANDURA, A., and WALTERS, R. H. Aggression. In *Child psychology: The sixty-second yearbook of the National Society for the Study of Education,* part I. Chicago: National Society for the Study of Education, 1963, pp. 364-415.

BERKOWITZ, L. The expression and reduction of hostility. *Psychol. Bull.,* 1958, *55,* 257-83.

———. *Aggression: a social psychological analysis.* New York: McGraw-Hill, 1962.

BUSS, A. H. *The psychology of aggression.* New York: Wiley, 1961.

BUSS, A. H., and DURKEE, ANN. An inventory for assessing different kinds of hostility. *J. consult. Psychol.,* 1957, *21,* 343-8.

FESHBACH, S. The drive-reducing function of fantasy behaviour. *J. abnorm. soc. Psychol.,* 1955, *50,* 3-11.

———. The catharsis hypothesis and some consequences of interaction with aggressive and neutral play objects. *J. Pers,.* 1956, *24,* 449-62.

———. The stimulating vs. cathartic effects of a vicarious aggressive activity. *J. abnorm. soc. Psychol.,* 1961, *63,* 381-5.

FERGUSON, G. A. *Statistical analysis in psychology and education.* New York: McGraw-Hill, 1959.

GELLERMAN, S. The effects of experimentally induced aggression and inhibition on word association response sequences. Unpublished doctoral dissertation, University of Pennsylvania, 1960.

HIMMELWEIT, HILDE T., OPPENHEIM, A. N., and VINCE, PAMELA. *Television and the child: an empirical study of the effect of television on the young.* Toronto: Oxford University Press, 1958.

KENNY, D. T. An experimental test of the catharsis theory of aggression. Unpublished doctoral thesis, University of Washington, 1952.

LÖVAAS, O. I. Effect of exposure to symbolic aggression on aggressive behaviour. *Child Develpm.,* 1961, *32,* 37-44.

MACCOBY, ELEANOR E., and WILSON, W. C. Identification and observational learing from films. *J. abnorm. soc. Psychol.,* 1957, *55,* 76-87.

MACCOBY, ELEANOR E. Testimony before the Subcommittee to investigate juvenile delinquency of the Committee on the Judiciary, United States Senate, Eighty-Fourth Congress. *S. Res. 62.* Washington, D.C.: U.S. Government Printing Office, 1955.

MCNULTY, J. A., and WALTERS, R. H. Emotional arousal, conflict, and susceptibility to social influence. *Canad. J. Psychol.,* 1962, *16,* 211-20.

MUSSEN, P. H., and RUTHERFORD, E. Effects of aggressive cartoons on children's aggressive play. *J. abnorm. soc. Psychol.,* 1961, *62,* 461-4.

ROSENBAUM, M. E., and DE CHARMS, R. Direct and vicarious reduction of hostility. *J. abnorm. soc. Psychol.,* 1960, *60,* 105-11.

SCHRAMM, W., LYLE, J., and PARKER, E. B. *Television in the lives of our children.* Toronto: University of Toronto Press, 1961.

SEARS, R. R. Relation of early socialization experiences to aggression in middle childhood. *J. abnorm. soc. Psychol.,* 1961, *63,* 466-92.

SIEGEL, ALBERTA E. Film-mediated fantasy aggression and strength of aggressive drive. *Child Developm.,* 1956, *27,* 365-78.

THIBAUT, J. W., and COULES, J. The role of communication in the reduction of interpersonal hostility. *J. abnorm. soc. Psychol.,* 1952, *47,* 770-7.

WALTERS, R. H., LLEWELLYN THOMAS, E., and ACKER, C. W. Enhancement of punitive behaviour by audiovisual displays. *Science,* 1962, *136,* 872-3.

WALTERS, R. H., MARSHALL, W. E., and SHOOTER, J. R. Anxiety, isolation, and susceptibility to social influence. *J. Pers.,* 1960, *28,* 518-29.

41 / A Comparison of Personality Characteristics of Mennonites with Non-Mennonites[1]

Irmgard Thiessen, Morgan W. Wright, and George C. Sisler *University of Manitoba*

In Canada there are many sub-cultural groups, such as the Doukhobors, the Hutterites, and the Mennonites, which have managed to maintain relatively distinct systems of values and mores. Since environment is highly effective in shaping personality, it would be expected that members of such sub-cultures would display characteristics that are different from non-members. In this investigation the authors assessed personality characteristics of Mennonites living in Manitoba.

This study is the first in a series of investigations of the relationship between the value system of a particular cultural group, the Mennonites in Manitoba, and the types of symptoms developed at the time of mental illness, the subsequent course of the illness and the pattern of recovery.

The Mennonite group was selected for study, since it has attempted to maintain its cultural identity despite the social pressures to conform to the society surrounding it. As well, the term "Mennonite psychosis" has been used by psychiatrists to describe a particular complex of symptoms which this group appears to develop when mentally ill, and which appears with more frequency in Mennonite patients than in other cultural groups. This is a schizoaffective disturbance which is characterized by depressed affect, strong feelings of guilt, delusions of persecution, and emotional detachment. It has further been assumed that the nature of the "Mennonite psychosis" is at least partially a result of the influence of rigid standards and inflexible beliefs that make the Mennonite patient particularly vulnerable to feelings of sinfulness and self-condemnations. This view has support in the findings of Eaton and Weil (1955) who found that the Hutterite group, which has its origin in common with the Mennonites, tended to develop guilt feelings and depression to a greater extent than the general population when mentally ill. However, it has not to the authors' knowledge been established that (a) such a syndrome does exist for the Mennonite group or (b) should it exist, whether this can be attributed to the cultural values of the Mennonite community.

Preliminary to studying mentally ill patients, it was considered important to attempt an objective assessment of the value system of a sample of healthy Mennonites in the community. In this way it was thought possible to establish a "normal" base line against which the results obtained with patients might then be compared. If it could be demonstrated that Mennonite young people have a tendency towards greater self-blame than non-Mennonites because of their moral standards, then such differences could be examined in relationship to mental illness. Certainly contemporary writers in both psychology (Pronko, 1964) and psychiatry (Szasz, 1961) have stressed the importance of viewing mental illness in its social context. What is considered irrational or "sick" in a given society is influenced by its values. Recent writers (Hunn, 1959; Mack, 1965; Oates, 1957) have emphasized the importance of taking the patient's individual value system into account when planning treatment and rehabilitation. If it can be demonstrated that a given cultural group has a value system differing from the norm of the larger cultural environment, then it would be important to take this into consideration in the treatment of its mentally ill.

Method

Subjects

The Mennonite group studied comprised 104 urban and 100 rural Mennonites. The urban Mennonite group included students drawn from two Bible Colleges, one representing a somewhat more, and another, a somewhat less orthodox Mennonite outlook. The rural Mennonite subjects came from a rural Bible School and an older group drawn from a Mennonite farm community. The control group of 199 urban non-Mennonite subjects included students from a nursing school, a physiotherapy school, a technical training school, and from a Teacher's College.

The authors attempted to obtain three samples of subjects, one non-Mennonite and two Mennonite, which might be roughly equivalent with respect to age, intelligence, education and sex distribution. Ta-

[1]This study was assisted by funds provided by the Public Health Research Grant (Project No. 606-7-126) of the National Health Grants Program.

Reprinted, by permission, from *Canadian Psychologist*, 1969, *10*, 129-137.

Table I – Distribution of age, intelligence and education of Mennonite and non-Mennonite groups

Group	N Male	N Female	Age Mean	Age S.D.	Otis I.Q. Mean	Otis I.Q. S.D.	Education Mean Grade
Urban Mennonites							
Bible College No. 1	13	17	23	3.4	119	11.2	12.0
Bible College No. 2	30	36	22	4.8	117	10.1	12.0
Students (Teacher's College)	5	3	21	5.7	118	7.6	12.0
Total Means	48	56	22	4.2	118	10.6	12.0
Rural Mennonites							
Provincial Bible School	26	39	20	3.6	109	10.3	10.0
Rural Community	22	13	37	11.1	95	10.2	8.0
Total Means	48	52	25	6.5	104	10.3	9.1
City Non-Mennonite or Control							
Teacher's College	4	12	22	5.0	118	6.9	12.0
Physiotherapy Student	0	54	19	0.9	121	7.4	12.0
Nurses in Training	4	60	20	2.7	114	6.5	11.5
Technical Students	65	0	20	2.6	114	13.3	12.0
Total Means	73	126	20	2.4	117	8.5	11.8

ble I outlines the three groups studied. It can be seen that the urban Mennonite and Control groups are similar in terms of age, educational level, and intelligence, whereas the rural Mennonite group is on the average, less well educated, and achieves a lower intelligence rating.

Since most of the urban and rural Mennonite subjects were Bible College students, it might be assumed that they would represent a biased sample of the Mennonite community. However, because many Mennonites attend Bible School either after having finished professional training or before entering, it was assumed that the sample would give a reasonable cross section of young Mennonites in Manitoba. The justification for such an assumption is supported by the fact that there was no significant difference between the Mennonite Bible School subjects and Mennonite non-Bible School subjects with respect to their religious responses to the tests.

Tests and procedures

A battery of five psychological tests was administered. These included three objective tests, the Otis Test of Mental Ability (Otis, 1922), Edwards Personal Preference (Edwards, 1959), and the George Washington Social Intelligence Test (Moss, Hunt, Omwake, and Woodward, 1955); and two projective tests, the Incomplete Sentences Test and the Thematic Apperception Test, (Murray, 1943). The tests were selected so as to provide a broad coverage of attitudes and abilities. As far as it was possible, uniform testing conditions were maintained. All tests were given on a voluntary basis and conducted in group sessions. Standard instructions were used in the administration of the tests with confidentiality assured. It was not possible to obtain a complete battery of five tests from all the Control subjects because of academic commitments which prevented them from attending some of the test periods. One hundred and forty-five Control subjects completed the Edwards Personal Preference and 131 completed the Incomplete Sentences Test.

Standard scoring procedures were used with the three objective tests. The two projective tests called for a special scoring system related to the problem. In both cases, the system devised was a simple procedure for categorizing the subject's responses.

The Incomplete Sentences Test was devised by the authors to include a number of incomplete sentences that might relate to values and religion. From a total of 67 incomplete sentences, 19 were selected for analysis. Twelve of the 19 incomplete sentences were neutral with respect to evoking religious or cultural responses. Such incomplete sentences included here were "The biggest difficulty in my home life------------" or "I feel I might have failed------------." The remaining items were directed towards the need for a religious value system (3 items), guilt with respect to religious value standards (2 items), perceiving the father as omnipotent and patriarchal (1 item), feeling uncomfortable in the presence of the minister (1 item). The sentence completions were independently evaluated by one author and another rater with respect to the number of completions indicating a religious orientation, guilt feelings about failure to meet religious standards, view of father as patriarchal, and feelings towards the minister. Using this system of categorizing the individual's responses to the incomplete sentences in terms of manifest content, an agreement of 90 per cent was established between the two interpreters.

Seven cards from the Thematic Apperception Test were employed: cards 2, 6BM, 7BM, 13B, 14, 19GF and 12M. All responses were analyzed for guilt, punishment, religious and violence themes. The variable "Religion" was scored if the content of the story involved praying, thinking of God, ministers, missionaries, conversions, or Biblical phrases. "Pun-

Table II – Comparison of the City Mennonite and the control groups on the Incomplete Sentences Test and the Thematic Apperception Test

Incomplete Sentences Test	City Mennonite (N=103)	Control (N=131)	P*
Religious responses to 12 general items	41%	0%	.001
Father experienced as omnipotent, patriarchal	37%	25%	.10
Insecurity feelings towards minister	15%	7%	.10
Guilt re religious standards	67%	16%	.001
Need for a religious value system			
"My personal goal in life . . ."	38%	1%	.001
"My most important responsibility in life . . ."	51%	0%	.001
Religious concept of sex	20%	2%	.001
Feelings towards non-Mennonites			
Neutral	7%	No corresponding item for the control group.	
Feelings freer with non-Mennonites	12%		
Marked difference	38%		
Inferiority feelings	12%		
Thematic Apperception Test	**City Mennonite (N=91)**	**Control (N=193)**	**P**
Religion	60%	22%	.001
Punishment	53%	37%	.02
Guilt	47%	33%	.05
Violence	30%	28%	n.s.

*Based on Chi-square test of significance, df = 1.

ishment" was scored if the protagonist did something against authoritative decision and consequently met unhappiness or was taken to jail or committed suicide as self-punishment. Included also was a threat of being punished, spanked or scolded for doing something wrong. "Guilt" was scored if the hero expressed shame for his deed, blamed himself, apologized or asked forgiveness. "Violence" included strangling, rape, and murder. The TAT cards were projected in a semi-dark room and the subjects spent from five to ten minutes writing a story for each. Their stories were analyzed according to the frequency of specific themes appearing in them. To check the reliability of the scoring system on the TAT, 210 stories were randomly selected and independently scored by two investigators. An agreement of 88 percent was found which would indicate a reasonably high degree of reliability for this simple non-interpretive scoring system.

Analyses and Results

The Chi-square test of significance was employed to differentiate responses to the TAT, the Incomplete Sentences and the Edwards Personal Preference Schedule (EPPS). Table II provides figures showing the proportion of City Mennonite and Control subjects making certain types of responses to the TAT and the Incomplete Sentence test. It will be noted that the City Mennonites made significantly more religious responses to 12 general items of the Incomplete Sentences Test, also to those evoking guilt with respect to religious standards. More City Mennonites indicated insecurity in the presence of Ministers, and experienced the fatherly authority as patriarchal and domineering than do the Control subjects. They expressed a stronger need for a religious value system and viewed sex more in a religious context. On this test there was one item which related to the Mennonites' attitude towards non-Mennonites. There was no similar item for the Control group. On this item, 38% of the Mennonites indicated a feeling of marked difference from non-Mennonites, 12% felt inferior, 7% expressed a neutral attitude, and 12% indicated that they felt more free with non-Mennonites than with members of their own group. With respect to the TAT, the City Mennonites wrote stories involving significantly more religious themes, punishment for wrong doing and guilt with respect to wrong doing.

Table III provides a comparison of scores from the EPPS between a sample of 42 male City Mennonite students and 70 Control male students. Also compared were 56 female City Mennonites and 75 female Controls. It may be noted that of 15 variables from the EPPS, four showed significant differences between the Mennonite male group and the Control group. Mennonite men indicated a greater need to be of assistance to others (nurturance), to defer to the opinions of others (deference), to feel guilty when things go wrong (abasement), and to feel less need to engage in heterosexual activity. City female Mennonites showed a greater need to feel guilty for wrong doing and also less interest in association with the opposite sex than the female Control group.

No differences were found between 97 City Mennonite subjects and 90 Control subjects on the Social

Table III – Comparison of the City Mennonite and the control groups on the Edwards Personal Preference Test

Variable	Criterion Score*	Male City Mennonite Group (N=42)	Male Control Group (N=70)	P**
Nurturance	% above 13	71%	42%	.01
Deference	" " 11	76%	31%	.001
Abasement	" " 15	72%	44%	.01
Heterosexuality	" " 15	21%	72%	.001
		Female City Mennonite Group (N=56)	Female Control Group (N=75)	
Abasement	% above 13	82%	65%	.05
Heterosexuality	" " 14	24%	57%	.001

Note–Only variables which significantly discriminate the two groups are shown.
*represents the median of the control group.
**based on the Chi-square test of significance, df=1.

Intelligence Test. This would suggest that at least in a hypothetical social situtlon the City Mennonite subjects were as able as the Control subjects to make the appropriate conventional response.

Table III summarizes the variables from all the tests found to differentiate City from Rural Mennonites. It is apparent that on the TAT City Mennonites more frequently give themes involving punishment and guilt. The EPPS test yielded three of 30 variables (male and female scales) which discriminate between the rural and City Mennonites. City female Mennonites showed less need to feel guilty than did rural Mennonites, and were inclined to be more dominant. Male City Mennonites expressed more dominance than rural. There was considerable difference in their responses to the Social Intelligence Test, but since the difference in intelligence noted in Table 1 was so great between the groups it was felt that their differing responses to the Social Intelligence Test could not be legitimately interpreted. Responses to the Incomplete Sentences did not significantly differentiate the two groups.

Discussion

On the basis of the findings there is little doubt that the Mennonite group studied does perceive its relationship to the environment in different terms from the non-Mennonite group. Depending on one's point of view, it can be said that they are more moral or more guilt ridden, have a greater feeling of responsibility to their community, or are more inflexible and rigid in their response to authority figures and concepts.

It is not apparent to what extent this is mentally healthy or unhealthy. From the psychological point of view it can be argued that there are both strengths and weaknesses in the absolute value system of the Mennonite community as compared to the non-Mennonite. To the extent that the Mennonite has faith in his religious values, then to this extent he is free from the anxiety of having to search for answers himself. However, as anxiety may be held in check by a conviction with respect to absolute values, so the possibility of guilt increases as one fails to measure up to such values.

Eaton and Weil (1955) in their study of a Hutterite community concluded that its members tended to take out their tensions on themselves, internalizing them as depressive or psycho-physiological responses. Within their highly structured social system, generalized anxiety reactions were rare. This, they believe, might change as acculturation progresses, the resulting shift being from depressive symptomatology to more generalized anxiety reactions.

Some confirmation of their predictions can be found in the present study. The Mennonite community in Manitoba is a culture in the process of change. The rural Mennonites still draw largely upon their tradition of isolation and religious fundamentalism; however, the city Mennonites are increasingly feeling the impact of modern society. It is apparent that the young urban Mennonite is beginning to challenge the convictions of his elders with respect to the sinfulness of dancing, wearing make-up, attending movies, etc. Possibly, as a result, the urban Mennonite is more socially dominant than his rural counterpart, while at the same time expressing a greater need for punishment. In other words, as the urban Mennonite moves in the direction of the larger society, he feels increasingly anxious about his moral worth.

The next phase of this research will consist of a comparative study of Mennonite and non-Mennonite mental hospital patients. Although the present results do not bear directly on the question of whether or not there is an identifiable psychiatric syndrome, "the Mennonite psychosis," they are consistent with the notion that the Mennonite patient may be particularly vulnerable to feelings of self-blame and hence to such symptoms as depression and withdrawal.

Abstract

The value system of 204 Mennonite young people was compared with a comparable control group of 200 non-Mennonites using a battery of five psychological tests. The findings suggest that Mennonites are more strongly motivated to interpret behaviour in "religious" terms, which includes feeling the need for punishment for wrong doing, being more concerned about moral issues, and having a greater need to orient their life around religious values. Urban Mennonites were found to be more dominant and to feel more guilt than rural Mennonites. The greater dominance of the urban Mennonites possibly reflects the result of being exposed to surrounding cultural pressure, which may then increase anxiety as the influence of the primary value system is challenged.

Résumé

Les auteurs comparent les systèmes de valeur d'un groupe de 204 jeunes Ménnonites et celui un groupe comparable de 200 non-Ménnonites, utilisant une batterie de cinq test psychologiques.

Les résultats suggèrent que les Ménnonites sont fortement motivés à interpréter le comportement en terms religeieux. Ceci inclus un besoin de châtiment pour iniquité, un souci des questions morales, et un désir approfondi d'orienter leur vie en termes de valeurs religieuses. Il est à remarquer que les Ménnonites urbains sont plus dominants et ressentent plus de culpabilité de conscience que les Mennonites ruraux. Cette constatation pourrait s'expliquer par le fait que les Ménnonites urbains sont exposés à des pressions culturelles plus sévères, ce qui suggère une hausse de leur niveau d'anxiété alors que l'influence de leur système de valeurs primaires est mis en contestation.

References

EATON, J. W., and WEIL, R. J. *Culture and Mental Disorders: A Comparative Study of the Hutterites and other Populations*. Glencoe, Illinois: Press Press, 1955.

EDWARDS, A. L. *Edwards Personal Preference Schedule Manual*. (Rev. ed.) New York: Psychological Corporation, 1959.

HUNN, K. W. Religious factors and values in counselling.

MACK, P. L. Efforts by the mentally ill to solve problems through religion: *Pastoral Counselor*, 1956, *3*, (2), 29-32.

MOSS, F. A., HUNT, T., OMWAKE, K. R., and WOODWARD, L. G. *George Washington University Series Social Intelligence Test Manual*. Washington: Centre for Psychological Service, 1955.

MURRAY, H. A. *Thematic Apperception Test Manual*. Cambridge: Harvard University, 1943.

OATES, W. E. *Religious Factors in Mental Illness*. New York: Association Press, 1957.

OTIS, A. S. *Otis Self-Administering Tests of Mental Ability Manual (Rev.) for Intermediate and Higher Examinations*. New York: Harcourt, Brace & World, 1922.

PRONKO, N. H. *Textbook of Abnormal Psychology*. Baltimore: The Williams & Wilkins Company, 1963.

SZASZ, T. S. *The Myth of Mental Illness;* Foundations of a theory of Personal Conduct. New York: Hoeber-Harper, 1961.

THIESSEN, IRMGARD. Values and personality characteristics of Mennonites in Manitoba. *The Mennonite Quart. Review*, 1966, *Jan.*, 48-61.

42 / Motivational and Attitudinal Characteristics of Indian School Children as Measured by the Thematic Apperception Test [1]

D. Sydiaha and J. Rempel *University of Saskatchewan and Centre for Community Studies, Saskatoon*

The Canadian Indian has one of the lowest standards of living of any group in Canada. Many people attribute this condition to the personality characteristics of the Indian. He is said to be ignorant of his condition and to lack aspirations to better his status. Are such conceptions valid? The present investigation explores the values and aspirations of contemporary Indian children by means of a projective technique.

The research reported here deals with the question of whether there are demonstrable differences in motives and attitudes of school children in Northern Saskatchewan who are of Indian ancestry, compared with those who are not. The purpose of the research was to ascertain whether special programs of social and economic development are required for the Indian population, as distinct from other underprivileged groups. Since, as a segment of the population, Métis-Indians constitute an underprivileged minority, the attitudes and motives which distinguish them from the rest of the population may be expected to have a significant bearing upon questions of social change in Saskatchewan communities.

The word "Métis" refers to persons of mixed Indian-non-Indian parentage. Although the word was originally restricted to persons of Indian and French language ancestry, the more general use of the word is to refer to all children of Indian-non-Indian marriages. Although the distinction between Indian and Métis is legally important in Federal government administration of "Indian" affairs, it is not a very important cultural or social distinction. It should also be understood that all Indian and Métis communities in Saskatchewan are relatively acculturated, such that the Indian culture of today is probably very different from that observed by the first white settlers in Saskatchewan.

The study was exploratory in nature and data covering a wide range of attitudinal and motivational categories were collected for analysis. To provide a frame of reference for the investigation, the following three questions were formulated as part of the research design:

Question I: Do Métis-Indian children exhibit greater awareness of poverty than non-Indian children? One might advance the argument, on grounds of cultural influence, that Métis-Indians are not aware of their poverty either because their communities have always experienced sub-standard living standards, or because their value system places little emphasis on a high living standard. To put the matter crudely, it is sometimes argued that the Métis-Indians are ignorant of the fact that there is any alternative pattern of life other than what they have experienced, and that they are "happy in their ignorance."

Question II: Do Métis-Indian children aspire to achievements and satisfactions other than those experienced by their parents? In describing the Métis-Indian cultural values, the statement is sometimes made that Métis-Indian parents are particularly permissive in managing their children, and that group loyalties acquire precedence over individual achievement. Extending this argument to the question of aspirations of the Métis-Indian child, it would seem to follow that, compared with the non-Indian child, he is less inclined to value achievement in school or to aspire to improve his lot.

On the other hand, if one rejects a cultural interpretation of aspirations, it might seem reasonable to suppose that, because the Métis-Indian is destitute, he is highly motivated to advance his standard of living.

Question III: Do Métis-Indians exhibit evidence of conflict with authority? Insofar as members of the Métis-Indian population are identified with the lower social class, authority figures in the community are readily identifiable as representing an out-group, since they are typically both non-Indian and middle class. Being identifiable obstacles preventing the satisfaction of the needs of the community, such socie-

[1]This research was financed by the Centre for Community Studies, University of Saskatchewan. P.M.Worsley initiated the work; A. K. Davis, and J. E. M. Kew contributed substantially to its execution. Mrs. Alaka Chandrasekar assisted in the scoring of TAT protocols.

Reprinted, by permission, from *Canadian Psychologist*, 1964, *5*, 139-148.

tal authority figures might be expected to be seen in unfavorable terms by Métis-Indian subjects. At the same time, one might expect favorable attitudes to be shown toward parental authority figures, since such figures reflect sources of security to the individual member of the subordinate minority.

Since the above analysis may be seen as applying to Métis-Indians of all age levels, some explanation is warranted as to the reasons for restricting the research to children attending school. First of all, there are a number of strictly pragmatic reasons: school children are the most accessible subjects in a community, and they may be assumed to be least inhibited in providing the imaginative material required by the TAT. Furthermore, it may be taken for granted that of all members of the community, children are among those least exposed to societal constraints or prejudice. Thus, the effects of the school in moulding positive attitudes and motives may be expected to show most clearly in children. Finally, the use of children as subjects for study is consistent with the emphasis given to education as being one of the most effective ways of achieving social change. There is probably little argument against the proposition that every child, including the Métis-Indian child, has the right to an education to the extent of his ability. Consequently, if education is to contribute to the development of the socio-economic status of the Métis-Indian community, it is essential for educators and public policymakers to know how Métis-Indian children are motivated.

Procedure

A modified form of the TAT was used to elicit stories from subjects, and the stories obtained were submitted to a method of content analysis specifically developed for this study. The TAT as a technique was selected because of ease of administration, and because it permitted some degrees of comparability with other cross-cultural studies (Lindzey, 1961). It was also considered more appropriate to ask children to write stories than to complete an attitude questionnaire. Furthermore, it was reasoned that a projective technique was particularly appropriate since it enabled the investigators to circumvent the barriers of silence, evasion, habits of assent and deliberate falsification which often impede communication between Métis-Indians and non-Indians.

Nine pictures were used, and these were selected so as to elicit themes relevant to the questions described above. Three pictures were drawn from the original set of TAT cards (numbers 2, 7BM, 13B); one from the work of McClelland *et al.* (1953, picture number 8); and two from the Michigan study (numbers 102 and 103), described by Atkinson (1958, p. 834). The remaining three were specifically prepared for this study. Of these, two were sketches of groups of people, some of whom had Indian facial characteristics. The third picture was a photograph of three men with Indian-like facial features dressed in winter working clothes, seated on a bench in a waiting room.

Administration

In order to standardize the presentation of the pictures, the method described by McClelland was used (Atkinson, 1958, p. 837). Reproductions of the pictures were prepared as 35 mm. photographic slides; these were projected on a screen. A separate sheet of paper was provided for each picture, and each sheet contained four sets of questions to prompt Ss in the event they could not readily think of a story. The questions were: 1. What is happening? Who are the persons? 2. What has led up to the situation? That is, what has happened in the past? 3. What is being thought? What is wanted? By whom? 4. What will happen? What will be done?

Exposure time was 20 seconds for each picture, with four minutes for writing each story. This writing time was extended whenever it appeared that several students wanted to write more. It was reasoned that a precise time limit was not a necessary control in this study, and that it would be desirable to obtain as many long stories as possible.

The pictures were administered by one of the writers (Rempel), a non-Indian male school teacher, who was employed by the Centre for Community Studies to assist in the research. The study was introduced in each of the eight participating schools as "educational" in nature, in that the test was described as having been designed to discover how persons in different parts of the country wrote different stories about the same pictures. At the conclusion of the test, the children were shown films. This was assumed to emphasize the "educational" nature of the visit, as well as to reward the children for their help.

Subjects

Protocols were obtained from 248 Ss, drawn from eight schools in Saskatchewan. Six of these schools were situated in northern parts of the province, and were attended by Métis-Indian children, two being attended exclusively by Métis-Indian children. Of the 55 schools in northern Saskatchewan serving Métis-Indian communities, the six schools were selected on the basis of relative accessibility by car. In all cases, previous contact had been made by personnel of the Centre for Community Studies with the communities concerned. The remaining two schools were located in Saskatoon (approximate population 100,000) and included only non-Indian children in grades seven and eight. These urban school Ss were included to assess regional differences in TAT variables among non-Indian children. The choice of classrooms were governed by two considerations: (1) children in grades seven and eight were used to roughly match the modal grade of the northern sample, and (2) the two schools represented children differing in social class: the first school was situated in one of the older, less attractive regions of the city, while the second was a new school situated in a recently developed suburb. These two urban samples are referred to as working- and middle-class children respectively.

Of the 248 Ss, 113 were Métis-Indian, 42 were northern non-Indian and 93 were urban non-Indian. The age distribution ranged from 11 to 18 with a median of 14 years. The distribution of grades was from 5 to 10, with a median of grade eight.

Scoring of protocols

The method of content analysis used to analyze the stories was suggested by Abt and Bellack (1950), but was revised to include categories relevant to this study. A total of 145 content categories were included in the analysis sheet although many of the categories were not included in the analysis reported here. The categories covered a wide range of content areas: situation of story, problems, outcome, roles, figures introduced, main hero or heroine, hero's attitude toward self, hero's aspirations, attitudes toward superiors, ethnic attitudes, understanding of superiority. Most of the categories were scored on the basis of presence or absence of the category, but for those categories which involved attitudes, a three-point rating scale was used, in order to provide some assessment of the intensity of the attitude being expressed. After all protocols were obtained, they were scrambled, and each set of nine stories was coded so as to conceal identifying information: name, age, sex, grade, school, ethnicity. For training purposes, twenty protocols were drawn at random and scored by two persons working in collaboration. On the basis of this initial attempt, discrepancies were compared, and ambiguous categories were clarified by appropriate definition of terms. The twenty protocols were then replaced in the sample, and all protocols were scored by one of two scorers. Consultation between scorers was maintained during the entire procedure in order to maintain consistency and to clarify problems of interpretation.

To estimate the reliability of scoring, one of the scorers (Rempel) repeated the scoring of a sample of twenty-five protocols. This was done approximately eight months after completion of the first attempt. The number of categories used for the second scoring was reduced from 145 to 125, since 20 of the categories yielded too few scores to warrant inclusion in the analysis. The correlation between scorings was calculated for all 125 categories (intra-class correlation) and differences in mean scores between first and second scoring were tested for constant error. The reliability coefficients obtained ranged from .091 to 1.000 with a median of .643. Of the 125 categories, 25 were not statistically different from zero, and 9 gave significant differences between first and second scoring. The 91 remaining categories were retained for analysis: the correlation coefficients ranged from .359 to 1.000 with a median of .696.

Categories Used

Each of the three general questions described in the introduction to this paper were related to specific content categories, as follows:

(1) Awareness of poverty (4 categories): themes of poverty and nurturance; security; money; employment.

(2) Aspirations involving achievement and satisfaction not experienced by parents (8 categories): themes of school work and examinations; aspirations involving high marks and education; service orientation; spending, possessing material goods; income; money; status and prestige; security, having better home, more food.

(3) Conflict with authority (41 categories): rejection and desertion by parents; child leaving home; conflict with parents; conflict with peers; frustration of hero; ethnicity; attitudes toward parental superiors (8 positive and 7 negative categories); attitudes toward societal superiors (5 positive and 8 negative categories); ethnic attitude (5 categories); understanding of superiority; happy personal relationships.

Effect of story length

Since TAT protocols vary in numbers of words employed, a problem is created by the possible magnification of scores assigned to Ss who wrote long stories. Particularly in this study where the three groups (Métis-Indian, northern non-Indian, urban non-Indian) are not comparable in age, the variable of length of story may be expected to confound results attributable to ethnicity.

In an attempt to evaluate this problem, all protocols were classified into one of four categories according to word length. Mean scores on each of the 125 variables used on the analysis sheet were then calculated for each of the word length categories and these means compared by the F-ratio. Results of this analysis indicated that 43 of the 125 variables were, in fact, positively correlated with word length. However, comparisons of the mean word length of groups of Ss failed to indicate any systematic differences between Métis-Indian and other children. Thus, while stories of middle-class children were significantly longer than those of Métis-Indian children, stories of Métis-Indian public school children were longer that those of northern non-Indian public school children.Also, girls wrote longer stories than did boys. Other specific comparisons did not give significant differences: working class vs. Métis-Indian children; northern high school Métis-Indian vs. non-Indian. In the absence of systematic overall differences, it was reasoned that word length of protocols was not a significant confounding variable.

Results

Awareness of Poverty

Of the four variables included to assess awareness of poverty, two gave higher mean scores for Métis-Indian Ss compared with Northern non-Indian Ss. (All differences in mean scores reported in this paper were tested with Student's t-test for independent samples, using two-tailed tests of statistical significance, at less than the 5 per cent level of confidence). These variables were the themes of security and poverty nurturance. Other group comparisons gave negative results: northern vs. urban non-Indians; working class vs. middle class; boys vs. girls. In other words, high scores for these variables were associated with Métis-Indian Ss specifically. The data support the notion that there is greater awareness of poverty among Métis-Indian school children than among non-Indian school children.

Aspirations

Of the eight variables selected to assess aspirations toward achievement and satisfactions not experienced by parents, three yielded higher scores for Métis-Indian Ss compared with northern non-Indian Ss. These variables were school work and examinations; good marks and education; security. But other group comparisons indicated that higher scores were also obtained for working class, compared with middle class children. The variables found to be significant were: good marks and education; service; spending money for material goods. To the extent that these two sets of categories overlap, the results suggest a resemblance between the values of Indian and urban working-class children, in that they apparently articulate a greater awareness of aspirations. Presumably the basis of such a resemblance might involve the fact both groups may be thought of as being in an inferior position, socially and economically, in their respective communites. But whatever the explanation of the results may be, the fact of similarity between these two groups clearly argues against a cultural interpretation of Métis-Indian vs. non-Indian differences in aspirations.

One incidental finding may be noted here: urban girls showed higher scores for "good marks, education" than boys, but there were no sex differences for Métis-Indian or northern non-Indian children.

Conflict

Of the 41 categories selected to assess conflict with superiors, only two were found to indicate differences between the Métis-Indian and northern non-Indian children. Since on the basis of chance occurence at least two differences would be expected to occur in 41 tests of significance, it was concluded that the results were negative.

Further analysis indicated that working-class urban children displayed characteristically higher scores on the conflict categories. Thus compared with northern non-Indian children, they had higher scores on a number of "negative" categories and low scores on "positive" categories. (High scores for conflict with peers; being independent and autonomous; superior and aggressive; non-conforming; total score for negative attitudes to societal superiors, being unafraid and confident. Low scores for being complaint and cooperative.) Similar results appeared for comparisons between working- vs. middle-class Ss with the former having the higher scores. A direct comparison between Métis-Indian and working-class children yielded significant differences for 16 of the 41 variables tested.

The conclusion suggested by these results is that Métis-Indian children do not display any particular patern of conflict. The fact that working-class children do exhibit differences would seem to suggest that a cultural interpretation of Métis-Indian reaction to frustration is not called for: to the extent that groups of non-Indian children show greater variability than do Métis-Indian in attitudes toward authority, the argument of Métis-Indian "cultural heritage" appears unjustified.

There was no support for the prediction that Métis-Indian Ss would show more positive attitude toward parental authorities, and negative attitudes toward societal authorities. Also, although nine of the 40 categories yielded sex differences, none of these were included among the 16 categories which gave significant results mentioned above.

Discussion

The results of this investigation are consistent with the view that Métis-Indian children do not have attitudes and motives distinguishable from those of other children living in north Saskatchewan. There is evidence of greater awareness of poverty among Métis-Indian children, but since there is objective evidence that such poverty exists for the Métis-Indian population, this awareness probably reflects a situational factor rather than a cultural bias. In terms of other attitudinal and motivational measures, it would appear that cultural factors are less important than social and geographical location.

These results would seem to have important implications for any plan designed to raise the standard of living of the Métis-Indian population. Assuming Métis-Indian and non-Indian values to be indistinguishable, as far as school work is concerned, a program of integrated education would seem to be called for since ethnicity does not appear to relate to any special problem of willingness to work, or of hostility toward authority. The results also suggest that if Métis-Indian, non-Indian differences do exist among adults, the explanation for such differences would probably involve situational and/or experiental factors following termination of formal schooling. Whether such differences do, in fact, exist can only be established by further research: Indians in employment would be expected to modify attitudes and motives of the person being discriminated against. But the picture suggested by the data reported here is that childhood experiences are such as to produce a fairly adequate pattern of adjustment.

Other Evidence

The imaginative responses of Ss to a set of ambiguous drawings are far removed from attitudes and motives displayed in concrete human situations. It is clearly beneficial to validate the TAT material if one is to make definitive statements about the problem.

Some evidence is provided in three reports, published by the Centre for Community Studies, as part of an economic and social survey of northern Saskatchewan (Kew, 1962; Buckley, 1962; Knill and Davis, 1963). Of direct relevance to this study was a content analysis of school essays written by Metis-Indian and non-Indian children on the theme of vocational aspirations ("What I want to be"). The results, in general, indicated few differences among Metis-Indian children: all children tended to express high aspirations. Considering the known distribution of occupational groups typically found in North America, such high aspirations must be considered unattainable for most of the children in the sample. That such aspirations may be typical of all school children is suggested by similar finding cited by Lifton (1961).

The high aspirations of Metis-Indian and working class urban children is supported by Phelps and Horrocks (1958) who show that working class adolescents, more than others, tend to have aspirations to go to college.

The economic survey by Buckley (1962) and the field observations of Kew (1962) document, in dramatic terms, the economic deprivation and inferior class position of the Metis-Indian population in northern Saskatchewan. The average income is considerably less than five hundred dollars per year, which is comparable to that of the more backward countries in Asia and Africa. It is also significant that government welfare payments (mean $128 per year) are the largest single source of income. The population of the region is increasing and the income is decreasing. Taking all of these facts into consideration, it seems not too inappropriate to think of the Indian problem in terms of "white colonialism." In view of such destitute circumstances which the Indian community faces, it is difficult to be convinced by the argument that Metis-Indian children are no different from others in their motives and attitudes.

This apparent inconsistency can only be resolved by further research. But one possible interpretation of this inconsistency is to view the school as being successful in shaping a positive orientation to life: although the Metis-Indian child knows he is poor, he is no different from any other child in his desire to work hard and to build a better life, while maintaining a favourable attitude toward society. Perhaps it is only after he leaves school and attempts to fulfill his aspirations that he becomes a victim of colonial barriers to progress. If this interpretation is correct, then the implication is clear: educational opportunities should be expanded so as to provide him with skills for raising his standard of living. If such opportunities are made available, the evidence reported here would suggest a willingness on the part of the Metis-Indian population to take advantage of such opportunities.

Abstract

A study was conducted to assess differences in attitudinal and motivational categories for TAT between Métis-Indian and non-Indian children living in northern Saskatchewan. Nine pictures were presented to 248 children in schools situated in northern settlements of the province as well as in a large urban city. A set of 145 scoring categories was devised for analysis of the stories. This number was reduced to 90 categories, on the basis of frequency of usage in scoring as well as test-retest reliability. The results indicated clear differences between Métis-Indian and northern non-Indian Ss only for categories related to awareness of poverty. Since Indians are objectively poorer than non-Indians living in the north, these differences were considered attributable to economic as well as to cultural influences. Examination of categories related to aspirations and conflicts with authority indicated that differences were not attributable to Métis-Indian – non-Indian differences, but rather to geographical and class variables. The results were interpreted as supporting the view that current educational practices support positive adjustment to adverse living conditions experienced by the Indian population. This suggests that barriers to economic and social development of Métis-Indians might stem from absence of opportunity rather than from motivational and attitudinal predisposition of the Métis-Indians themselves.

Résumé

Cette étude a pour but l'évaluation des différences d'attitudes et de motivation par rapport aux catégories du TAT entre des enfants Métis-Indiens et d'autres non-Indiens demeurant dans le nord de la Saskatchewan. Neuf images furent présentées à 248 enfants dans des écoles de villages du nord de la province aussi bien que dans une grande cité. Un total de 145 catégories furent préparées pour l'analyse des histoires. Ce nombre fut réduit à 90 catégories à cause de la fréquence de l'emploi de catégories et de leur stabilité d'un test à l'autre. Les résultats ont indiqué des différences valides entre les sujets, Métis Indiens et les sujets non-Indiens du nord seulement dans les catégories se rapportant à la perception de la pauvreté. Puisque les Indiens sont objectivement plus pauvres que les non-Indiens du nord, ces différences furent considérées attribuables aux influences économiques autant que culturelles. L'examen des catégories se rapportant aux aspirations et aux conflits avec l'autorité indiqua que les différences ne résultaient pas des différences entre Métis-Indiens et non-Indiens, mais étaient plutôt dues à des variables géographiques et de classes. Les résultats furent interprétés comme supportant le point de vue que les pratiques pédagogiques actuelles favorisent chez les Indiens un ajustement positif aux expériences de vie parmi des conditions adverses. Cela suggère que les barrières contre le dévelopement économique et social des Métis-Indiens résulte de l'absence de chances d'avancement plutôt que de prédispositions de motivation et d'attitudes chez les Métis-Indiens mêmes.

References

1. ABT, L. A., and BELLACK, L. *Projective psychology*. New York: Knopf, 1950.
2. ATKINSON, J. W. (ed.) *Motives in phantasy, action and society*. Princeton: Van Nostrand, 1958.
3. BUCKLEY, HELEN. *Trapping and fishing in the economy of northern Saskatchewan*. Report No. 3, Economic and Social Survey of Northern Saskatchewan. Saskatoon: Centre for Community Studies, 1962.
4. KEW, J. E. M. *Cumberland House in 1960*. Report No. 2, Economic and Social Survey of Northern Saskatchewan. Saskatoon: Centre for Community Studies, 1962.
5. KNILL, W., and DAVIS, A. K. *Saskatchewan public education north of 53*. Report No. 4, Economic and Social Survey of Northern Saskatchewan. Saskatoon: Centre for Community Studies, 1963.
6. LIFTON, W. M. *Working with groups*. New York: Wiley, 1961.
7. LINDZEY, G. *Projective techniques and cross-cultural research*. New York: Appleton-Century-Crofts, 1961.
8. PHELPS, H. R., and HORRICKS, J. E. Factors influencing informal groups of adolescents. *Child development*, 1958, *29*, 69-86.

NINE
DEVIANT BEHAVIOUR

43 / A Method for the Investigation of Somatic Response Mechanisms in Psychoneurosis[1]

Robert B. Malmo, Charles Shagass, and John F. Davis *Allan Memorial Institute of Psychiatry, McGill University*

This article describes an important technique used to study the neural mechanisms that underlie the exaggerated anxiety states characterizing the psychoneuroses.

Professor Malmo, who is the director of the Neuropsychology Laboratory, Allan Memorial Institute, McGill University and an internationally known physiological psychologist, is the author of over 65 scientific papers. He is the recipient of numerous honours and awards, including an LL.D. degree from the University of Manitoba.

The psychoneuroses are characterized by states, such as anxiety, which appear to be emotional responses of pathologically increased intensity and duration. Little is known concerning the neural processes that underlie these disorders of emotional experience in psychoneurosis, although recent investigations have indicated that they are accompanied by abnormally increased excitability in both the autonomic and the central nervous systems (8). This paper is concerned with the development of a method that could be used for experimental investigation of basic central nervous system processes involved in psychoneurosis.

Largely in response to the influence of Cannon and his school (1), physiological studies of emotion have centered upon the increased activity in the sympathetic division of the autonomic nervous system, for example, increased heart rate and blood pressure. That increased parasympathetic excitation may also occur during strong emotion, however, is clearly indicated by such phenomena as involuntary evacuation of the bowel and fainting. Further, although seldom the subject of experimental investigation, the important role of the central nervous system in states of emotional excitement has long been recognized from clinical observations of hyperreflexia; and the electromyographic studies of Jacobson (3) have provided objective evidence of increased muscular tension in emotional disturbance. Consequently, any concept that attempts to integrate the facts concerning the physiology of emotion must take into account the events occurring in all main divisions of the nervous system.

The most widely accepted integrating principles concerning the physiological aspects of emotion are Cannon's concepts of emergency reaction and homeostasis. From the standpoint of these concepts some emotions are viewed as states of preparation for fight or flight; and the autonomic changes that accompany these emotions have been interpreted as events designed to ensure appropriate bodily conditions during such activity as, for example, greater blood flow to the muscles provided by increased blood pressure. The attention directed toward the homeostatic role of the autonomic nervous system in emotions has unfortunately led to neglect of the part played by the central nervous system. Muscular tension changes in emotion cannot be fully understood in terms of increased supportive function by the autonomic nervous system. The somatic motor system is characterized by shorter latencies of reaction than the autonomic system. In some emotion-producing situations skeletal muscle tension may complete a cycle of rise and return to prestimulation level, well before autonomic homeostatic mechanisms have had time enough to complete their cycles. This makes it appear necessary to seek a homeostatic mechanism with direct control over *somatic* (skeletal) motor activities by the *central* nervous system.

Recent discoveries in the physiology of brainstem, thalamic, and cortical interrelationships have resulted in the description of the thalamic and brainstem reticular systems, which may provide the necessary mechanisms for "*somatic*" homeostasis (4, 7, 9). Jasper (4) has found that stimulation of the thalamic reticular system effectively eliminates cortical after-discharge resulting from sensory stimulation, and muscular afterdischarge produced by direct stimulation of the motor cortex. Moruzzi and Magoun (9) have shown that stimulation of the brainstem reticular system will produce similar effects. From this recent work Jasper has concluded as follows:

It seems, therefore, that there exists a separate

[1]This research was performed under Contract No. W-49-007-MD-422 between the Department of the U.S. Army, Office of the Surgeon General, and McGill University.
The authors wish to acknowledge gratefully the invaluable suggestions of H. H. Jasper, of the Montreal Neurological Institute, and the assistance of F. H. Davis and E. J. Martin.

Reprinted, by permission, from *Science*, Vol. 112 (September 22, 1950), pp. 325-328.

regulatory system involving thalamic and other brain stem structures which acts upon the cortex, controlling the form and rhythm of the background of cortical activity upon which afferent impulses must act, and regulating local and generalized excitatory states of the cortex as a whole (4, p. 418).

The reticular system thus seems to exert a regulatory (homeostatic) effect upon cortical and motor activity. Since pathological anxiety appears to involve an excess of excitation in the somatic motor mechanisms (8), it is conceivable that this could be due to defective regulatory action (inhibitory) of some somatic homeostatic mechanism, such as the thalamic or brain-stem reticular system.

The method described in this paper was designed to bring experimental data to bear upon the question of defective somatic regulatory action in pathological anxiety. The following features were sought in devising the method: (1) The physical characteristics of external stimulation should be subject to exact measurement and control. (2) Stimuli should be of nonpainful intensity so that avoidance movements would not be produced. (3) In order to simulate the simple conditions of neurophysiological stimulation experiments, no voluntary reaction to stimulation should be required. (4) Recordings should be made from the somatic motor system with an apparatus capable of following the rapid changes in this system and of providing exact measurements of activity. (5) Given all of these features, the method, to be useful for studies of pathological anxiety, must distinguish clearly between the physiological activity of patients with pathological anxiety, and that of normal subjects.

The purpose of the present preliminary study was to test the differentiative capacity of a method that satisfies the first four criteria. If the method were shown to discriminate effectively between psychoneurotics and normals, it would be useful as a basic tool for further investigations of somatic response mechanisms in psychoneurosis.

As a technique that appeared likely to satisfy the criteria outlined above, we selected a procedure similar to the one used by Davis (2) in his studies of electromyographic response to strong auditory stimuli. Davis showed, with normal subjects, that auditory stimulation produces measurable electromyographic responses, even when subjects are instructed not to respond to the stimulus.

The subjects were 10 psychiatric patients, 5 of each sex, and 10 controls drawn from the medical and secretarial staffs of the hospital and matched with the patients for age and sex. The patients were all psychoneurotics in whom severe pathological anxiety was a prominent symptom. In one case of severe anxiety there were also symptoms suggesting early schizophrenia.

During the experiment the subject lay on a hospital bed. Action potentials from the extensor muscles of the right forearm were recorded by one channel of an Offner (Type D) EEG from silver leads, one placed over the extensor crest and the other at the wrist. The right forearm was placed in the prone position, and the subject was instructed to hold a rubber bulb in the right hand and to maintain a constant pressure on it throughout the experiment. Apart from this, he was asked to relax as much as possible. Davis (2) showed that induced tension increases the electromyographic response to sound. (In preliminary experiments we found that the induced tension provided by the rubber bulb was necessary for responses of sufficient magnitude to be easily recorded by our equipment.)

The auditory stimulus was a 1,000-cycle tone of 3 seconds' duration which was kept at an electrically constant intensity. This intensity was approximately 80 decibels above threshold, as determined by having 8 subjects compare the tone with an audiometer standard. Stimuli were 90 seconds apart, and there were 10 stimuli during the test proper. These were transmitted to the subject through binaural earphones. It should be mentioned that a constant feature of the stimulus was a sharp "on-effect," which gave the impression of a click of very brief duration.

The subject was instructed that he would hear a tone in the earphones. He was asked to disregard this tone and to make no response of any kind. Reassurance regarding the experimental situation was given as needed before and during the test. In a trial period before the test proper, 3 stimuli of increasing intensity were administered, the last one being of the same intensity as that used in the test. The subject was told that the last tone was what he would hear from then on, and that no louder tones would come.

Analysis of the electromyographic tracings was carried out by a method similar to that of Davis. The time periods chosen for measurement were as follows: (a) 1 second preceding the stimulus; (b) the 3-second stimulus period; (c) the 1-second period 12-13 seconds after the start of stimulation. These periods were divided off into fifths of seconds. For each fifth second the largest muscle potential spike was selected. This spike was measured in millimeters, and the millimeter measurements were converted to microvolts by reference to d-c calibrations.[2] This phase of the analysis required 5,000 individual measurements.

In statistical treatment of the data for each subject the 10 stimuli were averaged for each fifth second, and the mean amplitude of the muscle spikes determined. For group averages the medians of these means were calculated, because means would have been unduly influenced by the extremely high poten-

[2]The largest spike in a given time period was selected for measurement in order to reduce the number of measurements required and to facilitate the actual measuring. The assumption was that total potential would parallel the largest spike. Frequency or spike duration was not measured because of methodological difficulties, and because previous studies with present recording methods have shown spike amplitude alone to be an adequate indicator of degree of muscular activity.

tials of 2 subjects in the patient group. The chi-square test was used for determination of statistical reliability.

Median amplitude curves for the patient and control groups are shown in Fig. 1. The median prestimulus tension level of the patient group (24.5μv) was somewhat higher than that of the controls 15.9 μv); however, this difference was not statistically reliable. In the first 0.2 second after onset of the stimulus, both patient and control groups showed approximately equal rise in tension. In the next fifth of a second (0.2-0.4 second), the control subjects' tension fell to approximately prestimulus level, whereas the potentials of the patients continued to rise, so that their response to stimulation was now double that in the first 0.2 second. For the remainder of the stimulus period, EMG amplitude for the controls showed steady tension at about prestimulus level, with only a slight increase in tension at about the 1-second mark (probably the "b-response" of Davis). On the other hand, the patients' curve, after reaching peak amplitude from 0.2 to 0.4 second after start of stimulation, began to descend relatively slowly, and with numerous oscillations. At the end of the 3-second stimulus period, it was still well above the prestimulus level. The measurements for the period, 12-13 seconds after onset of stimulation, revealed that complete recovery had taken place, and both patients and controls were at about their prestimulus tension levels.

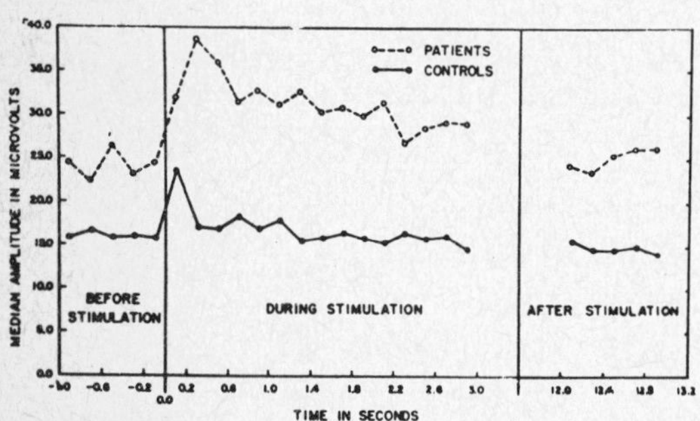

Fig. 1. Comparison of patients and controls with respect to median EMG amplitudes before, during, and after stimulation. Interval of measurement = 0.2 second.

The data shown in Figure 1 reveal a major difference in the response characteristic of the patients and controls. The initial tensional response (0-0.2 second) was equal in both groups, but, whereas the controls then returned to pre-existing tension levels, the patients showed further augmentation of response, and their response was prolonged over the entire period of auditory stimulation. Since the major qualitative and quantitative difference between the groups seemed to be evident particularly in the first second of stimulation, a more detailed analysis of this time period was carried out. The electromyograms for the half-second preceding stimulus onset and the first second of stimulation were remeasured for tenth-second intervals. These data for tenths of seconds were then averaged in the same way as those for fifths.

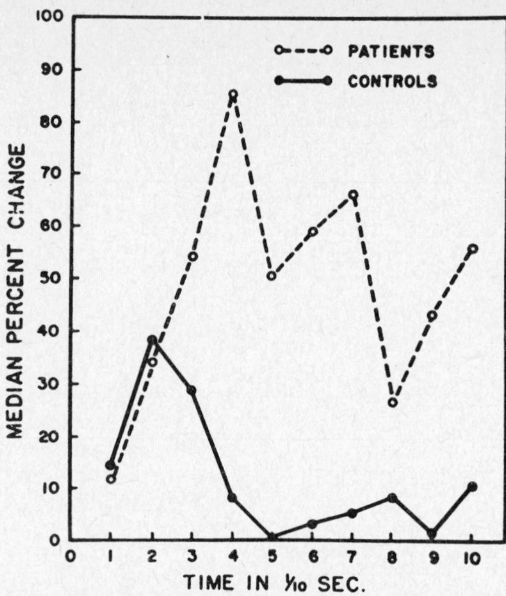

Fig. 2. Per cent change in EMG response during first second of stimulation. Interval of measurement = 0.1 second.

Figure 2 shows response curves for patients and controls during the first second of stimulation. The curves are plotted in terms of median per cent change from the average level preceding the stimulus. Percentages were used to avoid the possible influence of prestimulus tension differences on size of response. Figure 2 shows clearly the identical electromyographic response (change) of patients and controls during the first 0.2 second of stimulation. From 0.2 to 0.3 second the control curve falls, and that of the patients continues to rise, reaching a peak at a time when the controls are almost back to prestimulus level.

The significant difference between patients and controls was shown in two ways: (1) Although immediate electromyographic response (change) upon stimulation was approximately the same in both patient and control groups, after the first 0.2 second of stimulation the change was decidedly greater in the patients. (2) The peak response of the patients occurred much later than the peak response of the controls. The statistical reliability of these differences was determined as follows: (a) The median response of the entire subject group for the period from 0.2 to 0.6 second was determined; 8 of the 10 patients showed responses greater than the median, and 8 of the 10 controls showed responses less then the median. The difference was reliable at the 1 per cent level of confidence. (b) The tenth of a second during which the peak potential was reached during the first second of each stimulus was determined for each subject and for the group. Figure 3 shows how often peaks were observed during each tenth-second inter-

pal in the patient and control groups. Whereas in the control group 50 per cent of the peaks were found in the first 0.2 second, the patients showed only 13 per cent of their peaks from 0.2 to 0.6 second, whereas the controls had only 25 per cent of their peaks during this period. These differences were highly reliable statistically. Individual comparisons between matched patients and controls also yielded a highly reliable difference with respect to the frequency with which peak responses occurred during the first 0.2 second of stimulation.

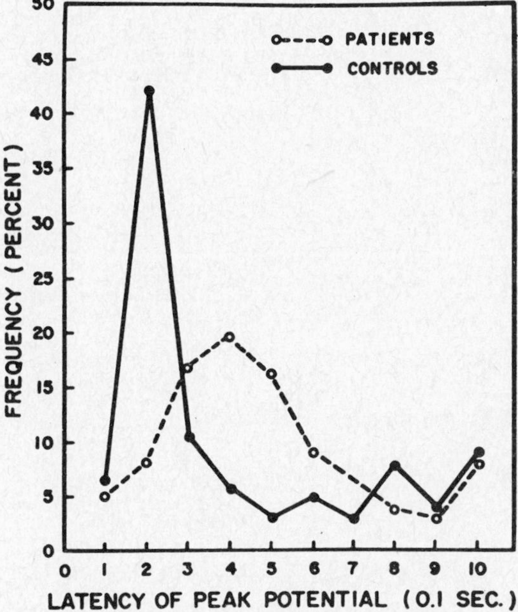

Fig. 3. Distribution curves showing that peak EMG responses in patients occurred most frequently after the normal latency for arm in the startle pattern (approximately 0.2 second).

Onset of tonal stimulation at high intensity and the click ("on-effect") appeared to constitute an effective startle stimulus for the subjects. According to Landis and Hunt (6, p. 30) the latencies for the arm in the startle pattern range from 125 to 195 milliseconds. It was during this interval in our experiment that per cent of change was approximately equal for patients and controls. This also agrees quite well with Davis' finding of what he calls the "a-response" (and which he relates to startle) with a peak at 0.2 second. It seems reasonable to assume, therefore, that the immediate startle reaction was approximately the same in patients and controls. The difference between the groups appeared *after* the 0.2-second period of reflex startle.

These results are what might have been expected from the hypothesis that, in anxiety, inhibition of cortical afterdischarge, through some regulatory mechanism, such as the reticular system (thalamic and/or brain-stem) is defective. The term afterdischarge is used on the assumption that *normally* the initial impact of click and tone has higher stimulating value (startle) than the continuation of the tone for the remainder of the 3-second stimulation interval. This assumption is based on our present finding with normal control subjects.

These positive findings make it seem worth while to proceed to a more detailed analysis of somatic response mechanisms in psychoneurosis. Kubie (5) has previously emphasized the importance of the factor of somatic overexcitation in anxiety. He has integrated observations from the clinical field, from Pavlovian conditioning, and from the work of Landis and Hunt on the startle pattern; and he has identified anxiety with the anticipation of explosive "irradiation" of excitation.

Present considerations suggest that the principal source of somatic overreaction in pathological states of anxiety may be defective somatic regulation by such a mechanism as the thalamocortical elaborative system. The present technique, modified according to the particular purpose of each separate experiment, appears a promising one for further investigations of somatic response mechanisms in psychoneurosis.

References

1. CANNON, W. B. *The wisdom of the body.* New York: Norton, 1939 (see esp. p. 227).
2. DAVIS, R. C. *J. exp. Psychol.*, 1948, *38*, 257.
3. JACOBSEN, E. *Progressive relaxation.* Chicago: Univ. Chicago Press, 1938.
4. JASPER, H. H. *EEG clin. Neurophysiol.*, 1949, *1*, 405.
5. KUBIE, L. S. *Psychosom. Med.*, 1941, *3*, 263.
6. LANDIS, C., and HUNT, W. A. *The startle pattern.* New York: Farrar and Rinehart, 1939.
7. LINDSLEY, D. B., BOWDEN, J. W., and MAGOUN, H. W. *EEG clin. Neurophysiol.*, 1949, *1*, 475.
8. MALMO, R. B., and SHAGASS, C. *Psychosom. Med.*, 1949, *11*, 9.
9. MORUZZI, G., and MAGOUN, H. W. *EEG clin. Neurophysiol.*, 1949, *1*, 455.

44 / Some Empirical Studies of Psychopathy

Robert D. Hare[1] *University of British Columbia*

The psychopath (or sociopath) frequently engages in antisocial, delinquent, or criminal acitivities. He does not exhibit neurotic or psychotic symptoms; yet he deviates from the accepted behavioural norms of his society. The psychopath is typified by the swindler, the "con" man, the habitual criminal, and the pathological liar. At the present time little is known about the causes or effective treatment of psychopathy but the research and speculations presented here by Professor Hare may represent a major advance in this area.

Psychopathy represents one of the most persistent and disruptive forms of abnormal behaviour. It is not surprising, therefore, that a great deal has been written about it. A recent and far from exhaustive bibliography contained over 800 relevant references.[2] What is surprising, however, is that only a small part of this literature is based upon empirical theory and research. The result is that instead of an extensive body of empirical data and comprehensive theories of psychopathy we have a number of mini-theories and hypotheses. All of them are incomplete or restricted to some specific aspect of psychopathy, and many of them are untestable and without empirical foundation. Fortunately this rather unhappy situation is changing rapidly, and I think that within the next few years the elements of a general theory of psychopathy will begin to emerge, largely as a result of the increasing use of procedures and conceptualizations derived from the behavioural and biological sciences.

Characteristics of the Psychopath

Perhaps at this point I should define what I mean by the term, "psychopathy." Briefly, the psychopath is a callous, egocentric, impulsive, frequently aggressive individual who lacks the ability to empathize and to form warm emotional relationships with others. He tends to treat people as objects rather than as persons, experiencing no guilt or remorse for having done so and for having used them to satisfy his own needs. His judgement is poor and his behaviour apparently guided by current, momentary needs. When caught in one of his frequent manipulations or social misadventures, his attempts to extricate himself from difficulty often result in an intricate and contradictory web of lies and rationalizations. These are coupled with theatrical and sometimes convincing explanations and promises to change.

One characteristic that has received some attention is the psychopath's apparent inability to delay the gratification of psychological and physiological needs no matter what the future consequences to himself or others. What other investigators and myself have tried to do is to account for this and related aspects of psychopathic behaviour within the framework of learning theory. In doing so we've made considerable use of the fact that "conditioned" or learned fear plays an important role in the motivation and regulation of behaviour. Learning to inhibit behaviour that is likely to have unpleasant consequences may be viewed as a two-stage process. In the first stage, for example, cues or stimuli associated with punished behaviour acquire the capacity (through Pavlovian or classical conditioning) to elicit fear responses. When next the behaviour begins to occur, anticipatory fear is elicited; and since fear is an unpleasant state the individual is motivated to reduce it. He does so by inhibiting the behaviour that produces the fear-arousing cues. This is the second stage, and it includes the reinforcement, by fear-reduction, of the tendency to inhibit the punished behaviour.

A Model of Psychopathy

The relevance of this is that psychopaths appear to lack the capacity to acquire conditioned anticipatory fear responses.[3] This has led to the suggestion that certain aspects of the psychopath's behaviour, including his apparent disregard for the future consequ-

[1]The author was the recipient of the CMHA 1969 National Mental Health Research Award of $25,000. Since 1966 his research in psychopathy has been financed by Public Health Research Grant 609-7-163, Canadian National Health Grants Program. His forthcoming book, *Psychopathy: Theory and Research* (Wiley, New York) is scheduled for early publication.

[2]R.D.Hare and A.S.Hare, Psychopathic Behaviour: A Bibliography, *Excerpta Criminologica*, 1967, *7*, 365-386.

Reprinted, by permission, from *Canada's Mental Health*, 1970, *18*, No. 1, 4-9, (the bi-monthly journal of the Department of National Health and Welfare, Ottawa).

[3]R.D.Hare, Acquisition and Generalization of a Conditioned-Fear Response in Psychopathic and Non-psychopathic Criminals, *J. of Psych.*, 1965, *59*, 367-370.
D.T.Lykken, A Study of Anxiety in the Sociopathic Personality, *J. of Abnormal and Soc. Psych.*, 1957, *55*, 6-10.

ences of his behaviour are related to the failure of cues (verbal, symbolic, kinesthetic, visual, etc.) associated with punishment to elicit sufficient anticipatory fear for the instigation of the appropriate avoidance behaviour. (By way of contrast, the neurotic may be seen as one who experiences too much anticipatory fear.) Several years ago, I incorporated this suggestion into a simple model of psychopathy which made use of the further assumption that the aversive events anticipated in the near future are generally more fear-arousing (and thus more capable of inhibiting behaviour) than are similar events more remote in time. This situation I described as "temporal gradient of fear-arousal" (and response-inhibition). The important thing here is that this "temporal gradient" is postulated to be much steeper for psychopaths than it is for normal persons. In effect, aversive events expected in the future have virtually no immediate emotional significance for the psychopath. One of my earlier studies provided some empirical support for these postulated gradients of fear-arousal. Subjects were told to expect a strong electric shock at a specific point in time. While the normal ones exhibited a considerable amount of anticipatory fear-arousal (as inferred from physiological recordings) well in advance of impending shock, the psychopathic subjects did not. Similar results in somewhat different contexts have recently been obtained by several other investigators.

It is obvious, of course, that expectation of punishment is not the only factor determining whether or not some specific behaviour will occur. Many responses or actions are ambivalent in nature, having both positive (rewarding) and negative (punishing) consequences. In effect, the individual is motivated to make the response and at the same time to inhibit it. Whether or not the response occurs then depends upon the relative weights subjectively assigned by the individual to the positive and negative consequences of his actions. His task, however, is complicated by the fact that the anticipated rewards and punishments are often located at different points in time. Thus a response may have immediate, rewarding features but delayed unpleasant consequences, or vice versa. The individual's task is therefore one of "temporal integration"[4] in which the relative value or utility of rewards and punishments (and their ability to influence behaviour) is determined by their remoteness in time. Originally I assumed that psychopaths and normal persons had similar "temporal reward gradients." However, on the basis of a recent study by a Ph. D. student of mine, Michael Quinn, as well as what is known about psychopathy clinically, I have recently proposed that the psychopath's temporal reward gradient, like his temporal gradient of fear arousal, is steeper than a normal person's. In other words, future rewards and punishments have little immediate emotional and motivational impact on the psychopath. Whereas the normal person's philosophy may be "live now – pay later," the psychopath's is more likely to be one of "live now – pay never."

The "Two-Dimensional" Person

Most clinical descriptions of the psychopath make some reference to his egocentricity, lack of empathy and feeling for others, and his inability to form warm emotional relationships. These characteristics apparently lead him to treat others as objects rather than as persons and prevent him from experiencing guilt and remorse for his social depredations. This "emotional shallowness," coupled with his normal physical and intellectual characteristics, has led Karpman[5] to refer to the psychopath as a "two-dimensional" person. Similarly, Cleckley[6] has suggested that the psychopath's verbalizations (e.g., "I'm sorry" or "If I do this I'll be caught," etc.) are devoid of appropriate emotional content, a situation referred to as *semantic dementia*. As someone else has put it, "he knows the words but not the music."

There is no doubt that these emotional anomalies have physiological correlates and that they are related to other aspects of the psychopath's behaviour – I've referred to some of them above. Not surprisingly, they have been the subject of a number of investigations concerned with uncovering the physiological (particular autonomic) correlates of psychopathy. In general, the results have been consistent with clinical statements about the psychopath's lack of anxiety, guilt and "emotional tension." That is, psychopaths tend to be autonomically hypo-responsive in a variety of situations that would ordinarily be considered emotion-provoking or stressful.[7] It is likely, for example, that their lack of empathy is associated with failure (or inability) to give the appropriate autonomic responses to the suffering and distress of others, and to situations involving the interpersonal exchange of such emotions as love, affection and remorse. To investigate this possibility, an experiment is being conducted (as part of a larger study, with Dr. Dan Craigen and Roger Brock of Matsqui Institute in British Columbia), on the psychophysiological dimensions of drug addiction in which subjects are required to administer shocks, under various conditions, to other subjects who have the opportunity to retaliate. Our prediction is that the more psychopathic subjects will verbally express concern and distress for the suffering of the others but that the appropriate autonomic correlates of this expression will be absent. We are also interested in whether the

[4]K.E.Renner, Conflict Resolution and the Process of Temporal Integration, *Psych. Reports,* Monograph Supplement No. 2, 1964, *15*, 423-438.

[5]B.Karpman, The Structure of Neurosis: With Special Differentials Between Neurosis, Psychosis, Homosexuality, Alcoholics, Psychopathy and Criminality, *Arch. of Criminal Psychodynamics*, 1961, *4*, 599-646.

[6]H.Cleckley, *The Mask of Sanity*. 4th ed. St. Louis, Mo: Mosby, 1964.

[7]R.D.Hare, Psychopathy, Autonomic Functioning, and the Orienting Response, *J. of Abnorm. Psychol.*, 1968, *73*, Monograph Supplement No. 3, Part 2.

psychopath is capable of "vicarious" conditioning to the cues associated with the rewards and punishments administered to others. If he is incapable of acquiring conditioned emotional responses vicariously, an important means of obtaining information and guidance from the contingencies in his social environment (e.g., observational learning, modelling, role-playing, etc.) would be denied him.

Some Treatment Programs

If part of the psychopath's difficulty is in experiencing the appropriate autonomic correlates of emotional behaviour, it may be possible to take some form of remedial action. For example, adrenalin increases the activity of the sympathetic branch of the nervous system. We might therefore expect that it could be used to increase the psychopath's capacity to experience anticipatory fear and thereby to avoid socially undesirable behaviour. That adrenalin can in fact enhance the psychopath's ability to avoid punishment (behaviour that I've earlier indicated is dependent upon anticipatory fear-arousal) has been nicely shown by Schacter and Latane.[8] In my opinion psychopaths tend to show rapid homeostatic recovery of autonomic activity following termination of a stressful episode. One of the consequences of this short-lived autonomic activity is that the emotional components of a stressful situation would be largely confined to the temporal period in which the situation occurs. As a result, the length of time during which autonomic activity could become conditioned to external and internal stimuli would be relatively short. This would mean that, compared with the normal person (and especially the neurotic) there would be few cues with the capacity to elicit the autonomic components of fear and anxiety. What I am suggesting is that the drugs such as adrenalin could perhaps be used to increase and prolong the psychopath's autonomic activity in selected social situations. This might thereby provide him with the opportunity of acquiring more effective emotional responses to a wider range of stimuli. In any case, it might seem worthwhile to set up a long-term experimental treatment program, somewhat like the "therapeutic communities" found in Denmark and Holland. But this might also include procedures designed to increase the motivating and guiding influence of fear and anxiety and to make social reinforcers more effective.

Psychopathic Arousal Levels

Much of the preceding has been based upon the recognition that the autonomic nervous system plays an important role in emotional behaviour. Some of my recent research has been concerned with the proposal that the psychopath's autonomic activity has implications for his cortical and sensory functioning. The proposal is based upon the rapidly accumulating evidence that complex interactive relationships exist between autonomic, cortical, sensory and behavioural processes. Very briefly, there is reason to believe that certain aspects of the psychopath's autonomic functioning are associated with a tendency towards cortical "underarousal" and a high sensory threshold. As used here, arousal is a dimension representing the physiological and psychological state of the individual. The low end of the dimension is characterized by deep sleep, complete loss of awareness, and a low level of physiological activity. As arousal increases, the individual's awareness of the environment and his behavioural efficiency also increase, but only up to a point. Beyond some optimal level of arousal, awareness and efficiency tend to break down, as for instance, in highly agitated states. A similar relationship probably exists between arousal and affective experience. Both high and low levels of arousal are less pleasant than some more moderate level. One implication of this latter relationship is that an individual in a low state of arousal will seek to increase it, while one who is in a heightened state of arousal will seek to decrease it. One of the most important determinants of arousal is stimulation. The sensory pathways send collaterals into the reticular formation which in turn sends diffuse excitatory impulses to the cortex of the brain. We would therefore expect an individual to either seek stimulation or to avoid it, depending upon whether he is below or above what is for him an optimal level of arousal for the particular situation in which he finds himself.

Now, it appears that the environmental conditions that permit a normal person to enjoy an optimal level of arousal tend to produce a state of cortical underarousal in the psychopath. As a consequence, he tends to be bored and restless and to seek stimulation that is exciting, novel, varied and unpredictable. He looks for activities that others would consider dangerous, foolish or frightening. He might also tend to resort to all forms of self-generated stimulation, including fantasy and daydreams, when appropriate sources of external stimulation are not available. Incidentally, I think that if we examine the content of his fantasies we will find that the psychopath is concerned with "exciting" themes rather than with mental planning. This would help to account for some of his poor judgement and lack of foresight, assuming that one of the functions of fantasy is to permit "vicarious trial and error" in which various sources of action and their possible consequences are run through mentally beforehand. Besides self-generated stimulation, a psychopath should show a marked preference for psychotomimetic drugs (e.g., *LSD-25*) and drugs that are psychomotor stimulants (e.g., amphetamine, methadrine).

Besides a tendency towards cortical and autonomic underarousal, psychopathy may be associated with a tendency for sensory input to be "gated out" or

[8]S.Schacter and B.Latane, Crime, Cognition and the Autonomic Nervous System. In M.R.Jones (ed.) *Nebraska Symposium on Motivation*, (Lincoln, Neb.: Univ. of Nebraska Press, 1964), pp. 221-275.

attenuated during transmission from the receptors to the higher cortical centers. If the psychopath's sensory input is in fact subject to a certain degree of attenuation during transmission, a given amount of stimulation would tend to move him a shorter distance up the arousal continuum than it would if he were a normal person. The result would be even more of a tendency to seek new and exciting sources of stimulation than if he were simply cortically underaroused. There could be other consequences of a general tendency to attenuate sensory input. For one thing, many of the cues essential for adequate social functioning are subtle and of low intensity. The psychopath's tendency to attenuate sensory input would mean that some of these cues would be below threshold and ineffective. In addition, in an attempt to attain an optimal level of arousal, he would actively seek intense stimulation, however, he would probably miss, or perhaps simply ignore, many social cues – cues that have important informational and emotional content, and that are needed for the guidance of social behaviour. As a result, the psychopath would ordinarily be little influenced by many of the cues emanating from other individuals such as signs of distress, approval or disapproval. If, however, these cues had special significance for him – as would be the case if he was trying to use others to satisfy his own needs – we might expect that a concerted effort would be made to attend to them more closely.

Towards Long-Term Research

Besides a general tendency to attenuate sensory input, it is possible that psychopaths are able to selectively "tune out" or at least greatly attenuate stimulation that is potentially disturbing, a process that some clinicians would perhaps refer to as a "defensive mechanism." What interests me here is that such processes appear to be psychophysiological in nature, with identifiable cortical and autonomic correlates. One consequence of an ability to "tune-out" potentially disturbing input, is that threats of punishment and cues warning of unpleasant consequences for misbehaviour would not have the same emotional impact that they would have for other individuals. Hopefully, some of our current and planned research will shed further light on these rather intriguing possibilities.

Finally, I should note that one of the limitations of research on psychopathy is that it has for the most part been carried out with adult subjects. What is needed, therefore, is a long-term study of the variables related to the development of the disorder. As an initial step in this direction, we are planning a study in which the psychophysiological characteristics of adolescent probationers will be subjected to intensive investigation. We hope that the results will provide us with a set of working hypotheses which will make it feasible to begin working with even younger children. Ultimately, when time and funds are available, I would hope to be able to begin a very long-term study in which a large number of children selected at random are thoroughly studied from birth. The aim would be to uncover the psychophysiological and experiential precursors of psychopathy and to determine whether early intervention is (at least theoretically) feasible.

45 / Future Time Perspectives in Alcoholics and Social Drinkers

Reginald G. Smart *Alcoholism and Drug Addiction Research Foundation, Toronto*

The ability to plan for the future and to foresee long-term consequences of present actions is characteristic of the well-integrated personality. Evidence is presented here to indicate that alcoholics exhibit shortened and distorted future time perspectives.

One of the most puzzling aspects of the alcoholic's behaviour has always been the persistence of frequently punished responses. Although the alcoholic can derive immediate anxiety reduction from drinking alcoholic beverages, his drinking is frequently punished by the occurrence of blackouts, hangovers, ill health, loss of employment, and disruption of family ties (Jellinek, 1946). Unlike the anxiety-reducing effects of alcohol, most of the punishments for drinking are delayed, if only for a few hours or days. Some of the most striking *sequelae* to alcoholic drinking, for example, liver cirrhosis and early death, are delayed as much as 15 or 20 years, while those of a social nature are less delayed but still not immediate.

One possible explanation for the alcoholic's ability to tolerate these punishments may be that he has developed a different time orientation than is usual in nonalcoholics. Chiefly, this orientation would be one which is deficient in future time perspective. It could be argued that the alcoholic does not respond to delayed punishments for drinking because they appear in a shortened and poorly perceived future in which present behaviour loses its usual consequences. Gliedman (1956) has suggested from clinical impressions that alcoholics seem to live in an "extended present" unaffected by past or future. This study is concerned with comparing the future time perspectives of alcoholics with those of a matched group of social drinkers.

Only one aspect of time orientation – that of future time perspective – is examined here. This concept has been defined by Wallace (1956) as "the timing and ordering of personalized future events." Two constituent aspects, extension and coherence, have been defined. Extension refers to "the length of the future time span which is conceptualized," and coherence to "the degree of organization of the events in the future time span."

Wallace (1956) has devised several tests which have been used (Barndt and Johnson, 1955; Wallace, 1956) to measure aspects of future time perspective. These tests involve (a) the description and organization of future events and (b) story-completion techniques. It is hypothesized here that alcoholics will show less extensive and less coherent future perspectives than social drinkers on these tasks. The correlation between extension and age of the alcoholics will also be investigated. Among alcoholic clinic patients age has a high positive correlation with length of drinking career ($r = .638$, $p < .0005$ for $n = 58$) (Smart, 1966).

Method

Subjects

The Alcoholic group consisted of 33 alcoholics attending the out-patient and day-care facilities of the Alcoholism and Drug Addiction Research Foundation. All of these alcoholics had a long history of uncontrolled drinking and previous attempts at therapy. They manifested the usual symptoms of alcoholism such as uncontrolled craving, frequent drunkenness, and inability to control their intake. None was overtly psychotic; all were diagnosed as neurotics or character disorders.

The Nonalcoholic group consisted of 33 social drinkers. It included people from employment agencies, people in skilled trades, and a few professionals from the Ontario College of Education and from the staff of the Alcoholism and Drug Addiction Research Foundation. None of the social drinkers had any convictions for public intoxication nor any previous treatment for a drinking problem. Their drinking frequency and quantity were within normal limits. The total number tested in this group was considerably larger than 33. The *S*s were chosen from this larger number so that the Social Drinker group would match the Alcoholic group in age, sex, marital status, and occupational category.

Procedure

The *S*s were required to do two tasks which were the same as those used by Wallace (1956) in studying

From Smart R. G. Future time perspectives in alcoholics and social drinkers. *J. abnorm. Psychol.*, 1968, *73*, 81-83.

the future perspectives of schizophrenics.[1] The third task used by Wallace was not used here as it required *S*s to tell at what ages various events might happen to them. This task seemed inappropriate for alcoholics who would be in their 40s and 50s and would have already experienced such events in their past – for example, birth of first grandchild, youngest child leaving home, reaching middle age.

Task I consisted of two parts, the first concerned with *extension* and the second with *coherence*. On the first part *E* gave the following instructions: "Tell me ten events that refer to things that may happen to you during the rest of your life." Each event was recorded on a separate card and after each event was given *E* asked: "And how old might you be when that happened?" The age given was also recorded but not on the cards.

Table I – Medians and sums of ranks for extension scores obtained by alcoholics and non alcoholics

Tasks	Alcoholics		Nonalcoholics		U	p
	Mdn	Sum of ranks	Mdn	Sum of ranks		
I Part I	5 yr.	821.0	22 yr.	1390.0	3.65	.00016
II Story A	1 ¾ hr.	979.0	2 hr.	1037.0	.179	.4325
Story B	2 hr.	1008.0	2 hr.	1137.0	.630	.2643
Story C	½ hr.	863.5	1 ¾ hr.	1281.5	2.53	.0057
Story D	½ hr.	683.5	1 hr.	1146.5	3.54	.0023

The second part of Task I was done after Task II had been completed. The 10 cards were returned to *S* and he was asked to "arrange these cards in the order in which they might occur." The ordering given was recorded.

The measure of extension in Task I was based on the range of years included between *S*'s actual age and the most distant event given by him. The coherence measure was the rank-order correlation between ranking of events based on age of occurrence in Part I with the order of events given in Part II.

Task II was concerned only with *extension*. It consisted of four story-completion items which were first used by Barndt and Johnson (1955) and revised by Wallace (1956).

The following instructions were given to *S*s:

Story A: "I want to see what kind of a story you can tell. I'll start one for you, and then let you finish it any way you wish. I'll start it now. At three o'clock one bright sunny afternoon in May, two men were walking near the end of town . . . Now you start there and finish the story for me."

Story B: "That was fine. Now I'll begin another story which, as before, you may finish any way you want to. Here it is: Ten o'clock one morning Al met his friend Jerry near the centre of town . . . Now you start there and finish it for me."

Story C: "That was pretty good. Now here is the start of another story which you may again finish in any way you wish. Joe is having a cup of coffee in a restaurant. He's thinking of the time to come when . . . Now you finish it for me."

Story D: "Here is the last story that I'll give you. I want you to finish it any way you wish, just like you did on the other stories. Here it is: After awakening Bill began to think about his future. In general he expected to . . . Now you start there and finish it for me."

All stories were recorded verbatim. After each story *E* asked, "How long a time was involved in this story – not in telling it, but in the action described?" A record was made of the time taken by each story and these were used as measures of extension.

Five separate measures of extension were obtained, one for Task I and four for Task II. There was no effort to sum or average these measures and the distributions for each were treated separately. It can be seen that Stories A and B contain explicit mentions of time while Stories C and D do not.

Results

The score distributions for extension showed some departures from normality so that statistical comparisons were made with a nonparametric technique. The Mann-Whitney *U* test (Siegel, 1956) was used to compare the alcoholics and social drinkers on the five measures of extension. Table I shows the medians and sums of the ranks for each group. The Alcoholic group shows significantly shorter extension than the social drinkers on three out of five measures. However, on the two stories (A and B) where specific mention of time was made there is no difference.

It proved to be extremely difficult to get adequate coherence scores for the alcoholics but no problem at all among the social drinkers. Only 12 out of 33 alcoholics were able to order completely or to assign ages to the 10 events of Task I. Some could order only a few events and could not imagine when the others would occur; others could give no ordering at all. It was surprising to find this task so difficult for nonpsychotic alcoholics, most of whom were employed or recently employed, living with families and functioning in a minimally adequate way in many non-drinking situations.

Complete rank-order correlations were obtained only for 12 alcoholics, and their coherence scores were compared with the social drinkers' scores. The Mann-Whitney test indicated that the 12 alcoholics who *could* order the future events had significantly lower coherence scores than did the social drinkers ($U = 2.07$, $p < .02$). Because this analysis leaves out all those alcoholics who could not generate coherence scores, this finding is a very conservative estimate of the difference between the groups.

As hypothesized, there was a significant negative correlation (Spearman $r = -.434$, $p < .001$) between age and extension on Task I for the alcohol-

[1]The author wishes to thank Susan Pepper and Marilyn Cooper for obtaining and processing the data.

ics. However, the correlation for social drinkers was nonsignificant ($r = -.20$, $p > .05$). Also, extension scores and number of years of drinking showed no correlation for the social drinkers ($r = .12$, $p > .05$).

Discussion

Striking differences were found between the alcoholics and social drinkers in two aspects of future time perspective. Alcoholics, when given unstructured tasks with no explicit mention of time, show far less extensive perspectives than do social drinkers. When given more structured tasks with specific mention of time, they show no difference compared with social drinkers.

Achieving a coherent ordering of future events seems almost unusually difficult for many alcoholics. Those who can achieve some ordering show less coherence than do social drinkers. The results for alcoholics are not too different from those for institutionalized schizophrenics (Wallace, 1956), although alcoholics seem to depart further from normals on extension, and much further on measures of coherence.

These findings do not clearly indicate whether the shortened and disordered future time perspective results from uncontrolled drinking or whether it is a prior selective factor in the development of alcoholism. However, the high negative correlation between extension and age (and presumably years of drinking) suggests that it may be a coping mechanism developed during uncontrolled drinking. Perhaps as their drinking gets increasingly out of control, and as the unpleasant consequences build up (e.g., difficulties with employment, family stability, and general health), the alcoholic perceives such a bleak future that he refrains from extending it or ordering what little future is perceived. An alternative explanation is that alcoholics cannot take account of the negative consequences of their drinking because to do so requires an elaborate time perspective. When the impulse to drink heavily occurs, it is readily acted upon because the lack of a future orientation prevents consideration of sanctions or other negative reinforcements contingent upon drunkenness.

It is interesting to speculate on the implications of these findings for treatment. They suggest that treatments emphasizing long-term changes and dire eventualities may be less effective than treatments focusing on the present. It would also be interesting to know if those alcoholics with extensive and coherent future perspectives continue longer in treatment than those without, and if they show greater improvement.

Abstract

The differences in future time perspective between alcoholics and social drinkers were investigated. 33 alcoholics and 33 social drinkers matched for age, sex, occupation, and marital status were compared using Wallace's method of measuring future time perspective. It was found that the alcoholics had substantially less extensive and less coherent perspectives. A correlation between age and extension for the alcoholics indicates that the deficiency may develop as a response to problem drinking rather than being a selective factor in its development.

References

BARNDT, R. J., and JOHNSON, D. M. Time orientation in delinquents. *Journal of Abnormal and Social Psychology,* 1955, *51,* 343-345.

GLIEDMAN, L. H. Temporal orientation and alcoholism. *Addictions,* 1956, *3,* 11-14.

JELLINEK, E. M. Phases in the drinking history of alcoholics. Analysis of a survey conducted by the official organ of Alcoholics Anonymous. *Quarterly Journal of Studies on Alcohol,* 1946, *7,* 1-88.

SIEGEL, S. *Nonparametric statistics for the behavioural sciences.* New York: McGraw-Hill, 1956.

SMART, R. G. Verbal conditioning with reward and punishment in alcoholics. Alcoholism and Drug Addiction Research Foundation. Substudy 28-7-66, 1966.

WALLACE, M. Future time perspective in schizophrenia. *Journal of Abnormal and Social Psychology,* 1956, *52,* 240-245.

46 / L.S.D.: Problems and Promise

Reginald G. Smart *Alcoholism and Drug Addiction Research Foundation, Toronto*

In the past decade there has been an unprecedented willingness on the part of adolescents and young adults to alter their experiences and emotions by means of drugs such as lysergic acid diethylamide (L.S.D.). Nevertheless, many are apprehensive about the long-term effects of L.S.D. Is L.S.D. addictive? Can it precipitate prolonged psychotic reactions? Can it cause genetic damage which might affect their future children? Evidence on such questions is slowly accumulating and Dr. Smart presents here a summation of our present knowledge about L.S.D.

It was Osler who said that "The desire to take medicine is perhaps the greatest feature which distinguishes man from animals." In itself perhaps this is not sinister, but what characterizes much of the modern approach to taking medicine is self-prescription for non-physical purposes. Many people are not merely content to take medicine for physical illnesses but they wish drugs to modify their feelings and emotions, their innermost thoughts, even their perceptions of the real world. One of the consequences of the great psychopharmacological revolution of the 1950's is the growing tendency of people to expect mood and perceptual modification from drugs. The newer drugs such as L.S.D. provide this in a most striking, almost terrifying manner. Their use has fewer medical than psychological implications – at least in the sense that L.S.D., at present, probably cannot be used to successfully treat any medical or psychiatric condition. What is most interesting about L.S.D. has to do with the people who use it and their motivations for doing so. This article will explore these motivations and examine some of the problems created by its use. L.S.D. also holds promise – albeit a limited one – but one plagued by the problems of its use and abuse, problems so great as to make it a drug of very questionable scientific worth.

Discovery of L.S.D.

The discovery of L.S.D. as a hallucinogen was made by Dr. Albert Hofmann and described in Stoll (1) in 1947. Lysergic acid has been known as a constituent of ergot, a parasitic fungus which affects rye in extremely wet weather. Only when Hofmann added diethylamide did it become hallucinogenic. Although he did this in 1938, he did not discover the psychic effects until 1943. The entry in his notes reads, "Last Friday, the 16th of April, I had to leave my work in the laboratory and go home because I felt strangely restless and dizzy. Once there, I lay down and sank into a not unpleasant delirium which was marked by an extreme degree of fantasy. In a sort of trance with closed eyes (I found the daylight unpleasantly glaring) fantastic visions of extraordinary vividness accompanies by a Kaleidoscopic play of intense colouration swirled around me. After two hours this condition subsided." Hofmann realized that his fantasy must have been due to accidental ingestion of L.S.D., later making studies to clarify its effects on himself. Having taken about 250 mcg, he experienced most of its acute effects.

L.S.D. is a drug which is extremely potent in small amounts – only 100 mcg is sufficient to produce a reaction in people who take it for the first time. When ingested, it is rapidly absorbed and passes quickly from the blood into the brain and other organs, and thence into the bile. (2) Studies of the metabolism of L.S.D. show that half of it has left the body in 35 minutes; after two hours only traces can be found.

Acute Effects

The major effects of L.S.D. are variable, depending on the person's mood, expectations and his previous experience with it. However, there are a few similarities that have been noted among almost all types of reactions. Probably the main effects are visual and emotional. Many people report a heightening of brightness and colour perception – colours seem absolutely saturated, intense and vivid. Bright objects appear brilliant, luminous or glowing. Objects are often fantastically distorted – either much too large or too small, or they are convoluted, wavy, distorted, or smashed up. Often there is the perception of movement in stationary objects. Some people report that walls pulse in and out, or undulate, and that stairs look like escalators and move continually. Frequently it is difficult to hear correctly after L.S.D. –

Reprinted, by permission, from *Canada's Mental Health*, Supp. No. 57, 1968 (the bi-monthly journal of the Department of National Health and Welfare, Ottawa).

people may seem to be shouting or whispering. Many feel that their attention becomes focused on some object during L.S.D. sessions. There are also difficulties in concentrating on intellectual tasks. People lose track of time and usually feel that it is passing more slowly than usual, although some find the opposite. Most people report that their bodies feel strange – particularly, they feel numbness, tingling, chills, nausea, and physical weakness, especially in the earliest stages. Dissociation of the person from his body and a melting of the body into the background is also common.

On an emotional level, the changes are complex and highly variable. Many people feel that they have lost control of their emotions – some become angry, some tearful and depressed, and a few silly and immature. L.S.D. may get people to relive childhood experiences, or promote transcendental or mystical experiences. It is also said to create self-awareness, an increased self-acceptance, and does away with the need for psychological defence mechanisms. Anxiety, psychological pain and suffering are said to disappear. Through L.S.D., rapid personality change is said to follow the mystical, transcendental or visionary experience.

Therapeutic Use

L.S.D. appears to have no scientifically warranted use in the treatment of any disorder. Even its occasional playful use may lead to a variety of complications. And with respect to the cultural context in which L.S.D. is so often taken, i.e., the hippy subculture of people who have "dropped out," "tuned in" and "turned on," whether this *really* creates a problem or not is uncertain – no doubt most "straight" people (non-drug users) would consider that it does.

Few drugs have had so much research interest focused on them as L.S.D. For more than 20 years researchers have been trying to find a use for it – a use in understanding schizophrenia, or in treating neurotics and alcoholics. The early conception that L.S.D. could be used to study schizophrenia because it produced a model psychosis, has long been given up. The L.S.D. psychosis does not sufficiently resemble the schizophrenic psychosis to tell us anything new about schizophrenia. Nor is L.S.D. useful in the treatment of the mentally ill. Where it has been carefully compared with existing treatments, it was not found to be superior(3) L.S.D. only seems to be useful where it is not compared with a control group treated in the same way, but not getting L.S.D. This is particularly true in the case of alcoholism; the Ontario Addiction Research Foundation has supported two studies which show that L.S.D. with psychotherapy is not better than psychotherapy without it. Another study (4) by a committed proponent of L.S.D. has also found that its supposed value with alcoholics disappears when carefully controlled studies are made. L.S.D., then, is a drug which can be used only for "kicks," self-exploration, or for religio-philosophical experiences but not for therapeutic purposes.

Unfavourable Reactions

The proponents of the therapeutic and psychedelic uses of L.S.D. have often said that it is relatively safe, but this lack of safety constitutes a most serious problem. Sometimes the dangers are made into a virtue, since Leary (5) has said that "it becomes necessary for us to go out of our minds in order for us to use our heads." Heard (6) tells us that "the hallucinogens are less harmful than aspirin or alcohol, less dangerous than riding in a motor car." Despite these assurances, it now appears that a variety of serious complications can result from both the therapeutic and non-therapeutic uses of L.S.D. Reports of these complications have grown from only a few prior to 1960, to six reports in 1966 and early 1967 containing 158 cases.

The most serious complications include prolonged psychotic reactions, recurrent L.S.D. experiences, disturbed non-psychotic reactions, and less frequently, suicide, homicide, and convulsions. It has also been suggested that the acute toxic effects of L.S.D. could lead to death. Without a clear demonstration, some persons have speculated that L.S.D. users could develop addiction or physical dependence and that they could be led to try drugs such as heroin or morphine. By June of 1967 there were 20 reports which contained the details of 225 adverse reactions to L.S.D.[1]

Toxic Reactions

With any drug having such striking physical and behavioural effects as L.S.D. there is always the question of lethal toxicity. Toxic effects from L.S.D. appear to be of minor importance, provided the drug is relatively pure and the dose taken is small (100 to 300 mcg). Poisonings from L.S.D. have not been reported in man except from morning glory seeds, and they contain a variety of substances in addition to L.S.D. The possibilities that ergotism (marked by vasoconstriction and peripheral coldness) can result from taking these seeds, have been described by Hoffer. (8)

The lethal dose of L.S.D. for man is not known, since no human death from an overdose has been reported. Almost all studies of lethal doses in non-human species have used acute intravenous doses and this provides a useful analogy to the therapeutic and experimental uses, but L.S.D. taken in unsupervised settings is usually eaten or dissolved in a drink. The intravenous and ingestive lethal doses might be rather different, as with drugs such as morphine. What is clear from all available lethality studies on non-hu-

[1]Much of the material on adverse effects is condensed from a longer review by Smart and Bateman.(7)

mans is that the acute lethal dose for man is probably many times the usual therapeutic or psychedelic dose of 100-300 mg. However, studies of the accumulation of toxic effects over a long series of doses have not been made with humans.

L.S.D. has been found by a few investigators to produce convulsions. (9), (10) If these convulsions are a true toxic reaction rather than a peculiar response of certain individuals, it is surprising that the reports are so infrequent.

Recently there have been studies of the genetic and fetal damage caused by L.S.D. Studies reported in 1967 (11) showed that a moderate amount of L.S.D. placed in tissue cultures of leucocytes created chromosome breaks during cell division. This occurred in 10 to 20 per cent of the cells treated with L.S.D. Chromosome breaks also occurred in a patient tested eight months after he had received 15 L.S.D. administrations. A later study (12) showed that six out of eight L.S.D. users, compared to only one out of nine controls, had chromosome abnormalities. However, the latest in this series of studies (13) found that chromosome breaks in users were not more frequent than those in non-users.

Studies have also been made of the fetal abnormalities resulting from L.S.D. use in pregnant females. A large variety of abnormalities such as spinal defects, brain hemorrhages, and edema in various body regions have been found. Three studies, done with rats, (14) mice, (15) and hamsters (16) have found unusually high rates of abnormalities in animals born to L.S.D.-treated mothers. However, a recently published study (17) found no effect of L.S.D. on the offspring of rats treated during pregnancy. As yet there are no extensive studies of these abnormalities in humans. In summary, the use of L.S.D. carries uncertain risks to chromosomes and offspring.

Prolonged Psychotic Reactions

There have been 138 cases of prolonged psychotic reactions to L.S.D., including those in therapeutic, experimental and unsupervised settings. The most typical symptoms seem to be paranoid delusions, schizophrenic-like hallucinations and overwhelming fear. The majority of these psychoses have required special tranquillizer medication or hospitalization lasting from a few days to several years. Psychiatrists in Los Angeles reported (18) that 68% of their 70 cases required more than one month of hospitalization, but five to six months is not unusual in isolated cases. Psychiatrists at the Bellevue Hospital in New York found (19) that 30 of 52 cases of prolonged psychosis became normal within 48 hours. A further 11 patients required two to seven days, and six more a longer period of time. Surprisingly, five of those six "had no psychiatric history or had previous psychiatric history but were adequately integrated." There can be no doubt that serious, prolonged psychoses may result from L.S.D. use.

It appears that *some* persons who experienced prolonged psychoses after illicit L.S.D. use had prior psychiatric diagnoses. Psychiatrists in Los Angeles found that 27 out of 70 persons with both mixed psychotic and non-psychotic reactions had previous psychiatric treatment; 25 (36%) had been diagnosed as psychotic before taking L.S.D. The Bellevue study contained only 12 out of 52 (23%) who were psychotic or schizoid personalities, and of these seven were "adequately integrated into society." It is clear that these rates of pre-L.S.D. psychoses are much higher than in the general population; however we are uncertain how many psychotics can take L.S.D. without a prolonged psychotic episode. A more important point is the L.S.D. is precipitating prolonged psychoses in many persons who cannot be diagnosed as psychotic, or who have only minor personality disturbances or none at all. In fact, about 77% of the prolonged psychoses from L.S.D. in the Bellevue study could *not* have been predicted from previous psychotic disturbances.

Spontaneous Recurrences

A further complication, for which there is no adequate explanation, is the spontaneous recurrence of parts of the L.S.D. experience.(20), (21). In at least 11 cases, frightening delusions or hallucinations have reappeared weeks or months after the last ingestion of L.S.D. and after an interval of normality.

The possible mechanisms for spontaneous recurrences are difficult to identify at present. There is a close connection between spontaneous recurrences and the frequency with which L.S.D. has been taken. In six of the 11 cases noted above, exact doses were reported and these persons had taken L.S.D. (or similar hallucinogens) on 10 to 12, 200 to 300, 25, 9, 15 and over 200 occasions. This is much more frequent than that found for persons experiencing only prolonged psychoses, about half of whom have taken it only once or on a few occasions. The connection between frequent L.S.D. taking and recurrent experiences suggests that L.S.D. itself, or some of its effects, may persist or build up over repeated administrations sufficiently to cause a recurring experience, particularly under stress.

Prolonged Non-Psychotic Reactions

In addition to psychoses and recurrent experiences, L.S.D. has resulted in a variety of disturbed reactions which are difficult to classify.(10, 22, 23) In all, 63 cases of non-psychotic prolonged reactions to L.S.D. have been described. These could be classified as 39 cases of acute panic or confused reactions, 17 cases marked by depression, five cases of antisocial or psychopathic behaviour, one case of a "motor-excitatory state," and one case of chronic anxiety. Virtually all of the non-psychotic reactions occurred in persons who took L.S.D. alone, or in unsupervised settings. The doses taken do not seem to be abnormally large, except for those who had psychopathic reactions. They tended to take large doses or to have taken it very frequently (up to 2,000 mcg weekly for 3 years, in the case described by Cohen). Where the information is given, most had previous personality disturbances.

Suicide

Depressions accompanied by suicide have often been reported as a complication from L.S.D. administrations. The first study of such suicides was made by Cohen(10) who queried 62 L.S.D. therapists about the complications seen. Only 44 replied; nonetheless, they had administered L.S.D or mescaline to 5,000 persons. Five attempted suicides had resulted, but four of these occurred many months after the L.S.D. session.

Since Cohen's questionnaire study there have been reports of 14 attempted and six successful suicides, and nine persons with possible suicidal intent.(22, 24, 19) The successful suicides were all males, two were college students and both had taken L.S.D. in an unprotected setting. Two of the successful suicides and four of the attempted suicides occurred during or soon after therapy with L.S.D.

In summary, suicide attempts are an important complication from L.S.D. administration. Some of them occur in persons who take L.S.D. in non-medical settings, although seven successful and twelve unsuccessful suicides have occurred as a result of therapy. There is, of course, a difficulty in attributing all of these suicides to L.S.D. therapy, since it is typically given to disturbed persons already prone to suicide. Probably no more than half of the suicides would be directly attributed to L.S.D. by the therapists involved.

It is difficult to specify further the conditions leading to L.S.D.-related suicides. The dosage likely to lead to attempted suicide cannot be specified, but it may be as low as 40 mcg for severly disturbed persons. Almost nothing is known about suicide *rates* among persons who take L.S.D. in unprotected settings, although rates for those given L.S.D. in therapy are low, if they have not been under-reported.

Homicide and Assault

Some persons have been found to react to L.S.D. with increased emotionality and aggressiveness. In at least four cases this has led to homicidal attempts or threats, and in one case to a completed homicide.

Only one case of successful homicide has occurred after treatment with L.S.D. Knudsen.(25) described a 25 year old woman who murdered her boy friend two days after the last of five L.S.D. sessions. The murder was not committed during the acute effects of L.S.D. but a close connection is apparent, since the desire to kill the boy friend was expressed during at least one L.S.D. session. In this patient, L.S.D. appeared to release aggressive drives and weaken self-control. She had been diagnosed as a psychopathic personality with chronic alcoholism, and prior disturbances may have contributed to her lack of control after L.S.D.

Addiction and Dependence

Addiction and dependence on L.S.D. have been mentioned as possible complications, with few indications that they actually occur. Farnsworth (26) has also stated that "until we know otherwise, it is prudent for us to assume ... that regular use of the hallucinogens will prepare individuals to 'move up' to other and more powerful drugs such as morphine or diacetylmorphine (heroin)." However, there is no evidence yet that L.S.D. users move up to heroin.

Addiction can be understood as a state of physical dependence marked by increased tolerance and physiological withdrawal symptoms. Tolerance to L.S.D. develops rapidly, but it also dissipates rapidly. Many volunteers for L.S.D. studies do not wish to take the drug again, particularly if it is not given as a therapeutic agent. Consequently, few would have the chance to develop tolerance to it. No studies of human L.S.D. use have studied tolerance over a long period of time (e.g., several years), but there are many reports of persons taking L.S.D. numerous times. So far, there are no reported cases of pharmacological addiction to L.S.D.

Questions have also been raised about long-term dependence on L.S.D. and about the creation of psychological or social damage (via personality changes, damage to employability, family relationships, moral and ethical controls, etc.). Again, clear cases of dependency over a long period of time have rarely been reported. Perhaps the only such case involved a woman who took L.S.D. 200 to 300 times in a year; she developed psychological dependence on it, but no withdrawal symptoms were described.(23) No studies have been made of the psychological or social damage resulting from long-term use.

The Basis for Unfavourable Reactions

The reported cases may appear to reflect a striking social problem to the observer, but it is uncertain what proportion of the total L.S.D. sessions result in adverse reactions. Several conditions are associated with unfavourable reactions. Most of the reactions in every category described occur most frequently in persons taking L.S.D. in unprotected settings – alone, with friends, or with other L.S.D. takers. About 17 per cent of the prolonged psychotic and virtually all of the non-psychotic reactions, were outside therapeutic and experimental use. Only three out of 11 recurrences came after therapeutic use. However, almost two-thirds of the suicidal attempts, and the only successful homicide, occurred in carefully protected settings; this poses an enigma for L.S.D. therapists. There have not been sufficiently detailed follow-up studies to be certain that L.S.D. therapy is as safe as reported earlier, particularly with regard to the precipitation of suicidal thoughts and behaviour.

Although many of those with prolonged psychotic reactions had previous personality disturbances, the proportion may be as low as 23 per cent. Spontaneous recurrences and psychopathic reactions appear almost exclusively in very heavy users, but many of the other reactions appear after a single, relatively moderate dose. Judging from the reactions reported so far, *no one is able to guarantee a safe dosage, a safe series of doses, or a personality which is certain to create no unfavourable reaction to L.S.D.* Many cases have been reported in which a single, moderate dose of L.S.D. led to a profoundly adverse reaction in otherwise normal persons, especially where that dose has been taken in an unprotected situation. Even where other persons have been with the L.S.D. taker, *supposedly* protecting him, suicide and psychotic reactions have occurred. As yet, we are uncertain about the dose being taken in unprotected settings – it could be similar to the therapeutic doses or much larger, depending on the quality control exercised by the supplier.

The users with adverse effects appear to be a young population of students, former students and college graduates. The majority are in their early 20's. Most of them are males – 132 out of 180 for whom sex is stated. At least half of the persons with adverse L.S.D. reactions are college students or former students. Unfortunately, we know very little of the motivations of these persons for taking L.S.D., or other details about their social class, life problems or coping mechanisms.

At present, illicit L.S.D. use is an urban phenomenon. All studies of unfavourable reactions have come from large cities – Los Angeles, New York, Boston – with the exception of a single report from a small university city, Chapel Hill.(24) It cannot be assumed that L.S.D. is being used only in these cities but its connection with urbanism and university facilities is probably not an artifact of the reporting done so far.

Much research on the adverse effects of L.S.D. remains to be done. More studies of the long-term effects are needed – studies of both the effects of long L.S.D. series, and of the development and progress of unfavourable reactions. It is also important to understand something of the attraction of L.S.D. for the male college population. Currently, we know very little of the reasons for taking L.S.D., nor do we know the personality and social needs which are served by the hallucinogens in general.

The Hippy Sub-Cultures

Current concern, even alarm, is focused in the subculture in which L.S.D. is most frequently used. In Toronto, for example, this is the hippy sub-culture of the Yorkville area. Does this sub-culture in itself create a problem? In a sense, every deviant subculture evokes scorn and disapproval within the larger society. Such sub-cultures tend to threaten and undermine the values, customs and morals of the larger society. They provide a place to break away to for young people and a forum for social criticism and social action against the larger society. Perhaps this is particularly true with Yorkville. Judging from "letters to editors," "man in the street interviews" and the like, many people would like to see the area razed and its inhabitants dispersed into the army, work camps, etc., after having been washed, shaved and appropriately dressed. There is the assumption that the hippies are merely lazy, dirty and socially delinquent.

But far broader questions than of mere delinquency are raised by Yorkville. One of these has to do with the social and cultural needs filled by hippy subcultures. Why do people go there? How did the subculture develop? Why should there be a need for Yorkville if all is well with society? What are the reasons for the extensive use of L.S.D. and other hallucinogens? Are present social realities so unpleasant for some as to require total withdrawal from society, even on the perceptual level?

For some of these questions the answers are only beginning to appear. Yorkville is a place where nonpolitical social rebellion occurs. Perhaps it is true that hippies are reacting to the artificiality and dishonesty inherent in much of modern social life. What information we have now suggests that the Yorkville hippies are highly intelligent – near the average college freshman. But they are under achievers – very few have been to college and most have left high school in grade 10 or 11. We could ask what it is about high school life that these persons find so aversive? Perhaps their psychological problems are too great for them to continue in school; but perhaps too, the high schools are not making sufficient efforts to hold such people. Also, we know that the Yorkville population is a young one – with the majority between 15 and 23. Most of the hippies have a limited stay in their sub-culture and leave within a few years. What happens to older hippies is anyone's guess but probably many rejoin society and resume conventional, middle-class values. Whether the hippy experience makes them more productive and more comfortable in that society cannot be answered at present. Perhaps the hippy sub-culture provides a place for monastic withdrawal, with an emphasis not on theology but on self-understanding and social philosophy.

What is most disturbing is the hippy emphasis on drug-taking. "Dropping out," particularly when so much of it is temporary, seems much less dangerous than "turning on." One of the chief "turn-on" drugs is L.S.D., followed closely by marijuana. However, amphetamines and barbiturates are also frequently used, with or without L.S.D. Lately, a new hallucinogen – S.T.P. – became available in Yorkville and it is reported to produce a four to five day "high" which is difficult to terminate with tranquillizers(27).

This drug was available on the black market and adverse reactions had occurred even before the Food and Drug Administration in Washington could give the chemical formula for it. At the time of writing, not a single scientific study has been made of its effects, but it can be bought in Yorkville. Prolonged adverse reactions from STP have occurred in Toronto, and at least one of them has lasted for several months. It is obvious that hippies are calling for stronger wine and louder music. In reality, they have merely scratched the surface when it comes to the stronger wine of novel drug experiences. There are reports now of new hallucinogens with 12 day "highs," of amphetamine and L.S.D. combinations, of marijuana impregnated with L.S.D. or DMT, and of ether swallowing on the West Coast of the U.S.A. The tendency to readily accept new drug experiences is one of the unique characteristics of the present hippy sub-culture.

What makes drug-taking so prevalent among young people today? Some have suggested that it is part of a search of meaning – a search for meaningful answers to the questions Who am I, What is my purpose in life, Where is the world going, How can I fit into it or change it? In typically North American fashion many people want to discover the answers very quickly. Some have argued that in a world with so much emphasis on achievement, on getting ahead and getting things done, there is little time to ask these questions and none to answer them adequately. The L.S.D. user does not want to discover answers to his questions slowly, over half a lifetime. He wants them now. If there is a value to the hallucinogenic drugs, then perhaps this is it – they might allow certain kinds of experiments with life styles, with the asking and answering of existential questions. These are experiments which have become difficult to do within the present social system. However, much of the current use of L.S.D. is of a mindless, senseless sort, about which nothing is being investigated, no important questions being asked.

Its Promise

What is the promise for L.S.D.? There are several areas of research which indicate that it could have a limited value. It may be that it will prove to be useful in developing or fostering creativity. The perceptual effects of L.S.D. might allow people to approach aesthetic problems with fresh and unique attitudes. Because of its visual effects, it might be thought that visual or plastic creativity might be especially enhanced. Both negative and positive results have been found, the latter in studies not as well controlled as desirable. A study by Zegans, Pollard and Brown(28) found no effect of L.S.D. on psychological tests of creative abilities when persons getting it were compared with those getting a placebo. In the study with positive findings, subjects worked on actual creative problems in their own environment, and many reported (29) finding post-L.S.D. solutions. But more closely controlled research is needed for, at present, we have no technology for producing creativity. Even in our technologically developed world, nobody can tell you how to get a good idea.

Another rather novel suggestion for L.S.D. research concerns its use with terminally ill patients. Kast(30) has argued that many terminal cancer patients become depressed and isolated in their last few weeks of life and that L.S.D. might give them some sort of training in preparing for death. In one of his studies, 80 patients who knew that they had only weeks or months to live volunteered for L.S.D., after having had an explanation of its effects. Kast reported that 72 of the patients gained insight, lucidity and the capacity for greater communication with the observer and with other patients. Explicit pain was considerably reduced and a happy, oceanic feeling was usually obtained. L.S.D. also improved the relationship between patients and their families, and created elevated moods and improved outlooks on death. These studies are interesting and worthy of more carefully controlled replications.

The future for L.S.D. appears black to me – there are far more problems than promise. The problems of adverse effects and lack of validated usefulness, appear to outweigh any promises. It may be useful in creativity and in certain cases of terminal illness, but it still appears a bad bargain for the user. It would be well if L.S.D. helped to create and promote a productive life-style for the hippies or, at least helped to solve some problem or other for them. Yet this is only a hope – and the risks they take in using L.S.D. seem very great, particularly if they obtain only a few hours of hallucinations and illusions from it.

References

1. Stoll, W. A. *Lysergsaure Diathylamid, ein Phantastikum aus der Mutterkorngruppe Schweiz. Arch. Neurol. and Psychiat.*, 1947, *60*, 279-323.
2. Rothlin, E. Lysergic Acid Diethylamide and Related Substances. *Ann. New York Acad. Sci.*, 1957, *66*, 668-676.
3. Smart, R. G., Storm, T., Baker, E. F. W., and Solursh, L. *Lysergic Acid Diethylamide in the Treatment of Alcoholism.* Toronto: University of Toronto Press, 1967.
4. Van Dusen, W., Wilson, W., Miners, W., and Hook, H. Treatment of Alcoholism with Lysergide. Pre-publication abstract. *Quart. J. Stud. Alc,.* 1966, *27*, 534.
5. Leary, T. Introduction to L.S.D., *The Consciousness Expanding Drug.* D. Solomon (ed.). New York: Putnam, 1964.
6. Heard, G. Can This Drug Enlarge Man's Mind?, *Horizon,* 1963, *5*, 115.
7. Smart, R. G., and Bateman, Karen. Unfavourable Reactions to L.S.D.: A Review and Analysis of the Available Case Reports, *Can. Med. Ass. J.*, 1967, *97*, 1214-1221.

8. Hoffer, A. D-lysergic Acid Diethylamide (LSD); A Review of its Present Status. *Clin. Pharmacol. & Therapeutics,* 1965, *6,* 183-255.
9. Baker, E. F. W. L.S.D. Psychotherapy—2nd Conference on Use of L.S.D. in Psychotherapy, Amityville, N.Y., 1965.
10. Cohen, S. Lysergic Acid Diethylamide: Side Effects and Complications. *J. Nerv. Ment. Dis.,* 1960, *130,* 30-39.
11. Cohen, M. M., Marinello, Michelle, and Back, N. Chromosomal Damage in Human Leukocytes, Induced by Lysergic Acid Diethylamide. *Science,* 1967, *155,* 1417-1419.
12. Irwin, S., and Egozcue, J. Chromosomal Abnormalities in Leukocytes from L.S.D.—25 Users. *Science,* 1967, *157,* 313-314.
13. Loughman, W. D., Sargent, T. W., and Israelstam, D. M. Leukocytes of Humans Exposed to Lysergic Acid Diethylamide: Lack of Chromosomal Damage. *Science,* 1967, *158,* 508-509.
14. Alexander, G. J., Miles, B. E., Gold, G. M., and Alexander, R. B., L.S.D.: Injection Early in Pregnancy Produces Abnormalities in Offspring of Rats.
15. Auerbach, R., and Rugowski, J. A. Lysergic Acid Diethylamide: Effect on Embryos. *Science,* 1967, *157,* 1325-1326.
16. Geber, W. Congenital Malformations Induced by Mescaline, Lysergic Acid Diethylamide, and Bromolysergic Acid in the Hamster. *Science,* 1967, *158,* 265-266.
17. Warkany, J., and Takacs, Eva. Lysergic Acid Diethylamide (L.S.D.): No Teratogenicity in Rats. *Science,* 1968, *159,* 731-7 32.
18. Ungerleider, J. T., Fraser, D. D., and Fuller, Marielle. The Dangers of L.S.D. *J. Amer. Med. Ass.,* VTFF, *197,* 109-112.
19. Subcommittee on Narcotics Addiction, Bellevue Hospital, New York. The Dangerous Drug Problem. *N.Y. Med.,* 1966, *22,* 3-8.
20. Frosch, W. A., Robbins, E. S., and Stern, M. Untoward Reactions to Lysergic Acid Diethylamide (L.S.D.) Resulting in Hospitalization. *New Eng. J. Med.,* 1965, *273,* 1235-1239.
21. Rosenthal, S. H. Persistent Hallucinosis Following Repeated Administration of Hallucinogenic Drugs. *Amer. J. Psychiat.,* 1964, *121,* 238-244.
22. Cohen, S. A Classification of L.S.D. Complications. *Psychosomatics,* 1966, *7,* 182-186.
23. Cohen, S., and Ditman, K. S. Prolonged Adverse Reactions to Lysergic Acid Diethylamide. *Arch. Gen. Psychiat.,* 1963, *8,* 475-480.
24. Keeler, H. M., and Reifler, C. B. Suicide During an L.S.D. Reaction. *Amer. J. Psychiat.,* 1967, *123,* 884-885.
25. Knudsen, K. Homocide After Treatment With Lysergic Acid Diethylamide. *Acta Psychiat. Scandinav.,* 1964, *180,* 289-395.
26. Farnsworth, D. Hallucinogenic Agents. *J. Amer. Med. Ass.,* 1963, *185,* 164-166.
27. Solarsh, L. P., and Clement, W. R. Hallucinogenic Drug Abuse: Manifestations and Management. *Can. Med. Ass. J.,* 1968, *98,* 407-410.
28. Zegans, L. S., Pollard, J. C., and Brown, D. The Effects of L.S.D.—25. On Creativity and Tolerance to Regression. *Arch. Gen. Psychiat.,* 1967, *16,* 740-749.
29. Harman, W., McKim, R. H., Mogar, R. E., Fadiman, J., and Stolaroff, M. J., Psychedelic Agents in Creative Problem Solving: A Pilot Study. *Psychol. Rep.,* 1966, *19,* 211-227.
30. Kast, E., L.S.D. and the Dying Patient. Paper presented at an L.S.D. Conference, University of California, San Francisco, 1966.

TEN
TREATMENT OF DEVIANT BEHAVIOUR

47 / Psychotherapy and the Recovery from Neurosis

Dalbir Bindra *McGill University*

Does psychotherapy work? Although this appears to be a straightforward question it is not easy to provide an adequate answer for it. For one thing the terms "psychotherapy" and "work" mean different things to different investigators. Also, there are various types of psychotherapy, which means that the technique used must be specified. In addition, personalities of the therapists themselves vary and controls must be provided for this factor. Finally, it must be ensured that the criteria employed to evaluate the therapy are valid and not subject to the biases of the therapist, the patient, or the researcher. This article represents one of the earliest attempts to clarify the conceptual and methodological issues involved in assessing the effectiveness of psychotherapy.

Both practically and theoretically, it is important to find out whether or to what extent psychotherapy is effective in the treatment of various behavioural disorders. This paper considers from a critical and broad viewpoint the problem of the efficacy of psychotherapy in the treatment of neurosis. It separates and clarifies the specific issues involved, and attempts to show what questions can or cannot be answered on the basis of available evidence.

Problem

Basically, the question is whether or not the proportion of recoveries is greater among neurotics who undergo psychotherapy than among neurotics who do not receive such therapy. Meehl, in his recent review of the literature on this subject(5), notes the lack of the type of controlled studies which would unequivocally answer this question. In the absence of adequate experimental evidence on this question, psychologists have tried to argue (e.g. 2, 3, 8) for or against the efficacy of psychotherapy on the basis of indirect evidence obtained from improperly controlled studies. In general these arguments reach one of two conclusions: "No one has yet demonstrated that psychotherapy is effective in treating neurosis," or "No one has yet demonstrated that psychotherapy is *not* effective in treating neurosis." Clearly, this question is amenable to experimental attack. With two groups of patients equated in terms of symptoms, severity of neurosis, motivation for therapy, socioeconomic status, intelligence, and the like, only one of the groups must receive psychotherapy. A comparison of the proportion of recoveries in the two groups will then indicate whether psychotherapy is effective.

Unfortunately, discussions of this rather straightforward empirical question can easily get complicated by certain theoretical preconceptions. In the thinking of many psychologists, the problem of the efficacy of psychotherapy is intimately tied up with the problem of the etiology of neurosis. The notion that life experiences play a dominant and crucial role in the onset of neurotic ailments is generally considered to support the view that psychotherapy can cure these ailments. And the view that neuroses arise primarily from organic or nonpsychological factors is considered to favour the view that psychotherapy is ineffective. No one has explicitly stated and defended this type of argument, but it is implicit in most reputable psychological discussions (e.g., 9). There is little justification, however, for this contention that etiology and therapy bear such a direct and clear-cut relation to each other. The only effective treatment of a disorder of organic origin (like cerebral palsy) may consist of some form of training or psychotherapy; on the other hand, a psychogenic disorder (like some insomnias) may be most effectively treated by medication. The mere knowledge of the etiology in these cases does not tell whether a particular treatment would be effective. Similarly, whether neurotic ailments result from psychological conflicts, environmental stresses, or some subtle chemical factors in the blood is quite irrelevant in determining the efficacy of psychotherapy in their treatment. I do not mean to imply that neurotic disorders can be identified in a way that excludes etiological concerns. Rather, the point here is simply that the effectiveness of psychotherapy is an issue that can be and should be decided without linking it with any specific conjecture about the etiology of neurotic ailments.

Clarity and explicitness are also necessary in defining neurosis. In the present discussion, *neurosis* or neurotic disorder refers to cases of persistent and

From Bindra, D. Psychotherapy and the recovery from neurosis. *J. abnorm. soc. Psychol.*, 1956, *53*, 251-254.

gross maladjustments involving some definite, palpable, behavioural peculiarities (or symptoms) such as anorexia, phobias, compulsive acts, demonstrable anxiety attacks, hysterical blindness, impotence, amnesias, and the like. It should be noted that this rough and arbitrary definition excludes minor maladjustments defined with reference only to subjective states such as "unhappiness," "anxiety," and "tension." It is true that "anxiety," "unhappiness," and "tension" are often (though not always) reported by neurotics, but they are also frequently reported by normals. Since these states are not a *sine qua non* of persistent and gross maladjustments unless accompanied by definite symptoms of the type listed above, they are excluded from the present definition of neurosis. Some psychologists believe that both neurosis and these minor maladjustments arise from the same type of etiological factors. Even if this view is correct, it does not necessarily imply that an effective treatment of minor maladjustments would also be effective in cases of neurosis, or vice versa. The concern here is primarily with recovery from neurosis.

A General Formulation

Recovery from neurosis means nothing more than a kind of behavioural change, a change in those aspects of the patient's behaviour that put him in the category of neurotics. Thus, the question of the effectiveness of psychotherapy is really a special case of the general problem of the extent to which psychotherapy can produce *personality change*. A clear formulation of this question requires a closer analysis of the concepts of "personality change" and "psychotherapy." Precise descriptions are needed of (a) the personality variables along which change is presumed to occur, and (b) the psychotherapeutic processes which are presumed to effect the change. The effect of a specified therapeutic process on a specified personality variable can then be investigated.

Personality variables can be specified easily enough. For present purposes, they can arbitrarily be categorized into five rough categories: (a) *cognitive variables*, such as general information, reasoning ability, and memory; (b) *attitude variables*, such as attitudes toward in- and outgroups, attitude toward oneself, and likes and dislikes; (c) *need variables* , such as introversion, super-ego, anxiety, and aggression; (d) *specific neurotic symptoms*, behavioural characteristics, such as hysterical or compulsive symptoms, which are used in defining persons as neurotics; (e) *personality variables (if any) that are causally related to neurotic ailments*. Intelligence tests, scales of attitudes, and "personality tests" could be used to measure changes along the first three types of personality variables. The last two categories are not at the same level of discourse as the first three, nor have they been adequately identified so far, but they are listed here to focus attention on the type of variables that are of direct concern in this discussion. Accepting this admittedly arbitrary categorization, the problem of the effect of psychotherapy on personality variables resolves itself into five separate questions. Does psychotherapy have any effect on (a) cognitive variables, (b) attitude variables, (c) need variables, (d) specific neurotic symptoms, and (e) personality variables (if any) that cause neurotic symptoms?

To answer these questions, it is necessary to specify the exact nature of psychotherapy.[1] Unfortunately, it is not possible to do so. Psychotherapy still has its mysterious aspects, and present knowledge is far from unraveling the essential nature of all that takes place in the therapist's office. But from all accounts, it appears that the therapist provides the patient with a friendly, permissive, and uncritical atmosphere, and then systematically makes use of "interpretation," suggestion, and catharsis. It is not clearly understood, however, exactly how these various processes operate in the psychotherapeutic situation. Ideally, empirical questions should be formulated in terms of specific psychoterapeutic processes. Thus, one could ask such questions as "Can suggestion change attitudes and needs?" or "Can interpretive analysis affect compulsive of hysterical symptoms?" or "Can catharsis relieve functional impotence?" Such questions, however cannot be answered unless psychotherapy is analyzed into its component processes rather than conceived as a unitary whole. The only point here is that if knowledge of exactly how psychotherapy produces whatever effects it does produce is to be gained, then an analysis of this type must be undertaken. From the point of view of the therapist, psychotherapy may well be considered as a unitary healing device, but for the researcher it is an analyzable complex of psychological processes. For the present, however, one is forced to discuss the issues without benefit of this kind of analysis. With this handicap in mind, questions concerning the effects of psychotherapy on the various categories of personality variables may now be considered.

Effects of Psychotherapy

Inasmuch as psychotherapy involves prolonged social interaction between the therapist and the patient, it is to be expected that the psychotherapeutic situation will produce change along at least some personality dimensions. It is known that interpersonal relations can affect behavior. Interests and tastes change through association with friends. Gestures of immigrants begin to conform to the typical gestures of their adopted communities (1). Exposure to conflict-

[1]This conception excludes the *incidental* "psychotherapy" that is sometimes said to have taken place when a neurotic gets some attention from a nurse or when he confides his innermost thoughts to his bartender, priest, or barber. Whether or not incidental "psychotherapy" has some of the same ingredients as psychotherapy proper (given by a qualified psychiatrist or clinical psychologist) is impossible to say until more is known about what is involved in the latter.

ing social influences may contribute to behavioural disturbances in juveniles (4). Attitudes can be changed, one way or the other, simply by showing a short movie to audiences (6). In view of the abundance of naturalistic and experimental evidence of this kind, it would be strange, indeed unbelievable, if the long and intimate social interaction between the therapist and his patient did not produce some change in the patient (and, indeed, in the therapist himself). The patient is likely to learn something about the work of the therapist, to increase his vocabulary, and to change his attitudes. Since he is the focus of attention in the therapeutic situation, the patient is particularly likely to learn more about himself and to evaluate himself rather differently. Also, the change from a nagging wife, a rude boss, and critical friends to the understanding and permissive therapist is likely to facilitate these new self-evaluations, and they may be more in keeping with the therapist's direct or indirect suggestions regarding what a normal person thinks of himself.

The recent studies of Rogers, Dymond and their collaborators (7) present direct evidence in support of these statements. They administered a number of personality tests to their patients before, during, and after psychotherapy. Comparable control data were obtained from normal subjects, who were not given therapy, and from patients who had to wait for therapy. The most impressive finding was that psychotherapy produced a significant change in self-perception or in the perception of the self-ideal. It was also found that responses of patients to the Thematic Apperception Test changed as a result of psychotherapy in the direction of greater judged personality integration and adjustment. The results on needs and changes in behaviour in everyday life situations were equivocal, and no change in attitudes toward others could be attributed to the treatment. No data are presented on the changes in specific neurotic systems. It seems appropriate to conclude that psychotherapy has some effect on the client's attitudes toward himself. That specific psychotherapy (as well as informal interpersonal relations generally) can produce behavioural changes does not, of course, diminish the need for analyzing "psychotherapy" into its component processes, as suggested in the last section. If one could identify the specific effective agents in the psychotherapeutic situation, it would be a step toward more efficient therapeutic procedures.

These demonstrations by Rogers, Dymond, and collaborators, important as they are, do not, of course, tell anything about the efficacy of psychotherapy in the cure of neurosis. These workers have shown that the attitudes of their patients changed, and that, *on the basis of test data,* they were said to become more "mature" and "better adjusted." But this does not indicate whether psychotherapy was effective in eradicating the specific neurotic symptoms of their clients. Even if psychotherapy demonstrably alleviates some minor maladjustments involving attitudes of different kinds, the issue of the effectiveness of psychotherapy in the treatment of the basic, gross, and persistent maladjustment ("primary neurotic symptoms") still remains unanswered. A neurotic with hysterical or compulsive symptoms may well become better adjusted as a result of psychotherapy without showing any change in his primary neurotic symptoms. Even a person who loses a leg may benefit from psychotherapy inasmuch as his life-goals and attitudes may change in a way that would be more consistent with his handicap, and in this sense he may become more mature, better adjusted, and happier. However, in order to demonstrate that psychotherapy is effective in curing neurosis, it must show that it diminishes or eradicates the symptoms that constitute the neurosis, quite apart from making the patient better adjusted, mature, or happier. Such a demonstration has not yet been made. Perhaps future research will show that certain psychoterhapeutic processes can be effective in the treatment of certain types of neurotic maladjustments.[2]

Even if it were demonstrated that psychotherapy can relieve neurotic ailments, there would still be no answer to the final question. Can psychotherapy produce a change in those processes or personality variables (if any) that are causally connected with neurosis? Evidence showing psychotherapy to be effective in eradicating neurotic symptoms would not indicate anything about the mechanism by which psychotherapy operated. In this connection, two types of treatments should be distinguished. One kind involves directly undoing the disease process analogous to treating streptococcal infections with penicillin. The other type of treatment is indirect and is aimed at something other than the disease process itself; an analogy is treating typhoid or tuberculosis with rest. In textbooks on psychiatry and abnormal psychology, it is generally implied that the effectiveness of psychotherapy results from directly undoing (through relearning) the processes that produce neurosis. However, there is no evidence for this belief, and there cannot be until we know the exact basis of neurosis. It is quite conceivable that, were psychotherapy shown to be effective in treating neurosis, its effectiveness could result from some indirect effects that are quite unrelated to the causes of neurosis.

In summary, available evidence suggests that psychotherapy can be effective in alleviating minor maladjustments characterized by such subjective states as "unhappiness," "anxiety," and "tension" that often accompany neurosis. But the evidence does not yet support the view that psychotherapy is effective in relieving those gross and persistent maladjustments (neuroses) that are characterized by definite, palpable symptoms. Whether it has any effect on these is a question which only future research can settle.

---

[2] Whether the recovery from neurosis could be more effectively produced by methods other than psychotherapy is an important question, but one that need not be raised in the present discussion.

References

1. Efron, D., and Foley, J. P. Gestural behaviour and social setting. In T. M. Newcomb and E. L. Hartley (eds.), *Readings in social psychology.* New York: Holt, 1947. Pp. 33-40.
2. Eysenck, H. J. The effects of psychotherapy: an evaluation. *J. consult. Psychol.*, 1952, *16*, 319-324.
3. ———. The effects of psychotherapy: a reply. *J. abnorm. soc. Psychol.*, 1955, *50*, 147-148.
4. Hunt, J. McV. An instance of the social origin of conflicts resulting in psychoses. In C. Kluckhohn and H. A. Murray (eds.), *Personality in nature, society and culture.* New York: Knopf, 1948. Pp. 367-374.
5. Meehl, P. E. Psychotherapy. *Annu. Rev. Psychol.*, 1955, *6*, 357-378.
6. Peterson, R. C., and Thurstone, L. L. *Motion pictures and the social attitudes of children.* New York: Macmillan, 1933.
7. Rogers, C. R., and Dymond, Rosalind F. (eds.), *Psychotherapy and personality change.* Chicago: Univer. of Chicago Press, 1954.
8. Rosenzweig, *S.* A transvaluation of psychotherapy —a reply to Hans Eysenck. *J. abnorm. soc. Psychol.*, 1954, *49*, 298-304.
9. White, R. W. *The abnormal personality.* New York: Ronald, 1948.

48 / Interaction and Insight in Group Psychotherapy[1]

W.H. Coons *Ontario Hospital and McMaster University, Hamilton*

It is commonly observed that in an ordinary problem-solving situation a solution is facilitated if one gains an insight into the critical relationships involved. From this it is often assumed that insight can also aid in the solution of personal emotional difficulties. However, the following study suggests that insight contributes little towards improvement in adjustment. The most favourable condition for improvement appears to be "a warm, acceptant, and permissive atmosphere in which patient-to-patient interaction was encouraged."

All major schools of psychotherapy have encountered difficulty in explaining how and why therapeutic changes occur during psychotherapy. Since Freud's development of psychoanalysis the primary stress in all systematic psychotherapies has been on insight as the core of adjustment. However, no unequivocal relationship between degree of insight and level of adjustment has yet been demonstrated. If insight is considered to be a cognitive act by which the significance of some pattern of relations is understood (12) clinical experience does not wholly support its use as an explanatory concept. Improved adjustment occurs in persons who have not shown evidence of increased insight; other persons who are thought to have gained insight remain seriously maladjusted. This suggests that there is a more basic explanation for behavioural changes which occur during psychotherapy.

The literature reveals two lines of evidence which converge to support the assumption that insight is not the crucial condition for change in behaviour. All major psychotherapeutic systems recognize that insight alone is ineffective and make careful provision for interpersonal interaction (1, 2, 5, 11, 13, 15). At the same time, current research on personality development suggests that understanding is not enough to assure adaptive learning, and that adjustment to reality depends on opportunities for the repeated trial and check of an individual's expectations (7, 10, 14). Both these trends suggest that opportunity for interpersonal interaction in a consistently warm and accepting social environment is central to psychotherapy.

From this theoretical orientation it was hypothesized that interaction rather than insight, is responsible for therapeutic improvement. Therefore, it was predicted that a technique of psychotherapy which stressed interpersonal interaction in the absence of insightful content would be superior, in effecting improved adjustment, to a technique which stressed insight with minimal interaction.

The present study was designed to test this hypothesis experimentally by comparing the effects on adjustment of two techniques of group psychotherapy. One of these (Interaction Therapy) fostered group interaction in the absence of the usual concern for imparting insight; the other (Insight Therapy) strove to impart insight while holding group interaction to a minimum. A control group which received no group psychotherapy was included in the study as an index of the absolute efficacy of the two therapeutic techniques.

Method

The Measures of Adjustment

For reasons outlined in the original report of the study (4), the Rorschach Technique of Personality Diagnosis (8) and the Wechsler-Bellevue Adult Intelligence Scales (16, 17) were chosen as the best available indices of adjustment.

The Rorschach. The Rorschach was administered to each of 64 research subjects before and after the period of therapy. Pre- and post-therapy protocols for each subject were analysed "blind" by an experienced Rorschach examiner.[2] The examiner knew only that each pair of protocols was from the same subject, and that one of the protocols was the pre-therapy, the other the post-therapy record. He did not know which was which, nor did he know in which type of group the subject had been. This procedure eliminated any personal biases due to acquaintance with the subject or active espousal of either therapeutic technique.

The examiner was instructed to select in each pair the protocol which represented the better level of

[1]Adapted from part of a thesis submitted in 1955 in partial fulfilment of the requirements for the degree of Doctor of Philosophy at the University of Toronto. The author is indebted particularly to Dr. J. N. Senn and Dr. C. R. Myers for their assistance in the conception and development of this study.

Reprinted, by permission, from *Canadian Journal of Psychology*, 1957, *11*, 1-8.

[2]K. G. Ferguson, Westminster Hospital, London, Ontario.

adjustment. When the protocol which he judged to be "better" was the post-therapy record, that subject was considered to have shown improved adjustment during the therapy period. The examiner was unable to distinguish differences between the protocols of eight patients. These patients were considered to have shown no improvement.

As a reliability check, another experienced Rorschach examiner[3] independently examined 20 of the 64 pairs of Rorschach protocols. His selections corresponded with those of the first examiner in 19 out of the 20 pairs.

The Wechsler-Bellevue Adult Intelligence Scales. Pre- and post-therapy intellectual efficiency was measured with Forms I and II of the Wechsler-Bellevue (16, 17). Since available evidence shows no significant difference between the Verbal Scale, Performance Scale, and Full Scale Intelligence Quotients of these two scales (6, 17), they were treated as equivalent, the two forms being administered alternately to each patient, i.e., when one form of the scale was used for the pre-therapy assessment, the other was used for the post-therapy assessment.

Research Design

The research involved the operation of two experimental units (one male, one female), each of which was composed of three different types of group:

1. *Interaction groups.* Members of this type of group were subject to the usual hospital routines with the addition for three hours each week of a type of group experience which will be referred to as interaction group psychotherapy. The technique used was designed to create a warm, acceptant, and permissive atmosphere in which patient-to-patient interaction was encouraged. Interaction was considered to be any type of verbal communication on any subject. There was little or no reference to the content usually associated with psychotherapy, and discussion ranged from the price of fur coats to the progress of industrial expansion in Newfoundland. Thus the interaction groups were characterized by emphasis on maximum interaction in the absence of insightful material.

2. *Insight groups.* Members of this type of group were subject to the usual hospital routines with the addition three times each week of a type of group experience which will be referred to as insight group psychotherapy. The technique involved directed discussion of the aetiology, manifestations, and control of psychological disturbances. Personal involvement of the part of each group member was encouraged. Each member was directively encouraged to examine his personal difficulties, their origins, and their solution. Emotional catharsis was common. The therapeutic climate might best be described as benignly authoritarian. Interaction was restricted to that between patient and therapist. Thus the insight groups were characterized by maximum emphasis on insight with minimum interaction.

3. *Control groups.* Members of the control groups received no planned group psychotherapy, but were subject to the usual hospital routines. They did not realize that they were considered as a group.

To ensure that the two types of therapy groups actually showed the difference in amount of interaction required by the research design, all available transcripts of the recordings of the therapy sessions were analysed after the method of Bovard (3) to derive "interaction ratios." These ratios confirm that the interaction group sessions were characterized by a high proportion of patient-to-patient interaction, and that this was largely absent in the insight group sessions. (The difference in ratios is highly significant: *C.R.* 12.8, *P* .001)

Subjects

A total of 66 patients at the Ontario Hospital, Hamilton, were used as research subjects. These were all the patients for whom complete, or nearly complete pre- and post-therapy data were available.

Selection. Each subject was selected on the basis of suitability for group psychotherapy. The selection procedures took no account of psychiatric nosology. The majority of the patients chosen turned out to be classified as Schizophrenic.

To reduce the possibility that any one group might be formed of patients with an especially favourable prognosis, patients selected for therapy were randomly assigned to each group of each unit. Comparison of the groups on such factors as economic status, occupational classification, nosological grouping, educational level, I.Q., age, duration of illness and hospitalization, number of E.C.T., etc., indicated that the randomization procedures were successful in producing comparable groups (4).

Replacement. Initially, 21 patients were selected for each unit and randomly assigned to the three groups comprising it. However, group members were subject to the ordinary hospital routines, including those regarding discharge. Thus, when a group member was considered suitable for release by the physician in charge, or when relatives insisted on taking him home, he was discharged from the hospital.

Replacements were taken in sequence as required, from a reserve of patients considered suitable for group psychotherapy. When a vacancy occurred in any group of a unit it was filled with the patient whose name headed the reserve list.

Procedure

The experimental procedure lasted for fifteen months, during which the composition of the six groups altered as patients were released and replaced by others (see above). At any given time there were seven members in each group, 21 in each experimental unit (male and female). Each psychotherapy group had three group sessions, each of one-hour

[3] F. W. Burd, Westminster Hospital, London, Ontario.

duration, each week. Two therapists were involved, one working with the male unit, the other with the female unit. All group sessions were recorded electrically and transcripts of samples made at regular intervals.

Duration of therapy. Owing to the fluid membership of the groups, duration of therapy was not the same for all subjects. However, no member was used as a research subject unless he had a minimum of eight hours of psychotherapy. The maximum number of hours for any subject was ninety. In this respect, members of the control groups were dealt with as though they were members of a group receiving therapy. That is, at any time they were considered to have had the number of sessions which they would have had if they had actually been assigned to a psychotherapy group when first included as a "control" subject. The average number of group sessions of patients in the Interaction Group was 27 (Range: 8-60), the Insight Group 32 (Range 9-87), and the Control Group 47 (Range: 12-90).

Testing. The Rorschach and Wechsler tests were administered individually before and after therapy by members of the psychological staff at the Ontario Hospital, Hamilton.

Statistical Analysis

The study was designed to permit comparison of the effects of three different types of experience: interaction group psychotherapy, insight group psychotherapy, and no group psychotherapy. Differences were held to be significant when they made possible the rejection of the null hypothesis at the 5 per cent level of confidence. Techniques, and methods of reporting results, follow McNemar (9). The devices used are: standard error of the difference between percentages, and analysis of variance for small samples. No *t*-scores are considered significant unless they occur in the context of significant over-all *F*-ratios.

Results

Rorschach

As is shown in Table I, 16 out of 23 subjects in the Interaction Group, 10 out of 23 subjects in the Insight Group, and 7 out of 19 subjects in the Control Group were rated as showing improved adjustment following the therapy period.

Table II shows that the percentage of improved subjects in the Interaction Group was significantly greater than the percentages of improved subjects in

Table I – Numbers of subjects in each group rated as improved and unimproved after therapy

Group	Improved	Unimproved	Total
Interaction	16	6	22
Insight	10	13	23
Control	7	12	19

either the Insight Group (P = .04) or the Control Group (P = .02). The difference between the Insight and Control Groups was not significant.

Table II – Differences in percentages of subjects showing improvement in interaction, insight, and control groups

Groups compared	Difference in per cent.	*D*p	*CR*	*P*
Interaction–Insight	31	14.7	2.1	0.04
Interaction–Control	37	15.5	2.4	0.02
Insight–Control	12	15.2	0.8	N.S.

Wechsler-Bellevue

Table III indicates that significant intergroup differences in the amount of change in Wechsler Full Scale IQ occurred during the therapy period (F = 5.3, P = .01). The Interaction Group showed improvement which was not approached by either the insight Group (t = 3.14, P = .003) or the Control Group (t = 2.63, P = .01). The difference in mean changes in IQ between the Insight and Control Groups was not significant.

No significant intergroup differences in change on the Verbal and Performance Scales of the test are evident. This suggests that the change in intellectual efficiency was a function of a general improvement on all sub-tests. For confirmation of this suggestion, the significance of the intergroup differences of mean changes on sub-test weighted scores was tested. The results show only two exceptions, the Comprehension and Digit Symbol sub-tests. The Interaction Group showed improvement on Comprehension which was significantly greater than that shown by the Insight Group (t = 2.57, P = .01). The change in performance of the Insight and Control Groups on this sub-test was not significant. On Digit Symbol, also, the Interaction Group showed greater improvement than did the Insight Group (t = 2.23, P = .03) or the Control Group (t = 2.21, P = .03).

In summary, the Interaction Group showed a generally greater improvement in intellectual efficiency, which was most marked in the areas of general comprehension and new learning ability.

Table III – Differences between pre- and post-therapy Wechsler-Bellevue IQ's of (a) interaction, (b) insight, and (c) control groups

	Mean change in I.Q.				t-scores of differences between means		
	(a)	(b)	(c)	F-ratio†	(a) & (b)	(a) & (c)	(b) & (c)
Verbal IQ	4.4	–0.5	1.7	2.0*	2.0	1.0	0.9
Performance IQ	7.6	2.1	1.0	2.2	1.7	1.9	0.3
Full IQ	9.0	0	1.0	5.3**	3.1**	2.6**	0.3

† With 2 and 62 degrees of freedom. *Significant at the 5% level. **Significant at the 1% level.

Discussion

We have found two indications that the interaction technique was more effective in producing improved adjustment than the insight technique. This evidence supports the hypothesis that it is interaction rather than insight that is the basis of psychotherapeutic change; it casts serious doubt on the generally accepted belief that the chief purpose of psychotherapy is to facilitate insight. It suggests that the interpersonal interaction which characterizes both individual and group psychotherapy may, in itself, be the crucial factor in the production of therapeutic change. If this is true, explicit recognition of interaction as the prime therapeutic agent would require reorientation of our therapeutic efforts.

Psychotherapists from Freud onward have found it necessary to deviate in practice from those parts of their theoretical systems which stressed insight as the medium of therapeutic change. While insight has been retained as the explanatory concept, actual practice has moved progressively towards techniques which maximize patient-to-therapist or patient-to-patient interaction, in special types of acceptant atmospheres. Modern group therapy has been the culmination of this trend. Rational man is loath to surrender voluntarily any aspect of his behaviour to a non-cognitive process, since this implies that he is not complete master of his fate. In theory, psychotherapists have (with some difficulty) resisted surrender; in practice, the surrender is becoming ever more complete. Practical considerations have thus resulted in the modification of therapeutic techniques along the lines suggested by the present study. Explicit recognition of interaction as basic to therapeutic changes could provide the foundation for further and much needed technical advances.

Summary

Sixty-six hospital patients were divided at random into three groups:

a) A group which experienced a technique of group psychotherapy which stressed interpersonal interaction in a warm, permissive, therapeutic climate and made no reference to personal difficulties;

b) A group which experienced a technique of group psychotherapy which stressed cognitive understanding of personal difficulties (insight) in a benignly authoritarian therapeutic climate;

c) A control group which experienced no group psychotherapy.

The first group showed significantly greater improvement in adjustment than did either of the other two groups.

From these results the following conclusions were drawn:

1) In group psychotherapy, greater improvement results from a technique which stresses interaction than from a technique which stresses insight.

2) Therapeutic change can and does occur as a result of controlled interaction in the absence of traditional insight methods of psychotherapy.

3) Since there were no apparent differences in results between an insight technique and "no treatment," interaction rather than insight seems to be the essential condition for therapeutic change.

References

1. ADLER, A. *The practice and theory of individual psychology.* (Transl. by P. RADIN.) London: Kegan Paul, Trench, Trubner & Co., 1927.
2. BACH, G. R. *Intensive group psychotherapy.* New York: Ronald Press, 1954.
3. BOVARD, E. W. Interaction record. Personal communication, 1954.
4. COONS, W. H. Interaction and insight in group psychotherapy. Unpub. doctor's disseration, Univer. of Toronto, 1955.
5. FREUD, S. *Collected papers.* Vol. II. (Transl. by JOAN RIVIERE.) London: Hogarth Press, 1924.
6. GIBBY, R. G. A preliminary survey of certain aspects of Form II of the Wechsler-Bellevue Scale as compared to Form I. *J. clin. Psychol.,* 1949, *5,* 165-169.
7. HILGARD, E. R. The role of learning in perception. In BLAKE, R. R., and RAMSEY, G. V. (eds.), *Perception: An approach to personality.* New York: Ronald Press, 1951.
8. KLOPFER, B., and KELLEY, D. *The Rorschach technique.* New York: World Book Co., 1942.
9. MCNEMAR, Q. *Psychological statistics.* London: Chapman & Hall, 1949.
10. PARSONS, T., and SHILS, E. A. (eds.) *Toward a general theory of action.* Cambridge, Mass.: Harvard Univer. Press, 1951.
11. RANK, O. *Will therapy and truth and reality.* (Transl. by JESSIE TAFT.) New York: Knopf, 1945.
12. REID, J. R., and FINESINGER, J. E. The role of insight in psychotherapy. *Amer J. Psychiat.,* 1952, *108,* 726-734.
13. ROGERS, C. R. *Client-centered therapy.* Boston: Houghton Mifflin, 1951.
14. ———. Perceptual reorganization in client-centered therapy. In BLAKE, R. R., and RAMSEY, G. V. (eds.), *Perception: An approach to personality.* New York: Ronald Press, 1951.
15. WASSERMAN, M. B. *The psychology of C. G. Jung.* Mimeographed lectures delivered to the Institute of Psychology, Univer. of Ottawa, 1953.
16. WECHSLER, D. *The measurement of adult intelligence.* Baltimore: Williams and Wilkins, 1944.
17. WECHSLER, D. *The Wechsler--Bellevue intelligence scale: Form II.* New York: Psychological Corporation, 1946.

49 / Operant Conditioning Treatment of Autistic and Mentally Retarded Children at the Manitoba Training School[1]

Garry L. Martin *St. Paul's College, University of Manitoba*

Since B.F. Skinner (1938) first demonstrated the power of operant conditioning techniques in modifying the behaviour of laboratory animals, many fundamental principles of behaviour control have been studied in detail, using lower organisms as subjects. These principles prescribe specific arrangements between the manipulatable environment and the observable behaviour of a subject so that specified behaviours of that subject may be developed, maintained, or eliminated. In the past decade these behavioural principles have been successfully applied to treat individual behaviour problems encountered with retardates, autistic children, schizophrenics, psychotics, neurotics, juvenile delinquents, alcoholics, stutterers, sexual deviants, delinquent soldiers, children with learning disabilities, brain-damaged children, emotionally-disturbed children, and normal children and adults.

During the past three years, Professor Martin has co-ordinated the operant conditioning program at the Manitoba Training School concerning behavioural research and treatment with autistic and retarded children. In the present paper he describes some of the fundamental principles of operant conditioning as they have applied to treat some autistic boys and a group of severely retarded girls.

In recent years a number of behavioural principles, collectively referred to as operant conditioning, have emerged from psychological laboratories. These principles and techniques have been used with surprising success to establish desirable behaviours and eliminate undesirable behaviours of autistic children (Risley and Wolf, 1967; Lovass *et al.*, 1967), retardates (Watson, 1967), and patients in mental hospitals (Ayllon and Azrin, 1968). These and other studies prompted the author to initiate an operant conditioning program with a group of 10 autistic children at the Manitoba Training School during the summer of 1967. At that time, undergraduate psychology students used operant conditioning, under the author's supervision, to teach the children behaviour previously thought by many to be beyond their abilities. The success of that program had led to the following developments:

1 An ongoing therapy and research program for the autistic children.
2 The expansion of operant conditioning to teach 30 severely retarded retarded girls (at Cedar Cottage) basic self-care, social and work skills.
3 A series of short courses on operant conditioning given by the author to small groups of nursing staff at the institution.
4 A training program for the cottage nursing staff designed to instruct them in the effective use of operant conditioning.
5 A training program for psychology students from the University of Manitoba in the use of operant conditioning techniques.

The purpose of this report is to describe some of the basic operant conditioning techniques as applied to train the autistic boys, and the severely retarded girls at Cedar Cottage. The program with the autistic children was described in detail by Martin *et al.* (1968), and Martin and Pear (in press, I).

Operant Conditioning of Autistic Children

The subjects were chosen at the start of the program primarily because of their availability and their diagnosis as "Infantile Autism." They varied from age eight to thirteen. According to institution records all subjects were considered untestable regarding I.Q., and were observed to display typical defining features of autism, namely, withdrawal, self-stimulation (such as constant rocking back and forth), and little or no verbal behaviour.

[1]Grateful acknowledgement is due to Dr. G. H. Lowther, Medical Superintendent, and the staff at the Manitoba School for Retardates for their excellent co-operation during the development of this program.
A modified version of this paper first appeared in the *Manitoba School Journal*, 1968, *1*, No. 3, 11-17.

One of the subjects, Peter, was nine years old when the project began. He had attended speech therapy, play therapy, and occupational therapy at the Saskatchewan Training School, with no success. On occasion he would echo words spoken to him, but most often he ignored those around him. He threw frequent and severe temper tantrums, which were often self destructive. He could not dress himself and frequently tore his shirts.

During the initial session with Peter and the other children, great emphasis was placed on the necessity of consistent application of two fundamental principles of operant conditioning, namely, positive reinforcement and extinction. *Positive reinforcement* refers to the presentation of a reinforcer or reward following the occurrence of a response. Each time the children engaged in a desirable response, such as sitting quietly or following a simple command, they were immediately reinforced with a candy and the approval of the experimenter. Positive reinforcement is probably the single most important aspect of the learning process, and the children soon learned to engage in the behaviour for which they were being reinforced.

Because the children were quickly satiated on candy and other food reinforcers, they were taught to work for token reinforcement. Tokens are tangible objects, such as poker chips, which, in and of themselves, have no reinforcing power. The tokens acquire reinforcing properties for the children because they can be traded for other reinforcers such as the noon meal dispensed in small amounts, candy, salty items like potato chips or pretzels, small amounts of soft drinks, raisins or toys. At first the children could earn the tokens for simple activities such as sitting quietly or perhaps mimicking a sound or a word (see Figure 1). When the children would reliably mimic some sounds and words, they were taught to use the words to name objects by a procedure called fading. Fading refers to the gradual change of the cues controlling a response until the response eventually occurs to a completed new set of cues. That is, if a certain amount of physical or verbal guidance is initially necessary in order to get a child to engage in a particular behaviour, then that guidance can be gradually eliminated over a number of reinforced trials. For example, in order to teach the children to name items of clothing, the student experimenters were instructed as follows:

a) Point to your shirt and say, "Shirt." Repeat this sequence until the subject correctly mimics "shirt," each time reinforcing the subject for the correct response.
b) When the subject correctly mimics "shirt," then gradually fade in new verbal prompts. That is, say, "What's this? Shirt," while pointing to the shirt. To this, the subject usually mimics, "Shirt." Then over a period of several trials, gradually decrease the intensity of "shirt" to zero, so that the subject eventually responds to the question, "What's this?" with the answer, "Shirt." Again, each appropriate response is to be reinforced.
c) If the name of the item is faded out too fast, so that the question, "What's this?" brings the wrong reply or none at all, wait five seconds and repeat the last step to which the subject did respond correctly.

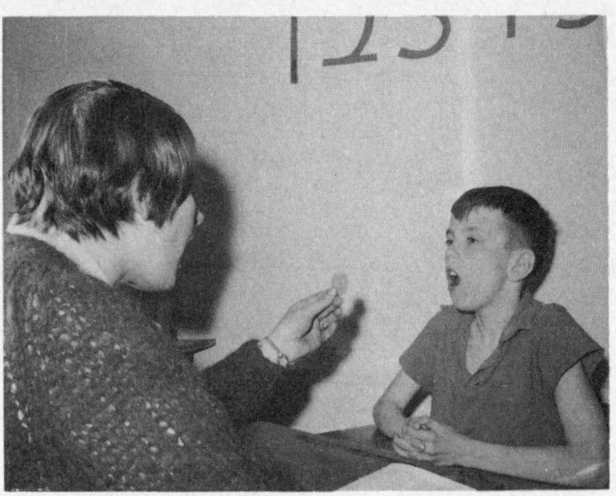

Fig. 1. A session on speech training. Gary, one of the autistic boys, is shown earning a token for correctly mimicking the experimenter. The tokens earned are kept in the cylindrical container shown on the table.

Fading was also used to teach the boys to respond with phrases to various questions, and to trace lines and copy simple patterns (for more detail see Martin *et al.*, 1968).

The second fundamental principle of operant conditioning, *extinction*, is a procedure for eliminating undesirable behaviour by removing the stimuli (such as candy or staff attention) that had been reinforcing the behaviour; in most cases what this amounts to is simply ignoring the behaviour. The principle of extinction states that a response that occurs frequently will begin to occur less often (and may eventually disappear) when that response ceases to be reinforced. For example, the undesirable tantrum behaviour of Peter was treated by extinction. With Peter, his tantrums were consistently accompanied by his saying, "cut, needle, doctor" and pointing to imaginary cuts on his arms. When Peter emitted these undesirable responses he was completely ignored until a brief period after the tantrum ceased. During the first session of this procedure Peter behaved quite badly, throwing one tantrum after another in an attempt to get the student's attention. However, during subsequent sessions, the tantrums began to decrease.

By the ninth session, this behaviour had dwindled to around zero. Peter still emitted the occasional "cut" or "doctor," but not more than once every three or four sessions. The nurses reported that the behaviour also decreased on the ward, although not to zero. The persistence of the undesirable behaviour on the ward appeared to be due to the reinforcement given by visitors and nurses who were not familiar with the program.

Three of the remaining subjects also emitted frequent tantrums and instances of whining and crying. These were handled by extinction and the extinction rates were comparable to Peter's.

The extinction procedure is most effective in eliminating some undesirable response if it is used in conjunction with positive reinforcement for some contrary but desirable response. For example, if one were attempting to extinguish instances of crying then that person should also reinforce the child for short periods of sitting quietly without crying.

Each of the learning programs for the autistic children involved techniques developed and studied in experimental laboratories, such as positive reinforcement, extinction, and fading. By the end of the summer of 1967, all the children would sit quietly in a classroom, attend to the teacher, and obey simple commands (e.g., shut the door). Seven of the children, all of whom emitted some mimicking behaviour initially, acquired a picture and object-naming repertoire and came to answer a variety of questions (e.g., "What's your name?" – "What colour is that?") with single-word answers.

During each summer since the initial program, the children have been worked with intensively by a small group of research assistants. During the winter months the program has continued on a less intense basis utilizing undergraduate psychology students as short term operant conditioners (for details see Martin and Pear, in press, I). Briefly, the students are given the opportunity of earning course credits by working with the children from 4:00 P.M. to 6:00 P.M. Monday through Friday, on structured and closely-supervised training programs.

At the time of this writing the progress has varied considerably from child to child. At one extreme, two of the children, who had no mimicking behaviour initially, have shown no progress whatsoever in speech development, although they have learned various motor tasks. At the other extreme, Peter, the most advanced child, can do such things as count to 199, read a portion of "Dick and Jane" kindergarten books, and several Grade I readers, tell time on the hour, half hour, and quarter hour, do simple arithmetic problems, and speak in phrases and sentences.

Several changes have occurred since the initial summer program. For example, the boys now must earn more than five tokens for back-up reinforcers, and they keep their tokens in token banks (see Figure 1). When they cash in their earnings they select what they want from the "store," provided that they have enough tokens to pay for their choices (see Figure 2).

It is too early to tell what the eventual outcome of the program will be. However, it appears that some of the children will acquire many of the academic skills demonstrated by normal grade school children as well as some basic self-care, social and work skills. Several factors have contributed greatly to the success of the program. Psychology student

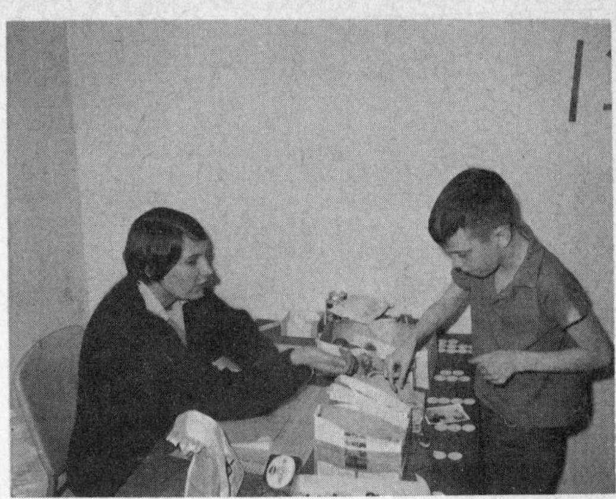

Fig. 2. Store time for the autistic program. Some sample items: a candy at a cost of 5 tokens; a glass of cool-aid at a cost of 15 tokens; two minutes of listening to a radio at a cost of 30 tokens.

volunteers have continued the program during the winter months. Also, during the regular academic year, the children have been taught kindergarten activities by the institutional teaching staff who are using a modified reinforcement program. Finally, the institutional staff are beginning to learn and apply operant conditioning when the children are back on the wards. Thus, while the students and teachers instruct the children in various social and classroom skills, the nursing staff emphasize basic self-care and work skills.

Operant Conditioning with the Severely Retarded Girls

In the summer of 1968, operant conditioning was extended to Cedar Cottage, a self-contained cottage unit with 30 severely retarded girls. At that time, students who had previously taught the autistic children, worked in co-operation with the cottage nursing staff to develop a token reinforcement program for the residents.

The residents in the cottage varied in age from six to twenty-one and in I.Q. from untestable to 26 on the Peabody Picture Vocabulary Test. Some of the girls are not toilet trained. Many had little or no speech, and, at the start of the program, could not dress themselves or wash themselves. Some of the girls were destructive to themselves and/or others and were frequently noisy and unruly.

As with the autistic program, the Cedar Cottage project is based on the premise that the receipt of a reward or reinforcer for some behaviour increases the probability that similar behaviour will occur in the future. The staff are continually watching for desirable behaviours to reinforce and they repeatedly attempt to ignore (i.e., extinguish) undesirable behaviours.

The program at the cottage consists of three general training categories: grooming or personal appearance; dressing, and work training. The tasks in these general categories are each broken down into small behavioural components. For example, bedmaking is sub-divided into 20 small steps, each step consisting of a single, simple behaviour such as placing a pillow on the bed or smoothing wrinkles on the bedspread.

Washing hands and face is broken into 15 small steps, including such steps as identifying the hot water tap, placing the plug in the sink, turning on the hot water, turning off the hot water, and so on. Initially the children are required to perform just one simple step of a task in order to earn a token reward which can be redeemed for candy, chewing gum, toys, or other rewarding items. As the children progress, they are required to perform more and more of the steps of a task for a token until finally they can complete the entire task without supervision.

Details of the grooming program were described in Treffry *et al.* (1969). At the start of this program, 11 girls were chosen for extra sessions, none of whom could completely wash and dry their hands and face without guidance. After nine weeks, six of the girls could wash and dry their hands and face without physical guidance, and were "graduated" to the other washroom at the cottage.

The tasks in the dressing program are also broken into small steps (for a more detailed report, see Martin *et al.*, 1969). Teaching a child to put on a sweater, for example, involves eight steps starting with the identification of "right side" and "wrong side" of the sweater (see Figure 3). Because of the complexity of the procedures and the importance of closely monitoring the residents' progress, the staff keep detailed records of the daily sessions. The daily data sheets provide an important source of reinforcement for the staff in terms of satisfaction from seeing progress, as well as necessary feedback on the basis of which unsuccessful procedures may be altered.

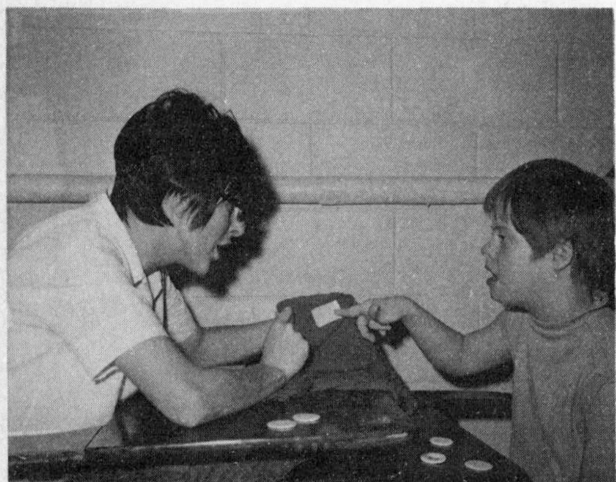

Fig. 3. A typical dressing session. The name tag on the sweater is the cue for the subject to say "Inside."

Three times per day the girls are allowed to spend their tokens in the cottage "store" (see Figure 4). The girls deposit their tokens in the appropriate slots and select the items of their choice within the range they can afford. If an expensive item (in terms of token cost) is desired, the girls are allowed to save their tokens until they have the required amount. The number of tokens spent and items purchased by each resident are recorded daily and tabulated weekly. The weekly totals provide a check to ensure that all the children are receiving appropriate consideration. Not all the girls at the cottage have learned the meaning of the store nor the value of the tokens. Only eight girls are aware of the different prices for the various back-up reinforcers. However, twenty-five of the thirty residents will now save their tokens earned during the day and cash them in at store time.

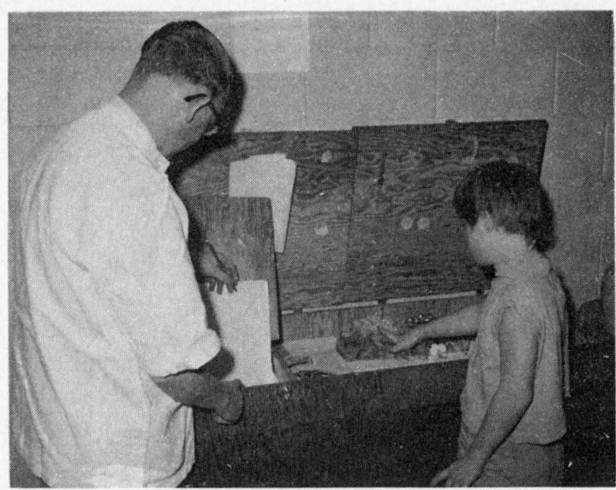

Fig. 4. Store time at Cedar Cottage. A psychiatric nurse at the cottage is shown recording the tokens spent and the items purchased by one of the residents.

The program at Cedar Cottage has been remarkably successful. The tasks for some of the residents now include such things as lacing and tying shoes appropriately, working as servers in the cottage dining room, and learning to spend tokens in the cottage "store." Dr. Lowther, Medical Superintendent, recently remarked that the children showed more progress during the first three months of the program than during their entire previous time in the institution. Since that time the author has worked closely with the Psychiatric Nurses at the Cottage, towards the goal of training the cottage staff, developing extensive recording procedures to monitor resident progress, and developing additional training procedures to increase the complexity of the tasks for some of the residents.

In many cases the change in staff performance is as remarkable as the resident's improvement. The exceptional performance of the staff is all the more impressive considering that it is indubitably more difficult to continually apply operant conditioning than to engage in limited custodial care of the children. One reason for this is that the staff must continually monitor their own behaviour as well as that of the residents in order to ensure that they are reinforcing and/or extinguishing the right responses at the right time. Another reason is that it often is much easier and quicker for a nurse to perform a task, such as dressing, for a resident rather than requiring her to perform that task for herself. Thus the nurse must patiently wait and operantly condition desirable behaviours rather than simply force or guide those behaviours.

Conclusion

It appears that operant conditioning has become an accepted and regular feature at the Manitoba Training School. The autistic and Cedar Cottage programs are continued year around by the regular nursing staff with full-time participation by psychology students during the summer, and part-time participation in the winter. The training programs are also being spread to other wards at the Manitoba Training School. Research is also emphasized in our programs (e.g., see Martin *et al.*, in press, II; Martin *et al.*, 1969; Steeves, *et al.*, in press, III). Recently, the author and Dr. J. Pear (from the University of Manitoba) received a $6,000 grant from the Medical Research Council to study operant conditioning procedures in order to determine which of the procedures are most effective. A growing body of evidence indicates that the systematic use of operant conditioning procedures provides a sufficient basis for establishing a variety of skills in autistic children and retardates. However, additional research is necessary to refine and improve upon the arsenal of techniques that are now available.

References

AYLLON, T., and AZRIN, N. H. *A token economy.* New York: Appleton-Century-Crofts, 1968.

LOVASS, O. I., FREITAS, L., NELSON, K., and WHALEN, C. The establishment of imitation and its use for the development of complex behaviour in schizophrenic children. *Behaviour Research and Therapy,* 1967, *5,* 171-181.

MARTIN, G. L., ENGLAND, G., KAPROWY, E., KILGOUR, K., and PILEK, V. Operant conditioning of kindergarten class behaviour in autistic children. *Behaviour Research and Therapy,* 1968, *6,* 281-294.

MARTIN, G. L., KEHOE, B., FERRIS, E., JENSEN, V., and DARBYSHIRE, M. Operant conditioning of dressing behaviour of severely retarded girls. Submitted to *Mental Retardation,* 1969 (a).

MARTIN, G. L., MCDONALD, S., and OMICHINSKI, M. An operant analysis of response interactions during meals with severely retarded girls. *American Journal of Mental deficiency.* In press, II.

MARTIN, G. L., MOIR, J., and SKINNER, M. A comparison of two time-outs as punishment for errors during a learning task with autistic and retarded children. Submitted to *Journal of Applied Behaviour Analysis,* 1969 (b).

MARTIN, G. L., and PEAR, J. J. Short term participation by 130 undergraduates as operant conditioners in an ongoing project with autistic children. *The Psychological Record.* In Press, I.

RISLEY, T., and WOLF, M. Establishing functional speech in echolalic children. *Behaviour Research and Therapy,* 1967, *5,* 73-88.

STEEVES, J. M., MARTIN, G. L., and PEAR, J. J. Self-imposed time-out by autistic children during an operant training program. *Behaviour Therapy.* In Press, III.

TREFFRY, D., MARTIN, G. L., SAMELS, J., and WATSON, C. Operant conditioning of grooming behaviour of severely retarded girls. Submitted to *Mental Retardation,* 1969.

WATSON, L. S. Application of operant conditioning techniques to institutionalized severely and profoundly retarded children. *Mental Retardation Abstracts,* 1967, *4,* 1-18.

50 / An Aversive Treatment for Addicted Cigarette Smokers: Preliminary Report

P. E. Gendreau and P. C. Dodwell *Queen's University*

The current emphasis on the harmful effects of cigarette smoking has led many individuals to try to break the habit. Various aids, such as drugs, have been used to ease the withdrawal process but none of these aids appears to be particularly effective in eliminating the addiction. This study describes a technique of treating addiction to cigarettes which is based on learning principles.

Introduction

Review of the behaviour therapy literature reveals an increasing use of aversive training techniques, which are designed to reduce the frequency of undesirable behaviour. However, the early results were not particularly encouraging (Grossberg, 1964). No doubt one reason for the lack of success was the general use of emetics as noxious agents, since these are notoriously difficult to administer effectively in a conditioning paradigm. More recently electric shock has been used as aversive stimulus, giving much better control of CS-UCS pairings. Some investigators (Blake, 1965, 1967; Sanderson, Campbell and Laverty, 1963; Solyom and Miller, 1965) report quite promising results with alcoholics and sexual deviants, but success is not uniform (MacCulloch, Feldman, Orford and MacCulloch, 1966). An overall evaluation of the findings is difficult, since a variety of situations and conditioning techniques has been used.

Aversive techniques have recently been applied to cigarette smoking but here again results are equivocal. Greene (1964) used white noise as an aversive UCS with questionable success. McGuire and Vallence (1964) claim success using shock, but with a single smoker. Wilde (1964, 1965) and Franks, Fried and Ashem (1966) attempted to treat smokers with a noxious stimulus of foul air. Wilde reported relapse some 60 days after treatment while Franks felt his data were too tentative to justify any solid conclusions. Koenig and Masters (1965) compared aversive treatment using shock, desensitization and supportive counselling treatments and found a 50% reduction in smoking rates although surprisingly all treatments were equally effective. A six month follow-up revealed that their subjects went back to almost their pre-treatment rates. Pyke, Agnew and Kopperud (1967) in a pilot study, also claim that desensitization treatment plus counselling are effective in attenuating cigarette smoking.

In summary previous research has failed to establish the promise of aversive techniques, including their use to reduce smoking.

The present study uses a modified classical conditioning paradigm with shock paired only with the act of inhalation.

Method

Thirteen subjects were used, and all were volunteers. Ten were inmates of the Maximum Security Prison at Kingston. Three were penitentiary staff. The experimental group (E) consisted of seven inmates and two staff. The control group (C) was made up of three inmates and one staff.

E group Ss had been smoking regularly for a mean period of 14 years at an average of about 35 cigarettes per day. Except when ill or locked up in isolation none of these Ss had ever voluntarily stopped smoking for more than 3 days at one time. The C group Ss had been smoking for a mean period of 12 years at an average rate of about 25 per day. The experimental Ss were, if anything, more heavily addicted than the controls.

A Reitar ECS machine was used for administering shock. Two semi-handcuff electrodes were attached to leads which, when extended, were 4 feet in length. The handcuff electrode apparatus was flexible and could be bent so that it could fit snugly over the subject's wrist or forearm.

Each S was seen individually, and the session proceeded as follows: S was seated at a table facing *E*, and was engaged in casual conversation. He was told he could start smoking when he wished. When he placed the cigarette in his mouth and inhaled, shock was applied, but was terminated when *S* got rid of the cigarette, or after two seconds. On 25% of the "trials" shock was omitted.

For group E, the initial shock level was set individually at just above pain threshold, and rapidly increased on subsequent trials (10 units increase on the Reitar machine each time) so that within comparatively few trials it reached a rather painful level. All *Ss* reported the shock as painful, and even terrifying. For group C the shock level was subliminal and constant from trial to trial. These Ss knew when

Reprinted, by permission, from *Canadian Psychologist*, 1968, *9*, 28-34.

they received a shock as its onset was signalled by a click of the on-switch in the Reitar machine. They put out their cigarettes on hearing the click.

Before the session began all Ss were told they were to undergo a treatment which might help them to quit smoking. They were allowed to ask questions about the experiment and were all told that they would receive shock for smoking. Control group Ss were told that the shock would be too slight to be noticed. They were assured that the treatment would nevertheless be quite effective. They accepted the explanation and were quite ready to try it. Group C was in effect a no-shock suggestion control group.

After the treatment session Ss were told they would be treated again if they so desired. Each S kept a record of the number of cigarettes smoked daily, following treatment. Penitentiary staff and inmate orderlies who had direct contact with Ss discreetly checked up on the validity of the smokers' results. Canteen records were also observed.

Experimental and Control Ss were seen equally often after treatment and any questions about the treatment and smoking were answered for them.

The first six *Ss* were all placed in the E group. As initial results were promising the next seven volunteers were assigned randomly to the E (3*Ss*) and C (4*Ss*) groups. These *Ss* were treated in the following two months. No secondary benefits (e.g. money, time off work, cell locations, recreation privileges) were gained for participating in the experiment. It is important to notice that the shock can be terminated by S. The situation is thus one of escape learning. A 75% partial reinforcement schedule was used in the hope that this might increase resistance to extinction. Since the session was voluntary, and *Ss* could avoid further shock by not lighting a cigarette, the design also has an avoidance feature over the session as a whole. Group C *Ss* were given about the same number of shocks as *Ss* in group E. Since no *S* requested further sessions, the treatment consisted of just one session in every case.

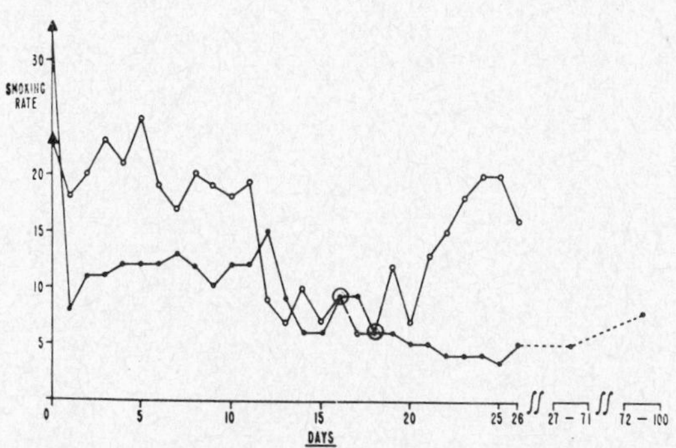

Fig. 1. Post-treatment smoking rates, both groups combined. ▲ *= Pre-treatment rate.* ● *= experimental group.* ○ *= control group. E group complete to day 9, C group to day 13. At day 26 E group has 8 Ss still recording, C group has 3.*

Results

Results are shown graphically in Figure I. A trend analysis was performed on the smoking rates for the first nine post-treatment days only, since on day ten one control subject stopped recording his rate. The scores analysed were the daily rates expressed as a proportion of the pre-treatment rate for each individual, and transformed to arcsine measures. For the first nine days, there was a significant difference between the groups ($F = 16.1$, df 1, 11; $p < .01$) but the effects over days and the interaction of days with treatments were not reliable.

The mean number of shock-smoking pairings for group E was 10 (range 8-11) and shock was terminated on every trial but two (involving different *Ss*) by putting out the cigarette. In these two instances *S* froze with the cigarette in his mouth, and thus received the full 2 sec. shock.

Five *Ss* in group E reported withdrawal symptoms (sweating, feelings of general uneasiness) after treatment, but these symptoms generally disappeared after about two weeks. Four *Ss* in this group increased eating, exercising, reading or gum chewing but such changes were transitory. In four cases it was stated that a temporary increase in smoking rate was connected with personal problems, but in each case *Ss* reported the rate declined as the personal crisis was resolved. Only one subject in group E failed to respond to treatment initially, and he – perversely – stated that he was going to "beat the treatment." The decline in rate was variable, being abrupt in some cases, quite gradual in others.

Discussion

There can be no reasonable doubt about the effectiveness of the aversive training on group E over the nine days following treatment. Group C subjects did not show a similar decline in smoking rate, so the effect can be attributed to the pairing of smoking with painful shock, and the escape from shock by stopping smoking. Although it was not possible to continue the investigation and analysis beyond day nine, since control Ss stopped recording their smoking rates, inspection of figure I suggests that a decreased rate was maintained by group E for at least 100 days. A supplementary investigation 250 days after treatment showed that two E group subjects had relapsed, 3 were smoking 5-10 cigarettes per day, and three had given up cigarette smoking altogether (one could not be contacted after 250 days, but after 100 days was abstinent). Thirty months after the treatment was given, four of the nine experimental *Ss* could be contacted, and three of the four controls. The latter were all smoking at about their pre-treatment rates. One of the experimental *Ss* was smoking heavily, and he was the one who had shown least effect immediately after treatment. Of the other three, one was completely abstinent, one was smoking about eight cigarettes a day (80% reduction) and one had cut his rate by 50% but had taken up pipe smoking. The longer-term findings are distinctly encouraging.[1] All group C subjects had reverted to their pre-treatment smoking rates, one by day 9, two at day 26 and two at day 42. Since they were seen as often as group E, and given as much verbal encouragement to stop smoking, the effective treatment again seems to have been the shock-smoking pairing. Incidentally the control group also provides some control against cheating over the first nine days post-treatment. Such cheating would be difficult anyway, at least for the fairly closely-watched prisoners.

It must be remembered that all *S*s were volunteers, and in fact anxious to co-operate in reducing or stopping their smoking. Even so the results are quite encouraging.

Interestingly enough the E group *S*s who cut their habit down to several cigarettes daily reported they could enjoy them without strain and avoid the unpleasant side effects of heavy smoking.

Although the design included partial reinforcement and an escape training procedure, it is possible that equally successful results could be obtained in other ways. It should be noted that Blake (1965, 1967) reported success using escape training. The escape procedure in this study was such that *S*s could escape from part of the shock, but future studies should investigate the relative merits of "full non-escape" in aversive treatment. It was unfortunate that more *S*s could not be obtained for the control group, but at the time of the study some restrictions on *S*s were enforced, Kingston Penitentiary being a maximum security prison. The control *S*s were certainly susceptible to suggestions to stop smoking but their attempts at reduction, albeit slightly effective, were negligible compared to those of the E group. A control to be considered for future research would be an unpaired shock control group or a yoked control with CS and UCS unpaired.

In conclusion, the results reported here, however promising, should be regarded as tentative. A larger program is presently underway with a much larger N to evaluate a number of the problems raised by this research.

Conclusion

Smoking rates amongst heavily addicted smokers can be drastically reduced, possibly in more than 50% of smokers, by appropriate aversive conditioning techniques. The technique used here was escape learning under partial reinforcement, with painful electric shock as aversive stimulus. There is no means of knowing at present whether this is the most efficient technique. The need for more adequate specification of the learning or conditioning paradigms used in aversion therapy is emphasised.

[1]Subsequent to the reported research 2 more *Ss* were treated in the same way and after 200 days one *S* had quit completely, the other maintained a habit reduced in amount by 70%.

Abstract

An aversive stimulus (electric shock) was paired with cigarette smoking in two groups of addicted smokers. In one group (E) it was made increasingly painful, in the other group (D) it was subliminal. In both groups shock was terminated when *S* put out his cigarette. Treatment was given in one session, with an average of 10 smoking – shock pairings per *S*. On 25% of trials shock was omitted. The treatment greatly reduced smoking in group E (9Ss) but not in group C (4Ss), and therefore has promise for the treatment of heavy smokers. Some subsidiary effects of the treatment were also noticed. More than two years after treatment there was evidence of reduced rates in some E group subjects.

Résumé

Les auteurs ont associé un stimulus aversif (choc électrique) avec l'habitude de fumer aupres de deux groupes de fumeurs invétérés. On intensifia le choc auprès d'un groupe (E) tandis qú auprès de l'autre on le rendit subliminal (C). Pour les deux groupes, on faisait cesser le choc dès que le S éteignait sa cigarette. En moyenne, les sujet reçurent 10 traitements chacun mais on omit le choc dans 25% des cas. L'habitude de fumer fut réduite sensiblement chez le groupe (E) mais non pas chez le groupe (C). Ainsi, il semble que le traitement puisse réduire l'habitude. Plus de 2 ans après le traitement, certain des sujets du groupe (E) fumaient encore moins qu'auparavant.

References

BLAKE, B. L. A follow up of alcoholism treated by behaviour therapy. *Beh. Res. Ther.*, 1967, *5*, 89-94.

———. The application of behaviour therapy to the treatment of alcoholics. *Behav. Res. Ther.*, 1965, *3*, p. 75-86.

FRANKS, CYRIL M., FRIED, ROBERT, and ASHEM, BEATRICE. An improved apparatus for aversive conditioning of cigarette smokers, *Beh. Res. Ther.*, 1966, *4*, 301-308.

GREENE, R. J. Modification of smoking in free operant conditioning methods, *Psychol. Rep.*, 1964, *16*, 171-178.

GROSSBERG, JOHN M. Behaviour Therapy: A Review. *Psychol. Bull.*, 1964, *62*, 73-88.

KOENIG, K., and MASTERS, J. Experimental treatment of habitual smoking. *Beh. Res. Ther.*, 1965, *3*, 234-243.

MACCULLOCH, M. J., FELDMAN, M. P., ORFORD, J. F., and MACCULLOCH, M. L. Anticipatory avoidance learning in the treatment of alcoholism: a record of therapeutic failure. *Beh. Res. Ther.*, 1966, *4*, 187-196.

MCGUIRE, R. J., and VALLENCE, M. Aversion therapy by electric shock: a simple technique. *Br. Med. J.*, 1964, *1*, 151-153.

PYKE, SANDRA, AGNEW, N. M., and KOPPERUD, JEAN. Modification of an overlearned maladaptive response through a re-learning program: a pilot study on smoking. *Ber. Res. Ther.*, 1966, *4*, 197-204.

SANDERSON, R. E., CAMPBELL, D., and LAVERTY, S. G. An investigation of a new aversive conditioning treatment for alcoholism. *Quart. Studies of Alcohol,* 1963, *24,* 261-275.

SOLYOM and MILLER, S. A differential conditioning procedure as the initial phase of the behaviour therapy of homosexuality. *Behav. Res. Ther.,* 1965, *3,* 147-160.

WILDE, G. J. S. Behaviour therapy for addicted cigarette smokers. *Behav. Res. Ther.,* 1964, *2,* 107-109.

———. Personal Communication, Queen's University, Kingston, Ontario, 1965.

51 / Tranquillizers and Perceptual Defensiveness[1]

W.H. Coons and Helen Annis *York University and Whitby Psychiatric Hospital*

Since 1950 tranquillizing drugs such as chlorpromazine and reserpine have been used extensively in the treatment of mental illness. These drugs have a calming and relaxing effect and frequently the patient appears to become more co-operative and communicative. It has been argued that tranquillizers also help to overcome the patient's defensiveness and hence hasten the process whereby he can "face his problems." This study is concerned with an experimental test of this hypothesis.

For over a decade now, tranquillizers have been used as an adjunct to psychotherapy in both private practice and clinical settings. Among psychotherapists of a variety of theoretical orientations, there is a widespread belief that tranquillizing drugs render an individual more receptive to ego-threatening stimuli and consequently more amenable to interpersonal relationships such as psychotherapy.

Within psychoanalytically-oriented literature, particularly, a number of psychodynamic effects have been attributed to these drugs. In general, it is asserted that tranquillizers help overcome resistances, alter defences, and facilitate the emergence of repressed material, thereby fostering communication and insight. Special attention has been focused on the relationship of tranquillizers to the defence process. Ostow (1960) advanced the theory that tranquillizers achieve their therapeutic effect by decreasing the reservoir of psychic energy available to the ego, thus demobilizing its defensive forces. Others (*e.g.*, Freed, 1958; Schmitt,1957; Winkelman, 1960a, 1960b) have hypothesized that tranquillizing drugs erect a protective barrier to the painfulness of external and internal stimuli so that the ego can tolerate more "undistorted derivatives." It is held that thoughts and ideas that were painful before lose their sting (*cf.* Schmitt, 1957); blind spots gradually become smaller, conflicts that were formerly avoided are investigated; more reality can be viewed without turning away (*cf.* Winkelman, 1960a).

In view of the wide acceptance of the usefulness of tranquillizing drugs in psychotherapy and the numerous psychodynamic formulations advanced on the effect of these drugs on the defence process, there is a surprising dearth of supporting experimental evidence. As a first step in submitting these ideas to controlled experimental scrutiny, the present study investigated the relationship between one of the most commonly used forms of tranquillizing medication, chlorpromazine, and receptivity to threatening stimuli. On the basis of the extensive literature, reviewed by MacKinnon and Dukes (1962), tachistoscopic recognition thresholds for personally emotion-arousing words were accepted as a sensitive index of an individual's reaction to threatening stimuli. Specifically, it was hypothesized that individuals who exhibit either of two defensive tendencies, "perceptual defence" (PD, longer recognition thresholds for emotional than for neutral words) or "perceptual vigilance" (PV, shorter recognition thresholds for emotional than for neutral words) will show a greater decrease in defensive responding on chlorpromazine medication than individuals receiving no drug or a placebo.

Method

Subjects

Ss for the study were 58 hospitalized female patients from the chronic wards of Whitby Psychiatric Hospital. Two criteria were used in selecting patients: (1) S had achieved an educational level of at least Grade VI and was presently able to read; (2) *S* was judged clinically suitable for tranquillizing medication by her psychiatrist. All but two of the 58 *S*s were receiving a major tranquillizer immediately prior to their inclusion in the study. The two exceptions had been on tranquillizers for long periods of time during their stay in hospital. Clinical diagnosis was not considered in the selection of *S*s.

Procedure

A word list of 35 six-letter words was drawn up following Richards (1964). All six-letter words of possible emotional connotation and a frequency of greater than 10 per million were drawn from the

[1]The research was supported by OMHF Grant No. 78. The authors are indebted particularly to Dr. P. G. Lynes and Dr. R. B. Kay for their support of the study, and to Poulenc Limited for supplying the necessary drugs and placebo.

Reprinted, by permission, from *Canadian Journal of Behavioural Science*, 1969, *1*, 106-112.

Thorndike-Lorge (1944) general word count. These words, omitting present and past participles and plurals, were rated for potential emotional connotation by three clinical psychologists and the 25 words producing the highest summed ratings were selected. To these were added 10 words of no obvious emotional connotation but similar in length, frequency, and grammatical form to the emotional words, producing a final list of 35 words.

The emotionality of each of the 35 words was idiosyncratically defined for each *S* in terms of her association time on a word association test. For each *S*, 18 words were selected; the 6 with the longest association times (defined as highly emotional stimuli for that subject), the 6 with the shortest association times, and the 6 with median association times.

Each of the 35 words, typed in capital letters, was mounted for presentation in a Gerbrands tachistoscope. In addition to the tachistoscope timer used for recognition threshold determinations, an interval timer connected to the manual operation permitted use of the tachistoscope in measuring word association times.

The 58 patients selected for study were taken off all medication for two weeks. Within the last two days of the two-week period, each subject was seen individually in two separate sessions. In session I, the subject was given the word association test; the experimenter presented the 35 words in random order in the tachistoscope at an illumination well above threshold and *S* was instructed to respond as quickly as possible with the first other word that came to her mind. In session II, *S* performed a recognition threshold task; each of her 18 chosen words (six long, six short, and six median association time words) arranged in random order, was shown at gradually increasing exposure durations until correct recognition occurred. Two defence modes were possible: PD (higher recognition thresholds for emotional words compared with *S*'s average recognition threshold) or PV (shorter recognition thresholds for emotional words compared with *S*'s average recognition threshold).

Following the two-week off-drug period, *S*s were randomly assigned to a four-week chlorpromazine, a no-drug, or a placebo condition. Each *S* in the chlorpromazine condition was placed on an individually prescribed dosage of the tranquillizer. *S*s in the placebo condition received their prescribed dosages in placebo tablets which were identical to the experimental drug in colour, shape, texture, and taste. A double-blind design was maintained throughout the study.

Within the last two days of the drug period, recognition thresholds were again determined for the same 18 words presented in a different random order.

Results

The comparability of the drug, placebo, and no-drug groups on a number of patient characteristics was first checked. As can be seen in Table I, the randomization procedures had largely equated the groups in terms of diagnosis, number of leucotomies, age, education, and frequency and length of hospitalization. The mean prescribed daily dosage of patients in the drug group was found to be 150 mg of chlorpromazine (range 75-300 mg). The mean daily dosage for the placebo group was 160 mg (range 25-400 mg). Since chlorpromazine and placebo were both dispensed in 25-mg capsules, patients in the drug and placebo groups received a comparable number of pills per day.

An "emotional response index" was calculated for each subject, both before and during the treatment period. The index was the standard score of the deviation of the mean threshold of highly emotional words for each subject from the mean recognition threshold for her 18 presented words. The first index reflected a subject's reaction to emotional stimuli while off medication; the second was an index of her reaction while on one of the 3 treatment conditions. In both cases, a positive index reflected a PD mode of defence, while a negative index reflected a PV mode of defence; the numerical value of the index gave the magnitude of the defensive tendency.

Table I – Diagnosis, age, education, leucotomy and hospitalization data for drug, placebo, and no-drug groups

	Group		
Patient characteristics	Drug group ($N = 18$)	Placebo group ($N = 21$)	No-drug group ($N = 19$)
Diagnosis			
Organic psychoses	2	2	3
Schizophrenia	9	13	14
Affective psychoses	0	0	1
Psychoneuroses	1	1	1
Involutional melancholia	1	1	0
Manic depressive psychoses	5	4	0
Leucotomy	0	3	3
Mean age (years)	52.1	45.1	44.8
Mean no. of admissions	2.6	3.1	2.2
Mean length of present hospitalization (mos.)	101.2	83.8	117.6
Mean grade education	10.5	10.0	10.1

Table II – Summary table of 2 X 2 partially hierarchial analyses of variance for each of the 3 drug groups on the "emotional response index"

Source	*df*	*SS*	*MS*	*F*	*P*
Drug Group					
Between *S*s	17				
Defensiveness	1	1.3862	1.3862	13.00	<0.01
Error	16	1.7048	0.1066		
Within *S*s	18				
Pretest–Post-test (T)	1	0	0	<1	ns
Def. X T	1	0.1978	0.1978	3.73	ns
Error	16	0.8490	0.0531		
Placebo Group					
Between *S*s	20				
Defensiveness	1	2.4544	2.4544	32.47	<0.01
Error	19	1.4366	0.0756		
Within *S*s	21				
Pretest–Post-test (T)	1	0.4912	0.4912	14.36	<0.01
Def. X T	1	0.6051	0.6051	17.69	<0.01
Error	19	0.6504	0.0342		
No-Drug Group					
Between *S*s	18				
Defensiveness	1	1.6394	1.6394	29.86	<0.01
Error	17	0.9347	0.0549		
Within *S*s	19				
Pretest–Post-test (T)	1	0.0819	0.0819	1.64	ns
Def. X T	1	0.5162	0.5162	10.34	<0.01
Error	17	0.8476	0.0499		

A one-way analysis of variance on the off-medication "emotional response index" for all subjects confirmed that there was no significant difference in reaction to emotional stimuli of subjects subsequently assigned to chlorpromazine, placebo, and no-drug treatments. Table II reports the separate analyses performed for drug, placebo, and no-drug groups over pre- to post-test scores. The means are presented in Table III.

The defensiveness X pre- post-test interaction is the term crucial to the testing of the experimental hypothesis. As can be seen in Table II, this term was not significant for the drug group but was significant for both the placebo and no-drug groups. It was therefore concluded that subjects on chlorpromazine did not show a decrease in defensiveness whereas subjects on placebo and no-drug conditions did show, upon retest, an over-all decrease in defensive responding. Further between-group orthogonal comparisons indicated a significantly greater decrease in defensiveness in the placebo and no-drug groups compared to the drug group for PD subjects ($F = 4.65$; $p < 0.05$) but not for PV subjects. There was no significant difference between placebo and no-drug groups.

Discussion

The results of the present study fail to support the hypothesis that the administration of chlorpromazine to long-term mental hospital patients increases their receptivity to personally threatening material. On the

Table III – Mean "emotional response index" of perceptually defensive (PD) and perceptually vigilant (PV) *S*s in each of the 3 drug groups

Group	Defence mode	*N*	Pretest (All groups off medication)	Post-test	Change
Drug	PD	8	+0.325	+0.195	–0.130
	PV	10	–0.176	–0.031	+0.145
Placebo	PD	11	+0.504	+0.059	–0.445
	PV	10	–0.220	–0.185	+0.035
No drug	PD	11	+0.427	+0.128	–0.299
	PV	8	–0.190	–0.046	+0.144

contrary, when compared with patients on no-drug and placebo treatments, patients receiving chlorpromazine showed impairment in their ability to perceive incoming stimuli in a less defensive way. This finding raises serious questions about the validity of the widespread belief that tranquillizers make an individual more amenable to psychotherapy by demobilizing defensive tendencies so that he is better able to explore painful areas of experience. The data indicate that, with long-term mental hospital patients, chlorpromazine reinforces defensive tendencies, at least of perceptually defensive individuals, thereby impairing reality-testing ability.

There is already substantial evidence that tranquillizing medication does not result in general improvement in the hospital adjustment of chronic patients (Annis and Coons, 1968; Coons, Boyd, and White, 1962). If the present results can be taken as representative, further limitations are imposed on the usefulness of tranquillizers. It would seem that, especially with perceptually defensive subjects, these drugs may actually impair reality-testing ability. A strengthened defensiveness to ego-threatening communications can be expected to immunize the patient from the potentially beneficial effects of benign social influences. As a consequence, ability to profit from psychotherapy, milieu therapy, and other planned educational experiences will be reduced.

It would appear that we no longer can confidently proceed on the blind assumption that tranquillizers give us the best of both worlds. When our predominant concern is the control of extremely agitated behaviour, tranquillizers may be a solution. However, when our goal is the creation of the optimal conditions for social learning, which depend on an openness on the part of the individual to perceive and test reality, the administration of tranquillizers may seriously undermine therapeutic attempts.

Abstract

This experiment is concerned with investigating the widespread belief that tranquillizing medication renders an individual more receptive to ego-threatening stimuli. It was hypothesized that mental hospital patients placed on chlorpromazine treatment would show a greater decrease in defensive responding than patients given no drug or a placebo. The results failed to support the hypothesis. Patients on chlorpromazine showed greater defensiveness than controls in the tachistoscopic perception of personally threatening material. Implications for the social re-education of patients are discussed.

Résumé

Les auteurs examinent la croyance bien répandue que les tranquillisants auraient pour effet de rendre le sujet plus sensible aux stimuli menaçant son égo. Les résultats ne confirment pas l'hypothèse voulant que des patients mentaux hospitalisés, soumis à une médication de chlorpromazine, montrent moins d'attitude défensive que des patients de contrôle (absence de drogue ou placebo). Les patients traités par le chlorpromazine montrent au contraire une attitude de défense plus marquée que les patients de contrôle dans la perception tachistoscopique d'un matériel à connotation menaçante pour l'égo. Incidences de telles données sur la rééducation sociale des patients sont discutées.

References

ANNIS, H. M., and COONS, W. H. Chlorpromazine and mental hospital patients. A paper presented at the Ontario Psychological Association Convention, Windsor, 1968.

COONS, W. H., BOYD, B. A., and WHITE, J. G. Chlorpromazine, trifluoperazine, and placebo with long-term mental hospital patients. *Canadian Psychiatric Association Journal*, 1962, *7*, 159-63.

FREED, H. On the combined use of trifluoperazine and electro-shock therapy. In H. BRILL, ed., *Trifluoperazine: clinical and pharmacological aspects*. Philadelphia: Lea and Febiger, 1958.

MACKINNON, D. W., and DUKES, W. F. Repression, In L. POSTMAN, ed., *Psychology in the making*. New York: Alfred A. Knopf, 1962.

OSTOW, M. The effects of the newer neuroleptic and stimulant drugs on psychic function. In G. J. SARWER-FONER, ed., *The dynamics of psychiatric drug therapy*. Springfield: Charles C. Thomas, 1960.

RICHARDS, B. S. Defensiveness in perception and self-description. An M.A. thesis submitted to the Faculty of Graduate Studies, Dalhousie University, 1964.

SCHMITT, R. J. The psychodynamics of the tranquillizing drugs. *Psychiatric Quarterly*, 1957, *31*, 17-30.

THORNDIKE, E. L., and LORGE, I. *The teacher's word book of 30,000 words*. New York: Columbia University Press, 1944.

WINKELMAN, N. W. Chlorpromazine and prochlorperazine during psychoanalytic psychotherapy. In G. J. SARWER-FONER, ed., *The dynamics of psychiatric drug therapy*. Springfield: Charles C. Thomas, 1960. (a)

———. The effect of phenothiazine compounds on the brain affecting psychic functions. In G. J. SARWER-FONER, ed., *The dynamics of psychiatric drug therapy*. Springfield: Charles C. Thomas, 1960. (b)

ELEVEN
SOCIAL GROUPS

52 / Ruhleben: A Prison Camp Society

J.Davidson Ketchum *University of Toronto*

At the outbreak of World War I, in 1914, four thousand men and boys – professors, scientists, bank directors, musicians, clerks, seamen, jockeys, and schoolboys – were taken from civilian life and placed in an internment camp (a former race track) in Ruhleben, a suburb of Berlin. No activities were prescribed for them and no direction was given to their communal life. In a relatively short period of time, this miscellaneous group of people, closed off from the world, created their own miniature society. One of the internees was a young Canadian, Davidson Ketchum, who was studying music in Germany in 1914 when he was caught by the war and interned for four years in the prison camp at Ruhleben. This experience led him to the study of social psychology and eventually to a distinguished career as a professor at the University of Toronto. Although Professor Ketchum worked sporadically, since 1932, on the material that he had collected at Ruhleben, it was not until late in 1950 that he was able to concentrate upon the final writing of his book entitled Ruhleben: A Prison Camp Society.

This selection from his book describes the nature of the prison camp as it existed nine months after its establishment. It is interesting to note that by this early date, the prisoners were already living in a very complex society whose social growth was complete. It was not, however, a "normal" society: it consisted only of males and it was not self-sustaining economically. These two factors, as will be seen, had important effects on its structure and character.

Professor Ketchum died in 1962 prior to the completion of his book. It was published posthumously by his friend and fellow-psychologist, Professor Robert MacLeod of Cornell University.

With the total organisation of Ruhleben in the summer of 1915 its social growth was complete; the prisoners were living in a full-grown society, with far-reaching results on their conduct and attitudes. These were most marked in the case of active men, whose lives were radically altered in character and tempo, but no one was unaffected by the new developments. This chapter, which closes the account of the period of expansion, will try to convey something of the summer's changed atmosphere, and then consider some obvious abnormalities in Ruhleben's social structure. As a concrete starting point, we may glance at the camp itself as it appeared nine months after its establishment, at six o'clock on the morning of Sunday, August 1, 1915.[1]

It is a clear, cool morning after four days of showers and thunderstorms, and the compound, seen from just inside the gate, looks fresh and not unattractive. Rain has laid the troublesome dust; the five trees in front of Barrack II are green against the brick stable, and flower beds along its walls are bright with nasturtiums and zinnias. Thousands of footprints in the damp sand suggest how heavily the stableyard is populated, but no prisoners are yet in sight; they are all in their bunks – though some, as Chapman's diary complains, have been wakened since 3.30 A.M. by the crowing of Barrack 12's pet rooster.

Reprinted from *Ruhleben: A Prison Camp Society*, by J. Davidson Ketchum, by permission of University of Toronto Press. Pp. 293-311. The photograph of the Ruhleben camp has been added to the article.

[1] The date has no special significance; it was chosen as being an ordinary Sunday, within the period desired, and reasonably well documented.

The boiler house in Trafalgar Square yields more evidence of a busy community; the traction engine is working on German farms for the summer, but the shed that housed it is covered with a mass of notices. The most conspicuous is an illuminated proclamation in Old English script, headed: "BOROUGH OF RUHLEBEN: PARLIAMENTARY BYE-ELECTION, 1915"; it announces with grandiose formality the mock political contest that will end on Tuesday with a Suffragette victory. At its head is the Ruhleben coat of arms, here making its first public appearance, but soon to adorn hundreds of souvenirs. Like the Ruhleben Song it reflects the camp's unchanging conception of itself; the quarterings contain a soup bowl, a black loaf, a German sausage, and a clog, with a rat and a mouse as supporters, and the steadfast if shopworn motto, *"Dum Spiro Spero."* Next to this grim self-portrait is yesterday's parcel list, with its hundreds of names in alphabetical order; it throws an ironic light on the symbolism of the coat of arms, for almost 25,000 food parcels have been received during July.

On a large board, labelled "OFFICIAL," a set of brusque instructions about laundering in the barracks, picking up paper, and general conduct is signed by Powell and headed by one of his pet phrases, "Play the Game!" (H). Below it the Sports Control Committee announces a Bank Holiday celebration on the field tomorrow; those who plan to operate shows and gambling devices must make written application for space (H). And at the top of the board a small typed notice states that nothing may be posted on the boiler house without being first stamped in the captains' office. A baize-covered board surmounted by a cross lists an elaborate programme of Anglican services on weekdays and Sundays, including Holy Communion this morning at seven. The Debating Society and several circles and associations have their own boards, and a poster high on the shed announces that the Ruhleben Dramatic Society will produce Galsworthy's *The Silver Box* on August 4 and the three following nights.

Miscellaneous advertisements are legion: for clogs and English tennis rackets, obtainable through the canteen; for tailors, a hairdresser, a carpenter, and the Ruhleben "Practicle" Laundry; for the books, music and war maps that Mr. Mussett orders from Berlin; and for the tempting salads, "made by a professor of the culinary art," procurable from I. Boyer & Co. (S). Teachers offer instruction in languages and London matric mathematics, while individuals advertise for lost note-books, fountain pens, and deck chairs, offer to buy text-books and razor blades, and announce meetings of organizations and informal groups. (It is reassuring to see that most of these individual notices have *not* been stamped by the captains.)

Outside Barrack 12 is a strange assortment of fowls and quadrupeds in a chicken-wire enclosure; the miniature zoo is the special pride of the barrack non-com, the amiable Corporal Pyro. Poor Pyro, though he does not know it, has only a fortnight more to spend in the comfort of Ruhleben; on August 17 his well-meant bootlegging activities will get him seventy-two hours' cells and transfer to front line duty.

Beyond Barrack 12 stands the hot-water house with its tall chimney; here are the first prisoners – three yawning seafarers stoking the boilers in preparation for the opening of business at 7.30 a.m. Across Bond Street, between Barracks 11 and 10, flies a banner reading "VOTE FOR BOSS!", and the hot-water house is plastered with boastful and vituperative election posters. The shops are closed and deserted, but they too bear traces of a lively population. Outside the grocery store, beside a list of what is in stock, an illustrated poster reads: "DON'T stand gaping, the notices are only ornamental, take no notice of them please! Come along now, ask questions, push, shove, help to keep customers away, we hate work!" (S). Scurrilous annotations have been added by waiting customers. And at the stall that serves tea and soft drinks a notice in blue pencil makes the double-barrelled appeal: "Will those persons who have absent-mindedly taken away our cups kindly return same as we are awfully short of them. *Why don't you bring that cup back, you cheap thief?*" (S). Employees in Ruhleben's shops and services were not unduly obsequious.

There is no early *Appell* on Sundays, but by half-past six the camp is coming to life. A policeman in striped arm-band unlocks the police station next to the outfitters' stores, early risers in pyjamas make their way to the latrines, and from the barracks come sounds of voices and running water. Camp workers in singlets and dungarees head towards the kitchens, where coffee is being brewed; two young men in suits, collars, and ties start for the grandstand to prepare altar and benches for the communion service, and another waits near the gate to meet the clergyman from Berlin.

From seven onwards there is an unbroken succession of public activities. As soon as the forty odd Anglicans vacate the hall it is taken over by Roman Catholics for eight o'clock mass; at eight, too, a party of golf professionals tees off on the field, while on the third grandstand Mr. Brose begins his second lecture on "The Dynamics of a Particle." He is followed at nine by Mr. Ford on *Richard III*, and at ten by Mr. Masterman on "The Development of England"; both draw large audiences. During the Shakespeare lecture sixty men are doing setting-up exercises on the field, and Masterman's listeners need only raise their eyes to see tennis games along the race-track and the start of a Lancashire-Yorkshire cricket match beyond them. This is a special event, and souvenir programmes are on sale for a penny. A second team match and various informal games also start this morning.

The stableyard meanwhile has been given over to domestic activities. The new wash-house is not finished, and the men still wash in the barrack corridor.

A large urn of German coffee is placed in the corridor by workers at 7.30 a.m.; prisoners who prefer their own tea line up at the hot-water house. The breakfast tables are plentifully if simply supplied with bread, butter, margarine, dripping, jam, and English sugar and condensed milk for the hot beverages. After the meal the messmate whose turn it is rinses the dishes under the tap, puts them away, and sweeps the box dirt into the corridor, where barrack cleaners are at work with brooms and pails.

Soon after eight Berlin Sunday papers go on sale, and those with no early appointments read them over their coffee. There is little war news today except from the east, where the Germans are close to Warsaw; the front pages are monopolized by the Kaiser's solemn proclamation on the war's first anniversary: "Before God and history my conscience is clear; I never willed this war!" The prisoners comment scornfully, "No, he never willed *this* war; what he wanted was a quick walk-over!" The *Ruhleben Daily News* with its page of English translations will not appear until the fall, and on the benches against the barrack walls men are translating the German papers to small groups of listeners.

By nine o'clock on this fine day almost everyone is out in the sun, and the camp has its typical crowded appearance. The largest numbers are watching the games or walking round and round the field, but there are many at lectures and meetings on the grandstands and the stableyard is far from empty. Hundreds of men have settled themselves in deck chairs, some merely reclining, but the majority reading, studying, or writing letters with the aid of little tables fastened to the chair arms. At 11.30 the kitchen parades begin and dinner-getting continues until nearly one. Each barrack marches off at an assigned time, which changes from day to day, so men consult the time-table before planning their morning activities. The soup is not exciting, but it is well studded with potatoes, and the little scrap of meat supplied on Sundays draws most of the men to the kitchens. Special arrangements exist for cricketers and others who cannot line up with their own barracks.

Many older men take a nap after dinner, but otherwise the afternoon is spent like the morning, with crowds on the field and tennis courts until they close at five and the rest of the men variously occupied. Nearly three hundred attend the 3.30 evensong, at which Mr. Williams, returning again from Berlin, preaches a carefully non-political sermon. The service is conducted with great formality; each worshipper is handed a prayer-book as he enters, responses are intoned, canticles chanted, and four hymns sung to harmonium accompaniment. Minister and congregation pay no attention to the occasional rounds of applause from the field, and a policeman restrains the irreligious from walking on the steel and concrete overhead. No concert is scheduled for this summer evening, and walks, cards, reading, and study pass the time from supper until *Appell* in the barracks at nine. By ten the men have settled down and another Ruhleben day is over.

What would most strike a visitor is the orderly, regulated nature of the camp's daily life. In contrast to the confusion and turbulence of November 1914, everything now seems to follow a schedule; all public activities are advertised in advance and take place as arranged. And the men's behaviour is correspondingly orderly. There is certainly some pushing and jostling around the parcel lists, and noisy arguments are often heard in the barracks, but the general picture is of a civilized population that has solved most of the social problems of its mixed and congested camp. The men sleep and wake, dress, eat, read, and write in their closely packed boxes with extraordinarily little friction, they appear on time for *Appell* and kitchen parades, and large crowds assemble and disperse several times a day with a minimum of disturbance.

Nor does this orderliness seem due to external discipline. The barrack soldiers and captains do some urging as they herd the men into line, a forgetful prisoner will be sharply told to take his pipe out of his mouth, and late arrivals run anxiously to their places. But they are usually less afraid of the German sergeant than of their barrack-mates, whose annoyance at being kept waiting is expressed in muttered booing. Everything, in fact, suggests that the men are conforming, not to military rules, but to a code of behaviour established by themselves. They never march smartly to the kitchens as the Germans wish, but walk there in ragged fours; when ordered off the field they leave leisurely, without breaking off their conversations; and at night they cease talking only after the guards have several times demanded silence. Occasionally a soldier loses his temper and marches some chosen delinquent to the cells, but in general an accommodation seems to have been reached on terms acceptable to the prisoners.

The Germans of course have nothing to do with the activities that occupy most of each day, and it is in these settings, where the men are entirely on their own, that their self-imposed orderliness is most conspicuous. As soon as the curtain rises or the conductor lifts his baton, silence falls in the grandstand hall; whispered remarks during a lecture bring immediate "shushing" from those around; the chairman's rulings are respected during the hottest debates; and even in bitterly contested games no umpire or referee is ever challenged. Self-restraint and mutual understanding are particularly evident in the long queues that form for theatre tickets or special canteen sales. After the wild race from morning *Appell* to be first in line, each man accepts his place without argument, though watching jealously that no late-comer edges in ahead of him. When all the seats are sold or the stock exhausted the disappointed ones walk quietly away. If the wait is a long one (theatre queues often lasted all morning) there is a tacit understanding that friends may alternate in holding a place, and that a man may absent himself long enough to go to

"Die Engländer holen ihr Mittagessen"—*Die Woche*, Berlin. September 11, 1915.
Ruhleben prisoners on their way to a mid-day meal.

the latrines without penalty. The policeman on duty seldom has anything to do; the accepted code covers most eventualities.

It was probably this spontaneous orderliness that Powell had in mind when he spoke of Ruhleben as "the best bit of corporate life" he had ever seen; it must have made government remarkably easy. And it was certainly this that moved the Commandant to approach the War Office in September and arrange for the removal of German guards; his own eyes had told him they were not needed.

What it meant, of course, was that the prisoners were under pervasive social control, applied when necessary by their fellows, but residing for the most part in the individual as a sense of "ought" or obligation. The control was a direct outcome of the organizing of the camp, which had changed each separate individual into a *member* of his box and barrack, of various associations, and always and above all of "Ruhleben" – an embattled outpost, proudly maintaining British standards in the face of the enemy. This conscious membership entailed sensitivity to the rights of others and binding obligations towards them, often crystallized in recognized codes of conduct. Thus the prisoner, in becoming a part of the camp and of many groups within it, had transcended his egocentric tendencies and become a socialized, civilized being.

This is not to suggest that Ruhleben gave its inhabitants their basic social training; they had acquired that, well or poorly, in early childhood. What the camp did was to tie them together in a great number of ways and so provide a context teeming with effective obligations. The first feeling of many prisoners on being interned had been one of *irresponsibility*, of freedom from social obligations; that it did not demoralize them was due to the prompt appearance of solidarity with its attendant norms of conduct. To this had then been added the community groups, associations, and numerous personal friendships, each involving the participants in further mutual responsibilities, until Ruhleben became for many of its inhabitants, the richest experience of attachments and obligations they were ever to have. As such it was, in actual fact, a school of social relations, broadening the sensitivities of those already well socialized, and supplementing the training of men whose early social experience had been defective.

The most obvious sign of effective social control was the almost complete absence of crime. [2] All sorts of dubious characters, from pimps, pickpockets, and petty swindlers to professional burglars, had been swept up in the internment, but Chapman, a member of the camp police during 1915, records not a single case of theft in his diary, and Mahoney, also a policeman, says flatly:

> Crime was unknown in Ruhleben . . . . More than one of our number had "done time" in England, but here the predatory instinct seemed to have become stifled. Now and again there was a slight outbreak of lawlessness, but these were few and quickly suppressed. Men who infringed the rules come to fear being ostracized by their comrades as much as, if not more than, being penalized by the German authorities. ([3?], p. 156).

Mahoney's statement needs but little qualification,

[2]Drunkenness and gambling, of course, were "crimes" only in the eyes of the Germans; those recognized by the prisoners were chiefly theft and extreme violence.

and its emphasis on social pressure is borne out by the temporal relations between offences against property and the growth of camp organization. In the early, chaotic days petty thieving was clearly prevalent; boxes were never left unattended except when everyone was on parade, and the familiar cry, "Stranger in the barrack!" was a necessary alarm signal. Hughes speaks of the early attitude towards property as resembling that in a boarding school: "If you didn't look out, someone bagged your towel" (p. 668). Mahoney also refers to towels being constantly guarded, and Henley, during his initial weeks in the grandstand, kept his soup bowl under his pillow at night. Solidarity at Ruhleben, as in the army and similar bodies, did not exclude the "adopting" of small but essential articles.

No serious losses are recorded, however, and with the organizing of the camp all types of theft dropped to a negligible level. A notice dated March 11, 1915, reads: "If the person who took the grey dinner can from the end of the corridor will call at Box 16 he may have the lid" (S), but only one other reference can be found before 1918, when the social structure was weakening. This is in Kendall's diary for April 6, 1916, and its content is startling: "Some day last week a man picked from the pocket of another a gold watch and sold it for M 30. He got three days, and will be kept in cells here for the rest of his internment." This drastic punishment (which must surely have been remitted) might suggest that crime was only controlled in Rhleben by the infliction of savage penalties. Its true significance, however, is quite different. The camp was peculiarly exposed to theft, for only the horse-boxes had doors, and these had no locks. The perpetual vigilance of the first week or so soon became impracticable, and the safeguarding of household goods and personal valuables had to depend on a collective recognition of their inviolability. Such an understanding, tacit but solemn, quickly emerged in response to the common need; it was part of the *mores* of Ruhleben, and so universally respected that when an infraction did occur, as in the case above, it was felt to be a heinous offence, the breaking of a strict taboo. The actual punishments were meted out by the Germans, but on this occasion, perhaps prompted by Powell, they evidently took the same view: the malefactor must be cut off from the camp. Thanks to this rigid code, surplus food in later years was stacked in the open corridors and never interfered with, deck chairs and other property were parked all over the camp, and lost wallets with considerable sums of money were regularly turned in by the finders to the police station.

There were, no doubt, more breaches of the taboo than are recorded, for habitual gamblers were sometimes in desperate straits for money, and some men's pilfering tendencies probably survived Ruhleben's severe moral climate. But to be exposed as a thief in this closely knit community was, as Mahoney implies, something to be dreaded by the most hardened, and the "pickings" available were scarcely worth such a risk.

No murder was committed in Ruhleben, but physical assault was fairly frequent, especially in the sailors' barracks. Chapman's diary contains half a dozen passing references to "fights" he witnessed. They were usually broken up by bystanders, but were not seriously regarded; only excessive violence and the use of weapons were taboo, and cases of these were almost invariably due to liquor or mental instability. Kendall reports several instances:

May 22, 1916. About 12.30 A.M. was awakened by a great row in Barracks 4 and 5. Wild Mac and some others ran amok. It seems they get a can full of wine in which they mix Spiritus to give it a "tang" and this sends them fighting mad. After laying out Cliff and several more they were mastered at 4 o'clock and put in cells. They got sentenced to 3 days dark cells and 28 days birdcage.[3]

Dec. 3, 1916. Man named S. in Barrack 9 went amok today, damaging Alex Hay badly. He was taken to sanatorium.

Nov. 28, 1917. A nigger from 12 slashed Bruce's neck with a razor. Collins, who was standing near, hit the blackie, who lay stunned for 45 minutes and was carried to lazarette.

As among schoolboys, a "fair fight" reflected no discredit on the participants, and was sometimes formally conducted. On January 13, 1916, Chapman was asked to act as second in a fight; next he met the other second to arrange details, and on January 15 he wrote:

At 7.30 A.M. went to Artists' Studio with White. Besides the two principals there was Smyllie and myself as seconds, White as referee and Egremont as doorkeeper. Sixteen rounds of 1½ minutes each were fought with no damage. They shook hands.

Episodes of violence were inevitable in a camp so mixed, so crowded, and exposed to so many strains; under the circumstances, the prisoners kept the peace remarkably well.

The pervasive effects of social control went much further than the discouragement of crime; by August 1915 conventional pressures were being felt in many directions. Leaders in camp institutions were being a little careful about their dress, decent language and manners were being cultivated in many boxes, strangers were being formally introduced. Sunbathing in trunks had been branded as immoral, and the Education Committee's banning of a debate on the legitimizing of "war-babies," though by no means generally supported, brought at least one approving letter to the magazine. Individuals were also having to remember their group affiliations; supermen were not seen in the stalls at music-hall shows, barrack officials were chary of criticizing the civil administration, and no one prominent in Protestant

[3]The "birdcage" or detention barrack was a section of Barrack 14 with a small wired-in enclosure for exercise. It supplemented the four punishment cells, and was controlled by German guards.

religious circles would dare to be seen gambling. (Nor would a recognized "tough" risk his reputation by appearing at a church service!)

The most unremitting control was exerted on the hundreds of men who kept Ruhleben running – captains and other unpaid officials, committee members, lecturers and teachers, actors and producers, conductors, orchestra players, and many others. All these men were now busily occupied with what was beginning to be called "work," held steadily at it by schedules reaching well into the future, and by a network of obligations to co-workers, institutions, and the camp as a whole. These obligations were rarely felt as burdensome in 1915, for organization was still fairly flexible, the self-chosen tasks were fresh and purposeful, and they brought many rewards in social stimulation and personal recognition. Indeed, the active men were the most contented in the camp. Merton, a senior barrack official, replying to the question, "What one thing did most to make life bearable or enjoyable?" wrote in 1933:

The fact that I had some definite duties to perform the neglect of which would react unfavourably upon others. Having accepted the responsibility for their performance, I was no longer wholly able to decide how I should spend my time. There was also the fact that the work was done in association with others, whose company was definitely entertaining and congenial.

This perceptively sums up the situation; the second sentence, however, is a two-edged one. It is true, as Merton implies, that prescribed duties kept men alert and free from boredom; on the other hand, the freedom to decide how to spend one's time is a boon that few are willing to dispense with indefinitely. In Ruhleben's later years there were clear indications that many active men were hankering for this freedom, and growing restive under the social control they had so gladly accepted.

The camp of 1915 was a very busy place. As the first review of music put it in June: "Function has followed function breathlessly. We have been swirled from concert to play, from play to lecture, from lecture to debate, and thence back again to the concert, to recommence the cycle anew" (*IRC* 1, p. 19). And, in spite of the hundreds of deck chairs to be seen, Sunday, August 1, was anything but a day of rest. All over the camp preparations were on foot for Monday's Bank Holiday celebration, when free beer, costumed performers, sideshows, games of chance, and an open-air concert and prize-giving would bring Hampstead Heath to the racecourse. Officials of the territorial societies were no doubt planning future strategy in the light of last Thursday's anti-medal meeting; the big-wigs of the R.D.S. were putting the final touches on a seven-point letter of protest against the Entertainments Committee; both the promenade orchestra and the cast of *The Silver Box* had morning rehearsals; the election candidates and their agents were canvassing for Tuesday's voting; Mr. Eric Swale, who had just organized the Technical Circle, was probably drumming up an audience for its first meeting next Thursday; and large numbers of men had lectures to prepare or homework to do over the weekend.

As the variety of occupations shows, the busy camp was also a highly differentiated one; while some men idly watched the cricket, others worked feverishly at constructing a ring-tossing game and still others sang hymns at the Anglican service. Differentiation had penetrated even to the homes; the early communicants, with their Sunday faces, had to dress silently to avoid waking their unsanctified boxmates, and the close family life of the winter was often disrupted by outside engagements. Denton wrote home on June 11, 1915: "I had a fine birthday yesterday, though the actual party cannot take place until Monday, for 'As you like it' is on every evening at present and the boys are all very busy from four o'clock on." Meetings and rehearsals might be called for almost any hour of the day, and members of the same box often ate at different times and on some occasions scarcely met until bedtime. And individuals who played more than one role were constantly involved in conflicts; a 1915 pencil notice reads: "Owing to dress rehearsal of orchestra Dr. Darbishire is obliged to postpone his second lecture on the manufacture of beet sugar till the following week" (H). The learned doctor was also a cellist.

Differentiation creates divisions, and Ruhleben was this summer a congeries of institutions, societies, and other formal and informal groups. Many of them were hotly competing for members, space, time, and power, and the camp, in spite of its orderly appearance, seethed with quarrels. The Extraordinary General Meeting of the A.S.U. in June was so acrimonious that the magazine issued a special supplement to cover it; on one speaker's suggestion that a certain proposal might cause friction with other bodies the report commented: "As if any Ruhleben Society ever existed without such friction."[4] In July the medal controversy split the camp for a fortnight; in August the entertaining bodies went on strike against the captains, and a long feud between the school and the A.S.U. culminated in their legal divorce. The supermen were a centre of dissension in every organization they belonged to, and Adler's supporters were loudly condemning the high-handedness of the musicians' society.

What had made the comradely Ruhlebenites so suddenly quarrelsome was again the organization of their camp, for in most of these disputes they were acting, not as simple individuals, but as members of groups with which they were strongly identified. Relations between the newly formed bodies were not yet stabilized by accepted conventions; each was in a large measure a law unto itself, pursuing its own interests as determinedly as nations in the modern

[4]*In Ruhleben Camp*, No. 1, Stop Press supplement (mimeographed).

world. Officials were playing their allotted parts in the social drama; however reasonable personally, they behaved like chauvinist politicians when organizational aims were at stake. Ruhleben, however, was more fortunate than the world of nations, for the representatives of all competing bodies spoke the same language and shared an over-riding loyalty to the camp as a whole. Hence, as contacts continued, conflicts were thrashed out, spheres of action delimited, and mutual relations put on a polite and conventional basis. The school and the A.S.U. were still quarrelling in 1916 – their fields were too similar for easy harmony – but otherwise there was little more friction except with that uncompromising body, the captains.

Closely akin to these inter-group quarrels was the extraordinary touchiness displayed by individuals in their new social roles. At the Mock Trial in March 1915 the camp police had been the targets of some witty shafts; to the astonishment of the Debating Society these were hotly resented, and a police strike was only prevented by a formal apology. It was the police, too, who turned in their badges in May when camp officials, after many complaints from private citizens, were deprived of the privilege of getting hot water at the head of the queue. A compromise was hurriedly reached and the police went back to work. Then in August a critical letter to the magazine about hot-water service was thought to reflect on the rectitude of the staff, who promptly "downed tools." A tea famine was averted by a personal apology from the letter-writer, followed by one from the editor in the next issue. The editor was having a rough time, for another item in the August issue got him into trouble with the redoubtable Tom Sullivan, an early pioneer in sports. Sullivan had been the subject of an imaginary interview centring around his predilection for cups and medals; he protested that his honour had been impugned, and did it so vigorously that the September issue carried apologies from the Education Committee, the editor, and the writer of the article.

A September reference to a cricket umpire was also resented by the victim, but this time there was no printed apology, and by October the editor had decided to stand his ground. A football report had criticized the play of two team members – caustically, but no more so than is commonplace in sports write-ups. Two leading sportsmen, however, wrote letters of complaint, and these were printed under the heading, "Should we criticize?", with rebuttals from the writer and the editor. The essence of the complaints was that sharp criticism was out of place "in a camp like this," and the phrase explains much of the first summer's touchiness. For Ruhleben was no longer what it once had been: a simple community in which social contacts were close and direct, relationships personal, and criticism accepted as "all in the family." A new dimension had been added to it, one characterized by formality and social distance, abstract, impersonal relations, and objective standards of judgment.[5] And the development had been so swift that many prisoners (and perhaps particularly sportsmen) had not yet adjusted to it. Though playing roles in the new society, they were still attuned to the old, and they found the remote impersonality of printed criticism deeply wounding, for it evaluated the comrades of the first winter as coldly as though they were strangers.

It was a drastic change, but irreversible, for Ruhleben had grown out of its crowd and community stages; it was now a public, and public life imposed its own conditions. As the editor put it: "It seems to us that if a man makes a public appearance, be it on the sports field, on the stage, or as a camp official he must as a matter of course be prepared to meet criticism" (*IRC* 10, p. 29).

The police and hot-water strikes revealed a sensitivity that extended beyond the individual to the groups to which he belonged. This too was most marked in 1915 when the associations first became dominant; the prisoner was then acutely conscious of his new group identifications, and the groups themselves were young and vulnerable. After 1915, however, injured feelings produced no more strikes and no more protests to the magazine. Criticism in 1916 was as severe as ever, but Ruhleben was a year older, organizations had weathered the storms and were solidly established, and individuals had accepted the new social conventions.

The letters written around August 1 were so dark with forebodings of a second winter that Chapter 9 spoke of the camp as generally depressed. In view of the busy activity since described, how should these letters be interpreted?. There is no doubt of the writers' sincerity, but there is also little doubt that these same men got great enjoyment from the games, theatre, and Bank Holiday revels. The prisoner writing home was for the moment in a different world from Ruhleben, one in which the cruelty of long separation often dominated his mind. He seldom remained there for long, however, but was soon caught up again in the concrete world about him. It is therefore pointless to ask whether the men were "happy" in their new society; all had their periods of elation and of depression, sometimes private, sometimes (as before another winter) widely shared. And during most of the time they were neither happy nor unhappy, but going about their business in a completely matter-of-fact way. For what the creative outburst of the spring had given them was something more vital than happiness; it was the chance to live a full, normal life on the racecourse. Like real life anywhere, it mixed its many satisfactions with plenty of pain, disappointment, and simple boredom; but it was also, as life always is, a source of inexhaustible interest, capturing and holding the attention of all who took part in it. And that was what mattered at Ruhleben.

[5]These distinctions were exhaustively analysed by Ferdinand Tonnies in *Gemeinschaft und Gesellschaft* (5th ed.; Berlin: K. Curtius, 1926).

The degree to which the prisoners were actually absorbed in camp affairs has perhaps been sufficiently indicated, but further light is thrown on it by the issue of *In Ruhleben Camp* that appeared on Sunday, August 1, and was sold out in a few hours. It was a Bank Holiday issue, but its content and tone were entirely typical. From a gaily coloured cover to the canteen advertisement on the back, the magazine is as oblivious of the outside world as its name suggests; Ruhleben is the sole reality. Illustrations make up a third of the content: there are drawings of camp landmarks, prominent cricketers, and theatrical casts and scenes; caricatures of medallists, sun-worshippers, and other notables; and some enticing but improbable views of the hidden glories of the Summer House. Scores of smaller drawings include a sketch of a mechanical man for standing in queues (he is set to move at one mile per year), and a close-up of Powell's refulgent arm-band, inscribed: "Captain of Captain, Lord of Lords, King of Kings, and only ruler of Camp."

The letterpress is similarly camp-centred; only once in the 48 pages is return to England mentioned even half-seriously. Sports are omitted from this number, but there is a chatty account of the Parcels Office, a humorous story of a man who was led to believe his release had been signed, a flippant debates report, and reviews, complimentary or cutting, of three recent plays. There are short notices of poetry and Dickens evenings, the Art Exhibition, and a concert of French music; Mr. Govett's "Phoebe" gets her first introduction to the quaint folkways of the camp, and "Ruhleben according to Otto" translates some of them into the stilted language of French exercises. "Answers to Correspondents" deals facetiously with lice, mosquitoes, and other plagues, while letters to the editor complain of high tennis fees, high theatre prices, and "agonizing sounds" from rehearsal sheds. There is much else, all of the same character.

What hundreds of Ruhlebenites were reading and chuckling about this morning was, then, their own camp, its amenities, celebrities, and shortcomings. But could the magazine have published anything different? Prison camp magazines are hard to come by, but Vischer's brochure (46) gives a partial answer with excerpts from journals got out by German and French prisoners, including the German civilians at Knockaloe. Many of these are painful reading; the tone is introspective, often self-pitying, and the emphasis is on the grinding monotony of camp life, the loathing of others induced by constant propinquity, the paralysing sense of powerlessness and sterility, and (from Knockaloe, be it noted) the utter worthlessness of everything achieved or learned behind barbed wire. It is true that Vischer's examples were selected, and selected to portray the strains of confinement; they may also have reflected literary convention or editorial bias. Typical or not, however, the fact remains that they were published, whereas they could never have been published in Ruhleben. Life there was sufficiently real and absorbing to cast a cloak of oblivion, not only over its trying aspects, but also over everything that lay beyond the barbed wire.

The fact needs no argument, for it was notorious in the camp and often joked about. In a skit in this same August magazine each member of the editorial staff has to write one wish on a piece of paper. All, it turns out, are identical: to have a pass to the Casino. Only the office boy, asked what his wish would have been, answers promptly, "To be released," at which the others exclaim, "Why, we never thought of that!" (*IRC* 4, p. 33). And a subsequent issue describes Hatfield as "the most practical man in Ruhleben" – so immersed in camp affairs that when asked, "Well, what d'ye think of the War?" he responded with a puzzled look, "War? What war?" (*IRC* 9, p. 14).

It is clear that the Ruhleben society "worked"; it performed its vital functions. It was, however, far from being a normal society, and particularly in two obvious respects: it consisted only of males, and it was not self-sustaining economically. Both facts had important effects on its structure and character.

The absence of women meant that it was biologically sterile, incapable of perpetuating itself, and also that it provided no legitimate sex outlets for its members. But the camp's unisexual character had positive aspects as well, and these deserve a moment's consideration. Suppose that British of both sexes had been interned at Ruhleben, with families, bachelors, and single women in different sections, but allowed to mingle during the day. How would the camp have developed? Certainly not as the deeply united body it actually became, but more probably as three separate communities, interacting but never blending, and each possessing its distinctive norms and atmosphere. Even in the opening days the sharing of emotion that gave birth to solidarity would have been impossible; with the women probably clinging to accepted conventions, and the married men playing their roles as husbands and fathers, no tides of common feeling and spontaneous behaviour could have swept through the camp.

And the rough and ready comradeship of Ruhleben would also have been impaired; it was characteristically a male comradeship, like that in the services, and could not have been extended to women. For sexual attraction with its possessiveness and jealousy, is inimical to purely social relationships; even the potentiality of it raises subtle barriers between man and man. As Freud wrote: "Sexual need does not unite men, it separates them."[6] Molony gives an interesting sidelight on this. After his escape from Ruhleben in 1916 he was sent to the "punishment camp" at Havelberg; it contained three hundred Russian women – segregated, of course, but occassionally accessible with a sentry's connivance. Mo-

[6] *Totem and Taboo*, tr. A.A.Brill (New York: New Republic, Inc., 1931), p. 250.

lony sensed a different atmosphere as soon as he arrived there:

The interest of our future co-prisoners in our plight soon wore off. In a gathering of men alone, many questions would have been asked. Some attempts at comradeship would have been made . . . . It was Bicycle Billy who enlightened us. He explained that there were women, that there were some 'nice little bits' among them, and that later he might require my assistance for sending them messages. (P. 174)

Thus the lack of women in Ruhleben, which some men felt acutely, was at least partly compensated by the warm relationships among the men.

Lacking its original solidarity, and with its general comradeship weakened, a "mixed" Ruhleben would have been very different – so different that there is no point in speculating on its later development. It would certainly have been a more "normal" community, and perhaps a more healthy one to live in, but there would have been no such creative outburst as occurred in 1915. The drive and enthusiasm that built the new city were not specifically sexual, though sexual deprivation no doubt contributed to their strength. But they were generated within a consciously homogenous body, in interactions unhampered by any differences as basic as those of sex, and untouched by its disturbing and divisive influences. The men were thus able to give themselves unitedly to constructive social pursuits.[7]

The most striking of Ruhleben's other abnormalities were economic. The camp was of course a parasitic community, producing nothing itself, but living on the surplus production of the German and British economies. In this it resembled a fashionable resort town, but the resemblance went no further, for it was also a singularly advanced "welfare state," whose inhabitants enjoyed almost complete economic security, whether or not they chose to work. And with security went a large measure of economic equality; nothing that an individual might do could have more than trifling effects on his standard of living.

[7]The creation of Ruhleben's social structure by men alone was of course typical rather than otherwise, for the popular belief that "society is built on the family" needs qualification. The family is actually in the paradoxical position of making wider forms of association possible by the social training of the young, and then contributing no further to them – if, indeed, it does not stand in their way by its demands on the interest and time of the male. These ideas were first developed by the German ethnologist, Heinrich Schurtz, who traced all non-familial associations back to the men's societies found in many primitive tribes, pointing out that most political, religious, legal, and educational institutions even in our own day still reflect their purely male origins (***Altersklassen und Männerbunde***; Berlin: Georg Reimer, 1902). Freud also saw the source of "social organization, moral restrictions and religion" in the revolt of a band of brothers" against their father (***Totem and Taboo***, pp. 247-8). Whether or not these views are valid, it seems obvious that societies do not represent the mere overflow or extension of familial relationships, but arise from associations uninfluenced by sex. Thus the speed with which Ruhleben was build may have been due, not only to the men's familiarity with social organization, but also to their relative freedom from conflicting family ties.

These utopian conditions were clearly reflected in the fact that Ruhleben's largest institutions were devoted, not to economic ends, but to games and cultural pursuits. They also had marked effects on the mental outlook of the prisoners, and explain in part the nostalgia with which some of them look back on their internment. For concern with earning a living was banished from its central position in consciousness, and replaced by interest in activities that were broadly recreational – pursued, that is, for their own sakes rather than as means to an end. Such pursuits became for many prisoners the real business of life, as important as work in office or on shipboard, and considerably more enjoyable.

There is no question that such a psychological shift took place; it is shown by the intense seriousness of camp activities, and by the fact that Ruhleben's most prominent citizens were scholars, actors, musicians, and sportsmen. And the dethronement of economic interests was also illustrated in ex-prisoners' answers to the question, "What one thing did most to make life there bearable or enjoyable?" Of 119 replies classified, 59 referred to such social values as friendship and comradeship, and 56 to camp activities – education, sport, theatre, and music, in that order. No one mentioned the canteen or other community services, and only four men referred to that indispensable economic item, parcels. One of them wrote argumentatively, "Parcels from home – obviously the only *truthful* answer to this question," and the rest, on consideration, might have had to agree; for if they had been actually starving, there would have been little sport or study. As things stood, however, the other answers were equally truthful; parcels sustained life, certainly, but it was having something to do, and a warm social context in which to do it, that made life worth living.

There is no need to labour the point; every holiday season shows how gladly men throw off their economic harness and give themselves to other pursuits. The inordinate length of the Ruhleben "holiday," however, makes the developments there relevant to some pressing social problems. There is first the paradoxical picture of men devoting four years of steady work to such organizations as the school, the orchestra, and the parcel post, without any economic rewards whatever. Earlier chapters suggested some of the incentives that replaced them: the men had a sense of belonging to a congenial group and enjoying full status within it; they were free to choose their work and determine, in consultation with others, how it should be done; and the work itself, though not always interesting, seemed to them of definite value to the community with which they were identified. The power of such incentives was long ago recognized by students of industrial morale; what Ruhleben does is to show it in high relief.

The economic peculiarities of the camp, however, have other and more controversial implications. Ruhleben was not only a complete welfare state; it was also a foretaste of the conditions to which industrial societies are rapidly moving, in which the time required for economic production and distribution will be so reduced that new employment must be found for the leisure time of millions. The gloomy views expressed in this connection are familiar: men will not work except when driven by fear of want; hence economic security will destroy any urge to accomplishment, and their increased leisure will be spent in watching television and similar occupations. On these shallow generalizations Ruhleben throws a considerable measure of doubt. It suggests rather that economic security and leisure can, under favourable circumstances, release new interests and aspirations, for which men will strive as hard as they do for subsistence, and with much greater satisfaction. "Suggests" is the most that can be said, for the Ruhleben informants were not representative of the population, and a large, relatively idle class existed after the first year or two. Even so, the camp picture is encouraging, for the only real difference between the idle and the active men – apart from age, infirmity, and similar handicaps – was one that a truly imaginative education could obliterate in a generation.

How to provide such an education for more than a tiny minority is of course the problem. We know little about how it is obtained except that it is almost certainly "caught" rather than taught – which raises the old question, "Where would we find teachers of such a calibre?" An even greater obstacle, however, lies in the character of current Western civilization. Ruhleben's "state socialism" left almost no place for the profit motive – a deprivation that was, incidentally, painless. Hence the motives of its eager band of students, teachers, performers, and organizers were precisely those that an enlightened education would foster: pleasure in the task itself, the satisfaction of accomplishment, stimulation from co-workers, concern for the wider community. We live, however, not in Ruhleben but in a society so dedicated to making and spending money that more social motives have little opportunity to develop. Those who control commercialized sport and entertainment do not ask the individual what he would like to do in his free time; they tell him. And the voice of the advertiser is so all-pervasive that the very existence of any values other than economic might well be questioned. The prospect of a society more in keeping with the full range of man's potentialities seems remote, but the struggle for it will go on, and it is not a hopeless struggle. For if Ruhleben shows anything at all, it is that work and achievement for their own sakes are as natural to the human being as eating or breathing. The desire to learn, strive, build, and create, in free association with others, does not have to be painfully inculcated; except when it has been stifled in childhood by economic need or mechanical education, it is already there, and will appear whenever it is given a chance.[8]

[8]Behaviourist psychology, with its original emphasis on "primary," physiological drives, tended to support the view that all human activity must be traced to hunger or sex. Since the middle of this century, however, many studies, both of animal behaviour and of brain function, have confirmed the importance of intellectual and constructive motives. Even monkeys will learn and work for no other reward than the satisfactions of seeing into the world about them or of solving a mechanical puzzle. See, for example, H. F. Harlow, in ***Learning Theory. Personality Theory, and Clinical Research; The Kentucky Symposium*** (New York; John Wiley and Sons, Inc., 1954) pp. 66-79.

53 / Leadership in a Student Mob

Frederick Elkin, Gerald Halpern, and Anthony Cooper
McGill University

In virtually every social group formed, certain persons emerge as leaders who initiate and direct action. It is often assumed that a leader has certain characteristics which others do not possess to as great a degree. The following is an example of the many studies that have been carried out to define the traits associated with leadership.

The experiment reported here concerns mob leadership in an organized group. Cantril (1941) distinguished the crude, low-status leader who directs the proletariat lynching from the respectable high-status leader who directs the bourbon lynching. Cantril also affirms that mob participants are defending values which they feel are under attack (p. 79), which suggests the hypothesis [1] that the leaders experience these values most strongly. Meier, Mennenga, and Stoltz (1941), in an experimental study in which students were given a running account of the capture of an alleged kidnapper, report that the potential mob participants tended to be extraverted, dominant, and less self-sufficient.

The subjects of this study were twenty fraternity pledges who met one evening a week for twenty-two weeks to learn the customs and ideology of the fraternity. In the thirteenth session, when the pledgemaster was out of the room, a mob situation was created. A fraternity brother burst into the room shouting that a rival fraternity had just stolen the fraternity's trophies. The story was embellished a few minutes later by another brother. The pledges lost interest in the business of the meeting and with considerable emotion discussed what to do. The pledge president could not maintain control and soon the entire pledge class dashed out to recapture the trophies.

The fraternity brothers who reported the theft and a participant observer, posing as a brother from an out-of-town chapter, noted who expressed the strongest feelings, advocated most direct and immediate action, and ran from the room first. They agreed that five pledges were most active and emotionally involved. By the nature of the experiment, it was impossible to rank the five according to their influence.

The list was compared with observations by the pledgemaster and a brother after a college football game in which the subjects, who attended as a group, stormed the field to tear down the goal posts. The same five, with one addition who was not present at the experiment, led this episode. In this report, all six are considered leaders.

Four hypotheses were tested.

Hypothesis 1. Mob leadership in an organized group is stable. As noted, except for an absentee in the experiment, the leaders were the same in both actions.

Hypothesis 2. Leaders in mob actions are not most popular under ordinary circumstances. The subjects, at the seventh session, were asked to choose the fellow pledges with whom they would most like to double-date, attend a football game, and write a school essay, and whom they would most like to introduce to their mothers.[2] Sociometric rankings were compiled on the basis of first choices. The first two items had a rank-order correlation of .85 and were grouped together as a measure of the social-relations choice. Items 3 and 4 also had a rank order correlation of .85 and were grouped together as a measure of the adult-value choice. The two sets of items were not correlated.

The mob leaders, as determined by the social-relations choices, may be divided into two groups of three: (1) A, B, and C, who were the 1st, 2nd, and 4th choices; and (2) X, Y, and Z who were 16th, 17th, and 18th. As adult-value choices, their rankings ranged from 12th to 20th, suggesting a low status in activities oriented towards the adult world.

Speculatively reconstructing the mob action, we distinguish two types of leaders. One, represented by A, B, and C, were "true" leaders, liked and enjoyed as companions by their fellow pledges. The other, X, Y, and Z were "pseudo" leaders who were a step ahead of the larger group and helped build a collective spirit, but who were not especially liked and

[1]Other hypotheses could also be derived from Cantril's statement, e.g., mob leaders, compared to followers (a) have a lower threshold for perceiving a group threat, or (b) are predisposed to react more quickly, aggressively, emotionally, or energetically.

Reprinted, by permission, from *Canadian Journal of Psychology*, 1962, *16*, 199-201.

[2]It is possible that the sociometric structure at the time of the mob action (13th week) was different from the structure when the measurements were made (7th week). However, using Newcomb's (1961) work as a guide, we have no reason to expect much change after six further weeks of contact.

would probably not have been followed in their own right. Their other activities and the comments of the pledgemaster support this distinction. Pledges A, B, and C were "very popular"; pledges, X, Y, and Z were "characters."

Hypothesis 3. Leaders of mobs have stronger feelings of loyalty to the reference group under attack than do followers. The subjects were given a questionnaire of 21 items, 14 concerning attitudes to fraternity values,and 7 presenting hypothetic situations putting fraternity *versus* competing sentiments. Each item was scored on a 5-point scale from strongly agree to strongly disagree.

Examples are: (1) Frater X does not want Frater Y to take out a girl he has been dating. Frater Y likes the girl and asks her anyway. How do you feel about his decision?; (2) A fraternity man in business should go out of his way to help a graduating Frater. No significant differences were found either between the "true" and "pseudo" leaders or the leaders and followers.

Hypothesis 4. Leaders of mobs are more extraverted and dominant and less self-reliant than followers. The subjects completed a Gordon Personal Profile (1953) which measures ascendancy, responsibility, emotional stability, and sociability and has been validated among college students. The results support Meier, *et al.* The mob leaders scored significantly higher than the followers on ascendancy and sociability, which might be interpreted to correspond to dominance and extraversion, and lower on emotional stability (Table I).

Table I – Gordon personal profile scores †

	N	Ascendancy		Responsibility		Emotional stability		Sociability	
		X	*SD*	X	*SD*	X	*SD*	X	*SD*
Leaders	6	8.5(75)	4.73**	4.5(53)	5.41	1(24)	3.56**	11(88)	3.83*
Followers	14	3.76(44)	3.62	8.1(76)	5.2	7.4(54)	6.52	5.2(54)	3.2

† Percentile equivalents are in parentheses. *Significantly different at 1% level. **Significantly different at 5% level.

References

CANTRIL, H. *The psychology of social movements.* New York: J. Wiley, 1941.

GORDON, L. V. *Gordon Personal Profile Manual.* Yonkers-on-Hudson, New York: World Book Co., 1953.

MEIER, N. C., MENNENGA, G. H., and STOLTZ, H. J. An experimental approach to the study of mob behaviour. *J. abnorm. soc. Psychol.*, 1941, *36*, 506-24.

NEWCOMB, T. M. *The acquaintance process.* New York: Holt, Rinehart and Winston, 1961.

54 / The Effect of Increased Salience of a Membership Group on Pain Tolerance

Wallace E. Lambert, Eva Libman, and Ernest G. Poser
McGill University

This experiment investigated the ability of Jewish and Christian subjects to tolerate pain. The results indicated that members of both groups increased their pain tolerance when they were informed that their religious group was inferior in this respect.

Membership in a group requires a certain amount of behavioural conformity to the rules, either explicit or implicit, which have been established by all members of that group. The concept of "group" itself signifies that there is some distinctive pattern of behaviours which characterizes members of a particular group and differentiates them from others. The fact that people are always members of more than one group indicates that their patterns of behaviour should vary as they take on particular roles in one group and temporarily shed the roles of another. While this generalization is verified in the every day experiences of most human beings, few experimental demonstrations are available of behavioural variations attributable to changes in one's roles or his feelings of identification with certain groups. Newcomb (1950, p. 275 ff.) has discussed the significance of this phenomenon and Charters and Newcomb (1958) have demonstrated how social attitudes vary when individuals' awareness of being members of religious groups is experimentally modified. In their research plan, some *S*s were made aware that they were expressing attitudes as Catholics (or Jews, or Protestants, depending on their actual religious affiliation) while other *S*s gave their attitudes as they assumed the role of university students. Those Catholic *S*s whose religious affiliation was made salient manifested a pattern of attitudes much more similar to the orthodox Catholic position than did control *S*s for whom religious affiliation was not made salient. The results for Jews and Protestants were less clear, suggesting that the two roles required of Catholic students (as Catholics and as students) are comparatively more dissimilar, at least in terms of the attitudes given consideration in the study.

The purpose of the present studies was to extend our understanding of the effect of group membership by paying attention to aspects of behaviour other than social attitudes. We attempted to vary experimentally the salience of religious-group membership and to observe changes in *S*s' responses to pain. Responses to pain have been related to religious affiliation by Chapman (1944) and Zborowski (1952). Chapman showed that samples of Jewish *S*s exhibited both lower pain perception and pain-tolerance thresholds than non-Jewish *S*s with North European ethnic backgrounds. Zborowski found that Jewish Americans tended to exaggerate their reactions and sensitivity to pain more than Americans of other religious or ethnic backgrounds. Social psychologists have become interested in the matter of pain tolerance since Moede (see Murphy and Murphy, 1931) demonstrated that thresholds for intolerable pain were increased when onlookers were present or when competition existed between *S*s.

In the two studies presented here, *S*s' pain-tolerance thresholds were measured, first when they were asked to assume the role of university students volunteering to assist in a scientific investigation, and then, after certain information was given them, as potential contributors to their own religious group's comparative standing in ability to tolerate pain. Between the two measurements for pain tolerance, *S*s were told that members of their religious groups had been found, on the average, to have a lower (in Experiment II, either lower or higher) pain-tolerance threshold when compared to other religious groups and that the objective of the experiment was to test the reliability of the evidence. We predicted that this procedure would prompt the experimental *S*s to compete against the hypothetical "other groups," as though we were manipulating an ethnocentric prestige motive, somewhat analogous to rivalry in Moede's study.

Experiment I

Method

The sample consisted of 40 Jewish and 40 Protestant *S*s, all women students ranging in age from 18 to 23 years. *S*s were selected from the McGill University library and other parts of the campus in the following manner: each individual was approach by *E* (E.L.) and asked if she would be willing to partici-

Reprinted, by permission of the senior author and the Duke University Press, from *J. of Personality*, 1960, *28*, 350-357.

pate in a short research project. Attention was paid to physical characteristics in order to estimate the religion of each *S*. At the time of testing, religious affiliation was verified and only the data from Jewish and Protestant *S*s are considered here. *S*s were alternately placed in experimental and control groups.

The instrument used for testing pain tolerance consisted of a clinical sphygmomanometer with sharp, hard rubber projections sewn into the pressure cuff. The cuff was adjusted with the hard rubber projections resting against the medial surface of the *S*'s upper arm, and the pressure was gradually increased at the rate of approximately 10 mm. Hg per sec. A pressure reading was taken at the moment when *S* first felt pain (this measure is not considered here) and then when the *S* pronounced the pain intolerable, the index of pain-tolerance level, measured as mm. of Hg on a standard sphygmomanometer gauge. Pressure was then released. This method has high reliability and correlates well with the usual methods for producing superficial pain (see Clark and Bindra, 1956). After the pain-tolerance level had been determined each *S* was told that she would be given a retest approximately five minutes later "for purposes of establishing reliability." During this period of time, the experimental *S*s were told in a casual manner (usually they asked about the purpose of the study at this time) that there was experimental evidence that Jews (Protestants) have a lower pain-tolerance level (take less pain) that non-Jews (other groups), and that the object of the experiment was to test the reliability of the evidence. Control *S*s simply waited for five minutes between their first and second measures of pain tolerance.

Results and Discussion

From Table I, it is clear that Jewish experimental *S*s significantly increased their pain-tolerance scores on retest while Jewish control *S*s showed an insignificant decrease. No difference was found between Protestant experimental and control *S*s: both groups showed hardly any change in pain-tolerance scores on retest. We conclude that the Jewish *S*s were clearly influenced by the interpolated statement which alluded to Jewish "inferiority" with regard to withstanding pain. The fact that an equivalent provoking statement had no apparent effect on Protestants can be interpreted as meaning that Protestantism does not function as a reference group in the same sense that Judaism does. It may well be, however, that the reference to own-group inferiority in comparison to non-Jews was more provocative for Jews in the sense that they very likely compared themselves with Christians and thought about the issue of Jewish-Christian prejudice. Protestants, on the other hand, were directed to compare their group's performance with other groups and they need not have interpreted this in terms of a Protestant-Jewish issue nor made any other comparison which would be emotionally involving. Following this reasoning, we predicted that an explicit comparison of Jews and Christians would be more equally provocative for members of both religious groups and that Christians receiving this information would display an increased pain-tolerance threshold.

Table I – Pain-tolerance scores for Jewish and Protestant Ss, experiment I

	Jewish				Protestant			
	Experimental (N=20)		Control (N=20)		Experimental (N=20)		Control (N=20)	
	Test 1	Test 2	Test 1	Test 2	Test 1	Test 2	Test 1	Test 2
Mean[a]	86	103	83	77	115	114	92	90
Mean Differences	+17		−6		−1		−2	
t		2.78*	n.s.		n.s.		n.s.	

[a] Units are in mm. Hg: the higher the score the greater the pain tolerance.
*p < .01, 2-tailed test for correlated data.

The change in the pain-tolerance threshold for the Jewish *S*s indicates that they were motivated to reduce the discrepancy between their group's purported pain sensitivity and that of non-Jews, but it is not clear whether they were interested in (a) surpassing non-Jews (thereby making their own group distinctive) or (b) merely closing the gap (thereby making their own group indistinguishable from non-Jews). If Jewish *S*s were told that their religious group reportedly could tolerate more pain than Christians, we could then determine the nature of their motivation: if motivated to surpass the Christians, their pain-tolerance thresholds should still increase, but if they reduced their pain-tolerance thresholds we could conclude that they were oriented to close the gap. The second experiment was carried out to investigate these extensions of the findings reported above.

Experiment II

Method

The *S*s were 160 women under-graduate students of McGill University; 80 were Jewish and 80 were Protestant. The same general procedure used in Experiment I was repeated with several modifications. A different sphygmomanometer and different (but supposedly identical) hard rubber projections were used in the second study. Two *E*s, one recognizably Jewish and the other recognizably not Jewish, were both present at each testing, either one applying the pressure cuff and giving the interpolated information, the other recording the results which were read out to her in code.[1]

[1] As will be seen by comparing Tables I and II, the means of the pain tolerance measures are markedly higher in the second study. We are unable to account fully for these differences. A different apparatus and different *E*s were used; furthermore, in the second study measurements were always taken with one *E* as an onlooker while the other conducted the study. Whatever the reason(s), the measures were higher in the second study, and in three or four cases *S*s were dropped because their pain perception thresholds were so high that the *E*s felt that there would be too little opportunity for change to be recorded after the experimental treatment.

Table II – Pain-tolerance scores for Jewish and Protestant Ss, experiment II

	Jewish						*Christian*					
Condition	*Take Less*		*Take More*		*Control*		*Take Less*		*Take More*		*Control*	
Test	*1*	*2*	*1*	*2*	*1*	*2*	*1*	*2*	*1*	*2*	*1*	*2*
Mean [a]	160	179	163	172	139	133	187	202	158	180	156	150
Mean Difference	+19		+9		−6		+15		+22		−6	
N	30		30		20		30		30		20	
t	2.74 [b]		1.21		.68		2.34		2.76		.88	
p	.02		n.s.		n.s.		.03		.01		n.s.	

[a] Units are in mm; Hg: the higher the score the greater the pain tolerance.
[b] Two-tailed tests of significance for correlated data are used throughout.

Between the first and second measures of pain tolerance, 30 Jewish *S*s were told that it had been reported in the literature that Jews as a group take less pain than Christians, and 30 were told that Jews take more pain than Christians. Two groups of 30 Christian *S*s were given the same information – for one group that Christians take less pain than Jews and for the other that Christians take more pain that Jews. Two control groups (one Jewish and one Christian) of 20 *S*s each were given no information between their two tests.

Results and Discussion

The results are presented in Table II. There is a clear replication of the findings of the first experiment in that the Jewish *S*s reliably increased their tolerance threshold upon being informed that Jews as a group take less pain than Christians. The Jewish control *S*s, who were given no interpolated information, show an insignificant decrease in their threshold, a finding that supports the conclusion that the change in threshold for the Jewish experimental *S*s is not due to taking the test twice nor to the unreliability of the measure. When Jewish *S*s are informed that Jews typically take more pain than Christians they tend to "hold the line" rather than reducing their thresholds ("closing the gap") or increasing their thresholds ("extending the differences"). Although this group does increase its mean tolerance threshold (from 163 to 172 units) this is not a reliable change. When the difference scores (subtracting the first from the second tolerance scores) for this group are compared with the difference scores for the Jewish control *S*s, again there is no reliable increase for that group, $t = 1.29$ with 48 *df*.

The Christian *S*s also are clearly affected by the interpolated information. There are significant increases in tolerance thresholds when they are informed that Christians typically take less pain or take more pain than Jews. We have evidence here that Christianity (which more clearly calls to mind the Christian – Jewish comparison) is a more effective reference group than Protestantism as used in the first experiment. We also have evidence that the Christian *S*s are motivated to extend the difference between Christians and Jews on pain tolerance in that they increase their threshold when informed that their religious group typically takes more pain than Jews.

In summary, the over-all findings suggest that *S*s do change their patterns of behaviour in meaningful ways when they alternately refer themselves to different membership groups, in this case first as university students contributing to a scientific investigation and then as members of a particular religious group. Samples of Jewish *S*s appear to be interested in both reducing any differences between their religious group and Christians with respect to ability to withstand pain as well as maintaining any superiority they may have in this regard (although the latter point is not clear from our data). Christian *S*s (but not "Protestants") appear ready to eliminate any inferiority their group may have in regard to pain tolerance when compared to Jews and to extend the difference between groups when they are led to believe their group is superior in withstanding pain.

Others working with pain sensitivity have reported differences attributable to religious affiliation (for example Chapman, 1944). We were able to compare our Jewish and Christian *S*s on their pain-tolerance thresholds (first test) since no experimental treatment was given to any *S* until after the first measure of pain tolerance. For the *S*s in Experiment I, the mean threshold for Jews was not reliably different from that of the Protestants, $t = 1.63$, $df = 78$, corrected for heterogeneous variances. For *S*s in Experiment II, the Jewish mean was again not reliably different from that of Protestants, $t = 1.08$, $df = 158$. We therefore offer no evidence for differences in pain sensitivity attributable to religious affiliation for Jewish and Protestant women. In both studies, however, we do find significantly less variance of pain-tolerance scores for Jewish in contrast to Christians *S*s, in Experiment I, $F = 3.15$ ($p = .01$) and Experiment II, $F = 1.56$ ($p < .05$). One explanation for this reliable finding comes from Zborowski's (1952) interpretation of the social and cultural significance of pain. He finds that Jewish patients typically search for the symptomatic meaning of pain and communicate their concern about their health and their family's welfare to family members and associates. Zborowski feels that this reaction pattern is acquired "by the individual members of the society from the earliest childhood along with other cultural attitudes and values which are learned from parents . . ." (p. 28). He argues that each culture develops an ideal pattern of attitudes and reactions to pain which are passed on during socialization. Our findings of more homogeneous reactions to pain among Jews would suggest that something like an ideal pattern of reactions to pain is either more standardized and/or more effectively communicated among Jews than Christians.

Summary

Jewish and Protestant female *S*s were tested for their tolerance of pain first when they were asked as students to participate in a scientific study and then, after their religious membership group was made salient to them by having them believe that scientific evidence indicated that their religious group characteristically is less able to withstand pain than others. The Jewish, but not the Protestant, *S*s showed a reliable increase in their mean pain-tolerance threshold after this information was given them.

In a second experiment subgroups of Jewish and Protestant *S*s were told either that their religious group typically takes less or more pain than other religious groups but in this case an explicit comparison was made between Jews and Chrstians. Both Jewish and "Christian" *S*s increased their pain tolerance when told their groups were typically inferior in regard to this variable. The Christain *S*s, similarly treated, showed no reliable change in their tolerance levels. The findings are conceptualized in terms of a theory of membership groups.

No evidence was found for the differences in normal pain-tolerance thresholds attributable to religious differences, although Jewish *S*s showed reliably less variability of pain-tolerance scores than did Protestant *S*s in both studies.

References

CHAPMAN, W. P. Measurements of pain sensitivity in normal control subjects and in psychoneurotic patients. *Psychosom. med.*, 1944, *6*, 252-257.

CHARTERS, W. W., and NEWCOMB, T. M. Some attitudinal effects of experimentally increased salience of a membership group. In MACCOBY, ELEANOR E., NEWCOMB, T. M., and HARTLEY, E. L. (eds.), *Readings in social psychology*. New York: Holt, Rinehart and Winston, 1958.

CLARK, J. W., and BINDRA, D. Individual differences in pain thresholds. *Canad. J. Psychol.*, 1956, *10*, 69-76.

NEWCOMB, T. M. *Social psychology*. New York: Holt, Rinehart and Winston, 1960.

MURPHY, G., and MURPHY, L. B. *Experimental social psychology*. New York: Harper & Row, 1931.

ZBOROWSKI, M. Cultural components in response to pain. *J. soc. Issues*, 1952, *8*, 16-30.

55 / Participation and Opinion-Change as a Function of the Sex of the Members of Two-Person Groups[1]

D.W. Carment *McMaster University*

In Canada, as in most societies, men and women are expected to assume different roles and behave in different ways. Generally speaking, men are expected to be dominating and aggressive while women are expected to be submissive. In this experiment, Professor Carment found that "while females may be submissive in direct verbal interaction with the male, this submissiveness may not be reflected in ultimate opinion-change."

It is generally accepted that North American culture assigns to the female role behaviours such as conformity to social norms, dependence, and submissiveness, especially in interaction with the male (Krech, Crutchfield, and Ballachey, 1962). It is not surprising, therefore, to find that in a variety of experimental situations females have shown greater susceptibility to influence than males (see Blake and Mouton, 1961; Krech, Crutchfield, and Ballachey, 1962; Secord and Backman, 1964). There have been a few exceptions to this generalization but, in most of these instances, the interaction of other variables such as the youth of the subjects (Abelson and Lesser, 1959), the sex-linked nature of the material being used (Coleman, Blake, and Mouton, 1958), or pre-influence information (Carment, Schwartz, and Miles, 1964) could account for the discrepancies reported.

However, degree of resistance to pressures toward conformity is only one aspect of the general syndrome of ascendance-submission in social relations. A number of studies of persuasive social interaction have revealed the covariation of likelihood of opinion-change and variables such as initiation of conversation, amount spoken, proportion of speech which supports or opposes the individual's point of view, as well as the tendency to stray from the topic (Carment, 1961; Carment, Schwartz, and Miles, 1963, 1964; Carment, Miles, and Cervin, 1965). Surprisingly, little is known about the effects of the sex of the participants in a persuasive dialogue on these additional reflections of social dominance. With this in mind the experiment reported here varied the sex of paired subjects who had been asked to debate a topic on which it was known they disagreed, with the purpose of arriving at a joint statement of agreement, compromise, or disagreement. Three kinds of pairs were observed: males paired with males, females paired with females, and females paired with males. The effects of these different combinations on amount of opinion-change, measures of participation, and content of discussion, as well as mutual social attraction or liking were examined.

Method

Subjects

Students in a summer session introductory psychology course had indicated in class, using 7 point Likert-type scales, the strength and nature of their opinions on a number of discussion topics. These topics were chosen to be of interest and included items such as "too much emphasis is being placed on university education today." Effort was made not to include items of direct political or religious significance.

It should be mentioned that the members of this population differed in many respects from the regular session undergraduates usually employed as subjects. These differences are best summed up by noting that the majority of the individuals in the population were school teachers with an average age of 26 years, whereas the average age of university freshmen is 19 years. Subjects were drawn from this population and pairs formed in which the participants were matched for age, and strength of opinion (strongly agree or disagree) on a topic on which their opinions were opposed. There were 10 male-male pairs, 10 female-female pairs, and 10 male-female pairs.

Procedure

On arrival at the laboratory the subjects were introduced (friends were not used) and then taken to the experimental room where they were seated at a table facing each other. Throat microphones were fitted and they were told to await further instructions without conversing. These instructions were given over the intercommunication system from the adjoining observation room as follows:

"In this experiment we are interested in observing people discussing various topics. You have indicated

[1]This research was supported by Grant Number APA-63 from the National Research Council of Canada.
Thanks are due to Arlene Vadum, F. van Fleet, D. Amoroso, A. Shulman and W. Norrison for assistance in the collection of data.

Reprinted, by permission, from *Acta Psychologica*, 1968, *28*, 84-91.

your opinions regarding a number of issues on this questionnaire you answered in class. I would like you to discuss one of these issues with the purpose of arriving at a common statement of your opinions, that is, until you reach some conclusion such as a common statement on agreement, compromise, or disagreement. You can talk as long as you want to. When you have reached a conclusion, ring the bell which is on the table. This will tell us that you have finished.

The topic I want you to discuss is on page –, number –.

In a few moments I'll knock on the window. This will be the signal for you to start talking. But it is very important that you DO NOT TALK until I knock. Do not say a word until then.

ANY QUESTIONS? Fine.

I will knock in a moment. Remember DON'T TALK."

Dependent Measures

1) Measures of Participation:

a) Initiation of conversation – which subject spoke first.

b) Amount spoken – the total lengths of each subject's utterances were recorded automatically on running-time meters by means of the throat microphones and a sound-sensitive relay system.

2) Measures of Content:

Observers, one for each subject, viewed the discussion via a one-way window and recorded on running-time meters the amounts of each subject's utterances which were:

a) positive – in favour of the subject's original opinion;

b) negative – opposed to the subject's original opinion;

c) neutral – unrelated to the topic.

3) Opinion-change:

Change of opinion was obtained in two ways:

a) Public – the subjects, while together, recorded their final opinions on the scale again.

b) Private – each of the subjects then recorded his opinion privately at a separate table.

Change was indicated by the number of steps the subject moved from his original opinion on the scale.

A subject who did not change his opinion received a score of 0, and a subject who switched to agree completely with his opponent received a score of 6, with decreasing scores for lesser degrees of change.

4) Interpersonal attraction:

The subjects, also privately, were given two additional scales designed to indicate the attraction each had for the other member of the pair:

a) Specific – whether, if they were requested to participate in a similar experiment again, they would prefer to have the same or a different opponent.

b) General – a seven-step social distance scale first used by Back (1951). The items range from "I would like to see (him, her) around campus sometime" to "I would discuss important personal problems with (him, her)."

Results

Where the data were subjected to an analysis of variance the main factors were a) sex of subject and b) sex of opponent. Since there were an unequal number of subjects in the cells an unweighted means solution was used (Winer, 1962).

1) Participation:

a) Initiation of conversation: the only meaningful comparison here is between the subjects in the male-female pairs. In 7 of these 10 pairs the male member spoke first. This is not a sufficient difference to reach an acceptable level of significance.

b) Total amount spoken: the over-all analysis of variance applied to these data revealed no significant effects. When only the male-female group is considered it is found that in 9 of the 10 pairs the male member spoke the most ($p = .01$, binomial).

2) Content:

a) Positive speech: again the analysis of variance showed no significant effects. However, in all 10 of the male-female pairs the male participant emitted the most positive statements ($p = .001$, binomial).

b) Negative speech: the analysis of variance indicated that, irrespective of the subject's own sex, a greater proportion of negative statements were emitted if the subject's opponent was male ($F = 4.71$, $p < .05$, 1 and 56 df). Also, in 8 of the 10 male-female pairs the female subject emitted the most negative statements ($p = .04$, binomial).

c) Neutral speech: the analysis of variance revealed a significant sex of subject by sex of opponent interaction ($F = 13.52$, $p < .01$, 1 and 56 df). Examination of the group means indicates that this interaction is attributable to males paired with females deviating most from the topic and the members of same-sex pairs, male or female, deviating least from the topic.

In addition, in 8 of the 10 male-female pairs, the male member emitted the most neutral statements ($p = .04$, binomial).

3) Opinion-change:

Since there was a correlation of + .94 between the public and private ratings of opinion, only the public data were analyzed.

The over-all analysis of variance of the amount each subject modified his opinion indicated no significant effects. On the other hand, a count of the number of pairs in which there was no change or compromise, and in which one subject changed more than the other, resulted in the distribution seen in Table I.

It can be seen that there are no differences between the cell frequencies of the male-male and female-female pairs which were combined. The χ^2 calculated from the resulting 2 x 2 table is 6.69 ($p < .01$, 1 df).

It also should be noted that the two instances of

Table I – Frequency of opinion change

	Male-Female	Male-male	Female-female	Total
No change and compromise	8	3	3	14
Change	2	7	7	16
Total	10	10	10	30

unequal change in the male-female pairs were both females.

4) Interpersonal attraction:

a) Specific: the frequencies with which subjects indicated whether they would prefer to have the same or a different opponent, if requested to participate again, are given in the Table II.

Table II – Frequency of rejection of opponent

	Males (paired with females)	Females (paired with males)	Males (paired with males)	Females (paired with females)	Total
Same Opponent	2	8	16	11	37
Another Opponent	8	2	4	9	23
Total	10	10	20	20	60

The χ^2 based on the total table is 11.99 ($p < .01$, 3 df). It can be seen that the males who were paired with females show the most rejection, while the opposite is the case for the females who were paired with these males, as well as for the males paired with males. Females paired with females also tend to be more rejecting.

b) General: the number of items checked was used as the subject's score on the social distance scale. The fewer the number of checks the greater the social distance indicated. The mean number of checks for the four categories of subjects are given in Table III.

Table III – Mean number of checks on social distance scale

	Males (paired with females)	Females (paired with males)	Males (paired with males)	Females (paired with females)
Mean number of checks	1.9	3.0	3.9	3.4

These data were subjected to an analysis of variance which resulted in a significant sex of subject by sex of opponent interaction ($F = 7.41$, $p < .01$, 1 and 56 df) based, for the most part, on the low score of males who were paired with females and the high scores of same-sex pairs.

Discussion

In terms of the content and amount of participation of the subjects in the mixed-sex pairs, this study supports the notion of the social submissiveness of women in this society. It was found that females, when interacting with males, spoke less, were less supportive of their own point-of-view, and more supportive of their opponent's point-of-view. There was also a tendency for the female to allow the male to initiate the interaction.

However, this submissiveness was not reflected in the change-of-opinion data. The most likely outcome of a male-female discussion was either compromise or no change, whereas same-sex pairs, whether male or female, showed a greater likelihood of one member of a pair changing opinion more than the other.

It should be emphasized that all the subjects initially felt strongly about the discussion topics. This would tend to anchor the opinions and reduce the likelihood of opinion change occurring. It is not known whether a similar distribution would be obtained if subjects had been selected who felt moderately or mildly about the issues in question.

It is of some interest to note that males paired with females were most likely to stray from the topic. This is in line with the suggestion (Carment, Schwartz and Miles, 1964) that this variable may reflect social discomfort, particularly since the least tendency to digress was found in same-sex pairs. Related to this are the social attraction data which show that as far as the specific experiment is concerned, as well as at the more general social level, males paired with females were most strenuous in their rejection of their female opponents. These opponents, on the other hand, do not seem to have been unsettled by the situation and were quite willing to participate in the experiment with the same individuals again. They were also willing to enter social relationships with the males and on this measure were not different from females paired with females.

To sum up, it appears that while females may be submissive in direct verbal interaction with the male, this submissiveness may not be reflected in ultimate opinion-change and that in the end the male may change opinion as much as the female. There is no evidence that, in terms of the present variables, females interacting with females behave differently than males interacting with males, except that males may be more friendly toward each other at the conclusion of the discussion. Finally, it seems that males are more uneasy in the mixed-sex condition than are the females with whom they are paired and that this is extended beyond the immediate situation to social relationships in general.

Summary

Subjects, in pairs which were either male-female, male-male, or female-female, were asked to debate a topic on which it was known they disagreed, with the purpose of arriving at a common statement on agreement, compromise, or disagreement. The effects of these different sex combinations on measures of participation, content of the debate, and interpersonal attraction were observed. It was found that, when paired with males, females were less supportive of their initial opinion, more supportive of the opposed opinion, and did not speak as much as the male. Less opinion-change occurred in the mixed-sex pairs than in the same-sex pairs. Males paired with females appeared more uneasy and rejected their opponents more than any of the other subjects.

References

ABELSON, R. P., and LESSER, G. S. A developmental theory of persuasibility. In C. HOVLAND and I. JANIS (eds.), *Personality and Persuasibility*. New Haven: Yale University Press,1959, 167-186.

BACK, K. Influence through social communication. *J. abnorm. soc. Psychol.*, 1951, *46*, 9-23.

BLAKE, R., and MOUTON, J. The experimental investigation of interpersonal influence. In. A. BIDERMAN and H. ZIMMER (eds.), *The Manipulation of Human Behaviour*. New York: Wiley, 1961, 216-276.

CARMENT, D. W. Ascendant-submissive behaviour in pairs of human subjects as a function of their emotional responsiveness and opinion strength. *Canad. J. Psychol.*, 1961, *15*, 45-51.

CARMENT, D. W., SCHWARTZ, F. S., and MILES, C. G. Persuasiveness and persuasibility as related to intelligence and emotional responsiveness. *Psychol. Rep.*, 1963, *12*, 767-772.

———. Participation and opinion change as related to cohesiveness and sex of subjects in two-person groups. *Psychol. Rep.*, 1964, *14*, 695-702.

CARMENT, D. W., SCHWARTZ, F. S., and CERVIN, V. B. Persuasiveness and persuasibility as related to intelligence and extraversion. *Brit. J. soc. clin. Psychol.*, 1965, *4*, 1-7.

COLEMAN, J., BLAKE, R., and MOUTON, J. Task difficulty and conformity pressures. *J. abnorm. soc. Psychol.*, 1958, *57*, 120-122.

KRECH, D., CRUTCHFIELD, R. S., and BALLACHEY, E. *Individual in Society*. New York: McGraw-Hill, 1962.

SECORD, P. F., and BACKMAN, C. W. *Social Psychology*. New York: McGraw-Hill, 1964.

WINER, B. J. *Statistical procedures in experiment design*. New York: McGraw-Hill, 1962.

TWELVE BELIEFS, ATTITUDES, AND PREJUDICES

56 / A Social Psychology of Bilingualism

Wallace E. Lambert *McGill University*

Even though both English and French have been the official languages of Canada since Confederation, it is only in recent years that the issue of bilingualism has been discussed in depth. Very often such discussions have focused on ideological, political, and economic issues with the result that psychological and social factors have been relatively neglected. Yet the psychological issues are of utmost importance. For example, does the very fact that English-Canadians and French-Canadians speak different languages produce social discord between the two groups? Does the English-speaking individual have a stereotyped impression of the French-speaking person and vice versa; and, if so, what is the nature of this stereotype and how does it develop? At a more practical level it is also necessary to determine to what extent the individual who becomes bilingual is faced with special social and psychological conflicts. An insight into these kinds of problems has been provided by a series of investigations conducted by Professor Lambert, Canada's foremost social psychologist, and his colleagues. The following report presents some of the major findings of some ten years of research into the problems of bilingualism.

Other contributions . . . have drawn attention to various aspects of bilingualism, each of great importance for behavioural scientists. For instance, we have been introduced to the psychologist's interest in the bilingual switching process with its attendant mental and neurological implications, and his interest in the development of bilingual skill; to the linguist's interest in the bilingual's competence with his two linguistic systems and the way the systems interact; and to the social-anthropologist's concern with the sociocultural settings of bilingualism and the role expectations involved. The purpose of the present paper is to extend and integrate certain of these interests by approaching bilingualism from a social-psychological perspective, one characterized not only by its interest in the reactions of the bilingual as an individual but also by the attention given to the social influences that affect the bilingual's behaviour and to the social repercussions that follow from his behaviour. From this perspective, a process such as language switching takes on a broader significance when its likely social and psychological consequences are contemplated, as, for example, when a language switch brings into play contrasting sets of stereotyped images of people who habitually use each of the languages involved in the switch. Similarly, the development of bilingual skill very likely involves something more than a special set of aptitudes because one would expect that various social attitudes and motives are intimately involved in learning a foreign language. Furthermore, the whole process of becoming bilingual can be expected to involve major conflicts of values and allegiances, and bilinguals could make various types of adjustments to the bicultural demands made on them. It is to these matters that I would like to direct attention.

Reprinted, by permission, from *Journal of Social Issues*, 1967, *22*, 91-109.

Linguistic Style and Intergroup Impressions

What are some of the social psychological consequences of language switching? Certain bilinguals have an amazing capacity to pass smoothly and automatically from one linguistic community to another as they change languages of discourse or as they turn from one conversational group to another at multilingual gatherings. The capacity is something more than Charles Boyer's ability to switch from Franco-American speech to Continental-style French when he turns from the eyes of a woman to those of a waiter who wants to know if the wine is of the expected vintage. In a sense, Boyer seems to be always almost speaking French. Nor is it the tourist guide's ability to use different languages to explain certain events in different languages. In most cases they are not fluent enough to pass and even when their command is good, their recitals seem to be memorized. Here is an example of what I do mean: a friend of mine, the American linguist, John Martin, is so talented in his command of various regional dialects of Spanish, I am told, that he can fool most

Puerto Ricans into taking him for a Puerto Rican and most Columbians into taking him for a native of Bogota. His skill can be disturbing to the natives in these different settings because he is a potential linguistic *spy* in the sense that he can get along too well with the intimacies and subtleties of their dialects.

The social psychologist wants to know how this degree of bilingual skill is developed, what reactions a man like Martin has as he switches languages, and what social effects the switching initiates, not only the suspicion or respect generated by an unexpected switch but also the intricate role adjustments that usually accompany such changes. Research has not yet gone far enough to answer satisfactorily all the questions the social psychologist might ask, but a start has been made, and judging from the general confidence of psycholinguists and sociolinguists, comprehensive answers to such questions can be expected in a short time.

I will draw on work conducted by a rotating group of students and myself at McGill University in Montreal, a fascinating city where two major ethnic-linguistic groups are constantly struggling to maintain their separate identities and where bilinguals as skilled as John Martin are not at all uncommon. Two incidents will provide an appropriate introduction to our work. One involves a bus ride where I was seated behind two English-Canadian ladies and in front of two French-Canadian ladies as the bus moved through an English-Canadian region of the city. My attention was suddenly drawn to the conversation in front wherein one lady said something like: "If I couldn't speak English I certainly wouldn't shout about it," referring to the French conversation going on behind them. Her friend replied: "Oh, well, you can't expect much else from them." Then one of the ladies mentioned that she was bothered when French people laughed among themselves in her presence because she felt they might be making fun of her. This was followed by a nasty interchange of pejorative stereotypes about French Canadians, the whole discussion prompted, it seemed, by what struck me as a humorous conversation of the two attractive, middle-class French-Canadian women seated behind them. The English ladies couldn't understand the French conversation, nor did they look back to see what the people they seemed to know so much about even looked like.

The second incident involved my daughter when she was about 12 years old. She, too, has amazing skill with English and two dialects of French, the Canadian style and the European style. One day while driving her to school, a lycée run by teachers from France, I stopped to pick up one of her friends and they were immediately involved in conversation, *French-Canadian* French style. A block or two farther I slowed down to pick up a second girlfriend when my daughter excitedly told me, in English, to drive on. At school I asked what the trouble was and she explained that there actually was no trouble although there might have been if the second girl, who was from France, and who spoke another dialect of French, had got in the car because then my daughter would have been forced to show a linguistic preference for one girl or the other. Normally she could escape this conflict by interacting with each girl separately, and inadvertently, I had almost put her on the spot. Incidents of this sort prompted us to commence a systematic analysis of the effects of language and dialect changes on impression formation and social interaction.

Dialect Variations Elicit Stereotyped Impressions

Over the past eight years, we have developed a research technique that makes use of language and dialect variations to elicit the stereotyped impressions or biased views which members of one social group hold of representative members of a contrasting group. Briefly, the procedure involves the reactions of listeners (referred to as judges) to the taped recordings of a number of perfectly bilingual speakers reading a two-minute passage at one time in one of their languages (e.g., French) and, later a translation equivalent of the same passage in their second language (e.g., English). Groups of judges are asked to listen to this series of recordings and evaluate the personality characteristics of each speaker as well as possible, using voice cues only. They are reminded of the common tendency to attempt to gauge the personalities of unfamiliar speakers heard over the phone or radio. Thus they are kept unaware that they will actually hear two readings by each of several bilinguals. In our experience no subjects have become aware of this fact. The judges are given practice trials, making them well acquainted with both versions of the message, copies of which are supplied in advance. They usually find the enterprise interesting, especially if they are promised, and receive, some feedback on how well they have done, for example, if the profiles for one or two speakers, based on the ratings of friends who know them well, are presented at the end of the series.

This procedure, referred to as the *matched-guise* technique, appears to reveal judges' more private reactions to the contrasting group than direct attitude questionnaires do (see Lambert, Anisfeld and Yeni-Komshian, 1965), but much more research is needed to adequately assess its power in this regard. The technique is particularly valuable as a measure of *group* biases in evaluative reactions; it has very good reliability in the sense that essentially the same profile of traits for a particular group appear when different samples of judges, drawn from a particular subpopulation, are used. Differences between subpopulations are very marked, however, as will become apparent. On the other hand, the technique apparently has little reliability when measured by test-retest ratings produced by the same group of judges; we believed this type of unreliability is due in large part to the main statistic used, the difference between an individual's rating of a pair of guises on a single trait. Difference scores give notoriously low test-retest reliability coefficients although their use for comparing means is perfectly appropriate (Bereiter, 1963; and Ferguson, 1959, 285*f*).

Several of our studies have been conducted since 1958 in greater Montreal, a setting that has a long history of tensions between English- and French-speaking Canadians. The conflict is currently so sharp that some French-Canadian (*FC*) political leaders in the Province of Quebec talk seriously about separating the Province from the rest of Canada, comprising a majority of English-Canadians (*EC*s). In 1958-59, (Lambert, Hodgson, Gardner and Fillenbaum, 1960) we asked a sizeable group of EC university students to evaluate the personalities of a series of speakers, actually the matched guises of male bilinguals speaking in Canadian style French and English. When their judgements were analyzed it was found that their evaluations were strongly biased against the *FC* and in favour of the matched *EC* guises. They rated the speakers in their *EC* guises as being better looking, taller, more intelligent, more dependable, kinder, more ambitious and as having more character. This evaluational bias was just as apparent among judges who were bilingual as among monolinguals.

We presented the same set of taped voices to a group of *FC* students of equivalent age, social class and educational level. Here we were in for a surprise for they showed the same bias, evaluating the *EC* guises significantly *more* favourably than the *FC* guises on a whole series of traits, indicating, for example, that they viewed the *EC* guises as being more intelligent, dependable, likeable and as having more character! Only on two traits did they rate the *FC* guises more favourably, namely kindness and religiousness, and, considering the whole pattern of ratings, it could be that they interpreted too much religion as a questionable quality. Not only did the *FC* judges generally downgrade representatives of their own ethnic-linguistic group, they also rated the *FC* guises much more negatively that the *EC* judges had. We consider this pattern of results as a reflection of a community-wide stereotype of *FC*s as being relatively second-rate people, a view apparently fully shared by certain subgroups of *FC*s. Similar tendencies to downgrade one's own group have been reported in research with minority groups conducted in other parts of North America.

Extensions of the Basic Study

The Follow-up Study.

Some of the questions left unanswered in the first study have been examined recently by Malcolm Preston (Preston, 1963). Using the same basic techniques, the following questions were asked: (a) Will female and male judges react similarly to language and accent variations of speakers? (b) Will judges react similarly to male and female speakers who change their pronunciation style or the language they speak? (c) Will there be systematic differences in reactions to *FC* and Continental French (*CF*) speakers?

For this study, 80 English Canadian and 92 French Canadian first year college students from Montreal served as judges. The *EC* judges in this study were all Catholics since we wanted to determine if *EC* Catholics would be less biased in their views of *FC*s than the non-Catholic *EC* judges had been in the original study. Approximately the same number of males and females from both language groups were tested, making four groups of judges in all: an *EC* male group, an *EC* female, a *FC* male and a *FC* female group.

The 18 personality traits used by the judges for expressing their reactions were grouped, for the purposes of interpretation, into three logically distinct categories of personality: (a) *competence* which included intelligence, ambition, self-confidence, leadership and courage; (b) *personal integrity* which included dependability, sincerity, character, conscientiousness and kindness; (c) *social attractiveness* which included sociability, likeability, entertainingness, sense of humour and affectionateness. Religiousness, good looks and height were not included in the above categories since they did not logically fit.

Results: Evaluative Reactions of English-Canadian Listeners.

In general it was found that the *EC* listeners viewed the female speakers more favourably in their French guises while they viewed the male speakers more favourably in their English guises. In particular, the *EC* men saw the *FC* lady speakers as more intelligent, ambitious, self-confident, dependable, courageous and sincere than their English counterparts. The *EC* ladies were not quite so gracious although they, too, rated the *FC* ladies as more intelligent, ambitious, self-confident (but shorter) than the *EC* women guises. Thus, *EC*s generally view *FC* females as more competent and the *EC* men see them as possessing more integrity and competence.

Several notions came to mind at this point. It may be that the increased attractiveness of the *FC* woman in the eyes of the *EC* male is partly a result of her inaccessibility. Perhaps also the *EC* women are cognizant of the *EC* men's latent preference for *FC* women and accordingly are themselves prompted to upgrade the *FC* female, even to the point of adopting the *FC* woman as a model of what a woman should be.

However, the thought that another group is better than their own should not be a comfortable one for members of any group, especially a group of young ladies! The realization, however latent, that men of their own cultural group prefer another type of women might well be a very tender issue for the *EC* woman, one that could be easily exacerbated.

To examine this idea, we carried out a separate experiment. The *S*s for the experiment were two groups of *EC* young women, one group serving as controls, the other as an experimental group. Both groups were asked to give their impressions of the personalities of a group of speakers, some using English, some Canadian-style French. They were, of course, actually presented with female bilingual speakers using Canadian French and English guises. Just before they evaluated the speakers, the experimental group was given false information about *FC* women, information that was designed to upset them. They heard a tape recording of a man reading supposedly authentic statistical information about the increase in marriages between *FC* women and *EC* men. They were asked to listen to this loaded passage twice, for practice only, disregarding the content of the message and attending only to the personality of the speaker. We presumed, however, that they would not likely be able to disregard the content since it dealt with a matter that might well bother them – *FC* women, they were told, were competing for *EC* men, men who already had a tendency to prefer *FC* women, a preference that they possibly shared themselves. In contrast, the control group received quite neutral information which would not affect their ratings of *FC*s in any way. The results supported the prediction: The experimental *S*s judged the *FC* women to be reliably more attractive but reliably less dependable and sincere than did the control *S*s. That is, the favourable reactions toward *FC* women found previously were evident in the judgements of the control group, while the experimental *S*s, who had been given false information designed to highlight the threat posed by the presumed greater competence and integrity of *FC* women, saw the *FC* women as men stealers – attractive but undependable and insincere. These findings support the general hypothesis we had developed and they serve as a first step in a series of experiments we are now planning to determine how judgements of personalities affect various types of social interaction.

Let us return again to the main investigation. It was found that *FC* men were not as favourably received as the women were by their *EC* judges. *EC* ladies liked *EC* men, rating them as taller, more likeable, affectionate, sincere, and conscientious, and as possessing more character and a greater sense of humour that the *FC* versions of the same speakers. Furthermore, the *EC* male judges also favoured *EC* male speakers rating them as taller, more kind, dependable and entertaining. Thus, *FC* male speakers are viewed as lacking integrity and as being less socially attractive by both *EC* female, and, to a less marked extent, *EC* male judges. This tendency to downgrade the *FC* male, already noted in the basic study, may well be the expression of an unfavourable stereotyped and prejudiced attitude toward *FC*s, but, apparently, this prejudice is selectively directed toward *FC* males, possibly because they are better known than females as power figures who control local and regional governments and who thereby can be viewed as sources of threat or frustation, (or as the guardians of *FC* women, keeping them all to themselves).

The reactions to Continental French *CF* speakers are generally more favourable although less marked. The *EC* male listeners viewed *CF* women as slightly more competent and *CF* men as equivalent to their *EC* controls except for height and religiousness. The *EC* female listeners upgraded *CF* on sociability and self-confidence, but downgraded *CF* men on height, likeability and sincerity. Thus, *EC* judges appear to be less concerned about European French people in general than they are about the local French people; the European French are neither downgraded nor taken as potential social models to any great extent.

Evaluative Reactions of French-Canadian Listeners.

Summarizing briefly, the *FC* listeners showed more significant guise differences than did their *EC* counterparts. *FCs* generally rated European French guises ***more*** favourably and Canadian French guises *less* favourably than they did their matched *EC* guises. One important exception was the *FC* women who viewed *FC* men as more competent and as more socially attractive than *EC* men.

The general pattern of evaluations presented by the *FC* judges, however, indicates that they view their own linguistic cultural group as ***inferior*** to both the English Canadian and the European French groups, suggesting that *FCs* are prone to take either of these other groups as models for changes in their own manners of behaving (including speech) and possibly in basic values. This tendency is more marked among *FC* men who definitely prefered male and female representatives of the *EC* and *CF* groups to those of their own group. The *FC* women, in contrast, appear to be guardians of *FC* culture at least in the sense that they favoured male representatives of their own cultural group. We presume this reaction reflects something more than a preference for *FC* marriage partners. *FC* women may be particularly anxious to preserve *FC* values and to pass these on in their own families through language, religion and tradition.

Nevertheless, *FC* women apparently face a conflict of their own in that they favour characteristics of both *CF* and *EC* women. Thus, the *FC* female may be safe-guarding the *FC* culture through a preference for *FC* values seen in *FC* men, at the same time as she is prone to change her own behaviour and values in the direction of one of two foreign cultural models, those that the men in her group apparently favour. It is of interest that *EC* women are confronted with a similar conflict since they appear envious of *FC* women.

The Developmental Studies.

Recently, we have been looking into the background of the inferiority reaction among *FC* youngsters, trying to determine at what age it starts and how it develops through the years. Elizabeth Anisfeld and I

(1964) started by studying the reactions of ten-year-old *FC* children to the matched guises of bilingual youngsters of their own age reading French and English versions of *Little Red Riding Hood*, once in Canadian-style French and once in standard English. In this instance, half of the judges were bilingual in English and half were essentially monolingual in French. Stated briefly, it was found that *FC* guises were rated significantly *more* favourable on nearly all traits. (One exception was height; the *EC* speakers were judged as taller.) However, these favourable evaluations of the *FC* in contrast to the *EC* guises were due almost entirely to the reactions of the monolingual children. The bilingual children saw very little difference between the two sets of guises, that is, on nearly all traits their ratings of the *FC* guises were essentially the same as their ratings of *EC* guises. The results, therefore, made it clear that, unlike college-age judges, *FC* children at the ten-year age level do not have a negative bias against their own group.

The question then arises as to where the bias starts after age ten. A recent study (Lambert, Franker and Tucker, 1966) was addressed to solving this puzzle. The investigation was conducted with 375 *FC* girls ranging in age from 9 to 18, who gave their evaluations of three groups of matched guises, (a) of some girls about their own age, (b) of some adult women, and (c) of some adult men. Passages that were appropriate for each age level were read by the bilingual speakers once in English and once in Canadian-style French. In this study attention was given to the social class background of the judges (some were chosen from private schools, some from public schools and to their knowledge of English (Some were bilingual and some monolingual in French). It was found that definite preferences for *EC* guises appeared at about age twelve and were maintained through the late teen years. There was, however, a marked difference between the private and public school judges: the upper middle class girls were especially biased after age 12, whereas the pattern for the working class girls was less pronounced and less durable, suggesting that for them the bias is short-lived and fades out by the late teens. Note that we probably did not encounter girls from lower class homes in our earlier studies using girls at *FC collèges* or *universités*.

The major implication of these findings is that the tendency for certain subgroups of college-age *FC*s to downgrade representatives of their own ethnic-linguistic group, noted in our earlier studies, seems to have its origin, at least with girls, at about age 12, but the ultimate fate of this attitude depends to a great extent on social-class background. Girls who come from upper middle class *FC* homes, and especially those who have become bilingual in English, are particularly likely to maintain this view, at least into the young adult years.

The pattern of results of these developmental studies can also be examined from a more psychodynamic perspective. If we assume that the adult female and male speakers in their *FC* guises represent parents or people like their own parents to the *FC* adolescent judges, just as the same-age speakers represent someone like themsleves, then the findings suggest several possibilities that could be studied in more detail. First, the results are consistent with the notion that teen-age girls have a closer psychological relation with their fathers than with their mothers in the sense that the girls in the study rated *FC* female guises markedly inferior to *EC* ones, but generally favoured or at least showed much less disfavour for the *FC* guises of male speakers. Considered in this light, social-class differences and bilingual skill apparently influence the degree of same-sex rejection and cross-sex identification: by the mid-teens the public school girls, both monolinguals and bilinguals, show essentially no rejection of either the *FC* female or male guises, whereas the private school girls, especially the bilinguals, show a rejection of both female and male *FC* guises through the late teens. These bilinguals might, because of their skill in English and their possible encouragement from home, be able to come in contact with the mothers of their *EC* associates and therefore may have developed stronger reasons to be envious of *EC* mothers and fathers than the monolingual girls would have.

Similarly, the reactions to "same-age" speakers might reflect a tendency to accept or reject one's peer-group or one's self, at least for the monolinguals. From this point of view, the findings suggest that the public school monolinguals are generally satisfied with their *FC* image since they favour the *FC* guises of the same-age speakers at the 16 year level. In contrast, the private school monolinguals may be expressing a marked rejection of themselves in the sense that they favour the *EC* guises. The bilinguals, of course, can consider themselves as being potential or actual members of both ethnic-linguistic groups represented by the guises. It is of interest, therefore, to note that both the public and particularly the private school bilinguals apparently favour the *EC* versions of themselves.

Two Generalizations

This program of research, still far from complete, does permit us to make two important generalizations, both relevant to the main argument of this paper. First, a technique has been developed that rather effectively calls out the stereotyped impressions that members of one ethnic-linguistic group hold of another contrasting group. The type and strength of impression depends on characteristics of the speakers – their sex, age, the dialect they use, and, very likely, the social-class background as this is revealed in speech style. The impression also seems to depend on characteristics of the audience of *judges* – their age, sex, socio-economic background, their bilinguality and their own speech style. The type of reactions and adjustments listeners must make to those who reveal, through their speech style, their likely ethnic group allegiance is suggested by the traits that listeners use to indicate their impressions. Thus, *EC* male and female college students tend to look down on the *FC* male speaker, seeing him as less intelligent, less dependable and less interesting than he would be seen if he had presented himself in an *EC* guise. Imagine the types of role adjustment that would follow if the same person were first seen in the *FC* guise and then suddenly switched to a perfect *EC* guise. A group of *EC* listeners would probably be forced to perk up their ears, reconsider their original classification of the person and then either view him as becoming too intimate in "their" language or decide otherwise and be pleasantly amazed that one of their own could manage the other group's language so well. Furthermore, since these comparative impressions are widespread throughout certain strata of each ethnic-linguistic community, they will probably have an enormous impact on young people who are either forced to learn the other group's language or who choose to do so.

The research findings outlined here have a second important message about the reactions of the bilingual who is able to convincingly switch languages or dialects. The bilingual can study the reactions of his audiences as he adopts one guise in certain settings and another in different settings, and receive a good deal of social feedback, permitting him to realize that he can be perceived in quite different ways, depending on how he presents himself. It could well be that his own self-concept takes two distinctive forms in the light of such feedback. He may also observe, with amusement or alarm, the role adjustments that follow when he suddenly switches guises with the same group of interlocutors. However, research is needed to document and examine these likely consequences of language or dialect switching from the perspective of the bilingual making the switches.

Although we have concentrated on a Canadian setting in these investigations, there is really nothing special about the Canadian scene with regard to the social effects of language or dialect switching. Equally instructive effects have been noted when the switch involves a change from standard American English to Jewish-accented English (Anisfeld, Bogo and Lambert, 1962); when the switch involves changing from Hebrew to Arabic for Israeli and Arab judges, or when the change is from Sephardic to Ashkenazic-style Hebrew for Jewish listeners in Israel (Lambert, Anisfeld and Yeni-Komshian, 1965). Our most recent research, using a modified approach, has been conducted with American Negro speakers and listeners (Tucker and Lambert, 1967). The same type of social effects are inherent in this instance, too: Southern Negroes have more favourable impressions of people who use what the linguists call *Standard Network Style* English than they do of those who speak with their own style, but they are more impressed with their own style than they are with the speech of educated, Southern whites, or of Negroes who become too "white" in their speech by exaggerating the non-Negro features and over-correcting their verbal output.

Social-Psychological Aspects of Second-Language Learning

How might these intergroup impressions and feelings affect young people living in the Montreal area who are expected by educators to learn the other group's language? One would expect that both French-Canadian youngsters and their parents would be more willing, for purely social psychological reasons, to learn English than *EC*s to learn French. Although we haven't investigated the French-Canadians' attitudes toward the learning of English, still it is very apparent that bilingualism in Canada and in Quebec has long been a one-way affair, with *FC*s much more likely to learn English than the converse. Typically, this trend to English is explained on economic grounds and on the attraction of the United States, but I would like to suggest another possible reason for equally serious consideration. *FC*s may be drawn away from Canadian-style French to English, or to bilingualism, or to European-style French, as a psychological reaction to the contrast in stereotyped images which English and French Canadians have of one another. On the other hand, we would expect *EC* students and their parents in Quebec, at least, to be drawn away from French for the same basic reasons. It is, of course, short-sighted to talk about groups in this way because there are certain to be wide individual differences of reaction, as was the case in the impression studies, and as will be apparent in the research to be discussed, but one fact turned up in an unpublished study Robert Gardner and I conducted that looks like a group-wide difference. Several samples of Montreal *EC*, high school students who had studied French for periods of up to seven years scored no better on standard tests of French achievement than did Connecticut high schoolers who had only two or three years of French training.

Instrumental and Integrative Motivation

When viewed from a social-psychological perspective, the process of learning a second language itself also takes on a special significance. From this viewpoint, one would expect that if the student is to be successful in his attempts to learn another social group's language he must be both able and willing to adopt various aspects of behaviour, including verbal behaviour, which characterize members of the other linguistic-cultural group. The learner's ethnocentric tendencies and his attitudes toward the other group are believed to determine his success in learning the new language. The orientation is *instrumental* in form if, for example, the purposes of language study reflect the more utilitarian value of linguistic achievement, such as getting ahead in one's occupation, and it is *integrative* if, for example, the student is oriented to learn more about the other cultural community, as if he desired to become a potential member of the other group. It is also argued that some may be anxious to learn another language as a means of being accepted into another cultural group because of dissatisfactions experienced in their own culture while other individuals may be as much interested in another culture as they are in their own. In either case, the more proficient one becomes in a second language the more he may find that his place in his original membership group is modified at the same time as the other linguistic-cultural group becomes something more than a reference group for him. Depending upon the compatibility of the two cultures, he may experience feelings of chagrin or regret as he loses ties in one group, mixed with the fearful anticipation of entering a relatively new group. The concept of *anomie* first proposed by Durkheim (1897) and more recently extended by Srole (1951) and Williams (1952), refers to such feelings of social uncertainty or dissatisfaction.

My studies with Gardner (1959) were carried out with English-speaking Montreal high school students studying French who were evaluated for their language learning aptitude and verbal intelligence, as well as their attitudes and stereotypes toward members of the French community, and the intensity of their motivation to learn French. Our measure of motivation is conceptually similar to Jones' (1949 and 1950) index of interest in learning a language which he found to be important for successful learning among Welsh students. A factor analysis of scores on these various measures indicated that aptitude and intelligence formed a common factor which was independent of a second one comprising indices of motivation, type of orientation toward language and social attitudes toward *FC*s. Furthermore, a measure of achievement in French taken at the end of a year's study was reflected equally prominently in both factors. This statistical pattern meant that French achievement was dependent upon both aptitude and verbal intelligence as well as sympathetic orientation toward the other group. This orientation was much less common among these students than was the instrumental one, as would be expected from the results of the matched-guise experiments. However, when sympathetic orientation was present it apparently sustained a strong motivation to learn the other group's language. Furthermore, it was clear that students with an integrative orientation were more successful in learning French than were those with instrumental orientations.

A follow-up study (Gardner, 1960)confirmed and extended these findings. Using a larger sample of *EC* students and incorporating various measures of French achievement, the same two independent factors were revealed, and again both were related to French achievement. But whereas aptitude and achievement were especially important for those French skills stressed in school training, such as grammar, the development of such skills, skills that call for the active use of the language in communicational settings, such as pronunciation accuracy and auditory comprehension, was determined in major part by measures of an integrative motivation to learn French. The aptitude variables were insignificant in this case. Further evidence from the intercorrelations indicated that this integrative motive was the converse of an authoritarian ideological syndrome, opening the possibliity that basic personality dispositions may be involved in language learning efficiency.

In this same study information had been gathered from the parents of the students about their own orientations toward the French community. These data suggested that integrative or instrumental orientations toward the other group are developed within the family. That is, the minority of students with an integrative disposition to learn French had parents who also were integrative and sympathetic to the French community. However, students' orientations were not related to parents' skill in French nor to the number of French acquaintances the parents had, indicating that the integrative motive is not due to having more experience with French at home. Instead the integrative outlook more likely stems from a family-wide attitudinal disposition.

Language Learning and Anomie

Another feature of the language learning process came to light in an investigation of college and postgraduate students undergoing an intensive course in advanced French at McGill's French Summer School. We were interested here, among other matters, in changes in attitudes and feelings that might take place during the six-week study period (Lambert, Gardner, Barik and Tunstall, 1961). The majority of the students were Americans who oriented themselves mainly to the European-French rather than the American-French community. We adjusted out attitude scales to make them appropriate for those learning European French. Certain results were of special interest. As the students progressed in French skill to the point that they said they "thought" in French, and even dreamed in French, their feelings of anomie also increased markedly. At the same time, they began to seek out occasions to use English even though they had solemnly pledged to use only French for the six-week period. This pattern of results suggests to us that these already advanced students experienced a strong dose of anomie when they commenced to *really* master a second language. That is, when advanced students became so skilled that they begin to think and feel like Frenchmen, they then became so annoyed with feelings of anomie that they were prompted to develop strategies to minimize or control the annoyance. Reverting to English could be such a strategy. It should be emphasized however, that the chain of events just listed needs to be much more carefully explored.

Elizabeth Anisfeld and I took another look at this problem, experimenting with ten-year-old monolingual and bilingual students (Peal and Lambert, 1962). We found that the bilingual children (attending French schools in Montreal) were markedly more favourable towards the "other" language group (i.e., the *EC*s) than the monolingual children were. Furthermore, the bilingual children reported that their parents held the same strongly sympathetic attitudes toward *EC*s, in contrast to the pro-*FC* attitudes reported for the parents of the monolingual children. Apparently, then, the development of second language skill to the point of balanced bilingualism is conditioned by family-shared attitudes toward the other linguistic-cultural group.

These findings are consistent and reliable enough to be of general interest. For example, methods of language training could possibly be modified and strengthened by giving consideration to the social-psychological implications of language learning. Because of the possible practical as well as theoretical significance of this approach, it seemed appropriate to test its applicability in a cultural setting other than the bicultural Quebec scene. With measures of attitude and motivation modified for American students learning French, a large scale study, very similar in nature to those conducted in Montreal, was carried out in various settings in the United States with very similar general outcomes (Lambert and Gardner, 1962).

One further investigation indicated that these suggested social psychological principles are not restricted to English and French speakers in Canada. Moshe Anisfeld and I (1961) extended the same experimental procedure to samples of Jewish high school students studying Hebrew at various parochial schools in different sectors of Montreal. They were questioned about their orientations toward learning Hebrew and their attitudes toward the Jewish culture and community, and tested for their verbal intelligence, language aptitude and achievement in the Hebrew language at the end of the school year. The results support the generalization that both intellectual capacity and attitudinal orientation affect success in learning Hebrew. However, whereas intelligence and linguistic aptitude were relatively stable predictors of success, the attitudinal measures varied from one Jewish community to another. For instance, the measure of a Jewish student's desire to become more acculturated in the Jewish tradition and culture was a sensitive indicator of progress in Hebrew for children from a particular district of Montreal, one where members of the Jewish subcommunity were actually concerned with problems of integrating into the Jewish culture. In another district, made up mainly of Jews who recently arrived from central Europe and who were clearly of a lower socio-economic level, the measure of desire for Jewish acculturation did not correlate with achievement in Hebrew, whereas measures of pro-Semitic attitudes or pride in being Jewish did.

Bilingual Adjustments to Conflicting Demands

The final issue I want to discuss concerns the socio-cultural tugs and pulls that the bilingual or potential bilingual encounters and how he adjusts to these often conflicting demands made on him. We have seen how particular social atmospheres can affect the bilingual. For example, the French-English bilingual in the Montreal setting may be pulled toward greater use of English, and yet be urged by certain others in the *FC* community not to move too far in that direction, just as *EC*s may be discouraged from moving toward the French community. (In a similar fashion, dialects would be expected to change because of the social consequences they engender, so that Jewish accented speech should drop away, especially with those of the younger generation in American settings, as should Sephardic forms of Hebrew in Israel or certain forms of Negro speech in America.) In other words, the bilingual encounters social pressure of various sorts: he can enjoy the fun of linguistic spying but must pay the price of suspicion from those who don't want him to enter too intimately into their cultural domains and from others who don't want him to leave his "own" domain. He also comes to realize that most people are suspicious of a person who is in any sense two-faced. If he is progressing toward bilingualism, he encounters similar pressures that may affect his self-concept, his sense of belonging and his relations to two cultural-linguistic groups, the one he is slowly *leaving* and the one he is *entering*. The conflict exists because so many of us think in terms of in-groups and out-groups, or of the need of showing an allegiance to one group or another, so that terms such as own language, other's language, *leaving* and *entering* one cultural group for another seem to be appropriate, even natural, descriptive choices.

Bilinguals and Ethnocentrism

Although this type of thought may characterize most people in our world, it is nonetheless a subtle form of group cleavage and ethnocentrism, and in time it may be challenged by bilinguals who, I feel, are in an excellent position to develop a totally new outlook on the social world. My argument is that bilinguals, especially those with bicultural experiences, enjoy certain fundamental advantages which, if capitalized on, can easily offset the annoying social tugs and pulls they are normally prone to. Let me mention one of these advantages that I feel is a tremendous asset.[1] Recently, Otto Klineberg and I conducted a rather comprehensive international study of the development of stereotyped thinking in children (Lambert and Klineberg, 1967). We found that rigid and stereotyped thinking about in-groups and out-groups, or about own groups in contrast to foreigners, starts during the pre-school period when children are trying to form a conception of themselves and their place in the world. Parents and other socializers attempt to help the child at this stage by highlighting differences and contrasts among groups, thereby making his own group as distinctive as possible. This tendency, incidentally, was noted among parents from various parts of the world. Rather than helping, however, they may actually be setting the stage for ethnocentrism with permanent consequences. The more contrasts are stressed, the more deep-seated the stereotyping process and its impact on ethnocentric thought appear to be. Of relevance here is the notion that the child brought up bilingually and biculturally will be less likely to have good versus bad contrasts impressed on him when he starts wondering about himself, his own group and others. Instead he will probably be taught something more truthful, although more complex: that differences among national or cultural groups of peoples are actually not clear-cut and that basic similarities among peoples are more prominent than differences. The bilingual child in other words may well start life with the enormous advantage of having a more open, receptive mind about himself and other people. Furthermore, as he matures, the bilingual has many opportunities to learn, from observing changes in other people's reactions to him, how two-faced and ethnocentric *others* can be. That is, he is likely to become especially sensitive to and leery of ethnocentrism.

Bilinguals and Social Conflicts

This is not to say that bilinguals have an easy time of it. In fact, the final investigation I want to present demonstrates the social conflicts bilinguals typically face, but, and this is the major point, it also demonstrates one particular type of adjustment that is particularly encouraging.

In 1943, Irving Child (1943) investigated a matter that disturbed many second-generation Italians living in New England: what were they, Italian or American? Through early experiences they had learned that their relations with certain other youngsters in their community were strained whenever they displayed signs of their Italian background, that is, whenever they behaved as their parents wanted them to. In contrast, if they rejected their Italian background, they realized they could be deprived of many satisfactions stemming from belonging to an Italian family and an Italian community. Child uncovered three contrasting modes of adjusting to these pressures. One subgroup rebelled against their Italian background, making themselves as American as possible. Another subgroup rebelled the other way, rejecting things American as much as possible while proudly associating themselves with things Italian. The third form of adjustment was an apathetic withdrawal and a refusal to think of themselves in ethnic terms at all. This group tried, unsuccessfully, to escape the conflict by avoiding situations where the matter of cultural background might come up. Stated in other terms, some tried to belong to one of their own groups or the other, and some, because of strong pulls from both sides, were unable to belong to either.

Child's study illustrates nicely the difficulties faced by people with dual allegiances, but there is no evidence presented of second-generation Italians who actually feel themselves as belonging to both groups. When in 1962, Robert Gardner and I (1962) studied another ethnic minority group in New England, the French-Americans, we observed the same types of reactions as Child had noted among Italian-Americans. But in our study there was an important difference.

We used a series of attitude scales to assess the allegiances of French-American adolescents to both their French and American heritages. Their relative degree of skill in French and in English were used as an index of their mode of adjustment to the bicultural conflict they faced. In their homes, schools and community, they all had ample opportunities to learn both languages well, but subgroups turned up who had quite different patterns of linguistic skill, and each pattern was conosonant with each subgroup's allegiances. Those who expressed a definite preference for the American over the French culture and who negated the value of knowing French were more proficient in English than in French. They also expressed anxiety about how well they actually knew English. This subgroup, characterized by a general rejection of their French background, resembles in many respects the rebel reaction noted by Child. A second subgroup expressed a strong desire to be identified as French, especially in comprehension of spoken French. A third group apparently faced a conflict of cultural allegiances since they were ambivalent about their identity, favouring certain features of the French and other features of the American culture. Presumably because they had not resolved the conflict, they were retarded in their command of both languages when compared to the other groups. This relatively unsuccessful mode of adjustment is very similar to the apathetic reaction noted in one subgroup of Italian-Americans.

A fourth subgroup is of special interest. French-American youngsters who have an open-minded, nonethnocentric view of people in general, coupled with a strong aptitude for language learning are the ones who profited fully from their language learning opportunities and became skilled in *both* languages.

[1]For present purposes, discussion is limited to a more *social* advantage associated with bilingualism. In other writings there has been a stress on potential intellectual and *cognitive* advantages, see Peal and Lambert (1962) and Anisfeld (1964); see also Macnamara (1964) as well as Lambert and Anisfeld (1966). The bilingual's potential utility has also been discussed as a linguistic mediator between monolingual groups because of his comprehension of the subtle meaning differences characterizing each of the languages involved, see Lambert and Moore (1966).

These young people had apparently circumvented the conflicts and developed means of becoming members of both cultural groups. They had, in other terms, achieved a comfortable bicultural identity.

It is not clear why this type of adjustment did not appear in Child's study. There could, for example, be important differences in the social pressures encountered by second-generation Italians and French in New England. My guess, however, is that the difference in findings reflects a new social movement that has started in America in the interval between 1943 and 1962, a movement which the American linguist Charles Hockett humorously refers to as a "reduction of the heat under the American melting pot." I believe that bicultural bilinguals will be particularly helpful in perpetuating this movement. They and their children are also the ones most likely to work out a new, non ethnocentric mode of social intercourse which could be of universal significance.

References

ANISFELD, ELIZABETH. A comparison of the cognitive functioning of monolinguals and bilinguals. Unpublished Ph.D. thesis, Redpath Library, McGill University, 1964.

ANISFELD, ELIZABETH, and LAMBERT, W. E. Evaluational reactions of bilingual and monolingual children to spoken language. *Journal of Abnormal and Social Psychology,* 1964, *69,* 89-97.

ANISFELD, M., BOGO, N., and LAMBERT, W. E. Evaluational reactions to accented English speech. *Journal of Abnormal and Social Phychology,* 1962, *65,* 223-231.

ANISFELD, M., and LAMBERT, W. E. Social and psychological variables in learning Hebrew. *ournal of Abnormal and Social Psychology,* 1961, *63,* 524-529.

BEREITER, C. Some persisting dilemmas in the measurement of change. In HARRIS, C. W. (ed.), *Problems in measuring change.* Madison: The University of Wisconsin Press, 1963.

CHILD, I. L. *Italian or American? The second generation in conflict.* New Haven: Yale University Press, 1943.

DURKHEIM, E. *Le suicide.* Paris: F. Alcan, 1897.

FERGUSON, G. A. *Statistical analysis in psychology and education.* New York: McGraw-Hill, 1959.

GARDNER, R. C., and LAMBERT, W. E. Motivational variables in second-language acquisition. *Canadian Journal of Psychology,* 1959, *13,* 266-272.

GARDNER, R. C. Motivational variables in second-language acquisition. Unpublished Ph.D. thesis, McGill University, 1960.

JONES, W. R. Attitude towards Welsh as a second language. A preliminary investigation. *British Journal of Educational Psychology,* 1949, *19,* 44-52.

JONES, W. R. Attitude towards Welsh as a second language, a further investigation. *British Journal of Educational Psychology,* 1950, *20,* 117-132.

LABOV, W. Hypercorrection by the lower middle class as a factor in linguistic change. Columbia University, 1964. (Mimeo).

LAMBERT, W. E., HODGSON, R. C., GARDNER, R. C., and FILLENBAUM, S. Evaluational reactions to spoken languages. *Journal of Abnormal and Social Psychology,* 1960, *60,* 44-51.

LAMBERT, W. E., GARDNER, R. C., OLTON, R., and TUNSTALL, K. A study of the roles of attitudes and motivation in second-language learning. McGill University, 1962. (Mimeo).

LAMBERT, W. E., GARDNER, R. C., BARIK, H. C., and TUNSTALL, K. Attitudinal and cognitive aspects of intensive study of a second language. *Journal of Abnormal and Social Psychology,* 1963, *66,* 358-368.

LAMBERT, W. E., ANISFELD, M., and YENI-KOMSHIAN, GRACE. Evaluational reactions of Jewish and Arab adolescents to dialect and language variations. *Journal of Personality and Social Psychology,* 1965, *2,* 84-90.

LAMBERT, W. E., FRANKEL, HANNAH, and TUCKER, G. R. Judging personality through speech: A French-Canadian example. *The Journal of Communication,* 1966, *16,* 305-321.

LAMBERT, W. E., and ANISFELD, ELIZABETH. A reply to John Macnamara. Mimeographed and submitted to *Studies,* 1966.

LAMBERT, W. E., and MOORE, NANCY. Word-association responses: Comparison of American and French monolinguals with Canadian monolinguals and bilinguals. *Journal of Personality and Social Psychology,* 1966, *3,* 313-320.

LAMBERT, W. E., and KLINEBERG, O. *Children's views of foreign peoples: A cross-national study.* New York: Appleton, 1967.

MACNAMARA, J. The Commission on Irish: Psychological aspects. *Studies,* 1964, 164-173.

McDAVID, R. I. The dialects of American English. In FRANCIS, W. N. (ed.), *The structure of American English.* New York: Ronald, 1958.

PEAL, ELIZABETH, and LAMBERT, W. E. The relation of bilingualism to intelligence. *Psychological Monographs,* 1962, *76,* Whole No. 546.

PRESTON, M. S. Evaluational reactions to English, Canadian French and European French voices. Unpublished M.A. thesis, McGill University, Redpath Library, 1963.

SROLE, L. Social dysfunction, personality and social distance attitudes. Paper read before American Sociological Society, 1951, National Meeting, Chicago, Ill. (Mimeo).

TUCKER, G. R., and LAMBERT, W. E., White and Negro listeners' reactions to various American-English dialects. McGill University, 1967. (Mimeo)

WILLIAMS, R. N. *American society.* New York: Knopf, 1952.

57 / Ethnic Stereotypes: A Factor Analytic Investigation[1]

R.C. Gardner, E. Joy Wonnacott and D.M. Taylor *University of Western Ontario.*

In the previous review article it was demonstrated that stereotypes of English Canadians and French Canadians exist and a brief description of these stereotypes was given. This study presents a more exhaustive analysis of the French-Canadian stereotype and attempts to specify the relationship between attitudes and stereotypes.

The term "stereotype" was originally suggested by Lippmann (1922) to refer to a "picture in the head" which organizes the individual's perception of the world. Although such a definition lacks precision, it emphasizes the fact that the concept of the stereotype is used to refer to images evoked by a particular label. This type of definition seems particularly appropriate for most studies of ethnic stereotypes where individuals are requested to check adjectives associated with an ethnic group label (cf. Harding, Kutner, Proshansky, and Chein, 1954).

The traditional method for assessing ethnic stereotypes was developed by Katz and Braly (1933) and resulted in an implicit extension to the definition, viz., that of consensus (cf. Secord and Backman, 1964). This technique requires subjects to select from a list of adjectives those which they feel characterize an ethnic group. The stereotype is defined in terms of those adjectives chosen most frequently, and thus implies consensus within the community concerning the type of image associated with a given ethnic group. Since this technique has been commonly used to define ethnic stereotypes (Harding *et al.*, 1954), consensual validation appears to be a necessary component of stereotypes, even though some researchers have noted the necessity of postulating "personal stereotypes" (cf. Secord and Backman, 1964).

The traditional method has many shortcomings. Foremost among these is the antagonism, noted by Gilbert (1951), that subjects feel toward the task. Although subjects object to choosing an adjective to characterize an ethnic group, it does not necessarily mean that they do not use stereotypes. Subjects may object to selecting an adjective and writing it down because this suggests finality and inclusiveness. The task might be too simple and categorical in these times when individual differences are expounded. Furthermore, this technique allows for only a listing of attributes generally chosen, and an index of the definiteness of the stereotype in the community. Individual difference measures of the extent to which subjects ascribe specific traits to the group in question cannot be determined.

Partly because of the techniques typically used to assess ethnic stereotypes, the relationship between attitudinal reactions and steretoyping is not clear. Buchanan (1951) demonstrated a relationship between the feeling of friendliness toward a country and the extent to which the stereotype contained favourable characteristics. Similar relationships are suggested by studies concerned with changes in stereotypes over time when attitudes are affected by international incidents. International conflict is reflected in the inclusion of negatively evaluative traits in the stereotype concerning protagonists (Dudycha, 1942; Meenes, 1943; Seago, 1947). These studies, however, do not clarify the relationship between individual attitudinal reactions and the content of stereotypical reactions. Such studies were not possible with the traditional technique for assessing stereotypes.

The present study was concerned with the application of the semantic differential technique (Osgood, Suci, and Tannenbaum, 1957) to the assessment of ethnic stereotypes. This technique seems appropriate to the determination of stereotypes since the scales require judgements of the extent to which one or the other end of a scale "is applicable or relevant" to the concept being rated. In addition, since individual judgements are made on each scale, this technique permits an evaluation of the correlates of the judgements. It may be, for example, that some scales are more highly correlated among themselves than with others because the ethnic label evokes a different type of image among some subjects. Moreover, by determining the relationship of reactions to individual scales with more traditional measures of attitudes, it may be possible to clarify the relation between attitudinal reactions and the propensity to ascribe various characteristics to members of an ethnic group.

The present study was carried out with subjects living in Ontario, Canada, and was concerned with

[1]The present study was supported in part by a grant from the Canada Council for research on the project: Bicultural Communication: The Significance of Stereotypes.

Reprinted, by permission, from *Canadian Journal of Psychology*, 1968, *22*, 35-44.

reactions toward French Canadians. This ethnic group was chosen because it has a particular relevance to these subjects. Attitudinal reactions between the English and French are probably as socially important here as are reactions between Negroes and whites in the United States.

Method

Subjects

Questionnaires were administered during a regular class period to 108 undergraduate students in an introductory course in psychology, though 11 *S*s did not complete all items on the questionnaire. The analysis summarized in Table I is based on the data from all *S*s, while the factor analysis is based on the data obtained from the 97 *S*s completing all items.

Materials

*S*s completed a questionnaire comprised of the following tests.

Semantic differential scales. The concept "French Canadians" was rated on 39 bipolar adjective scales (see Table I). The instructions were similar to those suggested by Osgood, *et al.* (1957), except that they were modified slightly to refer to ethnic groups. The 39 scales were selected for their potential relevance to French Canadians on the basis of other research (Lambert, Hodgson, Gardner, and Fillenbaum, 1960) and pilot studies conducted in this setting. Since the study was partly concerned with attitudinal reactions toward French Canadians it was necessary to determine the evaluative nature of the adjectives involved in the scales. Subsequent to the testing, five graduate students classified each of the 78 adjectives as "definitely positively evaluative," "definitely negatively evaluative," or "relatively neutral." A scale was considered evaluative if one of the bipolar adjectives was classified as "definitely positively evaluative" while the other was classified as "definitely negatively evaluative" by at least 4 of the 5 judges. Using this procedure, 16 of the scales (Variables 1,5,6,9,11,17,23,24,29,30,31,32,34,35,38,39) were adjudged evaluative.

The following three attitude scales were presented using a six-alternative Likert form.

California F-scale. Thirteen items which appeared most appropriate for a Canadian setting were selected from Forms 40 and 45 of the F-scale (Adorno, Frenkel-Brunswik, Levinson, and Sanford, 1950, p. 255) and were presented to the *S*s. A high score is indicative of authoritarian attitudes.

Ethnocentrism scale. Seven of the eight items from the Other Minorities and Patriotism section of the Ethnocentrism scale (Adorno *et al.*, 1950, p. 142) were used. The one item referring to "zootsuiters" was omitted and slight modifications were made in the wordings (i.e., "Canadians" substituted for "Americans") in some of the items to make them meaningful to the *S*s. A high score is indicative of ethnocentric attitudes.

French-Canadian Attitude scale. Fifteen positively worded items about French Canadians were presented. Items from this scale have been used in previous studies (Gardner and Lambert, 1959; Lambert, Gardner, Olton and Tunstall, 1960) to assess attitudes toward French Canadians. A typical item is: "French Canadians set a good example for us by their family life." A high score indicates favourable attitudes toward French Canadians.

Results and Discussion

Extremity of judgements of the concept "French Canadians" on each semantic differential scale was assessed by means of the *t*-distribution. Assuming an underlying normal distribution, the statistic $(\bar{X} - \mu)\sqrt{N}/s$ is distributed as t with $N - 1$ degrees of freedom. Stereotypy might be assumed present when the mean $(\bar{X})$ deviates significantly from an assumed neutral mean $(\mu) = 4$, since it suggests that there is a tendency for subjects to rate the concept toward one end of the scale. Table I presents the means, variances, and *t*s for each semantic differential scale; the scales are ranked in terms of the magnitude of the t statistic. It will be noted that 31 of the t values are significant at the 1 per cent level, three at the 5 per cent level, and that 5 are not significant.

In general, the magnitude of the t statistics reflect the extent of consensus among the subjects in their ratings (i.e., stereotyping); however, extreme agreement is not evident unless the mean deviates by at least one unit from the neutral position of 4. For example, the talkative-quiet scale has a mean rating of 1.99 and a t statistic of –21.93. The distribution of ratings for this scale demonstrated that 91 per cent of the subjects rated French Canadians on the talkative side of the neutral position, while 7 per cent rated them as neutral, and only 2 per cent rated them as slightly quiet. This contrasts with the reputable-disreputable scale ($\bar{X} = 3.44$, $t = -4.98$), which despite the significant t statistic evidences little consensus. Fifty per cent rated French Canadians toward the reputable pole, while 37 per cent rated them as neutral, and 13 per cent rated them on the disreputable side of the neutral position. Examination of the distributions for each scale suggested that those scales with a t statistic greater than $\pm$ 7.0 demonstrated appreciable polarity and in the following discussion such scales are referred to as evidencing extreme consensus.

The configuration obtained here is highly reliable. In a pilot study conducted last year, similar ratings were obtained from 90 subjects on the concept "French Canadians" on 37 scales in common with those used here. The Pearson product-moment correlation between the t values obtained from the two samples was .74 ($p < .01$), while the correlation between mean ratings was .97 ($p < .01$). Thus it is clear that a definite hierarchy of the characteristics is attributed to the French Canadians by English-speaking Canadians. It is not clear, however, even

Table I – Means, standard deviations, and tests of polarity of the 39 scales

Scale	Mean	Standard deviation	t	Rank
1. Honest–dishonest	3.32	1.21	−5.91**	21
2. Follower–leader	3.58	1.46	−2.97**	30
3. Religious–irreligious	1.89	1.16	−19.00**	4
4. Traditionalistic–modern	2.69	1.60	−8.55**	14
5. Hospitable–inhospitable	2.94	1.72	−6.39**	19
6. Reliable–unreliable	3.65	1.52	−2.41*	32
7. Emotional-rational	2.22	1.37	−13.49**	7
8. Short–tall	3.69	1.05	−3.04**	28
9. Knowledgeable–ignorant	3.90	1.28	−.83	37
10. Excitable–reserved	2.06	1.01	−19.96**	2
11. Active–passive	2.80	1.21	−10.31**	10
12. Stable–changeable	4.55	1.56	3.64**	25
13. Colourful–colourless	2.28	1.27	−14.13**	6
14. Humble–proud	6.00	1.07	19.47**	3
15. Sophisticated–naïve	4.15	1.25	1.23	36
16. Cultured–uncultured	3.50	1.52	3.42**	26
17. Reputable–disreputable	3.44	1.18	−4.98**	23
18. Tenacious–yielding	2.52	1.15	−13.41**	8
19. Complex–simple	3.54	1.73	−2.78**	31
20. Sensitive–insensitive	2.24	.99	−18.57**	5
21. Servile–haughty	4.57	1.22	4.82**	24
22. Neat–slovenly	3.75	1.29	−2.01*	34
23. Peace-loving–belligerent	4.22	1.38	1.67	35
24. Greedy–generous	4.34	1.19	2.98**	29
25. Eccentric–conventional	3.96	1.34	−.29	39
26. Talkative–quiet	1.99	.95	−21.93**	1
27. Impulsive–conservative	2.53	1.27	−12.04**	9
28. Artistic–inartistic	2.82	1.21	−10.07**	11
29. Disloyal–loyal	4.89	1.64	5.69**	22
30. Sociable–unsociable	2.82	1.36	−9.05**	12
31. Likable–unlikable	2.89	1.36	−8.47**	16
32. Pleasant–unpleasant	3.03	1.24	−8.14**	17
33. Affected–natural	4.86	1.43	6.26**	20
34. Tense–relaxed	3.94	1.59	−.36	38
35. Kind–unkind	3.12	1.28	−7.14**	18
36. Delicate–rugged	5.02	1.18	9.00**	13
37. Wealthy–poor	4.81	1.00	8.50**	15
38. Dependable–undependable	3.69	1.37	−2.32*	33
39. Stupid–intelligent	4.32	1.07	3.16**	27

**$p < .01$. *$p < .05$.

for the traits evidencing extreme consensus, that the image described reflects the stereotype of a unitary concept, French Canadian, or for that matter whether individuals differing in attitudes towards the French Canadians, or out-groups in general, share the same stereotype. In order to answer these questions, a factor analysis was performed on the correlations among the semantic differential scales and the three attitude scales.

Pearson product-moment correlation coefficients were computed among the semantic differential scales and the attitude measures. The resulting matrix was factor analysed using the Principal Axis solution.[2] Investigation of the eigenvalues indicated that four factors adequately reproduced the correlation matrix. The factor matrix was rotated by means of the Normalized Varimax solution. The rotated matrix is presented in Table II.

[2]Copies of the correlation matrix and the Principal Axis factor matrix are available from R.C.Gardner of D.M.Taylor.

Factor I receives appreciable loadings (i.e., greater than .30) from 19 variables and clearly describes an evaluative dimmension of reactions toward the French Canadians. Loadings of greater than .60 are received from six semantic differential scales (Variables 5, 24, 30, 31, 32, and 35) as well as the French Canadian Attitude scale. Each of these semantic differential scales was independently classified as evaluative by the judges, and the presence of the attitude scale on this factor supports the conclusion that it represents an attitudinal dimension. The other twelve loadings defining this factor are derived from 11 semantic differential scales and the Ethnocentrism scale. Seven of these scales were also adjudged evaluative, highlighting the attitudinal (affective) nature of this factor.

Factor I is defined as a *French Canadian Attitude* factor. The pattern of the loadings suggests that subjects with unfavourable attitudes toward the French Canadians, and with an ethnocentric orientation, rate the concept, French Canadians, toward the negative pole of evaluative scales. This appears to be

Table II – Rotated factor matrix

	I	II	III	IV
1. Honest-dishonest	0.307	0.003	0.300	-0.288
2. Follower–leader	0.125	-0.081	-0.472	0.204
3. Religious–irreligious	0.069	-0.439	-0.252	-0.060
4. Traditionalistic–modern	-0.153	-0.192	-0.258	0.085
5. Hospitable–inhospitable	0.638	-0.038	0.210	-0.120
6. Reliable–unreliable	0.437	0.150	0.384	-0.521
7. Emotional–rational	-0.006	-0.556	-0.271	0.047
8. Short–tall	0.004	-0.301	-0.250	0.286
9. Knowledgeable–ignorant	0.108	0.094	0.704	-0.069
10. Excitable–reserved	-0.029	-0.643	-0.247	-0.002
11. Active–passive	0.038	-0.482	0.388	-0.244
12. Stable–changeable	-0.049	0.062	0.113	-0.356
13. Colourful–colourless	0.377	-0.512	0.089	-0.109
14. Humble–proud	-0.095	0.571	0.002	0.045
15. Sophisticated–naive	0.173	0.021	0.702	0.082
16 Cultured–uncultured	0.257	-0.083	0.659	-0.055
17. Reputable–disreputable	0.393	-0.006	0.319	-0.368
18. Tenacious–yielding	-0.243	-0.368	0.100	-0.304
19. Complex–simple	0.112	-0.051	0.599	0.122
20. Sensitive–insensitive	0.112	-0.428	0.052	-0.003
21. Servile–haughty	0.302	0.486	0.030	0.152
22. Neat–slovenly	0.378	0.094	0.501	-0.153
23. Peace-loving–belligerent	0.577	0.216	0.212	0.083
24. Greedy–generous	-0.665	-0.083	-0.083	0.185
25. Eccentric–conventional	-0.289	-0.159	0.038	0.413
26. Talkative–quiet	0.088	-0.628	-0.135	0.093
27. Impulsive–conservative	-0.151	-0.568	-0.087	0.243
28. Artistic–inartistic	0.228	-0.501	0.217	0.075
29. Disloyal–loyal	-0.139	0.107	0.062	0.485
30. Sociable–unsociable	0.737	-0.084	0.243	-0.133
31. Likable–unlikable	0.787	-0.142	0.276	-0.093
32. Pleasant–unpleasant	0.813	-0.083	0.268	0.087
33. Affected–natural	-0.560	0.144	0.083	0.320
34. Tense–relaxed	-0.421	0.013	0.057	-0.016
35. Kind–unkind	0.748	-0.217	-0.029	-0.035
36. Delicate–rugged	-0.075	0.217	0.190	0.493
37. Wealthy–poor	-0.037	0.256	0.581	0.092
38. Dependable–undependable	0.474	0.009	0.291	-0.549
39. Stupid–intelligent	-0.296	0.078	-0.657	0.179
40. F-Scale	0.053	0.292	-0.032	0.004
41. E-Scale	0.372	0.009	0.009	-0.051
42. French Canadian Attitude scale	-0.609	-0.078	-0.349	0.358

true primarily for scales for which there is not strong consensus; only five of the scales included on this factor evidenced a high degree of consensus in the analysis of polarity discussed above. Moreover, on all but two of the 13 evaluative scales defining Factor I, the mean ratings of all subjects were toward the positively evaluative pole. Thus, although there is a general tendency for subjects to positively evaluate French Canadians, those with an anti-French Canadian ethnocentric orientation tend to disagree with this evaluation.

Factor II receives high loadings from 13 semantic differential scales (Variables 3, 7, 8, 10, 11, 13, 14, 18, 20, 21, 26, 27, and 28). The cluster of adjectives suggested by this factor describes French Canadians as excitable, talkative, proud, impulsive, emotional, colourful, artistic, haughty, active, religious, sensitive, tenacious, and short. Two striking features of the scales making up this factor are that only one of the scales is from those classified as evaluative (i.e., Variable 11, active-passive), and that eleven of them were from the highest eleven t values obtained in the analysis of polarity. The only two of these scales which did not evidence extreme polarity of ratings were Variable 8 (short-tall) and Variable 21 (servile-haughty). Consequently, Factor II appears to represent a stereotypical dimension of reactions to French Canadians. It will be noted that the scales are not clearly evaluative, and that individual differences in ratings on these scales are not related to attitudes toward the French Canadians (note the loading of Variable 42).

Factor II appears to reflect a stereotypical reaction, toward the French Canadians, which is commonly accepted by the community, and consequently is defined as a *French Canadian Stereotype* factor. In this definition, emphasis is placed on the consensual acceptance of the traits ascribed to the group. The configuration described here, furthermore, suggests that the tendency to adopt this community-wide stereotype is independent of attitudes toward French Canadians. This conclusion is not unwarranted on the basis of previous research even though it is generally accepted that a stereotype does reflect an attitudinal reaction (Allport, 1954; Harding *et al.*, 1954). Studies purporting to show a relationship between stereotypes and attitudes do so by indicating the presence of negative content in the stereotype of unfavourable groups (Dudycha, 1942; Meenes, 1943; Seago, 1947). They have not, however, demonstrated a relationship between an individual's attitude and his willingness to ascribe stereotyped traits to an ethnic group. Factor II indicates that individual differences in the extent to which the stereotype is adopted are independent of attitudes, a finding which might be expected since a stereotype presumably implies a community-wide acceptance of traits believed to characterize an ethnic group. There is the indication, however, that stereotyping is related to generalized prejudice reactions. It has been suggested (Adorno *et al.*, 1950) that authoritarians are predisposed to stereotyping. The low positive loading of the F-scale (Variable 40) suggests that individual differences in the tendency to ascribe stereotyped traits to French Canadians are characteristic of authoritarians; thus it is possible that individual differences in stereotyping are due not to specific attitudinal reactions but to generalized prejudice reactions.

Thirteen variables define Factor III, viz., 12 semantic differential scales and the French Canadian Attitude scale. Six of the semantic differential scales are clearly evaluative (Variables 1, 6, 9, 11, 17, and 39) and six are not (Variables 2, 15, 16, 19, 22, and 37). In general, the highest loadings are obtained from the non-evaluative scales. The configuration suggests that favourable attitudes toward the French Canadians are associated with ratings such as honest, reliable, knowledgeable, active, reputable, intelligent, sophisticated, cultured, complex, neat, wealthy, and leaderlike, while unfavourable attitudes toward the French Canadians tend to be associated with their polar opposites. That is, different images of the French Canadian seem to be associated with different attitudes toward them, and these images appear to involve both evaluative and non-evaluative traits. One image seems to describe an intelligent, sophisticated French Canadian, the other a somewhat unreliable, uncultured individual. The analysis of polarity indicated that there was consensus for most of the evaluative traits on this factor which were associated with favourable attitudes, but that there was some disagreement on the non-evaluative traits which were associated with favourable attitudes on this factor. Factor III therefore would appear to reflect a stereotype reaction toward French Canadians which is dependent upon affective reactions toward that group.

Factor IV receives appreciable loadings from 10 variables, nine semantic differential scales, and the French Canadian Attitude scale. In general, higher loadings are obtained from the four evaluative scales (Variables 6, 17, 29, and 38), and somewhat lower ones form the five non-evaluative scales (Variables 12, 18, 25, 33, and 36). Positive attitudes toward French Canadians are associated with traits such as dependable, reliable, loyal, reputable, rugged, conventional, stable, natural, and tenacious, while negative attitudes tend to be associated with their polar opposites. The analysis of polarity indicated consensus with all the positively evaluative traits, and with two of the non-evaluative ones. The factor pattern obtained suggests that subjects with favourable attitudes tend to adopt the same stereotypical reactions as most individuals, but that individuals with negative attitudes tend to reject them. This factor is similar to Factor III except for the traits involved. The configuration of these two factors would suggest that to some extent individuals with different affective reactions toward an ethnic group have slightly different images, or personal stereotypes, of that group in addition to the community-wide stereotype.

The results of this study suggest that a number of images are evoked by an ethnic group label and that, consequently, it is not meaningful to conceptualize an ethnic stereotype as a single relatively organized construct. There would appear to be a number of "stereotypes" associated with an ethnic group label, and each stereotype seems to involve a hierarchy of assumed attributes. In this study, endorsement of a community-wide stereotype was independent of attitudes toward the ethnic group, but was slightly related to authoritarian attitudes (Factor II). Since this stereotype is not clearly evaluative, it may be that such a relationship may not be replicated in other settings or with other ethnic groups. However, since there is community support for this reaction, it is reasonable to expect it to be independent of individual differences in attitudes toward the group. Specific group attitudes and an ethnocentric orientation are clearly related to the tendency to ascribe highly evaluative traits (Factor I) suggesting the role of attitudes in what might be termed an evaluative stereotype. Furthermore, attitudes are also related to other stereotypical reactions, but these appear to involve reactions only partly accepted by the general community (Factors III and IV). This supports the generalization that while attitudes influence stereotypical reactions, such an influence is limited to stereotypes not completely accepted by the community. In studies utilizing the traditional method for assessing stereotypes, this would appear to involve adjectives not evidencing high consensus.

Abstract

The semantic differential technique was employed to assess stereotypes of French Canadians. This technique provides a sensitive index of community-wide stereotypes as well as an individual difference measure of the extent to which such traits are attributed to the ethnic group. A factor analytic investigation suggested that community-wide stereotypes were independent of attitudinal reactions, though attitudes appeared to foster reactions not generally accepted by the community.

Résumé

Application de la méthode du différenciateur sémantique à l'évaluation des stéréotypes concernant les Canadiens français. La technique fournit un indice sensible des stéréotypes propres à une collectivité et indique également dans quelle mesure les individus attribuent certains traits au groupe ethnique concerné. L'analyse factorielle suggère que les stéréotypes propres à une collectivité sont indépendants des attitudes, quoique les attitudes semblent engendre certaines réactions partiellement acceptées par la collectivité.

References

ADORNO, T. W., FRENKEL-BRUNSWICK, ELSE, LEVINSON, D. J., and SANFORD, R. N. *The authoritarian personality*. New York: Harper & Row, 1950.

ALLPORT, G. W. *The nature of prejudice*. Cambridge, Mass.: Addison-Wesley, 1954.

BUCHANAN, W. Stereotypes and tensions as revealed by the UNESCO international poll. *Internat. soc. sci. J.*, 1951, *3*, 515-28.

DUDYCHA, G. J. The attitudes of college students toward war and the Germans before and during the Second World War. *J. soc. Psychol.*, 1942, *15*, 317-24.

GARDNER, R. C., and LAMBERT, W. E. Motivational variables in second-language acquisition. *Canad. J. Psychol.*, 1959, *13*, 266-72.

GILBERT, G. M. Stereotype persistence and change among college students. *J. abnorm. soc. Psychol.*, 1951, *46*, 245-54.

HARDING, J., KUTNER, B., PROSHANSKY, H., and CHEIN, I. Prejudice and ethnic relations. In G. LINDZEY, ed., *Handbook of social psychology*, Vol. 2, pp. 1021-61. Reading, Mass.: Addison-Wesley, 1954.

KATZ, D., and BRALY, K. W. Racial stereotypes of 100 college students. *J. abnorm. soc. Psychol.*, 1933, *28*, 280-90.

LAMBERT, W. E., GARDNER, R. C., OLTON, R., and TUNSTALL, K. A study of the roles of attitudes and motivations in second-language learning. Montreal: McGill Univer., 1961. (Mimeo).

LAMBERT, W. E., HODGSON, R. C., GARDNER, R. C., and FILLENBAUM, S. Evaluational reactions to spoken languages. *J. abnorm. soc. Psychol.*, 1960, *60*, 44-51.

LIPPMANN, W. *Public opinion*. New York: Harcourt, Brace, 1922.

MEENES, M. A comparison of racial stereotypes of 1935 and 1942. *J. soc. Psychol.*, 1943, *17*, 327-36.

OSGOOD, C. E., SUCI, G. J., and TANNENBAUM, P. H. *The measurement of meaning*. Urbana, Ill.: Univer. Illinois Press, 1957.

SEAGO, D. W. Stereotypes: before Pearl Harbor and after. *J. Psychol.*, 1947, *23*, 55-63.

SECORD, P. F., and BACKMAN, C. W. *Social psychology*. New York: McGraw-Hill, 1964.

58 / Ethnic and Party Affiliations of Candidates as Determinants of Voting

Leon J. Kamin *McMaster University*

The voter, who is confronted with a slate of candidates, bases his decision not only on relevant criteria such as party affilitation, leadership qualities, wisdom, and integrity but also on irrelevant factors including personal appearance, ethnic origin, and sex. The following article shows that, when the voter is not aware of relevant characteristics, his choice becomes highly influenced by irrelevant factors. It is also pointed out that "the ballot actually employed in Canadian parliamentary elections is of such a form as to maximize 'irrational' determinants of voting choices."

The process of electoral choice in a representative democracy ultimately confronts the voter with a ballot form presenting a number of alternative candidates among whom he must choose. The bases upon which such choices are made are an obvious concern of political theory and also a legitimate subject of psychological inquiry. Political theory tends to stress party affiliation as a rational determinant of such choices; political parties are said to represent distinctive programs of action, and the voter, by choosing the candidate of the appropriate party, expresses his preference among these programs. There are, however, many other factors which undoubtedly influence the voter's choice (e.g., 1, 2, 3).

Rationally irrelevant factors such as a candidate's personal appearance, mannerisms, and sex may influence voters in one direction or another. Another factor is perhaps of greater moment; practical politicians assert with confidence the importance of the ethnic affiliations of candidate and of voter. Voters of French descent are said to prefer candidates of French origin, voters of Jewish descent, Jewish candidates, and so on. The basis for such assertions lies largely in the analysis of actual election returns: French-speaking districts tend to return French-speaking candidates, Jewish districts Jewish candidates.

The study of such factors by analysis of actual elections suffers from inherent difficulties. Thus, if an Anglo-Saxon district traditionally returns an Anglo-Saxon Liberal, it is by no means clear whether this is because the candidate is Anglo-Saxon, is Liberal, wears a goatee, or all of these. We cannot, of course, intervene in actual elections to separate such confounded factors, but we can arrange artificial elections in such a way as to separate those factors whose effects we wish to study.

The essential technique of the present study was to approach voters in the context of a public opinion poll before an actual parliamentary election, and ask them to make a choice among fictitious candidates for a fictitious office. The personal characteristics of the "candidates" could obviously be of no influence in such a choice; hence, by varying in permutation their alleged ethnic and party affiliations, clear tests of the relative importance of these factors could be made. Although the conclusions drawn from the study are limited to the specific samples employed, the methodology may be of more general interest.

Method

The respondents' voting choices were obtained by door-to-door canvassing during May and June, 1957, before the June parliamentary election. The canvasser, carrying a cardboard "ballot box" and a sheaf of mimeographed ballot forms, asked the householder if he were a registered voter. If so, the canvasser explained that an attempt was being made to predict the outcome of the forthcoming election. The householder was asked to participate in the poll by accepting a ballot form, marking his choices, and depositing the ballot anonymously in the box. The refusal rate was very low and, in any event, has no bearing on the following analyses.

There were two separate polls, one conducted in the city of Kingston and one in the city of Cornwall. The Kingston canvasser was a native English speaker, and was instructed to avoid households with nameplates obviously suggesting French descent. The composition of the Kingston population makes it certain that very few of the respondents were ethnically French, and suggests that the majority were Scottish, English, and Irish. The Cornwall canvasser was a native French speaker, instructed to remain

[1]This research was supported by a grant form the Arts Research Committee of Queen's University, where the work was performed. Thanks are due to Messrs. J.W.S.Becker and Charles Hockman for assistance.

Reprinted, by permission, from *Canadian Journal of Psychology*, 1958, *12*, 205-212.

within a French-speaking neighbourhood. The Kingston ballots were in English, the Cornwall ballots in French. We shall refer to the respondents in the two cities as, respectively, "English" and "French."

The general form of the ballots employed is illustrated in Figure 1, which reproduces *one* of the forms used in Kingston. The ballot presents two separate contests. The first is genuine, giving the names and party affiliations of the actual candidates for parliament. The names and parties of the true candidates were never tampered with, though on some ballot forms there was no mention of political parties. The second contest, for "Federal Solicitor," is wholly fictitious. The parties attributed to the three fictitious candidates were permuted on different ballot forms. There were some ballot forms which made no mention of parties; on forms of this type the orders in which the three fictitious names appeared were permuted.

The canvasser was thus equipped with a number of different ballot forms. Within any given neighbourhood, he used the various forms in sequence as he progressed from house to house. The data analyses will be based on comparisons between different ballot forms, and for this purpose the technique assures equivalent samples for different forms. Independently of this, an attempt was made to sample geographic neighbourhoods in such a way as to be roughly representative of the entire city. The distribution of respondents' choices in the genuine contest, it may be noted, corresponded very closely to the votes later cast in the real election in the city.

The Public Opinion Centre

We are trying to predict the results of the next election. We are not interested in how you, as an individual, vote. But we would appreciate it greatly if you filled out this form and, in private, dropped it into the interviewer's box. Thank you.

If a federal election were to be held today for the following two offices, for which candidate would you vote?

FOR MEMBER OF PARLIAMENT, FROM KINGSTON:

HENDERSON, William J.	(LIBERAL)	____
KIDD, Thomas A.	(PROGRESSIVE CONSERVATIVE)	____
MILLARD, J. Allan	(C.C.F.)	____

FOR FEDERAL SOLICITOR, FROM KINGSTON:

CARTER, Stanley F.	(PROGRESSIVE CONSERVATIVE)	____
LAVOISIER, René	(LIBERAL)	____
McINTYRE, Robert H.	(C.C.F.)	____

Fig. 1. One form of the ballot employed in Kingston. Alternate forms omitted mention of political parties, rotated positions of fictitious candidates on the ballot, and permuted combinations of fictitious candidates and parties.

The Cornwall ballots were of the same general construction as the Kingston ballots, though the names of the true candidates for parliament were, of course, different. The fictitious office was termed "Conseilleur Juridique Federal." The three fictitious candidates, whose political parties and positions on the ballot were permuted, were Lucien Beaulieu, Robert H. Harris, and Rene Lavoisier. The canvasser made no attempt to obtain a representative sample of the city of Cornwall, remaining instead within a single French-speaking neighbourhood. In this neighbourhood different ballot forms were used in sequence to obtain equivalent samples.

When, as sometimes occurred, a respondent remarked that he had never heard of the office of "Federal Solicitor," or did not know the candidates, the canvassers remained non-committal. When pressed on this score – a rare occurrence – they explained that they merely worked for the polling agency, and were not familiar with details of the poll.The canvassers were instructed to give the name, address, and telephone of the experimenter to any respondent who requested a fuller explanation. The one respondent who asked for this information did not in fact contact the experimenter.

Within Kingston, it was assumed, the names Carter and McIntyre would be categorized as English, and the name Lavoisier as French. Within Cornwall, the names of Beaulieu and Lavoisier should be categorized as French, and Harris as English. The analyses will focus especially on votes for the odd, "contra-ethnic" candidate.

Results

The Kingston sample included six hundred individuals whose ballot forms made no mention of political parties. Thus, in the fictitious contest, any deviation of the choices of these respondents from a chance distribution must be attributed either to the names of the candidates or to the order in which the names appeared. To separate these possibilities the three names were presented equally often in each of the six possible permutations.

The first point of interest is that 241 (40) per cent) of these respondents, all of whom had indicated a choice in the true parliamentary contest, failed to vote in the fictitious contest. The following analysis is thus based on the 359 respondents who did vote. Table I indicates, in terms of both number and percentage of votes, the division of votes among the three candidates, with position on the ballot counterbalanced. There are, clearly, systematic preferences among the three fictitious names. The deviation of the votes from an even three-way division was assessed by chi-square. The chi-square, with 2 df, is 82.12, p much less than .001. The Lavoisier vote, as expected, is by far the smallest, however, when McIntyre and Carter alone are considered, McIntyre is selected insignificantly more often ($p < .01$).

Table I – Distribution of votes in Kingston sample with no parties on ballot

	Total vote	Percentage
Candidate		
Carter, Stanley F.	133	37.0
Lavoisier, Rene	44	12.3
McIntyre, Robert H.	182	50.7
Ballot position		
First	152	42.3
Second	128	35.7
Third	79	22.0

Table I also indicates, for the same respondents, the division of votes among the three ballot positions, with names of candidates counterbalanced. There is a marked effect of position on the ballot. The chi-square, assuming the theoretical model of an even three-way split among positions, is 23.33, with 2 df, $p < .001$. The main effect is a severe depression of the third ballot position, the difference between the first two positions alone falling short of significance.

The ballots of this sample had been so marked as to permit identification of the sex of the respondent. Analysis revealed no significant differences whatever between sexes as to preferences for names or for ballot positions.

There was an additional Kingston sample of three hundred whose ballots assigned political parties to each of the fictitious candidates. There were forty-three respondents (14 per cent) who failed to vote. Thus, in Kingston, more respondents vote in a fictitious election if candidates are assigned parties than if not ($p < .001$). The question of major interest, however, is whether systematic differences among candidates' names still occur when candidates are assigned parties. The critical candidate for analytic purposes is Lavoisier, who appeared on one hundred ballots as a Liberal, on one hundred as a Progressive Conservative, and on one hundred as a C.C.F. candidate, with ballot position held constant.

Table II presents, first, the proportion of votes for and against the Progressive Conservatives, both when Lavoisier is the Conservative candidate and when he is not. These proportions, submitted to a chi-square test, do not differ significantly. The table also indicates the proportion of votes for and against the Liberals, both when Lavoisier is the Liberal candidate and when he is not. These proportions do not differ significantly. These analyses indicate that the classifications by party and by candidate's name are independent. That is, the proportion of votes cast for a party is not significantly affected by the name of the party's candidate. This despite the fact that, in the absence of a party label, a clear order of preference exists among the names.

Table II – Analysis of votes of Kingston sample with parties on ballot

	Total vote		Percentage	
P.C. Candidate	For P.C.	Against P.C.	For P.C.	Against P.C.
Lavoisier	44	36	55.0	45.0
Carter or McIntyre	87	90	49.1	50.9
Liberal Candidate	For Libs.	Against Libs.	For Libs.	Against Libs.
Lavoisier	37	51	42.0	58.0
Carter or McIntyre	82	87	48.5	51.5

The C.C.F vote in the sample was so small (2 per cent) as to make an analysis for this party impossible. Parenthetically it may be noted that, in terms of votes for the genuine parliamentary contest, there were no significant differences among the various sub-samples to which different ballot forms were distributed.

In the French sample, in Cornwall, 126 people were given ballots which made no mention of parties. There were eighteen failures to vote in the fictitious contest (13 per cent). This percentage is smaller than that in Kingston, but no attempt was made to match the samples for socio-economic status or other variables. Table III indicates, for this sample, the distribution of votes among the candidates, with position on the ballot counterbalanced. There exists, as in Kingston, a systematic preference: the chi-square, with 2 df, is 54.06, $p < .001$. While Harris, as expected, polls the lowest vote, Lavoisier does not do significantly better; Beaulieu is by far the preferred candidate. Table III also indicates a significant effect of position on the ballot in Cornwall, similar to that in Kingston. The third position is significantly depressed; the chi-square, with 2 df, is 6.22, $p < .05$.

Table III – Distribution of votes in Cornwall sample with no parties on ballot

	Total vote	Percentage
Candidate		
Beaulieu, Lucien	72	66.7
Harris, Robert H.	17	15.7
Lavoisier, Rene	19	17.6
Ballot position		
First	40	37.0
Second	44	40.9
Third	24	22.2

There was an additional Cornwall sample of sixty-eight whose ballots assigned parties to the fictitious candidates. There were eleven failures to vote (16 per cent). This percentage does not differ significantly from the equivalent Kingston sample, or from

TABLE IV – Analysis of votes of Cornwall sample with parties on ballot

	Total vote		Percentage	
P.C. Candidate	For P.C.	Against P.C.	For P.C.	Against P.C.
Harris	0	19	0.0	100.0
Beaulieu or Lavoisier	5	33	13.2	86.8
Liberal candidate	For Libs.	Against Libs.	For Libs.	Against Libs.
Harris	14	3	82.4	17.6
Beaulieu or Lavoisier	37	3	92.5	7.5

the party-less Cornwall sample. Table IV presents, first, the proportion of votes for and against the Progressive Conservatives, both when Harris (now the critical candidate) is the Conservative candidate and when he is not. These proportions, submitted (because of the small *N* in some cells) to Fisher's exact test (4), do not differ significantly. The table also presents the proportion of votes for and against the Liberals when Harris is and is not the Liberal candidate; again, by Fisher's exact test, there is no significant difference between these proportions. There was only one C.C.F. vote in this sample, precluding any analysis. Thus, as with the English Kingston sample, the proportion of votes cast for a party is not affected by the name of the party's candidate, despite a marked preference among the names presented without parties.

Discussion

The over-all results of the study are clear. With both English and French samples, when respondents are requested to choose among fictitious candidates for a fictitious office, they are markedly influenced both by the candidates' names and by the order in which the names appear on the ballot. Within each ethnic group, a name with ethnic connotations opposite to the respondents' is under-chosen, as is the last name in a three-person list. When, however, the same names are presented but associated with political parties, both the English and French groups are guided by party identification of the candidate, and name as such cannot be demonstrated to have a significant effect.

The precise significance of the preference orders among names is difficult to specify. Although it does not seem surprising that Lavoisier fares poorly among the English, and Harris among the French, the preferences of the English for McIntyre over Carter and of the French for Beaulieu over Lavoisier were not expected. With hindsight, it seems reasonable to assume that Lavoisier, unlike Beaulieu, is not truly a *canadien* name; indeed, a few French respondents overtly remarked that, knowing none of the candidates, the "might as well vote for a *canadien*, Beaulieu." The English respondents volunteered no bases for their choices.

The candidates' names differ, of course, in terms of sheer familiarity to the respondents, as well as with regard to ethnic connotations. Although it is difficult to separate ethnic value and familiarity, it seems worthwhile to stress that there is no reason to equate preference orders among the names with ethnic *prejudice*. The vote distribution does not indicate an active rejection of opposite ethnic groups any more than it indicates an active "prejudice" against the third ballot position. Psychologically, these data are reminiscent of experimental studies of perception; the importance of minimal, irrelevant cues is exaggerated when the normally determining cues are deliberately excluded.

The results of this study are limited by the nature of the samples and conditions employed. Whether similar results would obtain in cities of different cultural composition, for other ethnic groups, in provincial and municipal elections, and so on, is an open question. The technique employed in this study, however, seems capable of answering many such questions, and may be of value both to social scientists and to practical politicians.

We should note, finally, that the ballot actually employed in Canadian parliamentary elections is of such a form as to maximize "irrational" determinants of voting choice. The ballot does not indicate the party affiliations of candidates, nor is position on the ballot counterbalanced. These, of course, are the conditions which maximize "ethnic voting" and the position effect. The present data, taken in conjunction with the political theory on which democracy rests, could support strong arguments for the inclusion of party affiliation on the ballot, and for counterbalancing of positions.

Summary

Within the context of a public opinion poll before a genuine parliamentary election, English- and French-speaking respondents were asked to choose among three fictitious candidates for a fictitious office. The candidates' names were varied with regard to ethnic connotations and to position on the ballot. Within both English and French groups there were marked tendencies to under-choose candidates whose names had "alien" ethnic connotations, or who appeared last on the ballot. When, however, with new samples, the same names were permuted with political parties, both English and French samples were guided by the candidates' party affiliations; name had no significant effect.

References

1. Bain, H. M., and Hecock, D. S. *Ballot position and voter's choice*. Detroit: Wayne State Univer. Press, 1957.
2. Campbell, A., and Cooper, H. C. *Group differences in attitudes and votes*. Ann Arbor: Survey Research Center, 1956.
3. Lazarsfeld, P. F., Berelson, B., and Gaudet, Hazel. *The people's choice*. New York: Columbia Univer. Press, 1948.
4. Siegel, S. *Nonparametric statistics for the behavioural sciences*. New York: McGraw-Hill, 1956.

59 / Anti-Semitism, Stress, and Anchor Effects on Interpersonal Judgements[1]

Donald Fischer and Brendan G. Rule *University of Alberta*

A prejudiced person displays a firmly fixed attitude of disapproval towards members of a particular racial, ethnic, or cultural group. One problem which has interested psychologists is how a prejudiced person reacts under stress, since it is under stress that most of the undesirable consequences of prejudice occur. In this experiment, individuals who varied in anti-semitism made judgements of neutral bystanders after being subjected to stress and either favourable or unfavourable ratings of themselves. Responses of moderately prejudiced subjects differed from those of either highly prejudiced or slightly prejudiced subjects.

The scapegoat theory of prejudice has received considerable experimental attention in the last decade. One particular focus of interest has been with delineating differences in hostility displacement by high- and low-prejudiced persons. In a series of studies, Berkowitz (1959, 1960, 1961) has reported that prejudiced individuals manifest different judgemental processes under stress than do their less-prejudiced peers. These studies indicated that under stress highly prejudiced individuals exhibit assimilation effects or make gross discriminations among stimuli, whereas low-prejudiced individuals exhibit contrast effects or make finer discriminations among stimuli. With respect to the kinds of judgements made, the highly prejudiced persons typically displayed assimilation effects by displacing hostility onto neutral bystanders. In other words, peers were included into the same category as an annoying experimenter, and hostility aroused by the latter was generalized to the former. In this case, the annoying experimenter served as a negative judgemental anchor.

However, when Berkowitz (1961) attempted to demonstrate the generality of his notions about the judgemental process of the high- and low-prejudiced persons by introducing a positive anchor, only partial confirmation of his hypotheses was obtained. Since his findings are ambiguous and restrict a judgemental process explanation for the behaviour of prejudiced persons, one purpose of the present study was to investigate the relevance of the anchor variable in an interpersonal situation rather than in the nonpersonal situation that characterized Berkowitz' study.

Furthermore, a very basic issue pertaining to displacement phenomena is whether high- and low-prejudiced groups do in fact differ from each other in the nature of their judgements. Recently, Rule (1966) found that judgemental effects for the high- and low-prejudiced individuals did not differ from each other but did differ from the moderately prejudiced persons. The extremists were more negative towards neutral strangers following stress than were the moderately prejudiced persons. The present study was designed also to provide further support for and extend Rule's findings regarding similarity of extremists' behaviour.

The discrepancy between Rule's and Berkowitz' findings was explained by differences in subject-selection criteria. Rule suggested that her moderately prejudiced group was comparable to Berkowitz' low-prejudiced group. Accounting for the inconsistency in findings in this way, it was possible to elaborate expectations consistent with both Berkowitz' and Rule's theoretical positions. It was expected that following stress high- and low-prejudiced persons would manifest similar judgemental processes, but would differ from moderately prejudiced persons. The extremists were expected to exhibit assimilation effects, and the moderately prejudiced persons were expected to exhibit contrast effects in judgements of neutral bystanders. According to Berkowitz' rationale, assimilation to a negative anchor should result in increased hostility, whereas assimilation to a positive anchor should result in increased favourability. Contrast to a negative anchor should be apparent in increased favourability, whereas contrast to a positive anchor should be apparent in increased hostility.

Method

Subjects

Subjects were 96 introductory psychology students

[1]From Fischer, D., and Rule, Brendan G. Anti-semitism, stress, and anchor effects on interpersonal judgements. *J. pers. soc. Psychol.*, 1967, *6*, 447-450.

[1]This paper is based in part on a master's thesis submitted to the University of Alberta by Donald Fischer. Portions of this research were reported in a paper read at the 1966 Canadian Psychological Association meeting.

who participated to meet course requirements. These subjects were selected from a pool of 639 students who had completed a questionnaire which included the 10-item Anti-Semitism and the 28-item F scales (Adorno, Frenkel-Brunswik, Levinson, & Sanford, 1950). For both scales item scores varied from 5 points for a response indicating strong agreement with an item to 1 point for a response indicating strong disagreement.

Median scores for subjects categorized as highly prejudiced, moderately prejudiced, and low prejudiced were Anti-Semitism, 29, F, 92; Anti-Semitism, 21, F, 82; Anti-Semitism, 14, F, 65, respectively.

Procedure

Subjects were run in 24 groups of 4 each. The groups were homogeneous with respect to sex and level of prejudice. Subjects were greeted and briefly introduced to each other. Each subject stated his or her name. No more communication was permitted. While subjects were in view of one another, the experimenter indicated seating arrangements. Subjects were then seated in cubicles which restricted their range of observation.

Subjects were told that there were two parts to the study. One task was to work out problems, the other was to provide information about first impressions of people. At the beginning of the session, subjects were given a rating scale consisting of a list of 13 bipolar adjectives. Each subject was asked to complete an evaluation of the person on his immediate right, with the exception of the person seated in the most extreme right cubicle who evaluated the person seated in the most extreme left cubicle. The experimenter collected these ratings ostensibly for distribution to the person rated, but in fact distributed substituted ratings which were either favourable or unfavourable. It was assumed that receiving an unfavourable evaluation of oneself from a peer would induce a negative anchor and receiving a favourable evaluation would induce a positive anchor. This procedure constituted manipulation of the anchor variable.

Subjects were then asked to solve a list of 13 difficult anagrams within an 18-minute period. The anagrams corresponded to the problems used by Sarason (1961). High- and low-stress induction was accomplished by instructions. High-stress instructions indicated that the performance on the task was directly related to intelligence and that high school students of above-average intelligence (IQ greater than 100) were able to successfully complete the task. Low-stress instructions indicated that the anagrams were difficult, and completion of all the anagrams was unlikely.

Subjects were given two rating scales identical to the one they had previously used and were asked to make successive judgements of the persons on their right and second from their left. It was intended that these ratings would depend only on the characteristics perceived during the subjects' brief introduction at the beginning of the session. Before leaving the experimental room, subjects were informed of the true nature of the experiment and asked to maintain secrecy until the completion of the experiment in about 1 month's time.

Results

To assess any possible differences between experimental groups in ability to solve anagrams, the mean number of anagrams correctly solved was examined. Results from an analysis of variance provided no evidence that high-, medium-, and low-prejudiced subjects differed in the number of correct solutions with 18 minutes time ($F = 2.34$, $df = 2/84$).

Evaluations given by the high-, medium-, and low-anti-Semitic subjects were examined. Data consisted of total scores over the 13 adjective scales for each of the two people described. Low scores indicated a favorable evaluation and high scores, an unfavorable evaluation. Data were analyzed using a 3 x 2 x 2 x 2 analysis of variance, split-split plot design. There were 3 levels of prejudice, 2 levels of stress, 2 levels of anchor, and 2 persons rated.

Results of the analysis indicated the following relationships. More negative ratings followed a negative anchor than a positive one ($F = 15.95$, $df = 1/84, p < .01$). The means were 3.16 and 2.67 for the negative and positive anchors, respectively. This indicates that the anchor manipulation was successful.

More hostility was expressed toward the first person evaluated than toward the second person ($F = 7.86$, $df = 1/85$, $p < .01$). The means were 3.07 and 2.82, respectively.

The high- and low-prejudiced persons were more favourable than the moderately prejudiced persons under mild stress, whereas the moderately prejudiced persons were more favourable than the extremists under severe stress ($F = 5.86$, $df = 2/84$, $p < .01$). Table I indicates the means for this interaction.

Prejudice, anchor, and person evaluated significantly interacted ($F = 4.31$, $df = 2/85$, $p < .01$). With respect to the first person evaluated, high- and low-prejudiced individuals increased in unfavourable evaluations as stress increased from mild to severe following a negative anchor and decreased in unfavourable evaluations following a positive anchor; the moderately prejudiced persons decreased in unfavourable evaluations as stress increased following both the positive and negative anchor. Thus, high- and low-prejudiced persons exhibited an assimilation to the anchor effect under stress, while the moderately prejudiced persons exhibited a contrast effect following the negative anchor and an assimilation effect only following the positive anchor.

With respect to the second person rated, as stress increased high- and low-prejudiced persons increased in unfavourable evaluations following a positive anchor, but the high-prejudiced individuals decreased in unfavourable evaluations following a negative anchor, and the low-prejudiced subjects increased in unfavourable ratings following the negative anchor. The moderately prejudiced invididuals decreased in negativity following both the positive and negative anchor as stress increased. Table II contains the mean evaluation scores for the conditions of this interaction. No other main effects or interactions were significant.

Discussion

Data supported Rule's findings that under stress extremely high- and extremely low-prejudiced persons are similar in their evaluations of other people, whereas the moderately prejudiced persons differ in reactions from the extremists. These findings lend further support to Rokeach's (1960) notion that the conceptual systems of extremists are similar. As previously suggested, it appears that as in Rule's study the high- and moderately prejudiced groups in this study compare to Berkowitz' high- and low-prejudiced groups, respectively. It is evident that a large number of subjects must be sampled to adequately specify the categories of high-, moderate-, and low-prejudiced persons.

Table I – Mean evaluation scores for the high-, moderate-, and low-prejudiced groups following mild and severe stress

Level of prejudice	Mild stress	Severe stress
Low	2.56	2.87
Moderate	3.36	2.76
High	2.98	2.96

Consistent with expectations, the results also indicated that stress served to broaden the categories of the high- and low-prejudiced persons so that more unfavourable evaluations were generalized to the first person described when a negative anchor was provided and more favourable evaluations were generalized when a positive anchor was provided. While the dependence of the high-prejudiced authoritarian individual on the external environment has long been recognized (Adorno *et al.*, 1950), this study demonstrated a similar dependence on external sources by the low-prejudiced person. These data also demonstrated that consistent judgemental effects operate for positive as well as negative stimuli. The implication for extremists is that, at least for the first person responded to, the effects of stress can be channeled into a favourable or unfavourable direction depending on the anchor stimuli provided in a particular situation.

Results regarding the second person evaluated did not form a consistent pattern. It appeared that the occurrence of the first evaluation altered the stimulus situation for the second evaluation. Since more negativity was expressed towards the first person rated, it is clear that hostility was reduced on the second rating. This could be accounted for in terms of catharsis, that is, a reduction in the instigation to hostility or in terms of aggression-anxiety – guilt or

Table II – Mean evaluation scores

Level of prejudice	1st person rated			
	Positive anchor		Negative anchor	
	Mild stress	Severe stress	Mild stress	Severe stress
Low	2.88	2.73	2.53	3.15
Moderate	3.21	2.48	3.62	3.23
High	2.91	2.61	3.25	3.50
Level of prejudice	**2nd person rated**			
	Positive anchor		Negative anchor	
	Mild stress	Severe stress	Mild stress	Severe stress
Low	2.30	2.79	2.53	2.80
Moderate	2.85	2.30	3.76	3.00
High	2.39	2.55	3.38	3.16

anxiety arousal which inhibited the expression of further hostility. Regardless of the mechanism involved in the hostility reduction, the conditions necessary to produce the expected judgemental effects in terms of assimilation and contrast did not appear to be present.

Of particular interest is the reaction of the moderately prejudiced person in terms of the nature of his judgements. The medium-prejudiced subjects reacted to increased stress with increased friendliness regardless of the anchor stimuli or persons evaluated. Stress seemed to establish a set to respond favourably regardless of other situational factors. The moderately prejudiced person appeared to respond more to internal evaluational cues rather than to external situational cues as did the extremists.

Abstract

Personality and situational factors related to evaluations of neutral bystanders following stress were investigated by varying prejudice, stress, anchor stimuli, and persons evaluated. Data indicated the following results: (a) Unfavourable evaluations were greater following a negative-anchor than following a positive-anchor condition; (b) more unfavourable evaluations were expressed toward the 1st person evaluated than toward the 2nd; (c) high- and low-prejudiced individuals were more favourable than were moderates towards others under mild stress, whereas the moderately prejudiced individuals were more favourable than the extremists under severe stress; (d) prejudice, stress, anchor, and the persons rated significantly interacted. Results supported the notion that the judgements of the high- and low-prejudiced persons are similar, while the moderately prejudiced individual differs from extremists in judgements. Furthermore, for the 1st person rated, an assimilation-contrast interpretation of the data partially confirmed Berkowitz' theoretical notions about judgemental effects in personality functioning.

References

ADORNO, T. W., FRENKEL-BRUNSWIK, E., LEVINSON, D. J., and SANFORD, R. N. *The authoritarian personality.* New York: Harper, 1950.

BERKOWITZ, L. Anti-Semitism and the displacement of aggression. *Journal of Abnormal and Social Psychology,* 1959, *59,* 182-187.

———. Judgemental processes in personality functioning. *Psychological Review,* 1960, *67,* 130-142.

———. Anti-Semitism, judgemental processes, and displacement of hostility. *Journal of Abnormal and Social Psychology,* 1961, *62,* 210-215.

ROKEACH, M. *The open and closed mind.* New York: Basic Books, 1960.

RULE, B. G. Anti-Semitism, stress, and judgements of strangers. *Journal of Personality and Social Psychology,* 1966, *3,* 132-134.

SARASON, J. G. The effects of anxiety and threat on the solution of a difficult task. *Journal of Abnormal and Social Psychology,* 1961, *62,* 165-168.

60 / Attitudes Towards Immigrants in a Canadian Community

Frank E. Jones and Wallace E. Lambert *McMaster University and McGill University*

The prefatory note for this article contained the following: "The displacement and migration of people has been a significant feature of the post-World War II world. The social relationships of immigrants in the communities in which they are settled present problems of extraordinary importance to social scientists as well as to community leaders. Here is a study of a town in Canada and its relationships with its recent immigrants."

Approximately one in nine persons in Canada is a postwar immigrant. As a result, the public is very much interested in immigrants and immigration policy. The complexity of the reactions to the current situation prompted us to undertake research that would allow description and analysis of the attitudes of native Canadians toward immigrants.[1]

We chose for the survey a town of 12,000 which had received a large number of immigrants after the war, chiefly from Holland and Germany. As the native population of the town was primarily of British origin, we observed a situation in which there would be little variation in the ethnic background of our subjects and little variation in the ethnic background of the immigrants. Because the town was small, the natives would be more likely to be aware of the immigrants than in a larger city.

While this research is directly relevant to the adjustment of immigrants and to their immigration into the community, it also provides a formulation of the relation of attitudes to certain basic characteristics of social systems which has broader applicability.

Theoretical Orientation

Previous studies of immigrants have emphasized the importance of the behaviour of the host population to immigrant adjustment or assimilation. Infeld regards the attitudes of native Americans as a main factor in the differential assimilation of his sample of German and Polish immigrants.[2] Taft has proposed that "the effect of social interaction becomes of greatest importance in assimilation,"[3] a view supported by Richardson in his theoretical statement on assimilation,[4] and in his report that the frequency of social participation between immigrants and natives is positively associated with assimilation.[5] Warner and Srole include frequency and kind of participation as major criteria for their Scale of Subordination and Assimilation.[6]

Our interest was consistent with the viewpoint expressed in the studies cited but we felt that it was worthwhile to direct attention to the relation between the attitudes toward immigrants held by the native population and the extent and kind of social participation these natives shared with immigrants. We took the view that a person's attitudes toward immigrants may be expected to vary in relation to the situation in which he interacts with immigrants.

Although several sets of questionnaire items previously employed in prejudice studies might have been used to measure attitudes toward immigrants, none of these satisfied the requirements made by our approach to the problem. The attitude schedule which we developed consisted of fifty-nine items constructed on the basis of Parsons' theory of social systems.[7] Item analysis[8] reduced to twenty-nine the

1See William Peterson, *Planned Migration: The Social Determinants of the Dutch-Canadian Movement*, Berkeley, Calif., University of California Press, 1955, Chaps. VI and VII, for a concise statement of the assumptions and group pressures which influence Canadian immigration policy.

2H.Infeld, The Aged in the Process of Ethnic Assimilation, *Sociometry*, 1940, *3*, 353-365.

3Ronald Taft, "The Shared Frame of Reference Concept Applied to the Assimilation of Immigrants," *Human Relations*, 1953, *6*, 45-55.

Reprinted, by permission of the authors and Columbia University Press, from *Public Opinion Quarterly*, 1959, *23*, 537-546.

4Alan Richardson, The Assimilation of British Immigrants in Australia, *Human Relations*, 1957, *10*, 157-166.

5Alan Richardson, Some Psycho-social Characteristics of Satisfied and Dissatisfied British Immigrant Skilled Manual Workers in Western Australia, *Human Relations*, 1957, *10*, 235-248.

6W.Lloyd Warner and Leo Srole, *The Social System of American Ethnic Groups*, New Haven, Yale University Press, 1945, pp. 288-289.

7Talcott Parsons, *The Social System*, Glencoe, Ill., Free Press, 1951; Talcott Parsons, Robert F.Bales, and Edward A.Shils, *Working Papers in the Theory of Action*, Glencoe, Ill., Free Press, 1952, Chaps. 3 and 5; Morris Zelditch Jr., A Note on the Analysis of Equilibrium Systems, Appendix B in Talcott Parsons and Robert F.Bales, *Family, Socialization, and Interaction Process*, Glencoe, Ill., Free Press, 1955.

8We used a procedure developed for this study by Professor George A. Ferguson, McGill University, whose generous assistance is gratefully acknowledged. A correlation coefficient, measuring the relation between responses to a specific item and the subjects' total scores, greater or equal to .50, and a variance, measuring variation in the distribution of responses in the five response categories of the item greater or equal to .90, were the arbitrary criteria for selection.

number of items with strong discriminatory power, and these provide the basis of our present analysis.[9] Preliminary study indicates support for our theoretically derived expectation that attitudes toward immigrants would vary in terms of the *functional dimensions* of social systems and in terms of the various *spheres of co-operative activity* in which immigrants and natives participated.[10] In this paper, however, we wish to present the results of an initial analysis in which variations in attitude were measured simply in terms of the subjects' total scores on the twenty-nine items, and in which attention is directed to the relation between (1) variations in attitude and certain personal characteristics of the subjects; and (2) variations in attitude and certain properties of the systems of social interaction in which natives and immigrants participated.

Validity of the Attitude Items

Usually acceptable evidence for the validity of attitude items consists in demonstrating that respondents, known through other measures of their behaviour to be favourable (or unfavourable) toward some object or event, are found to reveal favourable (or unfavourable) attitudes to the same object or event as measured by a set of items. A satisfactory procedure for validating our attitude items would be to have qualified judges observe and classify as favourable or unfavourable native Canadians who are in actual interaction with immigrants and then administer the questionnaire to the native Canadians. Plans to undertake this validation procedure in an industrial setting had, unfortunately, to be abandoned for reasons beyond our control. We can report, however, certain findings which suggest that our confidence in the attitude items is justified.

To our question, "In contrast to other Canadian communities, my community has received: too few immigrants, about the right number, or too many immigrants," 59 of the 78 respondents with favourable attitude scores on the Social System Items chose the first two categories as compared to 21 of the 79 with unfavourable attitude scores. This difference is statistically significant beyond the .001 level.[11]

Respondents who gave favourable responses to SSI reported more voluntary and active contacts with immigrants (34 such contacts as compared to 14 reported by those giving unfavourable responses), and more voluntary but passive contacts (52 as compared to 42), while those with unfavourable attitude scores on SSI have disproportionately more involuntary contacts (62 as compared to 53) with immigrants. Over all, these differences are statistically significant at approximately the .03 level.

Respondents who gave favourable responses to SSI judge more of their contacts with immigrants to be beneficial, while those with unfavourable attitude scores evaluate contacts with immigrants more often as a hindrance. The difference in the distributions of judgement of reported contacts is statistically significant beyond the .001 level.

Of 144 contacts with immigrants reported by respondents with favourable scores on SSI, 99 were judged to be enjoyable and 40 as unpleasant or a matter of indifference, while those with unfavourable attitude scores, reporting 124 contacts, judged 41 to be enjoyable and 80 as unpleasant or a matter of indifference (judgements on 8 contacts are lacking). The difference is statistically significant beyond the .001 level.

In summary, those respondents who score favourably on the questionnaire in contrast to the unfavourable scorers, do not feel that there are too many immigrants in their community, have more voluntary contacts with immigrants, more often see their contacts with immigrants as beneficial, and enjoy their contacts with immigrants. In short, the subjects' responses to SSI were consistent with their judgements and actions relative to immigrants.

Analysis revealed a high association between favourable wording of items and favourable responses and between unfavourable wording and unfavourable responses. However, the favourable-unfavourable split of 33-26 for the 59 items used in the original questionnaire and the 15-14 split for the 29 items finally selected for analysis provided an adequate safeguard against wording bias. As it seemed possible the subjects might find the questionnaire long, we took precautions to test for subject fatigue, but statistical analysis revealed that the order of item presentation did not influence results.

Samples and Field Procedure

The data were obtained from two probability samples[12] which will be referred to as Sample D, consisting of persons normally at home during the day, and Sample N, consisting of persons normally *not* at home during the day. In addition to the

[9]We shall refer to these items as the Social System Items, abbreviated as SSI. An example of one of the questionnaire items is: In social clubs to which Canadians and immigrants belong, the immigrants should have the same chance as Canadians to hold responsible positions. 1. Strongly agree, 2. Agree, 3. Undecided, 4. Disagree, 5. Strongly disagree.

[10]In this study, social system dimensions were: goals, means, status, and solidarity; the spheres of activity were: work, neighbourhood, social-recreational, commercial, family, religious, and educational. The theoretical rationale and the attitude questionnaire developed for this study will be published at a later date. See also, Frank E.Jones, A Sociological Perspective on Immigrant Adjustment, *Social Forces*, October, 1956, *35*, 39-47.

[11]Space limitations, unfortunately, preclude presentation of our data in tabular form. Mimeographed copies of the tables may be obtained from the authors.

[12]City blocks drawn at random from a complete listing, and systematic sampling from a random start within blocks in proportion to block population density, were the main features of the selection procedure. Where there was more than one eligible subject in a selected household, one was chosen on a random basis. No substitutions were permitted if the relevant household yielded no eligible subject.

We gratefully acknowledge assistance from the Dominion Bureau of Statistics, Ottawa, especially from Mr. Douglas Dale, in the design of the sample.

restriction concerning presence at home, each subject had to be Canadian-born or a naturalized Canadian citizen with fifteen years' residence in Canada. Sample D was composed primarily of housewives, although a few retired males and night-shift male workers were included. Sample N consisted primarily of married working males, although a few working females were included. The two samples yielded 157 subjects.

Collection of the data, undertaken by four interviewers[13] who resided in the community during the field period, required two weeks. The interview procedure required the interviewer to read each attitude item to the subject and to check the response on the schedule (the subject was provided with a copy of the schedule so that he could follow the oral presentation of the items) and, on completion of the attitude schedule, to obtain information, as directed by two additional schedules, concerning certain personal characteristics of the subject and the nature of his social contacts with immigrants. Approximately one hour was required to complete an interview. Most subjects readily agreed to be interviewed and showed a strong interest in the topic, usually volunteering opinions as well as responding to the prepared items.

Attitude Direction and Personal Characteristics

Although we collected information on certain personal characteristics of our subjects, such as age and education, we had no adequate theoretical basis for predicting association between variations in attitudes toward immigrants and such variables, except those which serve as indices of social class level. We regarded such analysis, therefore, as a sheerly empirical venture which might yield some useful findings. In this paper, we wish simply to summarize these results.

A clear difference in attitude direction[14] occurred between Sample D, which showed 49.8 per cent of responses to all 29 items as favourable, and Sample N, which showed 61.1 per cent favourable, a difference significant beyond the .001 level.[15] Sample N subjects were found to be consistently more favourable than Sample D subjects when the items were ordered in terms of social system dimensions and in terms of spheres of activity, the differences in percentages favourable being significant at or beyond the .02 level in one instance and at or beyond the 0.1 level in seven of the thirteen possible instances.

We can only speculate about the reasons for the difference between the samples. It is reasonable to suggest that housewives, since they report fewer contacts with immigrants, are simply fearful of the unknown, but separate analysis of each sample reveals no significant association between contact or lack of contact and attitude direction. The role of the housewife may restrict the range of activities of many women and be experienced as frustrating, possibly generating general hostility that in some circumstances can be directed against immigrants. Furthermore, since the wife is primarily dependent for her social-class position on her husband's occupational success, her relative incapacity to control her own destiny may be a source of stress which sharpens apprehensiveness toward her husband's possible occupational competitors. Unfortunately, we have no data to test such explanations.

Whatever the reason for the difference between the samples, separate analysis was clearly advisable, and the remaining findings will be reported separately for each sample.

The analysis showed little association between personal characteristics and attitude direction in either sample.[16] No association was found between attitudes toward immigrants and the subject's religious affiliation, ethnic origin, or length of residence in the community. No significant association was found between attitudes and the subject's age, sex, or marital status, although the data suggested a tendency for favourable attitudes to be associated with younger age groups, with married subjects, and with males.

A subject's level of education, occupation, and income were regarded as indices of social-class membership and, as we held that immigrants tend to enter a social system at its lower-class levels and are therefore a greater competitive threat to native members of such classes than to native members of higher social classes, we predicted a positive relation between attitude direction and social class. The data support our prediction, as significant associations between education,[17], occupation,[18] and income[19] were obtained.

Attitude Direction and Social Interaction

We assumed no necessary relation between attitude direction and the presence or absence of social contacts with immigrants in the sense that contacts nec-

[13] Professor Douglas Pullman, University of New Brunswick, Mr. G.A.Mendel, Ottawa, and the authors.

[14] "Attitude direction" is a term we shall use to refer to the assumed capacity of attitudes to vary from favourable to unfavourable. We recognize that in our analysis we may simply be reporting on variations in degrees of favourableness or unfavourableness, since we used no special technique, such as Guttman's intensity function (see S. A. Stouffer *et al., Measurement and Prediction,* Princeton, N.J., Princeton University Press, 1950, Chap. 7), to attempt to determine a zero point for each item.

[15] Unless otherwise stated, chi square was used to test for association between the frequencies of the various distributions. Miss Mildred Schwartz and Mr. Claude Doré, Ottawa, contributed materially to the research by undertaking the actual calculations.

[16] To analyze the attitude data, the distribution of scores for each sample was divided at the quartile points, which yielded four equal-sized groups of subjects ranked from most to least favourable.

[17] A marked trend in Sample D but not statistically significant; significant at the .03 level for Sample N.

[18] No association for housewives categorized in terms of husband's occupation; significant beyond the .01 level for Sample N.

[19] Significant beyond the .05 level for Sample D; beyond the .01 level for Sample N.

essarily generate positive or negative sentiments. It seemed more fruitful to think of social contacts between native Canadians and immigrants as occurring within systems of interaction and to analyze the attitude data in terms of selected properties of systems of interaction. We could not observe such systems directly, but with such analysis in mind we obtained from each subject information about the frequency of interaction, the number of spheres of activity in which interaction occurred, the subjects position in such interaction systems, and the rewards accruing from participation in such systems. Our prediction regarding the relation between attitude direction and the presence or absence of social contacts is supported by the data; they indicate that there is no association between absence of social contacts and attitude direction, although if contact has occurred there is a positive association, significant at the .02 level in Sample N, between attitude direction and the number of spheres of activity involved.

Frequency of interaction.

Our theoretical viewpoint led us to predict associations between certain characteristics of interaction systems and attitude direction, but among such characteristics of interaction we did not assume a necessary relation between frequency of interaction and attitude direction. As it is reasonable to expect persons to develop either positive or negative feelings toward one another with increased frequency of interaction, we predicted no association between these two variables. The data support our reasoning, as there is no statistically significant association in either sample, although there is a tendency for subjects reporting less frequent interaction with immigrants to have more favourable attitudes than subjects reporting more frequent interaction.

Spheres of activity and interaction.

We hold that the structures of interaction systems largely determine the actor's control of both frequency and initiation of interaction and that such control will be closely associated with each actor's attitudes to others in the system. In brief, we hypothesize a relation between the structure of interaction systems and attitude direction and specify the actor's control of the frequency and the initiation of interaction as two possible intervening variables.[20]

Data relevant to the control of interaction include information about the spheres of activity where interaction occurs, the relative positions of the subject and the immigrants with whom he interacts, the subject's evaluation of the numbers of immigrants in such interaction systems, and the subject's pattern of initiating actions. Analyses of these data, to be discussed separately below, provide a measure of support for our general hypothesis.

Among the interaction systems in the six spheres of activity for which information was obtained, the *work* sphere could be assumed to permit the individual the least control of interaction, while the neighbourhood, club, church, and school spheres of activity, in varying degree, permit the actor a greater control over his pattern of interaction and the conditions under which he interacts with others. To predict an association between attitude direction and participation in these various systems required knowledge of the actor's personal control of interaction for each sphere of activity that we did not possess, but we felt safe in predicting an association between unfavourable attitudes and interaction occurring in the work sphere, where personal control was assumed to be lowest. Analysis reveals that Sample D subjects with unfavourable attitudes have disproportionately more interaction in the work sphere, while subjects with favourable attitudes have disproportionately more interaction in the club sphere. Sample N subjects reveal a similar association between the work sphere and unfavourable attitudes, while favourable attitudes are associated with neighbourhood, business, and club spheres of activity. No statistically significant associations between spheres of activity and attitude direction, however, were found.

Voluntary and involuntary contact.

In any interaction system we may expect to find involuntary and voluntary contacts between members but we may also expect interaction systems to vary in terms of the relative opportunities for either type of contact. We have presented evidence bearing on the relation between attitude direction and different spheres of contact which support our prediction of a negative relation between favourable attitudes and involuntary contact. We tested this hypothesis further with data which bear directly on these types of contact and found an association in the predicted direction, significant beyond the .01 level for Sample D but not significant for Sample N.

Authority.

As superiors and inferiors may like or dislike each other, any association between the positions of incumbents, relative to the distribution of authority in interaction systems, and attitude direction must involve other variables. One such variable would likely be the actors' appraisals of the qualifications of incumbents of, or aspirants for, authoritative roles. In this respect, there is a general tendency for estab-

[20]A number of studies support the view that the actor's position in the structure of a given interaction system influences his attitudes. See, for example, the Bavelas-Leavitt studies of communication patterns in Alex Bavelas, "Communication Patterns in Task-oriented Groups," in Dorwin Cartwright and Alvin Zander, editors, *Group Dynamics*, Evanston, Ill., Row, Peterson, 1953, and in H.J.Leavitt, Some Effects of Certain Communication Patterns on Group Performance, *Journal of Abnormal and Social Psychology*, 1951, *46*, 38-50; W.F.Whyte, *Human Relations in the Restaurant Industry*, New York, McGraw-Hill, 1948, and *Street Corner Society*, Chicago, University of Chicago Press, 1945; George C.Homans, *The Human Group*, New York, Harcourt, Brace, 1950; and many studies which analyze the relation between attitudes and social-class membership.

lished members of a social system to be unwilling, under ordinary circumstances, to relinquish authority to new members. As actors who are in a superior authoritative position relative to others tend to control the initiation and intimacy of interaction with new members, we predicted that favourable attitudes would be more frequently reported by natives whose positions relative to immigrants were superior rather than inferior or equal. The data reveal no trend in the direction predicted for Sample D but a clear association in Sample N; there subjects whose attitudes are favourable report disproportionately more situations in which they hold superior positions in interaction with immigrants, while subjects whose attitudes are unfavourable report disproportionately more peer relations. The association between interaction position and attitude direction is significant at approximately the .03 level.

Rewards.

The distribution of rewards is a potential source of stress in any interaction system; this is especially true where it concerns new and established members of the system, as such contacts maximize the possibility of conflict between different conceptions of an appropriate distribution of rewards. In the present analysis, it is sufficient to observe that unless extraordinary circumstances prevail, the established members of a system define it as inappropriate for new members to have an equal or greater share of the available rewards until a considerable degree of socialization has occurred, and they tend to exclude new members from the exercise of authority. Interaction, therefore, in which one or more new members have the advantage with respect to rewards tends to be experienced as deprivational by the established members and to stimulate negative attitudes toward the new members. For our subjects, therefore, we predicted a positive association between position relative to rewards and attitude direction. We found, however, no consistent pattern of association between attitude direction and each subject's judgement of his job, his neighbourhood living conditions, and the privileges available to him in his clubs as compared to those available to immigrants with whom he participated in common interaction systems. Sample D subjects whose reward position relative to immigrants is "higher" or "lower" reveal unfavourable attitudes, while those whose attitudes are favourable tend to report equality with immigrants with respect to rewards. Sample N respondents in the extreme directions of attitude show a slight but nonsignificant trend in the predicted direction. Field experience, however, revealed that the required information was difficult to obtain, and there is good reason to doubt the reliability of the data which bear on rewards.

Evaluations of Proportions of Immigrants

Where social systems experience an influx of new members, the relative proportions of new and established members are likely to be a matter of concern to both categories of actor, since their proportionate numerical strengths have significance for the control of interaction and the distribution of rewards. On the basis of this assumption we were led to predict an association between attitude direction and our subjects' evaluations of the proportions of immigrants in the interaction systems in which both participated.[21] The data clearly reveal that subjects whose attitudes are favourable more frequently express the opinion that there are "less than enough" immigrants while those with unfavourable attitudes express the view that there are "more than enough." This association between attitude direction and the evaluation of proportions of immigrants is significant beyond the .01 level in Sample D and beyond the .001 level in Sample N. As an analysis of attitude direction and subjects' *estimates* of the proportions of immigrants present in given interaction systems showed a trend toward an association, although not statistically significant, between favourable attitudes and reports of small proportions of immigrants and between unfavourable attitudes and reports of large proportions of immigrants, we may suggest that attitude direction is more closely associated with the evaluation than with the actual numbers of proportions of new and established members.

Immigrants as Facilities Objects and Reward Objects

In interaction systems, actors may regard each other primarily as reward objects or primarily as facilities objects. This dichotomy can be applied to the orientations of native Canadians toward immigrants, where a tendency to regard immigrants as useful or valuable to the development of natural resources, to meet occupational shortages, to increase consumer demand (i.e., as facilities objects) can be observed as well as a tendency to regard immigrants as desirable simply as associates and friends (i.e., as reward objects). We hold that persons who regard immigrants primarily as facilities objects could hold favourable attitudes toward immigrants but, as the value of a facility object is a function of its utility in a given situation, there will be less stability or persistence in the attitude direction of such persons than among persons who regard immigrants primarily as reward objects. Our data do not permit us to compare our subjects in terms of these two actor orientations, but tests for association between each type of orientation and attitude direction show a clear positive association, significant beyond the .001 level in both samples, between these distributions, indicating a strong

[21]For reported contacts in a given sphere of activity, subjects were asked: "About how many immigrants are there as compared to the number of Canadians in this group?" Subjects were then asked if they would prefer to increase, decrease, or hold constant the stated proportion of immigrants to Canadians.

relation between the facilities and reward value of immigrants and attitudes toward them.

Summary

We have advanced the view that there is a systematic relation between attitude direction and the structure of interaction systems to which given attitudes are relevant. This approach appears to yield a better understanding of variations in attitude than the typical survey analysis approach, where it is usual to look for relations between attitudes and age, sex, residence, and similar personal characteristics of the subjects. Our argument is supported by the present analysis, which yielded no significant associations between attitude direction and the familiar personal characteristics except educational and income level, and the association between attitude direction and either of those two variables seemed better understood by interpretation in terms of the structure of interaction systems. On the other hand, in each sample we found four significant associations out of a possible nine between attitude direction and characteristics of interaction systems.

In summary, the analysis suggests that attitude direction is associated with the control of interaction and with the type and distribution of rewards in the relevant interaction system. We conclude that further study of this relation by survey analysis procedures and in experimental situations would contribute to the understanding of the determinants of attitudes.

THIRTEEN
APPLIED PROBLEMS

61 / Decision-Making in the Employment Interview[1]

Edward C. Webster *McGill University*

In the hiring process, personnel managers frequently place great reliance on the employment interview, despite its recognized lack of objectivity, reliability, and validity. This article describes some important experimental research on the employment interview and suggests some ways for obtaining a more accurate hiring decision.

Professor Webster is currently the Director of the Centre for Continuing Education, McGill University. He is also the author of the following books: Guidance for the High School Pupil, *1939;* Put Yourself to the Test, *1941;* Decision-Making in the Employment Interview, *1964; and* The Couchiching Report: Training in Professional Psychology in Canada, *1967.*

Much criticism has been directed at the traditional employment interview. The current concern with the interview in "how-to-do-it" books, manuals and articles indicates that many are questioning this most popular of appraisal methods.

Exactly what happens in the employment appraisal setting? Why are some applicants taken on the payroll and others left off? What is the role of the interviewer and of the interview in the whole process of building and maintaining a working force? Practically nothing in the technical literature throws light on these problems, although manuals do codify the lore of the past and include much that may be "common sense" in dealing with practical day-to-day problems of the modern employment office.

In a preliminary effort to determine what happens in an employment interview, we selected a student who appeared, in many respects, a good candidate for training as an army personnel officer (although certain things in his background were undoubtedly unfavourable). The necessary pre-enlistment documents were prepared for this young man and he passed through the normal army selection procedure – normal, that is, except that he was interviewed by six personnel selection officers rather than by only one. The usual documents were completed by each and no officer was aware of the fact that others were also involved. Each gave a short over-all appraisal and these read as follows:

Interviewing Officer	Over-all Appraisal
A	"I do not believe he is a suitable candidate for training as a personnel officer."
B	"He will do well."
C	"Good prospect for working as a personnel officer."
D	"Suitable."
E	"Suitable prospect on academic grounds for personnel selection work with militia unit. Doubtful risk as officer material."
F	"Not recommended."

Why these differences among experienced interviewers interviewing the same man for the same job? Examination of the detailed records of the interviews indicate that different examiners asked different questions and were interested in different aspects of the individual. They did not all "pay attention" to the same information. When they did, there was agreement in interpretation on certain points. Thus, all agreed he was intelligent because of his education and test scores.

Disagreement was in respect to such personality characteristics as emotional stability and maturity and here specific bits of information were given different interpretation and emphasis.

Perhaps additional training would bring about greater similarity of decision among these interviewers. But what kind of training is called for? They already had had far more than have most industrial interviewers. Something new is needed. It is suggested here that further improvement in employment interviewing may have to await research on the problem of decision making in this type of situation. We need to know much more about how the interviewer really arrives at his decisions. Only when this process is understood can we proceed to improve the accura-

[1] The research summarized in this article has been supported by grants-in-aid from the Defence Research Board, Department of National Defence, Ottawa.

cy of prediction through validity studies. Today we don't know enough about the variables that affect decisions to make effective generalizations from correlation coefficients or other statistics which indicate the relationship between a decision and the later success or failure of the candidate. Validity studies may be crucial, but they should come later.

We have been working on this problem of decision making for the past six years. Two Ph.D. theses and a number of unpublished studies have been produced while three Ph.D. investigations are currently under way. We have entered many blind alleys but some of our findings have been positive and we do appear to be understanding better what happens in the employment interview. This constitutes an interim report on the work completed so far.

American friends have informally but spontaneously rejected much of the work reported in this paper because, they claim, the decision making process in the Army recruiting situation is considerably less rigorous than in industry, and most of our work is within the Army setting. We know nothing of the situation in the United States but, in Canada, the Army is a small professional body of, it is hoped, career men. When we asked the Army for a criterion of successful recruitment, we were told the only meaningful measure is whether or not a man is invited to re-enlist at the end of his initial three years of service. Army personnel officers work against this criterion. We have close relations with personnel people in a large proportion of the larger Canadian firms and firmly believe that the Canadian Army selection procedures are just as rigorous as those in any company. Furthermore, very few companies have engineered into their appraisal procedures methods of checking interviewer reports and of referring back to the appropriate interviewer mistakes in judgement which only appear after the man is on the job. These are standard steps in Canadian Army selection.

Time to Reach a Decision

Many manuals on interviewing emphasize that a good interviewer holds himself apart from the interview, collects all relevant information, weighs this carefully and reaches a decision. Probably most interviewers consider this desirable.

A simple "experiment" which can be carried out in any employment office suggests that this seldom happens when plant or clerical help is being selected. Springbett (4) had interviewers draw a line across the centre of a sheet of paper and this line represented a completely neutral attitude. They were asked to examine a completed application form for a particular job and to place an "X" on the left hand side at some point above (favourable) or below (unfavourable) the neutral line. This X and the line provide anchor points. The applicant then entered the room and the interviewer started a hidden stop watch. Once the applicant was seated, and preliminary pleasantries were over, another "X" was placed on the chart in relation to the first to indicate the impression indicated up to that point. The interviewer thought he knew what his decision would be. He then placed a third "X" on the sheet and stopped the hidden watch. The interview continued until its normal ending when the final decision to hire or reject was recorded with a fourth "X".

With the co-operation of eight senior interviewers in six firms Springbett received reports on twenty interviews. Three unexpected findings emerged:

a) Nearly identical ratings at all stages of the interview were given in the case of 16 of the 20 applicants. Of four reversals in rating, three were from accept to reject, one from reject to accept.

b) The average "decision time" was under 4 minutes while the average interview time was 15 minutes. By the end of 4 minutes interviewers felt they had the information needed for a decision.

c) There was complete agreement in 19 of the 20 cases between the rating at the decision time and the final rating.

Springbett concluded that, in a large majority of interviews, ratings on an application form, appearance and a very short talk would produce results comparable to those obtained in a 15 minute session. This is disconcerting even though the experimental design has some obvious shortcomings and may not be conclusive.

Order of Input of Information

Various kinds of information are available to the interviewer – completed application form, auditory and visual cues from talking to and seeing the applicant, the interview content itself, a medical report, test scores, reports on references, etc. Springbett's major work (4) was a detailed experimental study of the effect upon the interviewer of receiving information in various orders of input. He concentrated upon three types of information: (a) the application form; (b) first impressions including visual and auditory cues; and (c) the content of the interview proper.

There is no need to describe his findings in detail as these have already been published (5). However, he had two sets of experiments: one involved 48 interviews for genuine jobs and were conducted by 12 industrial interviewers from 4 companies; the other was a laboratory study in which 18 experienced army personnel officers co-operated. While the industrial investigation was realistic in many respects the military laboratory study provided much better control of experimental variables.

The order of input of information to the interviewer was varied systematically in both experiments so that decisions were reached in some cases when the application form was studied before other information was available, in other instances the applicant was seen before the application forms were made available.

Results of the two studies were consistent and there were no serious discrepancies. Springbett (5) reports:

(a) *Where the interviewer first studies the application form and then "has a look at" the applicant the final outcome of the interview can be predicted from this information alone in 85% of cases.*

(b) *If either the application form or the first visual impression creates a negative reaction, there will be rejection of the applicant in 88% of cases.*

(c) *Where both the application form and the appearance are rated favourably, the chances of final acceptance are greater if the interviewer first studied the application form.*

These findings can be explained on the basis of mental set and the rewards and punishments affecting the interviewer. He operates in a social system where he is subject to criticism if he accepts an applicant who proves unsatisfactory, but a good prospect rejected remains unknown to others. Therefore, for his own protection he is likely to "play it safe" and turn down the doubtful case. Within this system of reward and punishment the interviewer develops a mental set or attitude as soon as he receives any information about the candidate. Initially, this set may be weak or strong but, once it becomes strong, the interviewer actively seeks supporting evidence and is more often swayed by negative than by positive information. A strong initial set is developed early in the appraisal situation if information is uncovered in which he has a high level of confidence (e.g., some of the data on the application form).

What the Interviewer Looks For

Springbett's research can be interpreted to suggest that the interviewer is assessing an applicant against a mental picture or a stereotype. There is support for this.

In one minor unpublished study 12 experienced interviewers from as many companies spent two hours discussing a job description in an attempt to have each obtain the same mental picture of the human requirements for a particular position in a hypothetical company. Each then interviewed several applicants for the position. Post-interview verbal reports indicated that, almost without exception, interviewers were unable to divorce their evaluations from the mental sets used on a day-to-day basis in their own companies. Apparently well established habits of the interviewer cannot be changed in a two-hour discussion.

The same thing was found in another minor experiment where typescript of an interview was rated. Post-experiment reports again indicated that the typescript had to be evaluated against conditions in the rater's place of work.

These studies are very inconclusive, but Sydiaha (6) obtained clear evidence of the existence of stereotypes in a major investigation of 257 interviews by 8 experienced Army personnel selection officers. Space does not permit a description of the rather complex research design but Sydiaha concludes:

The most important facts emerging from this investigation are that the decisions of personnel interviewers are highly correlated with fairly simple descriptive statements of applicant characteristics, and that these characteristics are equally correlated with the decisions of all interviewers. The results are consistent with the view that personnel interviewers tend to attach the same importance to systematic information such as biographical and test data and that they tend to support their decisions by referring to the same hypothetical attributes. Using the word stereotype in a nonevaluative sense it would appear that there is a stereotype of a good soldier which accounts for a great deal of decision-making. This stereotype is common to all interviewers (co-operating in this study) and serves as a standard against which applicants are matched for suitability to army service.

Contribution of the Interview Itself to Decision-Making

Springbett's work could be interpreted to mean that the interview contributes little to the interviewer's decision to hire or to reject and there are, of course, a number of other studies which support this view.

Sydiaha (6), however, has demonstrated rather conclusively that impressions formed during the interview itself do contribute quite definitely to the final decision to hire or to reject and much of the negative evidence may well be a result of the research design utilized.

The influence of the interview itself proved a most difficult area to explore. We have made attempts at content analysis but these did not pay off. In one study the content of 25 recorded interviews by one interviewer were examined against a criterion of accept-reject and 11 items were significantly related to decisions. However, only 3 of these remained significant when checked against another sample of 25 interviews by the same man (22 of the 50 interviews by this officer were rejects). The procedure was repeated with 20 interviews by a second interviewer and no items proved significant when checked against a holdout sample of 20 interviews (19 of the 40 interviews were rejects). These negative findings may result from the method of content analysis but they discouraged further work in this direction.

Bales (1) has developed a method of interaction process analysis. He has shown that groups of people engaged in problem solving activity show certain selected regularities in the types of interaction between separate individuals and that these regularities yield generalizations about the social structure of the group. Sydiaha, in an unpublished study, applied Bales' technique to 114 recorded employment interviews by 9 interviewers of whom six were Army and three industrial.

Results suggest that both applicants and interviewers react positively to supportive acts by the other. Interviews where the applicant is accepted are characterized by interaction showing agreement, satisfaction and solidarity between the interviewer and the candidate whereas rejection is accompanied by interaction showing disagreement, tension and antagonism. It is interesting to note that there is a tendency to reject the applicant who asks for clarification of something asked by the interviewer. It may be that an inability to understand questions asked by the interviewer is interpreted as clear evidence of lack of ability.

A McGill study by Malmo, Boag and Smith (3) relates closely to these findings although their work is not part of our series of studies. They obtained physiological recordings of muscle potentials from the neck and speech muscles, and a continuous recording of heartrate for 19 psychoneurotic females. Each patient told a story from a T.A.T. card to a psychologist who either praised or criticized her story, asked her to reply to his comments, then reassured her and informed her that Dr. N. would see her shortly. Dr. N. conducted an interview in which he first questioned the patient about her test, asked her other questions and finally reassured her. The physiological recordings secured for the patients were also obtained both for the psychologist examiner and for Dr. N.

Malmo summarizes their findings as follows:

The results revealed differential physiological reactions to supportive vs. threatening situations not only in the patients but also in the examiner. In brief rest intervals following praise, the speech muscle tension fell rapidly, in contrast to the nonfalling tension following criticism. This phenomenon of differential reaction was noted in the examiner as well as in the patients. That is, after he had been critical his tension remained high in contrast to the falling tension after he had praised. Related findings were obtained from the second part of the experiment (during the interview).

The examiner's diary notes over a three month period were used in studying the interaction of the examiner's feeling state with the patient's physiological reactions during the T.A.T. On the examiner's "bad" days the patient's mean heart rate rose significantly more than on the examiner's "good" days.

These findings clearly support the interaction process analysis.

Sydiaha, basing himself on the interaction process analysis, is inclined to believe that one of the factors contributing to the interviewer's decision is his perception of the social role performance displayed by the applicant. This would imply the presence of a characteristic sequence of acts or of appropriate responses to the stimulus of prior acts. 88 recorded interviews were analyzed to check this. The total number of acts occurring after a particular type of prior act was computed in each case for men accepted and for those rejected. Results were entirely negative and this line of attack was dropped although, for a time, a still more complex analysis was contemplated.

Flanagan (2) developed the critical incident method of studying situations and Sydiaha applied this in another unpublished study to the content of interviews. He interviewed interviewers immediately following interviews and found very few "critical incidents" as such; more commonly there were "critical impressions" which the interviewer associated with particular things done or said. The 114 interviews used in the interaction process analysis produced 157 critical incidents or impressions. A correlation of .39 between number of incidents reported and length of the interview suggests these bear some relation to decision-making; in any event they are not mere rationalizations made up by the interviewer on the spot to support a judgement that is wholly intuitive. Furthermore, in keeping with Springbett's findings, the critical incidents or impressions tended to occur in the early part of the interview. The mean length of time of the interviews was 19.3 minutes as contrasted with 8.3 minutes as the mean for the critical impressions.

These critical impressions were arranged as a 120 item Applicant Descriptive Check List which formed the basis for a study of the consistency of interviewer responses. Sydiaha had 8 army personnel officers complete this form following each of 257 interviews in which 173 men were accepted for service. Sydiaha developed two quantitative scores to predict acceptance-rejection of each individual in one half of his sample and applied his regression equations to the hold out half of the group. One score was based on 13 biographical and test data items, the other upon responses to 64 significant items on his check list. A comparison of the resulting data led him to conclude (6) "there is reason to believe that clinical-descriptive operations (impressions reported on the Applicant Descriptive Check List) involve the use of more information than is contained in systematically obtained biographical and test data." In other words, the interview, and the impressions derived from it, contribute to the decision to accept or reject a candidate.

Is this impression related to the phenomenon of empathy? When each of the 257 applicants had been interviewed, the candidate completed several documents for us. One of these was a personality questionnaire. The interviewer, following the interview, also completed this on the basis of "how he thought the applicant would reply." He also completed it as he saw himself. Crowell spent considerable time analyzing this material but results were almost entirely negative. There seemed to be no difference in ability to predict responses of those accepted and of those rejected. However, in keeping with interview "lore," those applicants "seen" as more similar to the interviewer tended to be accepted. These were the only findings. The whole problem is in process of being re-examined using different data.

Independent of this study Lambert and his students at McGill set out to determine the significance spoken language has for listeners by analyzing their evaluational reactions to French and English. They had French-speaking and English-speaking Canadians listen to four tape recordings of a passage read in the two languages by bilingual subjects. Listeners did not know that each subject read the passage in both languages at the time they were asked to evaluate 14 aspects of the "personality" of the speakers. Both French and English listeners rated the English voices more favourably than the French voices on most traits commonly considered necessary for social and economic success. This work will be reported in the *Journal of Social and Abnormal Psychology* under the title "Evaluational reactions to spoken languages" and we need only concern ourselves with its implications for the interview. It seems probable that, when the interview commences, certain attitudes that may be highly significant to the decision to accept or reject are "triggered" by the voice of the applicant and arm chair reasoning will not tell us accurately whether favourable or unfavourable mental sets will be established.

A number of other investigations into the factors affecting decision making are currently underway but results are not sufficiently definite to warrant description as yet.

Practical Implications

We are of the opinion that the work summarized has certain practical implications that could be acted upon to provide the interviewer with greater control over his initial bias to accept or reject a candidate. This would not necessarily lead to more valid selection but it is a necessary forerunner of any improvement. The practical implications and advice we are ready to offer now may be stated quite briefly:

1. Control the order of input of information to the interviewer. If the interviewer will conduct his interview without advance study of application forms, test scores, letters of reference or any other such aid in which he has confidence, he will try to base more of his judgement on the interview.

2. Develop an accurate picture of the kind of person desired in a particular job and train the interviewer to accept this stereotype. Such training may have to be prolonged. It is not enough to provide him with a job description.

3. Force an increase in the time required to reach a decision about an applicant. This can be done in many instances by re-engineering the selection procedure so that a final decision to hire cannot be reached until several good candidates for the same opening can be compared. Perhaps interviewing by two people and subsequent discussion between these would accomplish the same end.

4. Recognize that bias affecting the decision for or against an applicant may operate from the beginning of the interview (sound of voice, etc.) or may develop in the interview depending upon whether one feels at ease with the candidate. We have no information to suggest that such bias either increases or decreased the validity of predictions but we suspect that any unrecognized and uncontrolled influences on the decision to hire or to reject will tend to reduce validity.

References

1. BALES, R. E. *Interaction process analysis.* Cambridge: Addison-Wesley Press, 1950.
2. FLANAGAN, J. C. The critical incident technique. *Psychological Bulletin,* 1954, *51,* 327-358.
3. MALMO, R. B., BOAG, T. J., and SMITH, A. A. Physiological study of personal tension. *Psychosomatic Medicine,* 1957, *19,* 105-119.
4. SPRINGBETT, B. F. Series effect in the employment interview. Unpublished Ph.D. thesis. McGill University, 1954.
5. ———. Factors affecting the final decision in the employment interview. *Canadian Journal of Psychology,* 1958, *12,* 13-22.
6. SYDIAHA, D. The relation between actuarial and descriptive methods in personnel appraisal. Unpublished Ph.D. thesis, McGill University, 1958.

62 / Group vs. Individual Problem-Solving and Decision-Making[1]

G. A. Milton *University of Victoria*

In recent years, governments, large businesses, and corporations have become enthusiastic about a group approach to the solution of problems and the development of policy. The "brainstorming" technique involves the creation of new ideas and new solutions by several people operating in a group. The following experiment provides an empirical evaluation of the effectiveness of group solutions to policy problems.

A committee consists of the unwilling selected from the unsuitable to do the unnecessary.
-John Marsh
British Institute of Management

Although the introductory quotation may overstate the case, there is ample reason for serious empirical study of the virtues of committee work and group processes in general. At several stages in the process of administering governmental departments, the question of group vs. individual activity arises. The importance of research which leads to an understanding of this process has been noted by many administrators. For example, A. M. Williams has written, in the December, 1959, issue of *Canadian Public Administration*, "At the higher levels of administration one of the most vital activities is that of making decisions." The essential question is one of group vs. individual decision and problem-solving processes: *Will more decisions and solutions be produced by a group or by individuals?* This problem has important implications for both applied public administration and the theory of behaviour of groups.

There has been a popular trend in recent years for governmental, industrial, and military agencies to rely more and more heavily on group processes, such as the committee meeting, for the solution of problems.[2]

Although enthusiasm for group process has by no means been unanimous (see B. S. Benson, "Let's Toss This Idea Up . . ." in *Fortune*, Oct. 1957, pp. 145-146, and S. H. Mansbridge, "Organization Theory and Practice," in *Canadian Public Administration*, Sept. 1961, p. 262), group process may be said to have achieved wide acceptance as a means of producing creative decisions and solutions to problems. The enthusiasm for the group process has been facilitated by the advertising executive, Osborn, through his invention and popularization of the technique of "brainstorming,"[3] but is by no means confined to professional administrators. Some professional psychologists and sociologists have vigorously shared this enthusiasm.[4]

On the other hand, carefully controlled research is beginning to raise doubt about the supposed advantages of group process.[5] If group processes are not superior, a second important question is raised: *Why are group processes so enthusiastically supported?* The present research has been conducted in order to help answer these two questions.

Research on group vs. individual processes in problem-solving began with Shaw,[6] who interpreted her results as indicating that group performance was superior. Although her study has been followed by a number of experiments yielding similar conclusions, one basic flaw in the methodology of these studies has made their findings inconclusive. They usually follow the procedure of comparing the performance of a *group* (four or six individuals) with the performance of one individual. The performance of a group should be superior to that of an individual simply because of size, i.e., more individuals are working on a problem.

[1]This research was supported by the Institute of Public Administration of Canada, and conducted at the University of Victoria.

[2]*Time*, February 18, 1957.

Reprinted, by permission of the author and the Institute of Public Administration of Canada, from *Canadian Public Administration*, 1965, *8*, 301-306.

[3]A. F. Osborn, *Applied Imagination*. New York: 1957 (rev. ed.).

[4]I. Lorge, D. Fox, J. Davitz, and M. Breuner, A Survey of Studies Contrasting the Quality of Group Performance and Individual Performance. *Psychological Bulletin*, 1958, *55*, 337-370.

[5]D.W. Taylor, P.C. Berry, and C.H. Block, Does Group Participation When Using Brainstorming Facilitate or Inhibit Creative Thinking? *Administrative Science Quarterly*, 1958, *3*, 23-47; M.D. Dunnette, J. Campbell, and K. Jaasted, The Effect of Group Participation on Brainstorming Effectiveness for Two Industrial Samples. *J. Applied Psychology*, 1963, *47*, 30-37.

[6]M. E. Shaw, A Comparison of Individual and Small Groups in the Rational Solution of Complex Problems. *American Journal of Psychology*, 1932, *44*, 491-504. (Earlier studies contrasting group with individual thought processes did not use tasks of sufficient complexity to be called "problem solving." See, for example, G. B. Watson, Do Groups Think More Efficiently than Individuals? *Journal of Abnormal and Social Psychology*, 1928, *23*, 328-336.)

Lorge and Solomon[7] and Taylor[8] have independently noted this flaw and provided simple mathematical models for predicting group performance from knowledge of individual capability. Using these mathematical analyses, the conclusion that group productivity is superior to individual productivity seems dubious.

In a carefully designed study of the "brainstorming" technique, Taylor, *et al.*, use another procedure for controlling the error when comparing groups with individuals. Half of the subjects in their experiment were randomly assigned to "real" groups of four men each. The other half worked individually, but their scores were treated as if they had worked in "nominal" groups of four men each. The authors refer to this method of comparing group vs. individual productivity as the "nominal-real groups" method.

The study revealed that the average group performance was superior to the average individual performance when compared on an equal-time basis, but when group size was controlled by the "nominal-real groups" procedure the individuals working independently produced a greater total number of independent solutions and a greater number of creative solutions. The authors point out that the current enthusiasm for group solving processes may be due to the spurious apparent superiority of the group over any one individual performance when group size is not properly controlled.

A third question which must necessarily arise in any comparison of group vs. individual problem-solving is: *Which condition produces the more effective decision?* Productivity is not necessarily related to quality or effectiveness. The present research was designed to provide insight into this problem as well as into the problem of quantity and enthusiasm.

Despite the questionable validity of the assertion that group processes are superior to individual processes, enthusiasm for group process continues.[11] The present series of experiments was conducted in order to test the following predictions: (1) *On intellectual, problem-solving, and decision-making tasks, individual processes are superior to group processes.* (2) *Group members feel that group procedures are superior because each member feels that he is participating in all group solutions and decisions and therefore he feels that he is being more creative than when working independently.*

[7]Two Models of Group Behaviour in the Solution of Eureka-Type Problems. *Psychometrika*, 1955, *20*, 139-148.

[8] Problem Solving by Groups. *Proceedings of the Fourteenth International Congress of Psychology*. Amsterdam: 1955, pp. 218-219.

[9]Taylor, Berry, and Block, *op. cit.*, p. 26.

[10]Paradoxically enough, essentially this same method had been used in 1928 by Watson, *op. cit.* p. 328, but neither he nor subsequent investigators realised the significance of this correction. Watson referred to his procedure as "summation".

[11]C. J. Thomas and C. F. Fink, Effects of Group Size. *Psychological Bulletin*, 1963, *60*, 371-384.

The Experiment[12]

Subjects of this experiment were 48 men, ranging in age from 23 through 61 years, with a median age of 26 years. The executive responsibilities and experience of these men varied considerably, but all were currently involved in positions of some administrative responsibility in either business, industry, or government. Of the 48 subjects, 21 had primary responsibility in the area of personnel management, 10 were primarily office managers, 7 were in general business, 6 were involved in production and 4 were primarily responsible for sales. Although it was not possible to assign subjects randomly from each of these categories to nominal and real groups, care was taken to see that representatives from each category worked under each condition and no apparent bias resulted from this procedure.

Procedure

The experimenter presented an enthusiastic discussion of brainstorming methods followed by the instructions and a warm-up problem. Following the warm-up period, subjects were presented with a policy problem, and worked either in four-man groups or as individuals. Twenty-four of the subjects worked as group members, and twenty-four worked individually. The problem assigned to all participants was:

Each year a great many Canadian tourists go to visit the United States. But now suppose that our country wished to get many more U.S. citizens to come to visit Canada, particularly Vancouver Island; also, that we wished to attract more eastern Canadians to our island. What steps can you suggest that would get more tourists to visit Vancouver Island?

A twelve-minute time limit was observed for all subjects. After the problem-solving session, all subjects were asked to decide which idea was best and each subject was asked to fill out a brief questionnaire designed to measure his enthusiasm for the task: "How creative were these ideas?" (rated 1 through 5); "How much fun was this problem?" (rated 1 through 5).

Table I – Average number of solutions, effectiveness, and enthusiasm on the policy problem for the adult male sample

Group	Median Number of solutions	Median effectiveness score	Median enthusiasm score
Nominal	41.5	5.3	5.0
Real	28.0	3.7	7.7
Significance of difference (U-test)	Significant $p < .05$	Significant $p < .05$	Significant $p < .05$

[12]A previous experiment, also supported by the Institute of Public Administration, demonstrated essentially the same results for a population of university undergraduates (reported in a technical report to the IPA).

Results

The "nominal vs. real groups" method of analysing the results was used. The productivity of four individuals working independently (the "nominal group") was compared with the productivity of four men working in a group (the "real group"). Thus, six real groups were compared with six nominal groups. The transcripts of the experimental sessions for each nominal and real group were edited to eliminate duplicated ideas within the transcript for a single group. Real groups and nominal groups were compared with respect to number of solutions, enthusiasm, and effectiveness. The results, presented in Table I, confirm the prediction that individuals (when treated as a *nominal* group) produce more solutions and more effective decisions than groups. However, as predicted, groups produce more enthusiasm. In this latter connection, most of the men who participated in the group procedures in this experiment spontaneously commented to the experimenter on their enthusiasm for the group procedure and stated that they planned to introduce it in their organizations. The correlation between number of solutions and enthusiasm was .33, a statistically significant figure.

Discussion

This experiment confirms earlier investigations which indicate that group processes are inferior to individual processes when applied to intellectual problem-solving tasks. Although the finding applies most directly to the process known as brainstorming, the current study involved a simple decision task which suggests that the generalization may hold for any group procedures, and since the proponents of brainstorming regard that method as the superior group method, this generalization is further strengthened.

An additional important conclusion of the present research is that group processes produce greater enthusiasm for a task, despite their lower efficiency. This would seem to explain the growing enthusiasm for group procedures such as committees and group dynamics, and also to account for the mistaken conclusions drawn from some other psychological, political, and economic research projects. This finding also points to a potential value in using group procedures, even though they are less efficient intellectually.

The decision of whether to use group or individual procedures would seem to involve an evaluation of the primary purpose of any contemplated activity. If the primary purpose is one involving the emotional tone, good feelings, or enthusiasm of a number of individuals, then group processes provide a valuable way of arousing these non-intellectual responses. When problem solutions are required, of course, individual effort is to be preferred. When both enthusiasm and good problem solving are needed, a combination of individual and group activity may be required, possibly in that order. Dunnette has suggested that group procedures may also be used as a "warm-up" for individual effort.

The significant positive relationship between the number of solutions produced and the enthusiasm felt by members of a group provides a possible understanding of the enthusiasm for group procedures. An individual, when participating in group activity, is sharing in the production of more ideas that he alone would produce (although fewer than he would produce in a nominal group). Since enthusiasm seems to be tied to the number of solutions, his enthusiasm is higher because he adopts each group idea as being partially his production. When working individually in a nominal group, he has no knowledge of the ideas produced by other members of his nominal team and, of course, no feeling of participation in the total output.

The relative inferiority of group processes is suggested by both Taylor and Dunnette to be due to the tendency of group members to develop a directional set, or "fall in a rut' and pursue the same train of thought." This impression is borne out by inspection of the group discussion which followed the experimental sessions in the first of the current studies. Groups seemed to become so directed in their discussions that whole areas of solution were completely ignored. Also, some group members seemed to dominate and direct the discussions more than other members, further restricting the fullest exploration of alternative solutions.

An important possible limitation of the generality of these findings must be acknowledged. The time allotted to both groups and individuals for problem solutions – twelve minutes – was chosen because it was regarded as optimal on the basis of extensive pre-testing by Taylor. However, the enthusiasm engendered by the group processes may encourage greater perseverance by group members.

The evidence available at the present time suggests that individual processes are markedly superior to group processes when applied to problem-solving and decision-making. Group processes, on the other hand, produce greater enthusiasm among the participants.

63 / Psychological Factors in Industrial Organization affecting Employee Stability[1]

John C. Sawatsky *University of Toronto*

In order to maintain high productivity in industry, employee turnover and absenteeism must be minimized. Undoubtedly many of the factors which contribute to turnover and absenteeism are psychological in nature, yet the identification of these factors has not progressed rapidly. In the present study, employee turnover in different work situations is analyzed and some suggestions as to cause of turnover are offered.

This study represents an attempt to investigate the validity of the following hypothesis:

The manner in which work is organized in modern industrial settings has resulted in certain working conditions which contribute in varying degrees to instability of the working behaviour of employees. The inference is that differences in working conditions such as affect communication and teamwork among employees and their opportunities for personal recognition and identification will be reflected in differential rates of labour turnover and absenteeism.

Starting with objectively determined differences in labour turnover and absenteeism among various organizational divisions of a manufacturing plant, working conditions in these divisions are analyzed in order to make the discovered differences intelligible in terms of psychological factors related to work satisfaction.

Early researches, notably the early phases of the "Hawthorne Experiments" (7, 9, 11, 14, and 15) were designed primarily to test physiological fatigue hypothesis in repetitive industrial work. The results being mostly negative, later investigations were aimed to discover psychological implications of industrial work situations. The general outcome of the Hawthorne researches indicated that effective work performance and satisfying work experience on the part of employees were dependent not merely on financial reward, desirable circumstances regarding hours, physically comfortable working conditions, and health benefits, but particularly upon certain inter-personal relationships in the work setting. Elton Mayo's early independent study (8) of the mule-spinning department in a textile mill stressed the beneficial results which appeared to accrue from physical relaxation. Re-interpreting his findings later, Mayo suggested that the rest periods introduced also brought about a significant change in the inter-personal relationships among the workers. A study reported by Mayo and Lombard (10) indicates a high relationship between labour turnover and extent of teamwork which occurred in work situations of certain aircraft industries in California.

The hypothesis of the present study has a bearing on certain trends which have occurred in industry. The Industrial Revolution and subsequent developments have resulted in rapid expansion of the means of production. In the process of expansion, changes in production methods together with increase in the size of factories in terms of numbers of employees have resulted in changes in the organization of the work. Many of these changes have been made in accordance with the so-called principles of scientific management. The basis of these principles is division of labour with emphasis on the individual contribution of employees in terms of individual effort. Our hypothesis implies that this manner of organizing the work, with its emphasis on individual rather than joint contributions, results in the worker losing perspective. Being out of touch with fellow-workers he finds it difficult to see meaning in his effort.

The Setting

The data for the study were obtained chiefly from a wire and cable manufacturing company located in the vicinity of Toronto. The company employed approximately 1800 workers at the time and was considered to be a large organization by Canadian standards. Organizationally, it followed the pattern set by modern industry. This pattern, developed partly as a result of increasing scope of operations, consists of dividing the total production effort into various stages of operation. Thus the production organization consisted of twenty-nine departments each having a specialized function in the total process.

---

[1]This article represents a summary of a Ph.D. thesis based on a research project which the writer undertook as a graduate student in the Department of Psychology on a fellowship with the Institute of Industrial Relations, University of Toronto. The writer wishes to acknowledge particularly the helpful guidance and interest of Professor W. Line.

Reprinted, by permission, from *Canadian Journal of Psychology*, 1951, *5*, 29-38.

Procedure

Generally speaking, the procedure of the study was to examine all areas of the organization for the purpose of discovering psychological factors related to extent of labour turnover and absenteeism. Indices of labour turnover and absenteeism calculated over a twelve-month period were obtained for all twenty-nine departments. In view of the fact that departmental variations in labour turnover were found to correspond substantially to variations in absenteeism, (rank order = +.667 ±.073), subsequent analysis was confined primarily to examining the relationship of a number of variables with labour turnover.

Average age of employees in the various departments, marital status, number of dependents, educational level, and extent of earnings were not found to have a significant statistical relationship to extent of labour turnover. This also applied to size of department (in terms of number of employees) and the following job factors: mentality (intelligence), skill, mental application, and working conditions, as measured by the company's job evaluation system. However, the job evaluation factor of "responsibility" was found to correlate significantly with extent of labour turnover (rank order = −.538 ±.93).

Subsequent to this analysis the labour turnover of production departments was compared with that of the service departments. The production-service classification is an organizational break-down formally observed in the company records. Production departments, as their classification implies, are solely concerned with production; service departments are various work units which assist in mechanical and other maintenance functions related to the production departments. They keep the production departments supplied with materials, receive, store, and ship materials, etc. This specialization of function is the outcome of modern principles of scientific management. The emphasis is on division of labour, making each production unit responsible for a specific type or phase of manufacturing. Among other things this specialization of work results in differences in scope of operations. Employees in service departments, although limited in terms of function, tend to circulate in various areas of the plant wherever and whenever required. Production employees, on the other hand, are always confined to a particular scene of operations.

Table I indicates the percentages of labour turnover of production and service departments for comparative purposes. The difference of 28.35 per cent is statistically highly significant. Comparable data from three additional manufacturing plants indicated similar differences. Similarly significant differences in rates of absenteeism for the year were obtained, service departments showing decidedly lower rates.

In view of the foregoing results the study was focussed on production departments. The first procedure was to obtain a measure of labour turnover for each occupational classification, that is, for each job, in each of the fourteen production departments. To facilitate this analysis, the work activity in each of the production departments was examined and described and thus further information obtained about the situations in which differences in labour turnover occurred.

It was observed that there were two major types of occupations, "machine operating" and "non-machine operating." Machine operators, as their classification implies, are chiefly responsible for operating the equipment to which they have been assigned. Often their machines are "set up" or prepared by others. They bring their machines into operation, closely observing the product to insure uniform production. In case of breakage of threads or wires they do the required mending. They also make minor adjustments to the machines. Apart from lunch-hour shut down, trips to the wash-room, or stoppage for repair to their equipment, the operators are closely confined to their machines. Members of production departments whom we have classified as non-machine operators have a variety of functions. Some prepare or set up machines for operators, others oil the machines, supply operators with materials, etc. Generally speaking they perform a sort of service function for the operators and the varied nature of their duties naturally permits considerable mobility within the area of their departments.

Table II indicates that the labour turnover of machine operators is significantly higher than that of non-machine operators. Analysis of financial remuneration of these two groups indicated that this difference could hardly be attributed to earnings; in fact

Table I – Comparison of the total percentages of labour turnover in 14 production and 15 service departments in a twelve-month period

	Production Departments	Service Departments	Totals
Average Number Employed	818.38	410.06	1228.44
Number of Terminations	612.	190.	802.
Per cent Labour Turnover	74.78	46.33	65.29
σ	1.518	2.462	
σDp	2.184		
D	28.35		
$D/\sigma Dp$	12.98		

Table II – Comparison of labour turnover of "machine operators" and all "non-machine operators" in production departments

	"Machine Operators"	"Non-machine Operators"
Number Employed	530	319
Number of Terminations	414	167
Per cent of Labour Turnover	78.11	52.35
σ	1.795	2.795
σDp	2.46	
D	25.76	
$D/\sigma Dp$	10.47	

Table III – Comparison of labour turnover of departments assigned to three noise categories

	No. of Departments	Average No. Employed	No. of Terminations	Labour Turnover
1. Depts. in which extent of noise makes conversation difficult	4	341.93	291	85.11
2. Depts. in which extent of noise produces a medium range of difficulty of conversation	3	183.26	152	82.94
3. Depts. in which extent of noise does not appear to be a factor in possibility of conversation	7	293.19	169	57.64

the earnings of machine operators were somewhat higher.

The possible influence of a further variable in production departments – namely, the influence of noise – was examined. In some departments the noise was so great that conversation was difficult. Each of the fourteen departments was therefore rated jointly by the author and a competent company official in regard to the extent to which noise permits or prohibits conversation. The results of this analysis are presented in Table III. The labour turnover of departments in which noise makes conversation difficult is significantly higher than that of departments in which noise does not deter conversation.

Interpretation of Results

1. (a) Recent researches reported in the literature would lend weight to the explanation of differences in working regularity resulting from the influence of foremen and supervisors. Mayo and Lombard (10, p. 2) indicate that their research findings point to "the methods of first-line supervision as of critical importance to the control of absenteeism and labour turnover." The Hawthorne researches (7, 9, 11, 14, and 15) indicate the importance of the role of the supervisor in determining morale of employees. While the influence of supervision cannot be denied in the setting which has been studied here, evidence suggests that this influence does not account for the differences in labour turnover and absenteeism between service and production departments. In the first place, the data from all four companies investigated indicated similar differences, and it is highly improbable that a general difference in the effectiveness of supervision exists in all four situations. Secondly, examination of the labour turnover within production departments has indicated that machine operators within these departments have a higher incidence of turnover than other classifications of employees in the same departments. Within each department, machine operators and non-machine operators are influenced by the same foreman and supervisor. In other words, supervision appears to represent a constant variable in production departments.

(b) It is widely accepted that general employment conditions influence labour turnover in industry. Under conditions of labour scarcity and shifting demand for labour, overall labour turnover usually increases. It is conceivable that the general labour turnover of the four plants studied was affected by certain conditions prevailing during the time of the study. It is also possible that general conditions, whatever they may be, could have been responsible for differential rates of turnover in the settings investigated. Employees in production departments might conceivably have found it easier than employees in service departments to find employment elsewhere when the demand for labour was high. The validity of this interpretation could only be demonstrated by detailed study of the relationship of occupational labour turnover to the prevailing demand for labour. While possibility of some influence of external conditions is suggested here, our interpretation of the present findings tends to favour the significance of internal variables, that is, conditions within the organization.

(c) Another possible interpretation of the differential rates of labour turnover is that workers with different personality characteristics gravitate either to production or to service types of work. In spite of the findings that labour turnover did not correlate significantly with personal data such as age, education, etc., the validity or otherwise of this interpretation is difficult to establish within the limits of the present study. Further research into the work history of both production and service employees is warranted in this area.

2. Although the interpretations outlined above cannot be ruled out at the present stage of our knowledge, it seems justifiable to interpret our findings in terms of psychological factors related to variations in work organization. This interpretation is as follows:

(a) As stated above, employees in service departments, engaged in a variety of activities such as repairing and maintaining equipment, handling materials, and keeping the plant clean, have a service function mainly related to the entire plant. It is suggested that it is not difficult for individuals performing these functions to see themselves as having tangible day-to-day usefulness to fellow employees in production departments. The nature of service occupations is also such that, in general, their activities permit a relatively ***high degree of mobility*** within the plant. Mobility here is defined as movement within the plant area. Thus, the service function, because it necessitates discussion of current maintenance problems, etc., in the various areas of the plant, results in a good deal of personal contact. On the other hand, the activities of production department employees are confined to their various production areas.

Being relatively more mobile within the total plant area and apparently having more tangible evidence of usefulness to fellow workers, service department employees have greater *opportunity for obtaining recognition* of their efforts than production employees. Owing to the division of labour in the plant, each production department is responsible for only a fraction of the total production effort. In other words, the contribution of production employees is partial rather than whole. It is suggested that since they lack mobility and personal contact with others who are part of the production team, they find it relatively difficult to obtain recognition and a sense of participation.

This interpretation of the particular results of the present study appears to receive support from research findings and interpretations as reported in the literature. Some of these have already been referred to. T. N. Whitehead (15, p. 54) writes about the adjustment which came within the relay test group under experimental changes of the Hawthorne researches. When the members of the group were permitted to associate freely among themselves and when they began to realize that they were participating in a project which they as well as others regarded as important, they made a satisfactory adjustment. Their production output increased, their labour turnover and absenteeism became almost negligible, and the workers themselves indicated that they had achieved satisfaction in their work. As far as freedom of association was concerned, one of their former difficulties – lack of freedom to converse with one another – had been eliminated in the experimental situation. In writing about this group, Mayo (9, p. 72) suggests that the "individuals became a team and the team gave itself wholeheartedly and spontaneously to cooperation in the experiment." Mayo goes on to say that "the organization of working teams and the free participation of such teams in the task and purpose of the organization as it directly affects them in their daily rounds" deserves close attention.

On the basis of evidence which he presents, Whitehead suggests that one of the main social problems of industry is that "the immediate social routine activities are too few or unsatisfying" (15, p.95).

G. W. Allport has suggested (5, p. 258) that "the individual's desire for personal status is apparently insatiable. Whether we say that he longs for prestige, for self-respect, autonomy, or self-regard, a dynamic factor of this order is apparently the strongest of his drives." In the same article Allport goes on to say that when the individual is busily engaged in using his talents, understanding his work, and has a free and easy relationship with foreman and fellow workers, then he is "identified" with his work. He is "ego-involved," "participant." He suggests that when this process does not occur the "job-satisfaction" is low. "When the ego is not sufficiently engaged the individual becomes reactive." He finds outlets in complaints, strikes, etc. Our interpretation here, in Allport's frame of reference, is that production department employees, not having adequate opportunities of becoming ego-involved in their situation, become reactive; they absent themselves more frequently and terminate their employment more readily.

(b) Another aspect in which production and service functions appear to differ is related to *opportunity of exercising personal control of work effort.* Service employees are able to plan and vary their activities to a greater extent. The primary emphasis in their function is on *quality*. The activities of production employees, on the other hand, being more routine and in accordance with schedules, etc., emphasize quantity rather than quality of performance.

Again, in accordance with Allport's theory of personality needs, it seems entirely possible that this restriction in work function, brought about by the emphasis on quantity of work, produces loss of self-respect or self-regard on the part of production employees. Participation has been restricted to a narrow field of operations by the division of labour; that is, by the manner in which the work has been organized.

Labour Turnover Differences between Machine Operators and Non-Machine Operators within Production Departments. The results of the analysis of labour turnover within production departments have established that the relatively high labour turnover occurring in these departments stems largely from machine-operating occupations. It was further established that machine operators, because of the nature of their work are relatively confined to limited areas. Contrastingly, non-machine operators have a relatively high degree of freedom of movement within their department. At the same time the extent of noise in some of the departments was found to be such as to make conversation difficult. This particularly affected machine operators in these departments because of their proximity to the source of the noise.

It is suggested that the factors responsible for the difference in extent of labour turnover between machine operators and non-machine operators are very similar to those responsible for the production-service labour turnover differential. These findings tend to substantiate the results and the interpretation of obtained production-service differences. Non-machine operations are fairly comparable to service occupations. *The machine-operating individuals in the production departments appear to lack adequate opportunity of integrating themselves with other members of the production group.* If Allport's theory that a balanced personality needs deep-rooted participation has validity, machine operating in this particular setting does not afford opportunity to meet the need. Our interpretation here again is that under conditions of lack of opportunity to satisfy the social or psychological needs, the individual becomes frustrated, he becomes dissatisfied with the work situation and tends to withdraw. The manner in which the work schedule has been laid out for him does not meet the conditions of psychologically satisfying work experience.

The data which establish that there is a relationship between production department labour turnover and extent of noise in tems of conversation possibilities appear to support the interpretation. The Hawthorne relay test group tended to lose its social rigidity when conversation was freely permitted. Conversation, or communication generally, serves as a medium through which the worker becomes identified with other members of the work group. It serves the purpose of permitting him to become aware of his function, his participation in the work being done.

Responsibility. The examination of the influence of a number of variables in all twenty-nine departments has revealed that variations in extent of labour turnover corresponded rather closely to variations in extent of "responsibility" as defined by job evaluation in the setting. Although "responsibility" was rather narrowly defined as "the extent of coordination and alertness required where the relative chance of error is great and its probable cost high," this finding would appear to be significant to our interpretation of the general results of the study. Douglas McGregor (5, p. 49) has suggested that "a corollary of the desire for participation is a desire for responsibility." Employees in both service and production departments performing functions which the company regards as having relatively higher "responsibility," may have a greater awareness of their participating role. In being called upon to make decisions, to solve problems which are recognized as having importance, they obtain a measure of self-regard which results in personal satisfaction, and in stability of employment.

Summary

By way of examining the validity of the hypothesis that the manner in which work is organized in present-day industrial settings is conducive to employment instability through lack of work satisfaction on the part of employees, the present study includes: (a) a detailed demonstration of a number of differences in labour turnover and absenteeism among organizational divisions in the same industrial plant; (b) an attempt to interpret these differences in terms of psychological factors related to work satisfaction.

Interpretation of evidence implies making inferences from obtained data, and where, as here, these inferences involve psychological conditions not directly investigated, alternative interpretations cannot be finally excluded. Certain of the latter have been critically examined but it is possible that further research pertaining to some of the numerous variables operating in the situation may disclose additional explanatory factors.

However, on the basis of the facts at hand, it is the conclusion of the investigator that the interpretation suggested in this study is acceptable, because it renders the varied findings of the study intelligible, and because it is congruent with our present psychological knowledge and is supported by recent research in industrial psychology. Accepting this interpretation, it is concluded that the greater employment instability among production employees, and particularly among machine operators, is a function of the following conditions:

1. Their work is highly specialized; they have little mobility and opportunity of communicating with other members of the production staff.
2. As a result, their opportunity of obtaining social recognition of their contribution is reduced, particularly in its qualitative aspects.
3. They are thus less likely to become identified or ego-involved with other members of the work group or with the work as such.
4. Their work satisfaction is therefore low and they tend to absent themselves more frequently and terminate their employment more readily.

References

1. BARUCH, D. W. Why They Terminate. *Journal of Consulting Psychology,* 1944, *8,* 35-46.
2. FOX, J. B., and SCOTT, J. F. *Absenteeism, Management's Problem.* Boston: Harvard Business School, Division of Research, Business Research Studies, No. 29, 1943.
3. GARRETT, H. E. *Statistics in Psychology and Education.* Toronto: Longmans Green and Company, 1939.
4. HALL, P., and LOCKE, H. W. *Incentives and Contentment.* London: Sir Isaac Pitman and Sons, Ltd., 1938.
5. HOSLETT, S. D. *Human Factors in Management.* Parkville, Miss.: Park College Press, 1946.
6. KERR, W. A. Labour Turnover and its Correlates. *Journal of Applied Psychology,* 1947, *31,* 366-71.
7. MAYO, ELTON. *The Human Problems of an Industrial Civilization.* New York: The Macmillan Company, 1933.
8. ———. Revery and Industrial Fatigue. *Personnel Journal,* 1923-24, *3,* 273-81.
9. ———. *The Social Problems of an Industrial Civilization.* Boston: Harvard University, Graduate School of Business Administration, Division of Research, 1945.
10. MAYO, ELTON, and LOMBARD, G. F. F. *Teamwork and Labour Turnover in the Aircraft Industry of Southern California.* Boston: Harvard Business School, Division of Research, Business Research Studies, No. 32, 1944.
11. ROETHLISBERGER, F. J., and DIXON, W. J. *Management and the Worker.* Cambridge: Harvard University Press, 1939.
12. WATKINS, G. S., and DODD, P. A. *The Management of Labour Relations.* New York: McGraw-Hill Book Company, 1939.
13. WELCH, H. J., and MEYERS, C. S. *Ten Years of Industrial Psychology.* London: Sir Isaac Pitman and Sons, Ltd., 1932.
14. WHITEHEAD, T. N. *The Industrial Worker.* Cambridge: Harvard University Press, 1938.
15. ———. *Leadership in a Free Society.* Cambridge: Harvard University Press, 1937.

64 / The Effect of Magazine Page Size on Immediate Memory for Advertisements

Edward C. Webster and T.C. Bird *McGill University*

Since many large enterprises invest millions of dollars in advertising, there is a good deal of concern about the effectiveness of different advertising techniques. The following article represents one method of assessing such techniques. The authors sought to ascertain whether the size of an advertisement is an important variable in determining its effectiveness.

Over the past few years a number of pocket size magazines have appeared on the market and several periodicals have reduced their physical dimensions. What effect has this reduction in size on the effectiveness of advertisements? Page for page, does an advertisement make as great an impression on the reader if seen in a small magazine as if seen in a large magazine?

A considerable body of data indicates that, with a standard page size, attention and memory value within a magazine are related to the size of the advertisement. Can the further generalization be accepted that "the larger the magazine page, the greater is the memory value of the full page advertisement?"

Two experiments bearing directly on this problem were conducted in 1929 by Cutler (1), and Newhall and Heim (2). Neither found conclusive evidence to substantiate the hypothesis that large page advertisements were superior. While both reported negatively, their findings have been criticized on grounds of inadequate sampling. In any case, this problem is worthy of a further check if only to confirm the fact that no significant relationship exists between size of a full-page advertisement and its chance of being recalled.

In the spring of 1949 Spires and Leblanc (3) repeated the essential elements of the 1929 experiments and obtained results that suggested the present study which brings a new approach to the problem.

The Experiments

Two sets of dummy magazines – one a large, the other a small page size – were constructed. Each contained twenty full-page advertisements interspersed with pages of solid reading matter. Order of appearance and position on the right or left hand side of the double pages were the same in both large and small size booklets. Advertisements were identical except for: (a) *Size*: Small magazine size was that of "Reader's Digest" and "Coronet"; large magazine size was that of "Saturday Evening Post" and "Maclean's Magazine." (b) *Content*: In some instances the small advertisements did not contain all the content of the large although in every case the two were identical in respect to colour, principal theme, pictures, and layout of common content. Slides were prepared from photographs of the large page.

These dummies were used in three experiments.

First Experiment

The first study was a survey of 101 adults interviewed in their homes during July, 1949. A commercial market research organization divided this work among four experienced interviewers who selected English-speaking respondents on the basis of sex and residential area in Montreal. Individuals were classified as to socio-economic status and on the basis of a four-point scale. Each interviewer worked with a single size dummy and no interviewer or subject was aware of the fact that another size was available.

The interviewer presented a dummy magazine to the respondent with the following instructions: "Here is a sample magazine. Would you please look through it from beginning and end, page by page. Take as long as you wish, stop at whatever interests you, spend as much or as little time as you wish on each page. Don't bother about me. I just want to watch to see what interests you."

On completion of this task, the person interviewed was asked: (a) To name the brands or, failing that, the products advertised. No assistance was given and the responses represent achievement resulting from unaided recall. (b) To select from groups of five possible brand names presented on cards the one brand seen in the dummy. This recognition test followed immediately the unaided recall portion of the study and a card appropriate to each advertisement was used.

Results from the unaided recall and recognition tests are presented in Tables I and II respectively. Responses are classified both as to the size of dummy page and as to the socio-economic status of the individual interviewed.

Reprinted, by permission, from ***Canadian Journal of Psychology***, 1950, *4*, 115-121.

Table I – Number of advertisements spontaneously recalled

Socio-Economic Status	A		B		C		D		Total	
Page Size	Small	Large	Small	Large	Small	Large	Small	Large	Small	Large
Number of Interviewees	14	13	16	17	16	17	4	4	50	51
Mean Number of Ads. Recalled	4.9	3.3	3.6	4.9	4.6	3.9	4.0	2.7	4.3	4.0
S.D.	1.6	2.8	2.2	3.6	2.7	2.2	. .	. .	2.3	3.0

Comparing the mean memory scores for large and small full-page advertisements, it is evident that 8 out of the 10 differences favour the small size page. It is also evident that no consistent pattern exists when mean scores for the various socio-economic groups are examined. In view of the fact that such results are hardly to be expected, a more rigorous examination of these data is warranted. The results of an analysis of variance of data presented in Table I are shown in Table III.

Table II – Number of advertisements recognized

Socio-Economic Status	A		B		C		D		Total	
Page Size	Small	Large	Small	Large	Small	Large	Small	Large	Small	Large
Number of Interviewees	14	13	16	17	16	17	4	4	50	51
Mean Number of Ads. Recalled	10.1	7.2	8.9	8.5	8.1	8.4	8.0	7.0	8.9	8.0
S.D.	2.8	4.0	3.7	4.7	3.9	4.2	. .	. .	3.6	4.2

Table III – Analysis of variance of table I

Variance	D.F	Sum of Squares	Mean Square	F	Hypothesis
Page Size	1	1.473	1.473	4.754	Rejected
Socio-Economic Status	2	1.201	0.600	11.67	Rejected
Interaction	2	35.358	17.679	2.525	Rejected
Within Cells	95	665.266	7.003		
Total	100	703.298	7.033		

From this analysis it is noted that the f ratios are all non-significant at well below the 5 per cent level. More specifically, the f ratio between "interaction" and "within cells" is 2.5 for 95 x 2 df; between socio-economic status and "within cells" it is 4.75 for 95 x 1 df; and between page size and "within cells" it is 11.67 for 95 x 2 df. This can only mean that no discernable effect upon the recalling of brand names can be attributed either to page size or to socio-economic status.

A similar analysis of variance was made of Table II and is presented in Table IV. Here again the analysis strongly suggests that, taken separately or together, neither page size nor socio-economic status affects the responses obtained. Specifically, the f ratio between "interaction" and "within cells" is 1.42 for 95 x 2 df which produces a probability greater than 0.05. Between "within cells" and socio-economic status the f ratio is 1.83 which gives a probability greater than 0.05 for 95 x 1 df. In the same way the f ratio for "within cells" and page size is 2.29 for 95 x 2 df and this also gives a probability greater than 0.05.

Thus, this analysis of variance strongly suggests that the apparent superiority of small over large full-page advertisements results from chance factors and that the differences in mean scores when one socio-economic group is compared with another are also the result of chance.

Table IV – Analysis of variance of Table II

Variance	D.F.	Sum of Squares	Mean Square	F	Hypothesis
Page Size	1	32.216	32.216	1.829	Rejected
Socio-Economic Status	2	15.365	7.682	2.293	Rejected
Interaction	2	24.874	12.437	1.416	Rejected
Within Cells	95	1673.092	17.612		
Total	100	1745.547	17.455		

Second Experiment.
This was a laboratory experiment in which the subjects consisted of 44 adults. A majority, 31, were personnel department managers tested at a meeting attended for a purpose unrelated to the experiment. In terms of socio-economic status most of these subjects would be rated as 'B', a few as 'A', and a few as 'C'.

The experiment consisted of the following three stages:

(1) Twenty slides, each of a full-page advertisement not appearing in the dummy, were thrown by means of a tachistoscope on a screen for 1/10 second. The subject recorded the name of the brand advertised. The mean number of correct responses was 2.2. The purpose of this portion of the experiment was to accustom the subjects to the manner of responding.

(2) The group was divided on a chance basis into two samples, one of which examined a small page size dummy, the other a large page size dummy, for 4 minutes.

(3) Forty slides were presented for 1/10 second each. These included photographs of the 20 advertisements which appeared in the dummy. As each slide was shown the subject recorded the name of the advertisement and his score was the number correctly named from among those he had seen in the dummy.

The results confirm those of the first experiment. As will be seen from Table V, the mean number of advertisements correctly named is higher for the sample which examined the small dummy. Again, however, the differences are not statistically significant at the 5 per cent level for 42 df: t for the difference between means is 1.73.

Table V – Number of advertisements perceived correctly following tachistoscopic presentation

Page Size	Small Page	Large Page
Mean Number Perceived Correctly	10.1	7.6
S.D.	5.5	4.0
N	24	20

Third Experiment.
This laboratory study was a variation of the second experiment. The subjects were 32 final year medical students who, on a socio-economic scale, rate as either "A" or "B". Again, the experiment consisted of three steps:

(1) The groups were divided into two samples: one read a small, the other a large, page size dummy for 4 minutes. While the students knew that the experiment dealt with advertising, they were given no information as to its specific purpose or its technique.

(2) The name of a product (for example "sterling silver," "beer" and so on) was thrown on the screen for 15 seconds while the subject wrote the names of all brands of that product seen in the dummy. His score was the number of brand names correctly recalled.

(3) Twenty slides were then presented; each consisted of three or more pictures of trade names of one product advertised in the dummy. The subject was required to record any trade names he recognized and his score was the number of trade names which corresponded to brands appearing in the dummy.

Findings, as reported in Table VI, are essentially the same as in the second experiment. Thus:

(a) In the first part of the study there is a slight, although not significant, difference favouring the small page advertisement. The t of 0.29 for this difference between means is not significant at the 5 degree level for 30 degrees of freedom.

(b) In the second part, those who studied the large page dummy improved their responses so that the difference in mean scores favoured the large size page. However, this difference is not significant: "t" is 1.08 and, for 30 degrees of freedom, this is not significant at the 5 per cent level.

Table VI – Number of advertisements correctly named under conditions of directed recall and subsequent multi-choice recognition

	Recall			Recognition		
	Small Page	Large Page	Total	Small page	Large Page	Total
Mean No.	9.1	8.8	8.9	9.2	9.9	9.6
S.D.	3.0	2.8	2.9	2.0	1.8	1.9
N.	16	16	32	16	16	32

Discussion

It is evident that none of the five variations of this study of immediate memory for 20 full-page advertisements indicate significant differences favouring either the small full-page or the large full-page advertisement. Thus the investigation provides a general confirmation of three earlier experiments carried out with somewhat different procedures.

However, it has been noted that most of the comparisons between mean scores actually favoured the small advertisements. The question may be raised as to whether the consistency of such differences warrants the generalization that a small advertisement is better than a large one in spite of the lack of statistical significance in the differences. Ignoring all factors but page size, it was possible to investigate the responses to particular advertisements of persons interviewed in the first experiment.

It will be recalled that three measures of immediate memory were available for each of the 101 individuals interviewed: the number of brands and the number of products correctly named, and the number of brands correctly recognized.

The percentage of individuals who responded correctly to each large and small advertisement was determined for these three tests of memory. This permitted a comparison of the relative effectiveness of the 20 items. Advertisements were ranked from those best remembered in the small to those best remembered in the large page size dummy. As would be expected from the findings already reported the small page size dummy was more effective in most instances; however, a few advertisements were definitely superior in the large size.

An explanation of these differences was sought by arranging the actual advertisements according to memory scores and examining them for some underlying principle which would explain the order. This analysis was attempted by 15 persons including advertising men, professional psychologists, graduate and undergraduate students. None could see any consistent variable in the advertisements; even later when told the basis of the arrangement, they could see nothing. There was also no significant correlation between preference and order of presentation of the ads in the booklet.

We are left with the fact that some advertisements, for reasons which are not evident on the basis of visual examination, are more readily remembered when seen in a small full-page size, while the opposite is the case with others. This suggests that our general findings may have been determined by the choice of the particular set of 20 advertisements. Repetition of the experiment making use of different advertisements might be worth while. However, it is most unlikely that such a study would produce conclusive evidence favouring the large size page.

So far as generalizations may be made on the basis of this work and on the investigations of twenty years ago, it may be concluded that the decision to place an advertisement in a large page size or in a small page size magazine should be based on factors other than the absolute dimensions of the page.

References

1. CUTLER, T. H. The Effectiveness of Page Size in Magazine Advertising. *Journal of Applied Psychology,* 1929, *13,* 465-9.
2. NEWHALL, S. M., and HEIM, M. H. Memory Value of Absolute Size in Magazine Advertising. *Journal of Applied Psychology,* 1929, *14,* 62-75.
3. SPIRES, A. M., and LEBLANC, A. G. The Relative Effectiveness of Absolute Size in Advertisements. (Unpublished study, McGill University, 1949.

FOURTEEN
PHYSIOLOGICAL BASIS OF BEHAVIOUR

65 / Positive Reinforcement Produced by Electrical Stimulation of Septal Area and Other Regions of Rat Brain[1]

James Olds[2] and Peter Milner *McGill University*

This is the classic paper in which Olds and Milner demonstrate the existence of localized systems in the brain where electrical stimulation can act as a reward or punishment, the particular motivating effect being determined by the site of electrical stimulation. This experiment, which has precipitated an unprecedented volume of similar research on porpoises, pigeons, rats, cats, monkeys, and even man, has led to the clarification of the nature of the basic mechanisms underlying reward and punishment.

Professor Olds is now at the California Institute of Technology. Professor Milner is the author of the textbook Physiological Psychology, *1970.*

Stimuli have eliciting and reinforcing functions. In studying the former, one concentrates on the responses which come after the stimulus. In studying the latter, one looks mainly at the responses which precede it. In its reinforcing capacity, a stimulus increases, decreases, or leaves unchanged the frequency of preceding responses, and accordingly it is called a reward, a punishment, or a neutral stimulus (cf. 16).

Previous studies using chronic implantation of electrodes have tended to focus on the eliciting functions of electrical stimuli delivered to the brain (2, 3, 4, 5, 7, 10, 12, 14). The present study, on the other hand, has been concerned with the reinforcing function of the electrical stimulation.[3]

Method

General

Stimulation was carried out by means of chronically implanted electrodes which did not interfere with the health or free behaviour of *S*s to any appreciable extent. The *S*s were 15 male hooded rats, weighing approximately 250 gm. at the start of the experiment. Each *S* was tested in a Skinner box which delivered alternating current to the brain so long as a lever was depressed. The current was delivered over a loose lead, suspended from the ceiling, which connected the stimulator to the rat's electrode. The *S*s were given a total of 6 to 12 hr. of acquisition testing, and 1 to 2 hr. of extinction testing. During acquisition, the stimulator was turned on so that a response produced electrical stimulation; during extinction, the stimulator was turned off so that a response produced no electrical stimulation. Each *S* was given a percentage score denoting the proportion of his total acquisition time given to responding. This score could be compared with the animal's extinction score to determine whether the stimulation had a positive, negative, or neutral reinforcing effect. After testing, the animal was sacrificed. Its brain was frozen, sectioned, stained, and examined microscopically to determine which structure of the brain had been stimulated. This permitted correlation of acquisition scores with anatomical structures.

Electrode Implantation

Electrodes are constructed by cementing a pair of enameled silver wires of 0.010-in. diameter into a Lucite block, as shown in Figure 1. The parts of the wires which penetrate the brain are cemented together to form a needle, and this is cut to the correct length to reach the desired structure in the brain. This length is determined from Krieg's rat brain atlas (11) with slight modifications as found necessary by experience. The exposed cross section of the wire is the only part of the needle not insulated from the brain by enamel; stimulation therefore occurs only at the tip. Contact with the lead from the

---

[1]The research reported here was made possible by grants from the Rockefeller Foundation and the National Institute of Mental Health of the U.S. Public Health Service. The authors particularly wish to express their thanks to Professor D. O. Hebb, who provided germinal ideas for the research and who backed it with enthusiastic encouragement as well as laboratory facilities and funds. The authors are also grateful to Miss Joann Feindel, who performed the histological reconstructions reported here.

[2]National Institute of Mental Health Postdoctorate Fellow of the U.S. Public Health Service.

[3]The present preliminary paper deals mainly with methods and behavioural results. A detailed report of the locus of positive, negative, and neutral reinforcing effects of electrical brain stimulation is being prepared by the first author.

---

stimulator is made through two blobs of solder on the upper ends of the electrode wires; these blobs make contact with the jaws of an alligator clip which has been modified to insulate the two jaws from one another. A light, flexible hearing-aid lead connects the clip to the voltage source.

The operation of implantation is performed with the rat under Nembutal anaesthesia (0.88 cc/Kg) and held in a Johnson-Krieg stereotaxic instrument (11). A mid-line incision is made in the scalp and the skin held out of the way by muscle retractors. A small hole is drilled in the skull with a dental burr at the point indicated by the stereotaxic instrument for the structure it is desired to stimulate. The electrode, which is clamped into the needle carrier of the instrument, is lowered until the flange of the Lucite block rests firmly on the skull. Four screw holes are then drilled in the skull through four fixing holes in the flange, and the electrode, still calmped firmly in the instrument, is fastened to the skull with jeweler's screws which exceed the diameter of the screw holes in the skull by 0.006 in. The electrode is then released from the clamp and the scalp wound closed with silk sutures. The skin is pulled tightly around the base of the Lucite block and kept well away from the contact plates. A recovery period of three days is allowed after the operation before testing. Figure 2 is an X-ray picture of an electrode in place.

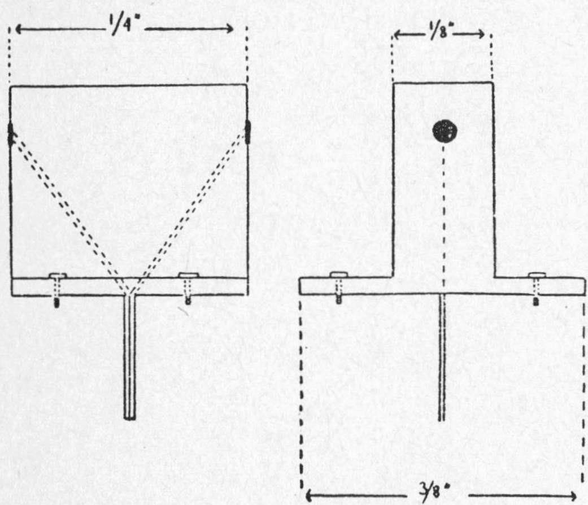

Fig. 1. Electrode design (see text for detailed description).

Testing

The testing apparatus consisted of a large-levered Skinner box 11 in. long, 5 in. wide, and 12 in. high. The top was open to allow passage for the stimulating lead. The lever actuated a microswitch in the stimulating circuit so that when it was depressed, the rat received electrical stimulation. The current was obtained from the 60-cycle power line, through a step-down transformer, and was adjustable between 0 and 10 v. r.m.s. by means of a variable potentiometer. In the experiments described here the stimulation continued as long as the lever was pressed, though for some tests a time-delay switch was incorporated which cut the current off after a predetermined interval if the rat continued to hold the lever down. Responses were recorded automatically on paper strip.

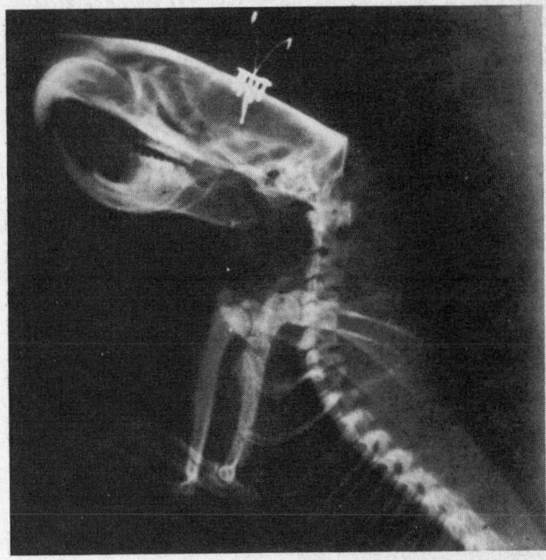
Fig. 2. X-ray showing electrode in place in intact animal. There are two wires insulated completely from each other, stimulating the brain with their tips.

On the fourth day after the operation rats were given a pretesting session of about an hour in the boxes. Each rat was placed in the box and on the lever by *E* with the stimulus set at 0.5 v. During the hour, stimulation voltage was varied to determine the threshold of a "just noticeable" effect on the rat's behaviour. If the animal did not respond regularly from the start, it was placed on the lever periodically (at about 5-min. intervals). Data collected on the first day were not used in later calculations. On subsequent days, *S*s were placed in the box for about 3½ hr. a day; these were 3 hr. of acquisition and ½ hr. of extinction. During the former, the rats were allowed to stimulate themselves with a voltage which was just high enough to produce some noticeable response in the resting animal. As this threshold voltage fluctuated with the passage of time, *E* would make a determination of it every half hour, unless *S* was responding regularly. At the beginning of each acquisition period, and after each voltage test, the animal was placed on the lever once by *E*. During extinction periods, conditions were precisely the same except that a bar press produced no electrical stimulation. At the beginning of each extinction period, animals which were not responding regularly were placed on the lever once by *E*. At first, rats were tested in this way for four days, but as there appeared to be little difference between the results on different days, this period was reduced to three and then to two days for subsequent animals. Thus, the first rats had about 12 hr. of acquisition after pretesting whereas later rats had about 6 hr. However, in computing the scores in our table, we have used only the first 6 hr. of acquisition for all animals, so the scores are strictly comparable. In behavioural curves, we have shown the full 12 hr. of acquistiion on the earlier animals so as to illustrate the stability of the behaviour over time.

At no time during the experiment were the rats deprived of food or water, and no reinforcement was used except the electrical stimulus.

Animals were scored on the percentage of time which they spent bar pressing regularly during acquisition. In order to find how much time the animal would spend in the absence of reward or punishment, a similar score was computed for periods of extinction. This extinction score provided a base line. When the acquisition score is above the extinction score, we have reward; when it is below the extinction score, we have punishment.

In order to determine percentage scores, periods when the animal was responding regularly (at least one response every 30 sec.) were counted as periods of responding; i.e., *intervals of 30 sec. or longer without a response were counted as periods of no responding*. The percentage scores were computed as the proportion of total acquisition or extinction time given to periods of responding.

Determination of Locus

On completion of testing, animals were perfused with physiological saline, followed by 10 per cent formalin. The brains were removed, and after further fixation in formalin for about a week, frozen sections 40 microns thick were cut through the region of the electrode track. These were stained with cresyl violet and the position of the electrode tip determined. Figure 3 is a photomicrograph showing the appearance of the electrode track in a stained and mounted brain section. [4]

Table I – Acquisition and extinction scores for all animals together with electrode placements and threshold voltages used during acquisition tests

Animal's No.	Locus of Electrode	Stimulation Voltage r.m.s.	Percentage of Acquisition Time Spent Responding	Percentage of Extinction Time Spent Responding
32	septal	2.2–2.8	75	18
34	septal	1.4	92	6
M-1	septal	1.7–4.8	85	21
M-4	septal	2.3–4.8	88	13
40	c.c.	.7–1.1	6	3
41	caudate	.9–1.2	4	4
31	cingulate	1.8	37	9
82	cingulate	.5–1.8	36	10
36	hip.	.8–2.8	11	14
3	m.l.	.5	0	4
A-5	m.t.	1.4	71	9
6	m.g.	.5	0	31
11	m.g.	.5	0	21
17	teg.	.7	2	1
9	teg.	.5	77	81

KEY: *c.c.*, *corpus callosum; hip.*, hippocampus; *m.l.*, medial lemniscus; *m.t.*, Mammillothalamic tract; *m.g.*, medial geniculate; *teg.*, tegmentum.

[4]Figure 3, "Photomicrograph showing the electrode track in a cresyl-violet-stained brain section," has been deleted.

Results

Locus

In Table I, acquisition and extinction scores are correlated with electrode placements. Figure 4 presents the acquisition scores again, this time on three cross-sectional maps of the rat brain, one at the forebrain level, one at the thalamic level, and one at the mid-brain level. The position of a score on the map indicates the electrode placement from which this acquisition score was obtained.

The highest scores are found together in the central portion of the forebrain. Beneath the *corpus callosum* and between the two lateral ventricles in section I of Figure 4, we find four acquisition scores ranging from 75 to 92 per cent. This is the septal area. The *S*s which produced these scores are numbered 32, 34, M-1, and M-4 in Table I. It will be noticed that while all of them spent more than 75 per cent of their acquisition time responding, they all spent less than 22 per cent of their extinction time responding. Thus the electrical stimulus in the septal area has an effect which is apparently equivalent to that of a conventional primary reward as far as the maintenance of a lever-pressing response is concerned.

If we move outside the septal area, either in the direction of the caudate nucleus (across the lateral ventricle) or in the direction of the *corpus callosum*, we find acquisition scores drop abruptly to levels of from 4 to 6 per cent. These are definitely indications of neutral (neither rewarding nor punishing) effects.

However, above the *corpus callosum* in the cingulate cortex we find an acquisition score of 37 per cent. As the extinction score in this case was 9 per cent, we may say that stimulation was rewarding.

At the thalamic level (section II of Fig. 4) we find a 36 per cent acquisition score produced by an electrode placed again in the cingulate cortex, an 11 per cent score produced by an electrode placed in the hippocampus, a 71 per cent score produced by an electrode placed exactly in the mammillo-thalamic tract, and a zero per cent score produced by an electrode placed in the medial lemniscus. The zero denotes negative reinforcement.

At the mid-brain level (section III of Fig. 4) there are two zero scores produced by electrodes which are in the posterior portion of the medial geniculate bodies; here again, the scores indicate a negative effect, as the corresponding extinction scores are 31 and 21 per cent. There is an electrode deep in the medial, posterior tegmentum which produces a 2 per cent score; this seems quite neutral, as the extinction score in this case is 1 per cent. Finally, there is an electrode shown on this section which actually stands 1 ½ mm. anterior to the point where it is shown; it was between the red nucleus and the posterior commissure. It produced an acquisition score of 77 per cent, but an extinction score of 81 per cent. This must be a rewarding placement, but the high extinction score makes it difficult to interpret.

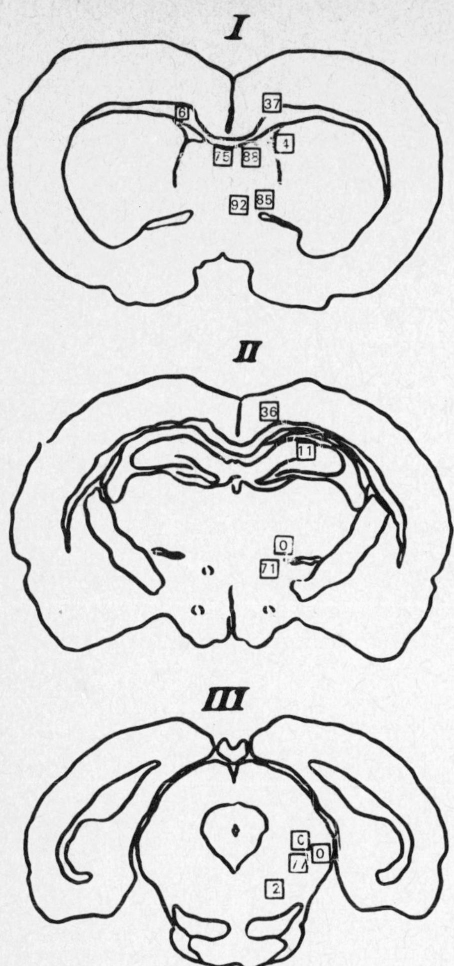

Fig. 4. *Maps of three sections, (I) through the forebrain, (II) through the thalamus, (III) through the mid-brain of the rat. Boxed numbers give acquisition percentage scores produced by animals with electrodes stimulating at these points. On section I the acquisition scores 75, 88, 92, 85 fall in the septal forebrain area. On the same section there is a score of 4 in the caudate nucleus, a score of 6 in the white matter below the cortex, and a score of 37 in the medial (cingulate) cortex. On section II the acquisition score of 36 is in the medial (cingulate) cortex, 11 is in the hippocampus, 71 is in the mammillothalamic tract, and 0 is in the medial lemniscus. On section III the two zeroes are in the medial geniculate, 2 is in the tegmental reticular substance, 77 falls 2 mm. anterior to the section shown – it is between the posterior commissure and the red nucleus.*

Behaviour

We turn our attention briefly to the behavioural data produced by the more rewarding electrode placements.

The graph in Figure 5 is a smoothed cumulative response curve illustrating the rate of responding of rat No. 32 (the lowest-scoring septal area rat) during acquisition and extinction. The animal gave a total of slightly over 3000 responses in the 12 hr. of acquisition. When the current was turned on, the animal responded at a rate of 285 responses an hour; when the current was turned off, the rate fell close to zero.

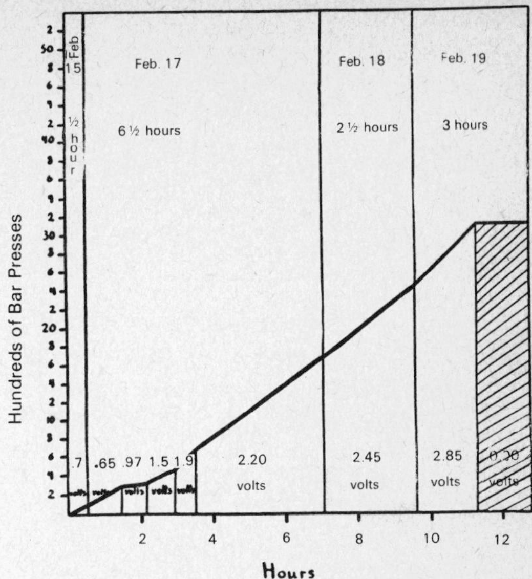

Fig. 5. *Smoothed cumulative response curve for rat No. 32. Cumulative response totals are given along the ordinate, and hours along the abscissa. The steepness of the slope indicates the response rate. Stimulating voltages are given between black lines. Cross hatching indicates extinction.*

The graph in Figure 6 gives similar data on rat No. 34 (the highest-scoring septal rat). The animal stimulated itself over 7500 times in 12 hr. Its average response rate during acquisition was 742 responses an hour; during extinction, practically zero.

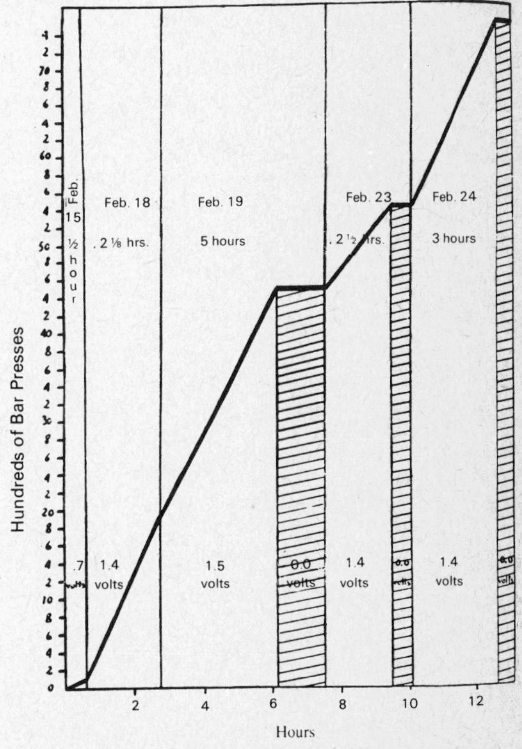

Fig. 6. *Smoothed cumulative response curve for rat No. 34.*

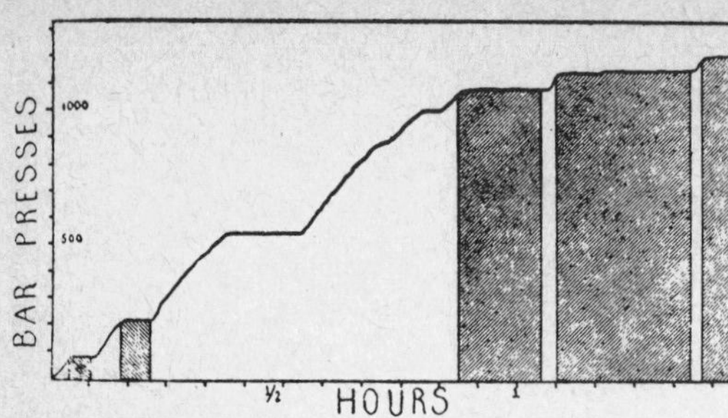

Fig. 7. Unsmoothed cumulative response curve showing about ¾ hr. of acquisition and ¾ hr. extinction for rat No. A-5. Shading indicates extinction.

Figure 7 presents an unsmoothed cumulative response curve for one day of responding for rat No. A-5. This is to illustrate in detail the degree of control exercised by the electrical reward stimulus. While this rat was actually bar pressing, it did so at 1920 responses an hour; that is, about one response for every 2 sec. During the first period of the day it responded regularly while on acquisition, extinguished very rapidly when the current was turned off, and reconditioned readily when the current was turned on again. At reconditioning points, *E* gave *S* one stimulus to show that the current was turned on again, but *E* did not place *S* on the lever. During longer periods of acquisition, *S* occasionally stopped responding for short periods, but in the long run *S* spent almost three-quarters of its acquisition time responding. During the long period of extinction at the end of the day, there was very little responding, but *S* could be brought back to the lever quite quickly if a stimulus was delivered to show that the current had been turned on again.

Discussion

It is clear that electrical stimulation in certain parts of the brain, particularly the septal area, produces acquisition and extinction curves which compare favourably with those produced by a conventional primary reward. With other electrode placements, the stimulation appears to be neutral or punishing.

Because the rewarding effect has been produced maximally by electrical stimulation in the septal area, but also in lesser degrees in the mammillothalamic tract and cingulate cortex, we are led to speculate that a system of structures previously attributed to the rhinencephalon may provide the locus for the reward phenomenon. However, as localization studies which will map the whole brain with respect to the reward and punishment dimension are continuing, we will not discuss in detail the problem of locus. We will use the term "reinforcing structures" in further discussion as a general name for the septal area and other structures which produce the reward phenomenon.

To provide an adequate canvass of the possible explanations for the rewarding effect would require considerably more argument than could possibly fit within the confines of a research paper. We have decided, therefore, to rule out briefly the possibility that the implantation produces pain which is reduced by electrical stimulation of reinforcing structures, and to confine further discussion to suggestions of ways the phenomenon may provide a methodological basis for study of physiological mechanisms of reward.

The possibility that the implantation produces some painful "drive stimulus" which is alleviated by electrical stimulation of reinforcing structures does not comport with the facts which we have observed. If there were some chronic, painful drive state, it would be indicated by emotional signs in the animal's daily behaviour. Our *S*s, from the first day after the operation, are normally quiet, nonaggressive; they eat regularly, sleep regularly, gain weight. There is no evidence in their behaviour to support the postulation of chronic pain. Septal preparations which have lived healthy and normal lives for months after the operation have given excellent response rates.

As there is no evidence of a painful condition preceding the electrical stimulation, and as the animals are given free access to food and water at all times except while actually in the Skinner boxes, there is no explicitly manipulated drive to be reduced by electrical stimulation. Barring the possibility that stimulation of a reinforcing structure specifically inhibits the "residual drive" state of the animal, or the alternative possibility that the first electrical stimulus has noxious after-effects which are reduced by a second one, we have some evidence here for a primary rewarding effect which is not associated with the reduction of a primary drive state. It is perhaps fair in a discussion to report the "clinical impression" of the *E*s that the phenomenon represents strong pursuit of a positive stimulus rather than escape from some negative condition.

Should the latter interpretation prove correct, we have perhaps located a system within the brain whose peculiar function is to produce a rewarding effect on behaviour. The location of such a system puts us in a position to collect information that may lead to a decision among conflicting theories of reward. By physiological studies, for example, we may find that the reinforcing structures act selectively on sensory or motor areas of the cortex. This would have relevance to current S-S versus S-R controversies (8, 9, 13, 16).

Similarly, extirpation studies may show whether reinforcing structures have primarily a quieting or an activating effect on behaviour; this would be relevant to activation versus negative feedback theories of reward (6, 13, 15, 17). A recent study by Brady and Nauta (1) already suggests that the septal area is a quieting system, for its surgical removal produced an extremely active animal.

Such examples, we believe, make it reasonable to hope that the methodology reported here should have important consequences for physiological studies of mechanisms of reward.

Summary

A preliminary study was made of rewarding effects produced by electrical stimulation of certain areas of the brain. In all cases rats were used and stimulation was by 60-cycle alternating current with voltages ranging from ½ to 5 v. Bipolar needle electrodes were permanently implanted at various points in the brain. Animals were tested in Skinner boxes where they could stimulate themselves by pressing a lever. They received no other reward than the electrical stimulus in the course of the experiments. The primary findings may be listed as follows:
(a) There are numerous places in the lower centres of the brain where electrical stimulation is rewarding in the sense that the experimental animal will stimulate itself in these places frequently and regularly for long periods of time if permitted to do so.
(b) It is possible to obtain these results from as far back as the tegmentum, and us far forward as the septal area; from as far down as the subthalamus, and as far up as the cingulate gyrus of the cortex.
(c) There are also sites in the lower centres where the effect is just the opposite; animals do everything possible to avoid stimulation. And there are neutral sites: animals do nothing to obtain or to avoid stimulation.
(d) The reward results are obtained more dependably with electrode placements in some areas than others, the septal area being the most dependable to date.
(e) In septal area preparations, the control exercised over the animal's behaviour by means of this reward is extreme, possibly exceeding that exercised by any other reward previously used in animal experimentation.

The possibility that the reward results depended on some chronic painful consequences of the implantation operation was ruled out on the evidence that no physiological or behavioural signs of such pain could be found. The phenomenon was discussed as possibly laying a methodological foundation for a physiological study of the mechanisms of reward.

References

1. BRADY, J. V., and NAUTA, W. J. H. Subcortical mechanisms in emotional behaviour: affective changes following septal forebrain lesions in the albino rat. *J. comp. physiol. Psychol.*, 1953, *46*, 339-346.
2. DELGADO, J. M. R. Permanent implantation of multilead electrodes in the brain. *Yale J. Biol. Med.*, 1952, *24*, 351-358.
3. ———. Responses evoked in waking cat by electrical stimulation of motor cortex. *Amer. J. Physiol.*, 1952, *171*, 436-446.
4. DELGADO, J. M. R., and ANAND, B. K. Increase of food intake induced by electrical stimulation of the lateral hypothalamus. *Amer. J. Physiol.*, 1953, *172*, 162-168.
5. DELL, P. Correlations entre le système vegetatif et le système de la vie relation: mesencephale, diencephale, et cortex cerebral. *J. Physiol.* (Paris), 1952, *44*, 471-557.
6. DEUTSCH, J. A. A new type of behaviour theory. *Brit. J. Psychol.*, 1953, *44*, 304-317.
7. GASTAUT, II. Correlations entre le système nerveux vegetatif et le système de la vie de relation dans le rhinencephale. *J. Physiol.* (Paris), 1952, *44*, 431-470.
8. HEBB, D. O. *The organization of behaviour.* New York: Wiley, 1949.
9. HULL, C. L. *Principles of behaviour.* New York: D. Appleton-Century, 1943.
10. HUNTER, J., and JASPER, H. H. Effects of thalamic stimulation in unanaesthetized animals. *EEG clin. Neurophysiol.*, 1949, *1*, 305-324.
11. KREIG, W. J. S. Accurate placement of minute lesions in the brain of the albino rat. *Quart. Bull., Northwestern Univ. Med. School*, 1946, *20*, 199-208.
12. MACLEAN, P. D., and DELGADO, J. M. R. Electrical and chemical stimulation of frontotemporal portion of limbic system in the waking animal. *EEG clin. Neurophysiol.*, 1953, *5*, 91-100.
13. OLDS, J. A. neural model for sign-gestalt theory. *Psychol. Rev.*, 1954, *61*, 59-72.
14. ROSVOLD, H. E., and DELGADO, J. M. R. The effect on the behaviour of monkeys of electrically stimulating or destroying small areas within the frontal lobes. *Amer. Psychologist*, 1953, *8*, 425-426. (Abstract).
15. SEWARD, J. P. Introduction to a theory of motivation in learning. *Psychol. Rev.*, 1952, *59*, 405-413.
16. SKINNER, B. F. *The behaviour of organisms.* New York: D. Appleton-Century, 1938.
17. WIENER, N. *Cybernetics.* New York: Wiley, 1949.

66 / Drinking Induced by Electrical Stimulation of the Lateral Hypothalamus

G.J. Mogenson and J.A.F. Stevenson[1] *University of Western Ontario*

Using an electrophysiological technique, evidence is presented for the existence of a central control system for water intake, the stimulation of which induces immediate drinking behaviour.

Introduction

It has been shown that the lateral hypothalamus plays an important role in controlling water intake. Lesions of this region of the brain produce adipsia (2, 7, 15) and stimulation, either electrical (9) or chemical (8, 10), elicits drinking.

In 1955, Greer (9) reported that electrical stimulation of the hypothalamus had caused one rat to drink over 400 ml of water per day. Since then, it had been noted during investigations of feeding behaviour that hypothalamic stimulation will elicit drinking in the rat (13, 16) but apparently there have been no quantitative studies of the effects of electrical stimulation of this region on water intake. While studying the behavioural effects of electrical stimulation of the lateral hypothalamus, it was observed in some rats that such stimulation readily elicited drinking of water. The drinking behaviour persisted for as long as the stimulation was maintained, for several hours a day, and was reproducible for several months.

Materials and Methods

Bipolar electrodes (Plastic Products Company, Roanoke, Virginia, MS-303-0.018) insulated except at the tips were placed stereotaxically (6) in the lateral hypothalamus (co-ordinates, A 5.0, L 1.6 to 1.9, V - 2.0 to - 3.0) of male Wistar rats anaesthetized with sodium pentobarbital. Several weeks later the rats were placed, one at a time, in a small chamber (15 x 30 x 30 cm) made of transparent Plexiglass and the effects of electrical stimulation of the hypothalamus were observed. A water spout from a graduated water bottle extended into the end of the chamber 6 cm above the floor. The source of electrical stimulation was a 60-cycle sine wave stimulator which delivered current in the range from 10-40 μamp. The intensity of current was monitored with an oscilloscope and its duration (1.2 sec) was controlled by means of an interval timer (Hunter Manufacturing Company, model 100C). The number of times stimulation was delivered was recorded on an impulse counter. The experimenter could apply electrical stimulation by external operation of a switch or the animal could press a level (Lehigh Valley Electronics, model 1535) located just below the water spout, which closed a switch and activated the stimulator. At the completion of the experiments, the rats were killed and the brains removed, fixed in 10% formalin and imbedded in paraffin. Sections cut at 15 μ were stained with cresyl violet to determine the locus of stimulation.

Results

Ten of sixty-five rats drank water when the lateral hypothalamus was stimulated electrically. Initial results obtained on four of these "drinkers" have been presented in a preliminary report (14). These rats were given additional tests two or three times per week for over 5 months and water intake was always induced by hypothalamic stimulation.

Six other rats, in which hypothalamic stimulation elicited drinking, have been studied for shorter periods (2-3 months). Figure 1 shows the quantity of water consumed by one of these rats during a 2-hr period of stimulation. For this rat the hypothalamic stimulation was controlled externally (the lever was removed from the chamber) and 1.2-sec. trains of current (20 μamp) were presented at the rate of 24 per min. Although the animal was satiated for water and food when the test began, it consumed 61 ml of water in 2 hr. After 25 min of stimulation and water intake, large quantities of dilute urine (specific gravity, 1.005 compared to a control of 1.030) were produced. Throughout the test the excess of water intake over water loss as urine was about 20 ml.

For most of the experiments the lever was present in the chamber, the stimulator being turned on whenever the animal pressed the level. Typically the animals were allowed to stimulate themselves for a period of 1 hr on a test day and during this time the volume of water intake varied from 10 to 48 ml

[1]This investigation was supported by grants from the Medical Research Council and the National Research Council of Canada. The authors wish to acknowledge the assistance of Charles Morgan with the surgery, of Martha Welsh with the histology and of Wayne Andrew and Mary Underhill with the 18- and 24-hour experiments.

(mean for the ten rats, 22.4 ml). Some of the sessions were continued for longer periods. The number of stimulations to the hypothalamus and the volumes of water intake and urine flow in a 4-hr experiment are shown in Figure 2. This rat stimulated its hypothalamus at a rate of 20.5 times per min and drank 64 ml of water during the 4-hr period. A similar experiment lasting 18 hrs is shown in Figure 3. In the first 12 hrs the animal stimulated itself 15,594 times and drank 217 ml of water. The volume of urine collected during this time was 176 ml. Allowing for the normal 12-hr extrarenal loss of water, the excess of intake over output was approximately 25 ml. After 12½ hrs the stimulator was shut off for 30 min during which the rat did not press the lever and ceased drinking water but urine flow continued (Fig. 3). The stimulator was turned on again at the beginning of the fourteenth hour. During the fifteenth hour the water spout was removed but lever-pressing for hypothalamic stimulation continued the urine flow was somewhat reduced because there was no water intake during this period. The water spout was replaced during the last 2 hr and the rat continued to stimulate its hypothalamus and drink.

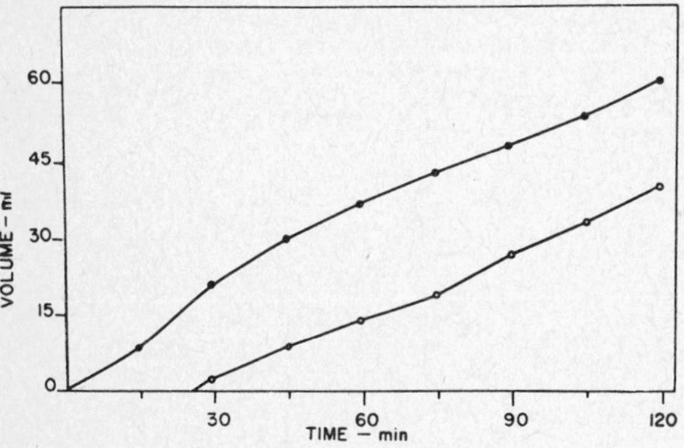

Fig. 1. Cumulative water intake (closed circles) and urine flow (open circles) for rat DE-8 receiving electrical stimulation of the lateral hypothalamus for a period of 2 hr. (for parameters of stimulation see text).

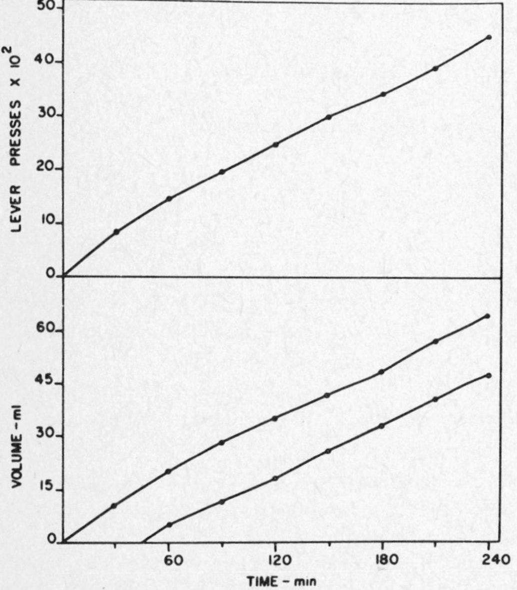

Fig. 2. Cumulative water intake (closed circles) and urine flow (open circles) for rat DE-6 stimulating its hypothalamus during a 4-hr. period. Each lever press (see top portion of figure) activated the stimulator for 1.2 sec. The current intensity was 25 µamp.

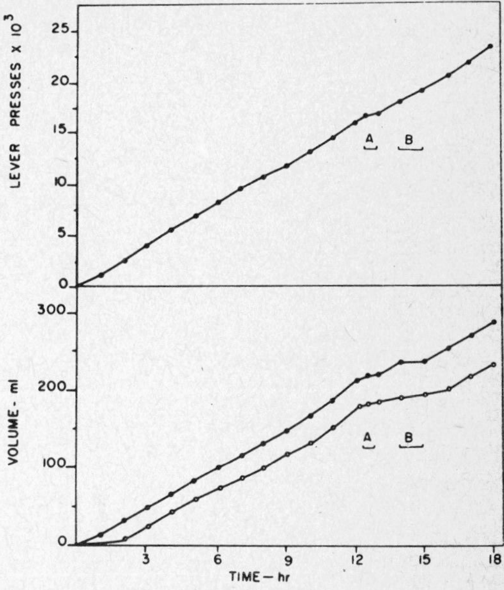

Fig. 3. Results obtained when rat DE-3 stimulated its lateral hypothalamus (current intensity 21 µamp) during an 18-hr. period. The cumulative number of lever presses is shown at the top and cumulative water intake (closed circles) and urine flow (open circles) are shown at the bottom. At A the stimulator was shut off for 30 min. Note that stimulation of the hypothalamus ceased and drinking no longer occurred. At B the water spout was removed from the chamber for 1 hr. The rat continued to stimulate its hypothalamus, but, of course, could not drink.

The results of an experiment in which an animal stimulated its lateral hypothalamus continuously for 24 hr are shown in Figure 4. The stimulator was activated 37,150 times which resulted in a water intake of 460 ml. Due to a defect in the system for collecting urine an accurate measurement was not obtained. However, large quantities of dilute urine were excreted (specific gravity, 1.003). During the test period this rat, as well as the previous one, stopped lever-pressing occasionally to eat. The quantity of food consumed did not appear to be abnormal; rat no. 13 ate 11 g in 18 hr and rat no. 15 ate 15 g in 24 hr; the normal intake on this diet is 12-17 g per day.

Although all electrodes were placed using the same stereotaxic co-ordinates, variation in their precise location was sufficient so that in only ten of the animals did electrical stimulation evoke drinking. As shown in Figure 5 the electrodes for nine of these ten rats terminated in a small region of the lateral hypothalamus dorsolateral to the fornix at 4.6 to 5.0 mm anterior to the intra-aural plane (6). A photomicrograph of the hypothalamic region of one of these animals is presented in Figure 6 and the electrode

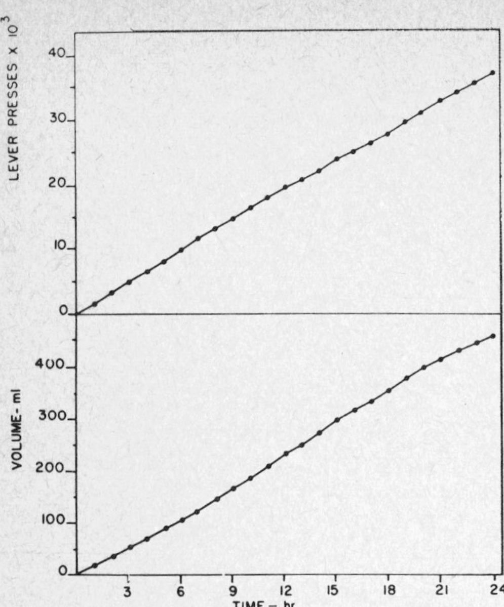

Fig. 4. Rat DE-4 stimulated its hypthalamus (current intensity 22 μamp) continuously for 24 hr. The stimulation induced a total water intake of 460 ml.

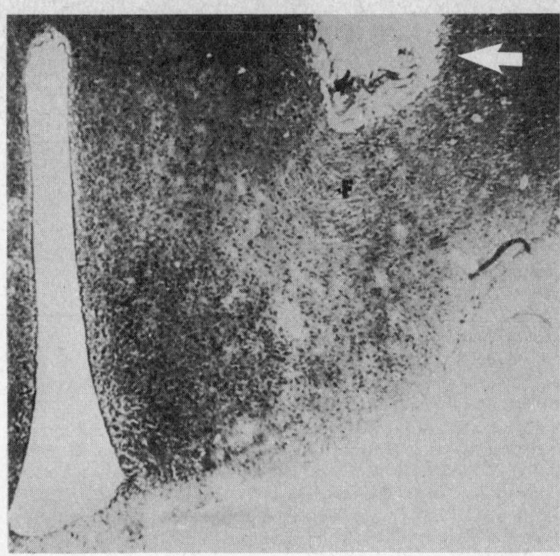

Fig. 6. Photomicrograph showing the termination of the electrode tract (marked by arrow) which was used to elicit drinking in one rat. The electrode was dorsal and slightly lateral to the fornix (F).

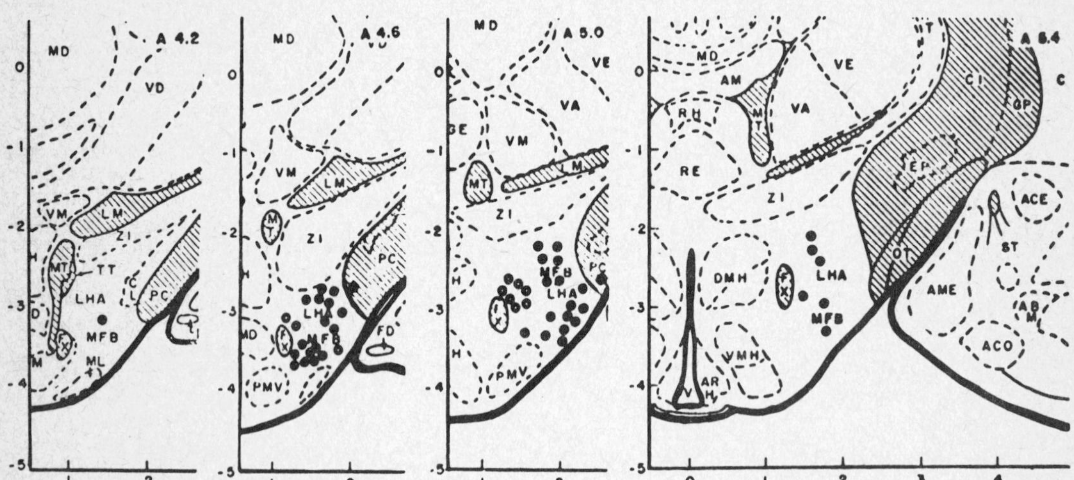

Fig. 5. The electrodes for the drinkers were in a small region of the hypothalamus dorsolateral to the fornix (F). The location of the electrode tips are shown on coronal sections of the rat hypothalamus. The electrode sites for the drinkers are indicated by open circles and for the nondrinkers by closed circles.

tract is seen to terminate near the fornix. The electrode of the other drinker was further lateral to the fornix at anterior 4.6. The stimulation sites of forty of the nondrinkers, for which histological verifications were made, also appear in Figure 5 and indicate that they terminated either above, below or lateral to what appears to be a critical focus for drinking behaviour near the fornix.

Discussion

The rats described in this report drank water as soon as electrical stimulation of the lateral hypothalamus was begun and stopped drinking when it ceased. Drinking after the electrical stimulation terminated, which was reported by Andersson, Larsson, and Persson (3) and described as an after-effect of the stimulation, was not observed. Perhaps this is because our train durations of stimulation were much shorter. The fact that they drank for some 20 min before an increase in urine flow was apparent indicates that the drinking was not secondary to a diuresis but was the result of stimulation of a central control system for water intake. This diuresis, secondary to water intake, permitted a new steady state of water exchange to be approached so that the animal could continue to drink water in response to the hypothalamic stimulation. This would not occur in an animal that fed in response to hypothalamic stimulation for absorption from the gastrointestinal tract and disposition of the ingested energy would not occur quickly enough (12).

Chemical stimulation with cholinergic agents has implicated various regions of the hypothalamus, amygdala, hippocampus and septum in a water intake control system (8, 11). However, the only region in which destruction has produced adipsia in the rat is in and perhaps near the lateral hypothalamus (2, 15). Apparently, cell assemblies essential to the control of water intake are located in this region, comprising a focus for the drinking system. It may be that the neurons involved in these assemblies are sufficiently concentrated in this region that electrical stimulation here may evoke drinking when it does not in other regions that respond to chemical stimulation. In the dog, goat and pigeon, other species in which drinking has been elicited by hypothalamic stimulation, the focus of the drinking system appears to be slightly more rostral and medial (1, 4, 5).

Both self-stimulation and drinking in response to such electrical stimulation in the lateral hypothalamus, when obtained, appeared likely to continue indefinitely. One of the rats stimulated its hypothalamus for 24 hr and drank over 450 ml of water. All ten of the rats in which hypothalamic stimulation induced drinking were avid self-stimulators. Thirty-nine of the remaining fifty-five rats were also self-stimulators, most of them at lower rates. None of these animals drank water either during self-stimulation or when hypothalamic stimulation was externally controlled.

It has been reported that rats will self-stimulate rather than eat available food even when they have been food-deprived for many hours (17, 18). In view of that obervation, it is interesting that the self-stimulating drinkers in this study would stop self-stimulation in order to eat. Whether this would occur in a self-stimulating drinker that was not consuming water is not known. It seems likely that it would since the rate of self-stimulation fell in these animals when water was not available.

Abstract

Rats received electrical stimulation through electrodes implanted chronically in the lateral hypothalamus. The stimulation, controlled either by the experimenter or by the rat pressing on a lever, elicited stimulus-bound drinking in several of the animals. In 1-hr tests the rats drank amounts which, in most cases, equalled or exceeded their normal 24-hr intakes. In longer tests, this induced drinking was quite constant; during a 24-hr period one rat drank 460 ml of water. About 20 to 30 min after stimulation was begun, diuresis was observed and during experiments extending over several hours the excess of water intake over water loss, allowing for the normal extrarenal loss of water, was 20 to 25 ml. In experiments repeated over several months in the same rats hypothalamic stimulation continued to induce water intake.

References

1. Akerman, B., Andersson, B., Fabricius, E., and Svensson, L. Observations on central regulation of body temperature and of food and water intake in the pigeon. *(Columbia livia). Acta Physiol. Scand.*, 1960, *50*, 328-336.
2. Anand, B. K., and Dua, S. Hypothalamic control over water consumption in the rat. *Indian J. Med. Res.*, 1958, *46*, 426-430.
3. Andersson, B., Larsson, S., and Persson, N. Some characteristics of the hypothalamic "drinking centre" in the goat as shown by the use of permanent electrodes. *Acta Physiol. Scand.*, 1960, *50*, 140-152.
4. Andersson, B., and McCann, S. M. A further study of polydipsia evoked by hypothalamic stimulation in the goat. *Acta Physiol. Scand.*, 1955, *33*, 333-346.
5. Andersson, B., and McCann, S. M. The effect of hypothalamic lesions on the water intake of the dog. *Acta Physiol. Scand.*, 1956, *35*, 312-320.
6. De Groot, J. The Rat Forebrain in Stereotaxic Co-ordinates. N-V Noord-Hollandsche Vitgevers Maatschapij, Amsterdam, 1959.
7. Epstein, A. N., and Teitelbaum, P. Severe and persistent deficits in thirst produced by lateral hypothalamic damage, pp. 395-410. In *"Thirst."* M. J. Wayner (ed.). Pergamon Press, New York, 1964.
8. Fisher, A. E., and Coury, J. M. Cholinergic tracing of a central neural circuit underlying the thirst drive. *Science*, 1962, *138*, 691-693.
9. Greer, M. A. Suggestive evidence of a primary "drinking centre" in the hypothalamus of the rat. *Proc. Soc. Exptl. Biol. Med.*, 1955, *89* 59-62.
10. Grossman, S. Eating or drinking elicited by direct adrenergic or cholinergic stimulation of the hypothalamus. *Science*, 1960, *132*, 301-302.
11. Grossman, S. P. Behavioural effects of chemical stimulation of the ventral amygdala. *J. Comp. Physiol. Psychol.*, 1964, *57*, 29-36.
12. Hoebel, B. G., and Teitelbaum, P. Hypothalamic control of feeding and self-stimulation. *Science*, 1962, *135*, 375-377.
13. Miller, N. E. Motivational effects of brain stimulation and drugs. *Federation Proc.*, 1960, *19*, 846-854.
14. Mogenson, G. J., and Stevenson, J. A. F. Drinking and self-stimulation with electrical stimulation of the lateral hypothalamus. *Physiol. Behav.*, 1966, *1*, 251-254.
15. Montemurro, D. G., and Stevenson, J. A. F. Adipsia produced by hypothalamic lesions in the rat. *Can. J. Biochem. Physiol.*, 1957, *35*, 31-37.
16. Morgane, P. J. Evidence of a "hunger motivational" system in the lateral hypothalamus of the rat. *Nature*, 1961, *191*, 672-674.
17. Routtenberg, A., and Lindy, J. Effects of availability of rewarding septal and hypothalamic stimulation on bar pressing for food under conditions of deprivation. *J. Comp. Physiol. Psychol.*, 1965, *60*, 158-161.
18. Spies, G. Food versus intracranial self-stimulation reinforcement in food-deprived rats. *J. Comp. Physiol. Psychol.*, 1965, *60*, 153-157.

67 / Stress: It's a G.A.S.

Hans Selye *University of Montreal*

Dr. Selye, the world's foremost expert on stress, summarizes the various physiological changes which occur when the organism is subjected to either physical or psychological stress. The evolution of the concept of the General Adaptation Syndrome (G.A.S.) is also described.

Dr. Selye is the Director, Institute of Experimental Medicine and Surgery, University of Montreal, and the author of over 600 scientific papers and 12 books. He is also the recipient of honorary degrees from numerous universities.

We can get high on our own stress hormones. Stress stimulates our glands to make hormones that can induce a kind of drunkenness. Who would consider it prudent to check his conduct as carefully during stress as he does during the cocktail hour? He should. I venture to say that this sort of drunkenness has caused much more harm to society than the other kind.

The concept of stress is very old. It must have occurred even to prehistoric man that there was something in common between the loss of vigour and the feeling of exhaustion that overcomes us after hard labour, prolonged exposure to cold or heat, loss of blood, agonizing fear or any kind of disease.

Man also must have found out long ago that we experience every unaccustomed task – be it swimming in cold water, lifting rocks or going without food – in three stages: at first it is a hardship, then we get used to it and finally we can't stand it any longer.

But it was not until some 30 years ago that we found that stress causes certain changes in the structure and chemical composition of the body, which can be accurately appraised. Some of these changes are merely signs of damage; others are the body's attempts to restore itself to normal, its mechanism of defense against stress.

Back in 1926, when stress was still a mystery and I was a second-year medical student, I first came across the stereotyped response. I wondered why the most diverse diseases produced so many common signs and symptoms. Whether a man suffers from severe blood loss, an infection, or advanced cancer, he loses his appetite, strength and ambition; usually he also loses weight and even his facial expression betrays his illness. I felt sure that the syndrome of just being sick, which is essentially the same no matter what disease we have, could be analyzed and expressed scientifically.

This possibility fascinated me and, with the enthusiasm of youth, I wanted to start work right away. But my background as a second-year medical student didn't reach far enough, and I got no farther than the formulation of an idea. And the more I learned about the details of medicine, the more I forgot my broad but imprecise plan to tackle the syndrome of just being sick.

Years later, under auguries more auspicious for research, I encountered the problem again. I was working as a young assistant in the biochemistry department of McGill University in Montreal, trying to find a new sex hormone in extracts of cattle ovaries. I injected the extracts into rats to see if their organs would show changes that could not be attributed to a known hormone.

Much to my satisfaction, the first and most impure extracts changed the rats in three ways: (1) the adrenal cortex became enlarged, (2) the thymus, the spleen, the lymph nodes and all other lymphatic structures shrank and (3) deep, bleeding ulcers appeared in the stomach and in the upper gut.

Because the three types of change were closely interdependent they formed a definite syndrome. The changes varied from slight to pronounced depending on the amount of extract I injected.

At first I ascribed all these changes to a new sex hormone in my extract. But soon I found that all toxic substances – extracts of kidney, spleen or even a toxin not derived from living tissue – produced the same syndrome. Gradually my classroom concept of the syndrome of just being sick came back to me. I realized that the reaction I had produced with my impure extracts and toxic drugs was an experimental replica of the syndrome of just being sick. Adrenal enlargement, gastrointestinal ulcers and thymicolymphatic shrinkage were the omnipresent signs of damage to the body when under disease attack. Thus the three changes became the objective indices of stress and the basis for the development of the entire stress concept.

My first paper on the syndrome of stress, "A Syndrome Produced by Diverse Nocuous Agents,"

Reprinted, by permission, from *Psychology Today*, September, 1969, pp. 25-26 and 56.

was published in the British journal, *Nature.* In this paper, I suggested *alarm reaction* for the animal's initial response because I thought that the syndrome probably represented a general call to arms of the body's defensive forces.

However, the alarm reaction evidently was not the entire response. My very first experiments showed that continuous exposure to any noxious agent capable of setting off this alarm reaction is followed by a stage of adaptation or resistance. Apparently disease is not just suffering, but a fight to maintain the homeostatic balance of our tissues when they are damaged. No living organism can exist continuously in a state of alarm. An agent so damaging that continuous exposure to it is incompatible with life causes death within hours or days of the alarm reaction. However, if survival is possible, the alarm reaction gives way to what we call the stage of resistance.

What happens in the resistance stage is, in many instances, the exact opposite of events in the alarm reaction. For instance, during the alarm reaction, the adrenal cortex discharges into the blood stream secretory granules that contain hormones. Consequently the gland depletes its stores. In the resistance stage, the cortex accumulates an abundant reserve of secretory granules. Again, in the alarm reaction, the blood volume diminishes and body-weight drops; but during the stage of resistance the blood is less concentrated and body-weight returns to normal.

Curiously, after prolonged exposure to any noxious agent, the body loses its acquired ability to resist, and enters the stage of exhaustion. This third stage always occurs as long as the stress is severe enough and is applied long enough, because the adaptation energy or adaptability of a living being is always finite.

All these findings made it necessary to coin an additional all-embracing name for the syndrome. I called the entire response the *General Adaptation Syndrome* (G.A.S.: *general,* because it is produced only by agents that have a general effect upon large portions of the body; *adaptive,* because it stimulates defense and thereby helps inure the body to hardship; *syndrome,* because its signs are co-ordinated and partly dependent on each other). This whole syndrome then evolves through three stages: (1) the alarm reaction, (2) the stage of resistance and (3) the state of exhaustion.

An important part of the defense mechanism in the resistance stage is the pituitary which secretes the so-called adrenocorticotrophic hormone (ACTH) that in turn stimulates the adrenal cortex to produce corticoids. Most important of these adaptive hormones are the glucocorticoids, such as cortisone, which inhibit tissue inflammation, and the mineralocorticoids, which promote inflammation. These hormones allow the body to defend its tissues by inflammation or to surrender them by inhibiting inflammation.

Various derangements in the secretion of adaptive hormones in the resistance stage lead to what we call diseases of adaptation. These diseases are not caused by any particular pathogen, but are due to a faulty adaptive response to the stress induced by some pathogen. For example, the excessive production of a pro-inflammatory hormone in response to some mild local irritation could damage organs far from the original site of an injury. In this sense, the body's faulty adaptive reactions seem to initiate or encourage various maladies. These could include emotional disturbances, headaches, insomnia, sinus attacks, high blood pressure, gastric and duodenal ulcers, certain rheumatic or allergic afflictions and cardiovascular and kidney diseases.

Over the years, we overcame two other obstacles to the concept of a single stereotyped response to stress. One obstacle was that qualitatively different types of stressors of the same stressor potency do not elicit exactly the same overall syndrome. For example, cold causes shivering, heat produces sweating, adrenalin increases blood sugar and insulin decreases it. All of these stressors have different specific effects. But their non-specific effects are essentially the same: they all elicit the G.A.S., i.e., adrenal cortex enlargement, shrinking of the thymus, deep bleeding ulcers.

The second obstacle was that the same stressor appeared to have different effects on different individuals. But we traced this difference to conditioning factors that can selectively enhance or inhibit a particular stress effect. This conditioning may be internal – genetic predisposition, age, sex – or external, resulting from certain hormone treatment, drugs or diet. Because of such conditioning, a normal tolerable degree of stress can adversely affect a predisposed region upon which a biologic agent acts, causing a disease of adaptation.

There is ample evidence that nervous and emotional stimuli (rage, fear, pain, etc.) can act as stressors, eliciting the G.A.S. Animals conditioned with corticoids and natrium-salts undergo heart failure when we expose them to purely nervous stimuli. On the other hand, pre-treatment with neurogenic stressors protects an animal's heart under nervous stimuli that otherwise prove fatal. Neurogenic stressors can also protect against inflammatory and hypersensitivity reactions, mainly through the pituitary-adrenocortical axis. Psychosomatic medicine shows that mental attitudes can produce bodily changes. Common examples are stomach ulcers or a heightened blood pressure caused by emotional upsets.

In a series of experiments, the Medical Research Group of the Swedish Army sought to determine whether psychologic stimuli can provoke biochemical and physiological reactions that lead to internal disorders. The Swedish experimenters subjected 32 senior officers (average age, 56) to the stress of alternating for 75 hours between staff work and three-hour sessions at an electronic shooting range. The officers were not allowed to relax or sleep, use stimulants, smoke or go for walks. Although the experiment provoked emotional reactions of only moderate intensity, the subjects underwent significant biochemical changes.

In a similar, considerably more trying experiment, 31 soldiers stayed at the shooting range for the entire 75 hours. Although their average age was only 29, their emotional and biochemical reactions were much more pronounced. One officer experienced temporary claustrophobia and panic. His adrenalin excretion was very high; he suffered headache, blurred vision, and palpitation; and his pulse exceeded 100 beats per minute.

In both experiments about 25 per cent of the subjects developed pathological electrocardiographic patterns. Only after several days of rest did their electrocardiographs return to normal. The experiments prove that relatively brief stints of stress, below the intensity that most people ordinary experience at some time in their lives, can provoke pathological changes in our body. If they are repeated often or are allowed to persist for long periods, they might cause disease.

On the opposite question of whether bodily changes and actions affect mentality, we have almost no systematic research. Of course, I do not refer to the potential psychological effects of physical brain damage. But it is a fact that looking fit helps us to be fit. A pale, unwashed unshaven tramp in dirty rags actually resists physical or mental stresses more effectively after a shave, some sun, a bath and a change into crisp new clothes.

My grandmother first introduced me to these truths when I was six. I no longer remember what I was so desperately crying about, but she looked at me with a particularly benevolent and protective look that I well remember and said, "Anytime you feel *that* low, just try to smile with your face, and you'll see . . . soon your whole being will be smiling," I tried it. It works.

None of this is new. Man has long been aware of physical and mental strain, the relationships between bodily and mental reactions and the importance of defensive adaptive responses. But stress first became meaningful to me when I found that we can dissect it by modern research methods and identify the components of the stress-response in chemical and physical terms. Then I was able to use the concept of stress to solve purely medical problems as well as problems of everyday life.

Everybody knows how it feels to be keyed up by nervous tension. It prepares us for peak accomplishment. On the other hand, the tingling sensations and jitteriness of being too keyed up impair our work and even prevent rest.

When we are overly alerted, tension has stimulated our adrenals to overproduce adrenaline and corticoids. We know that by injecting adrenaline or corticoids, we can key up and excite a person. A patient who takes large doses of cortisone for an allergy or rheumatism often can't sleep. He may slip into euphoria, or feel something closely akin to mild drunkenness. A sense of deep depression may follow.

It has long been known that mental excitement causes an initial excitement that is followed by depression. Examples include being caught up in a mob, or an individual act of violence as well as physical stressors – being burned or having an infectious fever. Now we can narrow the cause down to the hormones produced during the acute alarm-reaction phase of the G.A.S. They can stimulate us for action and then put us into a depression. This is of great practical value for the body: it is necessary to be keyed up for peak accomplishment and equally important to be let down – to let depression prevent us from carrying on too long at top speed. Of course hormones are not the only regulators of our emotional level, but knowing more about them may one day allow us to regulate our emotions.

What has stress research taught us about reaching a healthy balance between rest and work? Of course, all work and no play harms anyone at any age. The best advice, based on objective physiologic facts, is not to get keyed up more than is necessary to gain the momentum you need for your best self-expression. When we get excessively excited, especially late in the day, our stress-reaction may carry over into the night.

Nature likes variety. Our civilization forces people into highly specialized occupations that may become monotonous. We must remember that stress is the great equalizer of biologic activities. If we use the same parts of our bodies or minds over and over, nature has only stress with which to force us out of the rut.

68 / The Interpretive Cortex

Wilder Penfield *Montreal Neurological Institute, McGill University*

In this selection, Dr. Penfield, a world-famous neurosurgeon and medical scientist, describes some remarkable results which he has obtained through stimulation of the cortex. His discovery of the existence of "memory tapes" in the brain has brought us closer to an understanding of the problem of memory storage. Until his retirement in 1960, Dr. Penfield was the director of the Montreal Neurological Institute. He is the author of nine books and many scientific papers. He is also the recipient of over two dozen honorary degrees and numerous foreign decorations.

There is an area of the surface of the human brain where local electrical stimulation can call back a sequence of past experience. An epileptic irritation in this area may do the same. It is as though a wire recorder, or a strip of cinematographic film with sound track, had been set in motion within the brain. The sights and sounds, and the thoughts, of a former day pass through the man's mind again.

The purpose of this article is to describe, for readers from various disciplines of science, the area of the cerebral cortex from which this neuron record of the past can be activated and to suggest what normal contribution it may make to cerebral function.

The human brain is the master organ of the human race. It differs from the brains of other mammals particularly in the greater extent of its cerebral cortex. The gray matter, or cortex, that covers the two cerebral hemispheres of the brain of man is so vast in nerve cell population that it could never have been contained within the human skull if it were not folded upon itself, and refolded, so as to form a very large number of fissures and convolutions (Fig. 1). The fissures are so deep and so devious that by far the greater portion of this ganglionic carpet (about 65 per cent) is hidden in them, below the surface (Fig. 2).

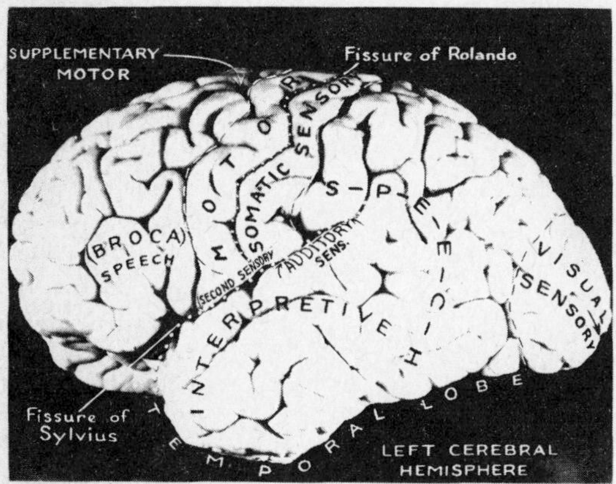

Fig. 1. Photograph of the left hemisphere of a human brain. The frontal lobe is on the left, the occipital lobe on the right. The major motor and sensory areas are indicated, as well as the speech areas and the interpretive area. [*Penfield and Roberts (18)*]

Reprinted, by permission, from *Science*, Vol. 129 (June 26, 1959), pp 1719-1725.

The portion that is labeled "interpretive" in Figures 1 and 3 covers a part of both temporal lobes. It is from these two homologous areas, and from nowhere else, that electrical stimulation has occasionally produced psychical responses which may be divided into (i) experiential responses and (ii) interpretive responses.

Experiential Responses

Occasionally during the course of a neurosurgical operation under local anaesthesia, gentle electrical stimulation in this temporal area, right or left, has caused the conscious patient to be aware of some previous experience (1). The experience seems to be picked out at random from his own past. But it comes back to him in great detail. He is suddenly aware again of those things to which he paid attention in that distant interval of time. This recollection of an experiential sequence stops suddenly when the electrical current is switched off or when the electrode is removed from contact with the cortex. This phenomenon we have chosen to call an experiential response to stimulation.

Case Examples (2)

The patient S. Be. observed, when the electrode touched the temporal lobe (right superior temporal convolution), "There was a piano over there and someone playing. I could hear the song you know." When the cortex was stimulated again without warning, at approximately the same point, the patient had a different experience. He said: "Someone speaking to another, and he mentioned a name but I could not understand it .... It was like a dream." Again the point was restimulated without his knowledge. He said quietly: "Yes, 'Oh Marie, Oh Marie'!

Someone is singing it." When the point was stimulated a fourth time he heard the same song again and said it was the "theme song of a radio program."

The electrode was then applied to a point 4 centimeters farther forward on the first temporal convolution. While the electrode was still in place, S. Be. said: "Something brings back a memory. I can see Seven-Up Bottling Company – Harrison Bakery." He was evidently seeing two of Montreal's large illuminated advertisements.

The surgeon then warned him that he was about to apply the electrode again. Then, after a pause, the surgeon said "Now," but he did not stimulate. (The patient has no means of knowing when the electrode is applied, unless he is told, since the cortex itself is without sensation.) The patient replied promptly, "Nothing."

A women (D.F.) (3) heard an orchestra playing an air while the electrode was held in place. The music stopped when the electrode was removed. It came again when the electrode was reapplied. On request, she hummed the tune, while the electrode was held in place, accompanying the orchestra. It was a popular song. Over and over again, restimulation at the same spot produced the same song. The music seemed always to begin at the same place nd to progress at the normally expected tempo. All efforts to mislead her failed. She believed that a gramophone was being turned on in the operating room on each occasion, and she asserted her belief stoutly in a conversation some days after the operation.

A boy (R.W.) heard his mother talking to someone on the telephone when an electrode was applied to his right temporal cortex. When the stimulus was repeated without warning, he heard his mother again in the same conversation. When the stimulus was repeated after a lapse of time, he said, "My mother is telling my brother he has got his coat on backwards. I can just hear them."

The surgeon then asked the boy whether he remembered this happening. "Oh yes," he said, "just before I came here." Asked again whether this seemed like a dream, he replied: "No, it is like I go into a daze."

J. T. cried out in astonishment when the electrode was applied to the temporal cortex; "Yes doctor, yes doctor. Now I hear people laughing – my friends in South Africa!"

When asked about this, he explained the reason for his surprise. He seemed to be laughing with his cousins, Bessie and Ann Wheliow, whom he had left behind him on a farm in South Africa, although he knew he was now on the operating table in Montreal.

Interpretive Responses

On the other hand, similar stimulation in this same general area may produce quite a different response.

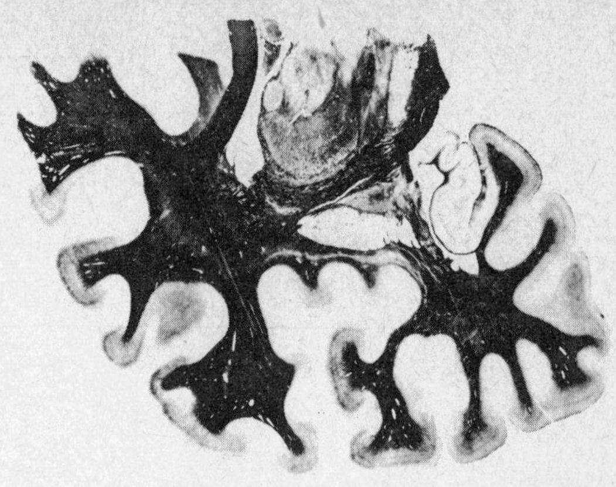

Fig. 2. Above is a photograph of a cross section of the left cerebral hemisphere [Jelgersma (19)]. The white matter is stained black and the gray matter is unstained. The major convolutions of the cerebral cortex and the subcortical masses of gray matter can be identified by reference to the diagram below. Below is a drawing of the cross section with additions. The surfaces and convolutions of the temporal lobe are identified, and the relationship of one hemisphere to the other and the relationship of the hemispheres to the brain stem and cerebellum are shown.

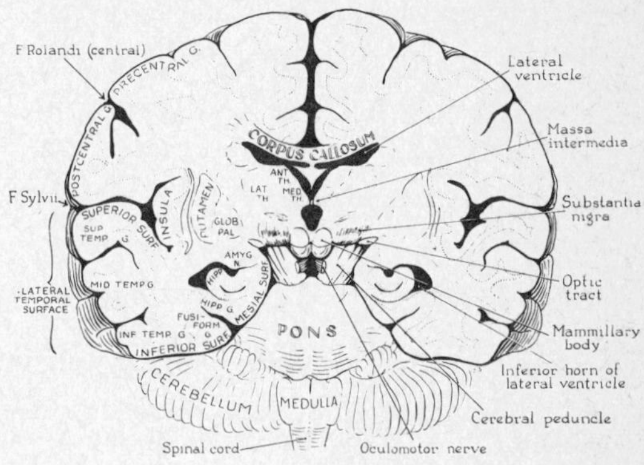

The patient discovers, on stimulation, that he has somehow changed his own interpretation of what he is seeing at the moment, or hearing or thinking. For example, he may exclaim that his present experience seems familiar, as though he had seen it or heard it or thought it before. He realizes that this must be a false interpretation. Or, on the contrary, these things may seem suddenly strange, absurd. Sights or sounds may seem distant and small, or they may come unexpectedly close and seem loud or large. He may feel suddenly afraid, as though his environment were threatening him, and he possessed by a nameless dread or panic. Another patient may say he feels lonely or aloof, or as though he were observing himself at a distance.

Under normal circumstances anyone may make such interpretations of the present, and these interpretations serve him as guides to action or reaction. If the interpretations are accurate guides, they must be based upon previous comparable experience. It is conceivable, therefore, that the recall mechanism

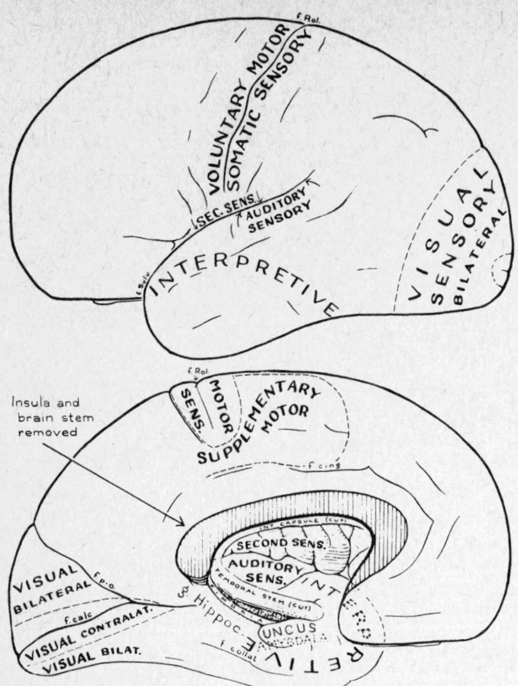

Fig. 3. The left cerebral hemisphere; the lateral surface is shown above and the mesial surface below. In the lower drawing the brain stem with the island of Reil has been removed to show the inner banks of the fissure of Sylvius and the superior surface of the temporal lobe. The interpretive cortex extends from the lateral to the superior surface of the temporal lobe. [*Penfield and Roberts (18)*]

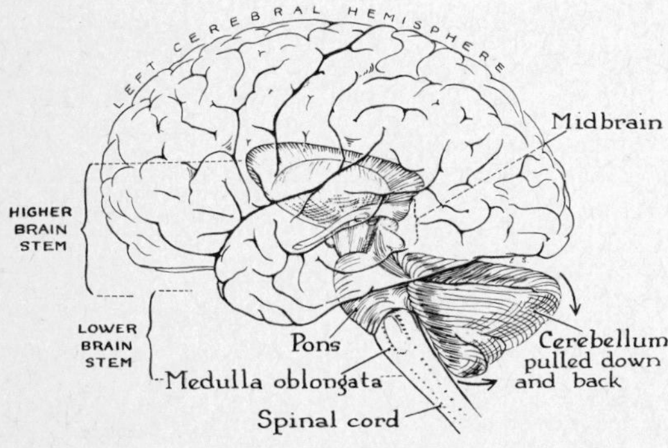

Fig. 4. Drawing of the left cerebral hemisphere, showing the higher brain stem, including the thalamus, within and the lower brain stem and spinal cord emerging below. The cerebellum is shown, attached to the lower brain stem. [*Penfield and Roberts (18)*]

which is activated by the electrode during an experiental response and the mechanism activated in an interpretive response may be parts of a common inclusive mechanism of reflex recognition or interpretation.

No special function had been previously assigned by neurologists to the area in each temporal lobe that is marked "Interpretive" in Figures 1 and 3, though some clinicians have suggested it might have to do with the recall of music. The term *interpretive cortex*, therefore, is no more than slang to be employed for the purposes of discussion. The terms *motor cortex, sensory cortex,* and *speech cortex* began as slang phrases and have served such a purpose. But such phrases must not be understood to signify independence of action of separated units in the case of any of these areas. Localization of function in the cerebral cortex means no more than specialization of function as compared with other cortical regions, not separation from the integrated action of the brain.

Before considering the interpretive cortex further, we may turn briefly to the motor and sensory areas and the speech areas of the cortex. After considering the effects of electrical stimulation there, we should be better able to understand the results of stimulation in the temporal lobes.

Specialization of Function in the Cortex

Evidence for some degree of localization within the brain was recognized early in the 19th century by Flourens. He concluded from experiment that functional subdivision of "the organ of the mind" was possible. The forebrain (4), he said (cerebral hemispheres and higher brain stem (figure. 4)) had to do with thought and will power, while the cerebellum was involved in the co-ordination of movement.

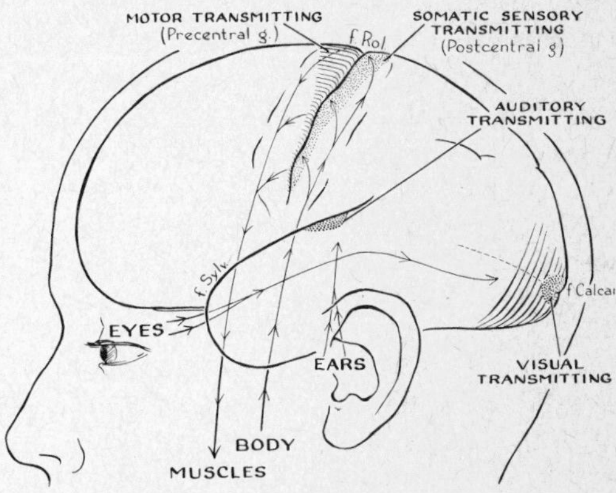

Fig. 5. Sensory and motor projection areas. The sensory areas are stippled, and the afferent pathways to them from eyes, ears, and body are indicated by entering arrows. The motor cortex is indicated by parallel lines, the efferent corticospinal tract is indicated by emerging arrows. [*Penfield and Roberts (18)*]

In 1861, Paul Broca showed that a man with a relatively small area of destruction in a certain part of the left hemisphere alone might lose only the power of speech. It was soon realized that this was the speech area of man's dominant (left) hemisphere. In 1870, Fritsch and Hitzig applied an electric current to the exposed cortex of one hemisphere of a lightly anaesthetized dog and caused the legs of the opposite side to move. Thus, an area of cortex called motor was discovered.

After that, localization of function became a research target for many clinicians and experimentalists. It was soon evident that in the case of man, the precentral gyrus (Fig. 5) in each hemisphere was related to voluntary control of the contralateral limbs and that there was an analogous area of motor cortex in the frontal lobes of animals. It appeared also that other separate areas of cortex (Fig. 1 and 5) in each hemisphere were dedicated to sensation (one for visual sensation, others for auditory, olfactory, and discriminative somatic sensation, respectively).

It was demonstrated, too, that from the "motor cortex" there was an efferent bundle of nerve fibres (the pyramidal tract) that ran down through the lower brain stem and the spinal cord to be relayed on out to the muscles. Through this efferent pathway, voluntary control of these muscles was actually carried out. It was evident, too, that there were separate sensory tracts carrying nerve impulses in the other direction, from the principal organs of special sense (eye, ear, nose, and skin and muscle) into separate sensory areas of the cortex.

These areas, motor and sensory, have been called "projection areas." They play a role in the projection of nerve currents to the cortex from the periphery of the body, and from the cortex to the periphery. This makes possible (sensory) awareness of environment and provides the individual with a means of outward (motor) expression. The motor cortex has a specialized use during voluntary action, and each of the several sensory areas has a specialized use, when the individual is seeing, hearing, smelling, or feeling.

Traveling Potentials

The action of the living brain depends upon the movement, within it, of "transient electrical potentials traveling the fibres of the nervous system." This was Sherrington's phrase. Within the vast circuits of this master organ, potentials travel, here and there and yonder, like meteors that streak across the sky at night and line the firmament with trails of light. When the meteors pass, the paths of luminescence still glow a little while, then fade and are gone. The changing patterns of these paths of passing energy make possible the changing content of the mind. The patterns are never quite the same, and so it is with the content of the mind.

Specialized areas in the cortex are at times active and again relatively quiet. But, when a man is awake, there is always some central integration and co-ordination of the traveling potentials. There must be activity within the brain stem and some areas of the cortex. This is centrencephalic integration (5).

Sensory, Motor, and Psychical Responses to Cortical Stimulation

My purpose in writing this article is to discuss in simple words (free of technical terms) the meaning of the "psychical" responses which appear only on stimulation of the so-called interpretive cortex. But before considering these responses let us consider the motor and sensory activity of the cortex for a moment.

When the streams of electrical potentials that pass normally through the various areas of sensory cortex are examined electrically, they do not seem to differ from each other except in pattern and timing. The essential difference is to be found in the fact that the visual stream passes to the visual cortex and then to one subcortical target and the auditory stream passes through the auditory cortex and then on to another subcortical target.

When the surgeon stimulates the intact sensory cortex he must be sending a current along the next "piece of road" to a subcortical destination. This electrode (delivering, for example, 60 "waves" per second of 2- millisecond duration and 1-volt intensity) produces no more than elementary sight when applied to visual cortex. The patient reports colours, lights, and shadows that move and take on crude outlines. The same electrode, applied to auditory cortex, causes him to hear a ringing or hissing or thumping sound. When applied to postcentral gyrus it produces tingling or a false sense of movement.

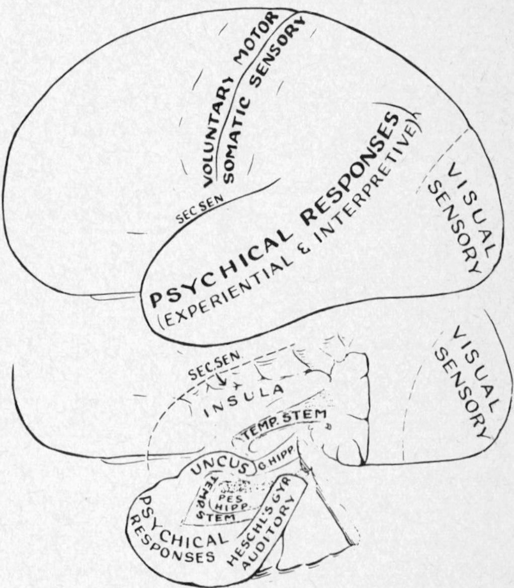

Fig. 6. The left cerebral hemisphere is shown with the temporal lobe cut across and turned down. The areas of cortex from which psychical responses have been elicited are indicated. [*Penfield (1)*]

Thus, sensation is produced by the passage inward of electrical potentials. And when the electrode is applied to the motor cortex, movement is produced by passage of potentials outward to the muscles. In each case positive response is produced by conduction in the direction of normal physiological flow – that is, by dromic conduction (6).

Responses to electrical stimulation that may be called "psychical," as distinguished from sensory or motor, have been elicited from certain areas of the human cortex (Fig. 6). But they have never been produced by stimulation in other areas. There are, of course, other large areas of cortex which are neither sensory nor motor in function. They seem to be employed in other neuron mechanisms that are also associated with psychical processes. But the function of these other areas cannot, it seems, be activated by so simple a stimulus as an electric current applied to the cortex.

Dreamy States of Epilepsy

"Epilepsy" may be defined, in Jackson's words, as "the name for occasional, sudden, excessive, rapid and local discharges of gray matter." Our aim in the operations under discussion was to remove the gray matter responsible for epileptic attacks if that gray matter could be spared. When the stimulating electrode reproduced the psychical phenomenon that initiated the fit, it provided the guidance sought (7).

During the 19th century clinicians had recognized these phenomena as epileptic. They applied the term *intellectual aura* to such attacks. Jackson substituted the expression *dreamy states* (see 8). These were, he said, "psychical states during the onset of certain epileptic seizures, states which are much more elaborate than crude sensations." And again, he wrote, "These are all voluminous mental states and yet of different kinds; no doubt they ought to be classified, but for my present purpose they may be considered together."

"The state," he said, "is often like that occasionally experienced by healthy people as a feeling of 'reminiscence.'" Or the patient has "dreamy feelings," "dreams mixing up with present thoughts," "double consciousness," a "feeling of being somewhere else," a feeling "as if I went back to all that occurred in my childhood," "silly thoughts."

Jackson never did classify these states, but he did something more important. He localized the area of cortex from which epileptic discharge would produce dreamy states. His localization was in the anterior and deep portions of the temporal lobes, the same area that is labeled "interpretative" cortex in Figure 3.

Case Example

Brief reference may be made to a specific case. The patient had seizures, and stimulation produced responses which were first recognized as psychical.

In 1936, a girl of 16 (J.V.) was admitted to the Montreal Neurological Institute complaining of epileptic attacks, each of which was ushered in by the same hallucination. It was a little dream, she said, in which an experience from early childhood was reenacted, always the same train of events. She would then cry out with fear and run to her mother. Occasionally this was followed immediately by a major convulsive seizure.

At operation, under local anaesthesia, we tried to set off the dream by a gentle electrical stimulus in the right temporal lobe. The attempt was successful. The dream was produced by the electrode. Stimulation at other points on the temporal cortex produced sudden fear without the dream. At still other points, stimulation caused her to say that she saw "someone coming toward me." At another point, stimulation caused her to say she heard the voices of her mother and her brothers (9).

This suggested a new order of cortical response to electrical stimulation. When the neighboring visual sensory area of the cortex is stimulated, any patient may report seeing stars of light or moving colours or black outlines but never "someone coming toward me." Stimulation of the auditory sensory cortex may cause any patient to report that he hears ringing, buzzing, blowing, or thumping sounds, perhaps, but never voices that speak. Stimulation in the areas of sensory cortex can call forth nothing more than the elements of visual or auditory or tactile sensation, never happenings that might have been previously experienced.

During the 23 years that have followed, although practically all areas of the cerebral cortex have been stimulated and studied in more than 1000 craniotomies, performed under local anaesthesia, psychical responses of the experiential or interpretive variety have been produced only from the temporal cortex in the general areas that are marked "psychical responses" in Figure 3 (10, 11).

Classification

It seems reasonable to subdivide psychical responses and psychical seizures (epileptic dreamy states) in the same way, classifying them as "interpretive" or "experiential," Interpretive psychical responses are those involving interpretations of the present experience, or emotions related to it; experiential psychical responses are re-enactments of past experiences. Interpretive seizures are those accompanied by auras and illusions; experiential seizures are those accompanied by auras and hallucinations.

The interpretive responses and seizures may be divided into groups (11) of which the commonest are as follows: (i) recognition, the illusion that things seen and heard and thought are familiar (*déjà vu* phenomenon); (ii) visual illusion, the illusion that things seen are changing – for example, coming nearer, growing larger (macropsia); (iii) auditory illusion, the illusion that things heard are changing – for example, coming near, going away, changing tempo; (iv) illusional emotion, the emotion of fear or, less often, loneliness, sorrow, or disgust.

Experiential phenomena (hallucinations) are an awareness of experiences from the past that come into the mind without complete loss of awareness of the present.

Discussion

What, then, is the function of the interpretive cortex? This is a physiological question that follows the foregoing observations naturally.

An electrode, delivering, for example, 60 electrical pulses per second to the surface of the motor cortex, causes a man to make crude movements. When applied to the various sensory areas of the cortex, it causes him to have crude sensations of sight or sound or body feeling. This indicates only that these areas have something to do with the complicated mechanism of voluntary action or conscious sensation. It does not reveal what contribution the cortex may make, or in what way it may contribute to skill in making voluntary movement or qualify the incoming sensory streams.

In the case of the interpretive cortex, the observations are similar. We may say that the interpretive cortex has something to do with a mechanism that can reactivate the vivid record of the past. It has also something to do with a mechanism that can present to consciousness a reflex interpretation of the present. To conclude that here is the mechanism of memory would be an unjustified assumption. It would be too simple.

What a man remembers when he makes a voluntary effort is apt to be a generalization. If this were not so, he might be hopelessly lost in detail. On the other hand, the experiential responses described above are detailed re-enactments of a single experience. Such experiences soon slip beyond the range of voluntary recall. A man may summon to mind a song at will. He hears it then in his mind, not all at once but advancing phrase by phrase. He may sing it or play it too, and one would call this memory.

But if a patient hears music in response to the electrode, he hears it in one particular strip of time. That time runs forward again at the original tempo, and he hears the orchestration, or he sees the player at a piano "over there." These are details he would have thought forgotten.

A vast amount of work remains to be done before the mechanism of memory, and how and where the recording takes place, are understood. This record is not laid down in the interpretive cortex, but it is kept in a part of the brain that is intimately connected with it.

Removal of large areas of interpretive cortex, even when carried out on both sides, may result in mild complaints of memory defect, but it does not abolish the capacity to remember recent events. On the other hand, surgical removals that result in bilateral interference with the underlying hippocampal zone do make the recording of recent events impossible, while distant memory is still preserved (12, 13).

The importance of the hippocampal area for memory was pointed out long ago in a forgotten publication by the Russian neurologist Bechterew (14).

The year before publication Bechterew had demonstrated the case before the St. Petersburg Clinic for Nervous and Mental Diseases. The man on whom Bechterew reported had "extraordinary weakness of memory, falsifications of memory and great apathy." These defects were shown at autopsy to be secondary to lesions of the mesial surface of the cortex of both temporal lobes. The English neurologists Glees and Griffith (15) reported similar defects, a half century later, in a patient who had symmetrical lesions of the hippocampus and of hippocampal and fusiform gyri on both sides.

The way in which the interpretive cortex seems to be used may be suggested by an example: After years of absence you meet, by chance, a man whose very existence you had forgotten. On seeing him, you may be struck by a sudden sense of familiarity, even before you have time to "think." A signal seems to flash up in consciousness to tell you that you've seen that man before. You watch him as he smiles and moves and speaks. The sense of familiarity grows stronger. Then you remember him. You may even recall that his name was Jones. The sight and the sound of the man has given you an instant access, through some reflex, to the records of the past in which this man has played some part. The opening of this forgotten file was subconscious. It was not a voluntary act. You would have known him even against your will although Jones was a forgotten man a moment before, now you can summon the record in such detail that you remark at once the slowness of his gait or a new line about the mouth.

If Jones had been a source of danger to you, you might have felt fear as well as familiarity before you had time to consider the man. Thus, the signal of fear as well as the signal of familiarity may come to one as the result of subconscious comparison of present with similar past experience.

One more example may be given from common experience. A sudden increase in the size of objects seen and in sounds heard may mean the rapid approach of something that calls for instant avoidance action. These are signals that, because of previous experience, we sometimes act upon with little consideration.

Summary

The interpretive cortex has in it a mechanism for instant reactivation of the detailed record of the past. It has a mechanism also for the production of interpretive signals. Such signals could only be significant if past records are scanned and relevant experiences are selected for comparison with present experience. This is a subconscious process. But it may well be that this scanning of past experience and selection from its also renders the relevant past available for conscious consideration as well. Thus, the individual may refer to the record as he employes other circuits of the brain.

Access to the record of the past seems to be as readily available from the temporal cortex of one side as from that of the other. Auditory illusions (or interpretations of the distance, loudness, or tempo of sounds) have been produced by stimulation of the temporal cortex of either side. The same is true of illusional emotions, such as fear and disgust.

But, on the contrary, visual illusions (interpretations of the distance, dimension, erectness, and tempo of things seen) are only produced by stimulation of the temporal cortex on the nondominant (normally, right) side of the brain. Illusions of recognition, such as familiarity or strangeness, were also elicted only from the nondominant side, except in one case.

Conclusion

"Consciousness," to quote William James (16), "is never quite the same in successive moments of time. It is a stream forever flowing, forever changing." The stream of changing states of mind that James described so well does flow through each man's waking hours until the time when he falls asleep to wake no more. But the stream, unlike a river, leaves a record in the living brain.

Transient electrical potentials move with it through the circuits of the nervous system, leaving a path that can be followed again. The pattern of this pathway, from neuron to neuron along each nerve-cell body and fibre and junction, is the recorded pattern of each man's past. That complicated record is held there in temporal sequence through the principle of durable facilitation of conduction and connection.

A steady stream of electrical pulses applied through an electrode to some point in the interpretive cortex causes a stream of excitation to flow from the cortex to the place where past experience is recorded. This stream of excitation acts as a key to the past. It can enter the pathway of recorded consciousness at any random point, from childhood on through adult life. But having entered, the experience moves forward without interference from other experiences. And when the electrode is withdrawn there is a likelihood, which lasts for seconds or minutes, that the stream of excitation will enter the pathway again at the same moment of past time, even if the electrode is reapplied at neighbouring points (17).

Finally, an electric current applied to the surface of what may be called the interpretive cortex of a conscious man (i) may cause the stream of former consciousness to flow again or (ii) may give him an interpretation of the present that is unexpected and involuntary. Therefore, it is concluded that, under normal circumstances, this area of cortex. must make some functional contribution to reflex comparison of the present with related past experience. It contributes to reflex interpretation or perception of the present.

The combination and comparison of present experience with similar past experience must call for remarkable scanning of the past and classification of similarities. What contribution this area of the temporal cortex may make to the whole process is not clear. The term *interpretive cortex* will serve for identification until students of human physiology can shed more light on these fascinating findings.

References

1. PENFIELD, W. *J. Mental Sci., 101,* 451 (1955).
2. These patients, designated by the same initials, have been described in previous publications in much greater detail. An index of patients (designated by initials) may be found in any of my books.
3. This case is reported in detail in W. PENFIELD and H. JASPER, *Epilepsy and the Functional Anatomy of the Human Brain* (Little, Brown, Boston, 1954) [published in abridged form in Russian (translation by N. P. GRASCHENKOV and G. SMIRNOV) by the Soviet Academy of Sciences, 1958].
4. The forebrain, or prosencephalon, properly includes the diencephalon and the telencephalon, or higher brain stem, and hemispheres. Flourens probably had cerebral hemispheres in mind as distinguished from cerebellum.
5. "Within the brain, a central transactional core has been identified between the strictly sensory or motor systems of classical neurology. This central reticular mechanism has been found capable of grading the activity of most other parts of the brain"—H. MAGOUN, *The Waking Brain* (Thomas, Springfield, Ill., 1958).
6. PENFIELD, W. *The Excitable Cortex in Conscious Man* (Thomas, Springfield, Ill., 1958).
7. It did more than this; it produced illusions or hallucinations that had never been experienced by the patient during a seizure.
8. TAYLOR, J., ed., *Selected Writings of John Hughlings Jackson* (Hodder and Stoughton, London, 1931), vol. 1, *On Epilepsy and Epileptiform Convulsions.*
9. Twenty-one years later this young woman, who is the daughter of a physician, was present at a meeting of the National Academy of Sciences in New York while her case was discussed. She could still recall the operation and the nature of the "dreams" that had preceded her seizures [W. PENFIELD, *Proc. Natl. Acad. Sci. U.S., 44,* 51 (1958)].
10. In a recent review of the series my associate, Dr. Phanor Perot, has found and summarized 35 out of 384 temporal lobe cases in which stimulation produced experiential responses. All such responses were elicited in the temporal cortex. In a study of 214 consecutive operations for temporal lobe epilepsy, my associate Sean Mullan found 70 cases in which interpretive illusion occurred in the minor seizures before operation, or in which an interpretive response was produced by stimulation during operation. In most cases it occurred both before and during operation.
11. MULLAN, S., and PENFIELD, W., *A.M.A. Arch. Neurol. Psychiat.,* 1959, *81,* 269.
12. This area is marked "Hipp" and "Hipp. G" in Fig. 2(bottom) and "g. Hippoc." and "amygdala" in Fig. 3.
13. PENFIELD, W., and MILNER, B. *A.M.A. Arch. Neurol. Psychiat.,* 1958, *79,* 475.
14. BECHTEREW, W. V. "Demonstration eines Gehirns mit Zerstorung der vorderen und inneren Theile der Hirnrinde beider Schlafenlappen," *Neurol. Zentralbl. Leipzig,* 1900, *19,* 990. My attention was called to this case recently by Dr. Peter Gloor of Montreal.
15. GLEES, P., and GRIFFITH, H. B. *Monatsschr. Psychiat. Neurol.,* 1952, *123,* 193.
16. JAMES, W. *The Principles of Psychology.* New York: Holt, 1910.

17. Thus, it is apparent that the beam of excitation that emanates from the interpretive cortex and seems to scan the record of the past is subject to the principles of transient facilitation already demonstrated for the anthropoid motor cortex [A. S. F. Grünbaum and C. Sherrington, *Proc. Roy. Soc.* (London), *72B,* 152 (1901); T. Graham Brown and C. S. Sherrington, *ibid., 85B,* 250 (1912)]. Similarly subject to the principles of facilitation are the motor and the sensory cortex of man [W. Penfield and K. Welch, *J. Physiol.* (London), *109,* 358 (1949)]. The patient D.F. heard the same orchestra playing the same music in the operating room more than 20 times when the electrode was reapplied to the superior surface of the temporal lobe. Each time the music began in the verse of a popular song. It proceeded to the chorus, if the electrode was kept in place.
18. PENFIELD, W., and ROBERTS, L. *Speech and Brain Mechanisms.* Princeton, N.J.: Princeton Univ. Press, 1959.
19. JELGERSMA, G. *Atlas anatomicum cerebri humani.* Scheltema and Holkema, Amsterdam.

69 / Psychological Defects Produced by Temporal Lobe Excision[1]

Brenda Milner *Montreal Neurological Institute, McGill University*

In 1938 Klüver and Bucy reported that bilateral removal of the temporal lobe in monkeys resulted in an inability to recognize familiar objects and a deficiency on various visual tasks. This discovery soon precipitated a considerable amount of animal research on the functions of the temporal lobe. At the present time, there are probably more scientific papers on this topic than on any other part of the cerebral cortex, with the possible exception of the frontal lobe. Dr. Milner's article is unique in two respects: first, the results are derived from human patients, and, second, a comparison is made of the function of the left and right temporal lobes – a problem which relates to the possible functional asymmetry of the two cerebral hemispheres.

Although experimental ablation studies in monkeys have failed to reveal any significant or consistent behavioural change after unilateral temporal lobectomy (in contrast to the marked deficits (10) which follow a bilateral lesion), in man the manifest non-equivalence of the two hemispheres, at least with respect to language, and the greater range and sensitivity of behavioural measures available encourage the search for clues to human temporal lobe function through a study of unilateral lesions. In fact we find that unilateral epileptogenic lesions of the temporal lobe dating from birth or early life are accompanied by certain cognitive defects which vary in kind depending on whether the lesion is in the dominant (left)[2] or non-dominant (right) temporal lobe. In such cases when unilateral partial temporal lobectomy is carried out for the relief of seizures, these characteristic defects persist and may even be accentuated, despite the fact that over-all intellectual efficiency is apt to increase if the patient is no longer having seizures. These specific defects form the main topic of the present paper.

During the last five years over a hundred patients with temporal lobe seizures have been subjected to formal psychological testing immediately before unilateral operation and again about 18 days later, at the time of the patient's discharge from hospital. Wherever possible, long-range follow-up studies have also been carried out, but these unfortunately have not been very numerous as yet. Twenty-two control cases consisting of patients with atrophic epileptogenic lesions of frontal or parietal cortex have been similarly studied before and after brain operation, in order to determine how far the deficits found are specific to the temporal lobe. All the patients in the series have been operated upon either by Dr. Wilder Penfield or by Dr. Theodore Rasmussen. In the course of the investigation the test battery has gradually changed and expanded, and we do not have complete data for all patients on all tests.

Temporal lobe seizures are notoriously difficult to control by anti-convulsant medication. In such cases unilateral partial temporal lobectomy constitutes a reasonably successful method of treatment. It is usually followed by upper quadrantic homonymous hemianopsia but by no other neurological deficit. As Penfield and Baldwin (14) have pointed out, the abnormal sclerotic area of cortex which must be removed usually lies deep to the surface in the most inferior and mesial portion of the temporal lobe, adjacent to the midbrain. It is believed that in most cases this sclerosis is produced by herniation through the incisura of the tentorium and compression of the arteries of supply at the time of birth (3), although seizures may not occur until much later. At operation the surgeon typically finds objective evidence of atrophy in the region of the uncus and anterior portion of the first temporal convolution and also in the hippocampus and hippocampal gyrus, and it is unusual to obtain lasting relief from seizures if these structures are spared. A typical removal is shown in Figure 1: the shading indicates abnormality of the hippocampal zone which was therefore excised together with the overlying cortex, the dotted line showing the total extent of excision. The fact that abnormality deep to the surface is typically found and that the excisions include both temporal neocortex and allocortex may well have an important bearing on the deficits seen.

[1]From the Department of Neurology and Neurosurgery and the Montreal Neurological Institute, McGill University.
[2]For the purpose of this study cases of right hemisphere speech representation are excluded.

Reprinted, by permission, from *Research Publs. Association for Research in Nervous and Mental Disease,* 1956, 36, 244-257.

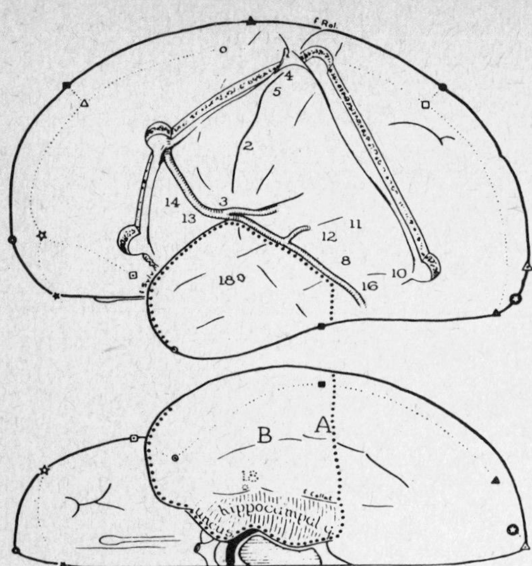

Fig. 1. Typical partial temporal lobectomy. The shading indicates abnormality of the hippocampal zone.

Results

General Intelligence

These patients with focal cortical epilepsy constitute a young group (the average age is 26 years, with a range from 14 to 45), and they are not intellectually retarded. During the last two years, in addition to more specialized tests, the Wechsler Intelligence Scale has been administered to all patients, Form I before operation and Form II after operation. Table I shows the mean intelligence ratings before operation for 30 consecutive temporal lobe cases, 15 left-sided and 15 right-sided, all with speech representation in the left hemishpere. The mean Full-Scale, Verbal and Performance I.Q. ratings all fall within the normal range, and there is no significant difference between the two groups on these various measures. There is, however, a significant difference ($t = 2.57$, $P < .05$) between the Verbal and Performance I.Q. ratings for the right temporal group, with the Performance Quotient (based on non-verbal tests) averaging 9 points lower than the Verbal. A relative inefficiency on non-verbal tests has been reported by various workers for miscellaneous lesions of the right hemishpere (1, 9, 11, 16, 20): our observations extend these findings to the right temporal lobe specifically, thus corroborating Hebb's findings in a single case of right temporal lobectomy (6).

After operation the patients were re-tested with Form II of the Wechsler scale which is a slightly harder test, yielding ratings lower rather than higher than Form I in a normal population (4). Thus practice effects can safely be ignored. Table II summarizes the findings three weeks after unilateral temporal lobectomy. There is no significant change in Full-Scale, Verbal, or Performance I.Q. ratings for the right temporal group. There were, however, some marked individual changes, a few patients improving by as much as 11 points in Full-Scale I.Q. rating and others showing a corresponding deterioration. The left temporal lobe group all showed some post-operative dysphasia due to the effects of cerebral edema upon neighbouring speech areas although of course no primary speech area had been destroyed. This dysphasia is a transient phenomenon, usually developing from one to three days after operation and beginning to clear by about the tenth postoperative day. Marked individual differences in the severity and duration of the dysphasia are found, and these are reflected in varying degrees of impairment on verbal tests three weeks after operation. Thus we see in Table II that the left temporal lobe group shows a pronounced postoperative deficit in Verbal I.Q. rating, and hence some deficit also in Full-Scale I.Q. rating, changes which are significant beyond the .001 level of probability. There is, however, no impairment on performance tests even during this dysphasic period. Furthermore when these patients return for follow-up study a year or more later, we find that the I.Q. rating has returned at least to the preoperative level, provided they are no longer having seizures. Thus we can conclude that no lasting impairment of general intelligence follows unilateral anterior temporal lobectomy in either hemisphere.

Table I – Preoperative mean I.Q. ratings

Group	N	Full Scale	Verbal	Performance
Left temporal	15	108.5 (86–129)	107.2 (87–122)	107.3 (87–133)
Right temporal	15	103 (87–127)	107.1 (94–143)	97.6 (78–117)

Table II – Mean fall in I.Q. rating 3 weeks after unilateral partial temporal lobectomy

Group	No. of Patients	Full Scale	Verbal	Performance
Left temporal	15	10.3	16.6	2.3
Right temporal	15	1.5	2.5	1.4

Specific Defects

Against this background of general intellectual competence certain specific deficits stand out: verbal for the left temporal lobe group, perceptual for the right. These deficits, which differentiate between right and left temporal lobe cases even before operation, will now be described.

a. Verbal Recall and the Left Temporal Lobe. Although before operation the patients with left temporal lobe lesions showed no consistent impairment on verbal intelligence tests and no dysphasia, it was possible to demonstrate a specific deficit in verbal learning and retention at this time. As a result of this specific deficit the Wechsler memory quotient fell far below the I.Q. level for the left temporal lobe group, whereas no difference was found for the right temporal lobe cases. Patients with frontal lobe lesions are intermediate between the two temporal lobe groups and do show some relative memory impairment before operation, but the deficit is both different in kind and less severe than that shown by patients with left temporal lobe lesions. Table III gives the mean intelligence and memory quotients for these three groups of patients before and after brain operation. Analysis of variance yielded F-values significant beyond the .001 level, and subsequent t-tests showed the three groups to differ significantly one from another both before and after operation, the left temporal lobe patients consistently showing the largest discrepancy between intelligence and memory quotients. The intergroup differences remain the same after operation, but Form II of the memory scale appears to be a somewhat easier test than Form I.

Table III – Comparison of mean intelligence and memory quotients (before and three weeks after operation) for left temporal, right temporal and frontal lobe cases

		Preoperative Means (Form I)			Postoperative Means (Form II)		
Group	N	I.Q.	M.Q.	I.Q.-M.Q.	I.Q.	M.Q.	I.Q.-M.Q.
Left temporal	9	106.6	91.2	15.4	95.1	77.4	17.7
Right temporal	12	102.5	102.2	0.3	102.8	107.8	-5.0
Frontal	9	101.6	94.8	6.8	93.0	92.6	0.4

The Wechsler memory quotient is based on a heterogeneous sample of subtests, not all of which show impairment in the left temporal lobe group. There is, for example, no impairment in the recall of geometrical drawings. Moreover, although the patients with left temporal lobe lesions tend to do poorly on all verbal memory tests, the defect shows up most clearly and characteristically when they are asked to recall simple prose passages (stories a mere paragraph in length) which have been read to them some time before. Such measures of delayed recall do not contribute to the conventional memory quotient, yet they provide our most valuable localizing sign. It is our current practice to read the patient the two stories of the Logical Memory subtest of the memory scale, obtaining immediate reproductions of each in the usual manner, and then about one and a half hours later and without any previous warning we ask the patient to tell us the stories once more. Under these conditions the left temporal lobe group makes very low scores, as can be seen from Table IV which gives the percentage of material recalled after an interval by the left temporal group as compared with a mixed group of frontal, parietal and right temporal lobe cases. The left temporal lobe patients remember only half as much of the stories as do patients with lesions in other areas, a difference which is significant well beyond the .001 level of probability. It is of interest that the patients with frontal lobe lesions showed no impairment on this particular memory task.

Table IV – Delayed recall of stories (preoperative)

Group	N	Per Cent Recall	
		Mean	Range
Left temporal	15	13	6–21
Others	29	25	8–42

All this is before operation, the effect of a focal epileptogenic lesion of the dominant temporal lobe. After operation these patients show the transient dysphasia noted above, at which time scores on all verbal tests, and not merely on verbal memory tests, are seriously impaired. But even after the dysphasia has cleared, the verbal memory difficulty persists, and there is now a detectable impairment even in the initial comprehension of stories. This is illustrated in Table V, which gives average scores for four patients tested before left anterior temporal lobectomy and again in follow-up study from one to three years later, at which time they were free of seizures and had achieved a mean I.Q. level slightly higher than before operation. All four patients show a residual postoperative impairment in the immediate recall of stories. Quantitatively this falling-off is significant ($P < .02$), and there are corresponding changes also, the postoperative versions being more fragmentary and losing the distinctive pattern of the original story. It appears that only a very limited amount of verbal material can be assimilated in one sequence although any specific sentence or question taken in isolation is readily understood. This is a defect of which a patient of good intelligence is well aware. A student will report that he cannot follow lectures; a stenographer that she cannot keep up with her dictation; a bank clerk that he cannot handle the rapid give-and-take of conversation in the business world. Such individuals are apt to be less successful in their work than their intelligence and high motivation would lead one to predict. It is interesting that Meyer and Yates (12), working with similar case material in England, have also emphasized the severe learning difficulty of patients undergoing partial temporal lobectomy in the dominant hemisphere. However they regard this primarily as a post-operative phenomenon, whereas the results of the present study show that there are marked verbal recall deficits present even before the operation. These differences in emphasis probably reflect differences in the measures used.

Table V – Specific postoperative impairment of story reproduction 1-3 years after partial left temporal lobectomy (means for 4 cases)

		Before Operation	Follow-up
Wechsler I.Q.		104	110
Story Recall (per cent)	Immediate...	30	20
	Delayed.......	13.8	9.2

b. Pictorial Comprehension and the Right Temporal Lobe. Patients with epileptogenic lesions of the right, non-dominant, temporal lobe have none of these verbal difficulties, but they show a clear, specific and reliable impairment on a pictorial test, the McGill Picture Anomaly Series. In this test the subject is shown a number of sketchily drawn scenes and has to point to what is most incongruous in each. A relatively easy item from this test is shown in Figure 2. In this instance the picture on the wall of the monkey's cage is immediately recognized as inappropriate by most normal subjects, and also by patients with lesions of frontal, parietal, or left temporal cortex. However, a patient with a right temporal lobe lesion might have difficulty identifying the various parts of the drawing and so might, for example, point to the woman's head in the foreground as "unidentifiable" and therefore "wrong." The error scores for the various groups on this test are shown diagrammatically in Figure 3, different forms of the test being used before and after operation to eliminate practice effects. The right temporal lobe patients make significantly more errors ($P < .01$), both before and after the operation, than other brain-injured subjects, who do not differ significantly from normal control subjects (a regrettably small group). It is particularly noteworthy that the patients with parietal lobe lesions made excellent scores. This pictorial test, whatever it measures, is not to be confused with tests such as Kohs Blocks which are primarily dependent upon spatial ability and are known to be peculiarly sensitive to parietal lobe injury (2,8).

Fig. 2. Representative item from the McGill Picture Anomalies test.

The Picture Anomalies test was originally intended as a power test only, time of response not being recorded; but it became increasingly clear that the right temporal lobe patients were abnormally slow and hesitant, and not merely inaccurate, in their responses, and therefore time scores for the test are now unobtrusively recorded. The results to date are shown in Figure 4. The right temporal group is

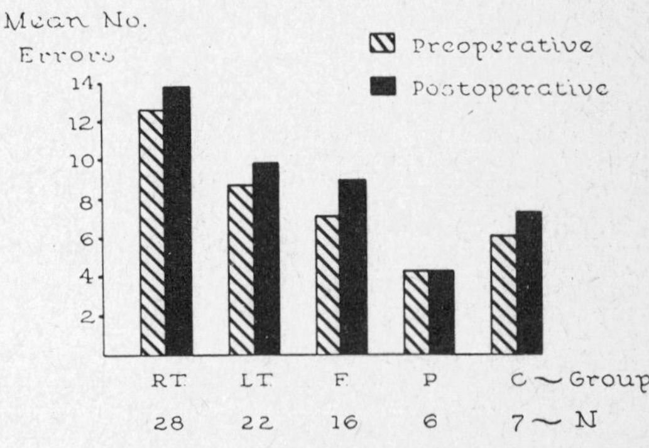

Fig. 3. Picture Anomalies test: error scores for right temporal (R.T.), left temporal (L.T.), frontal (F) and parietal lobe (P) cases before and after operation, and for normal control subjects (C) tested twice.

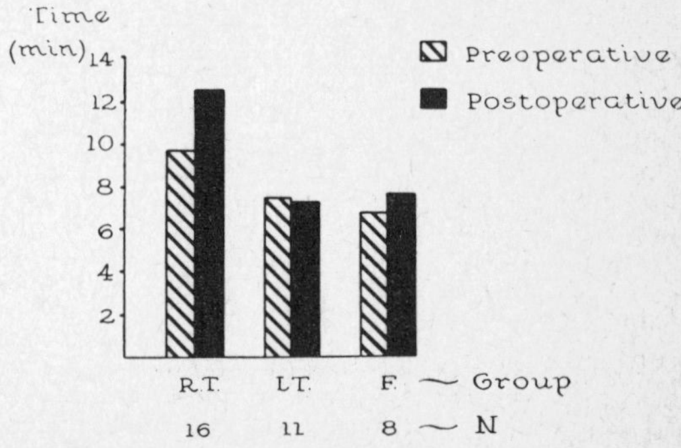

Fig. 4. Picture Anomalies test: time scores, showing significant postoperative slowing for the right temporal lobe group only.

slower than either the left temporal lobe or the frontal lobe groups even before operation, and after operation a significant further slowing occurs. Thus on this test we find a defect specific to the minor temporal lobe, and one which is heightened by removal of the epileptogenic area.

c. Auditory Discrimination – Preliminary Observations. The original test battery did not include any auditory tasks, but during the past year the Seashore tests of musical ability have been administered to all patients before and after operation. Despite the small number of cases, we already have some evidence of auditory deficits after unilateral temporal lobe excisions, the evidence so far being most clear for the right temporal lobe group. Unilateral temporal lobectomy, not necessarily including Heschl's gyrus, has consistently resulted in impairment on the Seashore tonal memory test, a test in which the subject listens to a simple melody of three or four notes played twice in rapid succession and has to indicate which note is changed at the second playing. After operation, scores of the right temporal group fall sharply on this test although other auditory tests, including simple pitch and intensity discrimination, may be unimpaired. In two patients seen for follow-up study this deficit was still present though not quite to the same degree. So far we do not see so consistent a deficit from the left temporal lobe, but the numbers are too small and the excision size too variable to permit any final conclusion to be drawn from this. Meanwhile it appears that right temporal lobectomy is in itself sufficient to cause a lasting deficit in the discrimination of tonal patterns. The fact that this deficit only appears after operation, wheras the visual difficulty is present even before the operation, suggests that different parts of the temporal cortex are implicated in the visual and auditory tasks.

General Versus Specific Defects and the Nociferous Effects of Epileptogenic Cortex

The data so far presented have emphasized specific effects shown by patients with long-standing epileptogenic lesions of one temporal lobe, defects which tend to increase rather than decrease when the epileptogenic area is excised. Apart from these specific defects, most patients show normal intellectual functioning both before and after operation. However there are marked individual differences in this respect, differences which may well be related to differences in degree of electrographic abnormality and seizure frequency before operation, though this has still to be demonstrated. Certainly some patients with unusually active electrographic foci before operation show general intellectual impairment which we attribute to widespread interference with cortical functioning rather than to the temporal lobe lesions specifically (7, p. 282). Unlike the specific defects, this more general intellectual inefficiency is apt to disappear after removal of the epileptogenic area. The following case is chosen to illustrate this point.

Case M.L. This 22-year-old man presented a life-long history of major and minor seizures, the latter occurring as often as 16 times a day. The attacks were ushered in by a warm, empty sensation in the umbilicus, followed by grunting, chewing and automatic behaviour for which there was subsequent amnesia. Repeated electroencephalographic studies showed a very clear right temporal focus which was extraordinarily active, with sharp waves and slow wave sequence present continuously. On December 16, 1953, Dr. Penfield carried out a right temporal lobectomy, finding marked abnormality beginning in the first temporal convolution deep anteriorly and extending into the uncus and hippocampus and along the inferior surface of the temporal lobe. The removal extended roughly 4 cm. along the first temporal convolution and 5.5 cm. along the inferior surface, including the anterior portion of the hippocampal gyrus. Since this operation failed to stop the patient's attacks, three weeks later Dr. William Feinderl extended the removal to include a further 1½ cm. of the hippocampus and adjacent inferior temporal cortex together with the insula. The patient has had no further seizures, and his family considers that his memory has improved greatly and that he is far less irritable than before.

Psychological findings. – Preoperative psychological examination on December 12, 1953, showed the characteristic right temporal lobe deficits. The Performance I.Q. rating was only 84, as compared with a Verbal I.Q. rating of 95, and he made poor time and error scores on the Picture Anomalies test. But in addition to these specific and expected deficits he showed abnormal variability on other tests, giving careless answers to simple questions, failing easy items on the mental arithmetic test only to succeed a moment later on more difficult ones, and showing a very restricted attention span. There was marked impairment on short term memory tests, resulting in a memory quotient of only 79, 10 points lower than the I.Q. rating. When tested for delayed recall of stories and drawings, further distortions and omissions occurred. We took these deficits as indicative of widespread interference with intellectual functioning due to the extremely active discharging lesion in the right temporal lobe, and hoped that improvement would follow surgical treatment. This in fact occurred. Fifteen days after the second operation the I.Q. level had risen from 89 to 99, the improvement being most marked on verbal tests. There was also a remarkable all-round improvement on short tests of memory and attention so that the memory quotient rose from 79 to 101, the most marked rise in the whole right temporal lobe group. Yet at the same time there was the typical further slowing on the Picture Anomalies test and also a falling off to chance scores on auditory discrimination tests, from which there has been little improvement to the present time.

This case has been selected to show the non-specific deficits which may result from an extremely active epileptogenic lesion in one temporal lobe. Removal of the epileptogenic focus in such a case may increase all round intellectual efficiency, as shown for example by an appreciable rise in I.Q. rating, but will at the same time tend to aggravate the deficits specific to the area removed. This same principle of course could have been illustrated equally well by a left temporal lobe lesion, but the specific deficits would have been different.

The Memory Defect in Bilateral Hippocampal Lesions

So far we have been considering only the effects of lesions strictly lateralized to one temporal lobe, cases in which the opposite temporal lobe is, we believe, functioning normally. In such cases only minor deficits are seen: a specifically verbal difficulty from the left temporal lobe, a perceptual difficulty from the right. But in two instances in our temporal lobe series unilateral partial temporal lobectomy in the dominant hemisphere was followed by a major impairment: a grave, persistent and totally unexpected loss of recent memory, fortunately unaccompanied by other changes of intellect or personality (15). In one instance the temporal lobe removal had been carried out in two stages, separated by a five-year period, and the memory loss followed the second operation only, at which time the uncus, hippocampus, and hippocampal gyrus alone were excised. Interestingly enough, although the patient has been aphasic for a time after the first operation, the second operation caused no language disturbance. The memory loss seen in these two cases appeared to be qualitatively quite distinct from the verbal learning difficulty normally seen in unilateral lesions of the dominant temporal lobe since it affected all postoperative events and not merely verbal material. We believe this distinction to be of fundamental importance.

Both these amnesic patients have continued to earn their living, one as a glove cutter, the other as a draughtsman; and their professional skills are well maintained. There is no defect of attention, concentration, or reasoning ability and no aphasia. Both patients show some retrograde amnesia for a period before the operation (four years in the first patient, three months in the second), but their memory for events before the period of retrograde amnesia is apprently normal. They show a very gross impairment of memory for all events subsequent to operation, and they are unable to recall test material after a lapse of five minutes or less if their attention has been diverted to another topic in the meantime. The retention difficulty is not specific to any one kind of material, but is quite general, affecting stories, drawings and numbers, and cutting across any distinction between verbal and perceptual material or between one sense modality and another.

To account for the severe memory loss in these two patients we have assumed that, in addition to the known epileptogenic lesion of the left hippocampal region, there was a second and preoperatively unsuspected destructive lesion of the opposite (right) hippocampal zone at the time of birth, so that when the surgeon removed the left hippocampal area, the patient was functionally deprived of that zone on both sides. And in fact both patients now show continuing electrographic abnormality in the unoperated temporal lobe. This view then attributes a key role to the hippocampal zone (hippocampus and hippocampal gyrus) in the retention and subsequent recall of current experience. A similar view was advanced by Glees and Griffith in 1952 (5) to account for memory loss seen in one patient with bilateral destruction of hippocampus and hippocampal gyrus by vascular accident. Strong and direct support for this interpretation comes from Dr. William Scoville who in 1954 (17) reported a grave loss of recent memory as a sequel to bilateral medial temporal lobe resection in one psychotic patient and one patient with intractable seizures. These operations had been radical ones, undertaken only when more conservative forms of treatment had failed. The removals extended posteriorly along the mesial aspect of the temporal lobes for a distance of about 8 cm. from the temporal tips, and the excisions were made by bisecting the tips of the temporal lobes and removing bilaterally the inferior portions of each temporal lobe which lay mesial to the inferior horn of the ventricle. These ablations must then have included the major portion of the hippocampus and hippocampal gyrus bilaterally, as well as uncus and amygdala[3], but of course spared the lateral neocortex. Dr. Scoville has very generously allowed us to study these patients, and they present exactly the same type of memory disturbance as our two cases had shown (18). Interestingly, I think, they do not have any perceptual difficulty or any disturbance of initial comprehension. The impairment is specifically one of retention.

Conclusions

What do these findings as a whole tell us of the normal function of the temporal lobes? The data on unilateral lesions show that the left temporal lobe contributes to the rapid understanding and subsequent retention of verbally expressed ideas. Deprived of this area a man is not dysphasic, but he remains an inefficient listener and a poor reader since he can assimilate less verbal information in one sequence than formerly and forgets this little abnormally quickly. The right, minor, temporal lobe, on the other hand, appears to be more critically involved in perceptual than in verbal skills.[4] When the right

[3]In his experience, bilateral removals limited to the uncal and amygdaloid regions cause no memory loss.

[4]Dr. Sean Mullan's observations, reported by Dr. Penfield (13) at these meetings, provide further evidence of the importance of the minor temporal lobe for perceptual functions. He finds that visual illusions of changes in the appearance of objects, whether occurring during epileptic discharge or as a result of cortical stimulation, arise almost invariably from the non-dominant rather than the dominant temporal lobe.

temporal lobe is removed, pictures and representational drawings lose some of their former distinctiveness, and the separate parts are less easily identified although there is never anything approaching a true visual agnosia. It seems that the right temporal lobe facilitates rapid visual identification, and that in this way it enters into the comprehension of pictorially expressed ideas.

These data on unilateral lesions have underlined the differences in function between the two temporal lobes, differences which relate to the functional asymmetry of the two hemispheres, the left being primarily concerned with verbal, the right with non-verbal skills. But it is clear that there must still be a considerable overlap of function between the two temporal lobes, the extent of which can only be revealed by bilateral lesions (19). We have no experience of bilateral lesions of the temporal neo-cortex, but the discovery of generalized memory loss, apparently independent of type of material or sense modality, after bilateral destruction of the hippocampus and hippocampal gyrus suggests that this hippocampal zone plays an essential part in the consolidation of the effects of current experience so that they endure beyond the moment of primary attention.

Summary

Formal psychological testing before and after unilateral partial temporal lobectomy in over 100 cases of temporal lobe epilepsy has yielded the following results.

1. Intelligence as measured by the Wechsler-Bellevue I.Q. rating is not permanently affected by these operations although there is a deficit on verbal subtests in the left temporal group during the period of postoperative dysphasia.

2. Long-standing epileptogenic lesions of the temporal lobe are associated with defects on certain specialized tests, these defects varying in kind depending on whether the lesion is in the dominant or non-dominant hemisphere.

3. Unilateral epileptogenic lesions of the dominant (left) temporal lobe are accompanied by difficulties in verbal recall although recall of non-verbal material is normal.

4. Unilateral epileptogenic lesions of the non-dominant (right) temporal lobe are accompanied by impairment in the comprehension of pictures although verbal skills are intact.

5. When unilateral partial temporal lobectomy is carried out for the relief of seizures, these specific deficits persist and in fact tend to be accentuated. This is true even in those cases which show a postoperative increase in I.Q. rating and complete cessation of seizures.

6. In contrast to the relatively mild deficits which accompany unilateral lesions, bilateral damage to the hippocampal zone causes profound and generalized loss of recent memory, unaccompanied by other intellectual changes.

7. These findings suggest that (a) the left temporal lobe contributes to the understanding and retention of verbally expressed ideas; (b) the right temporal lobe aids in rapid visual identification; (c) the hippocampus and hippocampal gyrus (either separately or together) play a crucial role in the retention of new experience.

References

1. ANDERSON, A. L. The effect of laterality localization of brain lesions on the Wechsler-Bellevue subtests. *J. Clin. Psychol.*, 1949, *7*, 149-153.
2. CRITCHLEY, M. The Parietal Lobes. Edward Arnold Ltd., London, 1953.
3. EARLE, K. M., BALDWIN, M., and PENFIELD, W. Incisural sclerosis and temporal lobe seizures produced by hippocampal herniation at birth. *Arch. Neurol. & Psychiat.*, 1953, *69*, 27-42.
4. GERBOTH, R. A study of the two forms of the Wechsler-Bellevue Intelligence Scale. *J. Consult. Psychol.*, 1950, *14*, 365-370.
5. GLEES, P., and GRIFFITH, H. B. Bilateral destruction of the hippocampus (cornu Ammonis) in a case of dementia. *Monatsschr. Psychiat. u. Neurol.*, 1952, *123*, 193-204.
6. HEBB, D. O. Intelligence in man after large removals of cerebral tissue; defects following right temporal lobectomy. *J. Gen. Psychol.*, 1939, *21*, 73-87.
7. HEBB, D. O. The Organization of Behaviour: a Neuropsychological Theory. New York: Wiley, 1949.
8. HECAEN, H., PENFIELD, W., BERTRAND, C., and MALMO, R. The syndrome of apractognosia due to lesions of the minor cerebral hemisphere. *Arch. Neurol. & Psychiat.*, 1956, *75*, 400-454.
9. HEILBRUNN, A. B., JR. Psychological test performance as a function of lateral localization of cerebral lesions. *J. Comp. & Physiol. Psychol.*, 1956, *49*, 10-14.
10. KLUVER, H., and BUCY, P. C. Preliminary analysis of functions of the temporal lobe in monkeys. *Arch. Neurol. & Psychiat.*, 1939, *42*, 979-1000.
11. MCFIE, J., and PIERCY, M. F. Intellectual impairment with localized cerebral lesions. *Brain*, 1952, *75*, 292-311.
12. MEYER, V., and YATES, A. J. Intellectual changes following temporal lobectomy for psychomotor epilepsy. *J. Neurol. Neurosurg. & Psychiat.*, 1955, *18*, 44-52.
13. PENFIELD, W. Functional localization in temporal and deep Sylvian areas. *Res. Publ. Assn. Res. Nerv. Ment. Dis.*, 1957.
14. PENFIELD, W., and BALDWIN, M. Temporal lobe seizures and the technique of sub-total temporal lobectomy. *Ann. Surg.*, 1952, *136*, 625-634.
15. PENFIELD, W., and MILNER, B. The memory deficit produced by bilateral lesions in the hippocampal zone. *Arch. Neurol. & Psychiat.*, 1957 (in press).

16. Reitan, R. M. Certain differential effects of left and right cerebral lesions in human adults. *J. Comp. & Physiol. Psychol.*, 1955, *48*, 474-477.
17. Scoville, W. B. The limbic lobe in man. *J. Neurosurg.*, 1954, *11*, 64-66.
18. Scoville, W. B., and Milner, B. Loss of recent memory after bilateral hippocampal lesions. *J. Neurol. Neurosurg. & Psychiat.*, 1957, *20*, 11-21.
19. Terzian, H., and Dalle Ore, G. Syndrome of Kluver and Bucy produced in man by bilateral removal of the temporal lobes. *Neurology*, 1955, *5*, 373-380.
20. Weisenberg, T., and McBride, K. Aphasia: A Clinical and Psychological Study. Commonwealth Fund, New York, 1936.

70 / Brain Response Correlates of Psychometric Intelligence [1]

John P. Ertl and Edward W.P. Schafer *Centre of Cybernetic Studies, University of Ottawa*

If a flash of light stimulates the eye, a distinct pattern of evoked electrical activity can be recorded from the scalp by means of an electroencephalograph. The time between the onset of the stimulus and various phases of the electrical activity (latency) can also be measured. In the present investigation, the remarkable finding was the presence of a relationship between the speed or latency of the electrical response of the human brain and psychometric intelligence. The more intelligent individuals exhibited a much shorter evoked potential latency than did the less intelligent individuals. Note the relationship of these findings to those reported in article 5.

Previous attempts to correlate electrophysiological variables with behavioural indices of intelligence have been inconclusive (1). Recent findings suggest that the average evoked potential (AEP) recorded from the human scalp may reflect the neural correlates of higher mental activity or information processing by the brain (2). The speed of this process, measured by the latency of sequential AEP components, could be the biological substrate of individual differences in behavioural intelligence. AEP latency data from cretinized rats (3), hypothyroid patients (4), ariboflavinotic children (5) and humans with differential intelligence (6) provide preliminary support for this hypothesis.

We now report evidence of a relationship between the time delays of the brain's electrical responses and psychometric intelligence. The latencies of sequential visual evoked potential components bear highly significant inverse correlations with IQ scores on three commonly used intelligence tests in a random sample of 573 primary school pupils. The visual AEP waveforms of high and low IQ subjects are characteristically distinct from each other.

The experimental sample comprised 317 male and 256 female pupils randomly selected from the population of 8,000 children attending grades 2, 3, 4, 5, 7 and 8 in the thirty-nine schools of the Ottawa separate school system.

The Wechsler intelligence scale for children (WISC), the primary mental abilities test (PMA) and the Otis quick-scoring mental ability test were used.

A visual AEP record was also obtained from each subject. The electroencephalograph (EEG) was recorded from bipolar scalp contact electrodes 6 cm apart, parallel with the midline and astride C4 in the 10-20 system with ground to the right earlobe (upward deflexion in reported data indicates negativity of the anterior electrode with respect to the posterior). The raw EEG was amplified to the required voltage in a bandwidth 3 dB down at 3 and 50 Hz and recorded on magnetic tape along with trigger pulses corresponding to the onset of flash stimuli. Subjects sat with eyes open in a darkened shielded room fixating a spot on a reflecting screen. Bright photic stimuli of microsecond duration were delivered according to a uniform stimulus interval distribution which ranged from 0.8 to 1.8 s. AEPs in response to 400 stimuli in a 625 ms interval after stimulation were extracted from the EEG by two methods – amplitude summation and zero-crossing analysis – using the Enhancetron *ND*-801 digital computer. These two techniques in combination facilitated objective identification of sequential AEP components.

Initially, the evoked potentials of each subject were amplitude averaged in alternate response sets of 200 and read out by XY recorder. Short term reliability assessments of the AEP and preliminary identification of its sequential components were made by visual cross-correlation from these graphs. A zero-crossing analysis technique was then used to confirm statistically the presence of sequential AEP components (7). The EEG was converted to pulses corresponding to zero-crossings where the EEG waveforms passed from positive to negative voltage. A histogram of zero-crossing occurrences against time, following 400 stimuli, was made by the Enhancetron

[1] This work was carried out in accordance with a contract with the US Department of Health, Education and Welfare, Office of Education. We also acknowledge the contribution of the Ontario Mental Health Foundation, the Educational Records Bureau of New York and the Ottawa Separate School Board.

Reprinted, by permission, from *Nature,* 1969, *223,* 421-422.

using its multiscaling mode across sixty-four channels (Fig. 1). The same EEG data were used to generate a control histogram by triggering the multi-scaler 400 times randomly with no time relation to experimental stimulation. The mean channel counts of both stimilated and control histograms were not statistically different. The standard deviation of the control histogram was also computed. If the number of zero-crossing counts in any channel of the stimulated histogram exceeded two standard deviations above its mean a statistically significant event was identified. The corresponding peaks of the summated AEP waveform were called sequentially E1, E2, E3 and E4 and their latencies from the onset of stimulus were measured with an error of measurement estimated to be plus or minus 5 ms. A statistically significant zero-crossing event was always accompanied by a visible component in the AEP record. Visible peaks in the AEP waveform not supported by significant zero-crossing events were rejected as sequential components.

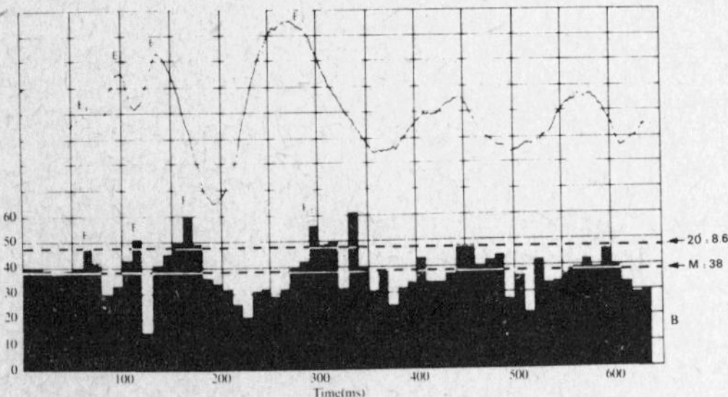

*Fig. 1. **A,** Average evoked potential resulting from amplitude summation of 400 responses to photic stimulation. **B,** Histogram of zero-crossing occurences in sixty-four channels following the same 400 photic stimuli as in **A.** Where the height of the histogram is greater than two standard deviations (computed from a control experiment in which no stimuli were given) above the mean, an AEP component is statistically identified.*

The latencies of the first four sequential AEP components detected in this manner were intercorrelated with the intelligence test scores using the Pearson *r* correlation coefficient across the entire sample.

Results, presented in Table I and illustrated in Figure 2, are evidence of a relationship between the electrical responses of the human brain and psychometric intelligence. The latencies of sequential components of the visual AEP bear highly significant inverse correlations with IQ scores from the three intelligence tests used (Table I). It would appear that AEP component latency is related to some common factor tapped by the highly intercorrelated intelligence tests.

IQ scores correlate higher with the late components (E3 and E4) of the visual AEP than with the early components (E1 and E2). This observation accords well with the generally accepted position that the late components of the AEP are more significant for conscious processes than the early primary components (8).

Table I – Pearson *r* correlation coefficients and descriptive statistics for psychometric and physiological variables

	Age (months)	WISC IQ	PMA IQ	Otis IQ	AEP latencies (ms) E1	E2	E3	E4
Age								
WISC IQ	–0.15							
PMA IQ	0.09	0.66						
Otis IQ	–0.07	0.61	0.75					
AEP: E1	–0.05	–0.18	–0.10	–0.14				
AEP: E2	–0.04	–0.30	–0.28	–0.29	0.59			
AEP: E3	–0.04	–0.35	–0.34	–0.35	0.43	0.78		
AEP: E4	–0.03	–0.33	–0.32	–0.35	0.34	0.65	0.83	
N	566.	566.	566.	538.	573.	573.	573.	573.
Mean	129.8	105.2	100.3	105.1	32.8	77.1	119.6	187.4
S.D.	26.5	13.1	13.9	13.3	13.6	15.8	26.7	45.0

With N of 566 Pearson *r* coefficients of 0.16 are significant at P=0.0001 level.

Specimen AEPs from ten high and ten low IQ subjects are shown in Figure 2. It is evident that these two sets of waveforms are internally consistent but distinct from each other. The AEPs of the high IQ subjects are more complex, characterized by high frequency components in the first 100 ms which are not observed in the AEPs of the low IQ subjects.

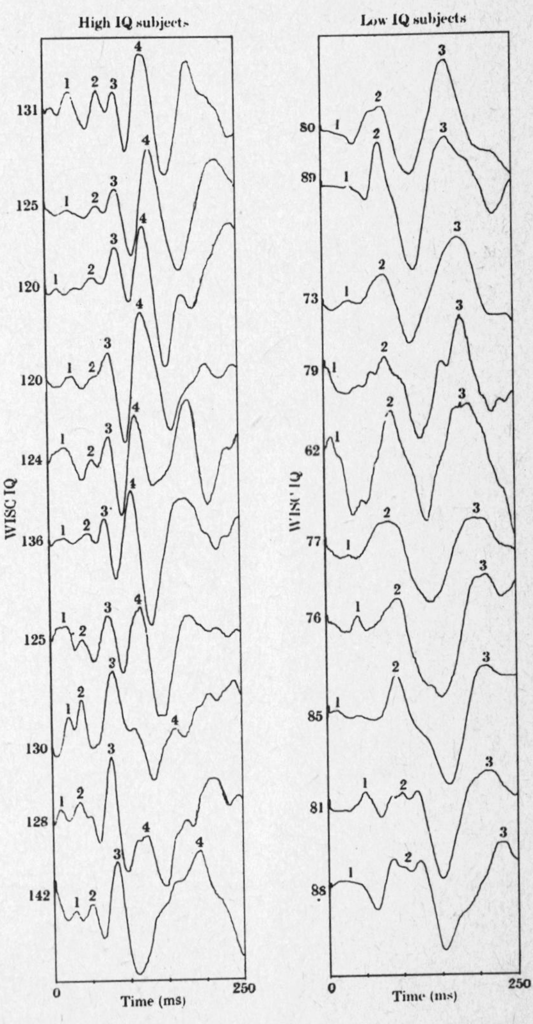

Fig. 2. Speciment visual average evoked potential waveforms for ten high and ten low IQ subjects. Components are sequentially labelled.

The ten high IQ subjects illustrated have a mean E3 (third sequential peak) latency of 88 ms. The ten low IQ subjects have a mean E3 latency of 194 ms.

The mean AEP component latencies for our entire sample correspond closely with normative data from other laboratories[9]. Our range of response latencies, however, is much greater, possibly because of the uncontrolled influence of intelligence and the visual and therefore subjective method of AEP component identification used in these other studies.

Several variables are known to affect the waveform of the visual AEP . The inter-subject AEP component latency differences noted in our sample, however, are much greater than any demonstrated latency changes attributable to potentially contaminating variables such as attention, arousal level, pupil diameter and so on. Furthermore, these potentially contaminating variables are not related to psychometric intelligence and are assumed to be randomly distributed in the population.

Reported intercorrelations between AEP component latency and IQ are not large but highly statistically significant. When attempting to relate variables in the psychological domain to variables in the physiological domain, it can be argued that even very small correlations, if statistically significant, could identify a fundamental relationship. Our findings suggest that evoked potentials, which reflect the time course of information processing by the brain, could be the key to understanding the biological substrate of individual differences in behavioural intelligence.

References

1. Vogel, W., and Broverman, D. M. *Psychol. Bull.*, 1964, *62,* 132.
2. Sutton, S., Tuetling, P., Zubin, J., and John, E. R. *Science,* 1967, *155,* 1436; John, E. R., Herrington, R. N., and Sutton, S., *ibid.*, 1967, *155,* 1439; Shevrin, H., and Fritzler, D. E., *ibid.*, 1968, *161,* 295. Cohen, J., and Walter, W. G., *Psychophysiology,* 1966, *3,* 187. Clynes, M., and Kohn, M., *EEG Clin. Neurophysiol.*, suppl. 26, 82, 1967.
3. Bradley, P. B., Eayrs, J. T., and Richards, N. M. *EEG Clin. Neurophysiol.*, 1964, *17,* 308.
4. Nishitani, H., and Kooi, K. A., *EEG Clin. Neurophysiol.*, 1968, *24,* 554.
5. Arakawa, T., Mizuno, T., Chiba, F., Sakai, K., Watanabe, S., Tamura, T., Tatsumi, S., and Coursin, D. B., *Tohoku J. Exp. Med.*, 1968, *94,* 327.
6. Chalke, F. C. R., and Ertl, J., *Life Sci.*, 1965, *4,* 1319; Ertl, J., in *Biocybernetics of The Central Nervous System* (edit. by Proctor, L. D.) (Little Brown, Boston, 1969); Whitaker, H. S., Osborne, R. T., and Nicora, B., *Trans. Amer. Neurol. Assoc.*, 1967, *92,* 194; Bennett, W. F., *Nature,* 1968, *220,* 1147; Rhodes, L. E., Dustman, R. E., and Beck, E. C., *EEG Clin. Neurophysiol.*, 1969, *26,* 237; Engle, R., and Butler, B. V., *EEG Clin. Neurophysiol.*, 1969, *26,* 237.
7. Ertl, J., *EEG Clin. Neurophysiol.*, 1965, *18,* 630; Krekule, I., *ibid.*, 1968, *25,* 175.
8. Libet, B., Alberts, W. W., Wright, Jun., E. W., and Feinstein, B., *Science,* 1967, *158,* 1597.
9. Kooi, K. A., and Bagehi, B. K. *Ann., N.Y. Acad. Sci.*, 1964, *112,* 254; Gastaut, H., and Regis, H. *NASA SP-72,* 7, 1965.
10. Beinhocker, G. D., Brooks, P. R., Anfenger, E., and Copenhaver, R. M. *IEEE Trans. Bio-Med. Eng.*, 1966, *13,* 11.

3 9004 01969900 5